THE NEW ANTHOLOGY OF AMERICAN POETRY

The New Anthology
of American Poetry

VOLUME ONE

*Traditions and Revolutions,
Beginnings to 1900*

✦   ✦   ✦   ✦   ✦   ✦   ✦   ✦   ✦   ✦   ✦   ✦   ✦

EDITED BY

Steven Gould Axelrod

Camille Roman

Thomas Travisano

RUTGERS UNIVERSITY PRESS
NEW BRUNSWICK, NEW JERSEY, AND LONDON

Second paperback printing, 2012

Library of Congress Cataloging-in-Publication Data

The new anthology of American poetry / edited by Steven Gould Axelrod,
    Camille Roman, and Thomas Travisano.
        p. cm.
        Vol. 1.
        Includes bibliographical references and index.
        Contents: v. 1. Traditions and revolutions, beginnings to 1900.
        ISBN 0-8135-3161-6 (cloth : alk. paper) — ISBN 0-8135-3162-4 (pbk. : alk. paper)
        1. American poetry.   I. Axelrod, Steven Gould, 1944–   II. Roman, Camille,
    1948–   III. Travisano, Thomas J., 1951–

PS586 .N49 2003
811.008 — dc21   2002070502

British Cataloging-in-Publication information is available from the British Library.

Produced by Wilsted & Taylor Publishing Services
    Copyediting: Melody Lacina
    Design and composition: Melissa Ehn

Manufactured in the United States of America

To Our Families and Students

CONTENTS

PART THREE: LATER NINETEENTH CENTURY

PREFACE

THE NEW ANTHOLOGY OF AMERICAN POETRY represents an evolving collaboration that began with its editors and publisher and now includes its readers. American poetry is in a continual state of evolution, and this anthology, too, is meant to be a work in perpetual progress. This book presents American poetry as a varied tapestry, like the New England quilt reproduced on its cover. It is a tree of life, with many branches, like the Iroquois poem that commences our text. American poetry also is a many-spirited, multicultural cornucopia, overflowing with poets representing different regions, races, ethnicities, classes, language traditions, and individual temperaments. This anthology, as it moves through historical and cultural time, confronts both a range of enduring traditions and what the poet Robert Lowell once called "a sequence of demolitions, the bravado of perpetual revolution." The story of American poetry is dialogical, including elements of cooperation, reciprocal learning, and mutual understanding and pleasure but also encompassing conflict — artistic competition, historical violence, and the marginalization and oppression of people who differ from those in power.

The poems brought together in these pages resemble nothing like a poetic consensus or mainstream. Rather, we present a series of artistic voices employing many different vocabularies, forms, and styles and representing as many different interests, perspectives, inheritances, and aims. Native-American poets alternate with European-American and African-American ones. By the nineteenth century, Asian-American poets, Latina/os, and others with identities too complicated to categorize easily make their presence felt. Gender also influences the poets' creative choices in multiple and unpredictable ways, as does region, with voices emerging and sometimes challenging one another from the North, from the South, from the East, and from a Western frontier that was moving ever westward.

Back in the nineteenth century, an informed discussion of American poetry might have focused on names such as William Cullen Bryant, Ralph Waldo Emerson, and Henry Wadsworth Longfellow. Toward the end of the century, some avant-garde readers might have wanted to insert Walt Whitman or the posthumously published Emily Dickinson into the discussion. By the middle of the twentieth century, the discussion would almost certainly have centered on Whitman and Dickinson as the two great figures in American poetic history. Ralph Waldo Emerson, Edgar Allan Poe, and Edwin Arlington Robinson might have been viewed as worthy but secondary poets of the century. Anne Bradstreet and Edward Taylor alone might have represented the earlier periods. F. O. Matthiessen's influential anthology of 1950, *The Oxford Book of American Verse*, did indeed propose a canon very much like the one just suggested.

The present collection includes all of the poets thus far mentioned, represented sympathetically and in depth, with particular attention paid to Whitman and Dickinson—and it includes many others besides. But the important point is that it offers a shift in the paradigm. This anthology does not present poems as part of a single "mainstream" or a uniform "canon." Rather, this anthology presents American poetry as a multiplicity of canons—a boisterous chorus of voices, some competing, some cooperating, and some in dialogue, though none of them hearing every one of the others. Instead of a mainstream, this anthology includes innumerable streams. Each of the poems reflects an effort by its creator to make language do something special. Yet each evokes the everyday life of its community as well: the social, political, economic, cultural, and aesthetic conditions that produced the poem and helped give that poem its meanings.

Some poems empathize with those who suffer historical injustice. Paul Laurence Dunbar eloquently wrote, "I know why the caged bird sings, alas!" Other poems evoke an anguish that is isolated and interior. Emily Dickinson observed, "One need not be a Chamber to be Haunted." Some poems anticipate a modest amount of recognition. Anne Bradstreet asked for only a "thyme or parsley wreath" to honor her artistry. Other poems strive for cultural redemption. The Iroquois poem opening this book with its image of a tree of life with many branches asserts:

> Roots have spread out from the Tree of the Great Peace. . . .
> the Great White Roots of Peace . . .
>
> Any man of any nation
> may trace the roots to their source and be welcome
> to shelter
> beneath the Great Peace. . . .

And some poems seem to speak directly from one vulnerable and soulful human being to another, perhaps across a very great distance in time. Walt Whitman wrote:

> Failing to fetch me at first keep encouraged,
> Missing me one place search another,
> I stop somewhere waiting for you.

This anthology begins with traditional Native-American texts, some of which may have preceded the arrival of Columbus on the shores of what was for Europeans, but not for those who already lived here, the "New World." The anthology ends as the nineteenth century flows into the twentieth. There are many cultural stories contained within these pages, and many astounding poems and songs that have changed the world and that may change yours. We greet you at the outset of an exciting adventure.

ACKNOWLEDGMENTS

WE WOULD LIKE TO BEGIN by thanking Professors Nina Baym, Paula Bernat Bennett, Emory Elliot, Anne Fountain, Richard Flynn, Lorrie Goldensohn, Cristanne Miller, Vivian Pollak, and Cheryl Walker for their expert help and advice along the way. We are deeply indebted to the numerous pathbreaking literary critics, historians, editors, and anthologists mentioned in our headnotes and the "Further Reading" sections. We thank the Center for Ideas and Society at the University of California, Riverside—and particularly Trudy Cohen, Laura Lozon, and our audience members—for giving us the opportunity to present our evolving ideas about anthologizing American poetry in a stimulating and congenial environment. We also thank our students at the University of California, Riverside, Washington State University, and Hartwick College for their lively sense of inquiry and their readiness to explore the unexpected.

Our special thanks go to Leslie Mitchner, our editor at Rutgers, for her enthusiasm, professionalism, and wise counsel. We are also grateful to the rest of the staff at the press, particularly Arlene Bacher, Marilyn Campbell, Alison Hack, Melanie Halkias, Adi Hovav, and Amy Rashap; and to Christine Taylor, Melody Lacina, and Melissa Ehn at Wilsted & Taylor Publishing Services, for their help and skill.

For her painstaking assistance with the "tree of life" quilt (ca. 1820) that appears on the cover, we thank Nancy Johnston, visual resource librarian at Old Sturbridge Village. The history of this quilt, with its European, Middle Eastern, and South Asian influences, highlights for us the transnational character of American culture.

Steven Gould Axelrod would like to thank Professors Melissa Axelrod, Rise B. Axelrod, Lucia Castello Branco, Jennifer Doyle, Donald Dyer, John Ganim, Jeffrey Gray, George Haggerty, Katherine Kinney, Cheryl Langdell, Tiffany Ana Lopez, Carole-Anne Tyler, and Traise Yamamoto for their good will and support. To Dr. Jeremiah B. C. Axelrod, historian par excellence, he owes more than he can say. He thanks his father, Dr. Bernard Axelrod, for wise counsel and the question, "How's the book coming along?" He gratefully acknowledges the help of his indefatigable and resourceful research assistant, Megan Fowler. He has learned a great deal about American poetry from his enthusiastic and knowledgeable graduate students, particularly Joy Barta, Kristin Brunnemer, Elston Carr, Liam Corley,

Richard Hishmeh, Deckard Hodge, Lauren Hollingsworth, Andrew Howe, Christina Mar, Amy Robbins, Christine Smedley, Kendall Smith, Craig Svonkin, Cassandra Van Zandt, Edith Vasquez, and Ryan Winters. Thanks are also due to the Research Committee of the University of California, Riverside, for financial assistance.

Camille Roman expresses her appreciation to Rise B. Axelrod and Chris D. Frigon for their astute collegial advice. She especially wishes to thank Chris D. Frigon, her husband and coeditor of Twayne's Music Book Series, for his knowledge of American music and his computer expertise, which contributed significantly to the development of this project. She acknowledges the invaluable and enthusiastic work of graduate research assistants Keely Kuhlman and Melissa Tennyson. She is most grateful to Victor Villanueva, chair of the Department of English, Washington State University, for much-needed financial assistance with permissions. She wishes to express her deep appreciation to Nancy Armstrong, chair, and the Department of English at Brown University for an invaluable appointment as visiting scholar during 1999–2000—and with it the unforgettable opportunity to peruse the university's inspiring library holdings in American poetry before 1900. For their warm hospitality, collegiality, and friendship during her time in Providence, she thanks Dottie Denniston, Mutlu Konuk, George Monteiro, Ruth Oppenheim, Tori Smith, Mark and Shelly Spilka, and Susanne Woods as well as staff members Lorraine Mazza and Marilyn Netter. She is especially grateful to Jane Betts-Stover, Thomas Disrud, associate minister, and the First Unitarian Church of Portland, Oregon, for a much-needed office during the copyediting and proofreading phases of this volume.

Thomas Travisano would like to thank research assistants Katherine Lomasney and Amy Norkus for their dedicated and enthusiastic efforts in support of the project. He thanks the reference department of the Hartwick College Library, especially Sue Stevens and Reagan Brumagen, for their energy and persistence in search of out-of-print books and other quaint and curious fragments of forgotten lore. He also thanks the board of trustees of Hartwick College and Susan Gotsch, Hartwick's vice-president for academic affairs and dean of the faculty, for their generous and ongoing support. And, of course, he thanks his wife, Elsa Travisano, for her computer expertise and literary judgment as well as her resilience, patience, good humor, and good counsel.

Each of the editors wishes to acknowledge the generous support and insight of the others in what has been, from start to finish, an extremely gratifying and enlightening collaboration.

Poems by Emily Dickinson: Reprinted by permission of the publishers and the Trustees of Amherst College from *The Poems of Emily Dickinson*, Ralph W. Franklin, ed., Cambridge, Mass.: The Belknap Press of Harvard University Press, Copy-

PART ONE

✦

*Pre-Columbian Period
to 1800*

INTRODUCTION

Poetry in what is now the United States began centuries before the English language was spoken or written here. It began with Native-American texts that were often, but not always, ceremonial or part of a ritual. Some of these songs, chants, and formulae mark particular historical occasions, such as the establishment of peace. Others speak lyrically of the love between human beings. Yet others are an enduring part of a culture, repeated in some evolving form to the present day. Native Americans produced the first great poetry of this place. Their poetry shows them building their relationship to the land, to their language, to their spirit, and to each other.

Next came a variety of European newcomers, especially those from Spain and from Britain, to live alongside and, too often, to seek to dominate or drive out the Native Americans. Soon Africans were added to the cultural mix, arriving as slaves or indentured servants and enduring as slaves or as free people trying to survive within very unjust social systems. Poetry in English arose with the first generation of British colonists. This anthology presents the three most prominent colonial poets. Anne Bradstreet, the first published poet living in the new land, displays an admirable verbal and intellectual dexterity while proving how surprisingly complex Puritan life could be. Her poetry presents a host of mixed feelings about the demands of the soul and the wishes of the body, the pleasures and self-doubts of creative production, and the loves, sorrows, and losses that mark a human life. Edward Taylor employs witty and complex imagery—derived in part from English metaphysical tradition and in part from the new world he inspected very closely— to ask the question that dominated Puritan thinking and feeling: "Am I saved?" Michael Wigglesworth, more simply, sought to frighten the "elect" away from Hell and toward salvation. Far less subtle or complicated than the poems by Bradstreet or Taylor, Wigglesworth's "Day of Doom" proved the most popular poem of its era.

By the eighteenth century, English-speaking culture had dramatically shifted. Puritanism no longer dominated daily life, even in New England, though many other varieties of faith flourished. Commerce arose to organize social life as well. The Bostonian Phillis Wheatley, an African-American slave who was freed at the age of fourteen, became the century's most powerful English-language poet on the continent. She pleaded in coded and, increasingly, in open ways for justice for blacks. She also spoke of an abiding Christian faith, and of her hopes for American independence and for equality for all. Other poets, such as Philip Freneau and Joel Barlow, wrote in very different ways about the relations of white male culture to the land and to native peoples and customs. Popular songs debated Revolutionary and loyalist identities, as the new nation broke away from its British colonizer and struggled for independent existence. If a previous generation had asked, "Am I saved?" a new generation was asking, "What does it mean to have this new identity as an 'American'?" The contradictions within that question would continue to haunt United States culture and poetry for centuries to come. Do Thomas Jefferson's eloquent phrases in the Declaration of Independence — "created equal," "life, liberty, and the pursuit of happiness" — apply to all or only to some? How and when can justice prevail? In poetry, the issue might be phrased: Who is permitted to speak and with how much freedom?

NATIVE-AMERICAN SONGS,
RITUAL POETRY, AND LYRIC POETRY
Pre-1492–1800

A̶PPROXIMATELY TEN MILLION Native Americans speaking three hundred fifty different languages were living in established societies throughout North America at the time of Christopher Columbus's arrival in 1492. They may have migrated from Asia roughly twenty-five thousand years ago, though this is not known with any certainty. Songs and poems played central roles in the customs and practices of Native Americans, indicating the existence of not only highly developed social communities but also rich and diverse cultures that shared common values: attachment to and love for the land, sustenance of communal harmony, belief in the continuance of life, and resistance to conquest. The poetic voices were not exclusively male; they were also significantly female. Dates for most of the songs and poems cannot be accurately ascertained. It is believed, however, that most were orally composed long before major European settlement.

Selections from the Iroquois, Zuni, Copper Eskimo, Aleut, Cherokee, Chippewa, and Seminole suggest the diverse poetic practices of the tribes and the wide-ranging geographical regions once populated solely by Native-American communities. While ritual poetry used for communal expression and ceremonies may seem to dominate traditional Native-American poetry, this preponderance may reflect a bias of the anthropological recorders themselves rather than reality. Lyric poetry or the individualized outpouring of a poet, while transcribed less frequently, is very diverse. Such poems range from evocations of pain and violence to contemplations of beauty and love. This heterogeneity suggests that lyric poetry was likely as valued as ritual poetry.

"The Tree of the Great Peace," the Iroquois selection that opens the anthology, offers an excellent example of how Native Americans have used poetry to commemorate historical events — in this case, the founding of the Iroquois confederation in about 1450. The Zuni ritual poem "Sayatasha's Night Chant" is a superb illustration of a long narrative drawing on a mythic subtext and employing formulae, conventionalized symbolic expressions in either phrases or lines. It is sung each December in New Mexico as part of an extensive eight-day Zuni ceremonial, called Shalako or "The Coming of the Gods." The ceremony reenacts the return of the kachinas, Zuni ancestral people and patron spirits of the earth, who bring moisture and seeds to renew life. For half of each year following the winter ceremonial, the kachinas are visible to the Zuni as they fulfill ritual obligations. Then in late summer, the kachinas return to Zuni heaven.

Among the other selections, the Copper Eskimo personal lyric voices express fear about kayaking; the Alaskan Aleut poem mourns love; and the Washington state Makah speaker repulses a vain lover. The two Cherokee selections are excellent examples of very short magic formulae used by medicine men in prescribed rituals, whereas the two Chippewa poems focus on intensely personal responses to a lover's parting and to war. Finally, the two Seminole entries reflect powerfully upon birth and death.

FURTHER READING

John Bierhorst, ed. *The Sacred Path: Spells, Prayers and Power Songs of the American Indians.* New York: William Morrow, 1983.
William Brandon, ed. *The Magic World: American Indian Songs and Poems.* New York: William Morrow, 1971.
Brian Swann. *Native American Songs: An Anthology.* Mineola, N.Y.: Dover Publications, 1996.
Paul Zolbrod. *Reading the Voice: Native American Oral Poetry on the Written Page.* Salt Lake City: University of Utah Press, 1995.

[IROQUOIS]   *The Tree of the Great Peace*

I am Dekanawideh and with the chiefs of the Five Nations[1]
I plant the Tree of the Great Peace. . . .

Roots have spread out from the Tree of the Great Peace. . . .
the Great White Roots of Peace . . .

Any man of any nation
may trace the roots to their source and be welcome
to shelter
beneath the Great Peace. . . .

I, Dekanawideh,
and the chiefs of our Five Nations of the Great Peace
we now uproot the tallest pine

Into the cavity thereby made
we cast all weapons of war

*   *   *

1. Dekanawideh (or Dekanawida), believed to have been a Huron, speaks for and with the chiefs of the five nations. In 1450 the five nations that made up the confederacy of the Iroquois—the Cayuga, Mohawk, Oneida, Onondaga, and Seneca—joined together under the leadership of Dekanawida and Hiawatha, a Mohawk. The Tuscarora also joined the confederacy. This poem commemorates their pledge to join together in peace and to bury their grievances against one another. Because they lived in the Northeast, mostly in New York, they were able to slow European settlement westward until about 1750.

Into the depths of the earth
into the deep underneath . . .

we cast all weapons of war
We bury them from sight forever. . . .
and we plant again the tree. . . .

Thus shall the Great Peace be established. . . .

1450

[ZUNI]

Sayatasha's Night Chant

And now indeed it has come to pass.
When the sun who is our father
Had yet a little ways to go to reach his left-hand altar,[1]

Our daylight father,
Pekwin of the Dogwood clan,
Desired the waters, the seeds
Of his fathers,
Priests of the masked gods.
Then our fathers,
Sharing one another's desire, sat down together
In the rain-filled room
Of those that first came into being.
Yonder following all the springs,
They sought those ordained to bring long life to man,
Those that stand upright,
But (like the waters of the world),
Springing from one root, are joined together fast.
At the feet of some fortunate one
Offering prayer meal,
Turquoise, corn pollen,
Breaking the straight young shoots,
With their warm human hands
They held them fast,[2]

1. The winter solstice. Most of the poem recounts all of the events leading up to the eighth night of Shalako. The Pekwin, or Sun Priest, begins preparations for the year's December Shalako a year before by gathering the priests in a kiva, a subterranean room for prayer and planning, called a "rain-filled room" in the poem because it symbol-izes the underwater world from which the Zuni first emerged onto the earth's surface. When the priests enter the kiva, they symbolically return to their point of origin or creation.

2. Willow shoots are gathered and made into prayer sticks that communicate Zuni needs to the kachinas, the ancestral spirits.

Taking the massed cloud robe of their grandfather, turkey man,
Eagle's mist garment,
The thin cloud wings and massed cloud tails
Of all the birds of summer,
With these four times clothing their plume wands,
They made the plume wands into living beings.
With the flesh of their mother,
Cotton woman,
Even a thread badly made,
A soiled cotton thread,
Four times encircling their wand they made their belts;
With rain-bringing prayer feathers
They made them into living beings.
When they said, "Let it be now,"
The ones who are our fathers
Commissioned with prayers
The prayer wands that they had fashioned.

When the sun who is our father
Had gone in to sit down at his ancient place,
Then over toward the south,
Whence the earth is clothed anew,
Our father, Käwulia Pautiwa,
Perpetuating what had been since the first beginning,
Again assumed human form.[3]
Carrying his father's finished plume wands,
He made his road come hither.
Wherever he thought, "Let it be here,"
Into his fathers' rain-filled room,
He made his road to enter.
And when our sun father
Had yet a little ways to go,
To go in to sit down at his ancient place,
Yonder from all sides
Rain-bringing birds,
Pekwin, priest
From where he stays quietly,
Made his road come forth.

3. Pautiwa is the pekwin of the kachinas, who live in an underwater social world known as Kothlu-wala, which parallels the Zuni tribal system. The impersonator of Pautiwa represents the human becoming god and the god assuming human form by donning a mask that is removed during Shalako.

Making his road come hither,
Into his fathers' rain-filled room,
He made his road to enter.
With his wings,
His fathers' cloud house he fashioned,
Their bed of mist he spread out,
Their life-giving road of meal he sent forth,
Their precious spring he prepared.[4]
When all was ready,
Our father, Käwulia Pautiwa,
Reaching his house chiefs,
His pekwin,
His bow priests,
He made his road to go in.
Following one road,
Sitting down quietly
A blessed night
The divine ones
With us, their children, came to day.

Next day, when our sun father
Had come out standing to his sacred place,
Saying, "Let it be now,"
Over there to the south,
Whence the earth is clothed anew,
Our father, Käwulia Pautiwa,
Perpetuating what had been since the first beginning,
Again assumed human form.
Carrying his waters,
Carrying his seeds,
Carrying his fathers' precious plume wands,
He made his road come forth.
He made his road come hither.
The country of the Corn priests,
Four times he made his road encircle.
Yonder wherever all his kiva children's rain-filled roads come out
His precious plume wands
He laid down.
Then turning he went back to his own country.

---

4. As the Zuni pekwin constructs an altar of sand-painted images in the kiva, Pautiwa visits the Zuni pueblo to select the impersonators of the kachinas, including Sayatasha, for the next year.

*   *   *

My father picked up the prayer plume,
And with the precious prayer plume
Me he appointed.
The moon, who is our mother,
Yonder in the west waxed large;
And when standing fully grown against the eastern sky,
She made her days,
For my fathers,
Rain maker priests,
Priests of the masked gods.
I fashioned prayer plumes into living beings.
My own common prayer plume,
I fastened to the precious prayer plume of my fathers.
At the place since the first beginning called "cotton hanging,"
I brought my fathers prayer plumes.
Drawing my prayer plumes toward them,
They spoke to those inside the place of our first beginning.[5]
Yonder following all the springs,
On all the mossy mountains,
In all the wooded places,
At the encircling ocean,
With my prayer plumes,
With my sacred meal,
With my sacred words,
They talked to those within.
Winter,
Summer,
Through the cycle of the months,
Though my prayer plumes were but poor ones,
There toward the south,
Wherever my fathers' roads come out
I continued to give them prayer plumes.

And when the cycle of months was at an end,[6]
My fathers made their rain roads come in

---

5. The Sayatasha impersonator visits all twenty-nine of the Zuni sacred springs and deposits prayer sticks at each spring to communicate to the spirits the Zuni need for rain.
6. After the months of ritual preparations, the intensive forty-nine-day preparation period for Shalako begins in mid-October, with each day marked by the untying of a knot on a knotted day-count cord.

To their fathers,
Their mothers,
Those that first came into being.
Sharing one another's desire, they sat down together.
With the flesh of their mother,
Cotton woman,
Even a cord badly made,
A soiled cotton cord,
With this four times
They made the day counts into living beings.
Saying, "Let it be now,"
They sent for me.
I came to my fathers,
Where they were waiting for me.
With their day count
They took hold of me fast.
Carrying their day count,
I came back to my house.
Saying, "Let it be now,"
And carrying the prayer plumes which I had prepared,
Yonder to the south
With prayers, I made my road go forth.
To the place ever since the first beginning called "Ants go in,"
My road reached.[7]
There where my fathers' water-filled roads come out,
I gave them plume wands;
I gave them prayer feathers;
There I asked for light for you.
That you may grow old,
That you may have corn,
That you may have beans,
That you may have squash,
That you may have wheat,
That you may kill game,
That you may be blessed with riches,
For all this I asked.
Then over toward the west
Where the road of my fathers comes in,
I gave them plume wands.

7. The man who impersonates Sayatasha verifies that he has visited all twenty-nine sacred springs.

✻   ✻   ✻

And now, when all of their days were past,[8]
Over toward the west,
Where the gray mountain stands,
And the blue mountain,
Where rain always falls,
Where seeds are renewed,
Where life is renewed,
Where no one ever falls down,
At the abiding place
Of those who are our children,
There I met them on their roads.
There where the one who is my father
Had prepared my seat
Four times my father sprinkled prayer meal.
On the crown of my head
Four times he sprinkled prayer meal.
And after he had sprinkled prayer meal on his rain seat,
Following him,
My prayer meal
Four times I sprinkled.
My father's rain seat
I stood beside.
My father took hold of me.
Presenting me to all the directions, he made me sit down.
When I had sat down,
My father
Took his grandson,
Reed youth.
Within his body,
He bored a hole going through him.
Four times drawing toward him his bag of native tobacco,
Into the palm of his hand
He measured out the tobacco.
Within his body
He placed mist.
He took his grandmother by the hand
And made her sit down in the doorway.

---

8. Sayatasha's impersonator visits the kachinas' underwater world or "Zuni heaven." There he is invested in his role through two rites, a smoking ritual signifying the breath of life, peace, and tribal harmony and a baptism with cornmeal symbolizing fertility.

Having made her sit in the doorway,
Four times inhaling, he drew the mist through.
With the mist
He added to the hearts
Of the rain maker priests of all directions.
It is well;
Praying that the rain makers
Might not withhold their misty breath,
With his prayers
He added to their hearts.
He handed it to me.
Four times inhaling,
Into my body
I made the mist pass through.
Then with the mist,
I added to the hearts of my fathers of all the directions.
When this was at an end,
We greeted one another with terms of kinship:
Father,
Son; elder brother, younger brother; uncle, nephew; grandfather, grandson;
    ancestor, descendant.
With this many words we greeted one another.
When all this was at an end,
My father questioned me:
"Yes, now indeed
You have passed us on our roads.
Surely you will have something to say, some words that are not too long."
Thus he spoke to me.

"Yes, indeed it is so.
Back at the New Year,
All my fathers,
Desiring something,
With their precious prayer plume
Appointed me.
Yonder toward the south,
At all the places where the roads of the rain makers come out,
I have continued to offer you prayer plumes.
Now that the cycle of your months is at an end,
Now that the counted number of your days has been told of,
Now that this many days
Anxiously we have awaited your day,

Now this day,
We have reached the appointed time.
Now I have passed you on your roads."
Thus I spoke to them.

When I had spoken thus,
Hurriedly, without delay,
My father took hold of me.[9]
From the very soles of my feet
Even to the crown of my head
He clothed me all over with all things needful.
When all this was at an end,
Then also with that which is called my belt,
His prayer meal,
He covered my navel.
With his bundle that covered it all over,
He took hold of me,
His bundle reached all around my body.
When all this was at an end,
Then also the different kinds of seeds four times he placed over my navel.
All different kinds of seeds his bundle contained:
The seeds of the yellow corn,
The seeds of the blue corn,
The seeds of the red corn,
The seeds of the white corn,
The seeds of the speckled corn,
The seeds of the black corn,
And also that by means of which you may have firm flesh,
Namely, the seeds of the sweet corn;
And also those which will be your sweet-tasting delicacies,
Namely, all the clans of beans—
The yellow beans,
The blue beans,
The red beans,
The white beans,
The spotted beans,
The black beans,
The large beans,

9. Sayatasha the kachina invests his impersonator by costuming him for the public ceremonial and empowering him to bless the people with fertility.

The small beans,
The little gray beans,
The round beans,
The string beans,
Then also those that are called the ancient round things—
The striped squash,
The crooked-neck squash,
The watermelons,
The sweet melons,
And also those which you will use to dip up your clear water,
Namely, the gourds;
And then also the seeds of the piñon tree,
The seeds of the juniper tree,
The seeds of the oak tree,
The seeds of the peach tree,
The seeds of the blackwood shrub,
The seeds of the first flowering shrub,
The seeds of the kapuli shrub,
The seeds of the large yucca,
The seeds of the small yucca,
The seeds of the branched cactus,
The seeds of the brown cactus,
The seeds of the small cactus;
And then also the seeds of all the wild grasses—
The evil-smelling weeds,
The little grass,
Tecukta,
Kucutsi,
O'co,
Apitalu,
Sutoka,
Mololoka,
Piculiya,
Small piculiya,
Hamato,
Mitaliko;
And then also the seeds of those that stand in their doorways,
Namely the cattails,
The tall flags,
The water weeds,
The watercress,

The round-leafed weed;
Across my navel
His bundle reached.
And then also, the yellow clothing bundle of the priest of the north,
The blue clothing bundle of the priest of the west,
The red clothing bundle of the priest of the south,
The white clothing bundle of the priest of the east,
The many-colored bundle of the priest of the above,
The dark-colored bundle of the priest of the below;
Across my navel
His bundle reached.

When all this was at an end,
My father spoke to me:[10]
"Thus you will go.
Your daylight fathers,
Your daylight mothers,
Your daylight children
You will pass on their roads.
And wherever you come to rest,
We shall come to you.
Assuredly none of us shall be left behind—
All the men,
Those with snow upon their heads,
With moss on their faces,
With skinny knees, no longer upright, and leaning on canes,
Even all of these;
And furthermore the women,
Even those who are with child,
Carrying one child on the back,
Holding another on a cradleboard,
Leading one by the hand,
With yet another going before,
Even all of us,
Our daylight fathers,
Our daylight mothers,
Our children,
We shall pass on their roads."

      ✳   ✳   ✳

10. When the impersonator of Sayatasha calls for the spirits of the ancestral dead to bring rain, they come.

Thus my father said.
Having spoken thus,
He took hold of me.
Presenting me to all the directions he made me arise.
With his prayer meal
Four times he sprinkled his water-filled ladder.[11]

After him,
Four times I sprinkled my prayer meal.
Taking four steps,
Four times striding forward,
Standing, I came out.
[Having come out standing,[12]
Yonder to all directions I looked;
I looked toward the north,
I looked toward the west,
I looked toward the south,
I looked toward the east.
Hither, toward the place of dawn,
I saw four roads going side by side.
Along the middle road,
Four times my prayer meal I sprinkled.
There I made the sound of the water-filled breath of the priest of the north.
Taking four steps,
Four times striding forward,
To the place known since the first beginning as Great Lake,[13]
My road came.

Where my father's road comes out
I stood in the doorway.
That which formed my belt,
My prayer meal,
Four times sprinkling inside,
I opened their curtain of scum.
After that,
Four times sprinkling prayer meal inside,

11. The priests enter the kiva through a ladder descending from a roof, so it is called "water-filled."
12. The bracket marks the beginning of the text that is repeated twenty-nine times as the Zuni visit all twenty-nine of their sacred springs. The Sayatasha impersonator also visits them to reenact the mythic search for the center of the world.

13. One of the twenty-nine springs visited. At each spring, the Sayatasha impersonator moves aside the algae scum, treating it as a door to the kiva, or "rain-filled room." The ritual smoking and baptism with cornmeal also occurs to seek the return of the ancestral spirits and their rainmaking powers.

Standing I came in.
When I came in standing,
My father,
Hurrying without delay
Where he had prepared his rain seat,
His prayer meal
Four times he sprinkled.
On the top of my head
His prayer meal
Four times he sprinkled.

After him,
Four times sprinkling my prayer meal,
My father's rain seat
I stood beside.
As I stood up beside it
My father took hold of me.
Yonder to all the directions presenting me,
He made me sit down.

Having seated me,
The one who is my father
Took the water-bringing cigarette which he had prepared.
Four times drawing it toward him,
He took his grandmother by the hand
And made her sit down in the doorway.
Four times inhaling, he drew the mist through.
With the mist
He added to the hearts of fathers,
Rain maker priests.
Thus it is well;
In order that the rain makers may not withhold their misty breath.
With mist he added to their hearts.
When all this was at an end,
My father handed it to me.
Four times inhaling, I drew the mist through.
Into my body drawing the misty breath,
With the mist
I added to the hearts of my fathers.
This is well;
In order that the rain makers may not withhold their misty breath,
With mist I added to their hearts.

When all this was at an end,
We greeted one another with terms of kinship:
Father,
Son; elder brother, younger brother; uncle, nephew; grandfather, grandson;
    ancestor, descendant.
With these words we greeted one another.

When all this was at an end,
My father questioned me:
"Yes, now at this time
You have passed us on our roads.
Surely you will have something to say, some word that is not too long,
If you let us know that,
I shall know it for all time."
Thus my father spoke.
When he had spoken thus, (I answered)
"Yes, indeed it is so.
Yonder to the south,
Following wherever your roads come out,
I have been bringing you prayer sticks,
I have been bringing you prayer feathers.
Now this day,
Having reached the appointed time,
I have passed you on your roads."
"Is that so. With plain words you have come to us.
We are clothed with your prayer sticks;
We hold your prayer meal;
With your prayer plumes in our hair we are sitting in here waiting.
Here where we are just standing around,
Where we are just sitting on our haunches,
You have come to us.[14]
When the sun who is our father
Has yet a little ways to go,
Before he goes in to sit down at his sacred place,
Nearby your daylight fathers,
Your daylight mothers,
Your children,
You will pass on their roads.
Wherever you come to rest,

14. The spirits await the request of the Zuni for assistance.

All together we shall come to you.
All the men,
Those with snow upon their heads, with moss upon their faces,
With skinny knees,
No longer upright but leaning on canes;
And the women,
Even those who are with child,
Carrying one upon the back,
Holding another on the cradleboard,
Leading one by the hand,
With yet another going before.
Yes, with all of these,
Your daylight fathers,
Your daylight mothers,
Your children,
You will pass on their roads,
And wherever you come to rest
We shall come to you."
Thus my father spoke.

When he had spoke thus,
He took hold of me.
Yonder to all the directions
Presenting me,
He made me arise.
After he had made me arise,
With his prayer meal
His water-filled ladder
He sprinkled.
After him, sprinkling my prayer meal,
Standing, I came out.][15]

Coming out standing,
Yonder to all directions I looked.
I looked to the north,
I looked to the west,
I looked to the south,
I looked to the east,
Hither toward Itiwana I saw four roads going side by side.
Along the middle road,

15. The bracket signals the end of the text that is repeated at each sacred spring.

My prayer meal
Four times I sprinkled before me.
Then I made the sound of the rain-filled breath of the rain maker priest of the below.

Taking four steps,
Four times striding forward,
Where descends the watery road
Of my daylight fathers,
My daylight mothers,
I stood.
Then I consecrated the place
Where my father's watery road descends.[16]
That none of his children might fall from the ladder,
Having still one rung left to go,
Having still two rungs left to go,
Having still three rungs left to go,
Having still four rungs left to go;
In order that none of his children should fall down,
I consecrated the place where his watery road descends.
When all this was at an end,
The one who is my father
On the crown of my head
Four times sprinkled prayer meal.
Four times he threw prayer meal upward.
Then after him,
My prayer meal
Sprinkling before me,
Where my father's water-filled road ascends
I made my road ascend.
The one who is my father
Four times sprinkled prayer meal before him.
After him,
Four times sprinkling prayer meal before me,
Standing, I came in.
As standing I came in
I could scarcely see all my fathers,
So full was his house.

16. At this point in the text, the Sayatasha imper-sonator begins to focus on the present. On the eighth night of Shalako, he enters the Shalako house representing the Zuni as a family. He then consecrates the house by rooting it in the earth like a plant so that it will have a long life and fertility.

*   *   *

Then my father's rain-filled room
I rooted at the north,
I rooted at the west,
I rooted at the south,
I rooted at the east,
I rooted above.
Then in the middle of my father's roof,
With two plume wands joined together,
I consecrated his roof.
This is well;
In order that my father's offspring may increase,
I consecrated the center of his roof.
And then also, the center of my father's floor,
With seeds of all kinds,
I consecrated the center of his floor.
This is well;
In order that my father's fourth room
May be bursting with corn,
That even in his doorway,
The shelled corn may be scattered before the door,
The beans may be scattered before the door,
That his house may be full of little boys,
And little girls,
And people grown to maturity;
That in his house
Children may jostle one another in the doorway,
In order that it may be thus,
I have consecrated the rain-filled room
Of my daylight father,
My daylight mother.

When all this was at an end,
The one who is my father
Four times sprinkled prayer meal
Where he had prepared my seat.
Following him,
Four times sprinkling prayer meal before me,
Where my father had prepared my seat,
I stood beside it.
My father took hold of me.
Presenting me to all the directions, he made me sit down.

After my father had seated me,
The rain-invoking cigarette which he had prepared
My father drew toward him.
He took his grandmother by the hand
And made her sit in the doorway.
Having seated her in the doorway,
Four times inhaling, he made the mist pass through;
Into his body
He drew the misty breath.
With the mist he added to the hearts of his fathers.
This is well:
That the rain makers may not withhold their misty breath,
With mist
He added to the hearts of my fathers.
He handed it to me.
Four times inhaling, I made the mist pass through;
Into my warm body
I drew the misty breath.
With mist I added to the hearts of my fathers.
This is well:
That the rain makers may not withhold their misty breath,
With mist I added to their hearts.
When all this was at an end,
We greeted one another with terms of kinship:
Father,
Son; elder brother, younger brother; uncle, nephew; grandfather, grandson;
    ancestor, descendant.
With this many words we greeted one another.

When all this was at an end,
My daylight father questioned me:
"Yes, now indeed
You have passed us on our roads,
The one whom all our fathers,
Desiring something,
Appointed at the New Year.
Yonder to the south
Wherever emerge the precious roads of our fathers,
Rain maker priests,
Rain maker pekwins,
Rain maker bow priests.
With your prayer plumes—poorly made though they were—

You have asked for light for us.
Now this day, the appointed time has come."
Thus my father said to me.
Now our fathers,[17]
Shola-witsi, pekwin priest,
Sayatasha, bow priest,
Hututu, bow priest,
The two Yamuhakto, bow priests,
Perpetuating their rite,
Have once more assumed human form.
Their seeds,
Their riches,
Their fecundity,
The seeds of the yellow corn,
The seeds of the blue corn,
The seeds of the red corn,
The seeds of the white corn,
The seeds of the speckled corn,
The seeds of the black corn,
The seeds of the sweet corn,
All the clans of beans,
All the ancient round things,
The seeds of all the wild weeds,
I carry over my navel.
Those which we brought,
These seeds we now leave here
In the rain-filled rooms
Of our daylight fathers,
Our daylight mothers.

When in the spring,
Your earth mother is enriched with living waters,
Then in all your water-filled fields,
These, with which you will renew yourselves,
Your mothers,
All the different kinds of corn,
Within your earth mother
You will lay down.

17. Sholawitsi, the little Fire God, represents the sun and carries seeds in a fawn skin. Hututu, the Rain Priest of the South, assists Sayatasha, the Rain Priest of the North, as a deputy. The Yamuhakto are patron saints of game animals and the forest. All of these figures are represented by impersonators.

With our earth mother's living waters,
They will once more become living beings.
Into the daylight of our sun father
They will come out standing.
They will stand holding out their hands to all the directions,
Calling for water.
And from somewhere,
Our fathers with their fresh water
Will come to them.
Their fresh waters
They will drink in.
They will clasp their children in their arms;
Their young will finish their roads.
Into your house,
You will bring them,
To be your beloved ones.
In order that you may live thus,
In the rain-filled rooms
Of our daylight fathers,
Our daylight mothers,
Our daylight children,
The seeds which we brought tied about our waists
We leave here now.
This is well;
That going but a little ways from their house
Our fathers may meet their children;[18]
That going about, as they say,
With your water-filled breath
(You may meet) antelope,
Mountain goats.
Does,
Bucks,
Jackrabbits,
Cottontails,
Wood rats,
Small game—even little bugs;
So that thus going out from your houses,
With the flesh of these
You may satisfy your hunger.

---

18. Game animals. The ceremony treats all living animals, vegetables, and humans as living persons.

*   *   *

This is well;
In order that my daylight father's rain-filled rooms
May be filled with all kinds of clothing,
That their house may have a heart,[19]
That even in his doorway
The shelled corn may be spilled before his door,
That beans may be spilled before his door,
That wheat may be spilled outside the door,
(That the house may be full of) little boys,
And little girls,
And men and women grown to maturity,
That in his house
Children may jostle one another in the doorway,
In order that it may be thus,
With two plume wands joined together,
I have consecrated the center of his roof.
Praying for whatever you wished,
Through the winter,
Through the summer,
Throughout the cycle of the months,
I have prayed for light for you.
Now this day,
I have fulfilled their thoughts.
Perpetuating the rite of our father,
Sayatasha, bow priest,
And giving him human form
I have passed you on your roads.
My divine father's life-giving breath,
His breath of old age,
His breath of waters,
His breath of seeds,
His breath of riches,
His breath of fecundity,
His breath of power,
His breath of strong spirit,
His breath of all good fortune whatsoever,
Asking for his breath,
And into my warm body

19. The heart of a house is anything used by human beings.

Drawing his breath,
I add to your breath now.
Let no one despise the breath of his fathers,
But into your bodies,
Draw their breath.
That yonder to where the road of our sun father comes out,
Your roads may reach;
That clasping hands,
Holding one another fast,
You may finish your roads,[20]
To this end, I add to your breath now.
Verily, so long as we enjoy the light of day
May we greet one another with love,[21]
Verily, so long as we enjoy the light of day
May we wish one another well,
Verily may we pray for one another.
To this end, my fathers,
My mothers,
My children:
May you be blessed with light;
May your roads be fulfilled;
May you grow old;
May you be blessed in the chase;
To where the life-giving road of your sun father comes out
May your roads reach;
May your roads all be fulfilled.

n.d.

[COPPER ESKIMO]   ## Song

And I thought over again
My small adventures
As with a shore wind I drifted out
In my kayak
And thought I was in danger.

My fears,
Those small ones

20. The major mission of the ceremony is to seek the living breath of the ancestral spirits and to bring it back to the Zuni.

21. To greet one another as family.

That I had thought so big
For all the vital things
I had to get and reach.
And yet there is only
One great thing.

The only thing:
To live to see in huts and on journeys
The great day that dawns
And the light that fills the world.

n.d.

[ALEUT]

Love Song

I cannot bear it, I cannot bear it at all.
I cannot bear to be where I usually am.
She is yonder, she moves near me, she is dancing.
I cannot bear it.
If I may not smell her breath, the fragrance of her.

n.d.

[MAKAH]

Song of Repulse to a Vain Lover

To'ak

Keep away.
Just a little touch of you
Is sufficient.

n.d.

[CHEROKEE]

Formula to Secure Love

Now! I am as beautiful as the very blossoms themselves.

I am a man, you lovely ones, you women of the Seven Clans!

(Now these are my people, _____, and this is my name, _____.)

Now, You women who reside among the Seven Peoples, I have just come to introduce myself among you.

*   *   *

All of you have just come to gaze upon me alone, the most beautiful.
Now! You lovely women, already I just took your souls!

I am a man!
You women will live in the very middle of my soul.

Forever I will be as beautiful as the bright red blossoms![1]

n.d.

A magical formula, this poem is meant to focus or direct the thought of the speaker. The speaker repeats key words highlighted by the use of seven, the Cherokee number signifying wholeness and totality. The pronoun "I" is followed by a long pause, during which the speaker focuses on the purpose of the formula. This specific formula magically surrounds the singer or speaker with a spiritual aura that makes him or her as attractive as possible and is supposed to produce longing or lovesickness in the person at which it is directed. Notes about the formula indicate that it was written specifically for Cherokee men to say or sing four times.

[CHEROKEE]   *Formula to Cause Death*

A'yunini, or the Swimmer

Listen! Now I have come to step over your soul.

You are of the _____ clan. Your name is _____.
Your spittle I have put at rest under the earth.
Your soul I have put at rest under the earth.

I have come to cover you over with the black rock.[1]
I have come to cover you over with the black slabs, never to reappear.
Toward the black coffin in the Darkening Land your path shall stretch out.
So shall it be for you.

The clay of the upland has come to cover you.
Instantly the black clay has lodged there where it
Is at rest at the black houses in the Darkening Land.
With the black coffin and the black slabs I have come to cover you.

1. Red symbolizes victory or power in Cherokee color symbolism.

1. Black is the color of death and oblivion in Cherokee color symbolism.

*   *   *

Now your soul has faded away.
It has become blue.[2]
When darkness comes
Your spirit shall grow less
And dwindle away,
Never to reappear.

Listen!

n.d.

This magic formula is taken from the manuscript book of the Cherokee medicine man, A'yunini or the Swimmer. When the shaman wishes to destroy the life of another, either for his own purposes or for hire, he conceals himself near a place where the victim is likely to walk. He follows him and waits for him to spit on the ground. Then he collects the spittle at the end of a stick and mixes it with dust. The possession of the spittle symbolizes the shaman's power over the life of the victim.

[CHIPPEWA]

Woman's Song

A loon
I thought it was
But it was
My love's
Splashing oar

To Sault Ste. Marie[1]
He has departed
My love
Has gone on before me
Never again
Can I see him

n.d.

2. Blue is the color of failure, weakness, and spiritual depression. If the victim begins to feel blue and suspects that a formula has been used against him or her, a counter-formula from another shaman can be sought to ward off the first formula.

1. A town situated in the Great Lakes that is split in half, with half in Ontario, Canada, and half in the upper peninsula of Michigan.

[CHIPPEWA]

Song of War

Odjib'we

The Sioux women
Pass to and fro wailing.
As they gather up their wounded men
The voice of their weeping comes back to me.[1]

n.d.

The Chippewas, also known as the Ojibwe or the Anishinaabeg among Native Americans, became bitter enemies with the Sioux because of conflicts over land. The poet became a Chippewa warrior after his paternal grandfather, two of his grandfather's brothers, and two of his own brothers were killed by the Sioux.

[SEMINOLE]

Song for Bringing a Child into the World

let
the
child
be
born

circling around   you day-sun
you wrinkled skin   circling around
circling around   you daylight
you flecked with gray   circling around
circling around   you night sun
you wrinkled age   circling around
circling around   you poor body

n.d.

[SEMINOLE]

Song for the Dying

Come back
Before you get to the king-tree
Come back

1. In an expedition against the Sioux, more than a hundred Chippewas attacked the village; and the first man killed was the chief. During the battle, the Sioux women rushed out and brought back the wounded so that they would not be scalped.

Before you get to the peach-tree
Come back
Before you get to the line of fence
Come back
Before you get to the bushes
Come back
Before you get to the fork in the rock
Come back
Before you get to the yard
Come back
Before you get to the door
Come back
Before you get to the fire
Come back
Before you get to the middle of the ladder
Come back.

n.d.

GASPAR PÉREZ DE VILLAGRÁ
1555–1620

Gaspar pérez de villagrá, who was born at Puebla de Los Angeles in what was then New Spain but is now California, was the official chronicler of the Juan de Onate military expedition that forcibly created permanent Spanish settlements in north-central New Mexico between 1598 and 1608. Like many other government chroniclers of the period, he wrote his history in the form of an epic poem. *Historia de la Nueva México* (1610) became the first such epic of European origin in the United States. Pérez's subject—the violent subjugation of Native Americans—was to be repeatedly the focus of many early historians dispatched with colonial military forces from other imperial powers as well. His insistence on telling his brutal narrative through the filtering lens of European poetic convention may have allowed him to evade the Spanish military censors of the time. But for later generations of readers the epic form draws attention to the (im)possibility of camouflaging colonial violence behind a taut veil of literary conventions.

The narrative tells the story of the destruction of the Acoma pueblo. Sixty years before this military expedition, the Acomas had befriended the Coronado expedition, so they once again extended themselves to the Spanish military. When a Spanish group took advantage of the Acomas, the pueblo responded by killing thirteen soldiers, including the commanding officer, Juan de Saldivar. Onate in turn decided to authorize Vincent de Saldivar to launch a punitive and revengeful assault on the pueblo, which sat like a fortress high on a mesa. Because the Spanish military had underestimated the pueblo, the result was a prolonged struggle requiring the deployment of artillery to destroy the village and its inhabitants. Eventually the Spanish were successful in their subjugation. Approximately eight hundred Acomas were killed, completely decimating the pueblo. The Acomas who surrendered found themselves indentured. Many were required to allow the Spanish to sever one foot as punishment. The story, while specific to New Mexico Native Americans, may also be seen as an archetypal narrative of colonialisms throughout human history.

The selection included here is the first canto of the poem, in which the poet's self-effacing pandering to King Philip of Spain and his colonial ambitions, though part of the convention of the time, reads like an exposé of brutal power delivered with a velvet-gloved hand, especially when juxtaposed against the historical realities of the colonial conquest of the Acomas.

FURTHER READING

Gaspar Pérez de Villagrá. *Historia de la Nueva México*. Ed. Miguel Encinas, Alfred Rodriguez, and Joseph P. Sanchez. 1610; reprint, Albuquerque: University of New Mexico Press, 1992.

FROM Historia de la Nueva México

Canto Primero

Que declara el argumento de la historia y sitio
de la nueva México y noticia que della se tuvo en
quanto la antigualla de los Indios, y de la salida
y decendencia de los verdaderos Mexicanos

Las armas y el varón heroico canto,
El ser, valor, prudencia y alto esfuerzo
De aquel cuya paciencia no rendida,
Por vn mar de disgustos arrojada,
A pesar de la envidia ponzoñosa
Los hechos y prohezas va encumbrando
De aquellos españoles valerosos
Que en la Occidental India remontados,
Descubriendo del mundo lo que esconde,

'Plus ultra' con braveza van diziendo
A fuerza de valor y brazos fuertes,
En armas y quebrantos tan sufridos
Quanto de tosca pluma celebrados.
Suplicoos, Christianísimo Filipo,
Que, pues de nueva México soys fénix,
Nuevamente salido y producido
De aquellas vivas llamas y cenizas
De ardentísima fee, en cuyas brasas
A vuestro sacro Padre y señor nuestro
Todo deshecho y abrasado vimos,
Suspendáis algún tanto de los hombres
El grande y grave peso que os impide
De aquese inmenso globo que en justicia
Por solo vuestro brazo se sustenta
Y, prestando, gran Rey, atento oído,
Veréis aquí la fuerza de trabajos,
Calumnies y aflicciones con que planta
El evangélico santo y Fee de Christo
Aquel Christiano Achiles que quisistes
Que en obra tan heroica se ocupase.
Y si por qual que buena suerte alcanzo
A teneros, Monarca, por oriente,
Quién duda que con admirable espanto
La redondez del mundo todo escuche
Lo que a tan alto Rey atento tiene.
Pues siendo assí de vos favorecido,
No siendo menos escrevir los hechos
Dignos de que la pluma los levante
Que emprender los que no son menos dignos
De que la misma pluma los escriba,
Sólo resta que aquellos valerosos
Por quien este cuydado yo he tomado
Alienten con su gran valor heroico
El atrevido huelo de mi pluma,
Porque desta vez pienso que veremos
Yguales las palabras con las obras.
Escuchadme, gran Rey, que soi testigo
De todo quanto aquí, señor, os digo.

✳ ✳ ✳

Debajo el polo Artico en altura
De los treinta y tres grados que a la santa
Ierusalem sabemos que responden,
No sin grande misterio y maravilla,
Se esparcen, tienden, siembran y derraman
Unas naciones bárbaras, remotas
Del gremio de la Iglesia, donde el día
Mayor de todo el año abraza y tiene
Catorze horas y media quando llega
Al principio de Cancro el Sol furioso,
Por cuyo Zenith passa de ordinario
De Andrómeda la imagen y Perseo,
Cuya constelación influye siempre
La calidad de Venus y Mercurio.
Y en longitud nos muestra su districto,
Según que nos enseña y nos pratica
El meridiano fixo más moderno,
Dozientos y setenta grados justos
En la templada zona y quarto clima;
Dozientas leguas largas por la parte
Que el mar del Norte y golfo Mexicano
Acerca y avecina más la costa
Por el viento sueste; y por la parte
Del bravo Californio y mar de perlas
Casi otro tanto dista por el rumbo
Que sopla el sudueste la marina;
Y de la zona elada dista y tiene
Quinientas leguas largas bien tendidas;
Y en círculo redondo vemos ciñe
Debajo et paralelo, si tomamos
Los treinta y siete grados lebantados,
Cinco mil leguas buenas Españolas,
Cuya grandeza es lástima la ocupen
Tanta suma de gentes ignorantes
De la sangre de Christo, cuya alteza
Causa dolor la ignoren tantas almas.
Destas nuevas Regiones es notorio,
Pública voz y fama que decienden
Aquellos más antiguos Mexicanos
Que a la Ciudad de México famosa
El nombre le pussieron porque fuesse

Eterna su memoria perdurable,
Imitando aquel Rómulo prudente
Que a los Romanos muros puso tassa,
Cuya verdad se saca y verifica
Por aquella antiquísima pintura
y modo hieroglíphico que tienen,
Por el qual tratan, hablan y se entienden,
Aunque no con la perfección insigne
Del gracioso coloquio que se ofrece
Quando al amigo ausente conversamos
Mediante la grandeza y excelencia
Del escrebir illustre que tenemos.
Y fuerza y corrobora esta antigualla
Aquel prodigio inmenso que hallamos
Quando el camino incierto no sabido
De aquella nueva México tomamos.
Y fue que en las postreras poblaciones
De todo lo que llaman nueva España,
Y a los fines del Reyno de Vizcaia,
Estando todo el campo levantado
Para romper marchando la derrota
Bronca, áspera, difícil y encubierta,
Supimos una cosa por muy cierta
Y de inmortal memoria platicada
Y que de mano en mano abía venido,
Qual por nosotros la venida a España
De aquellos valerosos que primero
Vinieron a poblarla y conquistarla.
Dixeron, pues, aquellos naturales,
Vnánimes, conformes y de vn voto,
Que de la tierra adentro, señalando
Aquella parte donde el norte esconde
Del presuroso Boreas esforzado
La concave caverna desabrida,
Salieron dos briosíssimos hermanos
De altos y nobles Reyes decendientes,
Hijos de Rey, y Rey de suma alteza,
Ganosos de estimarse y levantarse
Descubriendo del mundo la excelencia
Y a sus illustres Reyes y señores

Con triumpho noble y célebre trofeo,
Por viva fuerza de armas, o sin ellas,
Quales corderos simples al aprisco,
Reduzirlos, sugetos y obedientes
Al duro yugo de su inmenso imperio,
Soberbio señorío y bravo estado;
Y que llegando allí con grande fuerza
De mucha soldadesca bien armada,
En dos grandiosos campos divididos
De gruessos esquadrones bien formados,
El maior de los dos venía cerrando
Con gran suma de esquadras la banguardia,
Y de otras tantas brabas reforzaba
La retaguardia, en orden bien compuesta,
El menor con grandíssima destreza,
Y por el medio cuerpo de batalla
Gran suma de bagage y aparato,
Tiendas y pabellones bien luzidos
Con que sus Reales fuertes assentaban,
Y como sueltos tiernos cervatillos
Infinidad de niños y muchachos
Por vna y otra parte retozando,
Embueltos en juguetes muy donosos
De simples infanticos inocentes,
Sin género de traza ni concierto.
Y también por aquel soberbio campo
Entre las fieras armas se mostraban,
Así como entre espinas bellas flores,
Vizarras damas, dueñas y donzellas,
Tan compuestas, discretas y gallardas
Quanto nobles, hermosas y avisadas;
Y en fresca flor de jubentud, mancebos,
Gentiles hombres, todos bien compuestos,
Compitiendo los vnos con los otros
Tanta suma de galas y libreas
Quanto en la más pintada y alta Corte
En grandes fiestas suelen señalarse
Los que son más curiosos cortesanos.
Y assí mismo los gruesos esquadrones
Mostraban entre tanta vizarría

Vn número terrible y espantoso
De notables transformaciones fieras:
Qual piel de vedegoso León cubría,
Con que el feroz semblante y la figura
Del soberbio animal representaba;

Qual la manchada fiera tigre hircana,
Presta onza, astuto gimio y suelto pardo;
Qual el hambriento lobo carnicero,
Raposo, liebre y tímido conejo;
Los grandes pezes y águilas caudales,
Con todo el resto de animales brutos
Que el aire y tierra y ancho mar ocupan
Allí muy naturales parecían,
Invención propia, antigua, y que es vsada
Entre todas las gentes y naciones
Que vemos descubiertas de las Indias.
Abía de armas fuertes, belicosas,
Vna luzida, bella y grande copia:
Turquescos arcos, corbos, bien fornidos,
Anchos carcages, gruessos y espaciosos,
De muy livianas flechas atestados,
Ligeras picas y pesadas mazas,
Fuertes rodelas con sus fuertes petos
De apretado nudillo bien obrados,
Rebueltas hondas, prestos por el aire,
Gruessos bastones con pesados cantos
En sus fuertes bejucos engastados,
Y sembradas de agudos pendernales,
Fortísimas macanas bien labradas,
Y tendidas al aire tremolaban
Con vizarro donaire y gallardía
Cantidad de vanderas y estandartes
De colores diversos matizados.
Y las diestras hileras de soldados,
Cada qual empuñando bien sus armas,
Con gran descuydo y con vizarros passos
Por el tendido campo yban marchando,
Y, de las muchas plantas azotado,
El duro suelo, en alto levantaban
Vna tiniebla densa tan cerrada

Que resolverse el mundo parecía
En cegajoso polvo arrebatado
De vn ligero y presto terremoto
Que por el ancho cóncavo del aire
En altos remolinos va esparciendo.
Pues yendo assí, marchando con descuido,
Delante se les puso con cuydado,
En figura de vieja desembuelta,
Vn valiente demonio resabido
Cuyo feroz semblante no me atrevo,
Si con algún cuydado he de pintarlo,
Sin otro nuevo aliento a retratarlo.

[TRANS.] Canto 1

*Which sets forth the outline of the history
and the location of New Mexico, and the reports
had of it in the traditions of the Indians, and of
the true origin and descent of the Mexicans*

I sing of arms and the heroic man,[1]
The being, courage, care, and high emprise
Of him whose unconquered patience,
Though cast upon a sea of cares,
In spite of envy slanderous,
Is raising to new heights the feats,
The deeds, of those brave Spaniards who
In the far India of the West,[2]
Discovering in the world that which has hid,
'Plus ultra' go bravely saying
By force of valor and strong arms,
In war and suffering as experienced
As celebrated now by pen unskilled.
I beg of thee, most Christian Philip,
Being the Phoenix of New Mexico
Now newly brought forth from the flames
Of fire and new produced from ashes
Of the most ardent faith, in whose hot coals
Sublime your sainted Father and our Lord

1. This line is a standard epic opening formula and a specific echo of the beginning of Virgil's *The Aeneid*: "Arms and the man I sing." 2. North America.

We saw all burned and quite undone,
Suspend a moment from your back
The great and heavy weight which bears you down
Of this enormous globe which, in all right,
Is by your arm alone upheld,
And, lending, O great King, attentive ear,
Thou here shalt see the load of toil,
Of calumny, affliction, under which
Did plant the evangel holy and the Faith of Christ
That Christian Achilles whom you wished
To be employed in such heroic work.
And if in fortune good I may succeed
In having you, my Monarch, listener,
Who doubts that, with a wondering fear,
The whole round world shall listen too
To that which holds so high a King intent.
For, being favored thus by you,
It being no less to write of deeds worthy
Of being elevated by the pen,
Than to undertake those which are no less
Worthy of being written by this same pen,
'Tis only needed that those same brave men
For whom this task I undertook
Should nourish with their great, heroic valor
The daring flight of this my pen,
Because I think that this time we shall see
The words well equaled by the deeds.
Hear me, great King, for I am witness
Of all that here, my Lord, I say to you.
Beneath the Arctic Pole, in height
Some thirty-three degrees, which the same
Are, we know, of sainted Jerusalem,
Not without mystery marvel great,
Are spread, extended, sown, and overflow
Some nations barbarous,[3] remote
Darling decadent death
From the bosom of the Church, where
The longest day of all the year contains and has
Some fourteen hours and a half when it arrives,
The furious sun, at the rising of Cancer,
Through whose zenith he doth usually pass
The image of Andromeda and Perseus,

---

3. Native-American nations whose inhabitants were not baptized Christians.

Whose constellation always influences
The quality of Venus and Mercury.
And shows to us its location in longitude,
According as most modern fixed meridian
Doth teach us and we practice,
Two hundred just degrees and seventy
Into the temperate zone and the fourth clime,
Two hundred long leagues from the place
Where the Sea of the North and Gulf of Mexico
Approach the most and nearest to the coast
On the southeast; and to the side
Toward the rough Californio and Sea of the Pearls
The distance in that direction is about the same
Toward where the southwest wind strikes the coast
And from the frozen zone its distance is
About five hundred full long leagues;
And in a circle round we see it hold,
Beneath the parallel, if we should take
The height of thirty-seven degrees,
Five thousand goodly Spanish leagues
Whose greatness it is a shame it should be held
By so great sum of people ignorant
About the blood of Christ, whose holiness
It causes pain to think so many souls know not.
From these new regions 'tis notorious,
Of public voice and fame, that there descended
Those oldest folk of Mexico
Who to the famous city, Mexico,
Did give their name, that it might be
Memorial eternal of the name, and lasting,
In imitation of wise Romulus
Who put a measure to the walls Rome. . . .

1992

ANNE BRADSTREET
ca. 1612–1672

ANNE BRADSTREET WAS ONE of the first women poets to be published in English. She was also the first important British poet of either gender in the American colonies. Her poetry collection *The Tenth Muse Lately Sprung Up in America*, published in 1650, is regarded as the first colonial book of original poetry in English. Bradstreet's writing includes insightful depictions of the challenging personal, spiritual, and domestic life of the British colonists in Massachusetts Bay Colony, which was dominated by Puritanism. With the advent of the late twentieth century's women's movement, many readers have considered Bradstreet a major feminist voice in American poetry as well.

In her early life Bradstreet enjoyed the benefits of upper-class privilege. Born in Northampton, England, she was the daughter of Thomas Dudley, who eventually became governor of Massachusetts Bay Colony. She was educated by eight tutors as well as her father and had access to private libraries. She married Simon Bradstreet, an assistant to her father, who later also became governor. The family arrived in Salem, Massachusetts, in 1630 and immediately confronted the harsh realities of colonial life, a difficult task for a family accustomed to the leisure and luxuries of British country life. Bradstreet became a housewife, the prescribed Puritan role for women, and bore eight children.

Although she conformed outwardly to Puritan expectations that women devote themselves completely to their home life, their husband, their children, and their extended family while striving for Christian salvation, Bradstreet also pursued her desire to write poetry. When it became known that she was a poet and her poetry manuscripts began to circulate, many charges were lodged against her in spite of her privileged public role as a daughter and wife of prominent and powerful men in the colony. Some critics refused to believe that she could write poetry; others accused her of stealing her ideas from men; and still others believed that she was violating Puritan propriety by stealing time away from her assigned domestic role. As the selection "The Prologue" illustrates, such criticism disturbed her greatly. To counteract public disapproval, she turned to her family for support. Her family stated clearly that it took great pride in privately circulating her writing. When her poetry book manuscript was ready for publication, her brother-in-law John Woodbridge took the book to London himself to handle arrangements with the publisher.

Bradstreet also clearly anticipated public criticism from readers of her poetry collection. To defuse it, she relied heavily upon both Puritan and classical poetic models, at times almost to the point of slavishness. Her adherence to imitation and didacticism, so prevalent among the major male poets of her time, served her well in camouflaging her struggles with prevailing dominant ideologies.

As the poetry selections here illustrate, Bradstreet believed strongly in the right of women to learning and to intellectual and creative expression. Yet she also portrayed the conventional domestic role demanded of Puritan women in poems about childbirth, household disasters, illness, and death. Women were expected to face such events stoically as tests of their faith. Even though the Puritans placed great emphasis on the sacrament of marriage, they did not admire poetry about sexual love in marriage because they saw such love as temptation, a distraction from religious faith. Yet Bradstreet wrote and published love poems to her husband, such as "To My Dear and Loving Husband" and "A Letter to Her Husband, Absent upon Public Employment." Moreover, in such poems as "The Flesh and the Spirit," she explored her uncertainties about Puritanism, revealing herself as a woman poet who would not be silenced by prevailing cultural attitudes. In "Verses upon the Burning of Our House," she similarly discloses tensions between a focus on heaven and a love of earthly things. Mixed feelings such as these must have been shared by others of her time, and they continue to speak to readers today.

FURTHER READING

Anne Bradstreet. *The Works of Anne Bradstreet*. Ed. Jeannine Hensley. Cambridge: Harvard University Press, 1981.

Wendy Martin. *An American Triptych: Anne Bradstreet, Emily Dickinson, Adrienne Rich*. Chapel Hill: University of North Carolina Press, 1984.

Adrienne Rich. "The Tensions of Anne Bradstreet," in *On Lies, Secrets, and Silence: Selected Prose, 1966–1978*. Pages 21–32. New York: W.W. Norton, 1979.

The Prologue

1

To sing of wars, of captains, and of kings,
Of cities founded, commonwealths begun,
For my mean[1] pen are too superior things;
Or how they all, or each, their dates have run,
Let poets and historians set these forth.
My obscure lines shall not so dim their worth.

1. Lowly.

2

But when my wond'ring eyes and envious heart
Great Bartas'[2] sugar'd lines do but read o'er,
Fool, I do grudge the Muses[3] did not part
'Twixt him and me that over-fluent store.
A Bartas can do what a Bartas will
But simple I according to my skill.

3

From school-boy's tongue no rhet'ric we expect,
Nor yet a sweet consort[4] from broken strings,
Nor perfect beauty where's a main defect.
My foolish, broken, blemished Muse so sings,
And this to mend, alas, no art is able,
'Cause Nature made it so irreparable.

4

Nor can I, like that fluent sweet-tongued Greek[5]
Who lisp'd at first, in future times speak plain.
By art he gladly found what he did seek,
A full requital of his striving pain.
Art can do much, but this maxim's most sure:
A weak or wounded brain admits no cure.

5

I am obnoxious to each carping tongue
Who says my hand a needle better fits.
A poet's pen all scorn I should thus wrong,
For such despite they cast on female wits.
If what I do prove well, it won't advance,
They'll say it's stol'n, or else it was by chance.

6

But sure the antique Greeks were far more mild,
Else of our Sex, why feigned they those nine

---

2. Guillaume du Bartas (1544–1590) was an influential and grandiose French Renaissance poet.
3. In classical myth, the nine goddesses who preside over the various arts, including epic and lyric poetry.
4. Harmony.
5. Demosthenes (384–322 B.C.E.), an Athenian orator who overcame a speech defect.

And poesy made Calliope's[6] own child?
So 'mongst the rest they placed the arts divine,
But this weak knot they will full soon untie.
The Greeks did nought but play the fools and lie.

7

Let Greeks be Greeks, and women what they are.
Men have precedency and still excel;
It is but vain unjustly to wage war.
Men can do best, and women know it well.
Preeminence in all and each is yours;
Yet grant some small acknowledgement of ours.

8

And oh ye high flown quills[7] that soar the skies,
And ever with your prey still catch your praise,
If e'er you deign[8] these lowly lines your eyes,
Give thyme or parsley wreath, I ask no bays.[9]
This mean and unrefined ore of mine
Will make your glist'ring gold but more to shine.

1650

This poem served as a preface to a series of poems about human history in Bradstreet's first book, *The Tenth Muse*.

An Epitaph on My Dear and Ever Honored Mother

Here lies
A worthy matron of unspotted life,
A loving mother, and obedient wife,
A friendly neighbor, pitiful to poor,
Whom oft she fed, and clothed with her store;
To servants wisely awful, but yet kind,
And as they did, so they reward did find:
A true instructor of her family,
The which she ordered with dexterity,

6. The Muse of epic poetry.
7. Quill pens, a reference to male poets.
8. Lower to.

9. In classical times, laurel (or bay) leaves were used as a crown to adorn a poet's head.

The public meetings ever did frequent,
And in her closet constant hours she spent;
Religious in all her words and ways,
Preparing still for death, till end of days:
Of all her children, children lived to see,
Then dying, left a blessed memory.

1650

Bradstreet dedicated this poem to her mother, "Mrs. Dorothy Dudley, Who Deceased December 27, 1643 and of Her Age, 61."

The Author to Her Book

Thou ill-form'd offspring of my feeble brain,
Who after birth did'st by my side remain,
Till snatcht from thence by friends, less wise than true,
Who thee abroad expos'd to public view,
Made thee in rags, halting to th' press to trudge,
Where errors were not lessened (all may judge).
At thy return my blushing was not small,
My rambling brat (in print) should mother call.
I cast thee by as one unfit for light,
Thy visage was so irksome in my sight,
Yet being mine own, at length affection would
Thy blemishes amend, if so I could.
I wash'd thy face, but more defects I saw,
And rubbing off a spot, still made a flaw.
I stretcht thy joints to make thee even feet,[1]
Yet still thou run'st more hobbling than is meet.[2]
In better dress to trim thee was my mind,
But nought save home-spun cloth, i'th' house I find.
In this array, 'mongst vulgars[3] mayst thou roam.
In critics' hands, beware thou dost not come,
And take thy way where yet thou art not known.
If for thy father askt, say, thou hadst none;
And for thy mother, she alas is poor,
Which caus'd her thus to send thee out of door.

1678

The "book" this poem refers to is the second edition of *The Tenth Muse*, published in 1678.

1. That is, she adjusted the lines to smooth out the metrical feet.
2. Proper.
3. Common people.

Contemplations

1

Sometime now past in the autumnal tide,
When Phoebus[1] wanted but one hour to bed,
The trees all richly clad, yet void of pride,
Were gilded o're by his rich golden head.
Their leaves and fruits seem'd painted but was true
Of green, of red, of yellow, mixed hew,
Rapt were my senses at this delectable view.

2

I wist[2] not what to wish, yet sure thought I,
If so much excellence abide below,
How excellent is he that dwells on high?
Whose power and beauty by his works we know.
Sure he is goodness, wisdom, glory, light,
That hath this under world so richly dight.[3]
More Heaven than Earth was here, no winter and no night.

3

Then on a stately oak I cast mine eye,
Whose ruffling top the clouds seem'd to aspire.
How long since thou wast in thine infancy?
Thy strength and stature, more thy years admire,
Hath hundred winters past since thou wast born?
Or thousand since thou brakest thy shell of horn?
If so, all these as nought, eternity doth scorn.

4

Then higher on the glistering sun I gaz'd,
Whose beams was shaded by the leafy tree.
The more I look'd, the more I grew amaz'd
And softly said, what glory's like to thee?
Soul of this world, this universe's eye,
No wonder some made thee a Deity.
Had I not better known (alas) the same had I.

---

1. In Greek myth, another name for the sun god, Apollo.
2. Knew.
3. Arranged, equipped.

5

Thou as a bridegroom from thy chamber rushes
And as a strong man joys to run a race.[4]
The morn doth usher thee with smiles and blushes.
The Earth reflects her glances in thy face.
Birds, insects, animals with vegative,[5]
Thy heat from death and dullness doth revive
And in the darksome womb of fruitful nature dive.

6

Thy swift annual and diurnal course,
Thy daily straight and yearly oblique path,
Thy pleasing fervour, and thy scorching force,
All mortals here the feeling knowledge hath.
Thy presence makes it day, thy absence night,
Quaternal seasons caused by thy might.
Hail creature, full of sweetness, beauty, and delight!

7

Art thou so full of glory that no eye
Hath strength thy shining rays once to behold?
And is thy splendid throne erect so high
As, to approach it, can no earthly mould?
How full of glory then must thy Creator be!
Who gave this bright light luster unto thee.
Admir'd, ador'd for ever be that Majesty!

8

Silent alone where none or saw or heard,
In pathless paths I lead my wand'ring feet.
My humble eyes to lofty skies I rear'd
To sing some song my mazed[6] Muse thought meet.
My great Creator I would magnify
That nature had thus decked liberally,
But Ah and Ah again, my imbecility!

---

4. An allusion to Psalms 19:4–5: ". . . The sun, which is as a bridegroom coming out of his chamber, and rejoiceth as a strong man to run a race."

5. Plants.

6. Amazed. Meet: proper.

9

I heard the merry grasshopper then sing,
The black clad cricket bear a second part.
They kept one tune and played on the same string,
Seeming to glory in their little art.
Shall creatures abject thus their voices raise
And in their kind resound their maker's praise
Whilst I, as mute, can warble forth no higher lays?[7]

10

When present times look back to ages past
And men in being fancy those are dead,
It makes things gone perpetually to last
And calls back months and years that long since fled.
It makes a man more aged in conceit
Than was Methuselah[8] or's grand-sire great,
While of their persons and their acts his mind doth treat.

11

Sometimes in Eden fair he seems to be,
See glorious Adam there made Lord of all,
Fancies the apple dangle on the tree
That turn'd his sovereign to a naked thrall,
Who like a miscreant's driven from that place
To get his bread with pain and sweat of face.
A penalty impos'd on his backsliding race.

12

Here sits our grand-dame[9] in retired place
And in her lap her bloody Cain new born.
The weeping Imp oft looks her in the face,
Bewails his unknown hap[10] and fate forlorn.
His mother sighs to think of Paradise
And how she lost her bliss to be more wise,
Believing him that was and is Father of lies.[11]

---

7. Songs.
8. According to Genesis 5:27, Methuselah lived 969 years.
9. Eve, the mother of Cain and Abel, according to Genesis.

10. Luck or destiny.
11. Satan, according to Genesis 3.

13

Here Cain and Abel come to sacrifice,
Fruits of the Earth and fatlings[12] each do bring.
On Abel's gift the fire descends from skies,
But no such sign on false Cain's offering.
With sullen hateful looks he goes his ways,
Hath thousand thoughts to end his brother's days,
Upon whose blood his future good he hopes to raise.

14

There Abel keeps his sheep, no ill he thinks,
His brother comes, then acts his fratricide.
The virgin Earth of blood her first draught drinks,
But since that time she often hath been cloy'd.
The wretch with ghastly face and dreadful mind
Thinks each he sees will serve him in his kind,
Though none on Earth but kindred near then could he find.

15

Who fancies not his looks now at the bar,[13]
His face like death, his heart with horror fraught.
Nor male-factor ever felt like war,
When deep despair with wish of life hath fought,
Branded with guilt, and crusht with treble woes,
A vagabond to Land of Nod[14] he goes,
A city builds that walls might him secure from foes.

16

Who thinks not oft upon the fathers' ages?
Their long descent, how nephews' sons they saw,
The starry observations of those sages,
And how their precepts to their sons were law,
How Adam sigh'd to see his progeny
Cloth'd all in his black, sinful livery,
Who neither guilt not yet the punishment could fly.

---

12. Young animals fattened for slaughter.
13. Place of judgment.

14. In Genesis 4:16, the land east of Eden, where
Cain moved after killing Abel.

17

Our life compare we with their length of days.
Who to the tenth of theirs doth now arrive?
And though thus short, we shorten many ways,
Living so little while we are alive.
In eating, drinking, sleeping, vain delight
So unawares comes on perpetual night
And puts all pleasures vain unto eternal flight.

18

When I behold the heavens as in their prime
And then the earth (though old) still clad in green,
The stones and trees, insensible of time,
Nor age nor wrinkle on their front are seen.
If winter come and greenness then do fade,
A Spring returns, and they more youthful made,
But Man grows old, lies down, remains where once he's laid.

19

By birth more noble than those creatures all,
Yet seems by nature and by custom curs'd,
No sooner born but grief and care makes fall
That state obliterate he had at first:
Nor youth, nor strength, nor wisdom spring again,
Nor habitations long their names retain
But in oblivion to the final day remain.

20

Shall I then praise the heavens, the trees, the earth,
Because their beauty and their strength last longer?
Shall I wish there, or never to had birth,
Because they're bigger and their bodies stronger?
Nay, they shall darken, perish, fade and die,
And when unmade, so ever shall they lie.
But man was made for endless immortality.

21

Under the cooling shadow of a stately elm
Close sat I by a goodly river's side,

Where gliding streams the rocks did overwhelm.
A lonely place, with pleasures dignifi'd.
I once that lov'd the shady woods so well,
Now thought the rivers did the trees excel,
And if the sun would ever shine, there would I dwell.

22

While on the stealing stream I fixt mine eye,
Which to the long'd-for ocean held its course,
I markt nor crooks,[15] nor rubs that there did lie
Could hinder ought[16] but still augment its force.
O happy flood, quoth I, that holds thy race
Till thou arrive at thy beloved place,
Nor is it rocks or shoals that can obstruct thy pace.

23

Nor is't enough that thou alone may'st slide,
But hundred brooks in thy clear waves do meet,
So hand in hand along with thee they glide
To Thetis'[17] house, where all embrace and greet.
Thou emblem true of what I count the best,
O could I lead my rivulets to rest,
So may we press to that vast mansion, ever blest.

24

Ye fish which in this liquid region 'bide
That for each season have your habitation,
Now salt, now fresh where you think best to glide
To unknown coasts to give a visitation,
In lakes and ponds, you leave your numerous fry.[18]
So Nature taught, and yet you know not why,
You wat'ry folk that know not your felicity.

25

Look how the wantons frisk to task the air,
Then to the colder bottom straight they dive;
Eftsoon[19] to Neptune's glassy hall repair

15. Bends in the stream. Rubs: obstacles.
16. Anything.
17. In Greek myth, a sea nymph.
18. Young fish.
19. Soon. Neptune: the sea god in Roman myth.

To see what trade they, great ones, there do drive,
Who forage o'er the spacious sea-green field
And take the trembling prey before it yield,
Whose armour is their scales, their spreading fins their shield.

26

While musing thus with contemplation fed,
And thousand fancies buzzing in my brain,
The sweet-tongu'd Philomel[20] percht o'er my head
And chanted forth a most melodious strain
Which rapt me so with wonder and delight
I judg'd my hearing better than my sight
And wisht me wings with her a while to take my flight.

27

O merry Bird (said I) that fears no snares,
That neither toils nor hoards up in thy barn,
Feels no sad thoughts nor cruciating cares
To gain more good or shun what might thee harm—
Thy clothes ne'er wear, thy meat is everywhere,
Thy bed a bough, thy drink the water clear—
Reminds not what is past, nor what's to come dost fear.

28

The dawning morn with songs thou dost prevent,[21]
Sets hundred notes unto thy feathered crew,
So each one tunes his pretty instrument
And warbling out the old, begin anew,
And thus they pass their youth in summer season,
Then follow thee into a better region,
Where winter's never felt by that sweet airy legion.

29

Man at the best a creature frail and vain,
In knowledge ignorant, in strength but weak,
Subject to sorrows, losses, sickness, pain,
Each storm his state, his mind, his body break—

20. Nightingale, a European songbird (derived from the Greek myth of Philomela, an Athenian princess who was turned into a nightingale).

21. Foresee.

From some of these he never finds cessation
But day or night, within, without, vexation,
Troubles from foes, from friends, from dearest, near'st relation.

30

And yet this sinful creature, frail and vain,
This lump of wretchedness, of sin and sorrow,
This weather-beaten vessel wrackt with pain,
Joys not in hope of an eternal morrow.
Nor all his losses, crosses, and vexation,
In weight, in frequency and long duration
Can make him deeply groan for that divine Translation.

31

The mariner that on smooth waves doth glide
Sings merrily and steers his barque with ease
As if he had command of wind and tide
And now becomes great master of the seas,
But suddenly a storm spoils all the sport
And makes him long for a more quiet port,
Which 'gainst all adverse winds may serve for fort.

32

So he that faileth in this world of pleasure,
Feeding on sweets that never bit of th' sour,
That's full of friends, of honour, and of treasure,
Fond fool, he takes this earth ev'n for heav'ns bower,
But sad affliction comes and makes him see
Here's neither honour, wealth, or safety.
Only above is found all with security.

33

O Time the fatal wrack[22] of mortal things
That draws oblivion's curtains over kings,
Their sumptuous monuments, men know them not;
Their names with a record are forgot,
Their parts, their ports, their pomps all laid in th' dust.

22. Destroyer.

Nor wit, nor gold, nor buildings scape time's rust,
But he whose name is grav'd in the white stone[23]
Shall last and shine when all of these are gone.

1678

The Flesh and the Spirit

In secret place where once I stood
Close by the banks of Lacrim[1] flood,
I heard two sisters reason on
Things that are past and things to come.
One Flesh was call'd, who had her eye
On worldly wealth and vanity;
The other Spirit, who did rear
Her thoughts unto a higher sphere.

"Sister," quoth Flesh, "what liv'st thou on,
Nothing but meditation?
Doth contemplation feed thee so
Regardlessly to let earth go?
Can speculation satisfy
Notion without reality?
Dost dream of things beyond the Moon
And dost thou hope to dwell there soon?
Hast treasures there laid up in store
That all in th' world thou count'st but poor?
Art fancy-sick or turn'd a sot
To catch at shadows which are not?
Come, come. I'll show unto thy sense,
Industry hath its recompence.
What canst desire, but thou may'st see
True substance in variety?
Dost honour like? Acquire the same,
As some to their immortal fame;
And trophies to thy name erect
Which wearing time shall ne'er deject.
For riches dost thou long full sore?

23. An allusion to Revelation 2:17: "To him that overcometh will I give . . . a white stone."

1. *Lacrima* is Latin for tear; hence, river of tears.

Behold enough of precious store.
Earth hath more silver, pearls, and gold
Than eyes can see or hands can hold.
Affects[2] thou pleasure? Take thy fill.
Earth hath enough of what you will.
Then let not go what thou may'st find
For things unknown only in mind."

Spirit: "Be still, thou unregenerate part,
Disturb no more my settled heart,
For I have vow'd (and so will do)
Thee as a foe still to pursue,
And combat with thee will and must
Until I see thee laid in th' dust.
Sister we are, yea twins we be,
Yet deadly feud 'twixt thee and me,
For from one father are we not.
Thou by old Adam wast begot,
But my arise is from above,
Whence my dear father I do love.
Thou speak'st me fair but hat'st me sore.
Thy flatt'ring shows I'll trust no more.
How oft thy slave hast thou me made
When I believ'd what thou hast said
And never had more cause of woe
Than when I did what thou bad'st do.
I'll stop mine ears at these thy charms
And count them for my deadly harms.
Thy sinful pleasures I do hate,
Thy riches are to me no bait.
Thine honours do, nor will I love,
For my ambition lies above.
My greatest honour it shall be
When I am victor over thee,
And triumph shall, with laurel head,[3]
When thou my captive shalt be led.
How I do live, thou need'st not scoff,
For I have meat thou know'st not of.[4]

2. Seek.
3. That is, with a laurel crown, a symbol of victory, on her head.

4. In John 4:32, Jesus says to his followers, "I have meat to eat that ye know not of."

The hidden manna[5] I do eat;
The word of life, it is my meat.
My thoughts do yield me more content
Than can thy hours in pleasure spent.
Nor are they shadows which I catch,
Nor fancies vain at which I snatch
But reach at things that are so high,
Beyond thy dull capacity.
Eternal substance I do see
With which enriched I would be.
Mine eye doth pierce the heav'ns and see
What is invisible to thee.
My garments are not silk nor gold,
Nor such like trash which Earth doth hold,
But royal robes I shall have on,
More glorious than the glist'ring Sun.
My crown not diamonds, pearls, and gold,
But such as angels' heads enfold.
The City[6] where I hope to dwell,
There's none on Earth can parallel.
The stately walls both high and strong
Are made of precious jasper stone,
The Gates of Pearl, both rich and clear,
And angels are for porters there.
The streets thereof transparent gold
Such as no eye did e're behold.
A crystal river there doth run
Which doth proceed from the Lamb's throne.
Of Life, there are the waters sure
Which shall remain forever pure.
Nor Sun nor Moon they have no need
For glory doth from God proceed.
No candle there, nor yet torch light,
For there shall be no darksome night.
From sickness and infirmity
Forevermore they shall be free.
Nor withering age shall e're come there,
But beauty shall be bright and clear.

---

5. In Exodus 16:15, the spiritual food that God gave to the Jews to eat.

6. This passage alludes to the New Jerusalem described in Revelation 21–22.

This City pure is not for thee,
For things unclean there shall not be.
If I of Heav'n may have my fill,
Take thou the world, and all that will."

1678

"The Flesh and the Spirit" stages an interior debate between two sides of a human self, one side treasuring earthly fame and passion and the other devoted to divine and eternal rewards.

To Her Father with Some Verses

Most truly honored, and as truly dear,
If worth in me or ought[1] I do appear,
Who can of right better demand the same
Than may your worthy self from whom it came?
The principal might yield a greater sum,
Yet handled ill, amounts but to this crumb;
My stock's so small I know not how to pay,
My bond remains in force unto this day;
Yet for part payment take this simple mite,[2]
Where nothing's to be had, kings lose their right.
Such is my debt I may not say forgive,
But as I can, I'll pay it while I live;
Such is my bond, none can discharge but I,
Yet paying is not paid until I die.

1678

To My Dear and Loving Husband

If ever two were one, then surely we.
If ever man were lov'd by wife, then thee.
If ever wife was happy in a man,
Compare with me, ye women, if you can.
I prize thy love more than whole mines of gold
Or all the riches that the East doth hold.
My love is such that rivers cannot quench,
Nor ought[1] but love from thee give recompence.

1. Anything.
2. Very small sum.

1. Anything.

Thy love is such I can no way repay.
The heavens reward thee manifold, I pray.
Then while we live, in love let's so persever
That when we live no more, we may live ever.

1678

This poem is addressed to the poet's husband, Simon Bradstreet.

A *Letter to Her Husband, Absent upon Public Employment*

My head, my heart, mine eyes, my life, nay, more,
My joy, my magazine[1] of earthly store,
If two be one, as surely thou and I,
How stayest thou there, whilst I at Ipswich[2] lie?
So many steps, head from the heart to sever,
If but a neck, soon should we be together.
I, like the Earth this season, mourn in black,
My sun is gone so far in's zodiac,
Whom whilst I 'joyed, nor storms, nor frost I felt,
His warmth such frigid colds did cause to melt.
My chilled limbs now numbed lie forlorn;
Return, return, sweet Sol,[3] from Capricorn;
In this dead time, alas, what can I more
Than view those fruits which through thy heart I bore?
Which sweet contentment yield me for a space,
True living pictures of their father's face.
O strange effect! now thou art southward gone,
I weary grow the tedious day so long;
But when thou northward to me shalt return,
I wish my Sun may never set, but burn
Within the Cancer[4] of my glowing breast,
The welcome house of him my dearest guest.
Where ever, ever stay, and go not thence,
Till nature's sad decree shall call thee hence;
Flesh of thy flesh, bone of thy bone,
I here, thou there, yet both but one.

1678

1. Storehouse.
2. Ipswich, Massachusetts, where the Bradstreets lived from about 1635 to 1645.
3. The sun. Capricorn: the tenth sign of the zodiac, representing winter.

4. The fourth sign of the zodiac, representing summer.

Before the Birth of One of Her Children

All things within this fading world hath end,
Adversity doth still our joys attend;
No ties so strong, no friends so dear and sweet,
But with death's parting blow is sure to meet.
The sentence past is most irrevocable,
A common thing, yet oh, inevitable.
How soon, my Dear, death may my steps attend.
How soon't may be thy lot to lose thy friend,
We both are ignorant, yet love bids me
These farewell lines to recommend to thee,
That when that knot's untied that made us one,
I may seem thine, who in effect am none.
And if I see not half my days that's due,
What nature would, God grant to yours and you;
The many faults that well you know I have
Let be interred in my oblivious grave;
If any worth or virtue were in me,
Let that live freshly in thy memory
And when thou feel'st no grief, as I no harms,
Yet love thy dead, who long lay in thine arms,
And when thy loss shall be repaid with gains
Look to my little babes, my dear remains.
And if thou love thyself, or loved'st me,
These O protect from stepdame's injury.
And if chance to thine eyes shall bring this verse,
With some sad sighs honor my absent hearse;
And kiss this paper for thy love's dear sake,
Who with salt tears this last farewell did take.

1678

In Reference to Her Children

I had eight birds hatcht in one nest,
Four cocks were there, and hens the rest.
I nurst them up with pain and care,
No cost nor labour did I spare
Till at the last they felt their wing,
Mounted the trees and learned to sing.
Chief of the brood then took his flight

To regions far and left me quite.
My mournful chirps I after send
Till he return, or I do end.
Leave not thy nest, thy Dame and Sire,
Fly back and sing amidst this quire.
My second bird did take her flight
And with her mate flew out of sight.
Southward they both their course did bend,
And seasons twain they there did spend,
Till after blown by Southern gales
They Nor'ward steer'd with filled sails.
A prettier bird was no where seen,
Along the beach, among the treen.
I have a third of colour white
On whom I plac'd no small delight,
Coupled with mate loving and true,
Hath also bid her Dame adieu.
And where Aurora[1] first appears,
She now hath percht to spend her years.
One to the Academy flew
To chat among that learned crew.
Ambition moves still in his breast
That he might chant above the rest,
Striving for more than to do well,
That nightingales he might excel.
My fifth, whose down is yet scarce gone,
Is 'mongst the shrubs and bushes flown
And as his wings increase in strength
On higher boughs he'll perch at length.
My other three still with me nest
Until they're grown, then as the rest,
Or here or there, they'll take their flight,
As is ordain'd, so shall they light.
If birds could weep, then would my tears
Let others know what are my fears
Lest this my brood some harm should catch
And be surpris'd for want of watch
Whilst pecking corn and void of care
They fall un'wares in Fowler's[2] snare;

---

1. The Roman goddess of the dawn.   2. Bird hunter's; perhaps here, Satan's.

Or whilst on trees they sit and sing
Some untoward boy at them do fling,
Or whilst allur'd with bell and glass
The net be spread and caught, alas;
Or lest by lime-twigs they be foil'd;
Or by some greedy hawks be spoil'd.
O would, my young, ye saw my breast
And knew what thoughts there sadly rest.
Great was my pain when I you bred,
Great was my care when I you fed.
Long did I keep you soft and warm
And with my wings kept off all harm.
My cares are more, and fears, than ever,
My throbs such now as 'fore were never.
Alas, my birds, you wisdom want,[3]
Of perils you are ignorant.
Oft times in grass, on trees, in flight,
Sore accidents on you may light.
O to your safety have an eye,
So happy may you live and die.
Mean while, my days in tunes I'll spend
Till my weak lays[4] with me shall end.
In shady woods I'll sit and sing
And things that past, to mind I'll bring.
Once young and pleasant, as are you,
But former toys (no joys) adieu!
My age I will not once lament
But sing, my time so near is spent,
And from the top bough take my flight
Into a country beyond sight
Where old ones instantly grow young
And there with seraphim[5] set song.
No seasons cold, nor storms they see
But spring lasts to eternity.
When each of you shall in your nest
Among your young ones take your rest,
In chirping languages oft them tell

3. Lack.   5. Angels.
4. Songs.

You had a Dame that lov'd you well,
That did what could be done for young
And nurst you up till you were strong
And 'fore she once would let you fly
She show'd you joy and misery,
Taught what was good, and what was ill,
What would save life, and what would kill.
Thus gone, amongst you I may live,
And dead, yet speak and counsel give.
Farewell, my birds, farewell, adieu,
I happy am, if well with you.

1678

For Deliverance from a Fever

When sorrows had begirt me round,
And pains within and out,
When in my flesh no part was found,
Then didst Thou rid me out.
My burning flesh in sweat did boil,
My aching head did break,
From side to side for ease I toil,
So faint I could not speak.
Beclouded was my soul with fear
Of Thy displeasure sore,
Nor could I read my evidence
Which oft I read before.
"Hide not Thy face from me!" I cried,
"From burnings keep my soul.
Thou know'st my heart, and hast me tried;
I on Thy mercies roll."
"O heal my soul," Thou know'st I said,
"Though flesh consume to nought,
What though in dust it shall be laid,
To glory t'shall be brought."
Thou heard'st, Thy rod Thou didst remove
And spared my body frail,
Thou show'st to me Thy tender love,
My heart no more might quail.

O, praises to my mighty God,
Praise to my Lord, I say,
Who had redeemed my soul from pit,
Praises to Him for aye.[1]

1678

In Memory of My Dear Grandchild Elizabeth Bradstreet, Who Deceased August, 1665, Being a Year and Half Old

1

Farewell dear babe, my heart's too much content,
Farewell sweet babe, the pleasure of mine eye,
Farewell fair flower that for a space was lent,
Then ta'en away unto eternity.
Blest babe, why should I once bewail thy fate,
Or sigh thy days so soon were terminate,
Sith[1] thou art settled in an everlasting state.

2

By nature trees do rot when they are grown,
And plums and apples thoroughly ripe do fall,
And corn and grass are in their season mown,
And time brings down what is both strong and tall.
But plants new set to be eradicate,
And buds new blown to have so short a date,
Is by His hand alone that guides nature and fate.

1678

Verses upon the Burning of Our House

In silent night when rest I took,
For sorrow near I did not look,
I waken'd was with thund'ring noise
And piteous shrieks of dreadful voice.
That fearful sound of "fire" and "fire,"
Let no man know is my desire.
I, starting up, the light did spy,

---

1. Forever.   1. Since.

And to my God my heart did cry
To strengthen me in my distress
And not to leave me succourless.
Then coming out, beheld a space
The flame consume my dwelling place.
And when I could no longer look,
I blest his grace that gave and took,[1]
That laid my goods now in the dust.
Yea, so it was, and so 'twas just.
It was his own; it was not mine.
Far be it that I should repine,
He might of all justly bereft
But yet sufficient for us left.
When by the ruins oft I past
My sorrowing eyes aside did cast
And here and there the places spy
Where oft I sat and long did lie.
Here stood that trunk, and there that chest,
There lay that store I counted best,
My pleasant things in ashes lie
And them behold no more shall I.
Under the roof no guest shall sit,
Nor at thy table eat a bit.
No pleasant talk shall e'er be told
Nor things recounted done of old.
No candle e'er shall shine in thee,
Nor bridegroom's voice e'er heard shall be.
In silence ever shalt thou lie.
Adieu, adieu, all's vanity.[2]
Then straight I 'gin my heart to chide:
And did thy wealth on earth abide,
Didst fix thy hope on mould'ring dust,
The arm of flesh didst make thy trust?
Raise up thy thoughts above the sky
That dunghill mists away may fly.
Thou hast a house on high erect
Fram'd by that mighty Architect,

1. According to Job 1:21, "The Lord gave, and the Lord hath taken away; blessed be the name of the Lord."

2. According to Ecclesiastes 1:2, "Vanity of vanities, saith the Preacher, vanity of vanities; all is vanity."

With glory richly furnished
Stands permanent, though this be fled.
It's purchased and paid for too
By Him who hath enough to do.
A price so vast as is unknown,
Yet by his gift is made thine own.
There's wealth enough; I need no more.
Farewell, my pelf;³ farewell, my store.
The world no longer let me love;
My hope and treasure lies above.

                                        1867

Anne Bradstreet dated this poem July 10, 1666. Her son Simon copied it, and it was eventually published in a collected volume of her works over two centuries after its composition.

As Weary Pilgrim

As weary pilgrim, now at rest,
    Hugs with delight his silent nest,
His wasted limbs now lie full soft
    That mirey steps have trodden oft,
Blesses himself to think upon
    His dangers past, and travails done.
The burning sun no more shall heat,
    Nor stormy rains on him shall beat.
The briars and thorns no more shall scratch.
    Nor hungry wolves at him shall catch.
He erring paths no more shall tread,
    Nor wild fruits eat instead of bread.
For waters cold he doth not long
    For thirst no more shall parch his tongue.
No rugged stones his feet shall gall,
    Nor stumps nor rocks cause him to fall.
All cares and fears he bids farewell
    And means in safety now to dwell.
A pilgrim I, on earth perplexed
    With sins, with cares and sorrows vext,
By age and pains brought to decay,
    And my clay house¹ mold'ring away.

---

3. Possessions or riches.   1. That is, the body.

Oh, how I long to be at rest
   And soar on high among the blest.
This body shall in silence sleep,
   Mine eyes no more shall ever weep,
No fainting fits shall me assail,
   Nor grinding pains my body frail,
With cares and fears ne'er cumb'red be
   Nor losses know, nor sorrows see.
What though my flesh shall there consume,
   It is the bed Christ did perfume,
And when a few years shall be gone,
   This mortal shall be clothed upon.
A corrupt carcass down it lies,
   A glorious body it shall rise.
In weakness and dishonor sown,
   In power 'tis raised by Christ alone.
Then soul and body shall unite
   And of their Maker have the sight.
Such lasting joys shall there behold
   As ear ne'er heard nor tongue e'er told.
Lord make me ready for that day,
   Then come, dear Bridegroom,[2] come away.

1867

Bradstreet composed this poem on August 31, 1669, about three years before she died.

MICHAEL WIGGLESWORTH
1631–1705

As a small boy, Michael Wigglesworth sailed from his birthplace in Yorkshire, England, to settle with his family in the New England colonies. He grew up in New Haven, Connecticut, and attended Harvard. After becoming a Puritan minister in 1653, he preached first in Charlestown, Massachusetts, and then in Malden, Massachusetts, where he spent the last fifty years of his life. In 1662 he published *The Day of Doom*, a long, vigorous, and often lurid account of

2. Mark 2 refers to Christ as the "bridegroom" of the soul.

Judgment Day, written in the common meter of hymns. Intended to fortify his readers' emotional commitment to Calvinist Christianity, the poem was an immediate sensation. It remained the most popular English-language poem in the New World for at least the next hundred years.

FURTHER READING

Richard Drowder. *No Featherbed to Heaven: A Biography of Michael Wigglesworth.* East Lansing: Michigan State University Press, 1962.

Jeffrey Hammond. *Sinful Self, Saintly Self: The Puritan Experience of Poetry.* Athens: University of Georgia Press, 1993.

FROM *The Day of Doom*

1

The security of the world before Christ's coming to judgment.
Luk. 12:19

Still was the night, serene and bright,
　　when all men sleeping lay;
Calm was the season, and carnal reason
　　thought so 'twould last for aye.[1]
Soul, take thine ease, let sorrow cease,
　　much good thou hast in store:
This was their song, their cups among,
　　The evening before.

2

Mat. 25:5

Wallowing in all kind of sin,
　　vile wretches lay secure:
The best of men had scarcely then
　　their lamps kept in good ure.[2]
Virgins unwise, who through disguise
　　amongst the best were number'd,
Had clos'd their eyes; yea, and the wise
　　through sloth and frailty slumber'd.

3

Mat. 24:37, 38

Like as of old, when men grow bold
　　God's threat'nings to contemn,
Who stopt their ear, and would not hear,
　　when mercy warned them:

1. Forever.　　　　　　　　2. Condition.

But took their course, without remorse,
  till God began to pour
Destruction the world upon
  in a tempestuous shower.

4

They put away the evil day,
  and drown'd their care and fears,
Till drown'd were they, and swept away
  by vengeance unawares:

1 Thes. 5:3

So at the last, whilst men sleep fast
  in their security,
Surpris'd they are in such a snare
  as cometh suddenly.

5

The suddenness,
majesty, & terror of
Christ's appearing.
Mat. 25:6
2 Pet. 3:10

For midnight broke forth a light
  which turn'd the night to day,
And speedily an hideous cry
  did all the world dismay.
Sinners awake, their hearts do ache,
  trembling their loins surpriseth;
Amaz'd with fear, by what they hear,
  each one of them ariseth.

6

They rush from beds with giddy heads,
  and to their windows run,
Viewing this light, which shines more bright

Mat. 24:29, 30

  than doth the noon-day sun.
Straightway appears (they see't with tears)
  the Son of God most dread;
Who with his train[3] comes on amain
  to judge both quick[4] and dead.

7

Before his face the Heav'ns gave place,

2 Pet. 3:10

  and skies are rent asunder,

---

3. Attendants. Amain: in full force.   4. Living.

With mighty voice, and hideous noise,
 more terrible than thunder.
His brightness damps heav'n's glorious lamps
 and makes them hide their heads,
As if afraid and quite dismay'd,
 they quit their wonted steads.[5]

8

Ye sons of men that durst contemn
 the threat'nings of God's word,
How cheer you now? Your hearts, I trow,[6]
 are thrill'd as with a sword.
Now atheist blind, whose brutish mind
 a God could never see,
Dost thou perceive, dost now believe,
 that Christ thy Judge shall be?

9

Stout courages[7] (whose hardiness
 could death and Hell out-face)
Are you as bold now you behold
 your Judge draw near apace?
They cry, "No, no: Alas! And woe!
 our courage all is gone:
Our hardiness (fool hardiness)
 hath us undone, undone."

10

No heart so bold, but now grows cold
 and almost dead with fear:
Rev. 6:16 No eye so dry, but now can cry,
 and pour out many a tear.
Earth's potentates and pow'rful states,
 captains and men of might,
Are quite abasht, their courage dasht
 at this most dreadful sight.

---

5. Usual places.
6. Trust.
7. Brave souls.

11

Mean men lament, great men do rent
    their robes, and tear their hair:

Mat. 24:30

They do not spare their flesh to tear
    through horrible despair.
All kindreds wail: all hearts do fail:
    horror the world doth fill
With weeping eyes, and loud out-cries,
    yet knows not how to kill.

12

Rev. 6:15, 16

Some hide themselves in caves and delves,[8]
    in places under ground:
Some rashly leap into the deep,
    to scape by being drown'd:
Some to the rocks (O senseless blocks!)
    and woody mountains run,
That there they might this fearful sight,
    and dreaded Presence shun.

13

In vain do they to mountains say,
    "Fall on us, and us hide
From Judge's ire, more hot than fire,
    for who may it abide?"
No hiding place can from his face,
    sinners at all conceal.
Whose flaming eyes hid things doth 'spy,
    and darkest things reveal.

14

Mat. 25:31

The Judge draws nigh, exalted high
    upon a lofty throne,
Amidst the throng of angels strong,
    lo, Israel's Holy One!
The excellence of whose presence
    and awful majesty,
Amazeth nature, and every creature,
    doth more than terrify.

8. Pits in the ground.

15

Rev. 6:14

The mountains smoke, the hills are shook,
    the earth is rent and torn,
As if she should be clean dissolv'd,
    or from the center born.
The sea doth roar, forsakes the shore,
    and shrinks away for fear;
The wild beasts flee into the sea,
    so soon as he draws near.

16

Whose glory bright, whose wondrous might,
    whose power imperial,
So far surpass whatever was
    in realms terrestrial;
That tongues of men (nor angel's pen)
    cannot the same express,
And therefore I must pass it by,
    lest speaking should transgress.

17

1 Thes. 4:16
*Resurrection of
the Dead.*
John 5:28, 29

Before his throne, a trump[9] is blown,
    proclaiming th' Day of Doom:
Forthwith he cries, *Ye Dead arise,*
    and unto Judgment come.
No sooner said, but 'tis obey'd;
    sepulchres open'd are;
Dead bodies all rise at his call,
    and's mighty power declare.

18

Both sea and land, at his command,
    their dead at once surrender:
The fire and air constrained are
    also their dead to tender.
The mighty word of this great Lord
    links body and soul together
Both of the just, and the unjust,
    to part no more for ever.

9. Trumpet.

19

The living changed.

The same translates, from mortal states
    to immortality,
All that survive, and be alive,
    i' th' twinkling of an eye:

Luk. 20:36
1 Cor. 15:52

That so they may abide for aye
    to endless weal or woe;
Both the renate[10] and reprobate
    are made to die no more.

208

HELL.
Mat. 25:30
Mark 9:43
Isa. 30:33
Rev. 21:8

Whom having brought, as they are taught,
    unto the brink of Hell
(That dismal place far from Christ's face,
    where Death and Darkness dwell:
Where God's fierce ire kindleth the fire,
    and vengeance feeds the flame
With piles of wood, and brimstone flood,
    that none can quench the same).

209

*Wicked men and
devils cast into it for
ever.*
Mat. 22:13 and
25:46

With iron bands they bind their hands,
    and cursed feet together,
And cast them all, both great and small,
    into that lake for ever.
Where day and night, without respite,
    they wail, and cry, and howl
For tort'ring pain, which they sustain
    in body and in soul.

210

Rev. 14:10, 11

For day and night, in their despight,
    their torment's smoke ascendeth.
Their pain and grief have no relief,
    their anguish never endeth.
There must they lie, and never die,
    though dying every day:
There must they dying ever lie,
    and not consume away.

10. Reborn.

74   ◆   *Michael Wigglesworth*

219

The saints rejoice to
see Judgment
executed upon
the wicked world.

Ps. 58:10
Rev. 19:1, 2, 3

The saints behold with courage bold,
    and thankful wonderment,
To see all those that were their foes
    thus sent to punishment:
Then do they sing unto their King
    a song of endless praise:
They praise his name, and do proclaim
    that just are all his ways.

220

They ascend with
Christ into Heaven
triumphing.
Mat. 25:46
1 Joh. 3:2
1 Cor. 13:12

Thus with great joy and melody
    to Heav'n they all ascend,
Him there to praise with sweetest lays,
    and hymns that never end,
Where with long rest they shall be blest,
    and nought shall them annoy:
Where they shall see as seen they be,
    And whom they love enjoy.

221

Their eternal
happiness and
incomparable
glory there.

O glorious place! Where face to face
    Jehovah may be seen,
By such as were sinners whilere[11]
    And no dark veil between.
Where the sun shine, and light divine,
    Of God's bright countenance,
Doth rest upon them every one,
    With sweetest influence.

224

Heb. 12:23

For there the saints are perfect saints,
    And holy ones indeed,
From all the sin that dwelt within
    Their mortal bodies freed:
Made kings and priests to God through Christ's

Rev. 1:6 and 22:5

    dear love's transcendency,
There to remain, and there to reign
    With him eternally.

1662

11. Once.

EDWARD TAYLOR
ca. 1642–1729

EDWARD TAYLOR'S LIFE and poetic career offer many parallels with those of Emily Dickinson, another Massachusetts poet born almost two centuries later in the town of Amherst, just twenty-five miles northeast of the frontier village of Westfield, where Taylor served as minister for five decades. Like Dickinson, Taylor produced an extensive body of poetry that went virtually unpublished during his lifetime. And like Dickinson's, though much more belatedly, Taylor's work was recognized on its posthumous publication as the achievement of a unique and extraordinary poet. Taylor, again like Dickinson, created an imaginative and vibrantly learned meditative diary of the poet's emotional and spiritual life. Each poet was responding to a phase in the history of New England Calvinism. Taylor was responding eagerly to a Calvinism still closely linked to the first-generation Puritans' pioneer spirit and messianic zeal. Dickinson was responding more skeptically to a late-generation Calvinism moderated and tinctured by Emerson's Transcendentalism and by mid-nineteenth-century liberalism. Each poet built a powerfully expressive and flexible style on formal elements that might have been considered dated: Taylor worked freshly and spontaneously with the metaphysical poetics of Donne and Herbert, whose vogue had ended in England half a century before, while Dickinson created a virtuoso medium out of the traditional Protestant hymn stanza, a form which Robert Lowell would one day dismiss as "stiff quatrains shoveled out four-square" but which, in Dickinson's hands, lost its stiffness and gained a variety and expressivity that few have rivaled. Only a poet as unique as Dickinson can offer such extensive parallels to a poet as uncommon as Edward Taylor.

Taylor was born in Leicestershire, England. His writings suggest a man of extensive education, and Taylor pursued that education both in England (possibly at Cambridge University) and, after arriving in America at the age of twenty-six, at Harvard College. There he roomed with Samuel Sewall and associated with other prominent Puritans, including both Cotton and Increase Mather. Taylor had come to America in pursuit of religious freedom, having lost a teaching position in England after he refused to submit to the 1662 Act of Uniformity to the Anglican Church. Having begun his life in comparatively cultured surroundings in England and Boston, Taylor spent his final fifty-eight years as the spiritual leader of the frontier community of Westfield—a calling he initially resisted because he deemed this remote location "a howling wilderness." Yet he soon settled into Westfield life and became an indispensable member of its community, preaching weekly sermons, presiding at baptisms, marriages, and funerals, and also serving as the community's sole physician and lawyer. He married twice and fathered fourteen children, several of whom died in infancy.

In the midst of this active and productive frontier life, he also created an extensive body of poetry of remarkable beauty and power. This poetic life's work remained unpublished and all but unknown until a manuscript of the poems, which Taylor had left to his family after his death, was discovered in the Yale University Library in the 1930s by Thomas H. Johnson, who published a selection. (Johnson would later edit the first complete edition of Dickinson's poetry.)

Taylor's poetry centers on an intense and vibrantly human expression of religious feeling. Its style is modeled on the English school of metaphysical poetry. The metaphysical poets, particularly John Donne and George Herbert, Taylor's most important models, attempt to capture the mind in an active process of thought. Their poems, and Taylor's, depict a poet-speaker energetically thinking his way through an emotional and intellectual problem as the poet exploits paradoxes, puns, and the so-called "metaphysical conceit"—an extended metaphor extensively comparing two radically unlike things while making the case for an underlying profound likeness. Thus the poet captures the feeling of a mind wrestling actively with complexities and uncertainties. This drama of active thought is most obvious in Taylor's *Preparatory Meditations*, a series of poems he wrote over many years as spiritual preparations for the act of presenting his monthly sermons in celebration of the Lord's Supper—the communion service of his church. Each of Taylor's "Preparatory Meditations" focuses on the text (the brief quoted passage from the Bible) on which his sermon was to be based. And each poem works its way through a vivid process, with the poet beginning in a state of doubt or depression, beset by feelings of sinfulness or unworthiness. By working his way through the spiritually hopeful implications of his biblical text in language that mixes homely speech and images with a range of startling and unusual—but genuine—words (a single poem contains the words smaragdine, selvedge, and squitchen, all still to be found in a modern unabridged dictionary), Taylor discovers a logic of metaphor that leads toward ecstatic feelings of affirmation and joy in the presence of God's grace. Each of these "Preparatory Meditations" develops a series of such extended metaphors, so that in one poem Christ is considered extensively as the "bread of life" and the source of all spiritual nourishment whereas in another he is explored in the role of the divine lawyer, advocating for the sinner in the presence of God the father.

In Taylor's *Miscellaneous Poems* the metaphysical conceit is perhaps most fully and engagingly at work. Taylor starts with a common item from the physical world, such as "A Wasp Chilled with Cold" or "A Spider Catching a Fly," then explores the metaphorical relation between that common thing and the soul's journey toward God. Perhaps Taylor's wittiest and most fully developed conceit is found in "Huswifery," where a spinning wheel and loom, common objects in the seventeenth-century home, are transformed into analogies of the soul aspiring toward divine fulfillment.

Despite his links to the Puritan worthies of his generation and his many intriguing parallels to Emily Dickinson, Taylor remains a distinctive figure in American literature. Few Puritan poets have written with such sustained wit and imagination, and fewer still have produced a body of work so emotionally intense in expression or so persistently joyful in character.

FURTHER READING

Thomas M. Davis. *A Reading of Edward Taylor.* Newark: University of Delaware Press, 1992.

William J. Scheick. *The Will and the Word: The Poetry of Edward Taylor.* Athens: University of Georgia Press, 1974.

Edward Taylor. *The Poems of Edward Taylor.* Ed. Donald E. Stanford. New Haven: Yale University Press, 1960.

FROM Preparatory Meditations

Prologue

Lord, can a crumb of dust the earth outweigh,
    Outmatch all mountains, nay, the crystal sky?
Embosom in't designs that shall display
    And trace into the boundless deity?
    Yea hand a pen whose moisture doth gild ore
    Eternal glory with a glorious glore.[1]

If it its pen had of an angel's quill,
    And sharpened on a precious stone ground tight,
And dipped in liquid gold, and moved by skill
    In crystal leaves should golden letters write
    It would but blot and blur, yea, jag, and jar,[2]
    Unless Thou mak'st the pen, and scrivener.

I am this crumb of dust which is design'd
    To make my pen unto Thy praise alone,
And my dull fancy I would gladly grind
    Unto an edge on Zion's precious stone.[3]
    And write in liquid gold upon Thy name
    My letters till Thy glory forth doth flame.

1. Glory (Scottish).
2. It would mar the written page.
3. Sharpen my quill pen against a divine stone.

Zion was the hill on which the temple in Jerusalem was built.

*   *   *

Let not th'attempts break down my dust I pray
    Nor laugh Thou them to scorn but pardon give.
Inspire this crumb of dust till it display
    Thy glory through't: and then Thy dust shall live.
    Its failings then Thou'lt overlook I trust,
    They being slips slipped from Thy crumb of dust.

Thy crumb of dust breaths two words from its breast,
    That Thou wilt guide its pen to write aright
To prove Thou art, and that Thou art the best
    And show Thy properties to shine most bright.
    And then Thy works will shine as flowers on stems
    Or as in jewelry shops, do gems.

ca. 1682

Meditation 8 (First Series).
John 6.51. I am the living bread.[1]

I kenning through astronomy divine[2]
    The world's bright battlement, wherein I spy
A golden path my pencil cannot line,
    From that bright throne unto my threshold lie.
    And while my puzzled thoughts about it pore
    I find the bread of life in't at my door.

When that this bird of paradise[3] put in
    This wicker cage (my corpse) to tweedle praise
Had pecked the fruit forbad:[4] and so did fling
    Away its food; and lost its golden days;
    It fell into celestial famine sore:
    And never could attain a morsel more.

Alas! alas! Poor bird, what wilt thou do?
    The creatures field no food for souls e're gave.
    And if thou knock at angels' doors they show

1. Jesus said, "I am the bread which came down from heaven.... Verily, verily, I say unto you, He that believeth on me hath everlasting life. I am that bread of life" (John 6:41–48).
2. Studying (kenning) the stars (astronomy divine).
3. The soul.
4. That is, my soul mistakenly chose forbidden fruit rather than divine bread.

An empty barrel: they no soul bread have.
Alas! Poor bird, the world's white loaf is done.
And cannot yield thee here the smallest crumb.

In this sad state, God's tender bowels[5] run
    Out streams of grace: and He to end all strife
The purest wheat in heaven, His dear-dear son
    Grinds, and kneads up into this bread of life.
    Which bread of life from heaven down came and stands
    Dished on thy table up by angels' hands.

Did God mold up this bread in heaven, and bake,
    Which from His table came, and to thine goeth?
Doth He bespeak Thee thus, this soul bread take.
    Come eat thy fill of this thy God's white loaf?[6]
    Its food too fine for angels, yet come, take
    And eat thy fill. It's Heaven's sugar cake.

What grace is this knead in this loaf? This thing
    Souls are but petty things it to admire.
Ye angels, help: This fill would to the brim
    Heav'ns whelm'd-down[7] crystal meal bowl, yea and higher.
    This bread of life dropt in Thy mouth, doth cry.
    Eat, eat me, soul, and thou shalt never die.

                          1684

Meditation 16 (First Series).
Luke 7.16. A great prophet is risen up.[1]

Leaf gold, Lord of Thy golden wedge[2] o'relaid
    My soul at first, Thy grace in ev'ry part
Whose pert,[3] fierce eye Thou such a sight hadst made
    Whose brightsome beams could break into Thy heart
    Till Thy cursed foe[4] had with my fist mine eye
    Dashed out, and did my soul unglorify.

5. Here, the inner body, the seat of the tender emotions, the heart.
6. In Taylor's time, white flour was more expensive to refine than brown and thus associated with a higher social class.
7. Turned over.
1. Jesus was recognized as "a great prophet ... risen up among us" when he brought a dead man back to life (Luke 7:16).
2. When gilding, one applies small sheets of gold leaf to a surface. Here the sheets are wedge-shaped.
3. Sharp-eyed, alert.
4. Satan.

*   *   *

I cannot see, nor will Thy will aright.
    Nor see to wail my woe, my loss and hue
Nor all the shine in all the sun can light
    My candle, nor its heat my heart renew.
    See, wail, and will Thy will, I must, or must
    From heavens sweet shine to hells hot flame be thrust.

Grace then concealed in God himself, did roll
    Even snowball like into a sunball shine
And nestles all its beams bunched in Thy soul
    My Lord, that sparkle in prophetic lines.
    Oh! Wonder more than wonderful! this will
    Lighten the eye which sight divine did spill.

What art thou, Lord, this ball of glory bright?
    A bundle of celestial beams up bound
In graces band fixed in heavens topmost height
    Pouring Thy golden beams thence, circling round
    Which show Thy glory, and Thy glory's way
    And everywhere will make celestial day.

Lord, let Thy golden beams pierce through mine eye
    And leave therein an heavenly light to glaze
My soul with glorious grace all o're, whereby
    I may have sight, and grace in me may blaze.
    Lord ting⁵ my candle at Thy burning rays,
    To give a gracious glory to Thy praise.

Thou lightning eye, let some bright beams of thine
    Stick in my soul, to light and liven it:
Light, life, and glory, things that are divine;
    I shall be graced withal for glory fit.
    My heart then stuffed with grace, light, life, and glee
    I'll sacrifice in flames of love to Thee.

1685/86

---

5. Though ting more commonly means to make a ringing sound, here it perhaps means to light.

Meditation 22 (First Series).
Philippians 2.9. God hath highly exalted Him.[1]

When Thy bright beams, my Lord, do strike mine eye,
    Methinks I then could truly chide out right
My hide-bound soul that stands so niggardly
    That scarce a thought gets glorified by't.
    My quaintest[2] metaphors are ragged stuff,
    Making the sun seem like a mullipuff.[3]

It's my desire, Thou shouldst be glorified:
    But when Thy glory shines before mine eye,
I pardon crave, lest my desire be pride.
    Or bed Thy glory in a cloudy sky.
    The sun grows wan; and angels palefaced shrink,
    Before Thy shine, which I besmear with ink.

But shall the bird sing forth Thy praise, and shall
    The little bee present her thankful um?
But I who see Thy shining glory fall
    Before mine eyes, stand blockish, dull, and dumb?
    Whether I speak, or speechless stand, I spy,
    I fail Thy glory: therefore pardon cry.

But this I find; my rhymes do better suite
    Mine own dispraise than tune forth praise to Thee.
Yet being chid, whether consonant,[4] or mute,
    I force my tongue to tattle, as you see.
    That I Thy glorious praise may trumpet right,
    Be Thou my song, and make, Lord, me Thy pipe.

This shining sky will fly away apace,
    When Thy bright glory splits the same to make
Thy majesty a pass, whose fairest face
    Too foul a path is for Thy feet to take.
    What glory, then, shall tend Thee through the sky
    Draining the heavens much of angels dry?

What light then flame will in Thy judgment seat,
    'Fore which all men, and angels shall appear?

---

1. Jesus was made man, but in so doing, "God hath highly exalted him" (Philippians 2:9).
2. Cleverest.
3. Puffball.
4. Talkative.

How shall Thy glorious righteousness them treat,
    Rend'ring to each after His works done here?
  Then saints with angels Thou wilt glorify:
    And burn lewd[5] men, and devils gloriously.

One glimpse, my Lord, of Thy bright judgment day,
    And glory piercing through, like fiery darts,
All devils, doth make for grace to pray,
    For filling grace had I ten thousand hearts.
    I'd through ten hells to see Thy Judgment Day
    Wouldst Thou but gild my soul with thy bright ray.

                          1687

Meditation 39 (First Series).
1 John 2.1. *If any man sin, we have an advocate.*[1]

My sin! my sin, my God, these cursed dregs,
    Green, yellow, blue streaked poison, hellish, rank,
Bubs[2] hatched in nature's nest on serpent eggs,
    Yelp, chirp and cry; they set my soul a cramp.
    I frown, chide, strike and fight them, mourn and cry
    To conquer them, but cannot them destroy.

I cannot kill nor coop them up: my curb
    'S less than snaffle in their mouth: my reins
They as a twine thread, snap:[3] by hell they're spurred:
    And load my soul with swagging loads of pains.
    Black imps, young devils, snap, bite, drag to bring
    And pick[4] me headlong hell's dread whirlpool in.

Lord, hold Thy hand: for handle me Thou may'st
    In wrath: but, oh, a twinkling ray of hope
Methinks I spy Thou graciously display'st.
    There is an advocate:[5] a door is ope.
    Sin's poison swell my heart would till it burst,
    Did not a hope hence creep in't thus, and nursed.

---

5. Fallen, profane, unholy.
1. That is, Jesus will advocate with the Father for sinful man.
2. Pustules.

3. My sins, like a wild horse, cannot be controlled. They throw the bit and snap the reins.
4. Pitch, toss.
5. Specifically, a lawyer pleading one's case.

✻   ✻   ✻

Joy, joy, God's son's the sinners advocate
    Doth plead the sinner guiltless, and a saint.
But yet attorneys' pleas spring from the state
    The case is in: if bad it's bad in plaint.
    My papers do contain no pleas that do
    Secure me from, but knock me down to, woe.

I have no plea mine advocate to give:
    What now? He'll anvil arguments great store
Out of His flesh and blood to make thee live.[6]
    O dear bought arguments: good pleas therefore.
    Nails[7] made of heavenly steel, more choice than gold
    Drove home, well clenched, eternally will hold.

Oh! Dear bought plea, dear Lord, what buy't so dear?
    What with thy blood purchase, thy plea for me?
Take argument out of thy grave t'appear
    And plead my case with, me from guilt to free.
    These maul both sins, and devils, and amaze.
    Both saints, and angels; wreath their mouths with praise.

What shall I do, my Lord? what do, that I
    May have Thee plead my case? I fee Thee will
With faith, repentance, and obediently
    Thy service 'gainst satanic sins fulfill.
    I'll fight thy fields while live I do, although
    I should be hacked in pieces by thy foe.

Make me thy friend, Lord, be my surety:[8] I
    Will be thy client, be my advocate:
My sins make thine, thy pleas make mine hereby.
    Thou wilt me save, I will Thee celebrate.
    Thou'lt kill me sins[9] that cut my heart within:
    And my rough feet[10] shall thy smooth praises sing.

                          1690

6. Christ's sacrifice of his own flesh and blood is his ultimate argument for redemption.
7. The nails on Christ's cross drive home the case for salvation.
8. Legal security against loss or guarantee of the fulfillment of an obligation.
9. You will kill my sins for me.
10. Metrical units of poetry.

Meditation 42 (First Series).
Revelation 3.22. *I will give him to sit with me in my throne.*[1]

Apples of gold, in silver pictures shrined
    Enchant the appetite, make mouths to water.
And loveliness in lumps, tunned,[2] and enrined
    In jasper[3] cask, when tapped, doth briskly vapor:
    Brings forth a birth of keys t'unlock love's chest,
    That love, like birds, may fly to't from its nest.

Such is my Lord, and more. But what strange thing
    Am I become? Sin rusts my lock all o'er.
Though he ten thousand keys all on a string
    Takes out, scarce one is found unlocks the door.
    Which ope, my love crinched[4] in a corner lies
    Like some shrunk crickling:[5] and scarce can rise.

Lord, ope the door: rub off my rust, remove
    My sin, and oil my lock. (Dust there doth shelf.)
My wards[6] will trig before thy key: my love
    Then, as enlivened, leap will on Thyself.
    It needs must be, that giving hands receive
    Again receivers hearts furled in love wreath.

Unkey my heart; unlock thy wardrobe: bring
    Out royal robes: adorn my soul, Lord: so,
My love in rich attire shall on my king
    Attend, and honor on Him well bestow.
    In glory He prepares for His a place
    Whom He doth all beglory here with grace.

He takes them to the shining threshold clear
    Of His bright palace, clothed in grace's flame.
Then takes them in thereto, not only there
    To have a prospect, but possess the same.
    The crown of life, the throne of glory's place,
    The father's house blanched[7] o're with orient grace.

---

1. In Revelation (3:21) Jesus says, at the Last Judgment, "To him that overcometh will I grant to sit with me on my throne, even as I overcame, and am set down with my Father in his throne."
2. Placed in a casket, or tun. Enrined: rendered, melted down.
3. A precious stone. Cask: casket or small case.
4. Gnarled, shrunken.

5. A "crinkling": a withered apple. Thus: God's love is a golden apple clasped in a jasper casket. My love, by contrast, is a withered apple shut in a rusted case.
6. The lock edges that prevent a wrong key from entering. Trig: open.
7. Whitened, brightened.

* * *

Canaan[8] in golden print enwalled with gems:
    A kingdom rimmed with glory round: in fine
A glorious crown paled[9] thick with all the stems
    Of grace, and of all properties divine.
    How happy wilt Thou make me when these shall
    As a blessed heritage unto me fall?

Adorn me, Lord, with holy huswifery.[10]
    All blanch my robes with clusters of Thy graces:
Thus lead me to Thy threshold: give mine eye
    A peephole there to see bright glory's chases.[11]
    Then take me in: I'll pay, when I possess,
    Thy throne, to Thee the rent in happiness.

1691

Meditation 150 (Second Series). Canticles 7.3. Thy two breasts are like two young roes that are twins.[1]

My blessed Lord, how doth Thy beauteous spouse
    In stately stature rise in comeliness?
With her two breasts like two little roes that browse
    Among the lilies in their shining dress
    Like stately milk pails ever full and flow
    With spiritual milk to make her babes to grow.

Celestial nectar wealthier far than wine
    Wrought in the spirit's brew house and up tunned[2]
Within these vessels which are trust up fine
    Likened to two pretty neat twin roes that runned
    Most pleasantly by their dams sides like cades[3]
    And suckle with their milk Christ's spiritual babes.

Lord, put these nibbles then my mouth into
    And suckle me therewith I humbly pray,

---

8. The land God promised to Abraham.
9. Lined, ranked.
10. Clothes woven at home, the traditional housewife's task.
11. Settings for precious stones.
1. In Canticles 7:3 (also titled "The Song of Songs, which is Solomon's"), the speaker's beloved is so described. This description is commonly read as an allegory of the love of the human for the divine. Roes: deer.
2. Placed in a cask.
3. Pets.

Then with this milk Thy spiritual babe I'st grow,
   And these two milk pails shall themselves display
   Like to these pretty twins in pairs round and neat
   And shall sing forth Thy praise over this meat.

1719

FROM God's Determinations

The Preface

Infinity, when all things it beheld
In nothing, and of nothing all did build,
Upon what base was fixed the lathe, wherein
He turned this globe, and riggaled[1] it so trim?
Who blew the bellows of His furnace vast?
Or held the mold wherein the world was cast?
Who laid its cornerstone? Or whose command?
Where stand the pillars upon which it stands?
Who laced and filleted the earth so fine,
With rivers like green ribbons smaragdine?[2]
Who made the sea's its selvedge,[3] and its locks
Like a quilt ball within a silver box?[4]
Who spread its canopy? Or curtains spun?
Who in this bowling alley bowled the sun?
Who made it always when it rises set
To go at once both down and up to get?
Who th'curtain rods made for this tapestry?
Who hung the twinkling lanthorns[5] in the sky?
Who? who did this? or who is He? Why, know
Its only might almighty this did do.
His hand hath made this noble work which stands
His glorious handiwork not made by hands.
Who spake all things from nothing; and with ease
Can speak all things from nothing, if He please.
Whose little finger at His pleasure can
Out mete[6] ten thousand worlds with half a span:
   Whose might almighty can by half a looks

1. Grooved, as on a lathe.
2. Emeraldlike.
3. Border; literally, edge of woven material.
4. A ball of yarn shut up so it cannot unravel.
5. Lanterns.
6. Measure out, apportion.

Root up the rocks and rock the hills by th'roots.
Can take this mighty world up in His hand,
And shake it like a squitchen[7] or a wand.
Whose single frown will make the heavens shake
Like as an aspen leaf the wind makes quake.
Oh! what a might is this whose single frown
Doth shake the world as it would shake it down?
Which all from nothing fet,[8] from nothing, all:
Hath all on nothing set, lets nothing fall.
Gave all to nothing man indeed, whereby
Through nothing man all might Him glorify.
In nothing then embossed the brightest gem
More precious than all preciousness in them.
But nothing man did throw down all by sin:
And darkenéd that lightsome gem in Him.
    That now His brightest diamond is grown
    Darker by far than any coalpit stone.

n.d.

Taylor's "Preface" to *God's Determinations* introduces a collection of more than thirty-five poems that dramatize stages in the journey toward God experienced by a member of the Puritan elect: that is, those members of the church predestined for salvation. The full title is *God's Determinations Touching His Elect: and The Elects Combat in their Conversion, and Coming Up to God in Christ Together with the Comfortable Effects Thereof.*

FROM Miscellaneous Poems

Upon a Spider Catching a Fly

Thou sorrow, venom elf.
    Is this thy play,
To spin a web out of thyself
    To catch a fly?
      For why?

I saw a pettish[1] wasp
    Fall foul therein,
Whom yet thy whorl pins did not clasp
    Lest he should fling
      His sting.

---

7. A piece of bark (used in grafting); hence, a light stick, easily shaken.

8. Made.

1. Peevish.

*   *   *

But as afraid, remote
   Didst stand hereat
And with thy little fingers stroke
   And gently tap
      His back.

Thus gently him didst treat
   Lest he should pet,
And in a froppish,[2] waspish heat
   Should greatly fret
      Thy net.

Whereas the silly fly,
   Caught by its leg
Thou by the throat tookst hastily
   And 'hind the head
      Bite dead.

This goes to pot, that not
   Nature doth call.
Strive not above what strength hath got
   Lest in the brawl
      Thou fall.

This fray seems thus to us.
   Hell's spider gets
His entrails spun to whip cords thus
   And wove to nets
      And sets.

To tangle Adams race
   In's stratagems
To their destructions, spoiled, made base
   By venom things
      Damned sins.

But mighty, gracious Lord
   Communicate
Thy grace to break the cord, afford
   Us glory's gate
      And state.

*   *   *

2. Fretful, peevish.

> We'll nightingale sing like
> When perched on high
> In glories cage, Thy glory, bright,
> And thankfully,
> For joy.

n.d.

Upon a Wasp Chilled with Cold

The bear[1] that breaths the northern blast
Did numb, torpedo-like,[2] a wasp
Whose stiffened limbs encramped, lay bathing
In sol's warm breath and shine as saving,
Which with her hands she chafes and stands
Rubbing her legs, shanks, thighs, and hands.
Her petty toes, and fingers ends
Nipped with this breath, she out extends
Unto the sun, in great desire
To warm her digits at that fire.
Doth hold her temples in this state
Where pulse doth beat, and head doth ache.
Doth turn, and stretch her body small,
Doth comb her velvet capital.[3]
As if her little brain pan were
A volume of choice precepts clear.
As if her satin jacket hot
Contained apothecaries shop
Of natures receipts, that prevails
To remedy all her sad ails,
As if her velvet helmet high
Did turret rationality.
She fans her wing up to the wind
As if her petticoat were lined,
With reason's fleece, and hoises[4] sails
And humming flies in thankful gales
Unto her dun curled palace hall
Her warm thanks offering for all.

---

1. The Great Bear (Ursa Major), the constellation including stars that point to the North Star or polestar.
2. Like a stingray, or electric ray (*Torpedo nobiliana*).
3. Head.
4. Hoists.

* * *

Lord clear my misted sight that I
May hence view Thy divinity.
Some sparks whereof Thou up dost hasp
Within this little downy wasp
In whose small corporation[5] we
A school and a schoolmaster see
Where we may learn, and easily find
A nimble spirit bravely mind
Her work in ev'ry limb: and lace
It up neat with a vital grace,
Acting each part though ne'er so small
Here of this fustian animal.
Till I enravished climb into
The Godhead on this lather[6] do.
Where all my pipes inspired upraise
An heavenly music furred[7] with praise.

n.d.

Huswifery

Make me, O Lord, Thy spinning wheel[1] complete.
   Thy holy word my distaff[2] make for me.
Make mine affections Thy swift flyers[3] neat
   And make my soul Thy holy spool[4] to be.
   My conversation make to be Thy reel[5]
   And reel the yarn thereon spun on Thy wheel.

Make me Thy loom[6] then, knit therein this twine:
   And make Thy holy spirit, Lord, wind quills:[7]
Then weave the web Thyself. The yarn is fine.
   Thine Ordinances make my fulling mills.[8]
   Then dye the same in heavenly colors choice,
   All pinked[9] with varnished flowers of paradise.

5. Body, bodily organization.
6. Ladder.
7. Trimmed.
1. The device on which raw wool or flax was stretched into yarn or thread.
2. Part that holds the raw wool or flax.
3. Devices that twist the wool or flax into threads.
4. Cylinder on which the twisted threads are first wound.

5. Holder of the finished yarn.
6. Machine for weaving yarn into cloth.
7. Hollow reeds on which the yarn is wound.
8. Mills where cloth is beaten and cleansed with fuller's earth (or soap).
9. Decorated. Varnished: made to shine.

* * *

Then clothe therewith mine understanding, will,
    Affections, judgment, conscience, memory,
My words, and actions, that their shine may fill
    My ways with glory and Thee glorify.
    Then mine apparel shall display before ye
    That I am clothed in holy robes for glory.

n.d.

Before the rise of machine-made textiles during the earliest phase of the Industrial Revolution, housewives devoted a vast proportion of their time to the spinning and weaving of cloth, so that spinning and weaving themselves seemed to represent "huswifery."

Upon Wedlock, and Death of Children

A curious knot God made in paradise,
    And drew it out enameled neatly fresh.
It was the true-love knot, more sweet than spice
    And set with all flowers of grace's dress.
    Its wedden's[1] knot, that ne're can be untied.
    No Alexander's sword[2] can it divide.

The slips[3] here planted, gay and glorious grow:
    Unless an hellish breath do singe their plumes.
Here primrose, cowslips, roses, lilies blow
    With violets and pinks that void[4] perfumes.
    Whose beauteous leaves ore laid with honey dew.
    And chanting birds chirp out sweet music true.

When in this knot I planted was, my stock[5]
    Soon knotted, and a manly flower out brake.
And after it my branch again did knot,
    Brought out another flower its sweet breathed mate.
    One knot gave one tother the tothers place.
    Whence chuckling smiles fought in each others face.

But oh! a glorious hand from glory came
    Guarded with angels, soon did crop this flower[6]

1. Wedding's.
2. Alexander the Great cut the Gordian knot, famed as a knot that could not be untied, with a stroke of his sword.
3. Seedlings or, figuratively, children.
4. Breathe, exhale.
5. Tree graft.
6. That is, his second child, Elizabeth, who died, aged one year, in 1677.

Which almost tore the root up of the same
    At that unlooked for, dolesome, darksome hour.
    In prayer to Christ perfumed it did ascend,
    And angels bright did it to heaven tend.

But pausing on't, this sweet perfumed my thought,
    Christ would in glory have a flower, choice, prime,
And having choice, chose this my branch forth brought.
    Lord take't. I thank Thee, Thou takst ought[7] of mine,
    It is my pledge in glory, part of me
    Is now in it, Lord, glorified with Thee.

But praying ore my branch, my branch did sprout
    And bore another manly flower, and gay
And after that another, sweet, brake out,
    The which the former hand soon got away.
    But oh! the tortures, vomit, screechings, groans
    And six weeks fever would pierce hearts like stones.[8]

Grief o're doth flow: and nature fault would find
    Were not Thy will, my spell, charm, joy, and gem:
That as I said, I say, take, Lord, they're thine.
    I piecemeal pass to glory bright in them.
    I joy, may I sweet flowers for glory breed,
    Whether Thou getst them green, or lets them seed.

                 ca. 1683

Four of Taylor's children are mentioned in the poem: Samuel, "a manly flower" (b. 1675), survived to maturity; Elizabeth, "another flower," was born in 1676 and died a year later; James, "another manly flower," survived until maturity; Abigail, "another, sweet," was born in 1681 and died in 1683. Since Taylor's fifth child (Bathshuah, b. 1683 or 1684) is not mentioned, the poem probably dates from 1683. A passage from this poem was quoted by Cotton Mather: the only fragment of a Taylor poem to appear in his lifetime. The poem expresses a Puritan's acceptance of death as a sign of God's will.

7. Aught, or anything whatever.
8. Events in the traumatic illness and death of Taylor's fourth child, Abigail.

LUCY TERRY

ca. 1730 – 1821

Aᴌᴛʜᴏᴜɢʜ ᴘʜɪʟʟɪs ᴡʜᴇᴀᴛʟᴇʏ was the first African American to publish a book in the colonies and to earn an international reputation, Lucy Terry is now regarded as the first African American to write poetry. Her one known extant poem, the ballad "Bars Fight," about the last confrontation between Native Americans and the English in 1746 in the western Massachusetts village of Deerfield, was preserved in local oral memory until it was published in Josiah Holland's *History of Western Massachusetts* in 1855. The ballad is elusive, as is any text that comes from the oral tradition. Deerfield residents may have changed Terry's original text to promote the town's mythic participation on the English side in the four colonial wars against the French (1689–1763) for control of North America. Equally difficult to determine is whether Terry shared the dominant racist (English) view of the Native Americans who allied themselves with the French. As a slave bought by Ensign Ebeneezer Wells in Deerfield when she was about five years old, she knew that slaves were killed or captured and taken to Canada in the military struggles of their owners and therefore had no control over their destinies. Most likely the sharp reportorial language describing the conflict in the Deerfield section known as "the Bars," a colonial term for meadows, and the rhyming tetrameter couplets of the ballad are Terry's. Historian George Sheldon has called her description of this battle the best and most vivid in existence.

Terry was freed when Obijah Prince, a wealthy free African American from Vermont, married her in 1756 and bought her freedom. The couple lived in Vermont, where Terry's reputation as a raconteur grew. Eventually she achieved national recognition as a gifted orator. When Williams College rejected her oldest son, she delivered to the board of trustees a three-hour argument against the college's policy of racial discrimination. Unfortunately, her argument changed nothing. In 1797, however, in a dispute over her farmland in Vermont, she argued before the U.S. Supreme Court and won, becoming the first woman and possibly the first African American to argue before the court and earning high praise for her skilled presentation.

FURTHER READING

Josiah Holland. *History of Western Massachusetts.* 1855; reprint, Bowie, Md.: Heritage Books, 1994.

Richard Melvoin. *New England Outpost: War and Society in Colonial Deerfield.* New York: Norton, 1989.

George Sheldon. *A History of Deerfield, Sixteen Thirty-Six to Eighteen Eighty-Six.* Salem, Mass.: Higginson Books, 1989.

Bars Fight

August, 'twas the twenty-fifth,
Seventeen hundred forty-six,
The Indians did in ambush lay,
Some very valiant men to slay,
The names of whom I'll not leave out.
Samuel Allen like a hero fout,[1]
And though he was so brave and bold,
His face no more shall we behold.

Eleazer Hawks was killed outright,
Before he had time to fight, —
Before he did the Indians see,
Was shot and killed immediately.

Oliver Amsden he was slain,
Which caused his friends much grief and pain.
Simeon Amsden they found dead
Not many rods distant from his head.

Adonijah Gillet, we do hear,
Did lose his life which was so dear.
John Sadler fled across the water,
And thus escaped the dreadful slaughter.

Eunice Allen see the Indians coming,
And hopes to save herself by running;
And had not her petticoats stopped her,
The awful creatures had not catched her,
Nor tommy hawked her on the head,
And left her on the ground for dead.
Young Samuel Allen, Oh, lack-a-day!
Was taken and carried to Canada.

1746

1. Fought.

PHILIP FRENEAU
1752–1832

ONE OF PHILIP FRENEAU'S first poems, cowritten at the College of New Jersey (now Princeton University) with his friend Henry Brackenridge in 1771, when New Jersey was still one of Britain's thirteen colonies, is entitled "The Rising Glory of America." When, five years later, independence was declared, Freneau quickly became known throughout the rebellious colonies as the "poet of the American Revolution." After that revolution had succeeded, Freneau remained active as a poet, editor, and journalist. Allied with the emerging Democratic-Republican party led by Thomas Jefferson and Freneau's Princeton friend James Madison, Freneau was a persistent advocate of such Age of Enlightenment principles as reason and natural law and a critic of entrenched privilege and power. He also served—both in his poetry and as the editor of first the *Freeman's Journal* and later the *National Gazette*—as an insistent spokesman for democracy and the rights of such excluded peoples as slaves and Native Americans. He remained an outspoken adversary of the Federalist policies of George Washington's secretary of the treasury, Alexander Hamilton. Washington found his former ally's attacks on the rise of federal authority so disquieting that he termed him "that rascal Freneau."

Freneau was born in New York City in 1752 into the family of a wealthy wine importer and land investor. The young Freneau studied Latin and Greek, immersed himself in his family's extensive library, and associated with many leading figures in commerce and culture who were regular visitors to his family's home. The death of Freneau's father in 1767 marked a decline in the family fortunes, but Freneau was still able to begin his studies at Princeton in 1768. There he quickly became involved in pro-revolutionary politics, forming the American Whig Society with his friends Madison, Brackenridge, and others. He engaged in debates with the pro-Tory Cliosophic Society and wrote satirical attacks on royalism while also immersing himself in the study of literature, including the Latin and Greek classics and many modern English models. From his college days onward, Freneau's writings would show a linked preoccupation with the attainment of American political freedoms and the creation of a peculiarly American literature.

How far he succeeded in advancing the latter agenda has been the subject of some debate. Lewis Leary's influential 1941 biography, *That Rascal Freneau*, is subtitled *A Study in Literary Failure*. Leary contends that Freneau was so preoccupied with journalism that he never allowed himself to fully develop as a poet. Indeed, in Leary's view, "Freneau failed at almost everything he attempted." But many later American poets, including Poe and Whitman, worked extensively as journalists without notable loss to their creative work. Perhaps more significant is the schism between Freneau's radical rejection of England's royalist politics and his continued dependence, as a poet, on well-established English literary forms. In his political verse he shows that he has fully mastered the satirical deployment of the heroic couplet long established by Alexander Pope (1688–1744), who died eight years before Freneau was born. Freneau was able to create genuinely trenchant and still powerful poems in this medium, such as his denunciation of slave-holding, "To Sir Toby," and his still forceful meditations "On the Emigration to America and Peopling the Western Country" and "On Mr. Paine's Rights of Man." Still, it's not clear that Freneau has much to add stylistically to the literary models Pope created for the satiric poem and the poem of ideas a half century before. So, despite the radically American political viewpoint, complete with sharply expressed editorial positions and a great deal of fresh (and historically significant) subject matter, the literary template remains conservatively British. In his nature lyrics, such as "The Wild Honey Suckle," Freneau gravitates toward the rather more modern style of Thomas Gray (1716–1771) and William Collins (1721–1759), English poets of the Age of Sensibility who served as the forerunners of the great age of English romanticism. Yet here, too, it is debatable whether Freneau projects a truly individual voice. Some of his subject matter is fresh, but the tones remain close to those established by his English models. In the last years of his long life (he died in 1832 at the age of eighty), Freneau—his writing style no longer in vogue and himself impoverished and all but forgotten—fell silent as a poet and admitted that he was "out of the literary world."

Freneau's career illustrates that dramatic political changes, such as those brought about by the American Revolution, are often followed much more slowly by cultural changes. Though Freneau is rightly termed the poet of the American Revolution, he was—despite devoted career-long efforts—forced to leave to others the creation of a fully individual, and fully American, language for poetry.

FURTHER READING

Philip Freneau. *A Freneau Sampler*. Ed. Philip M. Marsh. New York: Scarecrow Press, 1963.
———. *The Poems of Philip Freneau*. Ed. Fred Lewis Pattee. 3 vols. New York: Russell & Russell, 1963.
Lewis Leary. *That Rascal Freneau: A Study in Literary Failure*. New Brunswick: Rutgers University Press, 1941.
Philip M. Marsh. *Philip Freneau: Poet and Journalist*. Minneapolis: Dillon Press, 1967.

To Sir Toby

A Sugar Planter in the interior parts of Jamaica,
near the City of San Jago de la Vega (Spanish town), 1784

> *The motions of his spirit are black as night,*
> *And his affections dark as Erebus.*
> SHAKESPEARE

If there exists a hell—the case is clear—
Sir Toby's slaves enjoy that portion here:
Here are no blazing brimstone lakes—'tis true;
But kindled Rum too often burns as blue;
In which some fiend, whom nature must detest,
Steeps Toby's brand, and marks poor Cudjoe's[1] breast.

Here whips on whips excite perpetual fears,
And mingled howlings vibrate on my ears:
Here nature's plagues abound, to fret and tease,
Snakes, scorpions, despots, lizards, centipedes—
No art, no care escapes the busy lash;
All have their due—and all are paid in cash—
The eternal driver keeps a steady eye
On a black herd, who would his vengeance fly.
But chained, imprisoned, on a burning soil,
For the mear avarice of a tyrant, toil!
The lengthy cart-whip guards this monster's reign—
And cracks, like pistols, from the fields of cane.

Ye powers! Who formed these wretched tribes, relate,
What had they done, to merit such a fate!
Why were they brought from Eboe's[2] sultry waste,
To see that plenty which they must not taste—
Food, which they cannot buy, and dare not steal;
Yams and potatoes—many a scanty meal!—

One, with a gibbet wakes his Negro's fears,
One to the windmill nails him by the ears;
One keeps his slave in darkened dens, unfed,
One puts the wretch in pickle ere he's dead:
This, from a tree suspends him by the thumbs,
That, from his table grudges even the crumbs!

O'er yond' rough hills a tribe of females go,

---

1. A common slave's name. Sir Toby is branding a slave to mark him as property.

2. A location in Senegal from which many inhabitants were taken as slaves.

Each with her gourd, her infant, and her hoe;
Scorched by a sun that has no mercy here,
Driven by a devil, whom men call overseer—
In chains, twelve wretches to their labors haste;
Twice twelve I saw, with iron collars graced!—

    Are such the fruits that spring from vast domains?
Is wealth, thus got, Sir Toby, worth your pains!—
Who would your wealth on terms, like these, possess,
Where all we see is pregnant with distress—
Angola's natives scourged by ruffian hands,
And toil's hard product shipp'd to foreign lands.

    Talk not of blossoms, and your endless spring;
What joy, what smile, can scenes of misery bring?—
Though Nature, here, has every blessing spread,
Poor is the laborer—and how meanly fed!—

    Here Stygian[3] paintings light and shade renew,
Pictures of hell, that Virgil's pencil drew:
Here, surly Charons[4] make their annual trip,
And ghosts arrive in every Guinea ship,
To find what beasts these western isles afford,
Plutonian[5] scourges, and despotic lords:—

    Here, they, of stuff determined to be free,
Must climb the rude cliffs of the Liguanee;[6]
Beyond the clouds, in skulking haste repair,
And hardly safe from brother traitors there.—

1784

Freneau's poem draws on details he observed while serving as a business agent on a West Indian plantation on the island of St. Croix from 1776 to 1778, where he experienced slavery and the slave trade firsthand.

3. In ancient Greek myth, the river Styx, which souls must cross to enter Hell.
4. The slave traders are compared to Charon, ferryman across the river Styx.
5. Relating to the Greek god of the underworld, Pluto.
6. As Freneau noted, "the mountains northward of Kingston."

On the Emigration to America and Peopling the Western Country

To western woods, and lonely plains,
Palemon[1] from the crowd departs,
Where Nature's wildest genius reigns,
To tame the soil, and plant the arts—
What wonders there shall freedom show,
What mighty states successive grow!

From Europe's proud, despotic shores
Hither the stranger takes his way,
And in our new found world explores
A happier soil, a milder sway,
Where no proud despot holds him down,
No slaves insult him with a crown.

What charming scenes attract the eye,
On wild Ohio's[2] savage stream!
There Nature reigns, whose works outvie
The boldest pattern art can frame;
There ages past have rolled away,
And forests bloomed but to decay.

From these fair plains, these rural seats,
So long concealed, so lately known,
The unsocial Indian far retreats,
To make some other clime his own,
Where other streams, less pleasing flow,
And darker forests round him grow.[3]

Great sire of floods! Whose varied wave
Through climes and countries takes its way,
To whom creating Nature gave
Ten thousand streams to swell thy sway!
No longer shall *they* useless prove,
Nor idly through forests rove;

Nor longer shall your princely flood
From distant lakes be swelled in vain,

---

1. An ancient Greek name that in English poetry was associated with the poet-shepherds of Arcadia. Freneau suggests that the poetic spirit is departing crowded Europe and migrating to beautiful and spacious America.

2. In 1785, the Ohio remained one of America's most western and least settled rivers.

3. Significantly, when Freneau's "unsocial Indian" is driven westward, he finds the new streams he encounters "less pleasing."

Nor longer through a darksome wood
Advance, unnoticed, to the main,
Far other ends, the heavens decree —
And commerce plans new freights for thee.

While virtue warms the generous breast,
There heaven-born freedom shall reside,
Nor shall the voice of war molest,
Nor Europe's all-aspiring pride —
There Reason shall new laws devise,
And order from confusion rise.

Forsaking kings and regal state,
With all their pomp and fancied bliss,
The traveler owns, convinced though late,
No realm so free, so blessed as this —
The east is half to slaves consigned,
Where kings and priests enchain the mind.

O come the time, and haste the day,
When man shall man no longer crush,
When Reason shall enforce her sway,
Nor these fair regions raise our blush,
Where still the *African* complains,[4]
And mourns his yet unbroken chains.

Far brighter scenes a future age,
The muse[5] predicts, these states will hail,
Whose genius may the world engage,
Whose deeds may over death prevail,
And happier systems bring to view,
Than all the eastern sages knew.

1785

The Wild Honey Suckle

Fair flower, that dost so comely grow,
Hid in this silent, dull retreat,
Untouched thy honeyed blossoms blow,

4. While white Americans might celebrate free-
dom, African Americans remained, with few ex-
ceptions, in a state of slavery.

5. Goddess who inspired poetry.

Unseen thy little branches greet:
 No roving foot shall crush thee here,
 No busy hand provoke a tear.

By Nature's self in white arrayed,
She bade thee shun the vulgar eye,
And planted here the guardian shade,
And sent soft waters murmuring by;
 Thus quietly thy summer goes,
 Thy days declining to repose.

Smit with those charms, that must decay,
I grieve to see your future doom;
They died—nor were those flowers more gay,
The flowers that did in Eden bloom;
 Unpitying frosts, and Autumn's power
 Shall leave no vestige of this flower.

From morning suns and evening dews
At first thy little being came:
If nothing once, you nothing lose,
For when you die you are the same;
 The space between, is but an hour,
 The frail duration of a flower.

      1786

The Indian Burying Ground

In spite of all the learned have said,
I still my old opinion keep;
The posture, that we give the dead,
Points out the soul's eternal sleep.

Not so the ancients of these lands—
The Indian, when from life released,
Again is seated with his friends,
And shares again the joyous feast.[1]

   ✳ ✳ ✳

---

1. "The North American Indians bury their dead in a sitting posture; decorating the corpse with wampum, the images of birds, quadrupeds, etc. And (if that of a warrior) with bows, arrows, tomahawks, and other military weapons" (Freneau's note).

His imaged birds, and painted bowl,
And venison, for a journey dressed,
Bespeak the nature of the soul,
Activity, that knows no rest.

His bow, for action ready bent,
And arrows, with a head of stone,
Can only mean that life is spent,
And not the old ideas gone.

Thou, stranger, that shalt come this way,
No fraud upon the dead commit —
Observe the swelling turf, and say
They do not lie, but here they sit.

Here still a lofty rock remains,
On which the curious eye may trace
(Now wasted, half, by wearing rains)
The fancies of a ruder race.

Here still an agèd elm aspires,
Beneath whose far-projecting shade
(And which the shepherd still admires)
The children of the forest played!

There oft a restless Indian queen
(Pale Sheba,[2] with her braided hair)
And many a barbarous form is seen
To chide the man that lingers there.

By midnight moons, o'er moistening dews,
In habit for the chase arrayed,
The hunter still the deer pursues,
The hunter and the deer, a shade!

And long shall timorous fancy see
The painted chief, and pointed spear,
And Reason's shelf shall bow the knee
To shadows and delusions here.

1787

2. The Arabian queen, noted for her beauty and sagacity, who put King Solomon's wisdom to the test (1 Kings 10).

On Mr. Paine's Rights of Man

Thus briefly sketched the sacred rights of man,
How inconsistent with the royal plan!
Which for itself exclusive honor craves,
Where some are masters born, and millions slaves.
With what contempt must every eye look down
On that base, childish bauble called a *crown*,
The gilded bait, that lures the crowd, to come,
Bow down their necks, and meet a slavish doom;
The source of half the miseries men endure,
The quack that kills them, while it seems to cure,
    Roused by reason of his manly page,
Once more shall Paine a listening world engage:
From Reason's source, a bold reform he brings,
In raising up *mankind*, he pulls down *kings*,
Who, source of discord, patrons of all wrong,
On blood and murder have been fed too long:
Hid from the world, and tutored to be base,
The curse, the scourge, the ruin of our race,
Their's was the task, a dull designing few,
To shackle beings that they scarcely knew,
Who made this globe the residence of slaves,
And built their thrones on systems formed by knaves
—Advance, bright years, to work their final fall,
And haste the period that shall crush them all.
    Who, that has read and scanned the historic page
But glows, at every line, with kindling rage,
To see by them the rights of men aspersed,
Freedom restrained, and Nature's law reversed,
Men, ranked with beasts, by monarchs willed away,
And bound young fools, or madmen to obey:
Now driven to wars, and now oppressed at home,
Compelled in crowds o'er distant seas to roam,[1]
From India's climes the plundered prize[2] to bring
To glad the strumpet, or to glut the king.
    Columbia,[3] hail! Immortal be thy reign:

1. The British navy was then manned to a signifi-
cant degree by impressed (or drafted) sailors,
often summarily forced into service against their
wills. The impressing of American merchant sea-
men into British naval service would later emerge
as one of the causes of the War of 1812.

2. Freneau alludes to the despoiling of India, then
Britain's largest and most lucrative Asian colony.
3. Freneau's frequent term for America.

Without a king, we till the smiling plain;
Without a king, we trace the unbounded sea,
And traffic round the globe, through each degree;
Each foreign clime our honored flag reveres,
Which asks no monarch, to support the stars:
Without a *king*, the laws maintain their sway,[4]
While honor bids each generous heart obey.
Be ours the task the ambitious to restrain,
And this great lesson teach—that kings are vain;
That warring realms to certain ruin haste,
That kings subsist by war, and wars are waste:
So shall our nation, formed on Virtue's plan,
Remain the guardian of the Rights of Man,
A vast republic, famed through every clime,
Without a king, to see the end of time.

1795

Thomas Paine (1737–1809), English-born pamphleteer for the American Revolution and author of *The Rights of Man* (1791), argued that human rights derive not from a monarch but from nature. Paine advanced his concept of "natural rights" in support of democratic government as a replacement for monarchial rule (which often used for justification an assertion of the ruler's "divine right"). In the context of the French Revolution, his book was viewed as seditious in England, where he was indicted for treason, and Paine was forced to flee England for revolutionary France.

PHILLIS WHEATLEY
ca. 1753–1784

THE FIRST AFRICAN AMERICAN to publish a book of poems, Phillis Wheatley was at an early age a celebrity in upper-class colonial and international circles. But this status does not mean that she escaped her African-American positioning. John Wheatley of Boston purchased her for his wife, Susanna, when Phillis arrived in Boston as a young child on a slave ship from West Africa. Because of her precocity and religious ardor, the Wheatleys educated Phillis and treated her almost as

---

4. Freneau mocks such English political theorists as Thomas Hobbes (1588–1679), who had argued that without a king's absolute authority a lawful and orderly society could not be sustained.

one of their own three children, though they did not adopt her. They did not even emancipate her until 1773 or perhaps even later. By then she was already writing and publishing poetry—her first poem was published in *The Newport Mercury* of Rhode Island on December 21, 1767. Although she published her first volume, *Poems on Various Subjects, Religious and Moral* in 1773, white supremacist attitudes made the publication very difficult. Attempts to publish the book in the colonies failed. Susanna Wheatley helped Phillis pursue patrons within her Methodist circle, locating an important supporter in the countess of Huntingdon in England, who arranged for publication in London and Phillis's promotion tour there. Wheatley's reputation continued to grow as she continued to write, and she attracted attention from such famous figures as George Washington, Benjamin Franklin, and Voltaire.

After the Wheatleys died, Phillis received no inheritance and was left destitute. She married John Peters, another free African American, in 1778, and the couple lived in poverty. Peters was forced to house Phillis and their three children in an African-American boardinghouse, where all three children died and Phillis, always frail, became very ill. Though penniless, she refused to sell the copy of Milton's *Paradise Lost* that Franklin had once given her. She died before she could raise enough money to publish her second volume of poems and was buried in an unmarked grave with her third child. Many of the poems and letters she wrote in her final years were lost.

Wheatley's poetry is often read as an imitation of the prevailing English poetry of her time. She so excelled in employing the eighteenth-century poetic idiom that supporters praised her for this talent while detractors doubted that the work was her own. She clearly understood how to reach her largely European-American audience. She wrote in a style and form that they valued and adapted a Christian rhetoric—based in Methodism—that they could embrace. During the 1830s the abolitionists reprinted her poetry because they found that it helped their antislavery cause.

Wheatley also inscribes a double-voiced quality into her poetry, revealing her consciousness of the cultural doubleness that W. E. B. Du Bois and, more recently, Henry Louis Gates, Jr., have identified with the position of African Americans in the United States. Poems that appeared submissive on the surface were rebellious in their depths. In her well-known early poem, "On Being Brought from Africa to America," for example, she writes in a conventional religious rhetoric in order to remind European Americans that Christ redeemed Africans. In addition, she chides readers for the un-Christian racism embodied in the statement "Their colour is a diabolic die," reminding them that their charges of paganism against Africans can apply as well to European Americans who fail to follow Christian principles.

Other poems also reveal Wheatley's subtle self-consciousness about her racial positioning. In "To the University of Cambridge, in New England," she tells Harvard students that she, an "Ethiop," wishes them to share in her Christian redemption, in effect lecturing her elite white male audience about Christianity. Moreover, by juxtaposing her so-called "land of errors" against the American slave colonies, she calls into question the latter's assumption of superiority through Christian rhetoric. Her poem for the English minister George Whitefield states very directly that Christ is an "impartial Savior" who desires the redemption of both Africans and Americans. In "On Imagination," she draws upon the *Iliad* story of the famed Memnon, the Ethiopian son of Aurora. Her poem to the earl of Dartmouth expresses her understanding of the colonial desire for freedom based on her own experience of being kidnapped from her parents and sold into slavery, focusing on the monstrous separation of parent and child. And in her poem to a young African painter, she portrays both him and herself as noble artists who must look to eternity for fair judgment.

Throughout all of this writing, Wheatley speaks in a forceful, though veiled, public voice. She refused to subordinate herself completely because of either her African-American identity or her gender.

FURTHER READING

Henry Louis Gates, Jr. *Figures in Black*. New York: Oxford University Press, 1987.

J. Saunders Redding. *To Make a Poet Black*. Chapel Hill: University of North Carolina Press, 1939.

Phillis Wheatley. *The Collected Works of Phillis Wheatley*. Ed. John C. Shields. New York and Oxford: Oxford University Press, 1988.

——. *Complete Writings*. Ed. Vincent Carretta. Harmondsworth, Eng.: Penguin, 2001.

On Being Brought from Africa to America

'Twas mercy brought me from my Pagan land,
Taught my benighted soul to understand
That there's a God, that there's a Saviour too:
Once I redemption neither sought nor knew.
Some view our sable[1] race with scornful eye,
"Their colour is a diabolic die."
Remember, Christians, Negroes, black as Cain,[2]
May be refin'd, and join th' angelic train.

1773

1. Black.
2. In these lines, Wheatley attempts to revise rac- ist associations of Africans with Cain (Genesis 4) by portraying the connection as transitory.

To the University of Cambridge, in New England

While an intrinsic ardor prompts to write,
The muses promise to assist my pen;
'Twas not long since I left my native shore
The land of errors,[1] and Egyptian gloom:
Father of mercy, 'twas thy gracious hand
Brought me in safety from those dark abodes.

Students, to you 'tis giv'n to scan the heights
Above, to traverse the ethereal space,
And mark the systems of revolving worlds.
Still more, ye sons of science ye receive
The blissful news by messengers from heav'n,
How Jesus' blood for your redemption flows.
See him with hands out-stretcht upon the cross;
Immense compassion in his bosom glows;
He hears revilers, nor resents their scorn:
What matchless mercy in the Son of God!
When the whole human race by sin had fall'n,
He deign'd to die that they might rise again,
And share with him in the sublimest skies,
Life without death, and glory without end.

Improve[2] your privileges while they stay,
Ye pupils, and each hour redeem, that bears
Or good or bad report of you to heav'n.
Let sin, that baneful evil to the soul,
By you be shunn'd, nor once remit your guard;
Suppress the deadly serpent in its egg.
Ye blooming plants of human race divine,
An Ethiop tells you 'tis your greatest foe;
Its transient sweetness turns to endless pain,
And in immense perdition sinks the soul.

1773

The university is Harvard College in Cambridge, Massachusetts, which was often referred to as the University of Cambridge or simply as Cambridge in the seventeenth and eighteenth centuries.

1. Theological errors, specifically, since Africa was not Christianized according to Western traditions. Egyptian gloom: "And Moses stretched forth his hand toward heaven; and there was a thick darkness in all the land of Egypt three days" (Exodus 10:22).
2. Take advantage of someone or a situation.

On the Death of the Rev. Mr. George Whitefield, 1770

Hail, happy saint, on thine immortal throne,
Possest of glory, life, and bliss unknown;
We hear no more the music of thy tongue,
Thy wonted[1] auditories cease to throng.
Thy sermons in unequall'd accents flow'd,
And ev'ry bosom with devotion glow'd;
Thou didst in strains of eloquence refin'd
Inflame the heart, and captivate the mind.
Unhappy we the setting sun deplore,
So glorious once, but ah! it shines no more.

Behold the prophet in his tow'ring flight!
He leaves the earth for heav'n's unmeasur'd height,
And worlds unknown receive him from our sight.
There Whitefield wings with rapid course his way,
And sails to Zion[2] through vast seas of day.
Thy pray'rs, great saint, and thine incessant cries
Have pierc'd the bosom of thy native skies.
Thou moon hast seen, and all the stars of light,
How he has wrestled with his God by night.
He pray'd that grace in ev'ry heart might dwell,
He long'd to see America excel;
He charg'd its youth that ev'ry grace divine
Should with full lustre in their conduct shine;
That Saviour, which his soul did first receive,
The greatest gift that ev'n a God can give,
He freely offer'd to the num'rous throng,
That on his lips with list'ning pleasure hung.

"Take him, ye wretched, for your only good,
"Take him ye starving sinners, for your food;
"Ye thirsty, come to this life-giving stream,
"Ye preachers, take him for your joyful theme;
"Take him my dear Americans," he said,
"Be your complaints on his kind bosom laid:
"Take him, ye Africans, he longs for you,

---

1. Accustomed. Auditories: listeners.
2. Here, indicating the city of God.

"Impartial Saviour is his title due:
"Wash'd in the fountain of redeeming blood,
"You shall be sons,[3] and kings, and priests to God."

Great Countess,[4] we Americans revere
Thy name, and mingle in thy grief sincere;
New England deeply feels, the Orphans mourn,
Their more than father will no more return.

But, though arrested by the hand of death,
Whitefield no more exerts his lab'ring breath,
Yet let us view him in th' eternal skies,
Let ev'ry heart to this bright vision rise;
While the tomb safe retains its sacred trust,
Till life divine re-animates his dust.

1773

George Whitefield (1714–1770) was a well-known English revivalist of the eighteenth century. A follower of John Wesley, Whitefield visited America several times and died in Newburyport, Massachusetts. He was not an abolitionist, however. He used slave labor to build an orphanage in Georgia.

On Imagination

Thy various works, imperial queen, we see,
How bright their forms! how deck'd with pomp by thee!
Thy wond'rous acts in beauteous order stand,
And all attest how potent is thine hand.

From Helicon's[1] refulgent heights attend,
Ye sacred choir, and my attempts befriend:
To tell her glories with a faithful tongue,
Ye blooming graces, triumph in my song.

3. Wheatley originally wrote, "He'll make you free," but was forced to substitute the present wording.

4. The countess of Huntingdon, Selina Shirley Hastings (1707–1791), who supported Whitefield and for whom Whitefield served as chaplain. She spent most of her fortune funding her dissident form of English Methodism. In 1773, Wheatley visited the countess in England when Hastings arranged for the publication of Wheatley's book of poetry, complete with an engraving of the poet on the frontispiece. Wheatley dedicated the book to the countess.

1. One of the many mountain homes of the Muses in Greek myth.

*   *   *

Now here, now there, the roving Fancy flies,
Till some lov'd object strikes her wand'ring eyes,
Whose silken fetters all the senses bind,
And soft captivity involves the mind.

Imagination! who can sing thy force?
Or who describe the swiftness of thy course?
Soaring through air to find the bright abode,
Th' empyreal palace of the thund'ring God,
We on thy pinions² can surpass the wind,
And leave the rolling universe behind:
From star to star the mental optics rove,
Measure the skies, and range the realms above.
There in one view we grasp the mighty whole,
Or with new worlds amaze th' unbounded soul.

Though Winter frowns, to Fancy's raptur'd eyes
The fields may flourish, and gay scenes arise;
The frozen deeps may break their iron bands,
And bid their waters murmur o'er the sands.
Fair Flora³ may resume her fragrant reign,
And with her flow'ry riches deck the plain;
Sylvanus⁴ may diffuse his honours round,
And all the forest may with leaves be crown'd:
Show'rs may descend, and dews their gems disclose,
And nectar sparkle on the blooming rose.

Such is thy pow'r, nor are thine orders vain,
O thou the leader of the mental train:
In full perfection all thy works are wrought,
And thine the sceptre o'er the realms of thought.
Before thy throne the subject-passions bow,
Of subject-passions sov'reign ruler Thou;
At thy command joy rushes on the heart,
And through the glowing veins the spirits dart.

Fancy might now her silken pinions try
To rise from earth, and sweep th' expanse on high;

2. Wings.
3. The Roman goddess of flowers.

4. The helper of woodspeople in Greek mythology.

From Tithon's[5] bed now might Aurora rise,
Her cheeks all glowing with celestial dies,
While a pure stream of light o'erflows the skies.
The monarch of the day I might behold,
And all the mountains tipt with radiant gold,
But I reluctant leave the pleasing views,
Which Fancy dresses to delight the Muse;
Winter austere forbids me to aspire,
And northern tempests damp the rising fire;
They chill the tides of Fancy's flowing sea,
Cease then, my song, cease the unequal lay.

1773

To the Right Honourable William, Earl of Dartmouth, His Majesty's Principal Secretary of State for North America, &c.

Hail, happy day, when, smiling like the morn,
Fair Freedom rose New-England to adorn:
The northern clime beneath her genial ray,
Dartmouth, congratulates thy blissful sway:
Elate with hope her race no longer mourns,
Each soul expands, each grateful bosom burns,
While in thine hand with pleasure we behold
The silken reins, and Freedom's charms unfold.
Long lost to realms beneath the northern skies
She shines supreme, while hated faction dies:
Soon as appear'd the Goddess[1] long desir'd,
Sick at the view, she[2] languish'd and expir'd;
Thus from the splendors of the morning light
The owl in sadness seeks the caves of night.

No more, America, in mournful strain
Of wrongs, and grievance unredress'd complain,

5. Also known as Tithonus. Tithon married Aurora (or Eos), the dawn goddess, and fathered her black son, Memnon, the heroic Ethiopian king whom Achilles killed in battle in Homer's *Iliad*.

1. Freedom.
2. Faction (personified).

No longer shall thou dread the iron chain,
Which wanton Tyranny with lawless hand
Had made, and with it meant t' enslave the land.

Should you, my lord, while you peruse my song,
Wonder from whence my love of Freedom sprung,
Whence flows these wishes for the common good,
By feeling hearts alone best understood,
I,[3] young in life, by seeming cruel fate
Was snatch'd from Afric's fancy'd happy seat:
What pangs excruciating must molest,
What furrows labour in my parent's breast?
Steel'd was that soul and by no misery mov'd
That from a father seiz'd his babe belov'd:
Such, such my case. And can I then but pray
Others may never feel tyrannic sway?

For favours past, great Sir, our thanks are due,
And thee we ask thy favours to renew,
Since in thy pow'r,[4] as in thy will before,
To sooth the griefs, which thou did'st once deplore.
May heav'nly grace the sacred sanction give
To all thy works, and thou for ever live
Not only on the wings of fleeting Fame,
Though praise immortal crowns the patriot's name,
But to conduct to heav'ns refulgent fane,[5]
May fiery coursers[6] sweep th' ethereal plain,
And bear thee upwards to that blest abode,
Where, like the prophet, thou shalt find thy God.

1773

William Legge, third earl of Dartmouth (1733–1801), for whom Dartmouth College is named, became the British Secretary of State for the Colonies and the President of the Board of Trade and Foreign Plantations in Lord North's administration in August 1772. Some thought that he was attentive to colonial grievances. He was sympathetic to Method-

3. This autobiographical passage rewrites Africa as a place in which she might have been happy, not a place from which she was mercifully delivered (as in "On Being Brought from Africa to America").

4. That is, it is in thy power.
5. Shining temple.
6. Horses. Ethereal plain: skies.

ists in England and was a friend of the countess of Huntingdon, Wheatley's patron. When Wheatley met the earl on her trip to England in 1773, he presented her with a copy of Tobias Smollett's translation of *Don Quixote*.

To S. M., a Young African Painter, on Seeing His Works

To show the lab'ring bosom's deep intent,
And thought in living characters to paint,
When first thy pencil did those beauties give,
And breathing figures learnt from thee to live,
How did those prospects give my soul delight,
A new creation rushing on my sight?
Still, wond'rous youth! each noble path pursue,
On deathless glories fix thine ardent view:
Still may the painter's and the poet's fire
To aid thy pencil, and thy verse conspire!
And may the charms of each seraphic[1] theme
Conduct thy footsteps to immortal fame!
High to the blissful wonders of the skies
Elate thy soul, and raise thy wishful eyes.
Thrice happy, when exalted to survey
That splendid city, crown'd with endless day,
Whose twice six gates[2] on radiant hinges ring:
Celestial Salem[3] blooms in endless spring.

Calm and serene thy moments glide along,
And may the muse inspire each future song!
Still, with the sweets of contemplation bless'd,
May peace with balmy wings your soul invest!
But when these shades of time are chas'd away,
And darkness ends in everlasting day,
On what seraphic pinions shall we move,
And view the landscapes in the realms above?
There shall thy tongue in heav'nly murmurs flow,
And there my muse with heav'nly transport glow:
No more to tell of Damon's[4] tender sighs,

1. Celestial or angelic.
2. According to Revelation 21, the new Heavenly Jerusalem, like the original earthly Jerusalem, has twelve gates, one for each of the tribes of Israel.
3. The Heavenly Jerusalem or Zion.
4. Refers to the classical myth in which Damon pledges his life for his friend Pythias.

Or rising radiance of Aurora's[5] eyes,
For nobler themes demand a nobler strain,
And purer language on th' ethereal plain.
Cease, gentle muse! the solemn gloom of night
Now seals the fair creation from my sight.

1773

S. M. was Scipio Moorhead, a slave of Rev. John Moorhead in Boston.

To His Excellency General Washington

Celestial choir! enthron'd in realms of light,
Columbia's[1] scenes of glorious toils I write.
While freedom's cause her anxious breast alarms,
She flashes dreadful in refulgent[2] arms.
See mother earth her offspring's fate bemoan,
And nations gaze at scenes before unknown!
See the bright beams of heaven's revolving light
Involved in sorrows and veil of night!
The goddess comes, she moves divinely fair,
Olive and laurel[3] bind her golden hair:
Wherever shines this native of the skies,
Unnumber'd charms and recent graces rise.

Muse! bow propitious while my pen relates
How pour her armies through a thousand gates,
As when Eolus[4] heaven's fair face deforms,
Enwrapp'd in tempest and a night of storms;
Astonish'd ocean feels the wild uproar,
The refluent surges beat the sounding shore;
Or thick as leaves in Autumn's golden reign,
Such, and so many, moves the warrior's train.
In bright array they seek the work of war,
Where high unfurl'd the ensign waves in air.
Shall I to Washington their praise recite?
Enough thou know'st them in the fields of fight.

---

5. The Roman goddess of dawn.
1. Wheatley's designation of America as "the land Columbus found" is thought to be the first printed instance of the phrase.

2. Brilliant and glorious.
3. Traditional symbols of victory.
4. Ruler of the winds.

Thee, first in peace and honours,—we demand
The grace and glory of thy martial band.
Fam'd for thy valour, for thy virtues more,
Hear every tongue thy guardian aid implore!

One century scarce perform'd its destined round,
When Gallic[5] powers Columbia's fury found;
And so may you, whoever dares disgrace
The land of freedom's heaven-defended race!
Fix'd are the eyes of nations on the scales,
For in their hopes Columbia's arm prevails.
Anon Britannia droops the pensive head,
While round increase the rising hills of dead.
Ah! cruel blindness to Columbia's state!
Lament thy thirst of boundless power too late.

Proceed, great chief, with virtue on thy side,
Thy ev'ry action let the goddess guide.
A crown, a mansion, and a throne that shine,
With gold unfading, WASHINGTON! be thine.

1776

Thomas Paine published this poem in *Pennsylvania Magazine*. George Washington invited Wheatley to meet him after she sent it to him in a letter.

JOEL BARLOW
1754–1812

JOEL BARLOW WAS BORN in the colony of Connecticut in 1754. After graduating from Yale, he served in the Revolutionary army and then worked as a lawyer and journalist. A member of a literary group called the Connecticut Wits, he wrote an epic poem about America called *The Vision of Columbus* (1787), later expanded and retitled *The Columbiad* (1807). Barlow, like others of his time, was concerned

5. French. This passage refers to the French and Indian War (1754–1763), the last of four campaigns waged between France and England, which ultimately ended France's colonial power in North America.

about producing a reputable national culture and literature that would comple-
ment the nation's new political independence.

Traveling with his wife to France, England, and North Africa, Barlow be-
friended Tom Paine and other political radicals and became committed to dem-
ocratic and egalitarian values. While in France, he composed his exuberant
mock-heroic poem called *The Hasty Pudding*. Beyond displaying an affable love of
gustatory pleasure, the poem makes a place for itself in an eighteenth-century tra-
dition of social humor. Like poems by Alexander Pope and others, it employs an
ironically elevated style to describe quite ordinary objects and behaviors. But *The
Hasty Pudding* possesses a serious side as well. It manifests a patriotic aim in cele-
brating a dish associated with the United States, a democratic ambience in prais-
ing a cornmeal mush common to the tables of poor people, and an awareness of
Native-American contributions to emerging national customs.

In 1811 President James Madison appointed Barlow minister to France. Sent to
negotiate a treaty with Napoleon in 1812, he was horrified by Napoleon's bloody
war on Russia and composed an angry protest poem about it called "Advice to a Ra-
ven in Russia." Shortly thereafter, Barlow fell ill of pneumonia and died near Cra-
cow, Poland.

FURTHER READING

Joel Barlow. *Works*. Vol. 2. Ed. W. K. Bottorff and A. L. Ford. Gainesville, Fla.: Scholars' Facsimi-
les and Reprints, 1970.
William C. Dowling. *Poetry and Ideology in Revolutionary Connecticut*. Athens: University of
Georgia Press, 1990.
Arthur L. Ford. *Joel Barlow*. New York: Twayne, 1971.
James Woodress. *A Yankee's Odyssey: The Life of Joel Barlow*. Philadelphia: Lippincott, 1958.

FROM *The Hasty Pudding*

Canto 1

Ye Alps audacious, though the heavens that rise,
To cramp the day and hide me from their skies;
Ye Gallic[1] flags that o'er their heights unfurled,
Bear death to kings, and freedom to the world,
I sing not you. A softer theme I choose,
A virgin theme, unconscious of the muse,
But fruitful, rich, well suited to inspire
The purest frenzy of poetic fire.

1. French.

✻ ✻ ✻

Despise it not, ye bards to terror steeled,
Who hurl your thunders round the epic field:
Nor ye who strain your midnight throats to sing
Joys that the vineyard and the still-house bring;
Or on some distant fair[2] your notes employ,
And speak of raptures that you ne'er enjoy.
I sing the sweets I know, the charms I feel,
My morning incense, and my evening meal—
The sweets of Hasty Pudding. Come, dear bowl,
Glide o'er my palate, and inspire my soul.
The milk beside thee, smoking from the kine,[3]
Its substance mingled, married in with thine,
Shall cool and temper thy superior heat,
And save the pains of blowing while I eat.

Oh! could the smooth, the emblematic song
Flow like thy genial juices o'er my tongue,
Could those mild morsels in my numbers[4] chime,
And, as they roll in substance, roll in rhyme,
No more thy awkward unpoetic name
Should shun the Muse, or prejudice thy fame;
But rising grateful the accustomed ear,
All bards should catch it, and all realms revere!

Assist me first with pious toil to trace
Through wrecks of time thy lineage and thy race;
Declare what lovely squaw,[5] in days of yore,
(Ere great Columbus sought thy native shore)
First gave thee to the world; her works of fame
Have lived indeed, but lived without a name.
Some tawny Ceres,[6] goddess of her days,
First learned with stones to crack the well-dried maize,
Through the rough sieve to shake the golden shower,
In boiling water stir the yellow flour:
The yellow flour, bestrewed and stirred with haste,
Swells in the flood and thickens to a paste,
Then puffs and wallops, rises to the brim,

2. Fair lady.
3. Cattle.
4. Verses.
5. Barlow here acknowledges the hasty pudding

as a Native-American invention that has enriched
the cuisine of all people who subsequently ar-
rived in the New World.
6. Roman goddess of agriculture.

Drinks the dry knobs that on the surface swim;
The knobs at last the busy ladle breaks,
And the whole mass its true consistence takes.

Could but her sacred name, unknown so long,
Rise, like her labors, to the son of song,
To her, to them, I'd consecrate my lays,[7]
And blow her pudding with the breath of praise,
If 'twas Oella,[8] whom I sang before,
I here ascribe her one great virtue more.
Not through the rich Peruvian realms alone
The fame of Sol's[9] sweet daughter should be known,
But o'er the world's wide climes should live secure,
Far as his rays extend, as long as they endure.

Dear Hasty Pudding, what unpromised joy
Expands my heart, to meet thee in Savoy!
Doomed o'er the world through devious paths to roam,
Each clime my country, and each house my home,
My soul is soothed, my cares have found an end,
I greet my long-lost, unforgotten friend.

For thee through Paris, that corrupted town,
How long in vain I wandered up and down,
Where shameless Bacchus,[10] with his drenching hoard,
Cold from his cave usurps the morning board.
London is lost in smoke and steeped in tea;
No Yankee there can lisp the name of thee;
The uncouth word, a libel on the town,
Would call a proclamation from the crown.[11]
For climes oblique, that fear the sun's full rays,
Chilled in their fogs, exclude the generous maize;
A grain whose rich luxuriant growth requires
Short gentle showers, and bright ethereal fires.

But here, though distant from our native shore,
With mutual glee we meet and laugh once more.
The same! I know thee by that yellow face,
That strong complexion of true Indian race,

Which time can never change, nor soil impair,
Nor Alpine snows, nor Turkey's morbid air;
For endless years, through every mild domain,
Where grows the maize, there thou art sure to reign.

But man, more fickle, the bold license claims,
In different realms to give thee different names.
Thee the soft nations round the warm Levant[12]
Polanta[13] call, the French of course *Polante*;
Ev'n in thy native regions, how I blush
To hear the Pennsylvanians call thee *Mush*!
On Hudson's banks, while men of Belgic spawn
Insult and eat thee by the name *Suppawh*.
All spurious appellations, void of truth;
I've better known thee from my earliest youth,
Thy name is *Hasty Pudding*! thus our sires
Were wont to greet thee fuming from their fires;
And while they argued in thy just defense
With logic clear, they thus explained the sense:
"In *haste* the boiling cauldron, o'er the blaze,
Receives and cooks the ready-powdered maize;
In *haste* 'tis served, and then in equal *haste*,
With cooling milk, we make the sweet repast,
No carving to be done, no knife to grate
The tender ear, and wound the stony plate;
But the smooth spoon, just fitted to the lip,
And taught with art the yielding mass to dip,
By frequent journeys to the bowl well stored,
Performs the hasty honors of the board."
Such is thy name, significant and clear,
A name, a sound to every Yankee dear,
But most to me, whose heart and palate chaste
Preserve my pure hereditary taste.

There are who strive to stamp with disrepute
The luscious food, because it feeds the brute;
In tropes[14] of high-strained wit, while gaudy prigs
Compare thy nursling, man, to pampered pigs;
With sovereign scorn I treat the vulgar jest,

12. The region that is now Syria, Lebanon, and Israel.

13. Polenta, an Italian cornmeal mush.

14. Figures of speech.

Nor fear to share thy bounties with the beast.
What though the generous cow gives me to quaff
The milk nutritious; am I then a calf?
Or can the genius of the noisy swine,
Though nursed on pudding, thence lay claim to mine?
Sure the sweet song, I fashion to thy praise,
Runs more melodious than the notes they raise.

My song resounding in its grateful glee,
No merit claims; I praise myself in thee.
My father loved thee through his length of days;
For thee his fields were shaded o'er with maize;
From thee what health, what vigor he possessed,
Ten sturdy freemen from his loins attest;
Thy constellation ruled my natal morn,
And all my bones were made of Indian corn.
Delicious grain! whatever form it take,
To roast or boil, to smother or to bake,
In every dish 'tis welcome still to me,
But most, my Hasty Pudding, most in thee.

Let the green succotash with thee contend,
Let beans and corn their sweetest juices blend,
Let butter drench them in its yellow tide,
And a long slice of bacon grace their side;
Not all the plate, how famed soe'er it be,
Can please my palate like a bowl of thee.

Some talk of hoe-cake, fair Virginia's pride,
Rich Johnny-cake this mouth has often tried;
Both please me well, their virtues much the same;
Alike their fabric, as allied their fame,
Except in dear New England, where the last
Receives a dash of pumpkin in the paste,
To give it sweetness and improve the taste.
But place them all before me, smoking hot,
The big round dumpling rolling from the pot;
The pudding of the bag, whose quivering breast,
With suet lined leads on the Yankee feast;
The Charlotte brown, within whose crusty sides
A belly soft the pulpy apple hides;
The yellow bread, whose face like amber glows,

And all of Indian that the bake-pan knows—
You tempt me not. My favorite greets my eyes,
To that loved bowl my spoon by instinct flies.

1796

Written in France, this poem praises America's "simplicity in diet," as the poet explained in his "Preface." More particularly, the poem nostalgically and genially pays tribute to the "hasty pudding," a cornmeal pudding of Native American origin that was a staple dish in much of the New World. Barlow adopts a humorously elevated style in which to laud a notoriously "plain dish."

SONGS OF THE AMERICAN REVOLUTION
AND NEW NATION

BOTH THE PATRIOTS AND the loyalists relied on songs and ballads to argue their causes to the colonial and British publics, distributing them through pamphlets, broadsides, newspapers, and other popular outlets in order to reach as many people in all classes as possible. During the war itself, both sides used often chauvinistic and propagandistic songs aimed at espousing the righteousness of their struggle to boost the morale of troops and the homefront. After the war, U.S. writers like Francis Hopkinson and Thomas Paine composed toasts to George Washington and John Adams, joining many patriots who turned to verse to honor the first leaders of the new nation and to mark official occasions. A selection of both patriot and loyalist poems and songs is included here to establish how both the new nation's leaders and the opposing colonial forces attempted to influence public opinion through popular and ephemeral lyrics.

FURTHER READING

Frank Moore, ed. *Songs and Ballads of the American Revolution.* 1856; reprint, Port Washington, N.Y.: Kennikat Press, 1964.

PATRIOT LYRICS

The "Liberty Song" and others in this group urge everyone to rally to the patriot cause.

The Liberty Song

Come join hand in hand, brave Americans all,
And rouse your bold hearts at fair Liberty's call;
No tyrannous acts shall suppress your just claim,
Or stain with dishonor America's name.

In freedom we're born, and in freedom we'll live;
Our purses are ready,
Steady, Friends, steady;
Not as slaves, but as freemen our money we'll give.

Our worthy forefathers—let's give them a cheer—
To climates unknown did courageously steer;
Thro' oceans to deserts, for freedom they came,
And, dying, bequeath'd us their freedom and fame.

Their generous bosoms all dangers despis'd,
So highly, so wisely, their birthrights they priz'd;
We'll keep what they gave, we will piously keep,
Nor frustrate their toils on the land or the deep.

The Tree, their own hands to Liberty rear'd,
They lived to behold growing strong and rever'd;
With transport then cried,—"Now our wishes we gain,
For our children shall gather the fruits of our pain."

How sweet are the labors that freemen endure,
That they shall enjoy all the profit, secure,—
No more such sweet labors Americans know,
If Britons shall reap what Americans sow.

Swarms of placemen and pensioners soon will appear,
Like locusts deforming the charms of the year:
Suns vainly will rise, showers vainly descend,
If we are to drudge for what others shall spend.

＊　＊　＊

Then join hand in hand, brave Americans all,
By uniting we stand, by dividing we fall;
In so righteous a cause let us hope to succeed,
For Heaven approves of each generous deed.

All ages shall speak with amaze and applause,
Of the courage we'll show in support of our laws;
To die we can gear,—but to serve we disdain,
For shame is to freemen more dreadful than pain.

This bumper I crown for our sovereign's health,
And this for Britannia's glory and wealth:
The wealth, and that glory immortal may be,
If she is but just, and we are but free.
  In freedom we're born.

1768

Chester

Let tyrants shake their iron rods,
and slav'ry clank her galling chains;
We fear them not, we trust in God—
New England's God forever reigns.

Howe and Burgoyne and Clinton, too,
With Prescott and Cornwallis joined
Together plot our overthrow,
In one infernal league combined

When God inspired us for the fight,
Their ranks were broke, their lines were forced;
Their ships were shattered in our sight,
Or swiftly driven from our coast.

The foe comes on with haughty stride;
Our troops advance with martial noise;
Their veterans flee before our youth,
And generals yield to beardless boys.

What grateful offering shall we bring?
What shall we render to the Lord?
Loud hallelujahs let us sing,
And praise his name on every chord.

1770

Alphabet

A, stands for Americans, who scorn to be slaves;
B, for Boston, where fortitude their freedom saves;
C, stands for Congress, which, though loyal, will be free;
D, stands for defence, 'gainst force and tyranny.
    Stand firmly, A and Z,
      We swear forever to be free!

E, stands for evils, which a civil war must bring;
F, stands for fate, dreadful to both people and king;
G, stands for George, may God give him wisdom and grace;
H, stands for hypocrite, who wears a double face.

J, stands for justice, which traitors in power defy,
K, stands for king, who should to such the axe apply;
L, stands for London, to its country ever true,
M, stands for Mansfield, who hath another view.

N, stands for North, who to the House the mandate brings,
O, stands for oaths, binding on subjects, not on kings;
P, stands for people, who their freedom should defend,
Q, stands for quere, when will England's troubles end?

R, stands for rebels, not at Boston but at home,
S, stands for Stuart, sent by Whigs abroad to roam,
T, stands for Tories, who may try to bring them back,
V, stands for villains, who have well deserved the rack.

W, stands for Wilkes, who us from warrants saved,
Y, stands for York, the New, half corrupted, half enslaved,
Z, stands for Zero, but means the Tory minions,
Who threatens us with fire and sword, to bias our opinions.
    Stand firmly, A and Z,
      We swear forever to be free!

1775

The King's own Regulars;
AND THEIR TRIUMPHS OVER THE IRREGULARS

Since you all will have singing, and won't be said, nay,
I cannot refuse where you so beg and pray;
So I'll sing you a song—as a body may say.
'Tis of the King's Regulars, who ne'er run way.
    O the old Soldiers of the King, and the King's own Regulars.

At Preston Pans we met with some Rebels one day,
We marshall'd ourselves all in comely array:
Our hearts were all stout, and bid our legs stray,
But our feet were wrong headed and took us away.
    O the old soldiers.

At Falkirk we resolv'd to be braver,
And recover some credit by better behaviour;
We would not acknowledge feet had done us a favour;
So feet swore they would stand, but—legs ran, however.
    O the old soldiers.

No troops perform better than we at reviews;
We march and wheel, and whatever you chuse.
George would see how we fight, and we never refuse;
There we all fight with courage—you may see it in the news.
    O the old soldiers.

To Monongehela with fifes and drums
We march'd in fine order, with cannon and bombs:
That great expedition cost infinite sums;
But a few irregulars cut us all into crumbs.
    O the old soldiers.

It was not fair to shoot at us from behind trees:
If they had stood open as they ought before our great Guns we
        should have beat them with ease.
They may fight with one another that way if they please;
But it is not regular to stand and fight with such rascals as these.
    O the old soldiers.

At Fort George and Oswego, to our great reputation,
We shew'd our vast skill in fortification;
The French fired three guns, of the fourth they had no occasion;
For we gave up those forts, not thro' fear—but mere persuasion.
    O the old soldiers.

*   *   *

To Ticonderoga we went in a passion,
Swearing to be revenged on the whole French nation.
But we soon turned tail, without hesitation
Because they fought behind trees, which is not the fashion.
    O the old soldiers.

Lord Loudon he was a fine regular General, they say;
With a great regular army he went his way
Against Louisbourg, to make it his prey;
But return'd without seeing it, for he did not feel bold that day.
    O the old soldiers.

Grown proud at reviews, great George had no rest,
Each grandsire, he had heard a rebellion supprest.
He wish'd a rebellion, look'd round and saw none,
So resolv'd a rebellion to make of his own—
    O the old soldiers.

The Yankees he bravely pitch'd on, because he thought they would not fight,
And so he sent us over to take away their right,
But least they should spoil our review clothes, he cried braver and louder,
"For God's sake, brother kings, don't sell the cowards any powder."
    O the old soldiers.

Our General with his council of war did advise,
How at Lexington we might the Yankees surprise.
We march'd—and we march'd—all surpris'd at being beat;
And so our wise General's plan of surprise was complete.
    O the old soldiers.

For fifteen miles they follow'd and pelted us, we scarce had time to pull a trigger;
But did you ever know a retreat perform'd with more vigour?
For we did it in two hours, which sav'd us from perdition,
'Twas not in going out but in returning consisted our expedition.
    O the old soldiers.

Says our General, we were forced to take to our arms in our own defence:
(For arms read legs, and it will be both truth and sense.)
Lord Percy (says He) I must say something of him in civility,
And that is, I can never enough praise him for his great—agility.
    O the old soldiers.

*   *   *

Of their firing from behind fences, he makes a great pother,
Ev'ry fence has two sides; they made use of one, and we only forgot to use the other.
That we turn'd our backs and ran away so fast, don't let that disgrace us;
'Twas only to make good what Sandwich said, "that the Yankees would not face us."
    O the old soldiers.

As they could not get before us, how could they look us in the face?
We took care they should not, by scampering away apace;
That they had not much to brag of, is a very plain case.
For if they beat us in the fight, we beat them in the race.
    O the old Soldiers of the King, and the King's own Regulars.

1776

The Irishman's Epistle to the Officers and Troops at Boston

By my faith, but I think ye're all makers of bulls,
With your brains in your breeches, your —— in your skulls,
Get home with your muskets, and put up your swords,
And look in your books for the meaning of words.
You see now, my honies, how much you're mistaken.
For Concord by discord can never be beaten.

How brave ye went out with your muskets all bright,
And thought to be-frighten the folks with the sight;
But when you got there how they powder'd your pums,[1]
And all the way home how they pepper'd your —— ,
And it is not, honies, a comical crack,
To be proud in the face, and be shot in the back.

How come ye to think, now, they did not know how
To be after their firelocks as smartly as you?
Why, you see now, my honies, 'tis nothing at all,
But to pull the trigger, and pop goes the ball.

And what have you got now with all your designing,
But a town without victuals to sit down and dine in;
And to look on the ground like a parcel of noodles,
And sing, how Yankees have beaten the Doodles.
I'm sure if you're wise you'll make peace for a dinner,
For fighting and fasting will soon make ye thinner.

1775

1. Most likely French slang for "head."

The Yankee's Return from Camp

Father and I went down to camp,
    Along with Captain Gooding,
And there we see the men and boys,
    As thick as hasty pudding.

CHORUS

    Yankee Doodle, keep it up,
    Yankee Doodle, dandy,
    Mind the music and the step,
    And with the girls be handy.

And there we see a thousand men,
    As rich as 'Squire David;
And what they wasted every day,
    I wish it could be saved.

The 'lasses they eat every day,
    Would keep an house a winter;
They have as much that, I'll be bound,
    They eat it when they're a mind to.

And there we see a swamping gun,
    Large as a log of maple,
Upon a deuced little cart,
    A load for father's cattle.

And every time they shoot it off,
    It takes a horn of powder,
And makes a noise like father's gun,
    Only a nation louder.

I went as nigh to one myself,
    As Siah's underpinning;
And father when as nigh again,
    I thought the deuce was in him.

Cousin Simon grew so bold,
    I thought he would cock'd it;
It scar'd me so, I shrink'd it off,
    And hung by father's pocket.

           ✻   ✻   ✻

And Captain Davis had a gun,
    He kind of clapt his hand on't,
And stuck a crooked stabbing iron
    Upon the little end on't.

And there I see a pumpkin shell
    As big as mother's basin;
And every time they touch'd it off,
    They scamper'd like the nation.

I see a little barrel too,
    The heads were made of leather,
They knock'd upon't with little clubs,
    And call'd the folks together.

And there was Captain Washington,
    And gentlefolks about him,
They say he's grown so tarnal proud,
    He will not ride without 'em.

He got him on his meeting clothes,
    Upon a slapping stallion,
He set the world along in rows,
    In hundreds and in millions.

The flaming ribbons in his hat,
    They look'd so taring fine ah,
I wanted pockily to get,
    To give to my Jemimah.

I see another snarl of men,
    A digging graves, they told me,
So tarnal long, so tarnal deep,
    They 'tended they should hold me.

It scar'd me so, I hook'd it off,
    Nor stop'd, as I remember,
Nor turn'd about, 'till I got home,
    Lock'd up in mother's chamber.

1778

The Public Spirit of the Women

Though age at my elbow has taken his stand,
And Time has stretch'd o'er me his wrinkling hand;
Our patriot fair like a charm can inspire,
In three-score-and ten, twenty's spirit and fire.
Derry down, down, hey derry down.

Boy, fill me a bumper! As long as I live,
The patriot fair for my toast must I give;
Here's a health to the sex of every degree,
Where sweetness and beauty with firmness agree.
Derry down, down, hey derry down.

No more will I babble of times that are past,
My wish is, the present forever may last;
Already I see sulky George in despair,
Should he vanquish the men, to vanquish the fair.
Derry down, down, hey derry down.

Could time be roll'd backward, and age become young,
My heart swell with ardor, my arm be new strung;
Under Washington's banner I'd cheerfully fight,
Where the smiles of the fair with glory untie.
Derry down, down, hey derry down.

Fill a bumper again, boy, and let it go round,
For the waters of youth in claret are found;
The younkers shall know, I've the courage to dare
Drink as deep as the best to the patriot fair.
Derry down, down, hey derry down.

1778

A Toast to Washington

Francis Hopkinson

'Tis Washington's health—fill a bumper around,
For he is our glory and pride;
Our arms shall in battle with conquest be crowned,
Whilst virtue and he's on our side.

*   *   *

'Tis Washington's health—loud cannons should roar,
And trumpets the truth should proclaim;
There cannot be found, search all the world o'er,
His equal in virtue and fame.

'Tis Washington's health—our hero to bless,
May heaven look graciously down!
Oh! Long may he live our hearts to possess,
And freedom still call him her own.

1791

Adams and Liberty

Thomas Paine

Ye sons of Columbia, who bravely have fought
For those rights which unstained from your sires have descended,
May you long taste the blessings your valour has bought
And your sons reap the soil which your fathers defended,
  Mid the reign of mild peace
  May your nation increase
With the Glory of Rome, and the wisdom of Greece;
And ne'er may the sons of Columbia be slaves,
While the earth bears a plant, or the sea rolls its waves.

In a clime whose rich vales feed the marts of the world
Whose shores are unshaken by Europe's commotion
The trident of Commerce should never be hurled,
To incense the legitimate powers of the ocean.
  But should pirates invade
  Though in thunder arrayed,
Let your cannon declare the free charter of Trade,
For ne'er shall the sons, &c.[1]

While France her huge limbs bathes recumbent in blood,
And society's base threats with wide dissolution;
May Peace, like the dove who returned from the flood,
Find an ark of abode in our mild Constitution!
  But though peace is our aim,

---

1. Signal to repeat the last two lines of the first verse.

Yet the boon we disclaim
If bought by our Sovereignty, Justice or Fame,
For ne'er shall the sons, &c.

Let our patriots destroy Anarch's pestilent worm,
Lest our Liberty's growth should be checked by corrosion,
Then let clouds thicken round us, we heed not the storm,
Our realm fears no shock, but the earth's own explosion.
    Foes assail us in vain
    Though their fleets bridge the main,
For our altars and laws with our lives we'll maintain.
And ne'er shall the sons, &c.

                                                            1798

LOYALIST LYRICS

The loyalists attempted to create a sense of solidarity based on their allegiance to
England.

When Good Queen Elizabeth Governed the Realm

When good Queen Elizabeth govern'd the realm,
And Burleigh's sage counsels directed the helm,
In vain Spain and France our conquest oppos'd;
For Valor conducted what Wisdom propos'd
    Beef and beer was their food;
    Love and Truth arm'd their band;
    Their courage was ready—
    Steady, boys, steady—
To fight and to conquer by sea and by land.

But since tea and coffee, so much to our grief,
Have taken the place of strong beer and roast beef,
Our laurels have wither'd, our trophies been torn;
And the lions of England French triumphs adorn.
    Tea and slops are their food;
    They unnerve every hand—
    Their courage unsteady
    And not always ready—
They often are conquer'd by sea and by land.

                    *   *   *

St. George views with transport our generous flame:
"My sons, rise to glory, and rival my fame.
Ancient manners again in my sons I behold
And this age must eclipse all the ages of gold."
    Beef and beer are our food;
    Love and Truth arm our band;
    Our courage is steady,
    And always is ready
To fight and to conquer by sea and by land.

While thus we regale as our fathers of old,
Our manners as simple, our courage as bold,
May Vigor and Prudence our freedom secure
Long as rivers, or ocean, or stars shall endure
    Beef and beer are our food;
    Love and Truth arm our band;
    Our courage is steady,
    And always is ready
To fight and to conquer by sea and by land.

1774

Song for a Fishing Party

How sweet is the season, the sky how serene;
On Delaware's banks how delightful the scene;
The Prince of the Rivers, his waves all asleep,
In silence majestic glides on to the deep.

Away from the noise of the fife and the drum,
And all the rude din of Bellona we come;
And a plentiful store of good humor we bring
To season our feast in the shade of Cold Spring.

A truce then to all whig and tory debate;
True lovers of freedom, contention we hate:
For the demon of discord in vain tries his art
To possess or inflame a true Protestant heart.

True Protestant friends to fair Liberty's cause,
To decorum, good order, religion and laws,
From avarice, jealousy, perfidy, free;
We wish all the world were as happy as we.

*   *   *

We have wants, we confess, but are free from the care
Of those that abound, yet have nothing to spare:
Serene as the sky, as the river serene,
We are happy to want envy, malice, and spleen.

While thousands around us, misled by a few,
The phantoms of pride and ambition pursue,
With pity their fatal delusion we see;
And wish all the world were as happy as we!

1776

Burrowing Yankees

Ye Yankees who, mole-like, still throw up the earth,
And like them, to your follies, are blind from your birth;
Attempt not to hold British troops at defiance,
True Britons, with whom you pretend an alliance.

Mistake not; such blood ne'er run in your veins,
'Tis no more than the dregs, the lees, or the drains;
Ye affect to talk big of your hourly attacks;
Come on! And I'll warrant, we'll soon see your backs.

Such threats of bravadoes serve only to warm
The true British hearts, you ne'er can alarm;
The Lion, once rous'd, will strike such a terror,
Shall show you, poor fools, your presumption and error.

And the time will soon come when your whole rebel race
Will be drove from the lands, nor dare show your face;
Here's a health to great George, may he fully determine,
To root from the earth all such insolent vermin.

1776

A Refugee Song

Here's a bumper, brave boys, to the health of our king,
Long may he live, and long may we sing,
In praise of a monarch who boldly defends
The laws of the realm, and the cause of his friends.

Then cheer up, my lads, we have nothing to fear,
While we remain steady and always keep ready
To add to the trophies of this happy year.

The Congress did boast of their mighty ally,
But George does both France and the Congress defy;
And when Britons unite, there's no force can withstand
Their fleets and their armies, by sea and on land.
Then cheer up, &c.

Thus supported, our cause we will ever maintain,
And all treaties with rebels will ever disdain;
Till reduced by our arms, they are forced to confess,
While ruled by Great Britain they ne'er knew distress.
Then cheer up, &c.

Then let us, my boys, Britain's right e'er defend,
Who regards not her rights, we esteem not our friend;
Then, brave boys, we both France and the Congress defy,
And we'll fight for Great Britain and George 'til we die.
Then cheer up, &c.

1779

PART TWO

✦

*Early to
Mid-Nineteenth Century*

INTRODUCTION

As THE NINETEENTH CENTURY progressed, the new nation expanded, flexed its muscles, and sought an identity, all the while being wracked by social inequities and economic contradictions that would, by 1861, threaten a violent dissolution. The nation acted as if it were self-confident, but beneath the surface lurked the institution of African-American slavery, continual wars of conquest against Native American nations, battles at the Mexican border, and often the extreme poverty of working and immigrant classes. Throughout this period, poetry in the United States embarked on a set of interconnected cultural, political, and aesthetic projects, all of them related to the nation's hopes and to what Randall Jarrell was later to call "the ruin of hopes."

The cultural enterprise of the period hummed with contradictory impulses. For example, poets identifying with European-American "high" culture often wished to forge a unified "American" literature, whereas poets and lyricists who identified with marginalized racial, ethnic, class, and gender groups often wrote works that preserved their group's separateness. They needed to console and fortify themselves for their struggles being waged within a nation they could not possess or adequately influence.

The poems and songs of this period were persistently and surprisingly political. Although the positions vary widely, the poets and lyricists recurrently addressed issues of racial justice, women's rights, wealth and poverty, civil liberties, unorthodox love, war and peace, national identity, and national symbology. It becomes difficult to find a poem that is not engaged with at least one of these issues, if not more. This observation pertains to traditionally canonical poets as well as to less recognized ones who are only emerging in our own era. Indeed, the varying political commitments of poets such as William Cullen Bryant, Ralph Waldo Emerson, Edgar Allan Poe, Herman Melville, and Walt Whitman become even clearer in the context of such poets as George Moses Horton, Elizabeth Oakes Smith, Julia Ward Howe, Frances Harper, and Rose Terry Cooke. And once the poems appeared, there was the politics of how they were interpreted and classified, celebrated or repressed, over successive generations.

African-American slave songs and work songs express the vitality of African culture as it developed and hybridized in the New World. They demonstrate spiritual and political fortitude. They also expose the toll in pain, desperation, and death that the system of white supremacy imposed on its victims. These songs play an important role in their period and lay the foundation for much of the vigor and originality of subsequent United States culture—and indeed world culture. Native-American songs, poems, and "ways" similarly represent a set of vital cultural traditions that were active throughout the century. When translated and disseminated into English-language culture, their influence grew. European-American poems and songs often sought to account for the African-American and Native-American presence, sometimes through a process of what the cultural critic Eric Lott has termed "love and theft." By mid-century, Asian immigrant voices were added to the mix, in Hawai'ian plantation work songs and songs of Gold Mountain, which have distinctive characteristics while bearing some striking resemblances to songs of other slave-class, working-class, and immigrant groups.

The aesthetic projects of the age interact with the cultural and political conditions in complex ways that involve both complicity and resistance. African-American poets such as Harper wrote poetry in popular narrative forms with the intent of changing a nation. Including stylistic and ideological elements derived from both African and European sources, these poems sought to move listeners and readers to public action as well as to inform and to stimulate an aesthetic response. The "fireside" European-American poets such as Henry Wadsworth Longfellow and John Greenleaf Whittier tried, with great popular success, to infuse traditional European models with typically American subject matter. Moreover, they joined with Harper in creating an influential antislavery poetic enterprise in the decades before the Civil War. Poe, in many ways a loner, explored his own haunted dreams and created, especially toward the end of his short life, amazingly complex and resonant verbal structures. Emerson, arguing that "America is a poem in our eyes," called for a revolutionary poetry that could include "our log-rolling, our stumps and their politics, our fisheries, our Negroes, and Indians, our boasts, and our repudiations, the wrath of rogues, and the pusillanimity of honest men, the northern trade, the southern planting, the western clearing, Oregon, and Texas." His own poems could not quite meet that challenge. But Whitman wrote poems that did. *Leaves of Grass*, his "epic of democracy," sought to define a nation and a world made up of "opposite equals"—men and women of diverse and contending conditions. Perhaps more than any other poet before or since, Whitman articulated and circulated the rebellious cultural, political, and aesthetic energies surging through a diverse nation—even as it confronted, endured, and survived a war that tested its very being.

AFRICAN-AMERICAN
SLAVE SONGS
1800–1863

BETWEEN 1619 AND 1860, according to historian Ronald Takaki, the African-American slave population grew to about four million, or about thirty-five percent of the South's population. Yet the slaves had no formal voice or power in European-American society. It is not surprising, then, that the slaves developed an oral culture of song to communicate among themselves upon their arrival in the colonies. They needed to talk without having their masters understand their messages, so they often created songs using what Henry Louis Gates, Jr., has called "signifyin(g)," or doubleness, as a coded language of resistance. Moreover, the slaves came from many regions in Africa and needed a common language that all could easily understand. Today these songs are part of the vernacular tradition in African-American literature, and many are familiar throughout the world. They are essential to the fabric of American poetry because of their large-scale continuing influence on poets, songwriters, and popular culture.

African-American slave spirituals, or sorrow songs, are especially valued for their reminder of past racism as well as for their inspiration in struggles against racial injustice. As nineteenth-century slave owners became more frightened by abolitionists and slave revolts, many slaves refused to be silenced. Instead, their songs became more encoded. "Many Thousand Gone," for instance, was first sung by the slaves when they were transported to Hilton Head and Bay Point, South Carolina, to build fortifications for the Civil War. While they toiled under the watchful eyes of their masters, they reminded one another of their coming emancipation.

The songs that appear here highlight the disparity between slave labor and the slave owner's profit, between subjugation and freedom. They also underscore the need for "talking back" by mobilizing physical, spiritual, and cultural resources. The resounding "no" that the slaves courageously sang is precisely the "no" that needs to be said continuously to various forms of oppression. Ancient African oral conventions, such as the repetitions and refrains used in the songs, not only provide a chant-like effect but also produce a politically charged emotional impact needed for a battle. Repetitions in these songs also serve as a reminder and recovery of history—so that the songs themselves can serve as weapons against historical amnesia about racism and colonialism.

Because these songs belong to an oral tradition, they have no definitive texts or exact dates of emergence, even when the songs are associated with specific historical "moments" or events. The lyrics evolved over time as communities sang and improvised them. The first known collection of slave vernacular lyrics appeared in 1801, but many slave communities undoubtedly developed their own collections of favorite songs, ballads, and hymns well before then.

FURTHER READING

William Francis Allen, Charles Pickard Ware, and Lucy McKim Garrison. *Slave Songs of the United States.* 1867; reprint, New York: Peter Smith, 1951.
Henry Louis Gates, Jr. *The Signifying Monkey: A Theory of African-American Literary Criticism.* Oxford: Oxford University Press, 1989.
James Weldon Johnson and J. Rosamond Johnson. *The Books of American Negro Spirituals.* 1925, 1926; reprint, New York: Da Capo Press, 1977.
Sterling Stuckey. *Slave Culture.* New York: Oxford University Press, 1987.
Ronald Takaki. *A Different Mirror: A History of Multicultural America.* Boston: Little, Brown and Company, 1993.

Go Down, Moses

Go down, Moses,
Way down in Egyptland
Tell old Pharaoh
To let my people go.

When Israel was in Egyptland
Let my people go
Oppressed so hard they could not stand
Let my people go.

Go down, Moses,
Way down in Egyptland
Tell old Pharaoh,
"Let my people go."

"Thus saith the Lord," bold Moses said,
"Let my people go;
If not I'll smite your firstborn dead
Let my people go.

"No more shall they in bondage toil,
    Let my people go;
Let them come out with Egypt's spoil,
    Let my people go."

*　*　*

The Lord told Moses what to do
    Let my people go;
To lead the children of Israel through,
    Let my people go.

Go down, Moses,
    Way down in Egyptland,
Tell old Pharaoh,
    "Let my people go!"

Many Thousand Gone

No more auction block for me,
No more, no more;
No more auction block for me,
Many thousand gone.

No more peck o' corn for me,
No more, no more;
No more peck o' corn for me,
Many thousand gone.

No more driver's lash for me,
No more, no more;
No more driver's lash for me,
Many thousand gone.

No more pint o' salt for me,
No more, no more;
No more pint o' salt for me,
Many thousand gone.

No more hundred lash for me,
No more, no more;
No more hundred lash for me,
Many thousand gone.

No more mistress' call for me,
No more, no more;
No more mistress' call for me,
Many thousand gone.

Michael Row the Boat Ashore

Michael row de boat ashore,
Hallelujah!

Michael boat a gospel boat,
Hallelujah!

I wonder where my mudder deh,
Hallelujah!

See my mudder on de rock gwine home,
Hallelujah!

On de rock gwin home in Jesus' name,
Hallelujah!

Michael boat a music boat,
Hallelujah!

Gabriel blow de trumpet horn,
Hallelujah!

O you mind your boastin' talk,
Hallelujah!

Boastin' talk will sink your soul,
Hallelujah!

Brudder, lend a helpin' hand,
Hallelujah!

Sister, help for trim dat boat,
Hallelujah!

Jordan stream is wide and deep,
Hallelujah!

Jesus stand on t' oder side,
Hallelujah!

I wonder if my maussa deh,
Hallelujah!

My fader gone to unknown land,
Hallelujah!

* * *

O de Lord he plant his garden deh,
Hallelujah!

He raise de fruit for you to eat,
Hallelujah!

He dat eat shall neber die,
Hallelujah!

When de riber overflow,
Hallelujah!

O poor sinner, how you land?
Hallelujah!

Riber run and darkness comin',
Hallelujah!

Sinner row to save your soul,
Hallelujah!

Nobody Knows the Trouble I've Had

REFRAIN

Nobody knows de trouble I've had,
    Nobody knows but Jesus
Nobody knows de trouble I've had,
    Glory hallelu.

One morning I was a-walking down,
    O yes, Lord!
I saw some berries a-hangin down,
    O yes, Lord!
    (Refrain)

I pick de berry and I suck de juice,
    O yes, Lord!
Just as sweet as the honey in de comb,
    O yes, Lord!
    (Refrain)

Sometimes I'm up, sometimes I'm down,
    O yes, Lord!

Sometimes I'm almost on de groun',
   O yes, Lord!
   (Refrain)

What make ole Satan hate me so?
Because he got me once and he let me go.
   (Refrain)

Roll, Jordan, Roll

My brudder sittin' on de tree of life,
An' he yearde when Jordan roll;
   Roll, Jordan, roll, Jordan, roll, Jordan, roll!
   O march de angel march, O march de angel march;
   O my soul arise in Heaven, Lord,
   For to year when Jordan roll.

Little chil'en, learn to fear de Lord,
And let your days be long;
   Roll, Jordan, roll, Jordan, roll, Jordan, roll!
   O march de angel march, O march de angel march;
   O my soul arise in Heaven, Lord,
   For to year when Jordan roll.

O, let no false nor spiteful word
Be found upon your tongue;
   Roll, Jordan, roll, Jordan, roll, Jordan, roll!
   O march de angel march, O march de angel march;
   O my soul arise in Heaven, Lord,
   For to year when Jordan roll.

There's a Meeting Here To-Night

I take my text in Matthew, and by de Revelation,[1]
I know you by your garment,
Dere's a meeting here to-night.

---

1. References to the books of Matthew and Revelation in the Bible's New Testament.

REFRAIN

Dere's a meeting here to-night (Brudder Tony),
Dere's a meeting here to-night (Sister Rina),
Dere's a meeting here to-night,
I hope to meet again.

Brudder John was a writer, he write de laws of God;
Sister Mary say to Brudder John, "Brudder John, don't write no more."
(Refrain)

NATIVE-AMERICAN SONGS, RITUAL POETRY, AND LYRIC POETRY
1800–1900

THE NINETEENTH CENTURY is a particularly painful period in the nation's relationship with Native-American peoples and cultures as the government moved to subjugate them and to place them in reservations. Many Native-American poets and writers eloquently protested the national policy. In addition, many European-American writers, scholars, ethnographers, and artists began investigating the indigenous cultures, transcribing the rituals and customs, and writing about them, often in collaboration with Native Americans themselves. As a result, many poems and songs became available to a large and interested reading public. Today many Native-American communities still sustain and celebrate their oral traditions as part of an ever-evolving culture. We should approach these writings as living presences, not as museum specimens of a now extinct world.

The ritual and lyrical songs and poems that appear here reveal not only highly developed social structures in spite of continual violence and struggle with late-coming settlers, but also rich and diverse cultures that share certain qualities: a love for the land, a sense of communal harmony, a reverence for life, and a resistance to oppression. The poetic voices are alternately male and female, communal and individual. The dates for most of the songs and poems cannot be accurately ascertained. Many of these texts were already a vital part of the cultures when ethnographers and scholars encountered them, and they therefore predate the transcription work.

Considerable attention focused on both the Navajo and Sioux religious rituals following the traumatic "Long Walk" and "Wounded Knee" battle, respectively, remembered in the same way that the Cherokees recall the "Trail of Tears." One of the earliest and most detailed versions of the Navajo "Night Chant" (or "Night Way," as it is also known in English), which involves a large number of complex prayers and invocations, was published by Dr. Washington Matthews, an army surgeon assigned to Fort Wingate, New Mexico, after the Navajos had been ordered onto their reservation. He published his first study of a Navajo ceremonial in 1887 and collaborated extensively with many tribal priests. James Mooney of the Bureau of American Ethnology studied the Sioux Ghost Dance religion and published his first work on the Ghost Dance songs in 1896, also in collaboration with tribal leaders.

Native-American songs, poems, and rituals broach a wide variety of topics and themes. In "The Dancing Speech of O-No'-Sa," for instance, the chief recalls the founding of the Iroquois confederation and its message of unity and harmony among the native peoples who wished to resist conquest. Other songs and poems are personal, introspective, or descriptive. As the "Six Dream Songs" of the Wintu illustrate, the lyric poetry is often highly evocative. Some readers may think these songs resemble Japanese haiku.

FURTHER READING

John Bierhorst, ed. *The Sacred Path: Spells, Prayers and Power Songs of the American Indians.* New York: William Morrow, 1983.

William Brandon, ed. *The Magic World: American Indian Songs and Poems.* New York: William Morrow, 1971.

A. LaVonne Brown Ruoff. *American Indian Literatures.* New York: Modern Language Association, 1990.

Brian Swann, ed. *Native American Songs and Poems: An Anthology.* Mineola, N.Y.: Dover Publications, 1996.

———. *On the Translation of Native American Literatures.* Washington, D.C.: Smithsonian Institution Press, 1992.

Paul Zolbrod. *Reading the Voice: Native American Oral Poetry on the Written Page.* Salt Lake City: University of Utah Press, 1995.

[NAVAJO]   FROM *The Mountain Chant*

One of the Awl Songs

The Maid Who Becomes a Bear walks far around.
On the black mountains, she walks far around.
Far spreads the land. It seems not far to her.
Far spreads the land. It seems not dim to her.

                        ✳   ✳   ✳

The Holy Young Woman walks far around.
On the blue mountains, she walks far around.
Far spreads the land. It seems not far to her.
Far spreads the land. It seems not dim to her.

Last Song of the Exploding Stick

Maid Who Becomes a Bear sought the gods and found them;
On the high mountain peaks she sought the gods and found them;[1]
Truly with my sacrifice she sought the gods and found them.
Somebody doubts it, so I have heard.

Holy Young Woman sought the gods and found them;
On the summits of the clouds she sought the gods and found them;
Truly with my sacrifice she sought the gods and found them.
Somebody doubts it, so I have heard.

ca. 1800s

"One of the Awl Songs": Called a chant because of its repetition, this song expresses pride
in the vastness of the Navajo lands, which at one time included much of the Southwest.

[NAVAJO]

FROM *The Night Chant*

Song in the Rock

I

In the House of the Red Rock,[1]
There I enter;
Halfway in, I am come.
The corn plants shake.

II

In the house of Blue Water,
There I enter;
Halfway in, I am come.
The plants shake.

1. The mountains are viewed as the place of the Navajo spirits; the speaker's sacrificial ritual was intended to ensure that she found the gods in her journey to them.
1. The night chant seeking a cure for a troubled person, called a patient, begins at sunset when the chanter enters the house of the patient and a crier enjoins the patient and the guests to participate.

Last Song in the Rock

I

At the Red Rock House it grows,[2]
There the giant corn plant grows,
With ears on either side it grows,
With its ruddy silk it grows,
Ripening in one day it grows,
Greatly multiplying grows.

II

At Blue Water House it grows,
There the giant squash vine grows,
With fruit on either side it grows,
With its yellow blossom it grows,
Ripening in one night it grows,
Greatly multiplying grows.

Prayer of First Dancers

In Tsegíhi,
In the house made of the dawn,
In the house made of the evening twilight,
In the house made of the dark cloud,
In the house made of the he-rain,
In the house made of the dark mist,
In the house made of the she-rain,
In the house made of pollen,
In the house made of grasshoppers,
Where the dark mist curtains the doorway,
The path to which is on the rainbow,
Where the zigzag lightning stands high on top,
Where the he-rain stands high on top,
Oh, male divinity!
With your moccasins of dark cloud, come to us.[3]
With your leggings of dark cloud, come to us.
With your shirt of dark cloud, come to us.
With your headdress of dark cloud, come to us.

2. Corn and squash are symbols of life and re-   3. A chant beseeching the god to come and cure.
newal, a cure for sickness.

With your mind enveloped in dark cloud, come to us.
With the dark thunder above you, come to us soaring.
With the shapen cloud at your feet, come to us soaring.
With the far darkness made of the dark cloud over your head, come to us soaring.
With the far darkness made of the he-rain over your head, come to us soaring.
With the far darkness made of the dark mist over your head, come to us soaring.
With the far darkness made of the she-rain over your head, come to us soaring.
With the zigzag lightning flung out on high over your head, come to us soaring.
With the rainbow hanging high over your head, come to us soaring.
With the far darkness made of the dark cloud on the ends of your wings, come to us
    soaring.
With the far darkness made of the he-rain on the ends of your wings, come to us soaring.
With the far darkness made of the dark mist on the ends of your wings, come to us
    soaring.
With the far darkness made of the she-rain on the ends of your wings, come to us
    soaring.
With the zigzag lightning flung out on high on the ends of your wings, come to us
    soaring.
With the rainbow hanging high on the ends of your wings, come to us soaring.
With the near darkness made of the dark cloud, of the he-rain, of the dark mist, and of
    the she-rain, come to us.
With the darkness on the earth, come to us.
With these I wish the foam floating on the flowing water over the roots of the great corn.
I have made your sacrifice.[4]
I have prepared a smoke for you.[5]
My feet restore for me.[6]
My limbs restore for me.
My body restore for me.
My mind restore for me.
My voice restore for me.
To-day, take out your spell for me.
To-day, take away your spell for me.
Away from me you have taken it.
Far off from me it is taken.
Far off you have done it.
Happily I recover.
Happily my interior becomes cool.

4. Ritual for the god.
5. Smoke ritual; smoke is a symbol of the breath of life, of rejuvenation.
6. The patient announces that a cure has taken place. After one to eight nights of chanted prayers, songs, and dances, the patient greets the dawn in newfound health and wholeness and with a restored connection to the community.

Happily my eyes regain their power.
Happily my head becomes cool.
Happily my limbs regain their power.
Happily I hear again.
Happily for me the spell is taken off.
Happily I walk.
Impervious to pain, I walk.
Feeling light within, I walk.
With lively feelings, I walk.
Happily abundant dark clouds I desire.
Happily abundant dark mists I desire.
Happily abundant passing showers I desire.
Happily an abundance of vegetation I desire.
Happily an abundance of pollen I desire.
Happily abundant dew I desire.
Happily may fair white corn, to the ends of the earth, come with you.[7]
Happily may fair yellow corn, to the ends of the earth, come with you.
Happily may fair corn of all kinds, to the ends of the earth, come with you.
Happily may fair plants of all kinds, to the ends of the earth, come with you.
Happily may fair goods of all kinds, to the ends of the earth, come with you.
Happily may fair jewels of all kinds, to the ends of the earth, come with you.
With these before you, happily may they come with you.
With these behind you, happily may they come with you.
With these below you, happily may they come with you.
With these above you, happily may they come with you.
With these all around you, happily may they come with you.
Thus happily you accomplish your tasks.
Happily the old men will regard you.
Happily the old women will regard you.
Happily the young men will regard you.
Happily the young women will regard you.
Happily the boys will regard you.
Happily the girls will regard you
Happily the children will regard you.
Happily the chiefs will regard you.
Happily, as they scatter in different directions, they will regard you.
Happily, as they approach their homes, they will regard you.
Happily may their roads home be on the trail of pollen.
Happily may they all get back.

7. The chanter praises the god for the healing.

In beauty I walk.
With beauty before me, I walk.
With beauty behind me, I walk.
With beauty below me, I walk.
With beauty above me, I walk.
With beauty all around me, I walk.
It is finished again in beauty,
It is finished in beauty,
It is finished in beauty,
It is finished in beauty.

ca. 1800s

[NAVAJO]

Song of the Earth

The earth is beautiful.
The earth is beautiful.
The earth is beautiful.

Below the East, the Earth, its face toward the East.
The top of its head is beautiful.
The soles of its feet are beautiful.
Its feet, they are beautiful.
Its legs, they are beautiful.
Its body, it is beautiful.
Its chest, its breast, its head feather,
They are beautiful.

Below the West, the Sky, it is beautiful, its face toward the West.
The top of its head is beautiful.
The soles of its feet are beautiful.
Its feet, they are beautiful.
Its legs, they are beautiful.
Its body, it is beautiful.
Its chest, its breast, its head feather,
They are beautiful.

Below the East, the Dawn, its face toward the East.
The top of its head is beautiful.
The soles of its feet are beautiful.
Its feet, they are beautiful.
Its legs, they are beautiful.

Its body, it is beautiful.
Its chest, its breast, its head feather,
They are beautiful.

Below the West, the afterglow of sundown, its face toward the West,
Is beautiful.
Below the East, White Corn, its face toward the East,
Is beautiful.
Below the South, Blue Corn, its face toward the South,
Is beautiful.
Below the West, Yellow Corn, its face toward the West,
Is beautiful.
Below the North, Varicolored Corn, its face toward the North,
Is beautiful.
Below the East, Sahanahray, its face toward the East,
Is beautiful.
Below the West, Bekayhozhon, its face toward the West,
Is beautiful.
Below the East, Corn Pollen, its face toward the East,
Is beautiful.
Below the West, the Corn Beetle, its face toward the West,
Is beautiful.

The Earth is beautiful.
The Earth is beautiful.
The Earth is beautiful.

n.d.

The main chant of praise for the beauty of the earth, "The Earth is beautiful," is supplemented by praising the earth in all four directions and associating the corn, a Navajo symbol of fertility, with the earth. The chant, reflecting the Navajos' deep attachment to their large Southwestern territory, is ironic, given their traumatic experiences with federal policies toward them and their lands. The United States took possession of most of the Southwest following the U.S.-Mexican War in 1848. In 1863, Kit Carson was hired by the federal government to destroy the Native Americans' crops and livestock in an effort to subjugate them. Shortly after this episode, many starving Navajos traveled to Fort Defiance in western Arizona. In 1864 approximately eight thousand were forced to make what is known as the "Long Walk" from Fort Defiance to Fort Sumner, three hundred miles east in east-central New Mexico, where they were imprisoned. In 1868 a new treaty established a reservation, and the people began to return to a portion of their lands. Today the Navajos constitute the most populous Native-American group in the United States in spite of food shortages, drought, and further land cessions to the United States.

[IROQUOIS] ## The Dancing Speech of O-No'-Sa

Many winters ago our wise ancestors predicted that a great
monster
with white eyes
would come from the east and consume the land.[1]

They advised their children to plant a tree
with four roots
to the north
to the south
to the east and to the west

and collecting under its shade
to dwell together in unity
and harmony.[2]

ca. 1850

SIX DREAM SONGS

[WINTU] ## You and I Shall Go

above
above
you and I shall go
you and I shall go
along the Milky Way
along the trail of flowers
you and I shall go
picking flowers on our way
you and I shall go

ca. 1800s

[WINTU] ## Minnows and Flowers

flowers droop
flowers rise back up

1. Refers to European settlement.
2. The founding of the confederation of the Iro- quois in about 1450, which was able to resist Euro- pean expansion westward until about 1750.

above
the place where
the minnow sleeps while
her fins move slowly
back & forward
forward
&
back

ca. 1800s

[WINTU]   *Sleep*

Where will you and I sleep?
At the down-turned jagged rim of the sky you
& I will sleep.

ca. 1800s

[WINTU]   *Dandelion Puffs*

above
rise
will   swaying
                                    like women
of people
The spirits
                                    while men dance,
swaying with dandelion puffs
                in their hands.

ca. 1800s

[WINTU]   *There Above*

                    spirits are wafted along the roof &
        at the Earthlodge of the South
there above
There above
                                    fall.
    Flowers bend heavily on their stems.

ca. 1800s

[WINTU]
Strange Flowers

Above
in the west, in the flat of the flowers
strange flowers bloom,
flowers with crests
bending to the east.

ca. 1800s

GHOST DANCE SONGS

[SIOUX]
[The Father Says So]

Who think you comes there?
Who think you comes there?
Is it someone looking for his mother?
Is it someone looking for his mother?
Says the father,
Says the father.

I love my children—Ye'ye'!
I love my children—Ye'ye'!
You shall grow to be a nation—Ye'ye'!
You shall grow to be a nation—Ye'ye'!
Says the father, says the father.
Haye'ye' Eyayo'yo! Haye'ye' E'yayo'yo'!

ca. 1880s–90s

This is a version of the opening song of the Sioux Ghost Dance, a response to defeat, poverty, and loss of land in the late nineteenth century. While singing it, all the dancers stand motionless with hands stretched out to the west, the country of the messiah Wovoka (an actual individual who combined elements of traditional Sioux beliefs with Christian motifs) and the location of the new spirit world. When the song ends, all cry together, after which they join hands and begin to circle to the left. The terms "father" and "grandfather" refer to the messiah in the Ghost Dance religion.

[SIOUX]
[Give Me Back My Bow]

Mother, come home; mother, come home.
My little brother goes about always crying,
My little brother goes about always crying.
Mother, come home; mother, come home.

⁎   ⁎   ⁎

Now they are about to chase the buffalo,[1]
Now they are about to chase the buffalo.
Grandmother, give me back my bow.
Grandmother, give me back my bow.
The father says so, the father says so.

ca. 1880s–90s

[SIOUX]   *[The Whole World Is Coming]*

A nation is coming, a nation is coming,[1]
The Eagle[2] has brought the message to the tribe.
The father says so, the father says so.[3]

Over the whole earth they are coming.
The buffalo are coming, the buffalo are coming,
The Crow[4] has brought the message to the tribe.
The father says so, the father says so.

It is I who make these sacred things,[5]
Says the father, says the father.
It is I who make the sacred shirt,[6]
Says the father, says the father.
It is I who make the pipe,[7]
Says the father, says the father.

ca. 1880s–90s

1. The hope of the Ghost Dance is to bring back the buffalo. The son wants to hunt with his bow and tells his grandmother that the messiah blesses his wish.
1. Refers to the return of both the buffalo and the dead.
2. A sacred bird.
3. The "father" refers to the messiah.
4. Another sacred bird.
5. Refers to all that the messiah has created.
6. A ritual shirt.
7. Refers to the pipe of peace and the breath of life.

LYDIA HOWARD HUNTLEY SIGOURNEY
1791–1865

LYDIA HOWARD HUNTLEY SIGOURNEY, arguably one of the most respected and most popular European-American woman poets of her generation, has been misread far too long as the much-satirized "Sweet Singer of Hartford." This oversimplification has led to a neglect of her considerable professional achievements at a time when respectable upper-class Christian women were supposed to shun what was viewed as the corrupting public sphere of writing. For years she wrote anonymously in order to protect her husband's status as well as the social standing of her patrons, who had taken her in as their protégée when she was a young child of servants. Eventually she signed her name to her writing, but not until after her husband's fortune fell. She ultimately wrote more than fifty books in a wide range of fields.

Sigourney's strongest poetry reveals her deft combination of the sentimental poetics of Christian domesticity, motherhood, and affections with her unyielding concerns about social justice. In "The Suttee," for example, she condemns the supposedly voluntary Hindu ritual then practiced in India in which a widow was immolated along with her husband's corpse. Sigourney portrays the ritual as being particularly monstrous because it destroys the mother-child relationship. Her poem "Indian Names" reflects on the irony of the U.S. government's attempt to annihilate Native-American peoples when the nation's geography bears Native-American names.

FURTHER READING

Mary G. De Jong. "Profile of Lydia Sigourney," in *Legacy* 5 (Spring 1988): 35–43.
Paul Kane. *Poetry of the American Renaissance: A Diverse Anthology from the Romantic Period.* New York: George Braziller, 1995.
Lydia Howard Huntley Sigourney. *Poems.* Philadelphia: Key and Biddle, 1834.
——. *Poems by the author of moral pieces in prose and verse.* Boston: S. G. Goodrich, 1827.

The Suttee

She sat upon the pile by her dear lord,
And in her full, dark eye, and shining hair
Youth revell'd. — The glad murmur of the crowd
Applauding her consent to the dread doom,
And the hoarse chanting of infuriate priests

She heeded not, for her quick ear had caught
An infant's wail. — Feeble and low that moan,
Yet it was answer'd in her heaving heart,
For the Mimosa in its shrinking fold
From the rude pressure is not half so true,
So tremulous, as is a mother's soul
Unto her wailing babe. — There was such woe
In her imploring aspect, — in her tones
Such thrilling agony, that even the hearts
Of the flame-kindlers soften'd, and they laid
The famish'd infant on her yearning breast.
There with his tear-wet cheek he lay and drew
Plentiful nourishment from that full fount
Of infant happiness, — and long he prest
With eager lip the chalice of his joy. —
And then his little hands he stretch'd to grasp
His mother's flower-wove tresses, and with smile
And gay caress embraced his bloated sire, —
As if kind Nature taught that innocent one
With fond delay to cheat the hour which seal'd
His hopeless orphanage. — But those were near
Who mock'd such dalliance, as that Spirit malign
Frown'd on our parents' bliss. — The victim mark'd
Their harsh intent, and clasp'd the unconscious babe
With such convulsive force, that when they tore
His writhing form away, the very nerves
Whose deep-sown fibres rack the inmost soul
Uprooted seem'd. —
           With voice of high command
Tossing her arms, she bade them bring her son, —
And then in maniac rashness sought to leap
Among the astonish'd throng. — But the rough cord
Compress'd her slender limbs, and bound her fast
Down to her loathsome partner. — Quick the fire
In showers was hurl'd upon the reeking pile; —
But yet amid the wild, demoniac shout
Of priest and people, mid the thundering yell
Of the infernal gong, — was heard to rise
Thrice a dire death-shriek. — And the men who stood
Near the red pile and heard that fearful cry
Call'd on their idol-gods, and stopp'd their ears,

And oft amid their nightly dream would start
As frighted Fancy echoed in her cell
That burning mother's scream.

1827

Indian Names

"How can the Red men be forgotten,
while so many of our states and territories,
bays, lakes and rivers, are indelibly stamped
by names of their giving?"

Ye say they all have passed away,
    That noble race and brave,
That their light canoes have vanished
    From off the crested wave;
That 'mid the forests where they roamed
    There rings no hunter shout,
But their names are on your waters,
    Ye may not wash it out.

'Tis where Ontario's billow
    Like Ocean's surge is curled,
Where strong Niagara's thunders wake
    The echo of the world.
Where red Missouri bringeth
    Rich tribute from the west,
And Rappahannock sweetly sleeps
    On green Virginia's breast.

Ye say their cone-like cabins,
    That clustered o'er the vale,
Have fled away like withered leaves
    Before the autumn gale,
But their memory liveth on your hills,
    Their baptism on your shore,
Your everlasting rivers speak
    Their dialect of yore.

Old Massachusetts wears it,
    Within her lordly crown,
And broad Ohio bears it,

Amid his young renown;
Connecticut hath wreathed it
Where her quiet foliage waves,
And bold Kentucky breathed it hoarse
Through all her ancient caves.

Wachusett hides its lingering voice
Within his rocky heart,
And Allegheny graves its tone
Throughout his lofty chart;
Monadnock on his forehead hoar
Doth seal the sacred trust,
Your mountains build their monument,
Though ye destroy their dust.

1838

WILLIAM CULLEN BRYANT
1794–1878

WILLIAM CULLEN BRYANT achieved fame first as a precocious young poet, then as a journalist, and finally as one of the country's eminent public intellectuals. One of his contemporaries, R. H. Stoddard, remarked that Bryant "enjoyed the dangerous distinction of proving himself a great poet at an early age." Indeed, he was the first highly successful poet in the United States and the first to earn international esteem. Many of Bryant's most memorable poems, such as his early masterpiece "Thanatopsis," meditate on the natural scene. Bryant, along with the landscape painters of his time, helped his readers appreciate the spiritual value of the American wilderness. Bryant also wrote political poems with egalitarian themes. These works opposed slavery and demonstrated a sympathetic, if limited, interest in Native Americans. Influenced by eighteenth-century English verse, Bryant's poetry always reflected its roots in the highly formal language and the moral and social emphases of that era. But his poetry also responded to the more recent innovations of English Romantic poets such as William Wordsworth, and it looked forward to the environmental imagination and the self-exploration that mark such later writers as Ralph Waldo Emerson, Henry David Thoreau, Walt Whitman, and Emily Dickinson. Poised between two traditions, one past and the other to come, Bryant's best work provides a powerful foretaste of what American poetry might achieve.

Bryant was born in western Massachusetts to a physician's family. He was brought up in a strict Calvinist religious tradition and with the Federalist political beliefs typical of his place and class. He had access to few books of poetry. But in his adult life he adopted less rigid religious beliefs, developed an abiding identification with the poor and the powerless, and devotedly read and wrote poetry. After a youthful year spent at Williams College, he studied law privately and was admitted to the bar at the age of twenty-one. Although he practiced law for a decade, he thoroughly disliked it, and at the age of thirty-one he moved with his wife, Frances, to New York to pursue a new career in literary journalism. At thirty-three, he became an editor of one of the nation's leading newspapers, the *New York Post*, and he remained editor (and ultimately part-owner) of the paper until his death at eighty-four.

Bryant published an early version of "Thanatopsis," the poem that established his reputation, when he was only twenty-three. "Thanatopsis" demonstrates how far he had already moved from the strict Calvinism of his youth. The poem finds consolation for death not so much in specifically Christian doctrine as in more general and melancholic notions of the reunification of the "individual being" with "the elements" and of the universal fellowship of the dead in "the great tomb of man." Other poems that Bryant published over the next decade, like "To a Waterfowl," pay the fauna and flora of the American landscape a passionate attention that was innovative for its time. His friend Stoddard noted that Bryant's social "sympathies were enlarged as the years went on." His later poems often address political issues with a sense of justice and empathy. He died at the age of eighty-four, several days after dedicating a statue in Central Park to the Italian revolutionary Giuseppe Mazzini. At the time of his death, Bryant was one of the best-known and most respected literary figures in the country.

William Cullen Bryant traveled a considerable distance in his life—from the insulated environment of his upbringing to a dynamic engagement with the social and intellectual currents circulating through national and international culture. In reconceiving himself, he helped to refashion American poetry as well.

FURTHER READING

William Cullen Bryant. *Poetical Works*. Introduction by R. H. Stoddard. New York: D. Appleton, 1878.

Bernard Duffey. *Poetry in America: Expression and Its Values in the Times of Bryant, Whitman, and Pound*. Durham, N.C.: Duke University Press, 1978.

Albert F. McLean. *William Cullen Bryant*, revised edition. Boston: Twayne, 1989.

Thanatopsis

To him who in the love of Nature holds
Communion with her visible forms, she speaks
A various language; for his gayer hours
She has a voice of gladness, and a smile
And eloquence of beauty, and she glides
Into his darker musings, with a mild
And healing sympathy, that steals away
Their sharpness, ere he is aware. When thoughts
Of the last bitter hour come like a blight
Over thy spirit, and sad images
Of the stern agony, and shroud, and pall,
And breathless darkness, and the narrow house,[1]
Make thee to shudder, and grow sick at heart;—
Go forth, under the open sky, and list[2]
To Nature's teachings, while from all around—
Earth and her waters, and the depths of air—
Comes a still voice[3]—Yet a few days, and thee
The all-beholding sun shall see no more
In all his course; nor yet in the cold ground,
Where thy pale form was laid, with many tears,
Nor in the embrace of ocean, shall exist
Thy image. Earth, that nourished thee, shall claim
Thy growth, to be resolved to earth again,
And, lost each human trace, surrendering up
Thine individual being, shalt thou go
To mix for ever with the elements,
To be a brother to the insensible rock
And to the sluggish clod, which the rude swain[4]
Turns with his share, and treads upon. The oak
Shall send his roots abroad, and pierce thy mould.

Yet not to thine eternal resting-place
Shalt thou retire alone, nor couldst thou wish
Couch more magnificent. Thou shalt lie down
With patriarchs of the infant world—with kings,
The powerful of the earth—the wise, the good,

---

1. That is, the coffin.
2. Listen.
3. Nature itself may be speaking the rest of the poem.

4. Country lad. "Rude" means unsophisticated rather than impolite. He is plowing the field with his "share" or plowshare.

Fair forms, and hoary seers of ages past,
All in one mighty sepulchre.[5] The hills
Rock-ribbed and ancient as the sun,—the vales
Stretching in pensive quietness between;
The venerable woods—rivers that move
In majesty, and the complaining brooks
That make the meadows green; and poured round all,
Old Ocean's gray and melancholy waste,—
Are but the solemn decorations all
Of the great tomb of man. The golden sun,
The planets, all the infinite host of heaven,
Are shining on the sad abodes of death,
Through the still lapse of ages. All that tread
The globe are but a handful to the tribes
That slumber in its bosom.—Take the wings
Of morning, pierce the Barcan[6] wilderness,
Or lose thyself in the continuous woods
Where rolls the Oregon,[7] and hears no sound,
Save his own dashings—yet the dead are there:
And millions in those solitudes, since first
The flight of years began, have laid them down
In their last sleep—the dead reign there alone.
So shalt thou rest, and what if thou withdraw
In silence from the living, and no friend
Take note of thy departure? All that breathe
Will share thy destiny. The gay will laugh
When thou art gone, the solemn brood of care
Plod on, and each one as before will chase
His favorite phantom; yet all these shall leave
Their mirth and their employments, and shall come
And make their bed with thee. As the long train
Of ages glides away, the sons of men,
The youth in life's green spring, and he who goes
In the full strength of years, matron and maid,
The speechless babe, and the gray-headed man—
Shall one by one be gathered to thy side,
By those, who in their turn shall follow them.

---

5. Grave.
6. Barca was a town near the Mediterranean coast in northeastern Libya. It is now called Al-Marj.

7. Native-American name for the Columbia River.

*   *   *

So live, that when thy summons comes to join
The innumerable caravan, which moves
To that mysterious realm, where each shall take
His chamber in the silent halls of death,
Thou go not, like the quarry-slave at night,
Scourged to his dungeon, but, sustained and soothed
By an unfaltering trust, approach thy grave,
Like one who wraps the drapery of his couch
About him, and lies down to pleasant dreams.

1817

The title means "view of death" or "meditation on death" in Greek. Decades after the poem's publication, Bryant explained to an inquirer, "It was written when I was seventeen or eighteen years old . . . and I believe it was composed in my solitary rambles in the woods. As it was first committed to paper, it began with the half-line—'Yet a few days, and thee' [line 17]—and ended with . . . the words—'And make their bed with thee' [line 66]. The rest of the poem—the introduction and the close—was added some years afterward, in 1821." Bryant published the early version in 1817, six years after he composed it, and then published the expanded version four years later. In structure the finished poem, written in blank verse, somewhat resembles a three-part sermon, with the first section stating the problem, the second revealing the solution, and the third making the application.

To a Waterfowl

Whither,[1] midst falling dew,
While glow the heavens with the last steps of day,
Far, through their rosy depths, dost thou pursue
    Thy solitary way?

Vainly the fowler's[2] eye
Might mark thy distant flight to do thee wrong,
As, darkly seen against the crimson sky,
    Thy figure floats along.

Seek'st thou the plashy[3] brink
Of weedy lake, or marge[4] of river wide,
Or where the rocking billows rise and sink
    On the chafed ocean-side?

1. Where.
2. Hunter of birds.

3. Marshy, splashing.
4. Margin, edge.

* * *

There is a Power whose care
Teaches thy way along that pathless coast—
The desert[5] and illimitable air—
   Lone wandering, but not lost.

All day thy wings have fanned,
At that far height, the cold, thin atmosphere,
Yet stoop not, weary, to the welcome land,
   Though the dark night is near.

And soon that toil shall end;
Soon shalt thou find a summer home, and rest,
And scream among thy fellows; reeds shall bend
   Soon o'er thy sheltered nest.

Thou'rt gone, the abyss of heaven
Hath swallowed up thy form; yet, on my heart
Deeply hath sunk the lesson thou hast given,
   And shall not soon depart.

He[6] who, from zone to zone,
Guides through the boundless sky thy certain flight,
In the long way that I must tread alone,
   Will lead my steps aright.

           1818

This poem resembles what M. H. Abrams identified as "the greater romantic lyric" as practiced by William Wordsworth and Samuel Taylor Coleridge, in which an observation of a natural scene or event leads to philosophical meditation. Bryant transfers this British form to the American landscape. He composed the poem in 1815, three years before it was published.

An Indian Story

"I know where the timid fawn abides
   In the depth of the shaded dell,
Where the leaves are broad and the thicket hides,
With its many stems and its tangled sides,
   From the eye of the hunter well.

   * * *

5. Deserted, empty.

6. The divine "Power" or Supreme Being.

"I know where the young May violet grows,
     In its lone and lowly nook,
On the mossy bank, where the larch-tree throws
Its broad dark boughs, in solemn repose,
     Far over the silent brook.

"And that timid fawn starts not with fear
     When I steal to her secret bower;
And that young May violet to me is dear,
And I visit the silent streamlet near,
     To look on the lovely flower."

Thus Maquon[1] sings as he lightly walks
     To the hunting-ground on the hills;
'Tis a song of his maid of the woods and rocks,
With her bright black eyes and long black locks,
     And voice like the music of rills.[2]

He goes to the chase—but evil eyes
     Are at watch in the thicker shades;
For she was lovely that smiled on his sighs,
And he bore, from a hundred lovers, his prize,
     The flower of the forest maids.

The boughs in the morning wind are stirred,
     And the woods their song renew,
With the early carol of many a bird,
And the quickened tune of the streamlet heard
     Where the hazels trickle with dew.

And Maquon has promised his dark-haired maid,[3]
     Ere eve shall redden the sky,
A good red deer from the forest shade,
That bounds with the herd through grove and glade,
     At her cabin-door shall lie.

The hollow woods, in the setting sun,
     Ring shrill with the fire-bird's lay;[4]

1. An imagined Native American who is the pro-
tagonist of this narrative. "Maquon" is Algonquin
for mussel shell.

2. Rivulets or brooks.
3. That is, his bride.
4. Song.

And Maquon's sylvan labors are done,
And his shafts are spent, but the spoil they won
   He bears on his homeward way.

He stops near his bower—his eye perceives
   Strange traces along the ground—
At once to the earth his burden he heaves;
He breaks through the veil of boughs and leaves;
   And gains its door with a bound.

But the vines are torn on its walls that leant,
   And all from the young shrubs there
By struggling hands have the leaves been rent,[5]
And there hangs on the sassafras, broken and bent,
   One tress of the well-known hair.

But where is she who, at this calm hour,
   Ever watched his coming to see?
She is not at the door, nor yet in the bower;
He calls—but he only hears on the flower
   The hum of the laden bee.

It is not a time for idle grief,
   Nor a time for tears to flow;
The horror that freezes his limbs is brief—
He grasps his war-axe and bow, and a sheaf
   Of darts made sharp for the foe.

And he looks for the print of the ruffian's feet
   Where he bore the maiden away;
And he darts on the fatal path more fleet
Than the blast hurries the vapor and sleet
   O'er the wild November sky.

'Twas early summer when Maquon's bride
   Was stolen away from his door;
But at length the maples in crimson are dyed,
And the grape is black on the cabin-side—
   And she smiles at his hearth once more.

But far in the pine-grove, dark and cold,
   Where the yellow leaf falls not,

5. Torn.

Nor the autumn shines in scarlet and gold,
There lies a hillock of fresh dark mould,
   In the deepest gloom of the spot.

And the Indian girls, that pass that way,
   Point out the ravisher's grave;
"And how soon to the bower she loved," they say,
"Returned the maid that was borne away
   From Maquon, the fond and the brave."

                          1821

A Scene on the Banks of the Hudson

Cool shades and dews are round my way,
And silence of the early day;
Mid the dark rocks that watch his bed,
Glitters the mighty Hudson spread,
Unrippled, save by drops that fall
From shrubs that fringe his mountain wall;
And o'er the clear still water swells
The music of the Sabbath bells.

All, save this little nook of land,
Circled with trees, on which I stand;
All, save that line of hills which lie
Suspended in the mimic sky—
Seems a blue void, above, below,
Through which the white clouds come and go;
And from the green world's farthest steep
I gaze into the airy deep.

Loveliest of lovely things are they,
On earth, that soonest pass away.
The rose that lives its little hour
Is prized beyond the sculptured flower.
Even love, long tried and cherished long,
Becomes more tender and more strong
At thought of that insatiate grave
From which its yearnings cannot save.

River! In this still hour thou hast
Too much of heaven on earth to last;

Nor long may thy still waters lie,
An image of the glorious sky.
Thy fate and mine are not repose,
And ere another evening close,
Thou to thy tides shalt turn again,
And I to seek the crowd of men.

1828

Hymn of the City

Not in the solitude
Alone may man commune with Heaven, or see,
　　Only in savage wood
And sunny vale, the present Deity;
　　Or only hear his voice
Where the winds whisper and the waves rejoice.

　　Even here do I behold
Thy steps, Almighty!—here, amidst the crowd
　　Through the great city rolled,
With everlasting murmur deep and loud—
　　Choking the ways that wind
'Mong the proud piles,[1] the work of human kind.

　　Thy golden sunshine comes
From the round heaven, and on their dwellings lies
　　And lights their inner homes;
For them thou fill'st with air the unbounded skies,
　　And givest them the stores
Of ocean, and the harvest of its shores.

　　Thy Spirit is around,
Quickening the restless mass that sweeps along;
　　And this eternal sound—
Voices and footfalls of the numberless throng—
　　Like the resounding sea,
Or like the rainy tempest, speaks of thee.

　　And when the hour of rest
Comes, like a calm upon the mid-sea brine,

---

1. That is, the tall buildings.

Hushing its billowy breast—
The quiet of that moment too is thine;
It breathes of Him who keeps
The vast and helpless city while it sleeps.

1830

The Death of Lincoln

Oh, slow to smite and swift to spare,
   Gentle and merciful and just!
Who, in the fear of God, didst bear
   The sword of power, a nation's trust!

In sorrow by thy bier[1] we stand,
   Amid the awe that hushes all,
And speak the anguish of a land
   That shook with horror at thy fall.

Thy task is done; the bond[2] are free:
   We bear thee to an honored grave,
Whose proudest monument shall be
   The broken fetters[3] of the slave.

Pure was thy life; its bloody close
   Hath placed thee with the sons of light,[4]
Among the noble host of those
   Who perished in the cause of Right.

1866

President Abraham Lincoln was assassinated on April 15, 1865, by John Wilkes Booth. Bryant composed this elegy in the weeks following Lincoln's death.

1. A stand bearing the coffin.
2. That is, the African-American slaves in the South, whom Lincoln liberated by issuing the Emancipation Proclamation.
3. Chains or shackles.
4. The Old Testament or Torah proclaims that "God divided the light from the darkness" (Genesis 1:4). According to Jewish tradition, the "sons of light" are the generation of the exodus from Egypt. According to Christian tradition, the "children of light" are those saved by Jesus Christ (John 12:36; 1 Thessalonians 5:5). Bryant uses the phrase to refer to those who died to abolish slavery or perhaps to achieve any just cause.

GEORGE MOSES HORTON
ca. 1797–1883

A SLAVE IN NORTH CAROLINA for sixty-eight years until he escaped in the closing year of the Civil War, George Moses Horton nonetheless achieved many outstanding distinctions as a poet. He was the first African-American male slave to publish a book in the South — *The Hope of Liberty* (1829) — and the only slave to earn a good income from his poetry. In addition, as Joan Sherman has written, Horton was the only slave to publish a book of poetry before learning to write (though he had taught himself to read). He published two books of poetry during bondage and one shortly after emancipation. His poetry attracted many elite European Americans, including newspapermen Horace Greeley and William Lloyd Garrison. The poem below was his first published poem and the first known poem at the time written by a slave. The antislavery author Caroline Lee Hentz, wife of a professor at the University of North Carolina, Chapel Hill, where Horton was a frequent visitor, sent it to her hometown newspaper, *The Lancaster Gazette*, in Massachusetts. The poem was published on April 18, 1829.

FURTHER READING

Joan R. Sherman, ed. *The Black Bard of North Carolina: George Moses Horton and His Poetry.* Chapel Hill: University of North Carolina Press, 1997.

On Liberty and Slavery

Alas! and am I born for this,
    To wear this slavish chain?
Deprived of all created bliss,
    Through hardship, toil and pain!

How long have I in bondage lain,
    And languished to be free!
Alas! and must I still complain
    Deprived of liberty.

Oh Heaven! and is there no relief
    This side the silent grave
To soothe the pain, to quell the grief
    And anguish of a slave?

*   *   *

Come Liberty, thou cheerful sound,
    Roll through my ravished ears!
Come, let my grief in joys be drowned,
    And drive away my fears.

Say unto foul oppression, Cease:
    Ye tyrants rage no more,
And let the joyful trump of peace,
    Now bid the vassal[1] soar.

Soar on the pinions[2] of that dove
    Which long has cooed for thee,
And breathed her notes from Afric's grove,
    The sound of Liberty.

Oh, Liberty! Thou holden prize,
    So often sought by blood —
We crave thy sacred sun to rise,
    The gift of nature's God!

Bid Slavery hide her haggard face,
    And barbarism fly:
I scorn to see the sad disgrace
    In which enslaved I lie.

Dear Liberty! Upon thy breast,
    I languished to respire;[3]
And like the Swan unto her nest,
    I'd like to thy smiles retire.

Oh, blest asylum — heavenly balm!
    Unto thy boughs I flee —
And in thy shades the storm shall calm,
    With songs of Liberty!

                                    1829

1. Slave.
2. Wings.   3. Breathe freely.

JANE JOHNSTON SCHOOLCRAFT
[BAME-WA-WA-GE-ZHIK-A-QUAY, WOMAN OF
THE STARS RUSHING THROUGH THE SKY]
1800–1841

JANE JOHNSTON SCHOOLCRAFT (Bame-wa-wa-ge-zhik-a-quay, Woman of the Stars Rushing through the Sky) has long been acknowledged for her collaboration with her husband, the ethnographer and explorer Henry Rowe Schoolcraft. Together they collected traditional Native-American narratives, most notably the myth of Hiawatha that Henry Wadsworth Longfellow used for his popular poem "The Song of Hiawatha." Jane Schoolcraft also wrote poetry, however, in both her native Ojibwa language and standard English. This work is of a quality that merits inclusion in the canon of American poetry. Schoolcraft contributed not only to mainstream English-language poetry but also to the establishment of a written Native-American literature.

Schoolcraft was Scotch, Irish, and Ojibwa. Her father was a fur trader, and her mother was the daughter of the renowned Ojibwa chief, Waub Ojeeg (White Fisher). Schoolcraft was educated at home by her father in Sault Sainte Marie, Michigan, and in private schools in Canada and later in Ireland. With her husband, Schoolcraft created the magazine *The Literary Voyager or Muzzeniegun* (a Chippewa word meaning a printed document), a successful publication that circulated in several cities, including New York. Her literary contributions in many genres brought her celebrity status as the "northern Pocahontas," drawing literary admirers and writers such as Harriet Martineau and Anna Jameson to visit her. Schoolcraft and her mother, Susan Johnston (Ozha-guscoday-way-quay, Woman of the Green Valley), were responsible for researching and compiling Ojibwa and other tribal texts, including the myth of Hiawatha, published first as *Algic Researches* in 1839 and then as a myth retold by her husband in 1856. Longfellow credited Schoolcraft in his notes to his reworking of the Hiawatha myth. The Schoolcrafts eventually settled in New York City, and she died there.

The two poems included here represent Jane Schoolcraft's work in both European-American and Native-American poetries. She wrote "To Sisters on a Walk in the Garden, After a Shower" in the poetics of sentimentality popular during the period, yet it also serves Schoolcraft's goal of bringing the two cultures together. Her address to "sisters" reflects her own cultural positioning in two of the American "spirits" or cultures. In addition, those poetics allow her to write a "double-voiced" discourse including European-American concerns with the private domestic world and personal relationships as well as the Ojibwa emphasis on

family responsibility and ties. The second selection, a Native-American plaintive
song excerpted from "The Forsaken Brother, a Chippewa Tale," emphasizes the
tragic outcome of placing one's personal desires before familial and tribal rela-
tionships.

FURTHER READING

Karen Kilcup, ed. *Native American Women's Writing, c. 1800–1924: An Anthology.* Oxford, Eng.:
Blackwell Publishers, 2000.

To Sisters on a Walk in the Garden, after a Shower

Come, sisters, come! The shower's past,
The garden walks are drying fast,
The Sun's bright beams are seen again,
And nought within, can now detain.
The rain drops tremble on the leaves,
Or drip expiring, from the eaves:
But soon the cool and balmy airs,
Shall dry the gems that sparkle there,
With whisp'ring breath shall shake ev'ry spray,
And scatter every cloud away.

Thus sisters! Shall the breeze of hope,
Through sorrow's clouds a vista ope;[1]
Thus, shall affliction's surly blast,
By faith's bright calm be still'd at last;
Thus, pain and care,—the tear and sigh,
Be chased from every dewy eye;
And life's mix'd scene itself, but cease,
To show us realms of light and peace.

1826

FROM The Forsaken Brother, a Chippewa Tale

Neesya, neesya, shyegwuh gushuh

Neesya, neesya, shyegwuh gushuh!
Ween ne myeengunish!
Ne myeengunish!

1. Open.

[TRANS.] My brother, my brother

My brother, my brother,
I am now turning into a Wolf! —
I am turning into a Wolf.

1827

SARAH HELEN WHITMAN
1803–1878

SARAH HELEN WHITMAN was the poet, well known in her own time, who inspired the second of Edgar Allan Poe's poems titled "To Helen." Born into the distinguished Power family in Rhode Island, Whitman at a young age lost her father, who deserted the family and went to sea in 1813, not reappearing until 1832. Known from an early age as Helen, she was educated at private schools in Providence and Long Island and soon showed a strong taste for literature. A transcendentalist and believer in psychic phenomena, she was described by her friends as beautiful, passionate, spiritual — yet level-headed. She married the Boston writer, editor, and attorney John Winslow Whitman in 1828. They had no children, and Helen Whitman was able to devote significant attention to literature, publishing her first poem in 1829 and following it with further poems praised for their refined imagination and delicacy and with essays on such Romantic authors as Goethe, Shelley, and Emerson. Her husband died in 1833. Her first book of verse, *Hours of Life and Other Poems*, was published in 1848. It went through several editions and was followed after her death by an enlarged collection titled simply *Poems* (1879).

Helen Whitman, in 1848 living in Providence, Rhode Island, was deeply impressed by Edgar Allan Poe's "The Raven" and composed a poetic tribute to the poem for a party in New York that she expected Poe to attend. Poe — still in mourning over the death of his young wife, Virginia, in January 1847 — was not, in fact, present, but he soon learned of the poem. In response, Poe, who had long been an admirer of Helen Whitman's writings and an avid listener to tales of her beauty, sensitivity, and charm, composed the second of his poems titled "To Helen" (1848), which evocatively recalls Poe's one previous meeting with Whitman, a brief glimpse of her in a rose garden at midnight some years before, following a gathering of a literary society in Providence at which Poe was the featured guest. An intense courtship followed, during which Poe produced a series of passionate and revealing love letters. Whitman was then forty-five—six years Poe's senior—but she had a reputation for having maintained her youthful beauty to an extraordinary degree. She was strongly drawn to Poe's imaginative genius, but when he proved unable to maintain his resolutions to avoid alcohol, Whitman, under pressure from friends, reluctantly broke off their engagement.

Poe died not long after, in 1849. He had made many enemies during a career marked by frequent literary quarrels and an aggressive reviewing style, and not all displayed the forbearance and insight of Longfellow, one of Poe's chief targets, who observed that "the harshness of his criticism I have always attributed to the irritation of a sensitive nature chafed by some indefinite sense of wrong." Several of these enemies now attacked Poe in print, particularly Poe's literary executor, Rufus Griswold, in a notorious memoir of Poe. To refute Griswold's "numerous misrepresentations, and mis-statements" and the "calumnious" yet untrue stories of others, Whitman produced in 1860 the brief book *Edgar Poe and His Critics*, a critical study that is still of value for its generous firsthand account of the complexity of Poe's character. There Whitman argues that "his proud reserve, his profound melancholy, his unworldliness—may we not say his *unearthliness* of nature—made his character one very difficult of comprehension to the casual observer." She writes with the ear of a fellow poet when she praises Poe as a "consummate master of language," one who had "sounded all the secrets of rhythm," who "understood . . . the balance and poise of syllables—the alternation of emphasis and cadence—of vowel-sounds and consonants—and all metrical sweetness of 'phrase and metaphrase.'" Though she recognized that "the peculiarities of Edgar Poe's organization and temperament doubtless exposed him to peculiar infirmities," she treats these in her account with a sympathy and understanding that is nearly unique in Poe criticism and sees these infirmities as inextricably linked with Poe's unique imaginative powers.

Given Whitman's preoccupation with Poe as man and poet, it should not surprise us that Whitman's own poetry, which, though always gracefully crafted, can today seem overly delicate or conventional, takes on an added resonance and power in the several poems she addressed to Poe during his lifetime and after.

FURTHER READING

Caroline Ticknor. *Poe's Helen*. New York: Scribner's, 1916.
Sarah Helen Whitman. *Edgar Poe and His Critics*. New York: Rudd & Carlton, 1860.
———. *Poems*. Boston: Houghton, Osgood & Co., 1879.

The Raven

Raven, from the dim dominions
    On the Night's Plutonian shore,
Oft I hear thy dusky pinions
    Wave and flutter round my door—
See the shadow of thy pinions
    Float along the moon-lit floor;

Often, from the oak-woods glooming
    Round some dim ancestral tower,
In the lurid distance looming—
    Some high solitary tower—
I can hear thy storm-cry booming
    Through the lonely midnight hour.

When the moon is at the zenith,
    Thou dost haunt the moated hall,
Where the marish flower greeneth
    O'er the waters, like a pall—
Where the House of Usher leaneth,
    Darkly nodding to its fall:

There I see thee, dimly gliding,—
    See thy black plumes waving slowly,—
In its hollow casements hiding,
    When their shadow yawns below,
To the sullen tarn confiding
    The dark secrets of their woe:—

See thee, when the stars are burning
    In their cressets, silver clear,—
When Ligeia's spirit yearning
    For the earth-life, wanders near,—
When Morella's soul returning,
    Weirdly whispers "I am here."

Once, within a realm enchanted,
    On a fair isle of the seas,
By unearthly visions haunted,
    By unearthly melodies,
Where the evening sunlight slanted
    Golden through the garden trees,—

✳   ✳   ✳

Where the dreamy moonlight dozes,
    Where the early violets dwell,
Listening to the silver closes
    Of a lyric loved too well,
Suddenly, among the roses,
    Like a cloud, thy shadow fell.

Once, where Ulalume lies sleeping,
    Hard by Auber's haunted mere,
With the ghouls a vigil keeping,
    On that night of all the year,
Came thy sounding pinions, sweeping
    Through the leafless woods of Weir!

Oft, with Prosperine[1] I wander
    On the Night's Plutonian shore,
Hoping, fearing, while I ponder
    On thy loved and lost Lenore—
On the demon doubts that sunder
    Soul from soul evermore;

Trusting, though with sorrow laden,
    That when life's dark dream is o'er,
By whatever name the maiden
    Lives within thy mystic lore,
Eiros, in that distant Aidenn,
    Shall his Charmion[2] meet once more.

1848

Whitman's "The Raven" contains many echoes of Poe's "The Raven," already a nationally famous poem, as well as numerous references to such Poe works as the stories "The Fall of the House of Usher," "Ligeia," and "Morella" and the poem "Ulalume."

---

1. In Greek myth, the goddess of spring, who dwelt during the winter months as Pluto's wife in the underworld.
2. Recalls Poe's mystical narrative "Eiros and Charmion," where the two souls, friends in life and parted by death, meet again in the afterworld (Aidenn).

FROM *Sonnets [to Poe]*

3

On our lone pathway bloomed no earthly hopes:
Sorrow and death were near us, as we stood
Where the dim forest, from the upland slopes,
Swept darkly to the sea. The enchanted wood
Thrilled, as by some foreboding terror stirred;
And as the waves broke on the lonely shore,
In their low monotone, methought I heard
A solemn voice that sighed, "Ye meet no more."
There, while the level sunbeams seemed to burn
Through the long aisles of red, autumnal gloom, —
Where stately, storied cenotaphs[1] inurn
Sweet human hopes, too fair on Earth to bloom, —
Was the bud reaped, whose petals pure and cold
Sleep on my heart till Heaven the flower unfold.

4

If thy sad heart, pining for human love,
In its earth solitude grew dark with fear,
Lest the high Sun of Heaven itself should prove
Powerless to save from that phantasmal sphere
Wherein thy spirit wandered, — if the flowers
That pressed around thy feet, seemed but to bloom
In lone Gethsemanes,[2] through starless hours,
When all who loved had left thee to thy doom, —
Oh, yet believe that, in that hollow vale
Where thy soul lingers, waiting to attain
So much of Heaven's sweet grace as shall avail
To lift its burden of remorseful pain,
My soul shall meet thee, and its Heaven forego
Till God's great love, on both, one hope, one Heaven bestow.

1879

These sonnets are from an elegiac sequence written after Poe's death.

1. A sepulchral monument erected to the memory of a deceased person entombed elsewhere.

2. Garden near Jerusalem where Jesus suffered agony and betrayal.

To ——

Vainly my heart had with thy sorceries striven:
It had no refuge from thy love,—no Heaven
But in thy fatal presence;—from afar
It owned thy power and trembled like a star
O'erfraught with light and splendor. Could I deem
How dark a shadow should obscure its beam?—
Could I believe that pain could ever dwell
Where thy bright presence cast its blissful spell?
Thou wert my proud palladium;—could I fear
The avenging Destinies when thou wert near?—
Thou wert my Destiny;—thy song, thy fame,
The wild enchantments clustering round thy name,
Were my soul's heritage, its royal dower;
Its glory and its kingdom and its power!

1879

This poem, dedicated to Poe, explores their relationship and its influence on her life.

RALPH WALDO EMERSON
1803–1882

Ralph waldo emerson articulated ways of thinking about poetry that have deeply embedded themselves in American poetic practice. His influence has been felt directly and through the work of poets he inspired, such as Walt Whitman and Emily Dickinson. In essays like "The Poet," Emerson asserted the primacy of spiritual and imaginative faculties in everyday life. He hoped that poetry could be a vehicle for transcendental experience, a medium connecting human beings with the holiness that he believed is always within and around us. In prose that is often as poetic as that found in any poem, he called for poets to break time-honored rules, to see themselves and their world with fresh eyes, to become prophets. His own poetry did not often attain the inspiration and power he sought. But his emphasis on poetic revolution helped create the conditions in which generations of poets would seek to renew and modernize their art.

Emerson was born on May 25, 1803, in Boston, the fourth of eight children. His father, a Unitarian minister, died when Emerson was only eight, and from then on the family was poor, supported by Emerson's mother, who ran a boardinghouse. Emerson attended Harvard, graduating in the middle of his class. After teaching school for several years, he returned to Harvard for a divinity degree and became a Unitarian minister himself. When his beloved wife Ellen died after two years of marriage, he underwent a crisis of faith. Rejecting Unitarianism's "pallid affirmations" and indeed all religious orthodoxy, he quit the ministry, moved from Boston to rural Concord, and began to chart his own spiritual journey, which involved a mystical belief in a divine and always present "Over-soul," a method of miraculous perception, and a quest for perpetual revelation. Influenced by such philosophers as Plato, Emanuel Swedenborg, and Immanuel Kant, and by such poets as George Herbert, Samuel Taylor Coleridge, and William Wordsworth, Emerson began to lecture to audiences about "the infinitude of the private man." Soon the "Sage of Concord" was the most famous lecturer in the United States.

Emerson remarried and with his wife Lydian had four children. To all appearances he lived a quite conventional life, but his mental world revolved around radical ideas and conjectures. Although better known for his lectures and his essays, he always thought of himself as a poet first. Like many poets today, he did not recognize strict boundary lines between poetry and other genres of writing. For him, all imaginative forms of writing were poetic. Emerson's first major publication was his prose study called *Nature* (1836), which argued that human beings could reunite with the divine spirit all around and within them by means of truly perceiving nature—not only with the eyes but with the heart as well. Just as he argued that words are symbolic of natural things, so he thought nature itself symbolic of the spirit. He sought to eliminate the gaps separating mind from nature and nature from divinity. He invited his readers to sense "the miraculous in the common" and to "build your own world."

Satirized as "Transcendentalists," Emerson and his friends readily accepted the name for their enterprise. Emerson wished to transcend ordinary reality and orthodox thinking. He expounded on his ideas in such later essays as "Self-Reliance" (1841) and "The Poet" (1844). In the former essay, he decried the social obstacles standing in the way of individualism. "Trust thyself," he proclaimed; "believe in your own thought." In "The Poet" (included in this volume), he addressed the centrality and profundity of the poet's task. According to Emerson, the poet is rightly a cultural hero. Such a poet should be willing to break formal rules in order to commune with the spirit that is in nature, to find the godlike power in the self, and to heal and transform the reader. For Emerson, the poet does not practice a craft. The poet is a "liberating god."

That is a tall order, and Emerson himself could not quite live up to it. Essays like "Experience" (1844) and "Fate" (1852) and poems like "Days" (1857)—the latter included in this anthology—communicate his later sense of incapacity and failed opportunity. Although the poems he published earlier in his career point toward imaginative freedom and power, he rarely achieved those qualities fully. He himself lamented that his poems spoke in a "husky" voice. Even if his poems did not become the transforming elements he wished them to be—perhaps Whitman accomplished that goal in his stead—they do achieve a great deal. Poems like "The Rhodora" and "The Snow-Storm" evoke the American landscape with remarkable vividness and feeling. The well-known "Concord Hymn" and the lesser-known "Voluntaries" prove that a patriotic poem can be both understated and moving. Poems such as "Hamatreya" initiated free verse as a viable mode of American poetry. In addition, "Hamatreya" and "Brahma" brought Hindu belief systems into the American mainstream. "Merlin" self-reflexively evokes Emerson's revolutionary aims for poetry and the poet. The "Ode, Inscribed to W. H. Channing" shows Emerson struggling to integrate his anger against slavery and other forms of political oppression into his aesthetic project. Ultimately the self-confident voice of "Merlin" and the vulnerability revealed in "Hamatreya" and "Days" complement each other, making Emerson a fascinating, inspiring, and heartbreaking figure to succeeding generations of readers and poets.

Emerson's first son, Waldo, died at the age of six, a tragedy from which the poet never fully recovered. Although Emerson opposed slavery and welcomed the freeing of the slaves, he found his optimism further sapped by the Civil War's incredible bloodshed. And in the last decades of his life he was haunted by declining powers. He traveled widely—to Yosemite under the guidance of John Muir, to Europe, and to the Middle East. But his later years were a process of increasing dementia and a descent into silence. By September 1866 he had lost his earlier, vitalizing sense of the spiritual unity of human beings and nature. He wrote in his *Journal*, "For every seeing soul there are two absorbing facts—*I and the Abyss.*" Emerson died on April 27, 1882, having changed the landscape of poetry.

FURTHER READING

Harold Bloom. *Agon*. New York: Oxford University Press, 1982.

Eduardo Cadava. *Emerson and the Climates of History*. Stanford: Stanford University Press, 1997.

Joel Porte and Saundra Morris, eds. *Emerson's Prose and Poetry*. New York: W.W. Norton, 2001.

Robert Richardson, Jr. *Emerson: The Mind on Fire*. Berkeley: University of California Press, 1995.

Pamela J. Schirmeister. *Less Legible Meanings: Between Poetry and Philosophy in the Work of Emerson*. Stanford: Stanford University Press, 2000.

Stephen E. Whicher. *Freedom and Fate: An Inner Life of Ralph Waldo Emerson*. Philadelphia: University of Pennsylvania Press, 1953.

R. A. Yoder. *Emerson and the Orphic Poet in America*. Berkeley: University of California Press, 1978.

Concord Hymn

By the rude bridge that arched the flood,[1]
    Their flag to April's breeze unfurled,
Here once the embattled farmers stood,
    And fired the shot heard round the world.

The foe long since in silence slept;
    Alike the conqueror silent sleeps;
And Time the ruined bridge has swept
    Down the dark stream which seaward creeps.

On this green bank, by this soft stream,
    We set today a votive[2] stone;
That memory may their deed redeem,
    When, like our sires, our sons are gone.

Spirit, that made those heroes dare
    To die, and leave their children free,
Bid Time and Nature gently spare
    The shaft we raise to them and thee.

1837

This poem was distributed and recited at the dedication of the monument commemorating the Revolutionary War battles of Lexington and Concord. Composed in traditional tetrameter quatrains, it balances small events with earth-changing ones, and time's passing with enduring memory.

Each and All

Little thinks, in the field, yon red-cloaked clown,[1]
Of thee from the hill-top looking down;
The heifer that lows[2] in the upland farm,
Far-heard, lows not thine ear to charm;
The sexton,[3] tolling his bell at noon,
Deems not that great Napoleon

1. That is, the river.
2. Offered in accordance with a vow.
1. Peasant. These first two lines derive from Emerson's memory of a visit to northern Italy.

2. Moos.
3. Church caretaker.

Stops his horse, and lists[4] with delight,
Whilst his files[5] sweep round yon Alpine height;
Nor knowest thou what argument
Thy life to thy neighbor's creed has lent.
All are needed by each one;
Nothing is fair or good alone.
I thought the sparrow's note from heaven,
Singing at dawn on the alder bough;
I brought him home, in his nest, at even;[6]
He sings the song, but it pleases not now,
For I did not bring home the river and sky—
He sang to my ear—they sang to my eye.
The delicate shells lay on the shore;
The bubbles of the latest wave
Fresh pearls to their enamel gave;
And the bellowing of the savage sea
Greeted their safe escape to me.
I wiped away the weeds and foam,
I fetched my sea-born treasures home;
But the poor, unsightly, noisome things
Had left their beauty on the shore,
With the sun, and the sand, and the wild uproar.
The lover watched his graceful maid,
As 'mid the virgin train she strayed,
Nor knew her beauty's best attire
Was woven still by the snow-white choir.
At last she came to his hermitage,
Like the bird from the woodlands to the cage—
The gay enchantment was undone,
A gentle wife, but fairy none.
Then I said, "I covet truth;
Beauty is unripe childhood's cheat;
I leave it behind with the games of youth."
As I spoke, beneath my feet
The ground-pine curled its pretty wreath,
Running over the club-moss burrs;
I inhaled the violet's breath;
Around me stood the oaks and firs;

4. Listens.   6. Evening.
5. Columns of soldiers.

Pine-cones and acorns lay on the ground,
Over me soared the eternal sky,
Full of light and of deity;
Again I saw, again I heard,
The rolling river, the morning bird—
Beauty through my senses stole;
I yielded myself to the perfect whole.

1839

The Rhodora

ON BEING ASKED, WHENCE IS THE FLOWER?

In May, when sea-winds pierced our solitudes,
I found the fresh Rhodora in the woods,
Spreading its leafless blooms in a damp nook,
To please the desert and the sluggish brook.
The purple petals, fallen in the pool,
Made the black water with their beauty gay;
Here might the red-bird come his plumes to cool,
And court the flower that cheapens his array.
Rhodora! If the sages ask thee why
This charm is wasted on the earth and sky,
Tell them, dear, that if eyes were made for seeing,
Then Beauty is its own excuse for being:
Why thou wert there, O rival of the rose!
I never thought to ask, I never knew;
But, in my simple ignorance, suppose
The self-same Power[1] that brought me there brought you.

1839

The rhodora is a variety of wild azalea that blooms in the New England countryside.

The Snow-Storm

Announced by all the trumpets of the sky,
Arrives the snow, and, driving o'er the fields,
Seems nowhere to alight: the whited air

---

1. Emerson believed in the inherent divinity of all things.

Hides hills and woods, the river, and the heaven,
And veils the farmhouse at the garden's end.
The sled and traveler stopped, the courier's feet
Delayed, all friends shut out, the housemates sit
Around the radiant fireplace, enclosed
In a tumultuous privacy of storm.

Come see the north wind's masonry.
Out of an unseen quarry evermore
Furnished with tile, the fierce artificer
Curves his white bastions with projected roof
Round every windward stake, or tree, or door.
Speeding, the myriad-handed, his wild work
So fanciful, so savage, nought cares he
For number or proportion. Mockingly,
On coop or kennel he hangs Parian[1] wreaths;
A swan-like form invests the hidden thorn;[2]
Fills up the farmer's lane from wall to wall,
Maugre[3] the farmer's sighs; and, at the gate,
A tapering turret overtops the work.
And when his hours are numbered, and the world
Is all his own, retiring, as he were not,
Leaves, when the sun appears, astonished Art
To mimic in slow structures, stone by stone,
Built in an age, the mad wind's night-work,
The frolic architecture of the snow.

1841

The Humble-Bee

Burly, dozing, humble-bee,
Where thou art is clime for me.
Let them sail for Porto Rique,[1]
Far off heats through seas to seek;
I will follow thee alone,

1. The snow shapes resemble wreaths sculpted from white marble quarried on the Greek isle of Paros.
2. Thorny shrub or small tree, such as the hawthorn.
3. Despite.
1. Emerson's brother Edward had gone to Puerto Rico in a vain effort to restore his health. He died there three years before Emerson composed the poem.

Thou animated torrid-zone![2]
Zigzag steerer, desert cheerer,
Let me chase thy waving lines;
Keep me nearer, me thy hearer,
Singing over shrubs and vines.

Insect lover of the sun,
Joy of thy dominion!
Sailor of the atmosphere;
Swimmer through the waves of air;
Voyager of light and noon;
Epicurean[3] of June;
Wait, I prithee,[4] till I come
Within earshot of thy hum —
All without is martyrdom.

When the south wind, in May days,
With a net of shining haze
Silvers the horizon wall,
And, with softness touching all,
Tints the human countenance
With a color of romance,
And, infusing subtle heats,
Turns the sod to violets,
Thou, in sunny solitudes,
Rover of the underwoods,
The green silence dost displace
With thy mellow, breezy bass.

Hot midsummer's petted crone,[5]
Sweet to me thy drowsy tone
Tells of countless sunny hours,
Long days, and solid banks of flowers;
Of gulfs of sweetness without bound
In Indian wildernesses found;
Of Syrian peace, immortal leisure,
Firmest cheer, and bird-like pleasure.

*   *   *

2. That is, the New England summer bee seems a
tropical zone in itself.
3. One with luxurious tastes; a lover of pleasure.
4. Pray thee.
5. The bee is already old by midsummer.

Aught[6] unsavory or unclean
Hath my insect never seen;
But violets and bilberry bells,[7]
Maple-sap, and daffodels,
Grass with green flag half-mast high,
Succory to match the sky,
Columbine with horn of honey,
Scented fern, and agrimony,
Clover, catchfly, adder's tongue,
And brier roses, dwelt among;
All beside was unknown waste,
All was picture as he passed.

Wiser far than human seer,
Yellow-breeched philosopher!
Seeing only what is fair,
Sipping only what is sweet,
Thou dost mock at fate and care,
Leave the chaff, and take the wheat.
When the fierce north-western blast
Cools sea and land so far and fast,
Thou already slumberest deep;
Woe and want thou canst outsleep;
Want and woe, which torture us,
Thy sleep makes ridiculous.

1846

"Humble-bee" is an alternative name for "bumblebee." Emerson composed this poem in May 1837, nearly a decade before publishing it. Suffering from a wave of depression, he looked to nature for comfort. In his *Journal* he observed, "The humble-bee and the pine-warbler seem to me the proper objects of attention in these disastrous times." His underlying anguish emerges in the final lines of this poem ostensibly about the joy of nature.

6. Anything.
7. Flowers of a native New England shrub. The following seven lines name other plants and flowers commonly found in the Massachusetts countryside.

Hamatreya

Bulkley,[1] Hunt, Willard, Hosmer, Meriam, Flint
Possessed the land which rendered to their toil
Hay, corn, roots, hemp, flax, apples, wool and wood.
Each of these landlords walked amidst his farm,
Saying, "'Tis mine, my children's and my name's.
How sweet the west wind sounds in my own trees!
How graceful climb those shadows on my hill!
I fancy these pure waters and the flags[2]
Know me, as does my dog: we sympathize;
And, I affirm, my actions smack[3] of the soil."

Where are these men? Asleep beneath their grounds:
And strangers, fond[4] as they, their furrows plough.
Earth laughs in flowers to see her boastful boys
Earth-proud, proud of the earth which is not theirs;
Who steer the plough, but cannot steer their feet
Clear of the grave.
They added ridge to valley, brook to pond,
And sighed for all that bounded their domain;
"This suits me for a pasture; that's my park;

We must have clay, lime, gravel, granite-ledge,
And misty lowland, where to go for peat.
The land is well—lies fairly to the south.
'Tis good, when you have crossed the sea and back,
To find the sitfast[5] acres where you left them."
Ah! The hot owner sees not Death, who adds
Him to his land, a lump of mold the more.
Hear what the Earth says:

EARTH-SONG

"Mine and yours;
Mine, not yours.
Earth endures;
Stars abide—

1. One of Emerson's ancestors was named Peter Bulkley. All of the names in this line refer to early settlers of Concord, Massachusetts. Some of the names have symbolic significance as well.
2. Any of several plants; in this case, probably a flower akin to an iris.
3. Taste.
4. Foolish, gullible, and also perhaps affectionate or doting.
5. Steadfast.

Shine down in the old sea;
Old are the shores;
But where are old men?
I who have seen much,
Such I have never seen.

"The lawyer's deed
Ran sure
In tail,[6]
To them, and to their heirs
Who shall succeed,
Without fail,
Forevermore.

"Here is the land,
Shaggy with wood,
With its old valley,
Mound and flood.
But the heritors?
Fled like the flood's foam.
The lawyer, and the laws,
And the kingdom,
Clean swept herefrom.

"They called me theirs,
Who so controlled me;
Yet every one
Wished to stay, and is gone.
How am I theirs,
If they cannot hold me,
But I hold them?"

When I heard the Earth-song
I was no longer brave;
My avarice cooled
Like lust in the chill of the grave.

1846

"Hamatreya" combines "hamadryad," a wood nymph or tree spirit in classical myth, with "Maitreya," a Hindu proper name meaning earth mother. The poem's reverence for the earth and its questioning of the idea of ownership derive from the Hindu scripture *Vishnu Purana* (Book 4). Emerson had begun to read Hindu texts seriously the year before. Poeti-

6. Entailed. The lawyer's deed has settled the estate on a specific line of heirs.

cally, the poem is marked by the variety of its diction as well as its movement, especially in the Earth-song, toward free verse. Although the Earth-song readily relinquishes meter, it cannot bear to forego irregular rhymes.

Merlin

1

Thy trivial harp will never please
Or fill my craving ear;
Its chords should ring as blows the breeze,
Free, peremptory, clear.
No jingling serenader's art,
Nor tinkle of piano strings,
Can make the wild blood start
In its mystic springs.
The kingly bard
Must smite the chords rudely and hard,
As with hammer or with mace;
That they may render back
Artful thunder, which conveys
Secrets of the solar track,
Sparks of the supersolar blaze.
Merlin's blows are strokes of fate,
Chiming with the forest tone,
When boughs buffet boughs in the wood;
Chiming with the gasp and moan
Of the ice-imprisoned flood;
With the pulse of manly hearts;
With the voice of orators;
With the din of city arts;
With the cannonade of wars;
With the marches of the brave;
And prayers of might from martyrs' cave.

Great is the art,
Great be the manners, of the bard.
He shall not his brain encumber
With the coil of rhythm and number;
But, leaving rule and pale forethought,
He shall aye[1] climb

1. Always; yes.

For his rhyme.
"Pass in, pass in," the angels say,
"In to the upper doors,
Nor count compartments of the floors,
But mount to paradise
By the stairway of surprise."

Blameless master of the games,
King of sport that never shames,
He shall daily joy dispense
Hid in song's sweet influence.
Things more cheerly live and go,
What time the subtle mind
Sings aloud the tune whereto
Their pulses beat,
And march their feet,
And their members are combined.

By Sybarites[2] beguiled,
He shall no task decline;
Merlin's mighty line
Extremes of nature reconciled—
Bereaved a tyrant of his will,
And made the lion mild.
Songs can the tempest still,
Scattered on the stormy air,
Mould the year to fair increase,
And bring in poetic peace.

He shall not seek to weave,
In weak, unhappy times,
Efficacious rhymes;
Wait his returning strength.
Bird, that from the nadir's floor
To the zenith's top can soar,
The soaring orbit of the muse exceeds that journey's length.
Nor profane affect to hit
Or compass that, by meddling wit,
Which only the propitious mind
Publishes when 'tis inclined.
There are open hours

2. A person devoted to pleasure and luxury; originally an inhabitant of Sybaris, an ancient Greek city in southern Italy.

When the God's will sallies free,
And the dull idiot might see
The flowing fortunes of a thousand years —
Sudden, at unawares,
Self-moved, fly-to the doors,
Nor sword of angels could reveal
What they conceal.

2

The rhyme of the poet
Modulates the king's affairs;
Balance-loving Nature
Made all things in pairs.
To every foot its antipode;[3]
Each color with its counter glowed
To every tone beat answering tones
Higher or graver;
Flavor gladly blends with flavor;
Leaf answers leaf upon the bough;
And match the paired cotyledons.[4]
Hands to hands, and feet to feet,
Coeval grooms and brides;
Eldest rite, two married sides
In every mortal meet.
Light's far furnace shines,
Smelting balls and bars,
Forging double stars,
Glittering twins and trines.[5]
The animals are sick with love,
Lovesick with rhyme;
Each with all propitious time
Into chorus wove.

Like the dancers' ordered band,
Thoughts come also hand in hand;
In equal couples mated,
Or else alternated;
Adding by their mutual gage,
One to other, health and age.

3. Exact opposite.   5. Groups of three.
4. A rudimentary leaf of the embryo of seed
plants.

Solitary fancies go
Short-lived wandering to and fro,
Most like to bachelors,
Or an ungiven maid,
Not ancestors,
With no posterity to make the lie afraid,
Or keep truth undecayed.
Perfect-paired as eagle's wings,
Justice is the rhyme of things;
Trade and counting use
The self-same tuneful muse;
And Nemesis,[6]
Who with even matches odd,
Who athwart[7] space redresses
The partial wrong,
Fills the just period,
And finishes the song.

Subtle rhymes, with ruin rife,
Murmur in the house of life,
Sung by the Sisters[8] as they spin;
In perfect time and measure they
Build and unbuild our echoing clay,
As the two twilights of the day
Fold us music-drunken in.

1846

The title refers to a legendary Welsh bardic poet, though it also reminds readers of the legendary English magician Merlin in Thomas Malory's fifteenth-century Arthurian romance, *Le Morte Darthur*. This poem, composed in an irregular rhythm punctuated by irregular rhymes, suggests the dynamic and godlike dimensions of Emerson's ideal poet. Emerson's twentieth-century editor Stephen Whicher suggests that the name "Merlin" meant to Emerson "a poet who sings with natural inspiration . . . and who, above all, has a potency that will change the hearts of men and direct their actions."

Ode, Inscribed to W. H. Channing

Though loath to grieve
The evil time's sole patriot,
I cannot leave

6. In classical myth, the goddess of divine retribution.
7. Across.
8. In classical myth, the Fates, who are three sisters, spin the threads of human destiny.

My honied thought
For the priest's cant,
Or statesman's rant.

If I refuse
My study for their politique,
Which at the best is trick,
The angry Muse
Puts confusion in my brain.

But who is he that prates
Of the culture of mankind,
Of better arts and life?
Go, blindworm, go,
Behold the famous States
Harrying Mexico[1]
With rifle and with knife!

Or who, with accent bolder,
Dare praise the freedom-loving mountaineer?
I found by thee, O rushing Contoocook![2]
And in thy valleys, Agiochook![3]
The jackals of the negro-holder.[4]

The God who made New Hampshire
Taunted the lofty land
With little men;
Small bat and wren
House in the oak:
If earth-fire cleave
The upheaved land, and bury the folk,
The southern crocodile would grieve.[5]

Virtue palters; Right is hence;
Freedom praised, but hid;
Funeral eloquence
Rattles the coffin-lid.

---

1. A reference to the U.S.-Mexican War (1846–48), then raging. Emerson, like Channing, opposed the war as an expansionary effort to increase slaveholding territories.
2. Native-American name for a branch of the Merrimack River in New Hampshire.
3. Native-American name for New Hampshire's White Mountains.

4. A reference to bounty hunters seeking escaped slaves in the free state of New Hampshire. It was common practice of the time not to capitalize the word "Negro."
5. That is, the Southern slaveholders would pretend to mourn, weeping crocodile tears.

What boots[6] thy zeal,
O glowing friend,
That would indignant rend
The northland from the south?
Wherefore? to what good end?
Boston Bay and Bunker Hill
Would serve things still;
Things are of the snake.

The horseman serves the horse,
The neatherd serves the neat,[7]
The merchant serves the purse,
The eater serves his meat;
'Tis the day of the chattel,[8]
Web to weave, and corn to grind;
Things are in the saddle,
And ride mankind.

There are two laws discrete,
Not reconciled,
Law for man, and law for thing;
The last builds town and fleet,
But it runs wild,
And doth the man unking.

'Tis fit the forest fall,
The steep be graded,
The mountain tunneled,
The sand shaded,
The orchard planted,
The glebe[9] tilled,
The prairie granted,
The steamer built.

Let man serve law for man;
Live for friendship, live for love,
For truth's and harmony's behoof;
The state may follow how it can,
As Olympus follows Jove.[10]

6. Profits.
7. Oxen.
8. Movable property, including slaves.
9. Field.

10. As the lesser gods on Mount Olympus follow Jove (or Jupiter), the supreme god in Roman myth.

*   *   *

Yet do not I implore[11]
The wrinkled shopman to my sounding woods,
Nor bid the unwilling senator
Ask votes of thrushes in the solitudes.
Every one to his chosen work;
Foolish hands may mix and mar;
Wise and sure the issues are.
Round they roll till dark is light,
Sex to sex, and even to odd;
The over-god
Who marries Right to Might,
Who peoples, unpeoples —
He who exterminates
Races by stronger races,
Black by white faces[12] —
Knows to bring honey
Out of the lion;[13]
Grafts scion[14]
On pirate and Turk.

The Cossack eats Poland,[15]
Like stolen fruit;
Her last noble is ruined,
Her last poet mute:
Straight, into double band
The victors divide;
Half for freedom strike and stand;
The astonished Muse finds thousands at her side.

1846

William Henry Channing (1810–1884), to whom this ode is dedicated, was a Unitarian cler-
gyman, a friendly critic of Emerson, and a fervent abolitionist. He wanted Emerson to work
on behalf of the whole human race rather than being solely concerned with the individual
self. In this ode, Emerson tried to defend his aesthetic and intellectual isolation while at the
same time taking a discernible step toward Channing's position of public engagement. In

11. Invite.
12. Another reference to slavery.
13. In the Bible, Samson, an Israelite judge, dis-
covers bees and honey in the carcass of a lion
(Judges 14:8).
14. Descendant.

15. Russia, peopled in part by Slavic warriors
called Cossacks, had annexed much of Poland in
the late eighteenth century. In the 1830s and
1840s, Poles rebelled and Russian officers muti-
nied, though both groups were unsuccessful.

subsequent years, he assumed an increasingly vocal antislavery position. By 1854, in "The Last of the Anti-Slavery Lectures," Emerson was writing that "it is not possible to extricate oneself from the questions in which our age is involved. . . . Liberty is the crusade of all brave and conscientious men."

Days

Daughters of time, the hypocritic Days,
Muffled and dumb like barefoot dervishes,[1]
And marching single in an endless file,
Bring diadems[2] and fagots in their hands.
To each they offer gifts after his will,
Bread, kingdoms, stars, and sky that holds them all.
I, in my pleached[3] garden, watched the pomp,
Forgot my morning wishes, hastily
Took a few herbs and apples, and the Day
Turned and departed silent. I, too late,
Under her solemn fillet[4] saw the scorn.

1857

Brahma

If the red slayer[1] thinks he slays,
    Or if the slain think he is slain,
They know not well the subtle ways
    I keep, and pass, and turn again.

Far or forgot to me is near;
    Shadow and sunlight are the same;
The vanished gods to me appear;
    And one to me are shame and fame.

They reckon ill who leave me out;
    When me they fly, I am the wings;
I am the doubter and the doubt,
    And I the hymn the Brahmin[2] sings.

*   *   *

1. Members of one of several Islamic orders who take vows of poverty and engage in ecstatic religious observances.
2. Jeweled crowns. Fagots: sticks.

3. Shaded with interwoven branches.
4. Headband.
1. Death.
2. A member of the Hindu priestly caste.

The strong gods pine for my abode,[3]
   And pine in vain the sacred Seven;[4]
But thou, meek lover of the good!
   Find me, and turn thy back on heaven.

1857

In Hinduism, Brahma is the Creator, the primal source and ultimate goal of all beings. He is the supreme impersonal deity in the Trimurti, which also includes Vishnu the Preserver and Shiva the Destroyer. According to Stephen Whicher, this poem "distills much of Emerson's Hindu reading; the subject is the 'doctrine of the absolute unity' that is central both to Hindu thought and Emerson's." A major source for the poem is the *Bhagavad Gita* (for example, 2:19 and 9:16–17).

FROM *Voluntaries*

In an age of fops[1] and toys,
Wanting wisdom, void of right,
Who shall nerve heroic boys
To hazard all in Freedom's fight—
Break sharply off their jolly games,
Forsake their comrades gay,
And quit proud homes and youthful dames,
For famine, toil, and fray?
Yet on the nimble air benign
Speed nimbler messages,
That waft the breath of grace divine
To hearts in sloth and ease.
So nigh is grandeur to our dust,
So near is God to man,
When Duty whispers low, *Thou must*,
The youth[2] replies, *I can*.

1867

A voluntary is a piece of music performed as a prelude. Emerson's poem, written during the height of the Civil War, praises the abolitionist and Unionist cause. The section of the poem reprinted here (part three of the five-part poem) portrays the heroism of ordinary young men willing to sacrifice their lives for the cause of freedom.

3. The Hindu gods Yama, Agni, and Indra yearn for oneness with Brahma.
4. The Hindu high saints.
1. Vain and excessively refined men. Toys: toylike or trifling men.
2. Specifically Robert Gould Shaw (1837–1863), the white commander of the Union army's first regiment of free black soldiers, the Massachusetts 54th. About half of the men, including Shaw, were killed at the battle of Fort Wagner, near Charleston, South Carolina, in July 1863. Emerson sent a copy of this poem to Shaw's father in September 1863.

PROSE

The Poet

Olympian bards who sung
Divine ideas below,
Which always find us young,
And always keep us so.[1]

Those who are esteemed umpires of taste are often persons who have acquired some knowledge of admired pictures or sculptures, and have an inclination for whatever is elegant; but if you inquire whether they are beautiful souls, and whether their own acts are like fair pictures, you learn that they are selfish and sensual. Their cultivation is local, as if you should rub a log of dry wood in one spot to produce fire, all the rest remaining cold. Their knowledge of the fine arts is some study of rules and particulars, or some limited judgment of color or form, which is exercised for amusement or for show. It is a proof of the shallowness of the doctrine of beauty, as it lies in the minds of our amateurs, that men seem to have lost the perception of the instant dependence of form upon soul. There is no doctrine of forms in our philosophy. We were put into our bodies, as fire is put into a pan, to be carried about; but there is no accurate adjustment between the spirit and the organ, much less is the latter the germination of the former. So in regard to other forms, the intellectual men do not believe in any essential dependence of the material world on thought and volition. Theologians think it a pretty air-castle to talk of the spiritual meaning of a ship or a cloud, of a city or a contract, but they prefer to come again to the solid ground of historical evidence; and even the poets are contented with a civil and conformed manner of living, and to write poems from the fancy, at a safe distance from their own experience. But the highest minds of the world have never ceased to explore the double meaning, or, shall I say, the quadruple, or the centuple, or much more manifold meaning, of every sensuous fact: Orpheus,[2] Empedocles, Heraclitus, Plato, Plutarch, Dante, Swedenborg, and the masters of sculpture, picture, and poetry. For we are not pans and barrows, nor even porters of the fire and torch-bearers, but children of the fire, made of it, and only the same divinity transmuted, and at two or three removes, when we know least about it. And this hidden truth, that the fountains whence all this river of Time,

1. This quatrain is from Emerson's "Ode to Beauty" (1843), lines 60–64.

2. The figure of the poet in classical myth. Empedocles and Heraclitus were Greek philosophers of the fifth and sixth centuries B.C.E.; Plato was the renowned Greek philosopher of the fourth century B.C.E.; Plutarch was a first-century biographer; Dante Alighieri was the thirteenth-century Italian poet who wrote *The Divine Comedy*; and Emanuel Swedenborg was an eighteenth-century mystical writer.

and its creatures, floweth, are intrinsically ideal and beautiful, draws us to the consideration of the nature and functions of the Poet, or the man of Beauty, to the means and materials he uses, and to the general aspect of the art in the present time.

The breadth of the problem is great, for the poet is representative. He stands among partial men for the complete man, and apprises us not of his wealth, but of the commonwealth. The young man reveres men of genius, because, to speak truly, they are more himself than he is. They receive of the soul as he also receives, but they more. Nature enhances her beauty, to the eye of loving men, from their belief that the poet is beholding her shows at the same time. He is isolated among his contemporaries, by truth and by his art, but with this consolation in his pursuits, that they will draw all men sooner or later. For all men live by truth, and stand in need of expression. In love, in art, in avarice, in politics, in labor, in games, we study to utter our painful secret. The man is only half himself, the other half is his expression.

Notwithstanding this necessity to be published, adequate expression is rare. I know not how it is that we need an interpreter; but the great majority of men seem to be minors, who have not yet come into possession of their own, or mutes, who cannot report the conversation they have had with nature. There is no man who does not anticipate a supersensual utility in the sun, and stars, earth, and water. These stand and wait to render him a peculiar service. But there is some obstruction, or some excess of phlegm[3] in our constitution, which does not suffer them to yield the due effect. Too feeble fall the impressions of nature on us to make us artists. Every touch should thrill. Every man should be so much an artist that he could report in conversation what had befallen him. Yet, in our experience, the rays or appulses[4] have sufficient force to arrive at the senses, but not enough to reach the quick, and compel the reproduction of themselves in speech. The poet is the person in whom these powers are in balance, the man without impediment, who sees and handles that which others dream of, traverses the whole scale of experience, and is representative of man, in virtue of being the largest power to receive and to impart.

For the Universe has three children, born at one time, which reappear, under different names, in every system of thought, whether they be called cause, operation, and effect; or, more poetically, Jove,[5] Pluto, Neptune; or, theologically, the Father, the Spirit, and the Son; but which we will call here, the Knower, the Doer, and the Sayer. These stand respectively for the love of truth, for the love of good, and for the love of beauty. These three are equal. Each is that which he is

---

3. Mucus, traditionally associated with apathy.
4. Conjunctions between celestial bodies.
5. In Roman myth, Jupiter (or Jove) was the su-
preme god. Pluto: the Roman god of the underworld. Neptune: the Roman god of the sea.

essentially, so that he cannot be surmounted or analyzed, and each of these three has the power of the others latent in him, and his own patent.

The poet is the sayer, the namer, and represents beauty. He is a sovereign, and stands on the centre. For the world is not painted, or adorned, but is from the beginning beautiful; and God has not made some beautiful things, but Beauty is the creator of the universe. Therefore the poet is not any permissive potentate, but is emperor in his own right. Criticism is infested with a cant of materialism, which assumes that manual skill and activity is the first merit of all men, and disparages such as say and do not, overlooking the fact, that some men, namely, poets, are natural sayers, sent into the world to the end of expression, and confounds them with those whose province is action, but who quit it to imitate the sayers. But Homer's words are as costly and admirable to Homer, as Agamemnon's victories are to Agamemnon.[6] The poet does not wait for the hero or the sage, but, as they act and think primarily, so he writes primarily what will and must be spoken, reckoning the others, though primaries also, yet, in respect to him, secondaries and servants; as sitters or models in the studio of a painter, or as assistants who bring building materials to an architect.

For poetry was all written before time was, and whenever we are so finely organized that we can penetrate into that region where the air is music, we hear those primal warblings, and attempt to write them down, but we lose ever and anon a word, or a verse, and substitute something of our own, and thus miswrite the poem. The men of more delicate ear write down these cadences more faithfully, and these transcripts, though imperfect, become the songs of the nations. For nature is as truly beautiful as it is good, or as it is reasonable, and must as much appear, as it must be done, or be known. Words and deeds are quite indifferent modes of the divine energy. Words are also actions, and actions are a kind of words.

The sign and credentials of the poet are that he announces that which no man foretold. He is the true and only doctor;[7] he knows and tells; he is the only teller of news, for he was present and privy to the appearance which he describes. He is a beholder of ideas, and an utterer of the necessary and causal. For we do not speak now of men of poetical talents, or of industry and skill in metre, but of the true poet. I took part in a conversation the other day, concerning a recent writer of lyrics, a man of subtle mind, whose head appeared to be a music-box of delicate tunes and rhythms, and whose skill, and command of language, we could not sufficiently praise. But when the question arose, whether he was not only a lyrist, but a poet, we were obliged to confess that he is plainly a contempo-

---

6. Agamemnon was the mythic king of Mycenae and commander of the Greek army, as portrayed in Homer's epic poem *The Iliad*.

7. The word here implies teacher as well as physician.

rary, not an eternal man. He does not stand out of our low limitations, like a Chimborazo[8] under the line, running up from the torrid base through all the climates of the globe, with belts of the herbage of every latitude on its high and mottled sides; but this genius is the landscape-garden of a modern house, adorned with fountains and statues, with well-bred men and women standing and sitting in the walks and terraces. We hear, through all the varied music, the ground-tone of conventional life. Our poets are men of talents who sing, and not the children of music. The argument is secondary, the finish of the verses is primary.

For it is not metres, but a metre-making argument, that makes a poem—a thought so passionate and alive, that, like the spirit of a plant or an animal, it has an architecture of its own, and adorns nature with a new thing. The thought and the form are equal in the order of time, but in the order of genesis the thought is prior to the form. The poet has a new thought: he has a whole new experience to unfold; he will tell us how it was with him, and all men will be the richer in his fortune. For, the experience of each new age requires a new confession, and the world seems always waiting for its poet. I remember, when I was young, how much I was moved one morning by tidings that genius had appeared in a youth who sat near me at table. He had left his work, and gone rambling none knew whither, and had written hundreds of lines, but could not tell whether that which was in him was therein told; he could tell nothing but that all was changed—man, beast, heaven, earth, and sea. How gladly we listened! how credulous! Society seemed to be compromised. We sat in the aurora of a sunrise which was to put out all the stars. Boston seemed to be at twice the distance it had the night before, or was much farther than that. Rome,—what was Rome? Plutarch and Shakespeare were in the yellow leaf,[9] and Homer no more should be heard of. It is much to know that poetry has been written this very day, under this very roof, by your side. What! that wonderful spirit has not expired! these stony moments are still sparkling and animated! I had fancied that the oracles were all silent, and nature had spent her fires, and behold! all night, from every pore, these fine auroras have been streaming. Every one has some interest in the advent of the poet, and no one knows how much it may concern him. We know that the secret of the world is profound, but who or what shall be our interpreter, we know not. A mountain ramble, a new style of face, a new person, may put the key into our hands. Of course, the value of genius to us is in the veracity of its report. Talent may frolic and juggle; genius realizes and adds. Mankind, in good earnest, have availed so far in understanding themselves and their work, that the foremost watchman on the peak announces his news. It is the truest word ever

---

8. A mountain in Ecuador, just south of the equator.
9. An allusion to Shakespeare's *Macbeth* (5.3.22–

23): "I have lived long enough: my way of life / Is fallen into the sere, the yellow leaf."

spoken, and the phrase will be the fittest, most musical, and the unerring voice of the world for that time.

All that we call sacred history attests that the birth of a poet is the principal event in chronology. Man, never so often deceived, still watches for the arrival of a brother who can hold him steady to a truth, until he has made it his own. With what joy I begin to read a poem, which I confide in as an inspiration! And now my chains are to be broken; I shall mount above these clouds and opaque airs in which I live — opaque, though they seem transparent — and from the heaven of truth I shall see and comprehend my relations. That will reconcile me to life, and renovate nature, to see trifles animated by a tendency, and to know what I am doing. Life will no more be a noise; now I shall see men and women, and know the signs by which they may be discerned from fools and satans. This day shall be better than my birth-day: then I became an animal: now I am invited into the science of the real. Such is the hope, but the fruition is postponed. Oftener it falls, that this winged man, who will carry me into the heaven, whirls me into the clouds, then leaps and frisks about with me from cloud to cloud, still affirming that he is bound heavenward; and I, being myself a novice, am slow in perceiving that he does not know the way into the heavens, and is merely bent that I should admire his skill to rise, like a fowl or a flying fish, a little way from the ground or the water; but the all-piercing, all-feeding, and ocular air of heaven, that man shall never inhabit. I tumble down again soon into my old nooks, and lead the life of exaggerations as before, and have lost my faith in the possibility of any guide who can lead me thither where I would be.

But leaving these victims of vanity, let us, with new hope, observe how nature, by worthier impulses, has ensured the poet's fidelity to his office of announcement and affirming, namely, by the beauty of things, which becomes a new, and higher beauty, when expressed. Nature offers all her creatures to him as a picture-language. Being used as a type, a second wonderful value appears in the object, far better than its old value, as the carpenter's stretched cord, if you hold your ear close enough, is musical in the breeze. "Things more excellent than every image," says Jamblichus,[10] "are expressed through images." Things admit of being used as symbols, because nature is a symbol, in the whole, and in every part. Every line we can draw in the sand has expression; and there is no body without its spirit or genius. All form is an effect of character; all condition, of the quality of the life; all harmony, of health (and, for this reason, a perception of beauty should be sympathetic, or proper only to the good). The beautiful rests on the foundations of the necessary. The soul makes the body, as the wise Spenser teaches:

> So every spirit, as it is most pure,
> And hath in it the more of heavenly light,

10. Iamblichus, a fourth-century Syrian philosopher.

So it the fairer body doth procure
To habit in, and it more fairly dight,
With cheerful grace and amiable sight.
For, of the soul, the body form doth take,
For soul is form, and doth the body make.[11]

Here we find ourselves, suddenly, not in a critical speculation, but in a holy place, and should go very warily and reverently. We stand before the secret of the world, there where Being passes into Appearance, and Unity into Variety.

The Universe is the externization of the soul. Wherever the life is, that bursts into appearance around it. Our science is sensual, and therefore superficial. The earth, and the heavenly bodies, physics, and chemistry, we sensually treat, as if they were self-existent; but these are the retinue of that Being we have. "The mighty heaven," said Proclus,[12] "exhibits, in its transfigurations, clear images of the splendor of intellectual perceptions; being moved in conjunction with the unapparent periods of intellectual natures." Therefore, science always goes abreast with the just elevation of the man, keeping step with religion and metaphysics; or, the state of science is an index of our self-knowledge. Since everything in nature answers to a moral power, if any phenomenon remains brute and dark, it is that the corresponding faculty in the observer is not yet active.

No wonder, then, if these waters be so deep, that we hover over them with a religious regard. The beauty of the fable proves the importance of the sense; to the poet, and to all others; or, if you please, every man is so far a poet as to be susceptible of these enchantments of nature: for all men have the thoughts whereof the universe is the celebration. I find that the fascination resides in the symbol. Who loves nature? Who does not? Is it only poets, and men of leisure and cultivation, who live with her? No; but also hunters, farmers, grooms, and butchers, though they express their affection in their choice of life, and not in their choice of words. The writer wonders what the coachman or the hunter values in riding, in horses, and dogs. It is not superficial qualities. When you talk with him, he holds these at as slight a rate as you. His worship is sympathetic; he has no definitions, but he is commanded in nature, by the living power which he feels to be there present. No imitation, or playing of these things, would content him; he loves the earnest of the north-wind, of rain, of stone, and wood, and iron. A beauty not explicable is dearer than a beauty which we can see to the end of. It is nature the symbol, nature certifying the supernatural, body overflowed by life, which he worships, with coarse, but sincere rites.

The inwardness, and mystery, of this attachment, drives men of every class to the use of emblems. The schools of poets, and philosophers, are not more

11. From English poet Edmund Spenser's "An Hymn in Honour of Beauty" (1596).

12. Fifth-century Greek philosopher.

intoxicated with their symbols than the populace with theirs. In our political par-
ties, compute the power of badges and emblems. See the great ball which they
roll from Baltimore to Bunker hill![13] In the political processions, Lowell[14] goes
in a loom, and Lynn in a shoe, and Salem in a ship. Witness the cider-barrel,[15]
the log-cabin, the hickory-stick, the palmetto, and all the cognizances of party.
See the power of national emblems. Some stars, lilies, leopards, a crescent, a
lion, an eagle, or other figure, which came into credit God knows how, on an old
rag of bunting, blowing in the wind, on a fort, at the ends of the earth, shall make
the blood tingle under the rudest, or the most conventional exterior. The people
fancy they hate poetry, and they are all poets and mystics!

Beyond this universality of the symbolic language, we are apprised of the
divineness of this superior use of things, whereby the world is a temple, whose
walls are covered with emblems, pictures, and commandments of the Deity,
in this, that there is no fact in nature which does not carry the whole sense of
nature; and the distinctions which we make in events, and in affairs, of low and
high, honest and base, disappear when nature is used as a symbol. Thought
makes every thing fit for use. The vocabulary of an omniscient man would
embrace words and images excluded from polite conversation. What would be
base, or even obscene, to the obscene, becomes illustrious, spoken in a new con-
nexion of thought. The piety of the Hebrew prophets purges their grossness. The
circumcision is an example of the power of poetry to raise the low and offensive.
Small and mean things serve as well as great symbols. The meaner the type by
which a law is expressed, the more pungent it is, and the more lasting in the mem-
ories of men: just as we choose the smallest box, or case, in which any needful
utensil can be carried. Bare lists of words are found suggestive, to an imaginative
and excited mind; as it is related of Lord Chatham,[16] that he was accustomed to
read in Bailey's Dictionary, when he was preparing to speak in Parliament. The
poorest experience is rich enough for all the purposes of expressing thought.
Why covet a knowledge of new facts? Day and night, house and garden, a few
books, a few actions, serve us as well as would all trades and all spectacles. We are
far from having exhausted the significance of the few symbols we use. We can
come to use them yet with a terrible simplicity. It does not need that a poem
should be long. Every word was once a poem. Every new relation is a new word.
Also, we use defects and deformities to a sacred purpose, so expressing our sense
that the evils of the world are such only to the evil eye. In the old mythology,

13. A stunt in the 1840 presidential campaign of
William Henry Harrison.
14. A town in Massachusetts that produced tex-
tiles. Lynn, Massachusetts, produced shoes. Sa-
lem, Massachusetts, was a shipping center.
15. The cider barrel and log cabin were associated
with Harrison's presidential campaign of 1840.
The hickory stick and palmetto were associated
with former President Andrew Jackson.
16. The British political leader William Pitt
(1708–1778), earl of Chatham.

mythologists observe, defects are ascribed to divine natures, as lameness to Vulcan, blindness to Cupid, and the like, to signify exuberances.

For, as it is dislocation and detachment from the life of God, that makes things ugly, the poet, who re-attaches things to nature and the Whole—re-attaching even artificial things, and violations of nature, to nature, by a deeper insight—disposes very easily of the most disagreeable facts. Readers of poetry see the factory-village, and the railway, and fancy that the poetry of the landscape is broken up by these; for these works of art are not yet consecrated in their reading; but the poet sees them fall within the great Order not less than the bee-hive, or the spider's geometrical web. Nature adopts them very fast into her vital circles, and the gliding train of cars she loves like her own. Besides, in a centred mind, it signifies nothing how many mechanical inventions you exhibit. Though you add millions, and never so surprising, the fact of mechanics has not gained a grain's weight. The spiritual fact remains unalterable, by many or by few particulars; as no mountain is of any appreciable height to break the curve of the sphere. A shrewd country-boy goes to the city for the first time, and the complacent citizen is not satisfied with his little wonder. It is not that he does not see all the fine houses, and know that he never saw such before, but he disposes of them as easily as the poet finds place for the railway. The chief value of the new fact is to enhance the great and constant fact of Life, which can dwarf any and every circumstance, and to which the belt of wampum, and the commerce of America, are alike.

The world being thus put under the mind for verb and noun, the poet is he who can articulate it. For, though life is great, and fascinates, and absorbs—and though all men are intelligent of the symbols through which it is named—yet they cannot originally use them. We are symbols, and inhabit symbols; workman, work, and tools, words and things, birth and death, all are emblems; but we sympathize with the symbols, and, being infatuated with the economical uses of things, we do not know that they are thoughts. The poet, by an ulterior intellectual perception, gives them a power which makes their old use forgotten, and puts eyes, and a tongue, into every dumb and inanimate object. He perceives the thought's independence of the symbol, the stability of the thought, the accidency and fugacity[17] of the symbol. As the eyes of Lyncaeus[18] were said to see through the earth, so the poet turns the world to glass, and shows us all things in their right series and procession. For, through that better perception, he stands one step nearer to things, and sees the flowing or metamorphosis; perceives that thought is multiform; that within the form of every creature is a force impelling it to ascend into a higher form; and, following with his eyes the life, uses the

17. Fleetingness, transience.
18. In Greek myth, one of the Argonauts who sailed with Jason to recover the Golden Fleece. He was noted for his keen vision.

forms which express that life, and so his speech flows with the flowing of nature. All the facts of the animal economy—sex, nutriment, gestation, birth, growth— are symbols of the passage of the world into the soul of man, to suffer there a change, and reappear a new and higher fact. He uses forms according to the life, and not according to the form. This is true science. The poet alone knows astronomy, chemistry, vegetation, and animation, for he does not stop at these facts, but employs them as signs. He knows why the plain, or meadow of space, was strown with these flowers we call suns, and moons, and stars; why the great deep is adorned with animals, with men, and gods; for, in every word he speaks he rides on them as the horses of thought.

By virtue of this science the poet is the Namer, or Language-maker, naming things sometimes after their appearance, sometimes after their essence, and giving to every one its own name and not another's, thereby rejoicing the intellect, which delights in detachment or boundary. The poets made all the words, and therefore language is the archives of history, and, if we must say it, a sort of tomb of the muses. For, though the origin of most of our words is forgotten, each word was at first a stroke of genius, and obtained currency, because for the moment it symbolized the world to the first speaker and to the hearer. The etymologist finds the deadest word to have been once a brilliant picture. Language is fossil poetry. As the limestone of the continent consists of infinite masses of the shells of animalcules, so language is made up of images, or tropes, which now, in their secondary use, have long ceased to remind us of their poetic origin. But the poet names the thing because he sees it, or comes one step nearer to it than any other. This expression, or naming, is not art, but a second nature, grown out of the first, as a leaf out of a tree. What we call nature is a certain self-regulated motion, or change; and nature does all things by her own hands, and does not leave another to baptize her, but baptizes herself; and this through the metamorphosis again. I remember that a certain poet[19] described it to me thus:

> Genius is the activity which repairs the decays of things, whether wholly or partly of a material and finite kind. Nature, through all her kingdoms, insures herself. Nobody cares for planting the poor fungus: so she shakes down from the gills of one agaric[20] countless spores, any one of which, being preserved, transmits new billions of spores tomorrow or next day. The new agaric of this hour has a chance which the old one had not. This atom of seed is thrown into a new place, not subject to the accidents which destroyed its parent two rods off. She makes a man; and having brought him to ripe age, she will no longer run the risk of losing this wonder at a blow, but she detaches from him a new self, that the kind may be safe from accidents to which the individual is exposed. So when the soul of the poet has come to ripeness of thought, she detaches

19. Emerson himself, in his persona of Orphic or   20. A family of fungi including mushrooms.
prophetic poet.

and sends away from it its poems or songs—a fearless, sleepless, deathless progeny, which is not exposed to the accidents of the weary kingdom of time: a fearless, vivacious offspring, clad with wings (such was the virtue of the soul out of which they came), which carry them fast and far, and infix them irrecoverably into the hearts of men. These wings are the beauty of the poet's soul. The songs, thus flying immortal from their mortal parent, are pursued by clamorous flights of censures, which swarm in far greater numbers, and threaten to devour them; but these last are not winged. At the end of a very short leap they fall plump down, and rot, having received from the souls out of which they came no beautiful wings. But the melodies of the poet ascend, and leap, and pierce into the deeps of infinite time.

So far the bard taught me, using his freer speech. But nature has a higher end, in the production of new individuals, than security, namely, *ascension*, or, the passage of the soul into higher forms. I knew, in my younger days, the sculptor who made the statue of the youth which stands in the public garden. He was, as I remember, unable to tell directly, what made him happy, or unhappy, but by wonderful indirections he could tell. He rose one day, according to his habit, before the dawn, and saw the morning break, grand as the eternity out of which it came, and, for many days after, he strove to express this tranquillity, and, lo! his chisel had fashioned out of marble the form of a beautiful youth, Phosphor,[21] whose aspect is such, that, it is said, all persons who look on it become silent. The poet also resigns himself to his mood, and that thought which agitated him is expressed, but *alter idem*,[22] in a manner totally new. The expression is organic, or, the new type which things themselves take when liberated. As, in the sun, objects paint their images on the retina of the eye, so they, sharing the aspiration of the whole universe, tend to paint a far more delicate copy of their essence in his mind. Like the metamorphosis of things into higher organic forms is their change into melodies. Over everything stands its daemon, or soul, and, as the form of the thing is reflected by the eye, so the soul of the thing is reflected by a melody. The sea, the mountain-ridge, Niagara, and every flower-bed, pre-exist, or super-exist, in pre-cantations,[23] which sail like odors in the air, and when any man goes by with an ear sufficiently fine, he overhears them, and endeavors to write down the notes, without diluting or depraving them. And herein is the legitimation of criticism, in the mind's faith, that the poems are a corrupt version of some text in nature, with which they ought to be made to tally. A rhyme in one of our sonnets should not be less pleasing than the iterated nodes of a sea-shell, or the resembling difference of a group of flowers. The pairing of the birds is an idyl, not tedious as our idyls are; a tempest is a rough ode, without falsehood or rant; a summer, with its harvest sown, reaped, and stored, is an epic song,

21. In Greek myth, a god of the morning star.
22. The same yet different (Latin).

23. Prophetic incantations.

subordinating how many admirably executed parts. Why should not the symmetry and truth that modulate these, glide into our spirits, and we participate the invention of nature?

This insight, which expresses itself by what is called Imagination, is a very high sort of seeing, which does not come by study, but by the intellect being where and what it sees, by sharing the path, or circuit of things through forms, and so making them translucid to others. The path of things is silent. Will they suffer a speaker to go with them? A spy they will not suffer; a lover, a poet, is the transcendency of their own nature,—him they will suffer. The condition of true naming, on the poet's part, is his resigning himself to the divine *aura* which breathes through forms, and accompanying that.

It is a secret which every intellectual man quickly learns, that, beyond the energy of his possessed and conscious intellect, he is capable of a new energy (as of an intellect doubled on itself), by abandonment to the nature of things; that, beside his privacy of power as an individual man, there is a great public power, on which he can draw, by unlocking, at all risks, his human doors, and suffering the ethereal tides to roll and circulate through him: then he is caught up into the life of the Universe, his speech is thunder, his thought is law, and his words are universally intelligible as the plants and animals. The poet knows that he speaks adequately, then, only when he speaks somewhat wildly, or, "with the flower of the mind;" not with the intellect, used as an organ, but with the intellect released from all service, and suffered to take its direction from its celestial life; or, as the ancients were wont to express themselves, not with intellect alone, but with the intellect inebriated by nectar. As the traveler who has lost his way throws his reins on his horse's neck, and trusts to the instinct of the animal to find his road, so must we do with the divine animal who carries us through this world. For if in any manner we can stimulate this instinct, new passages are opened for us into nature, the mind flows into and through things hardest and highest, and the metamorphosis is possible.

This is the reason why bards love wine, mead, narcotics, coffee, tea, opium, the fumes of sandal-wood and tobacco, or whatever other species of animal exhilaration. All men avail themselves of such means as they can, to add this extraordinary power to their normal powers; and to this end they prize conversation, music, pictures, sculpture, dancing, theatres, travelling, war, mobs, fires, gaming, politics, or love, or science, or animal intoxication, which are several coarser or finer *quasi*-mechanical substitutes for the true nectar, which is the ravishment of the intellect by coming nearer to the fact. These are auxiliaries to the centrifugal tendency of a man, to his passage out into free space, and they help him to escape the custody of that body in which he is pent up, and of that jailyard of individual relations in which he is enclosed. Hence a great number of such as were professionally expressors of Beauty, as painters, poets, musicians, and actors, have been more than others wont to lead a life of pleasure and indulgence; all but the few who received the true nectar; and, as it was a spurious mode of attaining freedom, as it was an emancipation not into the heavens, but into the freedom of baser places, they were punished for that advantage they won, by a dissipation and deterioration. But never can any advantage be taken of nature by a trick. The spirit of the world, the great calm presence of the creator, comes not forth to the sorceries of opium or of wine. The sublime vision comes to the pure and simple soul in a clean and chaste body. That is not an inspiration which we owe to narcotics, but some counterfeit excitement and fury. Milton[24] says that the lyric poet may drink wine and live generously, but the epic poet, he who shall sing of the gods, and their descent unto men, must drink water out of a wooden bowl. For poetry is not "Devil's wine," but God's wine. It is with this as it is with toys. We fill the hands and nurseries of our children with all manner of dolls, drums, and horses, withdrawing their eyes from the plain face and sufficing objects of nature, the sun, and moon, the animals, the water, and stones, which should be their toys. So the poet's habit of living should be set on a key so low and plain that the common influences should delight him. His cheerfulness should be the gift of the sunlight; the air should suffice for his inspiration, and he should be tipsy with water. That spirit which suffices quiet hearts, which seems to come forth to such from every dry knoll of sere grass, from every pine-stump, and half-imbedded stone, on which the dull March sun shines, comes forth to the poor and hungry, and such as are of simple taste. If thou fill thy brain with Boston and New York, with fashion and covetousness, and wilt stimulate thy jaded senses with wine and French coffee, thou shalt find no radiance of wisdom in the lonely waste of the pinewoods.

If the imagination intoxicates the poet, it is not inactive in other men. The metamorphosis excites in the beholder an emotion of joy. The use of symbols has a certain power of emancipation and exhilaration for all men. We seem to be touched by a wand, which makes us dance and run about happily, like children. We are like persons who come out of a cave or cellar into the open air. This is the effect on us of tropes, fables, oracles, and all poetic forms. Poets are thus liberating gods. Men have really got a new sense, and found within their world, another world, or nest of worlds; for, the metamorphosis once seen, we divine that it does not stop. I will not now consider how much this makes the charm of algebra and the mathematics, which also have their tropes, but it is felt in every definition; as when Aristotle defines *space* to be an immovable vessel, in which things are contained; or when Plato defines a *line* to be a flowing point; or *figure*

---

24. English poet John Milton, in his "Sixth Latin Elegy" (1629).

to be a bound of solid; and many the like. What a joyful sense of freedom we
have, when Vitruvius[25] announces the old opinion of artists, that no architect
can build any house well, who does not know something of anatomy. When
Socrates, in *Charmides*, tells us that the soul is cured of its maladies by certain
incantations, and that these incantations are beautiful reasons, from which
temperance is generated in souls; when Plato calls the world an animal; and
Timaeus[26] affirms that the plants also are animals; or affirms a man to be a
heavenly tree, growing with his root, which is his head, upward; and, as
George Chapman,[27] following him, writes,

> So in our tree of man, whose nervie root
> Springs in his top;

when Orpheus speaks of hoariness as "that white flower which marks extreme
old age;" when Proclus calls the universe the statue of the intellect; when Chau-
cer,[28] in his praise of "Gentilesse," compares good blood in mean condition to
fire, which, though carried to the darkest house betwixt this and the mount of
Caucasus, will yet hold its natural office, and burn as bright as if twenty thousand
men did it behold; when John[29] saw, in the apocalypse, the ruin of the world
through evil, and the stars fall from heaven, as the figtree casteth her untimely
fruit; when Aesop[30] reports the whole catalogue of common daily relations
through the masquerade of birds and beasts;—we take the cheerful hint of the
immortality of our essence, and its versatile habit and escapes, as when the gyp-
sies say, "it is in vain to hang them, they cannot die."

The poets are thus liberating gods. The ancient British bards had for the title
of their order, "Those who are free throughout the world." They are free, and
they make free. An imaginative book renders us much more service at first, by
stimulating us through its tropes, than afterward, when we arrive at the precise
sense of the author. I think nothing is of any value in books, excepting the tran-
scendental and extraordinary. If a man is inflamed and carried away by his
thought, to that degree that he forgets the authors and the public, and heeds only
this one dream, which holds him like an insanity, let me read his paper, and you
may have all the arguments and histories and criticism. All the value which
attaches to Pythagoras,[31] Paracelsus, Cornelius Agrippa, Cardan, Kepler, Swe-

25. Roman architect of the first century B.C.E.
26. The principal speaker in Plato's *Timaeus*.
27. English poet and translator (ca. 1559–1634). The quoted lines are from the dedication to his translation of Homer.
28. English poet Geoffrey Chaucer (ca. 1340–1400). The reference is to the Wife of Bath's Tale in *Canterbury Tales*.
29. Revelation 6:13.
30. Greek writer of fables (620–560 B.C.E.).

31. Greek mathematician of the sixth century B.C.E. Paracelsus (1493–1541) was a Swiss alchemist; Agrippa (1486–1535) was a German physician; Jerome Cardan (1501–1576) was an Italian mathematician; Johannes Kepler (1571–1630) was a German astronomer; Emanuel Swedenborg (1688–1772) was the Swedish philosopher who so influenced Emerson; Friedrich von Schelling (1775–1854) was a German philosopher; and Lorenz Oken (1779–1851) was a German naturalist.

denborg, Schelling, Oken, or any other who introduces questionable facts into his cosmogony, as angels, devils, magic, astrology, palmistry, mesmerism, and so on, is the certificate we have of departure from routine, and that here is a new witness. That also is the best success in conversation, the magic of liberty, which puts the world, like a ball, in our hands. How cheap even the liberty then seems; how mean to study, when an emotion communicates to the intellect the power to sap and upheave nature: how great the perspective! nations, times, systems, enter and disappear, like threads in tapestry of large figure and many colors; dream delivers us to dream, and, while the drunkenness lasts, we will sell our bed, our philosophy, our religion, in our opulence.

There is good reason why we should prize this liberation. The fate of the poor shepherd, who, blinded and lost in the snow-storm, perishes in a drift within a few feet of his cottage door, is an emblem of the state of man. On the brink of the waters of life and truth, we are miserably dying. The inaccessibleness of every thought but that we are in, is wonderful. What if you come near to it—you are as remote, when you are nearest, as when you are farthest. Every thought is also a prison; every heaven is also a prison. Therefore we love the poet, the inventor, who in any form, whether in an ode, or in an action, or in looks and behavior, has yielded us a new thought. He unlocks our chains, and admits us to a new scene.

This emancipation is dear to all men, and the power to impart it, as it must come from greater depth and scope of thought, is a measure of intellect. Therefore all books of the imagination endure, all which ascend to that truth, that the writer sees nature beneath him, and uses it as his exponent. Every verse or sentence, possessing this virtue, will take care of its own immortality. The religions of the world are the ejaculations of a few imaginative men.

But the quality of the imagination is to flow, and not to freeze. The poet did not stop at the color, or the form, but read their meaning; neither may he rest in this meaning, but he makes the same objects exponents of his new thought. Here is the difference betwixt the poet and the mystic, that the last nails a symbol to one sense, which was a true sense for a moment, but soon becomes old and false. For all symbols are fluxional; all language is vehicular and transitive,[32] and is good, as ferries and horses are, for conveyance, not as farms and houses are, for homestead. Mysticism consists in the mistake of an accidental and individual symbol for an universal one. The morning-redness happens to be the favorite meteor to the eyes of Jacob Behmen,[33] and comes to stand to him for truth and faith; and he believes should stand for the same realities to every reader. But the first reader prefers as naturally the symbol of a mother and child, or a gardener and his bulb, or a jeweller polishing a gem. Either of these, or of a myriad more,

---

32. Capable of transporting from the literal to the imaginative.

33. Jakob Boehme (1575–1624) was a German mystic.

are equally good to the person to whom they are significant. Only they must be held lightly, and be very willingly translated into the equivalent terms which others use. And the mystic must be steadily told, —All that you say is just as true without the tedious use of that symbol as with it. Let us have a little algebra, instead of this trite rhetoric—universal signs, instead of these village symbols—and we shall both be gainers. The history of hierarchies seems to show that all religious error consisted in making the symbol too stark and solid, and, at last, nothing but an excess of the organ of language.

Swedenborg, of all men in the recent ages, stands eminently for the translator of nature into thought. I do not know the man in history to whom things stood so uniformly for words. Before him the metamorphosis continually plays. Everything on which his eye rests, obeys the impulses of moral nature. The figs become grapes whilst he eats them. When some of his angels affirmed a truth, the laurel twig which they held blossomed in their hands. The noise which, at a distance, appeared like gnashing and thumping, on coming nearer was found to be the voice of disputants. The men, in one of his visions, seen in heavenly light, appeared like dragons, and seemed in darkness; but, to each other, they appeared as men, and, when the light from heaven shone into their cabin, they complained of the darkness, and were compelled to shut the window that they might see.

There was this perception in him, which makes the poet or seer, an object of awe and terror, namely, that the same man, or society of men, may wear one aspect to themselves and their companions, and a different aspect to higher intelligences. Certain priests, whom he describes as conversing very learnedly together, appeared to the children, who were at some distance, like dead horses; and many the like misappearances. And instantly the mind inquires, whether these fishes under the bridge, yonder oxen in the pasture, those dogs in the yard, are immutably fishes, oxen, and dogs, or only so appear to me, and perchance to themselves appear upright men; and whether I appear as a man to all eyes. The Brahmins[34] and Pythagoras propounded the same question, and if any poet has witnessed the transformation, he doubtless found it in harmony with various experiences. We have all seen changes as considerable in wheat and caterpillars. He is the poet, and shall draw us with love and terror, who sees, through the flowing vest, the firm nature, and can declare it.

I look in vain for the poet whom I describe. We do not, with sufficient plainness, or sufficient profoundness, address ourselves to life, nor dare we chaunt our own times and social circumstance. If we filled the day with bravery, we should not shrink from celebrating it. Time and nature yield us many gifts, but not yet the timely man, the new religion, the reconciler, whom all things await. Dante's

34. Hindu priestly caste. Emerson alludes here to the Hindu and Pythagorean belief in reincarnation.

praise is that he dared to write his autobiography in colossal cipher, or into universality. We have yet had no genius in America, with tyrannous eye, which knew the value of our incomparable materials, and saw, in the barbarism and materialism of the times, another carnival of the same gods whose picture he so much admires in Homer; then in the middle age; then in Calvinism. Banks and tariffs, the newspaper and caucus, methodism and unitarianism, are flat and dull to dull people, but rest on the same foundations of wonder as the town of Troy, and the temple of Delphos, and are as swiftly passing away. Our logrolling, our stumps and their politics, our fisheries, our Negroes, and Indians, our boasts, and our repudiations, the wrath of rogues, and the pusillanimity of honest men, the northern trade, the southern planting, the western clearing, Oregon, and Texas, are yet unsung. Yet America is a poem in our eyes; its ample geography dazzles the imagination, and it will not wait long for metres. If I have not found that excellent combination of gifts in my countrymen which I seek, neither could I aid myself to fix the idea of the poet by reading now and then in Chalmers's collection of five centuries of English poets.[35] These are wits, more than poets, though there have been poets among them. But when we adhere to the ideal of the poet, we have our difficulties even with Milton and Homer. Milton is too literary, and Homer too literal and historical.

But I am not wise enough for a national criticism, and must use the old largeness a little longer, to discharge my errand from the muse to the poet concerning his art.

Art is the path of the creator to his work. The paths, or methods, are ideal and eternal, though few men ever see them, not the artist himself for years, or for a lifetime, unless he come into the conditions. The painter, the sculptor, the composer, the epic rhapsodist, the orator, all partake one desire, namely, to express themselves symmetrically and abundantly, not dwarfishly and fragmentarily. They found or put themselves in certain conditions, as, the painter and sculptor before some impressive human figures; the orator, into the assembly of the people; and the others, in such scenes as each has found exciting to his intellect; and each presently feels the new desire. He hears a voice, he sees a beckoning. Then he is apprised, with wonder, what herds of daemons hem him in. He can no more rest; he says, with the old painter, "By God, it is in me, and must go forth of me." He pursues a beauty, half seen, which flies before him. The poet pours out verses in every solitude. Most of the things he says are conventional, no doubt; but by and by he says something which is original and beautiful. That charms him. He would say nothing else but such things. In our way of talking, we say, "That is yours, this is mine;" but the poet knows well that it is not his; that it is as strange and beautiful to him as to you; he would fain hear the like eloquence at

35. Alexander Chalmers's *Works of the English Poets* (1810).

length. Once having tasted this immortal ichor,[36] he cannot have enough of it, and, as an admirable creative power exists in these intellections, it is of the last importance that these things get spoken. What a little of all we know is said! What drops of all the sea of our science are baled up! and by what accident it is that these are exposed, when so many secrets sleep in nature! Hence the necessity of speech and song; hence these throbs and heart-beatings in the orator, at the door of the assembly, to the end, namely, that thought may be ejaculated as Logos, or Word.

Doubt not, O poet, but persist. Say, "It is in me, and shall out." Stand there, baulked and dumb, stuttering and stammering, hissed and hooted, stand and strive, until, at last, rage draw out of thee that *dream*-power which every night shows thee is thine own; a power transcending all limit and privacy, and by virtue of which a man is the conductor of the whole river of electricity. Nothing walks, or creeps, or grows, or exists, which must not in turn arise and walk before him as exponent of his meaning. Comes he to that power, his genius is no longer exhaustible. All the creatures, by pairs and by tribes, pour into his mind as into a Noah's ark, to come forth again to people a new world. This is like the stock of air for our respiration, or for the combustion of our fireplace, not a measure of gallons, but the entire atmosphere if wanted. And therefore the rich poets, as Homer, Chaucer, Shakespeare, and Raphael,[37] have obviously no limits to their works, except the limits of their lifetime, and resemble a mirror carried through the street, ready to render an image of every created thing.

O poet! a new nobility is conferred in groves and pastures, and not in castles, or by the sword-blade, any longer. The conditions are hard, but equal. Thou shalt leave the world, and know the muse only. Thou shalt not know any longer the times, customs, graces, politics, or opinions of men, but shalt take all from the muse. For the time of towns is tolled from the world by funereal chimes, but in nature the universal hours are counted by succeeding tribes of animals and plants, and by growth of joy on joy. God wills also that thou abdicate a manifold and duplex life, and that thou be content that others speak for thee. Others shall be thy gentlemen, and shall represent all courtesy and worldly life for thee; others shall do the great and resounding actions also. Thou shalt lie close hid with nature, and canst not be afforded to the Capitol or the Exchange. The world is full of renunciations and apprenticeships, and this is thine: thou must pass for a fool and a churl for a long season. This is the screen and sheath in which Pan[38] has protected his well-beloved flower, and thou shalt be known only to thine own, and they shall console thee with tenderest love. And thou shalt not be able

36. In Greek myth, the fluid that runs in the gods' veins.
37. Italian Renaissance painter (1483–1520).
38. In Greek myth, the god of forests and flocks, with the head of a man and the legs and horns of a goat.

to rehearse the names of thy friends in thy verse, for an old shame before the holy ideal. And this is the reward: that the ideal shall be real to thee, and the impressions of the actual world shall fall like summer rain, copious, but not troublesome, to thy invulnerable essence. Thou shalt have the whole land for thy park and manor, the sea for thy bath and navigation, without tax and without envy; the woods and the rivers thou shalt own; and thou shalt possess that wherein others are only tenants and boarders. Thou true land-lord! Sea-lord! Air-lord! Wherever snow falls, or water flows, or birds fly, wherever day and night meet in twilight, wherever the blue heaven is hung by clouds, or sown with stars, wherever are forms with transparent boundaries, wherever are outlets into celestial space, wherever is danger, and awe, and love, there is Beauty, plenteous as rain, shed for thee, and though thou shouldest walk the world over, thou shalt not be able to find a condition inopportune or ignoble.

1844

This essay, which began as a series of journal entries and a public lecture, redefines the role of the poet and the aim of a poem. Indebted to European romanticism as well as to European and Asian philosophy, it emphasizes the poet's visionary capacity. It progressively inflates the poet's role from being a representative human being with secrets to confess to being a seer, a namer, and finally "a liberating god." The essay also calls for an organic and democratic poetry. Rather than adhering to a preexistent form, the poem should have a thought "so passionate and alive" that it makes "an architecture of its own." The United States, Emerson believed, was calling out for the kind of poet he described. Indeed, the diverse and vigorous new nation was itself "a poem in our eyes."

Letter to Walt Whitman

Dear Sir—I am not blind to the worth of the wonderful gift of *Leaves of Grass*. I find it the most extraordinary piece of wit & wisdom that America has yet contributed. I am very happy in reading it, as great power makes us happy. It meets the demand I am always making of what seemed the sterile and stingy nature, as if too much handiwork, or too much lymph in the temperament, were making our western wits fat & mean.

I give you joy of your free & brave thought. I have great joy in it. I find incomparable things said incomparably well, as they must be. I find the courage of treatment which so delights us, & which large perception only can inspire.

I greet you at the beginning of a great career, which yet must have had a long foreground somewhere, for such a start. I rubbed my eyes a little, to see if this sunbeam were no illusion, but the solid sense of the book is a sober certainty. It has the best merits, namely, of fortifying & encouraging.

I did not know until I last night saw the book advertised in a newspaper that I could trust the name as real & available for a post-office. I wish to see my benefactor, & have felt much like striking my tasks, & visiting New York to pay you my respects.

1855

Emerson here responds with remarkable excitement and enthusiasm to Whitman's gift of a copy of *Leaves of Grass*. Emerson had never heard of Whitman before receiving the gift. Whitman used Emerson's letter to advertise his book and only responded to Emerson a year later, in a letter that he published but never sent.

ELIZABETH OAKES SMITH
1806–1893

LIKE MANY OTHER European-American middle- and upper-class women of her time, Elizabeth Oakes Smith was able to pursue her career as a poet, writer, and lecturer by aligning herself with a husband who was an editor and writer himself. After marrying Seba Smith, editor of the Portland, Maine, paper *The Eastern Argus*, and giving birth to six sons, she moved with her husband to New York, where in 1856 they established *Emerson's United States Magazine*. Smith was an early women's rights champion, but her public ambitions ended when Lucy Stone complained that the dress Smith wore to an early women's convention bared too much of her neck and arms. As Smith's strongest poems, like "The Unattained," reveal, she chafed at the limits of her female role within a male-dominated society. She expressed these feelings through a Romantic poetic that recalls such John Keats poems as "Ode on a Grecian Urn." Her writing anticipates the later outcries of female American poets in many cultural positions—from such writers as Alice Dunbar-Nelson, Edna St. Vincent Millay, and Amy Lowell to Sylvia Plath, Audre Lorde, Lorna Dee Cervantes, and Joy Harjo.

FURTHER READING

Elizabeth Oakes Smith. *The Sinless Child, and Other Poems*. Ed. John Keese. New York: Wiley & Putnam, 1843.

Cheryl Walker. *The Nightingale's Burden: Women Poets and American Culture before 1900*. Bloomington: Indiana University Press, 1982.

The Unattained

And in this life? and are we born for this?
To follow phantoms that elude the grasp,
Or whatso'er's secured, within our clasp,
To withering lie, as if each mortal kiss
Were doomed death's shuddering touch alone to meet.
O Life! has thou reserved no cup of bliss?
Must still the unattained beguile our feet?
The unattained with yearnings fill the breast,
That rob, for aye, the spirit of its rest?
Yes, this is Life; and everywhere we meet,
Not victor crowns, but wailings of defeat;

Yet faint thou not, thou dost apply a test,

That shall incite thee onward, upward still,
The present cannot sate, nor e'er thy spirit fill.

1843

HENRY WADSWORTH LONGFELLOW
1807–1882

Henry wadsworth longfellow was by far the most popular and widely praised American poet during his own lifetime. His best-known works, such as the narrative poems *Evangeline* (1847), *The Song of Hiawatha* (1855), and *The Courtship of Miles Standish* (1858), went through edition after edition on both sides of the Atlantic and reappeared in countless lyceum recitations, musical settings, and dramatizations before achieving, for succeeding generations, a new life as classroom staples. Together with such briefer early narratives as "The Wreck of the Hesperus," which swept the nation when it appeared in the 1841 *Ballads and Other Poems* and such later immensely popular narratives as "Paul Revere's Ride" from the three-volume series *Tales of a Wayside Inn* (1863), these poems helped to establish America's literary credibility with a doubtful Great Britain, where Longfellow outsold both Tennyson and Browning. They also helped to craft for America a national mythology that reinterpreted its early history in accord with liberal mid-nineteenth-century norms. Longfellow's contemporary critical success was as strong in England as in America, and he is the only American-born poet (with the exception of T. S. Eliot, who lived in England and became a British citizen) to have his name enshrined in Poet's Corner in England's great national monument, Westminster Abbey.

Yet, as Dana Gioia notes in his trenchant essay "Longfellow in the Aftermath of Modernism," with the emergence in the twentieth century of a new array of critical tools and standards designed to come to grips with the bristling complexities of a modernist poetics, Longfellow's reputation took a dramatic fall. His gift for lucid narrative, his metrical polish and inventiveness, his clear, directly expressive imagery, his vividly dramatized if sometimes all-too-conventional sentiment, and perhaps even his sheer accessibility were dismissed as out of date. What the critical fraternity now valued was the complexity, irony, formal challenge, and ambiguous depth to be found in Eliot, Ezra Pound, and Wallace Stevens as well as in such Longfellow contemporaries as Emily Dickinson, Walt Whitman, and Edgar Allan Poe—the latter Longfellow's most frequent and pointed contemporary critic. Moreover, Longfellow's message, which mixed a confident social progressivism with a peculiarly fatalistic view of individual emotional life, had dovetailed seamlessly with the spirit of his own times, but this same message came to seem badly out of joint with the culturally questioning yet emotionally assertive and self-exploratory spirit of the twentieth century, which Whitman and Dickinson had so brilliantly anticipated. Still, Longfellow, despite genuine limitations, remains a poet of real gifts whose work continues to be of great cultural and historical importance. For Longfellow was not just a vivid reflector of the spirit of his times but an important creator of that spirit. With the onset of the twenty-first century, the moment has surely come for a reassessment both of Longfellow's poetry and of his cultural standing.

Longfellow, the second of eight children, was born in Portland, Maine, in 1807 into a locally prominent family. The busy harbor life of Portland, its shorelines and subtle tidal variations, its frequent, violent storms, and its vast surrounding primeval forests would find recurrent expression in Longfellow's poetry. Longfellow's childhood was an unusually happy one for a poet. His mother, Zilpah, a woman of gentle spirit and imagination, supported his writing aspirations, while his father, a public-spirited lawyer who briefly served in Congress, provided an affirming presence as well as steady financial assistance that in his early years made possible Longfellow's college education and his crucial postgraduate travels in Europe. Admitted to Maine's Bowdoin College in 1821, when he was just fourteen, Longfellow excelled. Indeed, when he graduated in 1825, the college trustees offered this eighteen-year-old prodigy a newly established professorship in modern languages if he would prepare by undertaking a period of travel in Europe at his own expense. Accepting these terms, Longfellow departed in May 1826 and spent three years traveling through France, Spain, Italy, and Germany, where he perfected his command of several modern languages and began a lifelong dialogue with European literature and culture that contrasts strongly with Whitman's radical nativism.

Longfellow returned to Bowdoin College in 1829, where, at the age of twenty-two, he assumed his professorial duties. During his five years at Bowdoin, while establishing himself as a popular and influential teacher, Longfellow wrote little original poetry, but he did publish a series of translations of poems from many European languages and in 1833–34 the prose memoir *Outre-Mer: A Pilgrimage Beyond the Sea*. Longfellow, who had married Mary Storer Potter in 1831, accepted an endowed chair in modern languages at Harvard University in 1834. After leaving for Europe in April 1835 with his wife for further study of Germanic languages, Longfellow was stunned when his wife died in Holland in November due to complications from a miscarriage.

Following several months of deep mourning, Longfellow met Frances Appleton, the talented and sensitive daughter of a wealthy Bostonian, in Switzerland in the spring of 1836 and fell passionately in love. A difficult seven-year courtship followed, with Frances long resisting Longfellow's repeated entreaties. Finally, in 1843, Frances relented, and Longfellow and his longed-for bride entered into what one biographer describes as "one of the happiest marriages on record."

The years of his courtship and second marriage were also Longfellow's most productive years as a poet. His first book of original poems, *Voices in the Night*, appeared in 1839, followed quickly by *Ballads and Other Poems* (1841), *Poems on Slavery* (1842)—Longfellow was one of slavery's early opponents, though he shrank from the righteous intensity of the more radical abolitionists—and *The Belfry of Bruges and Other Poems* (1846). Each of these books was popular and warmly received, but it was the wildly successful *Evangeline*, followed by *The Song of Hiawatha* and *The Courtship of Miles Standish*, that established Longfellow, in the eyes of his contemporaries, as America's preeminent poet and most influential mythmaker.

Longfellow faced an overpowering personal tragedy when his much-beloved wife Fanny died in their home after her dress accidentally caught fire and Longfellow's attempts to extinguish the flames with his own body proved unsuccessful. He himself was badly injured, and, after hovering near death, he passed through a slow period of physical recovery and a longer period of deep despondency. Some of his writings from that period were so dark that he later destroyed them; surviving letters attest to their bleak mood. Though his face was deeply scarred—hence the long beard of his later years—he otherwise recovered physically. But he never entirely recovered from the psychic wounds of his wife's loss. His single poignant reference to the death of his wife in his poetry is "The Cross of Snow," a poem Longfellow considered too personal to publish during his lifetime.

The trend among recent anthologies of American poetry has been to shrink the representation of Longfellow's verse almost to the point of disappearance. But such an effort at erasure not only creates a skewed impression of nineteenth-century American literature and culture but also forces the omission of many of the most skillfully crafted, emotionally accessible, and widely read poems of that period. Longfellow, as a poet, was almost singularly incapable of ambiguity—that quality most prized by modernist critics. Moreover, both his formal language and the sentiment that pervades his poetry might best be described as *deeply* conventional. Yet he was a masterly creator of poetic atmosphere, in part because his virtuoso skill with meters enabled him to find the exact metrical equivalent to a particular mood, and he turned this skill to great advantage in a succession of beautifully turned lyrics, such as the early "Hymn to the Night" (1839) and "Mezzo Cammin" (1842). Moreover, the depth of his investment in and formation of the poetic, intellectual, and emotional conventions of his time makes him a nearly perfect reflector of the norms of mid-nineteenth-century progressivist culture. Still, despite his optimistic social progressivism, his emotional framework is melancholy—and this, too, struck a deep cord with his contemporaries, who often had to struggle with the sudden and early death of children, spouses, and friends even as they supported a public agenda of bourgeois expansionism.

Longfellow's earliest poetic "hit" was "A Psalm of Life" (1839). Its "good advice" in the guise of poetry, which became a target in the opening pages of Cleanth Brooks and Robert Penn Warren's influential text *Understanding Poetry,* has sometimes been taken to represent Longfellow's work as a whole. But its uncharacteristically urgent didacticism and stridently optimistic tone may most fruitfully be read as an effort by the temperamentally melancholy Longfellow to steel himself to renewed effort "at a time when I was rallying from depression" over the death of his first wife and the persistent refusals over many years of the woman who became his second. It reflected, as well, his frustration over what was, until then, a career-long failure to create original poetry.

Longfellow continued to compose elegantly atmospheric and increasingly austere nocturnal pieces like "The Day Is Done," "The Bridge," "Nature," and "The Tide Rises, the Tide Falls," culminating in the deeply melancholy resignation of "The Cross of Snow." Most of these poems concentrate on the meditative evocation of a single atmosphere as the poet's feeling merges with and is echoed by the natural scene, but Longfellow shows himself capable of considerably more complex effects in longer lyrics like "My Lost Youth" and "The Jewish Cemetery at Newport." Indeed, each stanza of "My Lost Youth" creates its own distinct physical and emotional atmosphere, which combine to paint a remarkably varied portrait both of Longfellow's native seaport town of Portland and of the fitfully contrasting emotional states of the remembered boy, whose "will" like "the wind's will" ranges from joyful inspiration to confused yet passionate urgency, and to deep anxiety and melancholy. On the other hand, "The Jewish Cemetery at Newport" displays a far more subtle and evocative didacticism than the early "Psalm of Life," exploring the sources and consequences of racial and religious prejudice as these forces pursued through life and even into death the now-resting inhabitants of the Jewish cemetery in Newport, Rhode Island. In each of these poems Longfellow's melancholy spirit dominates, to such an extent that one begins to think of him as the first and most delicate in that imposing line of New England poets of loss which extends through Edwin Arlington Robinson, Eliot, and Robert Frost to more recent poets like Robert Lowell, Elizabeth Bishop, and Sylvia Plath.

But, as indicated above, Longfellow's greatest popularity and fame in his lifetime lay in his narrative poems. These poems, though now unfashionable with professional critics, remain worthy of reexamination, both because they continue to be highly readable and effective and because they reveal a great deal about the needs and preconceptions of the mid-nineteenth-century Anglo-American and European culture that took these poems to their hearts. Such poems as "The Wreck of the Hesperus," which established Longfellow's popularity as a narrative poet, underline that culture's preoccupation with threats to fair-haired feminine innocence, from nature and from arrogant patriarchs like the schooner's captain. *Evangeline*, perhaps Longfellow's most extensive metrical tour de force, explores —with characteristic fatalism—both the violent destruction of an innocent pastoral community by impersonal political forces and the similarly violent separation of true but innocent lovers by impersonal politics and implacable fate. *Evangeline*'s famous prologue will offer some idea of the poem's evocative flavor. *The Song of Hiawatha*, on the other hand, invents and celebrates a Native American culture hero and in the process supplied American readers with a mythic history grounded in the then-talismanic figure of the noble savage. A similar impulse toward mythifying American history may be found in several of the *Tales of a Wayside Inn*, most popularly in "Paul Revere's Ride." What these narrative poems share with the lyrics is a direct and vivid approach and a strong sense of atmosphere. What they add is the invention of a mythic past that reflects an age's yearnings for cultural identity and meaningful history.

FURTHER READING

Newton Arvin. *Longfellow: His Life and Work*. Boston: Little, Brown, 1963.

Dana Gioia. "Longfellow in the Aftermath of Modernism," in *The Columbia History of American Poetry*. New York: Columbia University Press, 1993.

Henry Wadsworth Longfellow. *The Complete Poetical Works of Henry Wadsworth Longfellow* (Cambridge Edition). Boston: Houghton Mifflin, 1893.

A Psalm of Life

WHAT THE HEART OF THE
YOUNG MAN SAID TO THE PSALMIST

Tell me not, in mournful numbers,[1]
    Life is but an empty dream! —
For the soul is dead that slumbers,
    And things are not what they seem.

Life is real! Life is earnest!
    And the grave is not its goal;
Dust thou art, to dust returnest,
    Was not spoken of the soul.

Not enjoyment, and not sorrow,
    Is our destined end or way;
But to act, that each to-morrow
    Find us farther than to-day.

Art is long, and Time is fleeting,[2]
    And our hearts, though stout and brave,
Still, like muffled drums, are beating
    Funeral marches to the grave.

In the world's broad field of battle,
    In the bivouac of Life,
Be not like dumb, driven cattle!
    Be a hero in the strife!

Trust no Future, howe'er pleasant!
    Let the dead Past bury its dead![3]
Act, — act in the living Present!
    Heart within, and God o'erhead!

Lives of great men all remind us
    We can make our lives sublime,
And, departing, leave behind us
    Footprints on the sands of time;

1. Metrical syllables and, hence, poetic verses — from the tendency to count syllables in various metrical systems.
2. A sentiment perhaps first uttered by Hippocrates that emphasizes the length of time needed to master a difficult art (such as poetry or medicine) and the brevity of the life available to achieve that mastery. This sentiment has been echoed by Seneca, Chaucer, Goethe, Browning, and many others.
3. See Matthew 8:22: "But Jesus said to him, 'Follow me, and leave the dead to bury their own dead.'"

*   *   *

Footprints, that perhaps another,
    Sailing o'er life's solemn main,
A forlorn and shipwrecked brother,
    Seeing, shall take heart again.

Let us, then, be up and doing,
    With a heart for any fate;
Still achieving, still pursuing,
    Learn to labor and to wait.

1838

Longfellow recalled of this poem, "I kept it some time in manuscript, unwilling to show it to any one, it being a voice from my inmost heart, at a time when I was rallying from depression." The biblical psalms are predominantly mournful; hence Longfellow's affirmative "Psalm of Life" is a response both to biblical melancholy and to his own youthful experience of depression, linked in this case to the death of his first wife and his as-yet-unsuccessful pursuit of his second.

Hymn to the Night

Ἀσπασίη, τρίλλιστος[1]

I heard the trailing garments of the Night
    Sweep through her marble halls!
I saw her sable skirts all fringed with light
    From the celestial walls!

I felt her presence, by its spell of might,
    Stoop o'er me from above;
The calm, majestic presence of the Night,
    As of the one I love.

I heard the sounds of sorrow and delight,
    The manifold, soft chimes,
That fill the haunted chambers of the Night,
    Like some old poet's rhymes.

From the cool cisterns of the midnight air
    My spirit drank repose;
The fountain of perpetual peace flows there, —
    From those deep cisterns flows.

1. Homer, *Iliad* 8:488: "Welcome, three times prayed for [night]."

*   *   *

O holy Night! from thee I learn to bear
    What man has borne before!
Thou layest thy finger on the lips of Care,
    And they complain no more.

Peace! Peace! Orestes-like[2] I breathe this prayer!
    Descend with broad-winged flight,
The welcome, the thrice-prayed for, the most fair,
    The best-beloved Night!

                    1839

Longfellow recalled that this poem was composed in the summer of 1839, "while sitting at my chamber window, on one of the balmiest nights of the year. I endeavored to reproduce the impression of the hour and scene."

The Wreck of the Hesperus

It was the schooner Hesperus,
    That sailed the wintry sea;
And the skipper had taken his little daughtèr,
    To bear him company.

Blue were her eyes as the fairy-flax,
    Her cheeks like the dawn of day,
And her bosom white as the hawthorn buds,
    That ope in the month of May.

The skipper he stood beside the helm,
    His pipe was in his mouth,
And he watched how the veering flaw did blow
    The smoke now West, now South.

Then up and spake an old Sailòr,
    Had sailed to the Spanish Main,
"I pray thee, put into yonder port,
    For I fear a hurricane.

*   *   *

2. Orestes, according to Greek myth, murdered his mother and her lover to avenge their murder of his father, King Agamemnon. As the protago-nist of Euripides' *The Eumenides*, Orestes prays for and finds peace from his tormenting guilt.

"Last night, the moon had a golden ring,
　　And to-night no moon we see!"
The skipper, he blew a whiff from his pipe,
　　And a scornful laugh laughed he.

Colder and louder blew the wind,
　　A gale from the Northeast,
The snow fell hissing in the brine,
　　And the billows frothed like yeast,

Down came the storm, and smote amain
　　The vessel in its strength;
She shuddered and paused, like a frighted steed,
　　Then leaped her cable's length.

"Come hither! come hither! my little daughtèr,
　　And do not tremble so;
For I can weather the roughest gale
　　That ever wind did blow."

He wrapped her warm in his seaman's coat
　　Against the stinging blast;
He cut a rope from a broken spar,
　　And bound her to the mast.

"O father! I hear the church-bells ring,
　　Oh say, what it may be?"
"'T is a fog-bell on a rock-bound coast!" —
　　And he steered for the open sea.

"O father! I hear the sound of guns,
　　Oh say, what may it be?"
"Some ship in distress, that cannot live
　　In such an angry sea!"

"O father! I see a gleaming light,
　　Oh say, what may it be?"
But the father answered never a word,
　　A frozen corpse was he.

Lashed to the helm, all stiff and stark,
　　With his face turned to the skies,
The lantern gleamed through the gleaming snow
　　On his fixed and glassy eyes.

*　　*　　*

Then the maiden clasped her hands and prayed
    That savèd she might be;
And she thought of Christ, who stilled the wave,
    On the Lake of Galilee.

And fast through the midnight dark and drear,
    Through the whistling sleet and snow,
Like a sheeted ghost, the vessel swept
    Tow'rds the reef of Norman's Woe.

And ever the fitful gusts between
    A sound came from the land;
It was the sound of the trampling surf
    On the rocks and the hard sea-sand.

The breakers were right beneath her bows,
    She drifted a dreary wreck,
And a whooping billow swept the crew
    Like icicles from her deck.

She struck where the white and fleecy waves
    Looked soft as carded wool,
But the cruel rocks, they gored her side
    Like the horns of an angry bull.

Her rattling shrouds, all sheathed in ice,
    With the masts went by the board;
Like a vessel of glass, she stove and sank,
    Ho! ho! the breakers roared!

At daybreak, on the bleak sea-beach,
    A fisherman stood aghast,
To see the form of a maiden fair,
    Lashed close to a drifting mast.

The salt sea was frozen on her breast,
    The salt tears in her eyes;
And he saw her hair, like the brown seaweed,
    On the billows fall and rise.

Such was the wreck of the Hesperus,
    In the midnight and the snow!
Christ save us all from a death like this,
    On the reef of Norman's Woe!

                 1841

"The Wreck of the Hesperus," Longfellow's first major success in narrative poetry, was inspired by a disastrous winter storm off the New England coast on December 14, 1839. According to contemporary accounts, more than fifty ships were wrecked, dismasted, or carried to sea, and more than two hundred lives were lost. According to contemporary accounts, the actual *Hesperus* was docked in Boston harbor when it was hit by such strong winds that it sailed across the street into the third story of a building. The wreck from which many of the poem's details were obtained was actually the brig *Favorite*, wrecked on the Norman's Woe rocks just outside of Gloucester Harbor. *The Favorite* lost all on board, including a woman, perhaps forty-five years old, whose body was found washed ashore lashed to a mast. Longfellow's tale, composed at one sitting and without premeditation on the night of December 30, 1939, is thus an imaginative transformation of the storm's events.

Mezzo Cammin

Half of my life is gone, and I have let
 The years slip from me and have not fulfilled
 The aspiration of my youth, to build
 Some tower of song with lofty parapet.
Not indolence, nor pleasure, nor the fret
 Of restless passions that would not be stilled,
 But sorrow, and a care that almost killed,
 Kept me from what I may accomplish yet;
Though, half-way up the hill, I see the Past
 Lying beneath me with its sounds and sights, —
 A city in the twilight dim and vast,
With smoking roofs, soft bells, and gleaming lights. —
 And hear above me on the autumnal blast
 The cataract of Death far thundering from the heights.

1842

Longfellow's title alludes to the opening of Dante's *Divine Comedy*, which finds Dante "en mezzo cammin": in the middle of life's journey, since he is thirty-five (half the Bible's proverbial life span of seventy years). This point would be the start of Dante's mythic journey through hell, purgatory, and heaven. Longfellow, also thirty-five, a budding poet as yet uncertain of his fame—and still in apparently fruitless pursuit of Frances Appleton, his eventual second wife, after six years of courtship—views his life in terms of its unfulfilled yearnings and ambitions. Longfellow would later translate the complete *Divine Comedy*.

The Day Is Done

The day is done, and the darkness
    Falls from the wings of Night,
As a feather is wafted downward
    From an eagle in his flight.

I see the lights of the village
    Gleam through the rain and the mist,
And a feeling of sadness comes o'er me
    That my soul cannot resist:

A feeling of sadness and longing,
    That is not akin to pain,
And resembles sorrow only
    As the mist resembles the rain.

Come, read to me some poem,
    Some simple and heartfelt lay,
That shall soothe this restless feeling,
    And banish the thoughts of day.

Not from the grand old masters,
    Not from the bards sublime,
Whose distant footsteps echo
    Through the corridors of Time.

For, like strains of martial music,
    Their mighty thoughts suggest
Life's endless toil and endeavor;
    And to-night I long for rest.

Read from some humbler poet,
    Whose songs gushed from his heart,
As showers from the clouds of summer,
    Or tears from the eyelids start;

Who, through long days of labor,
    And nights devoid of ease,
Still heard in his soul the music
    Of wonderful melodies.

*   *   *

Such songs have power to quiet
    The restless pulse of care,
And come like benediction
    That follows after prayer.

Then read from the treasured volume
    The poem of thy choice,
And lend to the rhyme of the poet
    The beauty of thy voice.

And the night shall be filled with music,
    And the cares, that infest the day,
Shall fold their tents, like the Arabs,
    And as silently steal away.

1844

The Bridge

I stood on the bridge at midnight,
    As the clocks were striking the hour,
And the moon rose o'er the city,
    Behind the dark church-tower.

I saw her bright reflection
    In the waters under me,
Like a golden goblet falling
    And sinking into the sea.

And far in the hazy distance
    Of that lovely night in June,
The blaze of the flaming furnace
    Gleamed redder than the moon.

Among the long, black rafters
    The wavering shadows lay,
And the current that came from the ocean
    Seemed to lift and bear them away;

As, sweeping and eddying through them,
    Rose the belated tide,
And, streaming into the moonlight,
    The seaweed floated wide.

    ＊   ＊   ＊

And like those waters rushing
Among the wooden piers,
A flood of thoughts came o'er me
That filled my eyes with tears.

How often, oh how often,
In the days that had gone by,
I had stood on that bridge at midnight
And gazed on that wave and sky!

How often, oh how often,
I had wished that the ebbing tide
Would bear me away on its bosom
O'er the ocean wild and wide!

For my heart was hot and restless,
And my life was full of care,
And the burden laid upon me
Seemed greater than I could bear.

But now it has fallen from me,
It is buried in the sea;
And only the sorrow of others
Throws its shadow over me.

Yet whenever I cross the river
On its bridge with wooden piers,
Like the odor of brine from the ocean
Comes the thought of other years.

And I think how many thousands
Of care-encumbered men,
Each bearing his burden of sorrow,
Have crossed the bridge since then.

I see the long procession
Still passing to and fro,
The young heart hot and restless
And the old subdued and slow!

And forever and forever,
As long as the river flows,
As long as the heart has passions,
As long as life has woes;

*   *   *

The moon and its broken reflection
And its shadows shall appear,
As the symbol of love in heaven,
And its wavering image here.

1846

The poem's original title was "The Bridge over the Charles," the river separating Cambridge from Boston.

FROM *Evangeline*

[Prologue]

This is the forest primeval. The murmuring pines and the hemlocks,
Bearded with moss, and in garments green, indistinct in the twilight,
Stand like Druids of eld, with voices sad and prophetic,
Stand like harpers hoar, with beards that rest on their bosoms.
Loud from its rocky caverns, the deep-voiced neighboring ocean
Speaks, and in accents disconsolate answers the wail of the forest.

This is the forest primeval; but where are the hearts that beneath it
Leaped like the roe, when he hears in the woodland the voice of the huntsman?
Where is the thatch-roofed village, the home of Acadian farmers,—
Men whose lives glided on like rivers that water the woodlands,
Darkened by shadows of earth, but reflecting an image of heaven?
Waste are those pleasant farms, and the farmers forever departed!
Scattered like dust and leaves, when the mighty blasts of October
Seize them, and whirl them aloft, and sprinkle them far o'er the ocean.
Naught but tradition remains of the beautiful village of Grand-Pré.

Ye who believe in affection that hopes, and endures, and is patient,
Ye who believe in the beauty and strength of woman's devotion,
List to the mournful tradition, still sung by the pines of the forest;
List to a Tale of Love in Acadie, home of the happy.

1847

My Lost Youth

Often I think of the beautiful town[1]
    That is seated by the sea;
Often in thought go up and down
The pleasant streets of that dear old town,
    And my youth comes back to me.
        And a verse of a Lapland song
        Is haunting my memory still:
        "A boy's will is the wind's will,
And the thoughts of youth are long, long thoughts."[2]

I can see the shadowy lines of its trees,
    And catch, in sudden gleams,
The sheen of the far-surrounding seas,
And islands that were the Hesperides[3]
    Of all my boyish dreams.
        And the burden of that old song,
        It murmurs and whispers still:
        "A boy's will is the wind's will,
And the thoughts of youth are long, long thoughts."

I remember the black wharves and the slips,
    And the sea-tides tossing free;
And Spanish sailors with bearded lips,
And the beauty and mystery of the ships,
    And the magic of the sea.
        And the voice of that wayward song
        Is singing and saying still:
        "A boy's will is the wind's will,
And the thoughts of youth are long, long thoughts."

I remember the bulwarks by the shore,
    And the fort upon the hill;
The sunrise gun, with its hollow roar,

---

1. This poem is based on Longfellow's memories of Portland, Maine, "my native town, the city by the sea."
2. Longfellow's translation of lines from a Lapland folk song that he found in a German version of Gottfried von Herder's anthology of folk poetry, *Die Stimmen der Volker in Lieden* (1778–79). Upon completing "My Lost Youth," which he had been meditating on for some time, Longfellow noted in his diary, "Wrote the poem; and am rather pleased with it, and with the bringing in of the two lines of the old Lapland song:

    A boy's will is the wind's will,
    And the thoughts of youth are long,
        long thoughts."

3. Islands of the Blest, to be found in the western seas, according to Greek mythology.

The drum-beat repeated o'er and o'er,
    And the bugle wild and shrill.
        And the music of that old song
        Throbs in my memory still:
        "A boy's will is the wind's will,
And the thoughts of youth are long, long thoughts."

I remember the sea-fight far away,
    How it thundered o'er the tide!
And the dead captains, as they lay
In their graves o'erlooking the tranquil bay
    Where they in battle died.[4]
        And the sound of that mournful song
        Goes through me with a thrill:
        "A boy's will is the wind's will,
And the thoughts of youth are long, long thoughts."

I can see the breezy dome of groves,
    The shadows of Deering's Woods;
And the friendships old and early loves
Come back with a Sabbath sound, as of doves
    In quiet neighborhoods.
        And the verse of that sweet old song,
        It flutters and murmurs still:
        "A boy's will is the wind's will,
And the thoughts of youth are long, long thoughts."

I remember the gleams and glooms that dart
    Across the school-boy's brain;
The song and the silence in the heart,
That in part are prophecies, and in part
    Are longings wild and vain.
        And the voice of that fitful song
        Sings on, and is never still:
        "A boy's will is the wind's will,
And the thoughts of youth are long, long thoughts."

There are things of which I may not speak;
    There are dreams that cannot die;

4. In September 1813, when Longfellow was six, the American frigate *Enterprise* captured the British brig *Boxer* off the Maine coast. Both captains were killed in the battle and buried in a cemetery overlooking the bay.

There are thoughts that make the strong heart weak,
And bring a pallor into the cheek,
 And a mist before the eye.
  And the words of that fatal song
  Come over me like a chill:
  "A boy's will is the wind's will,
And the thoughts of youth are long, long thoughts."

Strange to me now are the forms I meet
 When I visit the dear old town;
But the native air is pure and sweet,
And the trees that o'ershadow each well-known street,
 As they balance up and down,
  Are singing the beautiful song,
  Are sighing and whispering still:
  "A boy's will is the wind's will,
And the thoughts of youth are long, long thoughts."

And Deering's Woods are fresh and fair,
 And with joy that is almost pain
My heart goes back to wander there,
And among the dreams of the days that were,
 I find my lost youth again.
  And the strange and beautiful song,
  The groves are repeating it still:
  "A boy's will is the wind's will,
And the thoughts of youth are long, long thoughts."

           1855

The Jewish Cemetery at Newport

How strange it seems! These Hebrews in their graves,
 Close by the street of this fair seaport town,
Silent beside the never-silent waves,
 At rest in all this moving up and down!

The trees are white with dust, that o'er their sleep
 Wave their broad curtains in the south-wind's breath,
While underneath these leafy tents they keep
 The long, mysterious Exodus[1] of Death.

---

1. Departure, emigration. The Bible's Book of Exodus describes the flight of the Israelites from Egypt through the wilderness in search of the promised land.

*   *   *

And these sepulchral stones, so old and brown,
    That pave with level flags their burial-place,
Seem like the tablets of the Law, thrown down
    And broken by Moses at the mountain's base.[2]

The very names recorded here are strange,
    Of foreign accent, and of different climes;
Alvares and Rivera[3] interchange
    With Abraham and Jacob of old times.

"Blessed be God, for he created Death!"
    The mourners said, "and Death is rest and peace;"
Then added, in the certainty of faith,
    "And giveth Life that nevermore shall cease."

Closed are the portals of their Synagogue,
    No Psalms of David now the silence break,
No Rabbi reads the ancient Decalogue[4]
    In the grand dialect the Prophets spake.

Gone are the living, but the dead remain,
    And not neglected; for a hand unseen,
Scattering its bounty, like a summer rain,
    Still keeps their graves and their remembrance green.

How came they here? What burst of Christian hate,
    What persecution, merciless and blind,
Drove o'er the sea—that desert desolate—
    These Ishmaels and Hagars[5] of mankind?

They lived in narrow streets and lanes obscure,
    Ghetto and Judenstrass,[6] in mirk and mire;
Taught in the school of patience to endure
    The life of anguish and the death of fire.

*   *   *

---

2. Moses broke the stone tablets on which the Ten Commandments were inscribed when he found the Israelites worshipping the golden calf of the false god Baal (Exodus 32:1–19).
3. Surnames of Portuguese and Spanish Jews, driven out of those countries, who migrated to New England in search of religious tolerance.
4. The Ten Commandments.

5. Hagar was Abraham's concubine. She and Ishmael, her son by Abraham, were cast into the wilderness after Abraham's lawful wife Sarah in her old age produced Isaac, a legitimate son and heir for Abraham (Genesis 16, 21).
6. Ghetto: a segregated quarter, originally one specifically for Jews. Judenstrasse: German for Street of the Jews.

All their lives long, with the unleavened bread
    And bitter herbs of exile and its fears,
The wasting famine of the heart they fed,
    And slaked its thirst with marah[7] of their tears.

Anathema maranatha![8] was the cry
    That rang from town to town, from street to street:
At every gate the accursed Mordecai[9]
    Was mocked and jeered, and spurned by Christian feet.

Pride and humiliation hand in hand
    Walked with them through the world where'er they went;
Trampled and beaten were they as the sand,
    And yet unshaken as the continent.

For in the background figures vague and vast
    Of patriarchs and of prophets rose sublime,
And all the great traditions of the Past
    They saw reflected in the coming time.

And thus forever with reverted look
    The mystic volume of the world they read,
Spelling it backward, like a Hebrew book,[10]
    Till life became a Legend of the Dead.

But ah! what once has been shall be no more!
    The groaning earth in travail and in pain
Brings forth its races, but does not restore,
    And the dead nations never rise again.

1852

Newport, Rhode Island, had the first Jewish cemetery in America.

7. Bitter, in Hebrew. Cf. "the bitter waters of Marah," a stream the Israelites found in the wilderness (Exodus 15:23).
8. "Let him be cursed; the Lord has come": a curse the apostle Paul uttered against anyone who has no love for Jesus (1 Corinthians 16:22).
9. Though cursed and threatened by the Babylonians, Mordecai remained faithful to the Jews and their welfare. Cf. the Old Testament's Book of Esther.
10. Hebrew, unlike English, is read from right to left.

from *The Song of Hiawatha*

V. *Hiawatha's Fasting*

You shall hear how Hiawatha
Prayed and fasted in the forest,
Not for greater skill in hunting,
Not for greater craft in fishing,
Not for triumphs in the battle,
And renown among the warriors,
But for profit of the people,
For advantage of the nations.

First he built a lodge for fasting,
Built a wigwam in the forest,
By the shining Big-Sea-Water,
In the blithe and pleasant Spring-time,
In the Moon of Leaves he built it,
And, with dreams and visions many,
Seven whole days and nights he fasted.

On the first day of his fasting
Through the leafy woods he wandered;
Saw the deer start from the thicket,
Saw the rabbit in his burrow,
Heard the pheasant, Bena, drumming,
Heard the squirrel, Adjidaumo,
Rattling in his hoard of acorns,
Saw the pigeon, the Omeme,
Building nests among the pine-trees,
And in flocks the wild-goose, Wawa,
Flying to the fen-lands northward,
Whirring, wailing far above him.
"Master of Life!" he cried, desponding,
"Must our lives depend on these things?"

On the next day of his fasting
By the river's brink he wandered,
Through the Muskoday, the meadow,
Saw the wild rice, Mahnomonee,
Saw the blueberry, Meenahga,
And the strawberry, Odahmin,
And the gooseberry, Shahbomin,
And the grape-vine, the Bemahgut,

Trailing o'er the alder-branches,
Filling all the air with fragrance!
"Master of Life!" he cried, desponding,
"Must our lives depend on these things?"
 On the third day of his fasting
By the lake he sat and pondered,
By the still, transparent water;
Saw the sturgeon, Nahma, leaping,
Scattering drops like beads of wampum,
Saw the yellow perch, the Sahwa,
Like a sunbeam in the water,
Saw the pike, the Maskenozha,
And the herring, Okahahwis,
And the Shawgashee, the crawfish!
"Master of Life!" he cried, desponding,
"Must our lives depend on these things?"
 On the fourth day of his fasting
In his lodge he lay exhausted;
From his couch of leaves and branches
Gazing with half-open eyelids,
Full of shadowy dreams and visions,
On the dizzy, swimming landscape,
On the gleaming of the water,
On the splendor of the sunset.
 And he saw a youth approaching,
Dressed in garments green and yellow,
Coming through the purple twilight,
Through the splendor of the sunset;
Plumes of green bent o'er his forehead,
And his hair was soft and golden.
 Standing at the open doorway,
Long he looked at Hiawatha,
Looked with pity and compassion
On his wasted form and features,
And, in accents like the sighing
Of the South-Wind in the tree-tops,
Said he, "O my Hiawatha!
All your prayers are heard in heaven,
For you pray not like the others;
Not for greater skill in hunting,
Not for greater craft in fishing,

Not for triumph in the battle,
Nor renown among the warriors,
But for profit of the people,
For advantage of the nations.
    "From the Master of Life descending,
I, the friend of man, Mondamin,
Come to warn you and instruct you,
How by struggle and by labor
You shall gain what you have prayed for.
Rise up from your bed of branches,
Rise, O youth, and wrestle with me!"
    Faint with famine, Hiawatha
Started from his bed of branches,
From the twilight of his wigwam
Forth into the flush of sunset
Came, and wrestled with Mondamin;
At his touch he felt new courage
Throbbing in his brain and bosom,
Felt new life and hope and vigor
Run through every nerve and fibre.
    So they wrestled there together
In the glory of the sunset,
And the more they strove and struggled,
Stronger still grew Hiawatha;
Till the darkness fell around them,
And the heron, the Shuh-shuh-gah,
From her nest among the pine-trees,
Gave a cry of lamentation,
Gave a scream of pain and famine.
" 'T is enough!" then said Mondamin,
Smiling upon Hiawatha,
"But tomorrow, when the sun sets,
I will come again to try you."
And he vanished, and was seen not;
Whether sinking as the rain sinks,
Whether rising as the mists rise,
Hiawatha saw not, knew not,
Only saw that he had vanished,
Leaving him alone and fainting,
With the misty lake below him,
And the reeling stars above him.

On the morrow and the next day,
When the sun through heaven descending,
Like a red and burning cinder
From the hearth of the Great Spirit,
Fell into the western waters,
Came Mondamin for the trial,
For the strife with Hiawatha;
Came as silent as the dew comes,
From the empty air appearing,
Into empty air returning,
Taking shape when earth it touches,
But invisible to all men
In its coming and its going.

    Thrice they wrestled there together
In the glory of the sunset,
Till the darkness fell around them,
Till the heron, the Shuh-shuh-gah,
From her nest among the pine-trees,
Uttered her loud cry of famine,
And Mondamin paused to listen.

    Tall and beautiful he stood there,
In his garments green and yellow;
To and fro his plumes above him,
Waved and nodded with his breathing,
And the sweat of the encounter
Stood like drops of dew upon him.

    And he cried, "O Hiawatha!
Bravely have you wrestled with me,
Thrice have wrestled stoutly with me,
And the Master of Life, who sees us,
He will give to you the triumph!"

    Then he smiled, and said: "To-morrow
Is the last day of your conflict,
Is the last day of your fasting.
You will conquer and o'ercome me;
Make a bed for me to lie in,
Where the rain may fall upon me,
Where the sun may come and warm me;
Strip these garments, green and yellow,
Strip this nodding plumage from me,
Lay me in the earth, and make it

Soft and loose and light above me.
　"Let no hand disturb my slumber,
Let no weed nor worm molest me,
Let not Kahgahgee, the raven,
Come to haunt me and molest me,
Only come yourself to watch me,
Till I wake, and start, and quicken,
Till I leap into the sunshine."
　And thus saying, he departed;
Peacefully slept Hiawatha,
But he heard the Wawonaissa,
Heard the whippoorwill complaining,
Perched upon his lonely wigwam;
Heard the rushing Sebowisha,
Heard the rivulet rippling near him,
Talking to the darksome forest;
Heard the sighing of the branches,
As they lifted and subsided
At the passing of the night-wind,
Heard them, as one hears in slumber
Far-off murmurs, dreamy whispers:
Peacefully slept Hiawatha.
　On the morrow came Nokomis,
On the seventh day of his fasting,
Came with food for Hiawatha,
Came imploring and bewailing,
Lest his hunger should o'ercome him,
Lest his fasting should be fatal.
　But he tasted not, and touched not,
Only said to her, "Nokomis,
Wait until the sun is setting,
Till the darkness falls around us,
Till the heron, the Shuh-shuh-gah,
Crying from the desolate marshes,
Tells us that the day is ended."
　Homeward weeping went Nokomis,
Sorrowing for her Hiawatha,
Fearing lest his strength should fail him,
Lest his fasting should be fatal.
He meanwhile sat weary waiting
For the coming of Mondamin,

Till the shadows, pointing eastward,
Lengthened over field and forest,
Till the sun dropped from the heaven,
Floating on the waters westward,
As a red leaf in the Autumn
Falls and floats upon the water,
Falls and sinks into its bosom.

And behold! the young Mondamin,
With his soft and shining tresses,
With his garments green and yellow,
With his long and glossy plumage,
Stood and beckoned at the doorway.
And as one in slumber walking,
Pale and haggard, but undaunted,
From the wigwam Hiawatha
Came and wrestled with Mondamin.

Round about him spun the landscape,
Sky and forest reeled together,
And his strong heart leaped within him,
As the sturgeon leaps and struggles
In a net to break its meshes.
Like a ring of fire around him
Blazed and flared the red horizon,
And a hundred suns seemed looking
At the combat of the wrestlers.

Suddenly upon the greensward
All alone stood Hiawatha,
Panting with his wild exertion,
Palpitating with the struggle;
And before him breathless, lifeless,
Lay the youth, with hair dishevelled,
Plumage torn, and garments tattered,
Dead he lay there in the sunset.

And victorious Hiawatha
Made the grave as he commanded,
Stripped the garments from Mondamin,
Stripped his tattered plumage from him,
Laid him in the earth, and made it
Soft and loose and light above him;
And the heron, the Shuh-shuh-gah,
From the melancholy moorlands,

Gave a cry of lamentation,
Gave a cry of pain and anguish!
    Homeward then went Hiawatha
To the lodge of old Nokomis,
And the seven days of his fasting
Were accomplished and completed.
But the place was not forgotten
Where he wrestled with Mondamin;
Nor forgotten nor neglected
Was the grave where lay Mondamin,
Sleeping in the rain and sunshine,
Where his scattered plumes and garments
Faded in the rain and sunshine.
    Day by day did Hiawatha
Go to wait and watch beside it;
Kept the dark mould soft above it,
Kept it clean from weeds and insects,
Drove away, with scoffs and shoutings,
Kahgahgee, the king of ravens.
    Till at length a small green feather
From the earth shot slowly upward,
Then another and another,
And before the Summer ended
Stood the maize in all its beauty,
With its shining robes about it,
And its long, soft, yellow tresses;
And in rapture Hiawatha
Cried aloud, "It is Mondamin!
Yes, the friend of man, Mondamin!"
    Then he called to old Nokomis
And Iagoo, the great boaster,
Showed them where the maize was growing,
Told them of his wondrous vision,
Of his wrestling and his triumph,
Of this new gift to the nations,
Which should be their food forever.
    And still later, when the Autumn
Changed the long, green leaves to yellow,
And the soft and juicy kernels
Grew like wampum hard and yellow,
Then the ripened ears he gathered,

Stripped the withered husks from off them,
As he once had stripped the wrestler,
Gave the first Feast of Mondamin,
And made known unto the people
This new gift of the Great Spirit.

XIV. Picture-Writing

In those days said Hiawatha,
"Lo! how all things fade and perish!
From the memory of the old men
Pass away the great traditions,
The achievements of the warriors,
The adventures of the hunters,
All the wisdom of the Medas,
All the craft of the Wabenos,
All the marvelous dreams and visions
Of the Jossakeeds, the Prophets!

"Great men die and are forgotten,
Wise men speak; their words of wisdom
Perish in the ears that hear them,
Do not reach the generations
That, as yet unborn, are waiting
In the great, mysterious darkness
Of the speechless days that shall be!

"On the grave-posts of our fathers
Are no signs, no figures painted;
Who are in those graves we know not,
Only know they are our fathers.
Of what kith they are and kindred,
From what old, ancestral Totem,
Be it Eagle, Bear, or Beaver,
They descended, this we know not,
Only know they are our fathers.

"Face to face we speak together,
But we cannot speak when absent,
Cannot send our voices from us
To the friends that dwell afar off;
Cannot send a secret message,
But the bearer learns our secret,

May pervert it, may betray it,
May reveal it unto others."
　Thus said Hiawatha, walking
In the solitary forest,
Pondering, musing in the forest,
On the welfare of his people.
　From his pouch he took his colors,
Took his paints of different colors,
On the smooth bark of a birch-tree
Painted many shapes and figures,
Wonderful and mystic figures,
And each figure had a meaning,
Each some word or thought suggested.
　Gitche Manito the Mighty,
He, the Master of Life, was painted
As an egg, with points projecting
To the four winds of the heavens.
Everywhere is the Great Spirit,
Was the meaning of this symbol.
　Mitche Manito the Mighty,
He the dreadful Spirit of Evil,
As a serpent was depicted,
As Kenabeek, the great serpent.
Very crafty, very cunning,
Is the creeping Spirit of Evil,
Was the meaning of this symbol.
　Life and Death he drew as circles,
Life was white, but Death was darkened;
Sun and moon and stars he painted,
Man and beast, and fish and reptile,
Forests, mountains, lakes, and rivers.
　For the earth he drew a straight line,
For the sky a bow above it;
White the space between for daytime,
Filled with little stars for night-time;
On the left a point for sunrise,
On the right a point for sunset,
On the top a point for noontide,
And for rain and cloudy weather
Waving lines descending from it.

Footprints pointing towards a wigwam
Were a sign of invitation,
Were a sign of guests assembling;
Bloody hands with palms uplifted
Were a symbol of destruction,
Were a hostile sign and symbol.

All these things did Hiawatha
Show unto his wondering people,
And interpreted their meaning,
And he said: "Behold, your grave-posts
Have no mark, no sign, nor symbol,
Go and paint them all with figures;
Each one with its household symbol,
With its own ancestral Totem;
So that those who follow after
May distinguish them and know them."

And they painted on the grave-posts
On the graves yet unforgotten,
Each his own ancestral Totem,
Each the symbol of his household;
Figures of the Bear and Reindeer,
Of the Turtle, Crane, and Beaver,
Each inverted as a token
That the owner was departed,
That the chief who bore the symbol
Lay beneath in dust and ashes.

And the Jossakeeds, the Prophets,
The Wabenos, the Magicians,
And the Medicine-men, the Medas,
Painted upon bark and deer-skin
Figures for the songs they chanted,
For each song a separate symbol,
Figures mystical and awful,
Figures strange and brightly colored;
And each figure had its meaning,
Each some magic song suggested.

The Great Spirit, the Creator,
Flashing light through all the heaven;
The Great Serpent, the Kenabeek,
With his bloody crest erected,

Creeping, looking into heaven;
In the sky the sun, that listens,
And the moon eclipsed and dying;
Owl and eagle, crane and hen-hawk,
And the cormorant, bird of magic;
Headless men, that walk the heavens,
Bodies lying pierced with arrows,
Bloody hands of death uplifted,
Flags on graves, and great war-captains
Grasping both the earth and heaven!

Such as these the shapes they painted
On the birch-bark and the deer-skin;
Songs of war and songs of hunting,
Songs of medicine and of magic,
All were written in these figures,
For each figure had its meaning,
Each its separate song recorded.

Nor forgotten was the Love-Song,
The most subtle of all medicines,
The most potent spell of magic,
Dangerous more than war or hunting!
Thus the Love-Song was recorded,
Symbol and interpretation.

First a human figure standing,
Painted in the brightest scarlet;
'T Is the lover, the musician,
And the meaning is, "My painting
Makes me powerful over others."

Then the figure seated, singing,
Playing on a drum of magic,
And the interpretation, "Listen!
'T Is my voice you hear, my singing!"

Then the same red figure seated
In the shelter of a wigwam,
And the meaning of the symbol,
"I will come and sit beside you
In the mystery of my passion!"

Then two figures, man and woman,
Standing hand in hand together
With their hands so clasped together

That they seemed in one united,
And the words thus represented
Are, "I see your heart within you,
And your cheeks are red with blushes!"
    Next the maiden on an island,
In the centre of an island;
And the song this shape suggested
Was, "Though you were at a distance,
Were upon some far-off island,
Such the spell I cast upon you,
Such the magic power of passion,
I could straightway draw you to me!"
    Then the figure of the maiden
Sleeping, and the lover near her,
Whispering to her in her slumbers,
Saying, "Though you were far from me
In the land of Sleep and Silence,
Still the voice of love would reach you!"
    And the last of all the figures
Was a heart within a circle,
Drawn within a magic circle;
And the image had this meaning:
"Naked lies your heart before me,
To your naked heart I whisper!"
    Thus it was that Hiawatha,
In his wisdom, taught the people
All the mysteries of painting,
All the art of Picture-Writing,
On the smooth bark of the birch-tree,
On the white skin of the reindeer,
On the grave-posts of the village.

                1855

In 1854 Longfellow determined on a plan for "a poem for the American Indians" that would "weave their beautiful traditions into a whole. I have hit upon a measure, too, which I think the right and only one for such a theme." Longfellow's measure was derived from the Finnish epic *Kalevala*, an ancient European saga that he found analogous in spirit to the Native American legends he had been reading. For the tale of Hiawatha and other stories, which he wove together into a single fabric featuring a single hero, Longfellow drew in particular on Jane Johnston Schoolcraft's compilations of Ojibwa myths.

The Landlord's Tale: Paul Revere's Ride

Listen, my children, and you shall hear
Of the midnight ride of Paul Revere,
On the eighteenth of April, in Seventy-five;
Hardly a man is now alive
Who remembers that famous day and year.

He said to his friend, "If the British march
By land or sea from the town to-night,
Hang a lantern aloft in the belfry arch
Of the North Church tower as a signal light, —
One, if by land, and two, if by sea;
And I on the opposite shore will be,
Ready to ride and spread the alarm
Through every Middlesex village and farm,
For the country folk to be up and to arm."

Then he said "Good-night!" and with muffled oar
Silently rowed to the Charlestown shore,
Just as the moon rose over the bay,
Where swinging wide at her moorings lay
The Somerset, British man-of-war;
A phantom ship, with each mast and spar
Across the moon like a prison bar,
And a huge black hulk, that was magnified
By its own reflection in the tide.

Meanwhile, his friend through alley and street
Wanders and watches with eager ears,
Till in the silence around him he hears
The muster of men at the barrack door,
The sound of arms, and the tramp of feet,
And the measured tread of the grenadiers,
Marching down to their boats on the shore.

Then he climbed the tower of the Old North Church,
By the wooden stairs, with stealthy tread,
To the belfry-chamber overhead,
And startled the pigeons from their perch
On the somber rafters, that round him made
Masses and moving shapes of shade, —
By the trembling ladder, steep and tall,

To the highest window in the wall,
Where he paused to listen and look down
A moment on the roofs of the town,
And the moonlight flowing over all.

Beneath, in the churchyard, lay the dead,
In their night-encampment on the hill,
Wrapped in silence so deep and still
That he could hear, like a sentinel's tread,
The watchful night-wind, as it went
Creeping along from tent to tent,
And seeming to whisper, "All is well!"
A moment only he feels the spell
Of the place and the hour, and the secret dread
Of the lonely belfry and the dead;
For suddenly all his thoughts are bent
On a shadowy something far away,
Where the river widens to meet the bay, —
A line of black that bends and floats
On the rising tide, like a bridge of boats.

Meanwhile, impatient to mount and ride,
Booted and spurred, with a heavy stride
On the opposite shore walked Paul Revere.
Now he patted his horse's side,
Now gazed at the landscape far and near,
Then, impetuous, stamped the earth,
And turned and tightened his saddle-girth;
But mostly he watched with eager search
The belfry-tower of the Old North Church,
As it rose above the graves on the hill,
Lonely and spectral and sombre and still.
And lo! as he looks, on the belfry's height
A glimmer, and then a gleam of light!
He springs to the saddle, the bridle he turns,
But lingers and gazes, till full on his sight
A second lamp in the belfry burns!

A hurry of hoofs in a village street,
A shape in the moonlight, a bulk in the dark,
And beneath, from the pebbles, in passing, a spark
Struck out by a steed flying fearless and fleet:

That was all! And yet, through the gloom and the light,
The fate of a nation was riding that night;
And the spark struck out by that steed, in his flight,
Kindled the land into flame with its heat.
He has left the village and mounted the steep,
And beneath him, tranquil and broad and deep,
Is the Mystic, meeting the ocean tides;
And under the alders that skirt its edge,
Now soft on the sand, now loud on the ledge,
Is heard the tramp of his steed as he rides.

It was twelve by the village clock
When he crossed the bridge into Medford town.
He heard the crowing of the cock,
And the barking of the farmer's dog,
And felt the damp of the river fog,
That rises after the sun goes down.

It was one by the village clock,
When he galloped into Lexington.
He saw the gilded weathercock
Swim in the moonlight as he passed,
And the meeting-house windows, black and bare,
Gaze at him with a spectral glare,
As if they already stood aghast
At the bloody work they would look upon.

It was two by the village clock,
When he came to the bridge in Concord town.
He heard the bleating of the flock,
And the twitter of birds among the trees,
And felt the breath of the morning breeze
Blowing over the meadows brown.
And one was safe and asleep in his bed
Who at the bridge would be first to fall,
Who that day would be lying dead,
Pierced by a British musket-ball.

You know the rest. In the books you have read,
How the British Regulars fired and fled, —
How the farmers gave them ball for ball,
From behind each fence and farmyard wall,
Chasing the red-coats down the lane,

Then crossing the fields to emerge again
Under the trees at the turn of the road,
And only pausing to fire and load.

So through the night rode Paul Revere;
And so through the night went his cry of alarm
To every Middlesex village and farm, —
A cry of defiance and not of fear,
A voice in the darkness, a knock at the door,
And a word that shall echo forevermore!
For, borne on the night-wind of the Past,
Through all our history, to the last,
In the hour of darkness and peril and need,
The people will waken and listen to hear
The hurrying hoof-beats of that steed,
And the midnight message of Paul Revere.

1860

This poem is the first and most popular of the *Tales of a Wayside Inn,* modeled on Chaucer's *Canterbury Tales,* with each guest at the inn telling a different story.

Aftermath

When the summer fields are mown,
When the birds are fledged and flown,
   And the dry leaves strew the path;
With the falling of the snow,
With the cawing of the crow,
Once again the fields we mow
   And gather in the aftermath.

Not the sweet, new grass with flowers
Is this harvesting of ours;
   Not the upland clover bloom;
But the rowen[1] mixed with weeds,
Tangled tufts from marsh and meads,
Where the poppy drops its seeds
   In the silence and the gloom.

1873

In its original meaning, the aftermath is a new growth of grass or hay following one or more previous mowings.

1. The second crop of grass or hay in a season.

Milton

I pace the sounding sea-beach and behold
   How the voluminous billows roll and run,
   Upheaving and subsiding, while the sun
   Shines through their sheeted emerald far unrolled,
And the ninth wave,[1] slow gathering fold by fold
   All its loose-flowing garments into one,
   Plunges upon the shore, and floods the dun
   Pale reach of sands, and changes them to gold.
So in majestic cadence rise and fall
   The mighty undulations of thy song,
   O sightless bard, England's Maeonides![2]
And ever and anon, high over all
   Uplifted, a ninth wave superb and strong,
   Floods all the soul with its melodious seas.

              1873

The blind English poet John Milton (1608–1674) is renowned for the weighty power of his poetic lines in the epics *Paradise Lost* and *Paradise Regained* and the dramatic poem *Samson Agonistes*. Longfellow compares this power to the "mighty undulations" of the sea.

Nature

As a fond mother, when the day is o'er,
   Leads by the hand her little child to bed,
   Half willing, half reluctant to be led,
   And leave his broken playthings on the floor,
Still gazing at them through the open door,
   Nor wholly reassured and comforted
   By promises of others in their stead,
   Which, though more splendid, may not please him more;
So Nature deals with us, and takes away
   Our playthings one by one, and by the hand
   Leads us to rest so gently, that we go

1. The most powerful wave in the series, according to folk wisdom.
2. Homer, the Greek epic poet who created the *Iliad* and the *Odyssey*, was so termed because his apparent homeland was Maeonia. Like Milton, Homer was blind, and his poetic lines have long been similarly celebrated for their "majestic cadence" and wave-like power.

Scarce knowing if we wish to go or stay,
Being too full of sleep to understand
How far the unknown transcends the what we know.

1876

Longfellow was sixty-nine years old when this poem was published. Though the poem suggests someone readying himself for death, he would live for another six years.

The Tide Rises, the Tide Falls

The tide rises, the tide falls,
The twilight darkens, the curlew calls;
Along the sea-sands damp and brown
The traveller hastens toward the town,
   And the tide rises, the tide falls.

Darkness settles on roofs and walls,
But the sea, the sea in the darkness calls;
The little waves, with their soft, white hands,
Efface the footprints in the sands,
   And the tide rises, the tide falls.

The morning breaks; the steeds in their stalls
Stamp and neigh, as the hostler calls;
The day returns, but nevermore
Returns the traveller to the shore,
   And the tide rises, the tide falls.

1879

The Cross of Snow

In the long, sleepless watches of the night,
  A gentle face—the face of one long dead—
  Looks at me from the wall, where round its head
  The night-lamp casts a halo of pale light.
Here in this room she died; the soul more white
  Never through martyrdom of fire was led
  To its repose;[1] nor can in books be read

1. Longfellow's wife Frances's "martyrdom of fire" began when her lacy Victorian dress caught fire from a drop of hot wax while she was sealing locks of her daughter's hair in packets—a most Victorian occupation. She ran toward Longfellow, her dress ablaze, and he, rising from the couch in his study on which he was resting, attempted to extinguish the flames with his own body. Longfellow was too late to save his wife and was left in dangerous condition from his own burns.

The legend of a life more benedight.[2]
There is a mountain in the distant West
     That, sun-defying, in its deep ravines
     Displays a cross of snow upon its side.
Such is the cross I wear upon my breast
     These eighteen years, through all the changing scenes
     And seasons, changeless since the day she died.

1886

This poem, composed in 1879, is a meditation on the loss of his beloved second wife, Frances, who died in the Longfellow home from burns after her dress caught fire in 1861. Longfellow deemed the poem too personal for print, and it remained unpublished until after his death.

JOHN GREENLEAF WHITTIER
1807–1892

JOHN GREENLEAF WHITTIER was initially known as "the slave's poet." Before the Civil War, the European-American Whittier wrote many poems forcefully opposing African-American slavery. After the war was fought and slavery abolished, he achieved new fame as a "household poet" with "Snow-Bound." This remarkably popular poem fostered a benevolent and nostalgic image of rural American family life. It helped to confirm an idealized notion of American innocence and stability that became tremendously influential at a time when the United States was in fact undergoing dramatic social and economic changes. Before the Civil War, therefore, Whittier helped to mobilize antislavery sentiment, and afterwards he provided an image that soothed the anxieties provoked by the war and its aftermath. Throughout Whittier's career, his poetry both mirrored and shaped American history.

Born in 1807, Whittier grew up on a poor and debt-ridden farm north of Boston, in Haverhill, Massachusetts. His Quaker family included a brother and two sisters. Quakers were no longer targets of discrimination in the nineteenth century, but they were still generally regarded as "different." Whittier, a studious and creative young boy, was often ill and had a distaste for farm labor. His formal education

---

2. Full of blessing.

essentially ceased with his graduation from the district school, though he did later attend Haverhill Academy for two terms. At the age of fourteen, he heard a recitation of poems by Robert Burns (1759–1796), the Scottish poet whose works emphasize democratic and rural Scottish values and often employ authentic Scottish vernacular. Following that lead, Whittier turned to the history, language, and public life of his native New England for his poetic inspiration. He was also shaped by a host of popular texts that he found morally uplifting: the Bible, Shakespeare's plays, John Bunyan's *Pilgrim's Progress*, John Milton's *Paradise Lost*, and later the poems of his contemporary, Henry Wadsworth Longfellow. Whittier sought to become a local poet who could articulate progressive social values in a way that a large audience would find acceptable.

When Whittier was nineteen, he met William Lloyd Garrison, the abolitionist editor and lecturer. Garrison encouraged him, as he was later to encourage the black abolitionist poet Frances Harper (also included in this anthology). Soon Whittier was publishing poems about political topics and local history in a wide variety of newspapers. He became editor of a Whig paper, *The American Manufacturer*, which supported business causes. After a mental breakdown in 1831, he resigned his editorship, returning to the family farm in Haverhill. Two years later Garrison paid him a visit and persuaded him to make abolition his primary poetic topic. Over the next several decades Whittier produced more than one hundred abolitionist poems of varying quality. Although he served one term in the Massachusetts state legislature, he did not have a serious career as an elected official. Nor did he marry, though he courted several wealthy, non-Quaker women. Rather, he devoted himself to writing poems that advocated the antislavery cause, such as "Massachusetts to Virginia" and "Ichabod!," and poems that reproduced New England legends and local color, such as "Skipper Ireson's Ride." He also engaged in nonstop activity as a political organizer, lecturer, and founder of the antislavery Liberty Party. In 1835 he was stoned by an anti-abolitionist mob, and in 1838 his office was burned. In the 1850s, however, his views received a much more favorable reception by a Northern public that had, by then, largely come around to his position.

When the Civil War was over, Whittier turned to the quieter, more personal and nostalgic themes that he had already broached in the prewar poem "Telling the Bees." That poem about a lost beloved may have reflected Whittier's grief over the death of his mother. Now he had also to mourn his cherished younger sister, Elizabeth, who died in 1865, the year the war ended. Whittier's profound sense of personal loss combined with a widely shared cultural desire to turn away from the conflict and mass death of the Civil War. "Snow-Bound" (1866), one of the most beloved poems of the century, invited readers to find comfort in idealized images of family, set in an earlier time that nostalgia reproduced as conflict-free. This poem of childhood memory has seemed sentimental to many later readers because of its well-worn imagery, its postabolitionist reversion to an all-white social world, and its erasure of inevitable family tensions. Nevertheless, the poem retains historical significance in revealing the postwar era's need for solace and healing. It satisfies that need by inventing a seemingly perfect family circle that also serves as a lost but recoverable image of national identity.

Moreover, the poem is psychologically fascinating. It discernibly attempts to repress conflicted feelings, yet its narrative fissures allow us to glimpse those feelings. Its central image of a farmhouse cut off from the world by snow vividly suggests a need to cocoon oneself, however briefly, from stormy events and emotions. Finally, the poem has enduring aesthetic power. Its language, rhythms, and yearnings possess vitality and beauty, if not always subtlety. Seen as a response to the unspeakable death and injury of the Civil War, and as the production of a troubled poet and audience driven to imagine a sheltering past, the poem intimates a poignant awareness of national suffering and mourning while mobilizing a vivid and consoling fantasy of security.

Whittier spent the final quarter century of his life widely revered as a great American poet. In the pre–Civil War period, he had used his medium to awaken his readers to the horrors of slavery. Immediately after the war, he tried to help his readers find relief from the national trauma. He initiated an effort to recover a lost (or nonexistent) American innocence by searching for it in the past.

FURTHER READING

Jayne K. Kribbs, ed. *Critical Essays on John Greenleaf Whittier.* Boston: G. K. Hall, 1980.

Edward Wagenknecht. *John Greenleaf Whittier: A Portrait in Paradox.* New York: Oxford University Press, 1967.

Robert Penn Warren. *John Greenleaf Whittier: An Appraisal and a Selection.* Minneapolis: University of Minnesota Press, 1971.

John Greenleaf Whittier. *Works.* 7 vols. Boston: Houghton Mifflin, 1892.

Massachusetts to Virginia

The blast from Freedom's Northern hills, upon its Southern way,
Bears greetings to Virginia from Massachusetts Bay—
No word of haughty challenging, nor battle bugle's peal,
Nor steady tread of marching files, nor clang of horsemen's steel.

No trains of deep-mouthed cannon along our highways go—
Around our silent arsenals untrodden lies the snow;
And to the land-breeze of our ports, upon their errands far,
A thousand sails of commerce swell, but none are spread for war.

*   *   *

We hear thy threats, Virginia! thy stormy words and high,
Swell harshly on the Southern winds which melt along our sky;
Yet, not one brown, hard hand foregoes its honest labor here,
No hewer of our mountain oaks suspends his axe in fear.

Wild are the waves which lash the reefs along St. George's bank[1] —
Cold on the shore of Labrador the fog lies white and dank;
Through storm and wave and blinding mist stout are the hearts which man
The fishing-smacks of Marblehead, the sea-boats of Cape Ann.

The cold north light and wintry sun glare on their icy forms,
Bent grimly o'er their straining lines or wrestling with the storms;
Free as the winds they drive before, rough as the waves they roam,
They laugh to scorn the slaver's threat against their rocky home.

What means the Old Dominion?[2] Hath she forgot the day
When o'er her conquered valleys swept the Briton's steel array?
How side by side, with sons of hers, the Massachusetts men
Encountered Tarleton's[3] charge of fire, and stout Cornwallis, then?

Forgets she how the Bay State, in answer to the call
Of her old House of Burgesses,[4] spoke out from Faneuil Hall?
When, echoing back her Henry's[5] cry, came pulsing on each breath
Of Northern winds, the thrilling sounds of "LIBERTY OR DEATH!"

What asks the Old Dominion? If now her sons have proved
False to their fathers' memory—false to the faith they loved,
If she can scoff at Freedom, and its great charter[6] spurn,
Must we of Massachusetts from truth and duty turn?

We hunt your bondmen,[7] flying from Slavery's hateful hell,
Our voices, at your bidding, take up the bloodhound's yell—
We gather, at your summons, above our fathers' graves,
From Freedom's holy altar-horns[8] to tear your wretched slaves!

---

1. St. George's bank and Labrador are in the Canadian North Atlantic. Marblehead and Cape Ann are on the Massachusetts coast.
2. Virginia. The "Bay State" in the next stanza is Massachusetts.
3. British general in the Revolutionary War, as was Cornwallis.
4. One of Virginia's legislative bodies. Faneuil Hall is the famous Boston meeting hall.
5. Patrick Henry (1736–1799), a Revolutionary-era Virginia statesman, famously exclaimed, "Give me liberty or give me death!"
6. The Declaration of Independence.
7. Slaves. Even before the Fugitive Slave Law of 1850 made escape more difficult, state laws required free states to return escaped slaves to slave-holding states.
8. In 1 Kings 1:50–53, the outcast Adonijah obtains mercy from Solomon by grasping the horns of a temple's altar.

*   *   *

Thank God! not yet so vilely can Massachusetts bow;
The spirit of her early time is with her even now;
Dream not because her Pilgrim blood moves slow and calm and cool,
She thus can stoop her chainless neck, a sister's slave and tool!

All that a *sister* State should do, all that a *free* State may,
Heart, hand, and purse we proffer, as in our early day;
But that one dark loathsome burden ye must stagger with alone,
And reap the bitter harvest which ye yourselves have sown!

Hold, while ye may, your struggling slaves, and burden God's free air
With woman's shriek beneath the lash, and manhood's wild despair;
Cling closer to the "cleaving curse"[9] that writes upon your plains
The blasting of Almighty wrath against a land of chains.

Still shame your gallant ancestry, the cavaliers of old.
By watching round the shambles[10] where human flesh is sold,
Gloat o'er the new-born child, and count his market value, when
The maddened mother's cry of woe shall pierce the slaver's den!

Lower than plummet soundeth, sink the Virginia name;
Plant, if ye will, your fathers' graves with rankest weeds of shame;
Be, if ye will, the scandal of God's fair universe—
We wash our hands forever of your sin and shame and curse.

A voice from lips whereon the coal from Freedom's shrine hath been,[11]
Thrilled, as but yesterday, the hearts of Berkshire's mountain men:
The echoes of that solemn voice are sadly lingering still
In all our sunny valleys, on every wind-swept hill.

And when the prowling man-thief came hunting for his prey
Beneath the very shadow of Bunker's shaft of gray,[12]
How, through the free lips of the son, the father's warning spoke;
How, from its bonds of trade and sect, the Pilgrim city[13] broke!

*   *   *

---

9. Deuteronomy 13:17.
10. Slaughterhouse, here a metaphor for the slave market.
11. In Isaiah 6:6–7 an angel lays a live coal from the altar on Isaiah's mouth, saying, "Thine iniquity is taken away, and thy sin purged."
12. The monument on Bunker Hill, site of an early Revolutionary War battle.
13. Boston.

A hundred thousand right arms were lifted up on high —
A hundred thousand voices sent back their loud reply;
Through the thronged towns of Essex[14] the startling summons rang,
And up from bench and loom and wheel her young mechanics sprang!

The voice of free, broad Middlesex — of thousands as of one —
The shaft of Bunker calling to that of Lexington —
From Norfolk's ancient villages, from Plymouth's rocky bound
To where Nantucket feels the arms of ocean close her round —

From rich and rural Worcester, where through the calm repose
Of cultured vales and fringing woods the gentle Nashua flows,
To where Wachuset's wintry blasts the mountain larches stir,
Swelled up to Heaven the thrilling cry of "God save Latimer!"

And sandy Barnstable rose up, wet with the salt sea spray,
And Bristol sent her answering shout down Narragansett Bay!
Along the broad Connecticut[15] old Hampden felt the thrill,
And the cheer of Hampshire's woodmen swept down from Holyoke Hill.

The voice of Massachusetts! Of her free sons and daughters —
Deep calling unto deep aloud[16] — the sound of many waters!
Against the burden of that voice what tyrant power shall stand?
No fetters in the Bay State! No slave upon her land!

Look to it well, Virginians! In calmness we have borne,
In answer to our faith and trust, your insult and your scorn;
You've spurned our kindest counsels — you've hunted for our lives —
And shaken round our hearths and homes your manacles and gyves![17]

We wage no war — we lift no arm — we fling no torch within
The fire-damps[18] of the quaking mine beneath your soil of sin;
We leave ye with your bondmen, to wrestle, while ye can,
With the strong upward tendencies and godlike soul of man!

But for us and for our children, the vow which we have given
For freedom and humanity is registered in heaven;
No slave-hunt in our borders — no pirate on our strand!
No fetters in the Bay State, — no slave upon our land!

1843

---

14. Whittier's home county. The following stanzas cite numerous other Massachusetts placenames to indicate the breadth of the opposition to Latimer's arrest.
15. River.
16. An allusion to Psalms 42:7: "Deep calleth unto deep."
17. Leg chains.
18. A combustible mixture of methane and other gases sometimes found in mines.

This poem refers to the notorious situation of George Latimer, a slave who had escaped and was arrested by authorities in Boston to be returned to his owner in Virginia. Whittier's poem, initially read at an antislavery convention and then published in the abolitionist paper *The Liberator*, played a major role in the effort to save Latimer. Ultimately he obtained his free papers for the sum of $400.

Ichabod!

So fallen! so lost! the light withdrawn
    Which once he wore![1]
The glory from his gray hairs gone
    Forevermore!

Revile him not—the Tempter hath
    A snare for all;
And pitying tears, not scorn and wrath,
    Befit his fall!

Oh! dumb be passion's stormy rage,
    When he who might
Have lighted up and led his age,
    Falls back in night.

Scorn! would the angels laugh, to mark
    A bright soul driven,
Fiend-goaded, down the endless dark,
    From hope and heaven!

Let not the land, once proud of him,
    Insult him now,
Nor brand with deeper shame his dim,
    Dishonored brow.

But let its humbled sons, instead,
    From sea to lake,
A long lament, as for the dead,
    In sadness make.

        ❉   ❉   ❉

1. These opening lines recall John Milton's *Paradise Lost*, book I, in which Satan exclaims to his fellow fallen angel Beelzebub, "[H]ow fall'n! how chang'd / From him who, in the happy realms of light, / Cloth'd with transcendent brightness didst outshine / Myriads though bright!" (84–87). Throughout Whittier's poem, the metaphor of a fallen angel and the imagery of light and dark evoke *Paradise Lost*.

Of all we loved and honored, naught
    Save power remains—
A fallen angel's pride of thought,
    Still strong in chains.

All else is gone; from those great eyes
    The soul has fled:
When faith is lost, when honor dies,
    The man is dead!

Then, pay the reverence of old days
    To his dead fame;
Walk backward, with averted gaze,
    And hide the shame![2]

1850

"Ichabod" in Hebrew means "inglorious." See 1 Samuel 4:21: "And she named the child Ichabod, saying, 'The glory is departed from Israel.'" Whittier's poem castigates and laments Senator Daniel Webster of Massachusetts, formerly an opponent of slavery, who changed sides by championing the Fugitive Slave Law as part of the Compromise of 1850. That law allowed European-American slave owners to pursue and capture African-American slaves who had escaped to the North. Whittier observed in a note to this poem, "This poem was the outcome of the surprise and grief and forecast of evil consequences which I felt on reading the Seventh of March speech of Daniel Webster in support of the 'Compromise,' and the Fugitive Slave Law. No partisan or personal enmity dictated it. On the contrary my admiration of the splendid personality and intellectual power of the great Senator was never stronger than when I laid down his speech, and, in one of the saddest moments of my life, penned my protest. I saw, as I wrote, with painful clearness its sure results—the Slave Power arrogant and defiant, strengthened and encouraged to carry out its scheme for the extension of its baleful system, or the dissolution of the Union, the guaranties of personal liberty in the free States broken down, and the whole country made the hunting-ground of slave-catchers. In the horror of such a vision, so soon fearfully fulfilled, if one spoke at all, he could only speak in tones of stern and sorrowful rebuke."

Skipper Ireson's Ride

Of all the rides since the birth of time,
Told in story or sung in rhyme—
On Apuleius's Golden Ass,[1]

2. This conclusion alludes to Genesis 9:20–25, in which Noah's children feel ashamed of their father, who has become drunk after the flood.
1. *The Golden Ass* is a fictionalized autobiography by Apuleius (born ca. 114). Transformed into an ass, the narrator witnesses many human follies until he is finally made human again by the goddess Isis.

Or one-eyed Calender's[2] horse of brass,
Witch astride of a human back,
Islam's prophet on Al-Borák[3] —
The strangest ride that ever was sped
Was Ireson's, out from Marblehead!
 Old Floyd Ireson, for his hard heart,
  Tarred and feathered and carried in a cart
   By the women of Marblehead!

Body of turkey, head of owl,
Wings a-droop like a rained-on fowl,
Feathered and ruffled in every part,
Skipper Ireson stood in the cart.
Scores of women, old and young,
Strong of muscle, and glib of tongue,
Pushed and pulled up the rocky lane,
Shouting and singing the shrill refrain:
 "Here's Flud Oirson, fur his horrd horrt,
  Torr'd an' futherr'd an' corr'd in a corrt
   By the women o' Morble'ead!"

Wrinkled scolds with hands on hips,
Girls in bloom of cheek and lips,
Wild-eyed, free-limbed, such as chase
Bacchus[4] round some antique vase,
Brief of skirt, with ankles bare,
Loose of kerchief and loose of hair,
With couch-shells blowing and fish-horns' twang,
Over and over the Mænads sang:
 "Here's Flud Oirson, fur his horrd horrt,
  Torr'd an' futherr'd an' corr'd in a corrt
   By the women o' Morble'ead!"

Small pity for him! — He sailed away
From a leaking ship, in Chaleur Bay[5] —
Sailed away from a sinking wreck,
With his own town's-people on her deck!
"Lay by! lay by!" they called to him.

2. A character in *The Arabian Nights*.
3. In Arabian tradition, the winged horse Al-Borák bore Mohammed from Mecca to the Seventh Heaven.
4. The Roman name for Dionysus, the Greek god of fertility and wine. Bacchus was generally surrounded by female worshipers called Mænads.
5. Located north of the Canadian province of New Brunswick and south of Quebec's Gaspé Peninsula.

Back he answered, "Sink or swim!
Brag of your catch of fish again!"
And off he sailed through the fog and rain!
  Old Floyd Ireson, for his hard heart,
    Tarred and feathered and carried in a cart
      By the women of Marblehead!

Fathoms deep in dark Chaleur
That wreck shall lie forevermore.
Mother and sister, wife and maid,
Looked from the rocks of Marblehead
Over the moaning and rainy sea —
Looked for the coming that might not be!
What did the winds and the sea-birds say
Of the cruel captain who sailed away? —
  Old Floyd Ireson, for his hard heart,
    Tarred and feathered and carried in a cart
      By the women of Marblehead!

Through the street, on either side,
Up flew windows, doors swung wide;
Sharp-tongued spinsters, old wives gray,
Treble lent the fish-horn's bray.
Sea-worn grandsires, cripple-bound,
Hulks of old sailors run aground,
Shook head, and fist, and hat, and cane,
And cracked with curses the hoarse refrain:
  "Here's Flud Oirson, fur his horrd horrt,
    Torr'd an' futherr'd an' corr'd in a corrt
      By the women o' Morble'ead!"

Sweetly along the Salem[6] road
Bloom of orchard and lilac showed.
Little the wicked skipper knew
Of the fields so green and the sky so blue.
Riding there in his sorry trim,
Like an Indian idol glum and grim,
Scarcely he seemed the sound to hear
Of voices shouting, far and near:

---

6. A Massachusetts seacoast town near Marblehead.

"Here's Flud Oirson, fur his horrd horrt,
Torr'd an' futherr'd an' corr'd in a corrt
    By the women o' Morble'ead!"

"Hear me, neighbors!" at last he cried —
"What to me is this noisy ride?
What is the shame that clothes the skin
To the nameless horror that lives within?
Waking or sleeping, I see a wreck,
And hear a cry from a reeling deck!
Hate me and curse me — I only dread
The hand of God and the face of the dead!"
    Said old Floyd Ireson, for his hard heart,
    Tarred and feathered and carried in a cart
        By the women of Marblehead!

Then the wife of the skipper lost at sea
Said, "God has touched him! — why should we!"
Said an old wife mourning her only son,
"Cut the rogue's tether and let him run!"
So with soft relentings and rude excuse,
Half scorn, half pity, they cut him loose,
And gave him a cloak to hide him in,
And left him alone with his shame and sin.
    Poor Floyd Ireson, for his hard heart,
    Tarred and feathered and carried in a cart
        By the women of Marblehead!

                    1857

When Whittier was a student at the Haverhill Academy, a fellow student from Marblehead, a coastal town north of Boston, had recited for him a "fragment of rhyme" that contained the gist of this poem. Whittier began to compose a version in 1828 but did not publish it until 1857. Twenty-two years later, Samuel Roads's *History of Marblehead* appeared, blaming the ship's crew rather than Captain Ireson himself for abandoning the disabled vessel. Whittier wrote to the historian that he had assumed the fragment his schoolmate had recited to him dated back at least a century. He added, "I am glad for the sake of truth and justice that the real facts are given in thy book. I certainly would not knowingly do injustice to any one, dead or living."

Telling the Bees

Here is the place; right over the hill
    Runs the path I took;
You can see the gap in the old wall still,
    And the stepping-stones in the shallow brook.

There is the house, with the gate red-barred,
    And the poplars tall;
And the barn's brown length, and the cattle-yard,
    And the white horns tossing above the wall.

There are the beehives ranged in the sun;
    And down by the brink
Of the brook are her poor flowers, weed-o'errun,
    Pansy and daffodil, rose and pink.

A year has gone, as the tortoise goes,
    Heavy and slow;
And the same rose blows, and the same sun glows,
    And the same brook sings of a year ago.

There's the same sweet clover-smell in the breeze;
    And the June sun warm
Tangles his wings of fire in the trees,
    Setting, as then, over Fernside farm.

I mind me how with a lover's care
    From my Sunday coat
I brushed off the burrs, and smoothed my hair,
    And cooled at the brook-side my brow and throat.

Since we parted, a month had passed—
    To love, a year;
Down through the beeches I looked at last
    On the little red gate and the well-sweep near.

I can see it all now—the slantwise rain
    Of light through the leaves,
The sundown's blaze on her window-pane,
    The bloom of her roses under the eaves.

       ❈   ❈   ❈

Just the same as a month before —
    The house and the trees,
The barn's brown gable, the vine by the door —
    Nothing changed but the hives of bees.

Before them, under the garden wall,
    Forward and back,
Went drearily singing the chore-girl small,
    Draping each hive with a shred of black.

Trembling, I listened: the summer sun
    Had the chill of snow;
For I knew she was telling the bees of one
    Gone on the journey we all must go!

Then I said to myself, "My Mary weeps
    For the dead to-day:
Haply her blind old grandsire sleeps
    The fret and the pain of his age away."

But her dog whined low; on the doorway sill,
    With his cane to his chin,
The old man sat; and the chore-girl still
    Sung to the bees stealing out and in.

And the song she was singing ever since
    In my ear sounds on: —
"Stay at home, pretty bees, fly not hence!
    Mistress Mary is dead and gone!"

                          1858

It was a rural New England custom, brought over from England, to tell the family's bees when a death occurred in the house and to drape the hives in black to keep the swarms from leaving. The farm depicted in this poem corresponds exactly to Whittier's childhood homestead. The story of Mary and her bereaved lover, however, is imagined.

Snow-Bound

A WINTER IDYL

To the Memory of the Household It Describes
This Poem is Dedicated by the Author

As the Spirits of Darkness be stronger in the dark, so Good Spirits,
which be Angels of Light, are augmented not only by the Divine light
of the Sun, but also by our common Wood Fire: and as the Celestial Fire
drives away dark spirits, so also this our Fire of Wood doth the same.
COR. AGRIPPA, *OCCULT PHILOSOPHY*, BOOK I, CH. V[1]

Announced by all the trumpets of the sky,
Arrives the snow, and, driving o'er the fields,
Seems nowhere to alight: the whited air
Hides hills and woods, the river and the heaven,
And veils the farm-house at the garden's end.
The sled and traveller stopped, the courier's feet
Delayed, all friends shut out, the housemates sit
Around the radiant fireplace, enclosed
In a tumultuous privacy of Storm.
EMERSON[2]

The sun that brief December day
Rose cheerless over hills of gray,
And, darkly circled, gave at noon
A sadder light than waning moon.
Slow tracing down the thickening sky
Its mute and ominous prophecy,
A portent seeming less than threat,
It sank from sight before it set.
A chill no coat, however stout,
Of homespun stuff could quite shut out,
A hard, dull bitterness of cold,
That checked, mid-vein, the circling race
Of life-blood in the sharpened face,
The coming of the snow-storm told.
The wind blew east:[3] we heard the roar

1. Heinrich Cornelius Agrippa (1486–1535), a German physician and student of the occult. "Snow-Bound" depicts Whittier's mother describing a sorcerer she knew in her youth who used Agrippa's *Three Books of Occult Philosophy* as his "conjuring book."
2. From Ralph Waldo Emerson's "The Snow-Storm" (1841). The complete poem appears in the Emerson selection in this anthology.
3. That is, from the east.

Of Ocean on his wintry shore,
And felt the strong pulse throbbing there
Beat with low rhythm our inland air.

Meanwhile we did our nightly chores —
Brought in the wood from out of doors,
Littered[4] the stalls, and from the mows
Raked down the herd's-grass for the cows;
Heard the horse whinnying for his corn;
And, sharply clashing horn on horn,
Impatient down the stanchion rows[5]
The cattle shake their walnut bows;
While, peering from his early perch
Upon the scaffold's pole of birch,
The cock his crested helmet bent
And down his querulous challenge sent.

Unwarmed by any sunset light
The gray day darkened into night,
A night made hoary[6] with the swarm
And whirl-dance of the blinding storm,
As zigzag, wavering to and fro,
Crossed and recrossed the wingèd snow:
And ere the early bed-time came
The white drift piled the window-frame,
And through the glass the clothes-line posts
Looked in like tall and sheeted ghosts.

So all night long the storm roared on:
The morning broke without a sun;
In tiny spherule[7] traced with lines
Of Nature's geometric signs,
In starry flake, and pellicle,[8]
All day the hoary meteor[9] fell;
And, when the second morning shone,
We looked upon a world unknown,

---

4. Put down straw for bedding. Mows: masses of hay stored in the barn.
5. Rows of stalls, each with a brace that loosely holds an animal's neck in place during feeding or milking. The brace is made of walnut wood and shaped like a bow.
6. Gray or white, as with age.
7. A small, round object.
8. Thin film.
9. Atmospheric phenomenon — that is, snow.

On nothing we could call our own.
Around the glistening wonder bent
The blue walls of the firmament,[10]
No cloud above, no earth below —
A universe of sky and snow!
The old familiar sights of ours
Took marvellous shapes; strange domes and towers
Rose up where sty or corn-crib stood,
Or garden-wall, or belt of wood;
A smooth white mound the brush-pile showed,
A fenceless drift what once was road;
The bridle-post an old man sat
With loose-flung coat and high cocked hat;
The well-curb had a Chinese roof;
And even the long sweep,[11] high aloof,
In its slant splendor, seemed to tell
Of Pisa's leaning miracle.

A prompt, decisive man, no breath
Our father wasted: "Boys, a path!"
Well pleased, (for when did farmer boy
Count such a summons less than joy?)
Our buskins[12] on our feet we drew;
With mittened hands, and caps drawn low,
To guard our necks and ears from snow,
We cut the solid whiteness through.
And, where the drift was deepest, made
A tunnel walled and overlaid
With dazzling crystal: we had read
Of rare Aladdin's wondrous cave,[13]
And to our own his name we gave,
With many a wish the luck were ours
To test his lamp's supernal powers.
We reached the barn with merry din,
And roused the prisoned brutes within.
The old horse thrust his long head out,
And grave with wonder gazed about;

10. Sky.
11. The well sweep, which is a pole used to raise the well bucket, resembles the leaning tower of Pisa in Italy.
12. Roughly hewn boots.
13. In the tale of Aladdin, the cave contains a magic lamp that Aladdin uses to become wealthy and to marry the sultan's daughter.

The cock his lusty greeting said,
And forth his speckled harem led;
The oxen lashed their tails, and hooked,
And mild reproach of hunger looked;
The hornèd patriarch of the sheep,
Like Egypt's Amun[14] roused from sleep,
Shook his sage head with gesture mute,
And emphasized with stamp of foot.

All day the gusty north-wind bore
The loosening drift its breath before;
Low circling round its southern zone,
The sun through dazzling snow-mist shone.
No church-bell lent its Christian tone
To the savage air, no social smoke
Curled over woods of snow-hung oak.
A solitude made more intense
By dreary-voicèd elements,
The shrieking of the mindless wind,
The moaning tree-boughs swaying blind,
And on the glass the unmeaning beat
Of ghostly finger-tips of sleet.
Beyond the circle of our hearth
No welcome sound of toil or mirth
Unbound the spell, and testified
Of human life and thought outside.
We minded that the sharpest ear
The buried brooklet could not hear,
The music of whose liquid lip
Had been to us companionship,
And, in our lonely life, had grown
To have an almost human tone.

As night drew on, and, from the crest
Of wooded knolls that ridged the west,
The sun, a snow-blown traveller, sank
From sight beneath the smothering bank,
We piled, with care, our nightly stack
Of wood against the chimney-back—
The oaken log, green, huge, and thick,

14. In Egyptian myth, a god with a ram's head.

And on its top the stout back-stick;
The knotty forestick laid apart,
And filled between with curious art
The ragged brush; then, hovering near,
We watched the first red blaze appear,
Heard the sharp crackle, caught the gleam
On whitewashed wall and sagging beam,
Until the old, rude-furnished room
Burst, flower-like, into rosy bloom;
While radiant with a mimic flame
Outside the sparkling drift became,
And through the bare-boughed lilac-tree
Our own warm hearth seemed blazing free.
The crane and pendent trammels[15] showed,
The Turks' heads[16] on the andirons glowed;
While childish fancy, prompt to tell
The meaning of the miracle,
Whispered the old rhyme: "*Under the tree,*
When fire outdoors burns merrily,
There the witches are making tea."

The moon above the eastern wood
Shone at its full; the hill-range stood
Transfigured in the silver flood,
Its blown snows flashing cold and keen,
Dead white, save where some sharp ravine
Took shadow, or the sombre green
Of hemlocks turned to pitchy black
Against the whiteness at their back.
For such a world and such a night
Most fitting that unwarming light,
Which only seemed where'er it fell
To make the coldness visible.

Shut in from all the world without,
We sat the clean-winged hearth about,
Content to let the north-wind roar
In baffled rage at pane and door,
While the red logs before us beat

15. Pothooks hanging on an iron arm extending   16. Turbanlike designs on the andirons.
into the fireplace.

The frost-line back with tropic heat;
And ever, when a louder blast
Shook beam and rafter as it passed,
The merrier up its roaring draught
The great throat of the chimney laughed.
The house-dog on his paws outspread
Laid to the fire his drowsy head,
The cat's dark silhouette on the wall
A couchant[17] tiger's seemed to fall;
And, for the winter fireside meet,[18]
Between the andirons' straddling feet,
The mug of cider simmered slow,
The apples sputtered in a row,
And, close at hand, the basket stood
With nuts from brown October's wood.

What matter how the night behaved?
What matter how the north-wind raved?
Blow high, blow low, not all its snow
Could quench our hearth-fire's ruddy glow.
O Time and Change! — with hair as gray
As was my sire's that winter day,
How strange it seems, with so much gone
Of life and love, to still live on!
Ah, brother![19] only I and thou
Are left of all that circle now —
The dear home faces whereupon
That fitful firelight paled and shone.
Henceforward, listen as we will,
The voices of that hearth are still;
Look where we may, the wide earth o'er,
Those lighted faces smile no more.
We tread the paths their feet have worn,
We sit beneath their orchard trees,
We hear, like them, the hum of bees
And rustle of the bladed corn;
We turn the pages that they read,
Their written words we linger o'er,

17. Crouching or lying.
18. Fitting, appropriate.
19. Younger brother Matthew Whittier (1812– 1883). This address to the family's only other surviving member culminates in one of the poem's eloquent passages of mourning.

But in the sun they cast no shade,
No voice is heard, no sign is made,
No step is on the conscious floor!
Yet Love will dream, and Faith will trust,
(Since He who knows our need is just,)
That somehow, somewhere, meet we must.
Alas for him who never sees
The stars shine through his cypress-trees!
Who, hopeless, lays his dead away,
Nor looks to see the breaking day
Across the mournful marbles[20] play!
Who hath not learned, in hours of faith,
The truth to flesh and sense unknown,
That Life is ever lord of Death,
And Love can never lose its own!

We sped the time with stories old,
Wrought puzzles out, and riddles told,
Or stammered from our school-book lore
"The Chief of Gambia's golden shore."[21]
How often since, when all the land
Was clay in Slavery's shaping hand,
As if a far-blown trumpet stirred
The languorous sin-sick air, I heard:
"Does not the voice of reason cry,
'Claim the first right which Nature gave,
From the red scourge of bondage to fly,
Nor deign to live a burdened slave!'"
Our father rode again his ride
On Memphremagog's[22] wooded side;
Sat down again to moose and samp[23]
In trapper's hut and Indian camp;
Lived o'er the old idyllic ease
Beneath St. François'[24] hemlock-trees;
Again for him the moonlight shone

20. Tombstones made of marble.
21. From "The African Chief," an antislavery poem by Sarah Wentworth Morton (1759–1846). The poem, which concerns an African prince captured by slave traders, was included in a schoolbook, *The American Preceptor*, by Caleb Bingham. The italicized quotation five lines below is also from this poem.
22. A lake between Vermont and Quebec that Whittier's father had visited.
23. He ate moose and cornmeal mush.
24. A village in Quebec.

On Norman cap and bodiced zone;[25]
Again he heard the violin play
Which led the village dance away,
And mingled in its merry whirl
The grandam and the laughing girl.
Or, nearer home, our steps he led
Where Salisbury's[26] level marshes spread
Mile-wide as flies the laden bee;
Where merry mowers, hale and strong,
Swept, scythe on scythe, their swaths along
The low green prairies of the sea.
We shared the fishing off Boar's Head,[27]
And round the rocky Isles of Shoals
The hake-broil[28] on the drift-wood coals;
The chowder on the sand-beach made,
Dipped by the hungry, steaming hot,
With spoons of clam-shell from the pot.
We heard the tales of witchcraft old,
And dream and sign and marvel told
To sleepy listeners as they lay
Stretched idly on the salted hay,
Adrift along the winding shores,
When favoring breezes deigned to blow
The square sail of the gundelow[29]
And idle lay the useless oars.

Our mother, while she turned her wheel
Or run the new-knit stocking-heel,
Told how the Indian hordes came down
At midnight on Concheco town,[30]
And how her own great-uncle bore
His cruel scalp-mark to fourscore.
Recalling, in her fitting phrase,
So rich and picturesque and free,
(The common unrhymed poetry
Of simple life and country ways,)

25. A cap in the style of Normandy, France, and a woman's waistband.
26. A town in Massachusetts.
27. A New Hampshire coastal town, near the Isles of Shoals.
28. Broiled cod.
29. Gondola, a flat-bottomed boat.
30. A village near Dover, New Hampshire.

The story of her early days —
She made us welcome to her home;
Old hearths grew wide to give us room;
We stole with her a frightened look
At the gray wizard's conjuring-book,[31]
The fame whereof went far and wide
Through all the simple country side;
We heard the hawks at twilight play,
The boat-horn on Piscataqua,[32]
The loon's weird laughter far away;
We fished her little trout-brook, knew
What flowers in wood and meadow grew,
What sunny hillsides autumn-brown
She climbed to shake the ripe nuts down,
Saw where in sheltered cove and bay
The ducks' black squadron anchored lay,
And heard the wild-geese calling loud
Beneath the gray November cloud.

Then, haply,[33] with a look more grave,
And soberer tone, some tale she gave
From painful Sewell's ancient tome,[34]
Beloved in every Quaker home,
Of faith fire-winged by martyrdom,
Or Chalkley's Journal,[35] old and quaint —
Gentlest of skippers, rare sea-saint! —
Who, when the dreary calms prevailed,
And water-butt and bread-cask failed,
And cruel, hungry eyes pursued
His portly presence mad for food,
With dark hints muttered under breath
Of casting lots for life or death,
Offered, if Heaven withheld supplies,
To be himself the sacrifice.
Then, suddenly, as if to save

31. Heinrich Cornelius Agrippa's *Occult Philosophy*, which "Snow-Bound" quotes in one of its epigraphs.
32. A New Hampshire river.
33. Perhaps.
34. *The History . . . of the Quakers* by William Sewell (1650–1725) recounted the persecution of the Quakers by the Puritans in seventeenth-century New England. The Whittiers were Quakers.
35. The *Journal* of Thomas Chalkley (1675–1741), a Quaker preacher and seafarer, was published in 1747.

The good man from his living grave,
A ripple on the water grew,
A school of porpoise flashed in view.
"Take, eat," he said, "and be content;
These fishes in my stead are sent
By Him who gave the tangled ram
To spare the child of Abraham."[36]

Our uncle, innocent of books,
Was rich in lore of fields and brooks,
The ancient teachers never dumb
Of Nature's unhoused lyceum.[37]
In moons and tides and weather wise,
He read the clouds as prophecies,
And foul or fair could well divine,
By many an occult hint and sign,
Holding the cunning-warded keys
To all the woodcraft mysteries;
Himself to Nature's heart so near
That all her voices in his ear
Of beast or bird had meanings clear,
Like Apollonius of old,[38]
Who knew the tales the sparrows told,
Or Hermes,[39] who interpreted
What the sage cranes of Nilus said;
A simple, guileless, childlike man,
Content to live where life began;
Strong only on his native grounds,
The little world of sights and sounds
Whose girdle[40] was the parish bounds,
Whereof his fondly partial pride
The common features magnified,
As Surrey hills to mountains grew
In White[41] of Selborne's loving view—

36. In Genesis 22:8–13, God provides Abraham with a ram to sacrifice in place of his son Isaac.
37. Public lecture hall or school. In his 1891 preface, Whittier explained that his uncle Moses "had many stories of hunting and fishing and some of witchcraft and superstition."
38. Apollonius of Tyana (3 B.C.E.–97 C.E.), a Greek philosopher and mystic who became a mythical hero to Roman pagans.
39. Hermes Trismegistus, a legendary Egyptian author of books on magic. Nilus: the Nile River.
40. Boundary.
41. Gilbert White (1720–1793), who lived in Selborne, in the county of Surrey in England, wrote *The Natural History and Antiquities of Selborne* (1789).

He told how teal[42] and loon he shot,
And how the eagle's eggs he got,
The feats on pond and river done,
The prodigies of rod and gun;
Till, warming with the tales he told,
Forgotten was the outside cold,
The bitter wind unheeded blew,
From ripening corn the pigeons flew,
The partridge drummed i' the wood, the mink
Went fishing down the river-brink.
In fields with bean or clover gray,
The woodchuck, like a hermit gray,
Peered from the doorway of his cell;
The muskrat plied the mason's trade,
And tier by tier his mud-walls laid;
And from the shagbark[43] overhead
The grizzled squirrel dropped his shell.

Next, the dear aunt, whose smile of cheer
And voice in dreams I see and hear—
The sweetest woman ever Fate
Perverse denied a household mate,
Who, lonely, homeless, not the less
Found peace in love's unselfishness,
And welcome wheresoe'er she went,
A calm and gracious element,
Whose presence seemed the sweet income
And womanly atmosphere of home—
Called up her girlhood memories,
The huskings and the apple-bees,
The sleigh-rides and the summer sails,
Weaving through all the poor details
And homespun warp of circumstance
A golden woof-thread of romance.
For well she kept her genial mood
And simple faith of maidenhood;
Before her still a cloud-land lay,
The mirage loomed across her way;
The morning dew, that dries so soon

42. A river duck. Loon: a fish-eating diving bird.   43. Hickory tree.

With others, glistened at her noon;
Through years of toil and soil and care,
From glossy tress to thin gray hair,
All unprofaned she held apart
The virgin fancies of the heart.
Be shame to him of woman born
Who hath for such but thought of scorn.

There, too, our elder sister[44] plied
Her evening task the stand beside;
A full, rich nature, free to trust,
Truthful and almost sternly just,
Impulsive, earnest, prompt to act,
And make her generous thought a fact,
Keeping with many a light disguise
The secret of self-sacrifice.
O heart sore-tried! thou hast the best
That Heaven itself could give thee — rest,
Rest from all bitter thoughts and things!
How many a poor one's blessing went
With thee beneath the low green tent
Whose curtain never outward swings!

As one who held herself a part
Of all she saw, and let her heart
Against the household bosom lean,
Upon the motley-braided mat
Our youngest and our dearest[45] sat,
Lifting her large, sweet, asking eyes,
Now bathed in the unfading green
And holy peace of Paradise.
Oh, looking from some heavenly hill,
Or from the shade of saintly palms,
Or silver reach of river calms,
Do those large eyes behold me still?
With me one little year ago: —
The chill weight of the winter snow
For months upon her grave has lain;

44. Mary Whittier (1806–1860).
45. Elizabeth Whittier (1815–1864). Her death oc-
curred a year before Whittier began composing
this poem. His grief may have generated his wish
to relive the past.

And now, when summer south-winds blow
And brier[46] and harebell bloom again,
I tread the pleasant paths we trod,
I see the violet-sprinkled sod
Whereon she leaned, too frail and weak
The hillside flowers she loved to seek,
Yet following me where'er I went
With dark eyes full of love's content.
The birds are glad; the brier-rose fills
The air with sweetness; all the hills
Stretch green to June's unclouded sky;
But still I wait with ear and eye
For something gone which should be nigh,
A loss in all familiar things,
In flower that blooms, and bird that sings.
And yet, dear heart! remembering thee,
Am I not richer than of old?
Safe in thy immortality,
What change can reach the wealth I hold?
What chance can mar the pearl and gold
Thy love hath left in trust with me?
And while in life's late afternoon,
Where cool and long the shadows grow,
I walk to meet the night that soon
Shall shape and shadow overflow,
I cannot feel that thou art far,
Since near at need the angels are;
And when the sunset gates unbar,
Shall I not see thee waiting stand,
And, white against the evening star,
The welcome of thy beckoning hand?

Brisk wielder of the birch and rule,
The master of the district school[47]
Held at the fire his favored place,
Its warm glow lit a laughing face
Fresh-hued and fair, where scarce appeared
The uncertain prophecy of beard.
He teased the mitten-blinded cat,

---

46. A prickly New England shrub. Harebell: an herb with blue, bell-shaped flowers.

47. George Haskell (died 1876), who had studied at Dartmouth College.

Played cross-pins on my uncle's hat,
Sang songs, and told us what befalls
In classic Dartmouth's college halls.
Born the wild Northern hills among,
From whence his yeoman father wrung
By patient toil subsistence scant,
Not competence and yet not want,
He early gained the power to pay
His cheerful, self-reliant way;
Could doff at ease his scholar's gown
To peddle wares from town to town;
Or through the long vacation's reach
In lonely lowland districts teach,
Where all the droll experience found
At stranger hearths in boarding round,
The moonlit skater's keen delight,
The sleigh-drive through the frosty night,
The rustic party, with its rough
Accompaniment of blind-man's-buff,
And whirling-plate,[48] and forfeits paid,
His winter task a pastime made.
Happy the snow-locked homes wherein
He tuned his merry violin,
Or played the athlete in the barn,
Or held the good dame's winding-yarn,
Or mirth-provoking versions told
Of classic legends rare and old,
Wherein the scenes of Greece and Rome
Had all the commonplace of home,
And little seemed at best the odds
'Twixt Yankee pedlers and old gods;
Where Pindus-born Arachthus[49] took
The guise of any grist-mill brook,
And dread Olympus[50] at his will
Became a huckleberry hill.

A careless boy that night he seemed;
But at his desk he had the look

---

48. A competitive game in which players spin plates on their edges.
49. A Greek river whose source is in the Pindus Mountains.
50. A Greek mountain that, according to myth, was the home of the gods.

And air of one who wisely schemed,
And hostage from the future took
In trainèd thought and lore of book.
Large-brained, clear-eyed,—of such as he
Shall Freedom's young apostles be,[51]
Who, following in War's bloody trail,
Shall every lingering wrong assail;
All chains from limb and spirit strike,
Uplift the black and white alike;
Scatter before their swift advance
The darkness and the ignorance,
The pride, the lust, the squalid sloth,
Which nurtured Treason's monstrous growth,
Made murder pastime, and the hell
Of prison-torture possible;
The cruel lie of caste refute,
Old forms remould, and substitute
For Slavery's lash the freeman's will,
For blind routine, wise-handed skill;
A school-house plant on every hill,
Stretching in radiate nerve-lines thence
The quick wires of intelligence;[52]
Till North and South together brought
Shall own the same electric thought,
In peace a common flag salute,
And, side by side in labor's free
And unresentful rivalry,
Harvest the fields wherein they fought.

Another guest[53] that winter night
Flashed back from lustrous eyes the light.
Unmarked by time, and yet not young,
The honeyed music of her tongue
And words of meekness scarcely told
A nature passionate and bold,
Strong, self-concentred, spurning guide,

51. That is, the schoolmaster is the kind of person who will continue to battle for full racial equality in the post–Civil War era.
52. Telegraph wires.
53. Harriet Livermore (died 1867). In his 1891 note, Whittier called her "a young woman of fine natural ability, enthusiastic, eccentric, with slight control over her violent temper, which sometimes made her religious profession doubtful." Her unflattering portrait here may expose the narrator's fear of assertive women.

Its milder features dwarfed beside
Her unbent will's majestic pride.
She sat among us, at the best,
A not unfeared, half-welcome guest,
Rebuking with her cultured phrase
Our homeliness of words and ways.
A certain pard-like,[54] treacherous grace
Swayed the lithe limbs and drooped the lash,
Lent the white teeth their dazzling flash;
And under low brows, black with night,
Rayed out at times a dangerous light;
The sharp heat-lightnings of her face
Presaging ill to him whom Fate
Condemned to share her love or hate.
A woman tropical, intense
In thought and act, in soul and sense,
She blended in a like degree
The vixen and the devotee,
Revealing with each freak or feint
The temper of Petruchio's Kate,[55]
The raptures of Siena's saint.[56]
Her tapering hand and rounded wrist
Had facile power to form a fist;
The warm, dark languish of her eyes
Was never safe from wrath's surprise.
Brows saintly calm and lips devout
Knew every change of scowl and pout;
And the sweet voice had notes more high
And shrill for social battle-cry.

Since then what old cathedral town
Has missed her pilgrim staff and gown,
What convent-gate has held its lock
Against the challenge of her knock!
Through Smyrna's[57] plague-hushed thoroughfares,
Up sea-set Malta's[58] rocky stairs,

---

54. Leopardlike.
55. The tempestuous heroine who is ultimately "tamed" by Petruchio in Shakespeare's *Taming of the Shrew*.
56. St. Catherine (1347–1380) of Siena, Italy.

57. A port city on the Aegean Sea, now called Izmir, Turkey.
58. A rocky island nation in the Mediterranean Sea.

Gray olive slopes of hills that hem
Thy tombs and shrines, Jerusalem,
Or startling on her desert throne
The crazy Queen of Lebanon[59]
With claims fantastic as her own,
Her tireless feet have held their way;
And still, unrestful, bowed, and gray,
She watches under Eastern skies,
With hope each day renewed and fresh,
The Lord's quick coming in the flesh,
Whereof she dreams and prophesies!

Where'er her troubled path may be,
The Lord's sweet pity with her go!
The outward wayward life we see,
The hidden springs we may not know.
Nor is it given us to discern
What threads the fatal sisters[60] spun,
Through what ancestral years has run
The sorrow with the woman born,
What forged her cruel chain of moods,
What set her feet in solitudes,
And held the love within her mute,
What mingled madness in the blood,
A life-long discord and annoy,
Water of tears with oil of joy,
And hid within the folded bud
Perversities of flower and fruit.
It is not ours to separate
The tangled skein[61] of will and fate,
To show what metes[62] and bounds should stand
Upon the soul's debatable land,
And between choice and Providence
Divide the circle of events;
But He who knows our frame is just,
Merciful and compassionate,

59. Lady Hester Lucy Stanhope (1776–1839), an English-born associate of Harriet Livermore, sought to establish a new faith in Lebanon composed of both Islam and Christianity.
60. In Greek myth, the three Fates are the goddesses of destiny. Named Clotho, Lachesis, and Atropos, they spin the thread of life and cut it off.
61. Yarn or thread wound on a reel.
62. Limits.

And full of sweet assurances
And hope for all the language is,
That He remembereth we are dust![63]

At last the great logs, crumbling low,
Sent out a dull and duller glow,
The bull's-eye watch[64] that hung in view,
Ticking its weary circuit through,
Pointed with mutely warning sign
Its black hand to the hour of nine.
That sign the pleasant circle broke:
My uncle ceased his pipe to smoke,
Knocked from its bowl the refuse gray,
And laid it tenderly away;
Then roused himself to safely cover
The dull red brands with ashes over.
And while, with care, our mother laid
The work aside, her steps she stayed
One moment, seeking to express
Her grateful sense of happiness
For food and shelter, warmth and health,
And love's contentment more than wealth,
With simple wishes (not the weak,
Vain prayers which no fulfilment seek,
But such as warm the generous heart,
O'er-prompt to do with Heaven its part)
That none might lack, that bitter night,
For bread and clothing, warmth and light.

Within our beds awhile we heard
The wind that round the gables roared,
With now and then a ruder shock,
Which made our very bedsteads rock.
We heard the loosened clapboards tost,
The board-nails snapping in the frost;
And on us, through the unplastered wall,
Felt the light sifted snow-flakes fall.
But sleep stole on, as sleep will do
When hearts are light and life is new;

63. An echo of Psalms 103:14: God "knoweth our frame; he remembereth that we are dust." 64. A globe-shaped watch or small clock.

Faint and more faint the murmurs grew,
Till in the summer-land of dreams
They softened to the sound of streams,
Low stir of leaves, and dip of oars,
And lapsing waves on quiet shores.

Next morn we wakened with the shout
Of merry voices high and clear;
And saw the teamsters[65] drawing near
To break the drifted highways out.
Down the long hillside treading slow
We saw the half-buried oxen go,
Shaking the snow from heads uptost,
Their straining nostrils white with frost.
Before our door the straggling train
Drew up, an added team to gain.
The elders threshed their hands a-cold,
Passed, with the cider-mug, their jokes
From lip to lip; the younger folks
Down the loose snow-banks, wrestling, rolled,
Then toiled again the cavalcade
O'er windy hill, through clogged ravine,
And woodland paths that wound between
Low drooping pine-boughs winter-weighed.
From every barn a team afoot,
At every house a new recruit,
Where, drawn by Nature's subtlest law,
Haply the watchful young men saw
Sweet doorway pictures of the curls
And curious eyes of merry girls,
Lifting their hands in mock defence
Against the snow-ball's compliments,
And reading in each missive tost
The charm with Eden never lost.

We heard once more the sleigh-bells' sound;
And, following where the teamsters led,
The wise old Doctor went his round,
Just pausing at our door to say,
In the brief autocratic way

65. Those who drive teams of horses or oxen, here in order to plow the snow.

Of one who, prompt at Duty's call,
Was free to urge her claim on all,
That some poor neighbor sick abed
At night our mother's aid would need.
For, one in generous thought and deed,
What mattered in the sufferer's sight
The Quaker matron's inward light,
The Doctor's mail of Calvin's creed?[66]
All hearts confess the saints elect
Who, twain in faith, in love agree,
And melt not in an acid sect
The Christian pearl of charity!

So days went on: a week had passed
Since the great world was heard from last.
The Almanac we studied o'er,
Read and reread our little store
Of books and pamphlets, scarce a score;
One harmless novel, mostly hid
From younger eyes, a book forbid,
And poetry, (or[67] good or bad,
A single book was all we had,)
Where Ellwood's[68] meek, drab-skirted Muse,
A stranger to the heathen Nine,
Sang, with a somewhat nasal whine,
The wars of David and the Jews.
At last the floundering carrier bore
The village paper to our door.
Lo! broadening outward as we read,
To warmer zones the horizon spread
In panoramic length unrolled
We saw the marvels that it told.
Before us passed the painted Creeks,[69]

66. That is, why should the sick neighbor care that the Quaker housewife and the Calvinist doctor have different religious beliefs, given that both are generous with their help?
67. Whether.
68. Thomas Ellwood (1639–1714), an English Quaker poet. His poetic muse, who has nothing in common with the nine Muses of classical myth, impelled him to write a boring epic poem called *Davideis* (1712).

69. The newspaper rather improbably tells of the defeat of the Creek Indians in Georgia and Alabama in 1813–14, the attempt by the Scottish adventurer Gregor MacGregor to colonize Costa Rica in 1819, and the victory of the Greek patriot Alexander Ypsilanti over Turkish warriors at Mt. Taygetos in 1820.

And daft McGregor on his raids
In Costa Rica's everglades.
And up Taygetos winding slow
Rode Ypsilanti's Mainote Greeks,
A Turk's head at each saddle-bow!
Welcome to us its week-old news,
Its corner for the rustic Muse,
Its monthly gauge of snow and rain,
Its record, mingling in a breath
The wedding bell and dirge of death:
Jest, anecdote, and love-lorn tale,
The latest culprit sent to jail;
Its hue and cry of stolen and lost,
Its vendue[70] sales and goods at cost,
And traffic calling loud for gain.
We felt the stir of hall and street,
The pulse of life that round us beat;
The chill embargo of the snow
Was melted in the genial glow;
Wide swung again our ice-locked door,
And all the world was ours once more!

Clasp, Angel of the backward look
And folded wings of ashen gray
And voice of echoes far away,
The brazen covers of thy book;
The weird palimpsest[71] old and vast,
Wherein thou hid'st the spectral past;
Where, closely mingling, pale and glow
The characters of joy and woe;
The monographs of outlived years,
Or smile-illumed or dim with tears,
Green hills of life that slope to death,
And haunts of home, whose vistaed trees
Shade off to mournful cypresses
With the white amaranths[72] underneath.
Even while I look, I can but heed

70. Auction.
71. A manuscript on which earlier writing has been partially erased and covered over with later writing.

72. A legendary, undying flower.

The restless sands' incessant fall,
Importunate hours that hours succeed,
Each clamorous with its own sharp need,
And duty keeping pace with all.
Shut down and clasp the heavy lids;
I hear again the voice that bids
The dreamer leave his dream midway
For larger hopes and graver fears:
Life greatens in these later years,
The century's aloe[73] flowers to-day!

Yet, haply, in some lull of life,
Some Truce of God which breaks its strife,
The worldling's eyes shall gather dew,
Dreaming in throngful city ways
Of winter joys his boyhood knew;
And dear and early friends—the few
Who yet remain—shall pause to view
These Flemish pictures[74] of old days;
Sit with me by the homestead hearth,
And stretch the hands of memory forth
To warm them at the wood-fire's blaze!
And thanks untraced to lips unknown
Shall greet me like the odors blown
From unseen meadows newly mown,
Or lilies floating in some pond,
Wood-fringed, the wayside gaze beyond;
The traveller owns the grateful sense
Of sweetness near, he knows not whence,
And, pausing, takes with forehead bare
The benediction of the air.

1866

This poem, composed in 1865–66 and published in 1866, immediately became one of the most popular poems in American history. The dedication was added in the 1891 edition. The poem recalls the members of the Whittier household, which included the poet himself, his mother and father, his brother and two sisters, an unmarried aunt and uncle, and the local schoolmaster, who was boarding with the family. In addition, a neighbor named

73. A Mexican agave plant that, according to erroneous legend, flowers once a century.
74. A comparison of this poem to highly realistic domestic paintings by seventeenth-century Flemish artists such as Adriaen Brouwer and David Teniers.

Harriet Livermore was "a not unfeared, half-welcome guest." In a prefatory note to the 1891 edition, Whittier commented, "In my boyhood, in our lonely farm-house, we had scanty sources of information; few books and only a small weekly newspaper. Our only annual was the Almanac. Under such circumstances story-telling was a necessary resource in the long winter evenings." The poem might be regarded as an exercise in nostalgia, an elegy for dead family members, a celebration of victory in the Civil War, or a consolation for the suffering caused by the war.

EDGAR ALLAN POE
1809–1849

EDGAR ALLAN POE WAS one of the most original literary minds America has produced and one of the nineteenth century's greatest literary innovators. Along with Nathaniel Hawthorne, whose work he deeply admired, Poe was a pioneer of the American short story. Such Poe classics as "The Fall of the House of Usher," "The Cask of Amontillado," "The Tell-Tale Heart," "Ligeia," and "The Black Cat" are among the most enduringly popular stories ever written, in part because he gave the rambling and improbable gothic tale an atmosphere, a concision, a relentless driving logic, and a psychological depth and inevitability hitherto undreamed of. Poe single-handedly invented the detective story. His "tales of ratiocination," beginning with "The Murders in the Rue Morgue" (1841) and featuring the master detective Auguste Dupin and an unnamed assistant who narrates the tales, set the model for a long line of sophisticated sleuthing teams, starting with Sherlock Holmes and Dr. Watson. Moreover, Poe's original and still controversial theoretical writings—including "The Philosophy of Composition," his account of the making of "The Raven"—placed new attention on the nature of literary form and the means of achieving literary effect.

As a poet, Poe focused most obviously on meter and rhyme. In contrast to the free-verse innovations of Whitman, who was ten years younger, Poe (like his near-contemporary Longfellow) was a tireless innovator and experimenter in more traditional forms. His most popular poem, "The Raven," is, significantly, also his most metrically inventive. Here he employs the comparatively uncommon trochaic rhythm (STRONG beat–weak beat; STRONG beat–weak beat)—later used to telling effect by Longfellow in *The Song of Hiawatha*—as the dominant meter of an uncommonly long sixteen-syllable line that creates a profoundly trancelike atmosphere. His six-line stanza employs an unusual pattern of internal rhymes that add variety and surprise to his long lines, in part by frequently breaking them in the middle. And that six-line stanza ends with a short line closing on the famously repeated word "Nevermore." That word, spoken by Poe's "ghastly grim and ancient raven," at first seems meaningless to the mournful narrator, but as the poem moves toward its dramatic climax, the word inevitably confirms the reality of the forlorn speaker's being "nevermore" reunited with his deceased love, that "rare and radiant maiden whom the angels name Lenore." Though Poe derived scant profit from "The Raven" (he sold the rights for about fifteen dollars), it became an overnight sensation when published in 1845 and was reprinted throughout the English-speaking world. Abraham Lincoln even discussed a parody of the poem in an 1846 letter to a literary friend. In the parody, Poe's raven was replaced with a polecat. (What the polecat "quoth" is not recorded.) Poe himself had emphasized his deliberate "introduction of some ludicrous touches amidst the serious and impressive," giving the poem a peculiar texture that lends itself to parody. Such ludicrous touches also appear in many Poe stories, such as "The Cask of Amontillado" and "The Tell-Tale Heart."

This blending of the somber and the ludicrous is a mark of Poe's ceaseless and original experimentation. Many of Poe's poems explore complex and at times contradictory emotional impressions—and they are marked, as well, by Poe's ongoing experimentation with meter, rhyme, and sound. Perhaps this effort is most conspicuous in "The Bells," which nearly abandons meaning in pursuit of novel musical and emotional effects. These experiments, supported by Poe's aesthetic theories, had a lasting impact on such important French symbolist poets as Charles Baudelaire, Paul Verlaine, and Stéphane Mallarmé.

Poe was from an early age a busy and widely published poet, journalist, fiction writer, critic, and editor. He achieved substantial national attention in 1843 with his prize-winning detective story "The Gold-Bug" and lasting international fame with "The Raven" two years later, but his life was never easy. Sorting fact from fiction in an account of Poe's life is also difficult. Rufus Griswold, a lifelong Poe enemy who claimed (perhaps fraudulently) to have been named Poe's literary executor, denounced Poe after his death, first in a pseudonymous and widely reprinted obituary and then in the introduction to what was for many years the standard edition of Poe's works—a set of volumes, often reprinted, that Griswold edited. Many of Griswold's most damaging claims were demonstrably false, and Poe was not without his defenders, including the poet Sarah Helen Whitman (also included in this anthology), whom Poe nearly married after the death of his beloved wife, Virginia, and whom he made the subject of the second of his poems entitled "To Helen." But Griswold's oft-printed claims, attached to Poe's own words, and assigning to Poe himself characteristics commonly found among his fictional narrators, took hold of the imagination of readers and still linger in many published accounts. At the same time, Poe was an inveterate storyteller and hoaxer, and his own accounts of his life are a mixture of fact and fabrication. Moreover, Poe's friends and his many enemies (Poe lived in a disputatious age and was a demanding editor and slashing critic) often painted radically different portraits of the man, the former whitewashing and the latter demonizing. Since even public records regarding Poe are sometimes in dispute, separating the man from the myths remains a genuine challenge.

It is worth looking at two of the most common attacks on Poe, both insisted on by Griswold. Griswold claimed, first, that Poe was a drug user and, second, that he was a chronic drunkard. The former charge is almost certainly false. Two doctors familiar with Poe, one a close friend and one a bitter enemy, both insisted that they had never known Poe to use or abuse opium or any of the other addictive drugs commonly available in America in the early nineteenth century. On the other hand, Poe certainly struggled with alcohol, though whether to term his condition alcoholism is a matter of interpretation. Poe had a limited tolerance for liquor, and a single drink could make him ill while still craving more alcohol. Some evidence implies that he was dealing with a hereditary medical disability, both because of his pronounced physical reaction to alcohol and because his father as well as his elder brother had a serious drinking problem. Poe was capable of long periods of abstinence, but his time was a hard-drinking age, and Poe lived with many stresses and uncertainties. Invariably, his good resolutions lapsed. His letters to friends and family are full of promises to give up alcohol and accounts of his long periods of sobriety. Near the end of his life he joined a temperance society, promising never to drink again. Many of the failures in his life may be linked to alcohol—he lost jobs, friends, and ultimately the chance to marry Sarah Helen Whitman as a result of it. And there are disputed claims that his death was brought on by an overdose of alcohol. One examining doctor thought he had been drinking. A second examining doctor found no trace of alcohol and concluded Poe had been beaten by thugs, a view made plausible by the observation of friends that Poe had been carrying a considerable sum in cash at the time, collected in support of his projected new magazine, *The Stylus*. Still, alcohol clearly was a problem with which Poe waged a lifelong struggle.

Even Poe's earliest struggles and losses may have been linked to paternal abuse of alcohol. Poe was born in Boston in 1809 to David and Elizabeth Poe, traveling stage actors. First his father and then his mother died, each in a different Virginia city, within a few months of one another in 1811, when Poe was two years old. Evidence suggests that Poe's father, struggling with alcoholism, had abandoned his wife and three small children a few months prior to his death. Poe was taken into the Richmond home of the childless John and Frances Allan, while his older brother and younger sister went to other families. Allan, a wealthy tobacco merchant, raised Poe as a son, and Poe accompanied the Allan family to London from 1818 to 1820, where he studied in a private school and may have imbibed elements of the European atmosphere that provides the Gothic setting for so many of his tales. Yet Poe was never formally adopted by John Allan, and this, in concert with later events, suggests that his position with the family remained insecure. Poe began studies at the University of Virginia in 1826. Although a successful student, he amassed substantial debts—at least in part because Allan sent him to the university with funds insufficient to pay his tuition and living expenses. There, according to some reports, Poe began to show the first signs of his struggle with alcohol. When John Allan refused to pay Poe's debts, a violent rupture between the two occurred that never healed. Poe enlisted in the army, where, praised for his good habits—he was, as indicated earlier, capable of long periods of sobriety—he was rapidly promoted to sergeant-major of artillery. In 1830, after obtaining an honorable discharge from his five-year enlistment, Poe enrolled in the West Point Military Academy. But he disliked the academy, perhaps because of its rigid discipline, and, refusing to attend classes, he forced his own expulsion in 1831. Some accounts indicate that he had again begun drinking.

When he left West Point in 1831, at the age of twenty-two, Poe had already published three overlapping volumes of poetry, beginning in 1827 with *Tamerlane and Other Poems*. His later writing career was prolific and varied, though he never knew much financial success or security. He produced short stories, journalism, and critical essays at a brisk rate and worked at various editorial positions with, among other journals, *The Southern Literary Messenger*, *The Gentleman's Magazine*, *Graham's Magazine* (which under Poe's editorship became for a time the most popular magazine in America), the *New York Evening Mirror*, and the *Broadway Journal*. Yet poetry remained a central preoccupation.

Though his most popular poem, "The Raven," creates a dark, somber, and psychologically charged atmosphere reminiscent of his best-liked stories, the main body of Poe's poetic work—including such poems as "Romance," "Israfel," the earlier poem entitled "To Helen," "The City in the Sea," and "The Haunted Palace" —is marked by an expression of yearning for an impossible-to-reach ideal, or for lost beauty, magnificence, or love. This aspect of his poetry perhaps receives its most poignant expression in "Annabel Lee," Poe's 1849 lament for his beloved wife, Virginia, who had lingered near death since 1842, finally dying in 1847. This emphasis on lost or unattainable joy and beauty should hardly surprise us, given Poe's sensitive and romantic nature and the many losses and difficulties he suffered, beginning with the early loss of both parents and later including his expulsion from the aristocratic world he knew during his time with the Allans. Poems such as "Israfel" and "Annabel Lee" treat these issues indirectly, in the form of romantic allegories.

Less well known are Poe's poems that more directly examine his experiences of isolation and loss. His early poem "Alone," for example, unpublished during his lifetime (it first appeared in 1875), begins with a declaration of his difference and sense of exclusion. This poignant, self-exploratory quality is maintained in such poems as "To My Mother," his verse tribute to Maria Clemm, his paternal aunt and the mother of his then recently deceased wife, Virginia.

The body of poetry Poe produced in his busy, all-too-brief life remains a unique accomplishment. Although the worlds Poe created in his poems carry us far away from early-nineteenth-century America, they speak to an unappeasable yearning for tangible security, acceptance, and happiness that many share. The verses remain alive as imaginative verbal experiments. And they reflect a desire for beauty and stability, which were especially compelling ideals in a life filled with misery and mutability.

FURTHER READING

Eric W. Carlson, ed. *A Companion to Poe Studies*. Westport, Conn.: Greenwood Press, 1996.
Thomas Ollive Mabbott, ed. *The Collected Works of Edgar Allan Poe—Volume I: Poems*. Cambridge: Harvard University Press, 1969.
A. Hobson Quinn. *Edgar Allan Poe: A Critical Biography*. New York: D. Appleton-Century, 1941.
www.eapoe.org/index.htm (website of The Edgar Allan Poe Society of Baltimore).

[Alone]

From childhood's hour I have not been
As others were—I have not seen
As others saw—I could not bring
My passions from a common spring—
From the same source I have not taken
My sorrow—I could not awaken
My heart to joy at the same tone—
And all I lov'd—*I* lov'd alone—
Then—in my childhood—in the dawn
Of a most stormy life—was drawn
From ev'ry depth of good and ill
The mystery which binds me still—
From the torrent, or the fountain—
From the red cliff of the mountain—
From the sun that 'round me roll'd
In its autumn tint of gold—
From the lightning in the sky
As it pass'd me flying by—
From the thunder, and the storm—
And the cloud that took the form
(When the rest of Heaven was blue)
Of a demon in my view—

1875

Untitled in manuscript, "[Alone]" was composed circa 1829.

Sonnet—To Science

Science! meet daughter of old Time thou art
   Who alterest all things with thy peering eyes!
Why prey'st thou thus upon the poet's heart,
   Vulture! whose wings are dull realities!
How should he love thee—or how deem thee wise
   Who woulds't not leave him, in his wandering,
To seek for treasure in the jewell'd skies
   Albeit, he soar with an undaunted wing?
Hast thou not dragg'd Diana[1] from her car,
   And driv'n the Hamadryad[2] from the wood
To seek a shelter in some happier star?
   The gentle Naiad[3] from her fountain-flood?
The elfin from the green grass? and from me
   The summer dream beneath the shrubbery?

                  1829

Romance

1

Romance who loves to nod and sing
With drowsy head and folded wing
Among the green leaves as they shake
Far down within some shadowy lake
To me a painted paroquet
Hath been—a most familiar bird—
Taught me my alphabet to say—
To lisp my very earliest word
While in the wild wood I did lie
A child—with a most knowing eye.

2

Of late, eternal Condor years
So shake the very air on high
With tumult, as they thunder by,
I hardly have had time for cares

---

1. The Roman goddess of the hunt, celebrated for her chastity and identified with the moon (her car).

2. A tree nymph, in Greek myth.
3. A nymph of a fountain or stream.

Thro' gazing on th' unquiet sky!
And, when an hour with calmer wings
Its down upon my spirit flings—
That little time with lyre and rhyme
To while away—forbidden things!
My heart would feel to be a crime
Did it not tremble with the strings!

1829

To Helen

Helen, thy beauty is to me
    Like those Nicean[1] barks of yore,
That gently, o'er a perfumed sea,
    The weary, way-worn wanderer bore
    To his own native shore.

On desperate seas long wont to roam,
    Thy hyacinth[2] hair, thy classic face,
Thy Naiad[3] airs have brought me home
    To the glory that was Greece,
And the grandeur that was Rome.

Lo! in yon brilliant window-niche
    How statue-like I see thee stand,
    The agate lamp within thy hand!
Ah, Psyche,[4] from the regions which
    Are Holy-Land!

1831

According to Greek myth, Helen of Troy was considered the most beautiful of all women. Poe's Helen here was a Richmond woman, Mrs. Jane Stith Stanard, whom Poe idolized and who died in 1824, when Poe was fifteen.

1. Several ancient Greek port cities are named Nicea. A bark is a small sailing ship.
2. A common Homeric epithet referring to black, glossy, curly hair.
3. A fountain nymph.
4. Greek goddess of the soul.

Israfel

And the angel Israfel, whose heart-strings are a lute,
and who has the sweetest voice of all God's creatures.
KORAN[1]

In Heaven a spirit doth dwell
   "Whose heart-strings are a lute;"
None sing so wildly well
As the angel Israfel,
And the giddy stars (so legends tell)
Ceasing their hymns, attend the spell
   Of his voice, all mute.

Tottering above
   In her highest noon,
   The enamoured moon
Blushed with love
   While, to listen, the red levin[2]
   (With the rapid Pleiads,[3] even,
   Which were seven,)
   Pauses in Heaven.

And they say (the starry choir
   And the other listening things)
That Israfeli's fire
Is owing to that lyre
   By which he sits and sings —
The trembling living wire
Of those unusual strings.

But the skies that angel trod,
   Where deep thoughts are a duty —
Where Love's a grown-up God —
   Where the Houri[4] glances are
Imbued with all the beauty
   Which we worship in a star.

*   *   *

1. Poe's actual source is not the Koran but George Sale's "Preliminary Discourse" to his translation of the Koran (1734), which Poe may have found quoted by Thomas Moore in a footnote to *Lalla Rookh* (1817).

2. Lightning.
3. The Pleiades, a cluster of seven stars located in the constellation Taurus.
4. Lovely virgins in the Islamic paradise for the devout.

Therefore, thou art not wrong,
   Israfeli, who despisest
An unimpassioned song;
To thee the laurels belong,
   Best bard, because the wisest!
Merrily live, and long!

The ecstasies above
   With thy burning measures suit —
Thy grief, thy joy, thy hate, thy love,
   With the fervour of thy lute —
   Well may the stars be mute!

Yes, Heaven is thine; but this
   Is a world of sweets and sours;
   Our flowers are merely — flowers,
And the shadow of thy perfect bliss
   Is the sunshine of ours.

If I could dwell
Where Israfel
   Hath dwelt, and he where I,
He might not sing so wildly well
   A mortal melody,
While a bolder note than this might swell
   From my lyre within the sky.

                1831

The City in the Sea

Lo! Death has reared himself a throne
In a strange city lying alone
Far down within the dim West,
Where the good and the bad and the worst and the best
Have gone to their eternal rest.
There shrines and palaces and towers
(Time-eaten towers that tremble not!)
Resemble nothing that is ours.
Around, by lifting winds forgot,
Resignedly beneath the sky
The melancholy waters lie.

*   *   *

No rays from the holy heaven come down
On the long night-time of that town;
But light from out the lurid sea
Streams up the turrets silently—
Gleams up the pinnacles far and free—
Up domes—up spire—up kingly halls—
Up fanes¹—up Babylon-like² walls—
Up shadowy long-forgotten bowers
Of sculptured ivy and stone flowers—
Up many and many a marvellous shrine
Whose wréathed friezes intertwine
The viol, the violet, and the vine.

Resignedly beneath the sky
The melancholy waters lie.
So blend the turrets and shadows there
That all seem pendulous in air,
While from a proud tower in the town
Death looks gigantically down.

There open fanes and gaping graves
Yawn level with the luminous waves;
But not the riches there that lie
In each idol's diamond eye—
Not the gaily-jewelled dead
Tempt the waters from their bed;
For no ripples curl, alas!
Along that wilderness of glass—
No swellings tell that winds may be
Upon some far-off happier sea—
No heavings hint that winds have been
On seas less hideously serene.

But lo, a stir is in the air!
The wave—there is a movement there!
As if the towers had thrust aside,
In slightly sinking, the dull tide—
As if their tops had feebly given

1. Temples.
2. In the Bible, a beautiful yet wicked and doomed city.

A void within the filmy Heaven.
The waves have now a redder glow—
The hours are breathing faint and low—
And when, amid no earthly moans,
Down, down that town shall settle hence,
Hell, rising from a thousand thrones,
Shall do it reverence.

1831

The Haunted Palace

In the greenest of our valleys
    By good angels tenanted,
Once a fair and stately palace—
    Radiant palace—reared its head.
In the monarch Thought's dominion—
    It stood there!
Never seraph[1] spread a pinion
    Over fabric half so fair!

Banners yellow, glorious, golden,
    On its roof did float and flow—
(This—all this—was in the olden
    Time long ago)
And every gentle air that dallied,
    In that sweet day,
Along the ramparts plumed and pallid,
    A wingéd odor went away.

Wanderers in that happy valley,
    Through two luminous windows, saw
Spirits moving musically,
    To a lute's well-tunéd law,
Round about a throne where, sitting,
    Porphyrogene,[2]
In state his glory well befitting
    The ruler of the realm was seen.

1. Angel of the highest order.
2. An offspring of royalty (*porphyro* is Greek for purple, the royal color).

   *   *   *

And all with pearl and ruby glowing
    Was the fair palace door,
Through which came flowing, flowing, flowing,
    And sparkling evermore,
A troop of Echoes whose sweet duty
    Was but to sing,
In voices of surpassing beauty,
    The wit and wisdom of their king.

But evil things, in robes of sorrow,
    Assailed the monarch's high estate.
(Ah, let us mourn!—for never morrow
    Shall dawn upon him, desolate!)
And round about his home the glory
    That blushed and bloomed,
Is but a dim-remembered story
    Of the old-time entombed.

And travellers, now, within that valley,
    Through the encrimsoned windows see
Vast forms that move fantastically
    To a discordant melody,
While, like a ghastly rapid river,
    Through the pale door
A hideous throng rush out forever
    And laugh—but smile no more.

               1838

The Raven

Once upon a midnight dreary, while I pondered, weak and weary,
Over many a quaint and curious volume of forgotten lore,
While I nodded, nearly napping, suddenly there came a tapping,
As of some one gently rapping, rapping at my chamber door.
" 'Tis some visiter," I muttered, "tapping at my chamber door—
           Only this, and nothing more."

Ah, distinctly I remember it was in the bleak December,
And each separate dying ember wrought its ghost upon the floor.
Eagerly I wished the morrow;—vainly I had sought to borrow

From my books surcease of sorrow — sorrow for the lost Lenore —
For the rare and radiant maiden whom the angels name Lenore —
    Nameless here for evermore.

And the silken sad uncertain rustling of each purple curtain
Thrilled me — filled me with fantastic terrors never felt before;
So that now, to still the beating of my heart, I stood repeating
" 'Tis some visiter entreating entrance at my chamber door —
Some late visiter entreating entrance at my chamber door; —
    This it is, and nothing more."

Presently my soul grew stronger; hesitating then no longer,
"Sir," said I, "or Madam, truly your forgiveness I implore;
But the fact is I was napping, and so gently you came rapping,
And so faintly you came tapping, tapping at my chamber door,
That I scarce was sure I heard you" — here I opened wide the door; —
    Darkness there and nothing more.

Deep into that darkness peering, long I stood there wondering, fearing,
Doubting, dreaming dreams no mortal ever dared to dream before;
But the silence was unbroken, and the darkness gave no token,
And the only word there spoken was the whispered word, "Lenore!"
This I whispered, and an echo murmured back the word, "Lenore!" —
    Merely this, and nothing more.

Back into the chamber turning, all my soul within me burning,
Soon I heard again a tapping somewhat louder than before.
"Surely," said I, "surely that is something at my window lattice;
Let me see, then, what thereat is, and this mystery explore —
Let my heart be still a moment and this mystery explore; —
    'Tis the wind and nothing more!"

Open here I flung the shutter, when, with many a flirt and flutter,
In there stepped a stately raven of the saintly days of yore;
Not the least obeisance made he; not an instant stopped or stayed he;
But, with mien of lord or lady, perched above my chamber door —
Perched upon a bust of Pallas[1] just above my chamber door —
    Perched, and sat, and nothing more.

Then this ebony bird beguiling my sad fancy into smiling,
By the grave and stern decorum of the countenance it wore,
"Though thy crest be shorn and shaven, thou," I said, "art sure no craven,

---

1. Pallas Athena, Greek goddess of wisdom.

Ghastly grim and ancient raven wandering from the Nightly shore—
Tell me what thy lordly name is on the Night's Plutonian[2] shore!"
                    Quoth the raven "Nevermore."

Much I marvelled this ungainly fowl to hear discourse so plainly,
Though its answer little meaning—little relevancy bore;
For we cannot help agreeing that no living human being
Ever yet was blessed with seeing bird above his chamber door —
Bird or beast upon the sculptured bust above his chamber door,
                    With such name as "Nevermore."

But the raven, sitting lonely on the placid bust, spoke only
That one word, as if his soul in that one word he did outpour.
Nothing farther then he uttered—not a feather then he fluttered—
Till I scarcely more than muttered "Other friends have flown before—
On the morrow *he* will leave me, as my hopes have flown before."
                    Then the bird said "Nevermore."

Startled at the stillness broken by reply so aptly spoken,
"Doubtless," said I, "what it utters is its only stock and store
Caught from some unhappy master whom unmerciful Disaster
Followed fast and followed faster till his songs one burden bore—
Till the dirges of his Hope that melancholy burden bore
                    Of 'Never—nevermore.'"

But the raven still beguiling all my sad soul into smiling,
Straight I wheeled a cushioned seat in front of bird, and bust and door;
Then, upon the velvet sinking, I betook myself to linking
Fancy unto fancy, thinking what this ominous bird of yore—
What this grim, ungainly, ghastly, gaunt and ominous bird of yore
                    Meant in croaking "Nevermore."

This I sat engaged in guessing, but no syllable expressing
To the fowl whose fiery eyes now burned into my bosom's core;
This and more I sat divining, with my head at ease reclining
On the cushion's velvet lining that the lamplight gloated[3] o'er,
But whose velvet violet lining with the lamplight gloating o'er,
                    She shall press, ah, nevermore!

Then, methought, the air grew denser, perfumed from an unseen censer
Swung by Angels whose faint foot-falls tinkled on the tufted floor.

2. Of the realm of Pluto, Roman god of the king-   3. Rare term for refracted light.
dom of death.

"Wretch," I cried, "thy God hath lent thee—by these angels he hath sent thee
Respite—respite and nepenthe[4] from thy memories of Lenore;
Quaff, oh quaff this kind nepenthe and forget this lost Lenore!"
                    Quoth the raven, "Nevermore."

"Prophet!" said I, "thing of evil!—prophet still, if bird or devil!—
Whether Tempter sent, or whether tempest tossed thee here ashore,
Desolate yet all undaunted, on this desert land enchanted—
On this home by Horror haunted—tell me truly, I implore—
Is there—*is* there balm in Gilead?[5]—tell me—tell me, I implore!"
                    Quoth the raven, "Nevermore."

"Prophet!" said I, "thing of evil—prophet still, if bird or devil!
By that Heaven that bends above us—by that God we both adore—
Tell this soul with sorrow laden if, within the distant Aidenn,[6]
It shall clasp a sainted maiden whom the angels name Lenore—
Clasp a rare and radiant maiden whom the angels name Lenore."
                    Quoth the raven, "Nevermore."

"Be that word our sign of parting, bird or fiend!" I shrieked, upstarting—
"Get thee back into the tempest and the Night's Plutonian shore!
Leave no black plume as a token of that lie thy soul hath spoken!
Leave my loneliness unbroken!—quit the bust above my door!
Take thy beak from out my heart, and take thy form from off my door!"
                    Quoth the raven, "Nevermore."

And the raven, never flitting, still is sitting, still is sitting
On the pallid bust of Pallas just above my chamber door;
And his eyes have all the seeming of a demon's that is dreaming,
And the lamp-light o'er him streaming throws his shadow on the floor;
And my soul from out that shadow that lies floating on the floor
                    Shall be lifted—nevermore!

                                                            1845

Our text is taken from the poem's first book publication, in *The Raven and Other Poems*
(1845). See "The Philosophy of Composition" for Poe's account of the origins of "The
Raven."

4. In Homer and Milton, a magic potion that   6. Variant spelling of Eden.
makes persons forget their woes.
5. See Jeremiah 8:22: "Is there no balm in
Gilead?"

Ulalume

A BALLAD

The skies they were ashen and sober;
    The leaves they were crispéd and sere —
    The leaves they were withering and sere;
It was night in the lonesome October
    Of my most immemorial[1] year;
It was hard by the dim lake of Auber,
    In the misty mid region of Weir[2] —
It was down by the dank tarn[3] of Auber.
    In the ghoul-haunted woodland of Weir.

Here once, through an alley Titanic,
    Of cypress, I roamed with my Soul —
    Of cypress, with Psyche,[4] my Soul.
These were days when my heart was volcanic
    As the scoriac[5] rivers that roll —
    As the lavas that restlessly roll
Their sulphurous currents down Yaanek[6]
    In the ultimate climes of the pole —
That groan as they roll down Mount Yaanek
    In the realms of the Boreal[7] Pole.

Our talk had been serious and sober,
    But our thoughts they were palsied and sere —
    Our memories were treacherous and sere —
For we knew not the month was October,
    And we marked not the night of the year —
    (Ah, night of all nights in the year!)
We noted not the dim lake of Auber —
    (Though once we had journeyed down here) —
We remembered not the dank tarn of Auber,
    Nor the ghoul-haunted woodland of Weir.

      *   *   *

1. Impossible to be remembered precisely. Poe stretches the standard denotation ("extending back beyond historical memory").
2. Auber and Weir, like Ulalume, are poetic names apparently invented by Poe, though they were possibly inspired by the names of Romantic composer Daniel Auber and landscape artist Robert Weir.
3. Small mountain lake or pool.
4. Greek personification of the soul.
5. Scoriaceous, that is, slag and cinderlike, lava.
6. An active volcano (the name is Poe's invention).
7. Northern.

And now, as the night was senescent[8]
  And star-dials pointed to morn—
  As the star-dials hinted to morn—
At the end of our path a liquescent
  And nebulous lustre was born,
Out of which a miraculous crescent
  Arose with a duplicate horn—
Astarte's[9] bediamonded crescent
  Distinct with its duplicate horn.

And I said—"She is warmer than Dian:[10]
  She rolls through an ether of sighs—
  She revels in a region of sighs:
She has seen that the tears are not dry on
  These cheeks, where the worm never dies,
And has come past the stars of the Lion[11]
  To point us the path to the skies—
  To the Lethean[12] peace of the skies—
Come up, in despite of the Lion
  To shine on us with her bright eyes—
Come up through the lair of the Lion
  With Love in her luminous eyes."

But Psyche, uplifting her finger,
  Said—"Sadly this star I mistrust—
  Her pallor I strangely mistrust:—
Oh, hasten!—oh, let us not linger!
  Oh, fly!—let us fly!—for we must."
In terror she spoke, letting sink her
  Wings till they trailed in the dust—
In agony sobbed, letting sink her
  Plumes till they trailed in the dust—
  Till they sorrowfully trailed in the dust.

I replied—"This is nothing but dreaming:
  Let us on by this tremulous light!
  Let us bathe in the crystalline light!

---

8. Growing old, aging.
9. Phoenician goddess of love and the moon, known by her crescent horn.
10. Diana, chaste goddess of the moon in Roman mythology.
11. Constellation Leo (the Lion), here suggesting a danger in the zodiac.
12. Promoting forgetfulness. In Greek myth, Lethe was a river in Hades. Those who drank from it forgot their earthly existence.

Its Sybillic[13] splendor is beaming
　　With Hope and in Beauty to-night:—
　　See!—it flickers up the sky through the night!
Ah, we safely may trust to its gleaming,
　　And be sure it will lead us aright—
We safely may trust to a gleaming
　　That cannot but guide us aright,
　　Since it flickers up to Heaven through the night."

Thus I pacified Psyche and kissed her,
　　And tempted her out of her gloom—
　　And conquered her scruples and gloom:
And we passed to the end of the vista,
　　And were stopped by the door of a tomb—
　　By the door of a legended tomb;
And I said—"What is written, sweet sister,
　　On the door of this legended tomb?
She replied—"Ulalume—Ulalume—
　　'Tis the vault of thy lost Ulalume!"

Then my heart it grew ashen and sober
　　As the leaves that were crispéd and sere—
　　As the leaves that were withering and sere,
And I cried—"It was surely October
　　On *this* very night of last year,
　　That I journeyed—I journeyed down here—
That I brought a dread burden down here—
　　On this night of all nights in the year,
　　Ah, what demon has tempted me here?
Well I know, now, this dim lake of Auber,
　　This misty mid region of Weir—
Well I know, now, this dank tarn of Auber,
　　In the ghoul-haunted woodland of Weir."

Said *we*, then—the two, then—"Ah, can it
　　Have been that the woodlandish ghouls—
　　The pitiful, the merciful ghouls—
To bar up our way and to ban it
　　From the secret that lies in these wolds[14]—

13. Prophetic. In Greek myth, the Sibyl was a　14. An open, hilly district.
prophetess able to predict the future.

From the thing that lies hidden in these wolds—
Had drawn up the spectre of a planet
From the limbo[15] of lunary souls—
This sinfully scintillant[16] planet
From the Hell of the planetary souls?"

1847

Ulalume, pronounced "yóu-la-loom," is a name invented by Poe that may echo the Latin *ululare*: to wail. The poem may be read purely as a metrical experiment, but it may also be read as an imaginative re-creation of the disorientation and depression caused by his wife's death earlier in the year of its composition, 1847.

Eldorado

Gaily bedight,[1]
A gallant knight,
In sunshine and in shadow,
Had journeyed long,
Singing a song,
In search of Eldorado.[2]

But he grew old—
This knight so bold—
And o'er his heart a shadow
Fell, as he found
No spot of ground
That looked like Eldorado.

And, as his strength
Failed him at length,
He met a pilgrim shadow—
"Shadow," said he,
"Where can it be—
This land of Eldorado?"

*　*　*

15. In Dante's *Inferno*, a place on the outer rim of hell containing the souls of the just but unbaptized.
16. Glittering, sparkling.
1. Appareled, dressed.
2. Literally, *el dorado* means, in Spanish, the golden or the gilded; figuratively, the place of gold or the golden city. In 1542 the Spanish explorer Hernando de Soto, already immensely wealthy from his leadership role in the conquest of the Incas, died of fever during an expedition through the American South—from present-day Florida to Louisiana and Texas—in search of a mythic city of gold.

"Over the Mountains
       Of the Moon,
Down the Valley of the Shadow,
       Ride, boldly ride,"
       The shade replied,—
"If you seek for Eldorado!"

                    1849

To Helen

I saw thee once—once only—years ago:
I must not say how many—but not many.
It was a July midnight; and from out
A full-orbed moon, that, like thine own soul, soaring,
Sought a precipitate pathway up through heaven,
There fell a silvery-silken veil of light,
With quietude, and sultriness, and slumber,
Upon the upturned faces of a thousand
Roses that grew in an enchanted garden,
Where no wind dared to stir, unless on tiptoe—
Fell on the upturn'd faces of these roses
That gave out, in return for the love-light,
Their odorous souls in an ecstatic death—
Fell on the upturn'd faces of these roses
That smiled and died in this parterre, enchanted
By thee, and by the poetry of thy presence.

Clad all in white, upon a violet bank
I saw thee half reclining; while the moon
Fell on the upturn'd faces of the roses,
And on thine own, upturn'd—alas, in sorrow!
Was it not Fate, that, on this July midnight—
Was it not Fate, (whose name is also Sorrow,)
That bade me pause before that garden-gate,
To breathe the incense of those slumbering roses?
No footstep stirred: the hated world all slept,
Save only thee and me. (Oh, Heaven!—oh, God!
How my heart beats in coupling those two words!)

Save only thee and me. I paused—I looked—
And in an instant all things disappeared.
(Ah, bear in mind this garden was enchanted!)

The pearly lustre of the moon went out:
The mossy banks and the meandering paths,
The happy flowers and the repining trees,
Were seen no more: the very roses' odors
Died in the arms of the adoring airs.
All—all expired save thee—save less than thou:
Save only the divine light in thine eyes—
Save but the soul in thine uplifted eyes.
I saw but them—they were the world to me!
I saw but them—saw only them for hours,
Saw only them until the moon went down.
What wild heart-histories seemed to lie enwritten
Upon those crystalline, celestial spheres!
How dark a woe, yet how sublime a hope!
How silently serene a sea of pride!
How daring an ambition; yet how deep—
How fathomless a capacity for love!

But now, at length, dear Dian² sank from sight,
Into a western couch of thunder-cloud;
And thou, a ghost, amid the entombing trees
Didst glide away. Only thine eyes remained;
They would not go—they never yet have gone;
Lighting my lonely pathway home that night,
They have not left me (as my hopes have) since;
They follow me—they lead me through the years.
They are my ministers—yet I their slave.
Their office is to illumine and enkindle—
My duty, to be saved by their bright light,
And purified in their electric fire,
And sanctified in their elysian fire.
They fill my soul with Beauty (which is Hope),
And are far up in Heaven—the stars I kneel to
In the sad, silent watches of my night;
While even in the meridian glare of day
I see them still—two sweetly scintillant
Venuses, unextinguished by the sun!

1849

2. Diana, Roman goddess of the moon.

The poem is addressed to Sarah Helen Whitman, a widowed poet noted for her bea whom Poe courted after the death of his wife, Virginia. When Poe wrote the poem and scribed their one fleeting encounter in a moon-lit rose garden after Poe had given a read ... to a literary society in her native city of Providence, Rhode Island, he had not seen Helen, as she was known to her friends, for many years. Poe was aware of Whitman's potential interest because of her poem in tribute to his "The Raven," included in this anthology. After Poe sent "To Helen" to Whitman, they began a romance that led to their engagement, which Whitman later broke off when Poe could not keep his vows of temperance. But she retained a strong sense of loyalty to Poe and his poetry and became his most eloquent defender after his death.

To My Mother

Because I feel that, in the Heavens above,
    The angels, whispering to one another,
Can find, among their burning terms of love,
    None so devotional as that of "Mother,"
Therefore by that dear name I long have called you—
    You who are more than mother unto me,
And fill my heart of hearts, where Death installed you
    In setting my Virginia's spirit free.
My mother—my own mother, who died early,
    Was but the mother of myself; but you
Are mother to the one I loved so dearly,
    And thus are dearer than the mother I knew
By that infinity with which my wife
    Was dearer to my soul than its soul-life.

1849

Poe lost his birth mother when he was two years old, and many of his poems and stories suggest the search for a maternal figure. This poem is addressed to Poe's beloved mother-in-law and aunt, Maria Clemm, with whom he continued to share a cottage in Fordham, New York, after the death of his wife, Virginia.

The Bells

1

Hear the sledges with the bells—
    Silver bells!
What a world of merriment their melody foretells!
    How they tinkle, tinkle, tinkle,

In the icy air of night!
While the stars that oversprinkle
All the Heavens, seem to twinkle
With a crystalline delight:
Keeping time, time, time,
In a sort of Runic rhyme,
To the tintinabulation that so musically wells
From the bells, bells, bells, bells,
Bells, bells, bells—
From the jingling and the tinkling of the bells.

2

Hear the mellow wedding bells—
Golden bells!
What a world of happiness their harmony foretells!
Through the balmy air of night
How they ring out their delight!—
From the molten-golden notes
And all in tune,
What a liquid ditty floats
To the turtle-dove that listens while she gloats
On the moon!
Oh, from out the sounding cells
What a gush of euphony voluminously wells!
How it swells!
How it dwells
On the Future!—how it tells
Of the rapture that impels
To the swinging and the ringing
Of the bells, bells, bells!—
Of the bells, bells, bells, bells,
Bells, bells, bells—
To the rhyming and the chiming of the bells!

3

Hear the loud alarum bells—
Brazen bells!
What tale of terror, now, their turbulency tells!
In the startled ear of Night
How they scream out their affright!
Too much horrified to speak,

They can only shriek, shriek,
Out of tune,
In a clamorous appealing to the mercy of the fire—
In a mad expostulation with the deaf and frantic fire,
Leaping higher, higher, higher,
With a desperate desire
And a resolute endeavor
Now—now to sit, or never,
By the side of the pale-faced moon.
Oh, the bells, bells, bells!
What a tale their terror tells
Of despair!
How they clang and clash and roar!
What a horror they outpour
In the bosom of the palpitating air!
Yet the ear, it fully knows,
By the twanging
And the clanging,
How the danger ebbs and flows:—
Yes, the ear distinctly tells,
In the jangling
And the wrangling,
How the danger sinks and swells,
By the sinking or the swelling in the anger of the bells—
Of the bells—
Of the bells, bells, bells, bells,
Bells, bells, bells—
In the clamor and the clangor of the bells.

4
Hear the tolling of the bells—
Iron bells!
What a world of solemn thought their monody compels!
In the silence of the night
How we shiver with affright
At the melancholy meaning of their tone!
For every sound that floats
From the rust within their throats
Is a groan.
And the people—ah, the people
They that dwell up in the steeple

> All alone,
> And who, tolling, tolling, tolling,
> In that muffled monotone,
> Feel a glory in so rolling
> On the human heart a stone—
> They are neither man nor woman—
> They are neither brute nor human,
> They are Ghouls:—
> And their king it is who tolls:—
> And he rolls, rolls, rolls, rolls
> A Paean from the bells!
> And his merry bosom swells
> With the Paean of the bells!
> And he dances and he yells;
> Keeping time, time, time,
> In a sort of Runic rhyme,
> To the Paean of the bells—
> Of the bells:—
> Keeping time, time, time,
> In a sort of Runic rhyme,
> To the throbbing of the bells—
> Of the bells, bells, bells—
> To the sobbing of the bells:—
> Keeping time, time, time,
> As he knells, knells, knells,
> In a happy Runic rhyme,
> To the rolling of the bells—
> Of the bells, bells, bells:—
> To the tolling of the bells—
> Of the bells, bells, bells, bells,
> Bells, bells, bells—
> To the moaning and the groaning of the bells.

1849

Annabel Lee

> It was many and many a year ago,
> In a kingdom by the sea,
> That a maiden there lived whom you may know
> By the name of Annabel Lee;—
> And this maiden she lived with no other thought
> Than to love and be loved by me.

* * *

I was a child and *she* was a child,
    In this kingdom by the sea;
But we loved with a love that was more than love—
    I and my Annabel Lee—
With a love that the wingéd seraphs in Heaven
    Coveted her and me.

And this was the reason that, long ago,
    In this kingdom by the sea,
A wind blew out of a cloud, chilling
    My beautiful Annabel Lee;
So that her highborn kinsmen came
    And bore her away from me,
To shut her up in a sepulchre
    In this kingdom by the sea.

The angels, not half so happy in heaven,
    Went envying her and me—
Yes!—that was the reason (as all men know,
    In this kingdom by the sea)
That the wind came out of the cloud by night,
    Chilling and killing my Annabel Lee.

But our love it was stronger by far than the love
    Of those who were older than we—
    Of many far wiser than we—
And neither the angels in Heaven above,
    Nor the demons down under the sea,
Can ever dissever my soul from the soul
    Of the beautiful Annabel Lee:—

For the moon never beams, without bringing me dreams
    Of the beautiful Annabel Lee;
And the stars never rise, but I feel the bright eyes
    Of the beautiful Annabel Lee:—
And so, all the night-tide, I lie down by the side
Of my darling—my darling—my life and my bride,
    In her sepulchre there by the sea—
    In her tomb by the sounding sea.

1849

PROSE

Many critics have doubted the literal accuracy of Poe's following account of the composition of "The Raven," and he himself conceded privately that it was largely fictional. But Poe's essay remains important. As a description of many effects that Poe strove for and achieved in "The Raven," it remains richly suggestive. It also shows an attention to the interconnection of the details of literary form that was at the time rare in criticism. And it gives us insight into the way in which Poe wished to be perceived—as a calculating, highly rational creator who was in complete control of the works he created.

The Philosophy of Composition

Charles Dickens, in a note now lying before me, alluding to an examination I once made of the mechanism of "Barnaby Rudge," says—"By the way, are you aware that Godwin wrote his 'Caleb Williams' backwards?[1] He first involved his hero in a web of difficulties, forming the second volume, and then, for the first, cast about him for some mode of accounting for what had been done."

I cannot think this the *precise* mode of procedure on the part of Godwin—and indeed what he himself acknowledges, is not altogether in accordance with Mr. Dickens' idea—but the author of "Caleb Williams" was too good an artist not to perceive the advantage derivable from at least a somewhat similar process. Nothing is more clear than that every plot, worth the name, must be elaborated to its *dénouement* before any thing be attempted with the pen. It is only with the *dénouement* constantly in view that we can give a plot its indispensable air of consequence, or causation, by making the incidents, and especially the tone at all points, tend to the development of the intention.

There is a radical error, I think, in the usual mode of constructing a story. Either history affords a thesis—or one is suggested by an incident of the day—or, at best, the author sets himself to work in the combination of striking events to form merely the basis of his narrative—designing, generally, to fill in with description, dialogue, or autorial comment, whatever crevices of fact, or action, may, from page to page, render themselves apparent.

I prefer commencing with the consideration of an *effect*. Keeping originality *always* in view—for he is false to himself who ventures to dispense with so obvious and so easily attainable a source of interest—I say to myself, in the first place,

---

1. Dickens had been much impressed by Poe's ability to guess, in print, the ending of the former's serialized romantic novel *Barnaby Rudge* (1841) before it appeared. Poe quotes from their subsequent correspondence about novelistic construction. *Caleb Williams* (1794), a novel by William Godwin, was an early work in the field of crime and detection. Godwin was the father (and Mary Wollstonecraft the mother) of Mary Shelley, author of *Frankenstein* (1818).

"Of the innumerable effects, or impressions, of which the heart, the intellect, or (more generally) the soul is susceptible, what one shall I, on the present occasion, select?" Having chosen a novel, first, and secondly a vivid effect, I consider whether it can best be wrought by incident or tone—whether by ordinary incidents and peculiar tone, or the converse, or by peculiarity both of incident and tone—afterward looking about me (or rather within) for such combinations of event, or tone, as shall best aid me in the construction of the effect.

I have often thought how interesting a magazine paper might be written by any author who would—that is to say, who could—detail, step by step, the processes by which any one of his compositions attained its ultimate point of completion. Why such a paper has never been given to the world, I am much at a loss to say—but, perhaps, the autorial vanity has had more to do with the omission than any one other cause. Most writers—poets in especial—prefer having it understood that they compose by a species of fine frenzy—an ecstatic intuition—and would positively shudder at letting the public take a peep behind the scenes, at the elaborate and vacillating crudities of thought—at the true purposes seized only at the last moment—at the innumerable glimpses of idea that arrived not at the maturity of full view—at the fully matured fancies discarded in despair as unmanageable—at the cautious selections and rejections—at the painful erasures and interpolations—in a word, at the wheels and pinions—the tackle for scene-shifting—the step-ladders, and demon-traps—the cock's feathers, the red paint and the black patches, which, in ninety-nine cases out of the hundred, constitute the properties of the literary *histrio*.

I am aware, on the other hand, that the case is by no means common, in which an author is at all in condition to retrace the steps by which his conclusions have been attained. In general, suggestions, having arisen pell-mell, are pursued and forgotten in a similar manner.

For my own part, I have neither sympathy with the repugnance alluded to, nor, at any time, the least difficulty in recalling to mind the progressive steps of any of my compositions; and, since the interest of an analysis, or reconstruction, such as I have considered a *desideratum*, is quite independent of any real or fancied interest in the thing analysed, it will not be regarded as a breach of decorum on my part to show the *modus operandi* by which some one of my own works was put together. I select "The Raven" as most generally known. It is my design to render it manifest that no one point in its composition is referrible either to accident or intuition—that the work proceeded step by step, to its completion with the precision and rigid consequence of a mathematical problem.

Let us dismiss, as irrelevant to the poem *per se*, the circumstance—or say the necessity—which, in the first place, gave rise to the intention of composing *a* poem that should suit at once the popular and the critical taste.

We commence, then, with this intention.

The initial consideration was that of extent. If any literary work is too long to be read at one sitting, we must be content to dispense with the immensely important effect derivable from unity of impression—for, if two sittings be required, the affairs of the world interfere, and every thing like totality is at once destroyed. But since, *ceteris paribus*, no poet can afford to dispense with *any thing* that may advance his design, it but remains to be seen whether there is, in extent, any advantage to counterbalance the loss of unity which attends it. Here I say no, at once. What we term a long poem is, in fact, merely a succession of brief ones— that is to say, of brief poetical effects. It is needless to demonstrate that a poem is such, only inasmuch as it intensely excites, by elevating the soul; and all intense excitements are, through a psychal necessity, brief. For this reason, at least, one half of the "Paradise Lost" is essentially prose—a succession of poetical excitements interspersed, *inevitably*, with corresponding depressions—the whole being deprived, through the extremeness of its length, of the vastly important artistic element, totality, or unity, of effect.

It appears evident, then, that there is a distinct limit, as regards length, to all works of literary art—the limit of a single sitting—and that, although in certain classes of prose composition, such as "Robinson Crusoe," (demanding no unity), this limit may be advantageously overpassed, it can never properly be overpassed in a poem. Within this limit, the extent of a poem may be made to bear mathematical relation to its merit—in other words, to the excitement or elevation— again in other words, to the degree of the true poetical effect which it is capable of inducing; for it is clear that the brevity must be in direct ratio of the intensity of the intended effect:—this, with one proviso—that a certain degree of duration is absolutely requisite for the production of any effect at all.

Holding in view these considerations, as well as that degree of excitement which I deemed not above the popular, while not below the critical, taste, I reached at once what I conceived the proper *length* for my intended poem— a length of about one hundred lines. It is, in fact, a hundred and eight.

My next thought concerned the choice of an impression, or effect, to be conveyed: and here I may as well observe that, throughout the construction, I kept steadily in view the design of rendering the work *universally* appreciable. I should be carried too far out of my immediate topic were I to demonstrate a point upon which I have repeatedly insisted, and which, with the poetical, stands not in the slightest need of demonstration—the point, I mean, that Beauty is the sole legitimate province of the poem. A few words, however, in elucidation of my real meaning, which some of my friends have evinced a disposition to misrepresent. That pleasure which is at once the most intense, the most elevating, and the most pure, is, I believe, found in the contemplation of the beautiful. When, indeed, men speak of Beauty, they mean, precisely, not a quality, as is supposed, but an effect—they refer, in short, just to that intense and pure elevation of *soul—not* of intellect, or of heart—upon which I have commented, and which is experienced in consequence of contemplating "the beautiful." Now I designate Beauty as the province of the poem, merely because it is an obvious rule of Art that effects should be made to spring from direct causes—that objects should be attained through means best adapted for their attainment—no one as yet having been weak enough to deny that the peculiar elevation alluded to, is *most readily* attained in the poem. Now the object, Truth, or the satisfaction of the intellect, and the object Passion, or the excitement of the heart, are, although attainable, to a certain extent, in poetry, far more readily attainable in prose. Truth, in fact, demands a precision, and Passion, a *homeliness* (the truly passionate will comprehend me) which are absolutely antagonistic to that Beauty which, I maintain, is the excitement, or pleasurable elevation, of the soul. It by no means follows from any thing here said, that passion, or even truth, may not be introduced, and even profitably introduced, into a poem—for they may serve in elucidation, or aid the general effect, as do discords in music, by contrast—but the true artist will always contrive, first, to tone them into proper subservience to the predominant aim, and, secondly, to enveil them, as far as possible, in that Beauty which is the atmosphere and the essence of the poem.

Regarding, then, Beauty as my province, my next question referred to the *tone* of its highest manifestation—and all experience has shown that this tone is one of *sadness*. Beauty of whatever kind, in its supreme development, invariably excites the sensitive soul to tears. Melancholy is thus the most legitimate of all the poetical tones.

The length, the province, and the tone, being thus determined, I betook myself to ordinary induction, with the view of obtaining some artistic piquancy which might serve me as a key-note in the construction of the poem—some pivot upon which the whole structure might turn. In carefully thinking over all the usual artistic effects—or more properly *points*, in the theatrical sense—I did not fail to perceive immediately that no one had been so universally employed as that of the *refrain*. The universality of its employment sufficed to assure me of its intrinsic value, and spared me the necessity of submitting it to analysis. I considered it, however, with regard to its susceptibility of improvement, and soon saw it to be in a primitive condition. As commonly used, the *refrain*, or burden, not only is limited to lyric verse, but depends for its impression upon the force of monotone—both in sound and thought. The pleasure is deduced solely from the sense of identity—of repetition. I resolved to diversify, and so vastly heighten, the effect, by adhering, in general, to the monotone of sound, while I continually varied that of thought: that is to say, I determined to produce continuously novel effects, by the variation *of the application* of the *refrain*—the *refrain* itself remaining, for the most part, unvaried.

These points being settled, I next bethought me of the *nature* of my *refrain*.

Since its application was to be repeatedly varied, it was clear that the *refrain* itself must be brief, for there would have been an insurmountable difficulty in frequent variations of application in any sentence of length. In proportion to the brevity of the sentence, would, of course, be the facility of the variation. This led me at once to a single word as the best *refrain*.

The question now arose as to the *character* of the word. Having made up my mind to a *refrain*, the division of the poem into stanzas was, of course, a corollary: the *refrain* forming the close to each stanza. That such a close, to have force, must be sonorous and susceptible of protracted emphasis, admitted no doubt: and these considerations inevitably led me to the long *o* as the most sonorous vowel, in connection with *r* as the most producible consonant.

The sound of the *refrain* being thus determined, it became necessary to select a word embodying this sound, and at the same time in the fullest possible keeping with that melancholy which I had predetermined as the tone of the poem. In such a search it would have been absolutely impossible to overlook the word "Nevermore." In fact, it was the very first which presented itself.

The next *desideratum* was a pretext for the continuous use of the one word "nevermore." In observing the difficulty which I had at once found in inventing a sufficiently plausible reason for its continuous repetition, I did not fail to perceive that this difficulty arose solely from the pre-assumption that the word was to be so continuously or monotonously spoken by a *human* being—I did not fail to perceive, in short, that the difficulty lay in the reconciliation of this monotony with the exercise of reason on the part of the creature repeating the word. Here, then, immediately arose the idea of a *non*-reasoning creature capable of speech; and, very naturally, a parrot, in the first instance, suggested itself, but was superseded forthwith by a Raven, as equally capable of speech, and infinitely more in keeping with the intended *tone*.

I had now gone so far as the conception of a Raven—the bird of ill omen—monotonously repeating the one word, "Nevermore," at the conclusion of each stanza, in a poem of melancholy tone, and in length about one hundred lines. Now, never losing sight of the object *supremeness*, or perfection, at all points, I asked myself—"Of all melancholy topics, what, according to the *universal* understanding of mankind, is the *most* melancholy?" Death—was the obvious reply. "And when," I said, "is this most melancholy of topics most poetical?" From what I have already explained at some length, the answer, here also, is obvious "When it most closely allies itself to *Beauty*: the death, then, of a beautiful woman is, unquestionably, the most poetical topic in the world—and equally is it beyond doubt that the lips best suited for such topic are those of a bereaved lover."

I had now to combine the two ideas, of a lover lamenting his deceased mistress and a Raven continuously repeating the word "Nevermore"—I had to combine these, bearing in mind my design of varying, at every turn, the *application* of the word repeated; but the only intelligible mode of such combination is that of imagining the Raven employing the word in answer to the queries of the lover. And here it was that I saw at once the opportunity afforded for the effect on which I had been depending—that is to say, the effect of the *variation of application.* I saw that I could make the first query propounded by the lover—the first query to which the Raven should reply "Nevermore"—that I could make this first query a commonplace one—the second less so—the third still less, and so on—until at length the lover, startled from his original *nonchalance* by the melancholy character of the word itself—by its frequent repetition—and by a consideration of the ominous reputation of the fowl that uttered it—is at length excited to superstition, and wildly propounds queries of a far different character—queries whose solution he has passionately at heart—propounds them half in superstition and half in that species of despair which delights in self-torture—propounds them not altogether because he believes in the prophetic or demoniac character of the bird (which, reason assures him, is merely repeating a lesson learned by rote) but because he experiences a phrenzied pleasure in so modeling his questions as to receive from the *expected* "Nevermore" the most delicious because the most intolerable of sorrow. Perceiving the opportunity thus afforded me—or, more strictly, thus forced upon me in the progress of the construction—I first established in mind the climax, or concluding query—that to which "Nevermore" should be in the last place an answer—that in reply to which this word "Nevermore" should involve the utmost conceivable amount of sorrow and despair.

Here then the poem may be said to have its beginning—at the end, where all works of art should begin—for it was here, at this point of my preconsiderations, that I first put pen to paper in the composition of the stanza:

> "Prophet," said I, "thing of evil! prophet still if bird or devil!
> By that heaven that bends above us—by that God we both adore,
> Tell this soul with sorrow laden, if within the distant Aidenn,
> It shall clasp a sainted maiden whom the angels name Lenore—
> Clasp a rare and radiant maiden whom the angels name Lenore."
> Quoth the raven—"Nevermore."

I composed this stanza, at this point, first that, by establishing the climax, I might the better vary and graduate, as regards seriousness and importance, the preceding queries of the lover—and, secondly, that I might definitely settle the rhythm, the metre, and the length and general arrangement of the stanza—as well as graduate the stanzas which were to precede, so that none of them might surpass this in rhythmical effect. Had I been able, in the subsequent composition, to construct more vigorous stanzas, I should, without scruple, have purposely enfeebled them, so as not to interfere with the climacteric effect.

And here I may as well say a few words of the versification. My first object (as usual) was originality. The extent to which this has been neglected, in versification, is one of the most unaccountable things in the world. Admitting that there is little possibility of variety in mere *rhythm*, it is still clear that the possible varieties of metre and stanza are absolutely infinite—and yet, *for centuries, no man, in verse, has ever done, or ever seemed to think of doing, an original thing*. The fact is, originality (unless in minds of very unusual force) is by no means a matter, as some suppose, of impulse or intuition. In general, to be found, it must be elaborately sought, and although a positive merit of the highest class, demands in its attainment less of invention than negation.

Of course, I pretend to no originality in either the rhythm or metre of the "Raven." The former is trochaic—the latter is octametre acatalectic, alternating with heptameter catalectic repeated in the *refrain* of the fifth verse, and terminating with tetrameter catalectic. Less pedantically—the feet employed throughout (trochees) consist of a long syllable followed by a short: the first line of the stanza consists of eight of these feet—the second of seven and a half (in effect two-thirds)—the third of eight—the fourth of seven and a half—the fifth the same—the sixth three and a half. Now, each of these lines, taken individually, has been employed before, and what originality the "Raven" has, is in their *combination into stanza*; nothing even remotely approaching this combination has ever been attempted. The effect of this originality of combination is aided by other unusual, and some altogether novel effects, arising from an extension of the application of the principles of rhyme and alliteration.

The next point to be considered was the mode of bringing together the lover and the Raven—and the first branch of this consideration was the *locale*. For this the most natural suggestion might seem to be a forest, or the fields—but it has always appeared to me that a close *circumscription of space* is absolutely necessary to the effect of insulated incident:—it has the force of a frame to a picture. It has an indisputable moral power in keeping concentrated the attention, and, of course, must not be confounded with mere unity of place.

I determined, then, to place the lover in his chamber—in a chamber rendered sacred to him by memories of her who had frequented it. The room is represented as richly furnished—this in mere pursuance of the ideas I have already explained on the subject of Beauty, as the sole true poetical thesis.

The *locale* being thus determined, I had now to introduce the bird—and the thought of introducing him through the window, was inevitable. The idea of making the lover suppose, in the first instance, that the flapping of the wings of the bird against the shutter, is a "tapping" at the door, originated in a wish to increase, by prolonging, the reader's curiosity, and in a desire to admit the incidental effect arising from the lover's throwing open the door, finding all dark, and thence adopting the half-fancy that it was the spirit of his mistress that knocked.

I made the night tempestuous, first, to account for the Raven's seeking admission, and secondly, for the effect of contrast with the (physical) serenity within the chamber.

I made the bird alight on the bust of Pallas, also for the effect of contrast between the marble and the plumage—it being understood that the bust was absolutely *suggested* by the bird—the bust of *Pallas* being chosen, first, as most in keeping with the scholarship of the lover, and, secondly, for the sonorousness of the word, Pallas, itself.

About the middle of the poem, also, I have availed myself of the force of contrast, with a view of deepening the ultimate impression. For example, an air of the fantastic—approaching as nearly to the ludicrous as was admissible—is given to the Raven's entrance. He comes in "with many a flirt and flutter."

> Not the *least obeisance made he*—not a moment stopped or stayed he,
> *But with mien of lord or lady*, perched above my chamber door.

In the two stanzas which follow, the design is more obviously carried out:—

> Then this ebony bird beguiling my sad fancy into smiling
> By the *grave and stern decorum of the countenance it wore*,
> "Though thy *crest be shorn and shaven* thou," I said, "art sure no craven,
> Ghastly grim and ancient Raven wandering from the nightly shore—
> Tell me what thy lordly name is on the Night's Plutonian shore!"
> Quoth the Raven—"Nevermore."

> Much I marvelled *this ungainly fowl* to hear discourse so plainly,
> Though its answer little meaning—little relevancy bore;
> For we cannot help agreeing that no living human being
> *Ever yet was blessed with seeing bird above his chamber door*—
> *Bird or beast upon the sculptured bust above his chamber door*,
> With such name as "Nevermore."

✦ ✦ ✦

The effect of the *dénouement* being thus provided for, I immediately drop the fantastic for a tone of the most profound seriousness:—this tone commencing in the stanza directly following the one last quoted, with the line,

> But the Raven, sitting lonely on that placid bust, spoke only, etc.

From this epoch the lover no longer jests—no longer sees any thing even of the fantastic in the Raven's demeanor. He speaks of him as a "grim, ungainly, ghastly, gaunt, and ominous bird of yore," and feels the "fiery eyes" burning into his "bosom's core." This revolution of thought, or fancy, on the lover's part, is intended to induce a similar one on the part of the reader—to bring the mind into a proper frame for the *dénouement*—which is now brought about as rapidly and as *directly* as possible.

With the *dénouement* proper—with the Raven's reply, "Nevermore," to the lover's final demand if he shall meet his mistress in another world—the poem, in its obvious phase, that of a simple narrative, may be said to have its completion. So far, every thing is within the limits of the accountable—of the real. A raven, having learned by rote the single word, "Nevermore," and having escaped from the custody of its owner, is driven, at midnight, through the violence of a storm, to seek admission at a window from which a light still gleams—the chamber-window of a student, occupied half in poring over a volume, half in dreaming of a beloved mistress deceased. The casement being thrown open at the fluttering of the bird's wings, the bird itself perches on the most convenient seat out of the immediate reach of the student, who, amused by the incident and the oddity of the visiter's demeanor, demands of it, in jest and without looking for a reply, its name. The raven addressed, answers with its customary word, "Nevermore"—a word which finds immediate echo in the melancholy heart of the student, who, giving utterance aloud to certain thoughts suggested by the occasion, is again startled by the fowl's repetition of "Nevermore." The student now guesses the state of the case, but is impelled, as I have before explained, by the human thirst for self-torture, and in part by superstition, to propound such queries to the bird as will bring him, the lover, the most of the luxury of sorrow, through the anticipated answer, "Nevermore." With the indulgence, to the utmost extreme, of this self-torture, the narration, in what I have termed its first or obvious phase, has a natural termination, and so far there has been no overstepping of the limits of the real.

But in subjects so handled, however skilfully, or with however vivid an array of incident, there is always a certain hardness or nakedness, which repels the artistical eye. Two things are invariably required—first, some amount of complexity, or more properly, adaptation; and, secondly, some amount of suggestiveness—some under current, however indefinite of meaning. It is this latter, in especial, which imparts to a work of art so much of that *richness* (to borrow from colloquy a forcible term) which we are too fond of confounding with *the ideal*. It is the *excess* of the suggested meaning—it is the rendering this the upper instead of the under current of the theme—which turns into prose (and that of the very flattest kind) the so called poetry of the so called transcendentalists.

Holding these opinions, I added the two concluding stanzas of the poem—their suggestiveness being thus made to pervade all the narrative which has preceded them. The under-current of meaning is rendered first apparent in the lines—

> "Take thy beak from out *my heart*, and take thy form from off my door!"
> Quoth the Raven "Nevermore!"

It will be observed that the words, "from out my heart," involve the first metaphorical expression in the poem. They, with the answer, "Nevermore," dispose the mind to seek a moral in all that has been previously narrated. The reader begins now to regard the Raven as emblematical—but it is not until the very last line of the very last stanza, that the intention of making him emblematical of *Mournful and Never-ending Remembrance* is permitted distinctly to be seen:

> And the Raven, never flitting, still is sitting, still is sitting,
> On the pallid bust of Pallas just above my chamber door;
> And his eyes have all the seeming of a demon's that is dreaming,
> And the lamplight o'er him streaming throws his shadow on the floor;
> And my soul *from out that shadow* that lies floating on the floor
> Shall be lifted—nevermore.

1846

OLIVER WENDELL HOLMES
1809–1894

A PROMINENT BOSTON PHYSICIAN and a distinguished professor of medicine at Dartmouth College (1838–40) and Harvard Medical School (1847–82), Holmes was also a popular and witty lecturer, and a versatile and skillful poet whose career in verse did not really hit its stride until he was nearly fifty. Holmes's literary qualities developed particularly in the context of Boston's literary "Saturday Club," which featured such luminaries as Longfellow, William Dean Howells, and James Russell Lowell. He was thus a member of that mid-nineteenth-century intellectual aristocracy that he himself first humorously termed the Boston Brahmins. Skepticism, empiricism, and witty detachment were keynotes of Holmes's character. Moreover, both his life and his writing emphasized the freedom to constantly grow and change like the "chambered nautilus"—which, as one of his most famous poems notes, is forever "leaving [its] outgrown shell by life's unresting sea." This was not merely a fanciful image but the expression of a personal philosophy that valued ongoing exploration of life. Holmes's worldview embodied a considered rejection of the Calvinist orthodoxy of his own father, the minister of Boston's famed First Church and a Puritan believer in the old style whose faith had emphasized predestination and unquestioning commitment to the literal verity of scripture.

After a brief early dabbling in writing that included the poem "Old Ironsides" (1830), which is largely credited with the preservation of the famous frigate U.S.S. *Constitution* (which remains afloat and on display in Boston Harbor), Holmes devoted most of his authorial energies to medical publications and lectures. Then in 1857 J. R. Lowell requested that Holmes contribute to a newly created magazine, *The Atlantic Monthly,* which centered on the Saturday Club authors and for which Holmes himself supplied the title. Holmes responded by producing the enormously popular series of witty conversational essays and poems collected as *The Autocrat of the Breakfast Table* (followed by several sequels). Holmes recalled that "Lowell woke me from a kind of literary lethargy in which I was half slumbering, to call me to active service." Holmes's literary awakening led to four volumes of verse between 1862 and 1887. Despite the detailed knowledge of underwater life displayed in "The Chambered Nautilus" and the astronomical lore in "The Flâneur," Holmes's verse remains conversationally accessible and engaging. And in "The Deacon's Masterpiece, or The Wonderful One Hoss-Shay," Holmes combines humor and seriousness to create an enduring example of popular folk poetry that may also be read as a veiled allegory on the sudden collapse of Calvinism in New England.

Holmes's intellectual legacy of skeptical, open-minded questioning was passed on to his son Oliver Wendell Holmes, Jr. (1841–1935), one of the most distinguished and long-serving justices in the history of the United States Supreme Court.

FURTHER READING

Oliver Wendell Holmes. *Complete Poetical Works.* Boston: Houghton Mifflin, 1923.
Edwin P. Hoyt. *The Improper Bostonian: Dr. Oliver Wendell Holmes.* New York: Morrow, 1979.

Old Ironsides

Ay, tear her tattered ensign down!
Long has it waved on high,
And many an eye has danced to see
That banner in the sky;
Beneath it rung the battle shout,
And burst the cannon's roar;
The meteor of the ocean air
Shall sweep the clouds no more.

Her deck, once red with heroes' blood,
Where knelt the vanquished foe,
When winds were hurrying o'er the flood,

And waves were white below,
No more shall feel the victor's tread,
Or know the conquered knee;
The harpies of the shore shall pluck
The eagle of the sea!

Oh, better that her shattered bulk
Should sink beneath the wave;
Her thunders shook the mighty deep,
And there should be her grave;
Nail to the mast her holy flag,
Set every threadbare sail,
And give her to the god of storms,
The lightning and the gale!

1830

About "Old Ironsides" Holmes wrote, "This was the popular name by which the frigate *Constitution* was known. The poem was first printed in the *Boston Daily Advertiser*, at the time when it was proposed to break up the old ship as unfit for service. I subjoin the paragraph which led to the writing of the poem. It is from the *Advertiser* of Tuesday, September 14, 1830: 'Old Ironsides.—It has been affirmed upon good authority that the Secretary of the Navy has recommended to the Board of Navy Commissioners to dispose of the frigate *Constitution*. Since it has been understood that such a step was in contemplation we have heard but one opinion expressed, and that in decided disapprobation of the measure. Such a national object of interest, so endeared to our national pride as Old Ironsides is, should never by any act of our government cease to belong to the Navy, so long as our country is to be found upon the map of nations. In England it was lately determined by the Admiralty to cut the *Victory*, a one-hundred gun ship (which it will be recollected bore the flag of Lord Nelson at the battle of Trafalgar), down to a seventy-four, but so loud were the lamentations of the people upon the proposed measure that the intention was abandoned. We confidently anticipate that the Secretary of the Navy will in like manner consult the general wish in regard to the *Constitution*, and either let her remain in ordinary or rebuild her whenever the public service may require.'—New York *Journal of Commerce*."

The Chambered Nautilus

This is the ship of pearl, which, poets feign,
  Sails the unshadowed main,—
  The venturous bark that flings
On the sweet summer wind its purpled wings
In gulfs enchanted, where the Siren sings,
  And coral reefs lie bare,
Where the cold sea-maids rise to sun their streaming hair.

*   *   *

Its webs of living gauze no more unfurl;
   Wrecked is the ship of pearl!
   And every chambered cell,
Where its dim dreaming life was wont to dwell,
As the frail tenant shaped his growing shell,
   Before thee lies revealed,—
Its irised[1] ceiling rent, its sunless crypt unsealed!

Year after year beheld the silent toil
   That spread his lustrous coil;
   Still, as the spiral grew,
He left the past year's dwelling for the new,
Stole with soft step its shining archway through,
   Built up its idle door,
Stretched in his last-found home, and knew the old no more.

Thanks for the heavenly message brought by thee,
   Child of the wandering sea,
   Cast from her lap, forlorn!
From thy dead lips a clearer note is born
Than ever Triton blew from wreathèd horn![2]
   While on mine ear it rings,
Through the deep caves of thought I hear a voice that sings:—

Build thee more stately mansions, O my soul,[3]
   As the swift seasons roll!
   Leave thy low-vaulted past!
Let each new temple, nobler than the last,
Shut thee from heaven with a dome more vast,
   Till thou at length art free,
Leaving thine outgrown shell by life's unresting sea!

                1858

The chambered nautilus is a spiral-shelled mollusk whose weblike membranes were imagined to act as sails. It is particularly known for its tendency to leave behind outgrown versions of its coiled shell and to form new and larger ones. Holmes wrote, "I have now and

1. That is, curved in shape and "purpled" in color like the iris flower.
2. Son of Poseidon, the god of the sea in Greek mythology. Triton was a merman often depicted as blowing on a conch shell, as on a horn.

Holmes's line echoes the close of Wordsworth's sonnet "The World Is Too Much with Us."
3. Cf. John 14:2: "In my Father's house are many mansions."

then found a naturalist who still worried over the distinction between the Pearly Nautilus and the Paper Nautilus, or Argonauta. As the stories about both are mere fables, attaching to the Physalia, or Portuguese man-of-war, as well as to these two mollusks, it seems over-nice to quarrel with the poetical handling of a fiction sufficiently justified by the name commonly applied to the ship of pearl as well as the ship of paper."

The Deacon's Masterpiece, or The Wonderful One-Hoss Shay
A LOGICAL STORY

Have you heard of the wonderful one-hoss shay,
That was built in such a logical way
It ran a hundred years to a day,
And then, of a sudden, it—ah, but stay,
I'll tell you what happened without delay,
Scaring the parson into fits,
Frightening people out of their wits,—
Have you ever heard of that, I say?

Seventeen hundred and fifty-five.
Georgius Secundus[1] was then alive,—
Snuffy old drone from the German hive.
That was the year when Lisbon-town
Saw the earth open and gulp her down,[2]
And Braddock's army was done so brown,
Left without a scalp to its crown.[3]
It was on the terrible Earthquake-day
That the Deacon finished the one-hoss shay.

Now the building of chaises, I tell you what,
There is always *somewhere* a weakest spot,—
In hub, tire, felloe,[4] in spring or thill,
In panel, or crossbar, or floor, or sill,
In screw, bolt, thoroughbrace,[5]—lurking still,
Find it somewhere you must and will,—

1. George II, king of England (1683–1760).
2. The Lisbon earthquake took place November 1, 1755, and took as many as 60,000 lives.
3. Edward Braddock (1695–1755), British general killed by a French and Indian army near Fort Duquesne, Pennsylvania.
4. The wheel-rim. Thills: a pair of shafts that attach the horse to the vehicle.
5. Leather braces that connect the front and back C-springs of the coach and hold it up.

Above or below, or within or without,—
And that's the reason, beyond a doubt,
A chaise *breaks down*, but doesn't *wear out.*

But the Deacon swore (as Deacons do,
With an "I dew vum," or an "I tell *yeou*")
He would build one shay to beat the taown
'N' the keounty 'n' all the kentry raoun';
It should be so built that it *could n'* break daown:
"Fur," said the Deacon, "'t's mighty plain
Thut the weakes' place mus' stan' the strain;
'N' the way t' fix it, uz I maintain,
Is only jest
T' make that place uz strong uz the rest."

So the Deacon inquired of the village folk
Where he could find the strongest oak,
That could n't be split nor bent nor broke,—
That was for spokes and floor and sills;
He sent for lancewood to make the thills;
The crossbars were ash, from the straightest trees,
The panels of white-wood, that cuts like cheese,
But lasts like iron for things like these;
The hubs of logs from the "Settler's ellum,"[6]—
Last of its timber,—they couldn't sell 'em,
Never an axe had seen their chips,
And the wedges flew from between their lips,
Their blunt ends frizzled like celery-tips;
Step and prop-iron, bolt and screw,
Spring, tire, axle, and linchpin too,
Steel of the finest, bright and blue;
Thoroughbrace bison-skin, thick and wide;
Boot, top, dasher, from tough old hide
Found in the pit when the tanner died.
That was the way he "put her through."
"There!" said the Deacon, "naow she'll dew!"

Do! I tell you, I rather guess
She was a wonder, and nothing less!
Colts grew horses, beards turned gray,
Deacon and deaconess dropped away,

6. The original elms harvested by the settlers.

Children and grandchildren—where were they?
But there stood the stout old one-hoss shay
As fresh as on Lisbon-earthquake-day!

EIGHTEEN HUNDRED;—it came and found
The Deacon's masterpiece strong and sound.
Eighteen hundred increased by ten;—
"Hahnsum kerridge" they called it then.
Eighteen hundred and twenty came;—
Running as usual; much the same.
Thirty and forty at last arrive,
And then come fifty, and FIFTY-FIVE.
Little of all we value here
Wakes on the morn of its hundredth year
Without both feeling and looking queer.
In fact, there's nothing that keeps its youth,
So far as I know, but a tree and truth.
(This is a moral that runs at large;
Take it.—You're welcome.—No extra charge.)

FIRST OF NOVEMBER,—the Earthquake-day,—
There are traces of age in the one-hoss shay,
A general flavor of mild decay,
But nothing local, as one may say.
There couldn't be,—for the Deacon's art
Had made it so like in every part
That there wasn't a chance for one to start.
For the wheels were just as strong as the thills,
And the floor was just as strong as the sills,
And the panels just as strong as the floor,
And the whipple-tree neither less nor more,
And the back crossbar as strong as the fore,
And spring and axle and hub *encore*.
And yet, *as a whole*, it is past a doubt
In another hour it will be *worn out*!

First of November, 'Fifty-five!
This morning the parson takes a drive.
Now, small boys, get out of the way!
Here comes the wonderful one-hoss shay,
Drawn by a rat-tailed, ewe-necked bay.[7]

7. A brown horse.

"Huddup!"[8] said the parson. — Off went they.
The parson was working his Sunday's text, —
Had got to *fifthly*, and stopped perplexed
At what the — Moses — was coming next.
All at once the horse stood still,
Close by the meet'n'-house on the hill.
First a shiver, and then a thrill,
Then something decidedly like a spill, —
And the parson was sitting upon a rock,
At half past nine by the meet'n'-house clock, —
Just the hour of the Earthquake shock!
What do you think the parson found,
When he got up and stared around?
The poor old chaise in a heap or mound,
As if it had been to the mill and ground!
You see, of course, if you're not a dunce,
How it went to pieces all at once, —
All at once, and nothing first, —
Just as bubbles do when they burst.

End of the wonderful one-hoss shay.
Logic is logic. That's all I say.

1858

A "one-hoss shay" is a wooden chaise or carriage drawn by a single horse. Holmes wrote, "'The Wonderful One-Hoss Shay' is a perfectly intelligible conception, whatever material difficulties it presents. It is conceivable that a being of an order superior to humanity should so understand the conditions of matter that he could construct a machine which should go to pieces, if not into its constituent atoms, at a given moment of the future. The mind may take a certain pleasure in this picture of the impossible. The event follows as a logical consequence of the presupposed condition of things.

"There is a practical lesson to be got out of the story. Observation shows us in what point any particular mechanism is most likely to give way. In a wagon, for instance, the weak point is where the axle enters the hub or nave. When the wagon breaks down, three times out of four, I think, it is at this point that the accident occurs. The workman should see to it that this part should never give way; then find the next vulnerable place, and so on, until he arrives logically at the perfect result attained by the deacon."

8. Giddap, "get up," get moving.

The Flâneur

BOSTON COMMON,[1] DECEMBER 6, 1882
DURING THE TRANSIT OF VENUS[2]

I love all sights of earth and skies,
From flowers that glow to stars that shine;
The comet[3] and the penny show,[4]
All curious things, above, below,
Hold each in turn my wandering eyes:
I claim the Christian Pagan's line,
Humani nihil,[5] — even so, —
And is not human life divine?
When soft the western breezes blow,
And strolling youths meet sauntering maids,
I love to watch the stirring trades
Beneath the Vallombrosa[6] shades
Our much-enduring elms bestow;
The vender and his rhetoric's flow,
That lambent stream of liquid lies;[7]
The bait he dangles from his line,
The gudgeon[8] and his gold-washed prize.
I halt before the blazoned sign
That bids me linger to admire
The drama time can never tire,
The little hero of the hunch,
With iron arm and soul of fire,
And will that works his fierce desire, —
Untamed, unscared, unconquered Punch![9]
My ear a pleasing torture finds
In tones the withered sibyl grinds,[10] —

1. Large public park in central Boston.
2. A rare astronomical event during which Venus, interposed between the sun and the Earth, appears in the form of a small disk that makes a transit across the face of the sun. This phenomenon is only observable through a telescope. Since the orbits of the Earth and Venus are on different planes and rarely align, no transit of Venus would again occur—following the event Holmes observed—until June 8, 2004.
3. A still rarer astronomical event, the "Great September Comet," had appeared three months earlier in 1882. This comet will not again be observable from Earth until 2641.
4. A cheap entertainment at fairs or carnivals, such as a Punch-and-Judy show.

5. "Nothing human." Holmes cites Terence's *Heauton Timoroumenos*, "Homo sum; humani nihil a me alienum puto" (I am a man; I count nothing human as alien to me).
6. Literally "shady valley," specifically an Italian valley near Florence known for its stately trees.
7. Falsehoods verbally advertised by a seller of patent medicines.
8. Small baitfish or a person easily duped.
9. A puppet husband who ludicrously battles his puppet wife Judy in the most persistently popular of all "penny shows."
10. A sibyl is an ancient Greek prophetess or fortune-teller; here her voice is linked to the organ-grinder's tune.

The *dame sans merci*'s broken strain,[11]
Whom I erewhile, perchance, have known,
When Orleans filled the Bourbon throne,[12]
A siren singing by the Seine.[13]

But most I love the tube that spies
The orbs celestial in their march;
That shows the comet as it whisks
Its tail across the planet's disks,
As if to blind their blood-shot eyes;
Or wheels so close against the sun
We tremble at the thought of risks
Our little spinning ball may run,
To pop like corn that children parch,
From summer something overdone,
And roll, a cinder, through the skies.

Grudge not to-day the scanty fee
To him who farms the firmament,
To whom the milky way is free;[14]
Who holds the wondrous crystal key,
The silent Open Sesame[15]
That Science to her sons has lent;
Who takes his toll, and lifts the bar
That shuts the road to sun and star.[16]
If Venus only comes to time,
(And prophets say she must and shall,)
To-day will hear the tinkling chime
Of many a ringing silver dime,
For him whose optic glass supplies
The crowd with astronomic eyes,—
The Galileo of the Mall.[17]

---

11. See Keats's dangerous enchantress in "La Belle Dame Sans Merci." This "beautiful lady without pity" enthralls men with her ravishing song.

12. Louis Philippe, king of France from 1830 to 1848, was from the house of Orleans. Previously, the French throne had been held for generations by the house of Bourbon.

13. Siren: a singer in Greek mythology who enchants sailors to their doom. Seine: the river that runs through Paris.

14. Our own galaxy, viewed from the earth, ap-pears as a broad band of stars and "milky" light spanning the night sky.

15. Ali Baba's magical command that opens the robbers' secret door in the rock in the tale "Ali Baba and the Forty Thieves."

16. As noted, the transit of Venus is a rare event visible only through a telescope.

17. Galileo Galilei (1564–1642), the Italian astron-omer and physicist, did not invent the refracting telescope, but he was the first to use it to observe the heavens, beginning in 1609.

*   *   *

Dimly the transit morning broke;
The sun seemed doubting what to do,
As one who questions how to dress,
And takes his doublets from the press,
And halts between the old and new.
Please Heaven he wear his suit of blue,
Or don, at least, his ragged cloak,
With rents that show the azure through!

I go the patient crowd to join
That round the tube my eyes discern,
The last new-comer of the file,
And wait, and wait, a weary while,
And gape, and stretch, and shrug, and smile,
(For each his place must fairly earn,
Hindmost and foremost, in his turn,)
'Till hitching onward, pace by pace,
I gain at last the envied place,
And pay the white exiguous[18] coin:
The sun and I are face to face;
He glares at me, I stare at him;
And lo! my straining eye has found
A little spot that, black and round,
Lies near the crimsoned fire-orb's rim.
O blessed, beauteous evening star,[19]
Well named for her whom earth adores,—
The Lady of the dove-drawn car,—
I know thee in thy white simar;[20]
But veiled in black, a rayless spot,
Blank as a careless scribbler's blot,
Stripped of thy robe of silvery flame,—
The stolen robe that Night restores
When Day has shut his golden doors,—
I see thee, yet I know thee not;
And canst thou call thyself the same?

A black, round spot,—and that is all;
And such a speck our earth would be

18. Small, of little value.
19. Venus.
20. A woman's light garment.

If he who looks upon the stars
Through the red atmosphere of Mars
Could see our little creeping ball
Across the disk of crimson crawl
As I our sister planet see.

And art thou, then, a world like ours,
Flung from the orb that whirled our own
A molten pebble from its zone?
How must thy burning sands absorb
The fire-waves of the blazing orb,
Thy chain so short, thy path so near,
Thy flame-defying creatures hear
The maelstroms of the photosphere![21]
And is thy bosom decked with flowers
That steal their bloom from scalding showers?
And hast thou cities, domes, and towers,
And life, and love that makes it dear,
And death that fills thy tribes with fear?

Lost in my dream, my spirit soars
Through paths the wandering angels know;
My all-pervading thought explores
The azure ocean's lucent[22] shores;
I leave my mortal self below,
As up the star-lit stairs I climb,
And still the widening view reveals
In endless rounds the circling wheels
That build the horologe[23] of time.
New spheres, new suns, new systems gleam;
The voice no earth-born echo hears
Steals softly on my ravished ears:
I hear them "singing as they shine"[24]—
—A mortal's voice dissolves my dream:
My patient neighbor, next in line,
Hints gently there are those who wait.
O guardian of the starry gate,
What coin shall pay this debt of mine?

21. Outer surface of the sun.
22. Shining.
23. Timekeeping device, such as a clock or sundial.

24. Holmes echoes Joseph Addison's "Ode" (1712), "For ever singing, as they shine, / 'The Hand that made us is Divine.'"

Too slightly thy claim, too small the fee
That bids thee turn the potent key
The Tuscan's[25] hand had placed in thine.
Forgive my own the small affront,
The insult of the proffered dime;
Take it, O friend, since this thy wont,
But still shall faithful memory be
A bankrupt debtor unto thee,
And pay thee with a grateful rhyme.

1882

Flâneur is French for stroller, promenader.

ABRAHAM LINCOLN
1809–1865

LIKE FELLOW MOUNT RUSHMORE immortals Thomas Jefferson and Theodore Roosevelt, Abraham Lincoln was not only an admired president of the United States but also a distinguished writer of prose. Moreover, his best prose writing is often rhythmically poised and boldly metaphoric, so it should not surprise us that Lincoln also tried his hand at poetry. He first established himself on the national stage through his writings. His antislavery speeches during his 1858 senatorial campaign against Stephen Douglas made him a leading figure in the emerging Republican party. Following Lincoln's election as president, his Gettysburg Address in 1863, which dedicated a famous battlefield and in the process succinctly defined American democracy ("a government of the people, by the people, and for the people"), and his magnanimous Second Inaugural Address of 1865 ("with malice toward none, with charity for all; with firmness in the right, as God gives us to see the right, let us strive on to finish the work we are in") established him as one of the most eloquent writers of his time. Though Lincoln was raised in Kentucky and Illinois, which were then frontier states, and though he received only a rudimentary formal education, he was an omnivorous reader who, through an intense effort of self-education, became first a surveyor and then a lawyer—and in the process acquired a memorable and highly persuasive prose style.

25. Galileo was from the Tuscan region of Italy.

Always politically active at the local level, in the 1840s Lincoln felt himself drawn increasingly into national politics, particularly through his opposition to slavery. After eight years in the Illinois state assembly, Lincoln was elected as a Whig to a single term in Congress in 1846, then returned to Illinois where he focused for several years on an increasingly successful law practice. As a lawyer, and later as a political orator, Lincoln knew how to carry his points by alternating homespun but well-pointed humor with plainspoken yet incisive logical arguments, elevated at times by a lofty quasi-biblical rhetoric. In each of these modes, Lincoln customarily employed metaphorical language that was vivid, clear, and memorable. Indeed, in the essay "How Lincoln Won the War with Metaphors," the noted historian James McPherson argued that one major advantage favoring the Union cause was that Lincoln handled verbal communication—and figurative language in particular—much more adroitly than did Confederate president Jefferson Davis, whose stilted and diffuse manner of expression was less effective in rallying popular support than Lincoln's acute and engaging precision. Because Lincoln could state his ideas more clearly and eloquently, he was able to win and unify the support of an initially divided North, and he was able to maintain that allegiance as the war dragged on, as casualties mounted, and as Union war goals changed.

Lincoln was moved to write poetry after he returned to his childhood home in Hardin County, Kentucky, in 1846, when he was a thirty-seven-year-old Illinois lawyer. There Lincoln saw, as he acknowledged humorously to a literary friend, "the neighborhood in that State in which I was raised, where my mother and only sister were buried, and from which I had been absent almost fifteen years. That part of the country is, within itself, as unpoetical as any spot on earth; but still, seeing it and its objects and inhabitants aroused feelings in me which were certainly poetry; though whether my expression of those feelings is poetry is quite another question."

Lincoln's poetical effort "My Childhood Home I See Again," which he enclosed in the above letter to his friend and which remained unpublished during his lifetime, may not rival the originality and force of his later prose, but it does show an easy, if somewhat conventional, handling of rhyme, meter, and stanza form. It also expresses a range of feelings, from joyful reacquaintance with familiar scenes to candidly melancholy reflections on the death or departure of friends, with the unaffected clarity and directness that were so characteristic of Lincoln as a writer and human being.

FURTHER READING

Roy P. Basler, ed. *Abraham Lincoln: His Speeches and Writings*. New York: World Publishing, 1946.

James McPherson. "How Lincoln Won the War with Metaphors," in *Abraham Lincoln and the Second American Revolution*. New York: Oxford University Press, 1990.

My Childhood Home I See Again

[1]

My childhood home I see again,
    And gladden with the view;
And still as mem'ries crowd my brain,
    There's sadness in it too.

O memory! Thou mid-way world
    'Twixt Earth and Paradise,
Where things decayed, and loved ones lost
    and dreamy shadows rise.

And freed from all that's gross or vile,
    Seem hallowed, pure and bright,
Like scenes in some enchanted isle,
    All bathed in liquid light.

As distant mountains please the eye,
    When twilight chases day—
As bugle-tones, that, passing by,
    In distance die away—

As leaving some grand water-fall
    We ling'ring, list its roar,
So memory will hallow all
    We've known, but know no more.

Now twenty years have passed away,
    Since here I bid farewell
To woods, and fields, and scenes of play
    And school-mates loved so well.

Where many were, how few remain
    Of old familiar things!
But seeing these to mind again
    The lost and absent brings.

The friends I left that parting day—
    How changed, as time has sped!
Young childhood grown, strong manhood gray,
    And half of all are dead.

        *   *   *

I hear the lone survivors tell
    How naught from death could save,
Till every sound appears a knell,
    And every spot a grave.

I range the fields with pensive tread,
    And pace the hollow rooms;
And feel (companions of the dead)
    I'm living in the tombs.

[II]
A[nd] here's an object more of dread,
    Than aught the grave contains—
A human-form, with reason fled,
    While wretched life remains.

Poor Mathew! Once of genius bright,—
    A fortune-favored child—
Now locked for aye, in mental night,
    A haggard mad-man wild.

Poor Mathew! I have ne'er forgot
    When first with maddened will,
Yourself you maimed, your father fought,
    And mother strove to kill;

And terror spread, the neighbors ran,
    Your dang'rous strength to bind;
And soon a howling crazy man,
    Your limbs were fast confined.

How then you writhed and shrieked aloud,
    Your bones and sinews bared;
And fiendish on the gaping crowd,
    With burning eye-balls glared.

And begged, and swore, and wept, and prayed,
    With maniac laughter joined—
How fearful are the signs displayed,
    By pangs that kill the mind!

       *   *   *

And when at length, the drear and long
    Time soothed your fiercer woes—
How plaintively your mournful song,
    Upon the still night rose.

I've heard it oft, as if I dreamed,
    Far-distant, sweet, and lone;
The funeral dirge it ever seemed
    Of reason dead and gone.

To drink its stains, I've stole away,
    All silently and still,
Ere yet the rising god of day
    Had streaked the Eastern hill.

Air held his breath; the trees all still
    Seemed sorr'wing angels round.
Their swelling tears in dew-drops fell
    Upon the list'ning ground.

But this is past, and naught remains
    That raised you o'er the brute.
Your mad'ning shrieks, and soothing strains
    Are like forever mute.

Now fare thee well: more thou the cause
    Than subject now of woe.
All mental pangs, by time's kind laws,
    Hast lost the power to know.

O death! thou awe-inspiring prince,
    That keepst the world in fear;
Why dost thou tear more blest ones hence,
    And leave him ling'ring here?

And now away to seek some scene
    Less painful than the last—
With less of horror mingled in
    The present and the past.

The very spot where grew the bread
    That formed my bones, I see.
How strange, old field, on thee to tread
    And feel I'm part of thee!

1846

MARGARET FULLER
1810–1850

MARGARET FULLER WAS one of the most powerful voices for the legal, educational, and emotional rights of women in the first half of the nineteenth century. Born on the outskirts of Boston and tutored by her father, a Harvard-educated lawyer who later served in both the state legislature of Massachusetts and the U.S. Congress, Fuller was a precocious child who emerged as a lifelong reader and a passionate, deeply inquisitive writer. Her famous seminar-like "Conversations," held in Boston with middle- and upper-middle-class women (many drawn from "Brahmin" circles), allowed her to explore their common gender experiences and inspired her most important book, *Woman in the Nineteenth Century* (1845), a major feminist manifesto that in turn inspired the Seneca Falls Declarations of 1848. Her travel book, *Summer on the Lakes* (1844), questioned environmental abuses, policies toward Native Americans, and the lot of pioneer women. Traveling to Europe in 1846, as a foreign correspondent for Horace Greeley's *New York Tribune*, Fuller became deeply involved in the cause of European emancipation that erupted with the revolutions of 1848. Fuller covered the revolutions against foreign domination that sprang up in Italy for the *Tribune*, consistently articulating the cause of the forces for Italian emancipation and unification. She had a child by an Italian aristocrat and revolutionary, Marchese Giovanni Angelo Ossoli (whether they were ever formally married remains in dispute). She died a tragic early death in 1850 when she, Ossoli, and their child were lost at sea during a storm while returning to America.

Fuller's concerns, however, were as much literary as political. She was an ardent Romantic who was drawn at an early age to the poetry of Novalis, Goethe, and Schiller. She taught herself German to read Goethe in the original and seriously contemplated writing his biography. She made important contributions to literature as the editor of the Transcendentalist Club's chief organ, *The Dial*, from 1840 to 1842 and from 1844 to 1846 as a literary critic and feature writer for the *New York Tribune*. Her critical writings were collected in *Papers on Literature and Art* (1846). In Emerson she found a friend and collaborator, and she conversed and corresponded with many of the leading literary figures of her time, both in America and abroad, including Carlyle in England. She inspired such powerful ambivalence in Nathaniel Hawthorne that he re-created her fictionally in Zenobia, the brilliant and magnetic yet morally ambiguous female protagonist of his novel *The Blithedale Romance*.

In 1836 Fuller published the essay "Modern British Poets," which praised Wordsworth and Coleridge—neither of whom was as yet widely popular with

American audiences—for achieving a historic change in the nature of poetry. According to Fuller, their poetry had the power to express not only "the passions or heart-emotions of their fellow men" but also their "thoughts or mind-emotions." For Fuller, Wordsworth and Coleridge emerged as two of the "pilot-minds of the age." Fuller herself was a writer powerfully moved by "mind-emotions," and she aspired to achieve the status of a pilot-mind in her own right. In her 1833 "Meditations," written when she was twenty-three, Fuller shows through her lithely flowing, conversationally musing blank verse that she had already thoroughly absorbed the poetic language and intellectual movement of the Wordsworthian meditative lyric. Yet she gives the form a decided tincture of her own. This rare example of Fuller's early verse reveals her sensitive ear and keenly observant eye, and one wishes she had found more time in her productive and brief life for the writing of poetry.

FURTHER READING

Charles Capper. *Margaret Fuller: An American Romantic Life (The Private Years)*, vol. 1. New York: Oxford University Press, 1992.

Margaret Fuller. *The Essential Margaret Fuller*. Ed. Jeffrey Steele. New Brunswick: Rutgers University Press, 1992.

Meditations

Sunday, 12 May 1833

The clouds are marshalling across the sky,
Leaving their deepest tints upon yon range
Of soul-alluring hills. The breeze comes softly,
Laden with tribute that a hundred orchards
Now in their fullest blossom send, in thanks
For this refreshing shower. The birds pour forth
In heightened melody the notes of praise
They had suspended while God's voice was speaking,
And his eye flashing down upon his world.
I sigh, half-charmed, half-pained. My sense is living,
And, taking in this freshened beauty, tells
Its pleasure to the mind. The mind replies,
And strives to wake the heart in turn, repeating
Poetic sentiments from many a record
Which other souls have left, when stirred and satisfied
By scenes as fair, as fragrant. But the heart

Sends back a hollow echo to the call
Of outward things,—and its once bright companion,
Who erst would have been answered by a stream
Of life-fraught treasures, thankful to be summoned,—
Can now rouse nothing better than this echo;
Unmeaning voice, which mocks their softened accents.
Content thee, beautiful world! and hush, still busy mind!
My heart hath sealed its fountains. To the things
Of Time they shall be oped no more. Too long,
Too often were they poured forth: part have sunk
Into the desert; part profaned and swollen
By bitter waters, mixed by those who feigned
They asked them for refreshment, which, turned back,
Have broken and o'erflowed their former urns.
So when ye talk of *pleasure*, lonely world,
And busy mind, ye ne'er again shall move me
To answer ye, though still your calls have power
To jar me through, and cause dull aching *here*.

Not so the voice which hailed me from the depths
Of yon dark-bosomed cloud, now vanishing
Before the sun ye greet. It touched my centre,
The voice of the Eternal, calling me
To feel his other worlds; to feel that if
I could deserve a home, I still might find it
In other spheres,—and bade me not despair,
Though 'want of harmony' and 'aching void'
Are terms invented by the men of this,
Which I may not forget.
                    In former times
I loved to see the lightnings flash athwart
The stooping heavens; I loved to hear the thunder
Call to the seas and mountains; for I thought
'Tis thus man's flashing fancy doth enkindle
The firmament of mind; 'tis thus his eloquence
Calls unto the soul's depths and heights; and still
I defied the creature, nor remembered
The Creator in his works.
                    Ah now how different!
The proud delight of that keen sympathy
Is gone; no longer riding on the wave,

But whelmed beneath it: my own plans and works,
Or, as the Scriptures phrase it, my *'inventions'*
No longer interpose 'twixt me and Heaven.

Today, for the first time, I felt the Deity,
And uttered prayer on hearing thunder. This
Must be thy will, —for finer, higher spirits
Have gone through this same process, —yet I think
There was religion in that strong delight,
Those sounds, those thoughts of power imparted. True,
I did not say, 'He is the Lord thy God,'
But I had a feeling of his essence. But
' 'Twas pride by which the angels fell.' So be it!
But O, might I but see a little onward!
Father, I cannot be a spirit of power;
May I be active as a spirit of love,
Since thou hast ta'en me from that path which Nature
Seemed to appoint, O deign to ope another,
Where I may walk with thought and hope assured;
'Lord, I believe; help thou mine unbelief!'
Had I but faith like that which fired Novalis,[1]
I too could bear that the heart 'fall in ashes,'
While the freed spirit rises from beneath them,
With heavenward-look, and Phoenix-plumes[2] upsoaring!

1833

---

1. The pen name of Baron Friedrich von Hardenberg (1772–1801), a German Romantic poet noted for his religious, mystical leanings and his keen love of nature.
2. A fabled bird in Greek mythology, with brilliant gold and reddish-purple feathers. Only one existed at a time, and when its moment came to die, it burned itself on a funeral pyre, and a new phoenix rose from the ashes with renewed beauty and youth.

FRANCES SARGENT LOCKE OSGOOD
1811–1850

THE LARGELY OBSCURE poetry of Frances Sargent Locke Osgood reveals that nineteenth-century European-American women poets have not been sufficiently recognized for experimenting with the witty, satirical, and erotic poetic voices that readers associate more readily with modern female poets such as Edna St. Vincent Millay and Dorothy Parker. Indeed, Osgood's writing stands out boldly against the prevailing popular poetics of sentimentality that treated women as objects of desire, as saints devoid of sexuality, or as spiritual mothers. Her status as one of the nation's most popular published women poets—as well as one of the most sought-after New York literary salon poets—suggests that she succeeded in adding gender politics, sexual temptation, and romance to the narrow list of approved subjects for the woman poet.

Osgood's career proves that membership in the era's upper-class society brought with it many literary advantages. She was born into an elite Boston family, then mentored and published by the well-known writer and editor Lydia Maria Child, and married in 1834 to the coterie portrait artist Samuel Osgood, with whom she spent five years in England among the social and intellectual aristocracy. When she arrived at New York City literary and artistic salons with her husband, she brought with her a much-desired cosmopolitanism. She also brought the first of three published volumes of poetry—a collection entitled *A Wreath of Wild Flowers from New England*.

Although the mother of three children, Osgood did not permit domestic duties to interrupt her avid pursuit of literary success. She published in all of the popular venues of print culture open to her: books, magazines such as the *Ladies Home Companion* and *Godey's Lady Book*, pamphlets, anthologies, and newspapers, including the *New York Tribune*. Equally important, she developed a remarkable reputation as a sophisticated urban salon poet who wrote witty—and sometimes openly erotic and scandalous—verses for friends that circulated only in manuscript form and were frequently discarded. She impressed such elite writers and editors as Margaret Fuller and Horace Greeley. Her most important patron, however, was Edgar Allan Poe, who befriended her and published many of her poems in the *Broadway Journal* while he was editor.

The selections here suggest the range of Osgood's wit. "The Maiden's Mistake," published in the *Ladies Home Companion*, offers a woman's wry view of courtship. "The Wraith of the Rose" reveals Osgood's talents as a salon poet of playful impromptu verse in her social circle. In the satirical political poem "Lines," which

she published in the *New York Tribune*, Osgood responds to the announcement
that a bill for the protection of the property of married women had passed both
houses of the New York state legislature. Osgood's friendship with Poe surfaces as
an important influence in her composition of "The Hand That Swept the Sound-
ing Lyre," with its teasing eroticism and use of the refrain "nevermore" from "The
Raven," which he had published at about the time they first met.

FURTHER READING

Frances Sargent Locke Osgood. *Poems*. Boston: Abel Tompkins, 1846.
———. *Poems*. Philadelphia: Carey and Hart, 1850.
———. *A Wreath of Wild Flowers from New England*. London: Edward Churton, 1838.

The Maiden's Mistake

That his eyebrows were false—that his hair
    Was assumed, I was fully aware;
I knew his moustache of a barber was bought.
And that Cartwright provided his teeth;—but I thought
    That his heart was, at least, true and fair!

I saw that the exquisite glow,
    Spreading over the cheek of my beau,
From a carmine-shell[1] came;—and I often was told,
That his "gras de la jambe,"[2] by the tailor was sold;
    I dreamed not his love was but show!

I was sure, I could easily tell,
    That the form, which deluded each belle,
Was made over his own;—but I could not believe,
That his flattering tongue, too, was taught to deceive;
    That his fortune was humbug, as well!

I had made up my mind to dispense
    With a figure, hair, teeth, heart and sense—
"La jambe" I'd o'erlook, were it ever so small!
But to think that he is not a Count, after all,
    That's a not-to-be pardoned offence!

1839

1. Source of red dye.   2. Calf of the leg (French).

The Wraith of the Rose

An impromptu written on a visiting card

The magic of that name is fled,
The music of that dream is dead,
Long since Love's rose, its perfume, shed,
　　And what art thou to me?
If you have come to clasp again,
The fetter of that fairy chain,
You'd better far at home remain,
　　And save your time—and knee!
And yet that dream was strangely dear,
And yet that name awakes a tear,
The wraith of Love's sweet Rose is here,
　　It haunts me everywhere!
I wish the chain were still unbroken,
I wish those words again were spoken,
I wish I'd kept that last fond token,
　　And had not burned your hair!
I wish your voice still sounded sweet,
I wish you dared Love's vow repeat,
I wish you were not all deceit,
　　And I so fickle-hearted!
I wish we might go back again,
I wish you could reclasp the chain!
I wish—you hadn't drank champagne,
　　So freely since we parted!
Alas! While Flattery baits your line,
You fish in shallower hearts than mine!
You'll never find a pearl divine
　　Like that my spirit wasted!
But should you catch a seeming prize,
A flying fish you'll see it rise,
Away—beyond your wicked eyes,
　　Before the treasure's tasted!
Oh! if those eyes were splendid now,
As when they spoke the silent vow!
Oh! if the locks that wreath your brow,
　　Were not—but this is idle!
My wish shall be with kindness rife,

I'll wish you all the joys of life,
A pleasant home—a peerless wife,
　　Whose wishes, Sense shall bridle!
　　　　　　　　n.d.

Lines

Oh, ye who in those Houses hold
　　The scepter of command!
Thought's scepter, sunlit, in the soul,
　　Not golden, in the hand!

Was there not one among ye all,
　　No heart, that Love could thrill,
To move some slight amendment there,
　　Before you passed the bill?

Ye make our gold and lands secure;
　　Maybe you do not know,
That we have other property,
　　We'd rather not forego.

There are such things in woman's heart,
　　As fancies, tastes, affections;—
Are no encroachments made on these?
　　Do they need no "protections"?

Do we not daily sacrifice,
　　To our lords—and Creation's
Some darling wish—some petted whim,
　　Ah, me! in vain oblations![1]

These "cold realities" of life,—
　　These men, with their intrusions;
Do they not rob us, one by one,
　　Of all our "warm illusions"?

These highway robbers, prowling round,
　　Our "young affections" stealing,
Do they not take our richest store
　　Of Truth and Faith and Feeling!

1. Offerings to a deity.

*   *   *

Our "better judgment," "finer sense,"
    We yield with souls that falter,—
A costly, dainty holocaust,
    Upon a tyrant's altar;

We waste on them our "golden" hours,
    Our "real estate" of Beauty,
The bloom of Life's young passion-flowers—
    And still they talk of "Duty."

Alas for those, whose all of wealth
    Is in their souls and faces,
Whose only "rents" are rents in heart,
    Whose only tenants—graces.

How must that poor protection bill
    Provoke their bitter laughter,
Since they themselves are leased for life,
    And no pay-day till after!

By all the rest you fondly hope,
    When ends this lengthened session,
That household peace, which Woman holds
    Thank Heaven! at her discretion.

If a light of generous chivalry,
    This wild appeal arouses,
Present a truer, nobler bill!
    And let it pass—all houses!

                    1848

The Hand That Swept the Sounding Lyre

The hand that swept the sounding lyre
    With more than mortal skill,
The lightning eye, the heart of fire,
    The fervent lip are still!
No more, in rapture or in woe,
    With melody to thrill,
      Ah! nevermore!

*   *   *

Oh! bring the flowers he cherish'd so,
    With eager childlike care;
For o'er his grave they'll love to grow,
    And sigh their sorrow there:
Ah me! no more their balmy glow
    May soothe his heart's despair,
        No! nevermore!

But angel hands shall bring him balm
    For every grief he knew,
And Heaven's soft harps his soul shall calm
    With music sweet and true,
And teach to him the holy charm
    Of Israfel[1] anew,
        For evermore!

Love's silver lyre he play'd so well
    Lies shatter'd on his tomb;
But still in air its music-spell
    Floats on through light and gloom,
And in the hearts where soft they fell,
    His words of beauty bloom
        For evermore!

1850

ADA [SARAH LOUISA FORTEN]
ca. 1814–1898

WRITING UNDER THE PEN NAME of "Ada," Sarah Louisa Forten devoted her poetry to the abolition of slavery. A member of one of the most prominent free African-American families in Philadelphia, she established the importance of women's activist poetry in the African-American and European-American abolitionist cultures of the time. Both her writing and her social activism forcefully encouraged the creation of biracial opposition to slavery in the North while reaching

1. In Islamic myth, the angel of music who will announce the end of the world. Osgood surely alludes as well to Poe's 1831 poem "Israfel" (in- cluded in this anthology), and thus the poem may be read as an elegy for her friend Poe, who died in 1849.

out to slaves and European-American women in the South. She and her mother and two sisters were charter members of the first biracial women's abolitionist organization, the Philadelphia Female Anti-Slavery Society, founded in 1823. In addition to forging links among black abolitionists, Forten allied herself closely with such white feminist antislavery writers as Angelina Emily Grimké and urged all women to actively oppose slavery in spite of popular opposition to women speaking in public. With her entire family, she helped to either found or finance at least six other abolitionist organizations and worked directly with such leaders, intellectuals, and writers as John Greenleaf Whittier and William Lloyd Garrison.

The two poems here represent Forten's dramatization of the cruelties of slavery as well as her strategic use of the popular poetics of sentimentality. "The Slave Girl's Farewell" was suggested by an actual incident in which a young girl living with her mother in the West Indies was unconscious of her status as a slave. When their legal master moved to Louisiana, he separated the mother and daughter by taking the daughter with him. In "The Slave," Forten rebukes the nation for failing to free the slaves when it gained its independence from England and also positions herself as an outsider.

FURTHER READING

Janet Gray, ed. *She Wields a Pen: American Women Poets of the Nineteenth Century.* Iowa City: University of Iowa Press, 1997.
Dorothy Sterling, ed. *We Are Your Sisters: Black Women in the Nineteenth Century.* New York: Norton, 1997.
www.unl.edu/legacy/bio.htm (website of the Nineteenth-Century American Women Writers Web Etext Library: Sarah Louisa Forten).

The Slave Girl's Farewell

Mother, I leave thee—thou hast been
Through long, long years of pain
The only hope my fond heart knew;
Or e'er shall know again.
The sails are set—my master waits
To bear me far from thee;
I linger—can I give thee up,
And cross the fearful sea?
Oh, let me gaze! how bright it seems
As busy memory flies
To view those scenes of other days,
Beneath those bright blue skies.
The little hut where I have played

In childhood's fearless hours—
The murmuring stream—the mossy bank,
Where I have gathered flowers.
I knew not then I was a slave,
Or that another's will,
Save thine, could bend my spirit's pride;
Or bid my lips be still.
Who now will soothe me at my toil,
Or bathe my weary brow?
Or shield me when the heavy lash
Is raised to give the glow?
Thy fond arms press me—and I feel
Thy tears upon my cheek;
Tears are the only language now
A mother's love can speak.
Think of me, mother, as I bend
My way across the sea;
And midst thy tears, a blessing waft,[1]
To her who prays for thee.

1832

The Slave

Our sires who once in freedom's cause,
Their boasted freedom sought and won
For deeds of glory gained applause,
When patriot feelings led them on.
And can their sons now speak with pride,
Of rights for which they bled and died,—
Or while the captive is oppressed,
Think of the wrongs they once redress'd?
Oh, surely they have quite forgot,
That bondage once had been their lot;
The sweets of freedom now they know,
They care not for the captive's woe.
The poor wronged slave can bear no part
　　In feelings dearest to his heart;
　　He cannot speak on freedom's side,

1. Float through the air.

Nor dare he own a freeman's pride.
His soul is dark, ay dark as night,
O'er which is shed no gleam of light;
A cloud of error, doubt and fear,
O'er him is ever hovering near;
And sad and hard his lot must be,
To know that he can ne'er be free;
To feel that his is doomed to be
A life, and death, of slavery.
But will not justice soon arise,
And plead the cause of the despised?
For oh! my country, must it be,
That they still find a foe in thee?

1831

HENRY DAVID THOREAU
1817–1862

Henry david thoreau was one of the most imaginative writers about nature, spirit, and the self that the United States has ever produced. Throughout his life he kept his *Journal*, which Sharon Cameron has called "the great nineteenth-century American meditation on nature." His most notable work published in his lifetime, *Walden*, described his adventure living in a cabin on the shore of Walden Pond in rural Massachusetts. In that book, he used beautiful detail to evoke his effort to "live deliberately," to "simplify, simplify." He pondered the problem of "how to make the getting our living poetic; for if it is not poetic it is death we get, not life." Eliminating modern conveniences and abandoning all regular work, he sought to discover values he could live by in an age that seemed to have lost its way. He felt more of a bond with the Native Americans he encountered in the woods than with the European-American culture in which he had grown up. In other writings, including "Civil Disobedience" and "Life without Principle," he contemplated the proper relation of an individual to society—and particularly how one could combat such obvious evils as slavery and war.

Although Thoreau is best known as a writer of prose, he also wrote vivid poems. Most of these date from the 1840s, when Thoreau was in his twenties. In "Sic Vita," we observe his desire to know himself and to develop his spiritual insight. In

"Haze," "Smoke," and "Mist," we see his drive to perceive phenomena clearly and his wish to connect himself and his language to the world. These poems helped originate what is now called eco-poetry—a poetry that explores and treasures the natural environment.

Thoreau was born and lived most of his life in Concord, Massachusetts, a small town west of Boston. Never married, he alternately resided with his family, with his friend and mentor Ralph Waldo Emerson (included in this anthology), and by himself in the woods. A teacher by training, he quit working in Concord schools because of his opposition to corporal punishment. He then worked in a series of odd jobs—as private schoolmaster, tutor, surveyor, handyman for the Emerson family, pencil manufacturer, lecturer, and, most importantly, writer. "Civil Disobedience" (also called "Resistance to Civil Government") appeared in 1849, and *Walden* in 1854. By 1862, when *Walden* was reissued, Thoreau's fame was just beginning to spread. But in that year he died peacefully in his sleep of tuberculosis. On his deathbed he wrote that the autumn leaves "teach us how to die." When asked if he had made his peace with God, he replied, "I did not know we had ever quarreled." Slipping into delirium, he spoke his last words: "moose" and "Indian."

FURTHER READING

Lawrence Buell. *The Environmental Imagination: Thoreau, Nature Writing, and the Formation of American Culture*. Cambridge: Harvard University Press, 1996.

Walter Harding. *The Days of Henry Thoreau*. Princeton: Princeton University Press, 1993.

Robert Richardson. *Henry Thoreau: A Life of the Mind*. Berkeley: University of California Press, 1986.

Henry David Thoreau. *Collected Poems*. Ed. Carl Bode. Baltimore: Johns Hopkins University Press, 1964.

Sic Vita

I am a parcel of vain strivings tied
By a chance bond together,
Dangling this way and that, their links
Were made so loose and wide,
Methinks,
For milder weather.

A bunch of violets without their roots,
And sorrel intermixed,
Encircled by a wisp of straw
Once coiled about their shoots,
The law
By which I'm fixed.

*   *   *

A nosegay which Time clutched from out
Those fair Elysian fields,[1]
With weeds and broken stems, in haste,
Doth make the rabble rout
That waste
The day he yields.

And here I bloom for a short hour unseen,
Drinking my juices up,
With no root in the land
To keep my branches green,
But stand
In a bare cup.

Some tender buds were left upon my stem
In mimicry of life,
But ah! the children will not know,
Till time has withered them,
The woe
With which they're rife.

But now I see I was not plucked for naught,
And after in life's vase
Of glass set while I might survive,
But by a kind hand brought
Alive
To a strange place.

That stock thus thinned will soon redeem its hours,
And by another year,
Such as God knows, with freer air,
More fruits and fairer flowers
Will bear,
While I droop here.

1841

Thoreau's poem employs the Latin phrase "Thus life" for its title. Eight years after the poem's original publication, Thoreau reprinted it (without the title) in his account of *A Week on the Concord and Merrimack Rivers* (1849). There he introduced the poem, "It is

1. Paradise in Greek mythology.

but thin soil where we stand; I have felt my roots in a richer ere this. I have seen a bunch of violets in a glass vase, tied loosely with straw, which reminded me of myself." Suggesting an identity crisis, the poem remains ambiguously poised between hope and dejection.

Haze

Woof[1] of the sun, ethereal gauze,
Woven of nature's richest stuffs,
Visible heat, air-water, and dry sea,
Last conquest of the eye;
Toil of the day displayed, sun-dust,
Aerial surf upon the shores of earth,
Ethereal estuary,[2] firth of light,
Breakers of air, billows of heat,
Fine summer spray on inland seas;
Bird of the sun, transparent-winged,
Owlet of noon, soft-pinioned,[3]
From heath[4] or stubble rising without song;
Establish thy serenity o'er the fields.

1843

Thoreau originally called this poem one of his "Orphics." That is, he thought it cast a spell or contained a spiritual mystery, as did the poems and songs ascribed to Orpheus in Greek myth.

Smoke

Light-winged Smoke, Icarian[1] bird,
Melting thy pinions[2] in thy upward flight,
Lark without song, and messenger of dawn,
Circling above the hamlets at thy nest;
Or else, departing dream, and shadowy form
Of midnight vision, gathering up thy skirts;
By night star-veiling, and by day

1. Cross-threads.
2. An estuary or a firth is the river's mouth, where the current meets the tide.
3. Soft-feathered.
4. Wild land with low shrubs. Stubble: the stumps or cut stalks of plants.

1. In Greek myth, Icarus attempted to escape an island by attaching wings to his arms with wax; but when he flew too near the sun, the wax melted, and he fell to his death in the sea.
2. Wings or feathers.

Darkening the light and blotting out the sun;
Go thou my incense upward from this hearth,
And ask the gods to pardon this clear flame.

1843

Thoreau also called this poem "Orphic."

My life has been the poem I would have writ

My life has been the poem I would have writ,
But I could not both live and utter it.

1849

Mist

Low-anchored cloud,
Newfoundland air,
Fountain-head and source of rivers,
Dew-cloth, dream drapery,
And napkin spread by fays;[1]
Drifting meadow of the air,
Where bloom the daisied banks and violets,
And in whose fenny labyrinth[2]
The bittern[3] booms and heron wades;
Spirit of lakes and seas and rivers,
Bear only perfumes and the scent
Of healing herbs to just men's fields!

1849

Between the traveller and the setting sun

Between the traveller and the setting sun,
Upon some drifting sand heap of the shore,
A hound stands o'er the carcass of a man.

n.d.

1. Fairies.
2. Boggy maze.
3. North American marsh bird, a variety of heron, whose song is booming.

JULIA WARD HOWE
1819–1910

THE AUTHOR OF the "Battle Hymn of the Republic"—which became the anthem of the Union cause during the Civil War—was born in New York City, the daughter of a prominent banker, Samuel Ward, and an unpublished poet, Julia Rush (Cutler) Ward. Though her mother died when she was five, Julia Ward was raised in a cultured home by her father and received, through governesses and private schooling, an unusual degree of education for a woman of her time. In 1843, she married Dr. Samuel Gridley Howe, a passionate social reformer and champion of the underdog. They became deeply involved in the antislavery cause and together edited the abolitionist paper *Commonwealth*. After the slaves were freed, Howe emerged as a leading figure in the battle for women's suffrage. Along with being known for her devotion to causes, Howe began to make a name for herself as a poet, publishing the volume *Passion Flowers* in 1854. Touring the encampments of the Union army around Washington with her husband and their friend Reverend James Freeman Clarke in November 1861, she was pondering what she could do personally for the Union cause when her party heard some soldiers singing "John Brown's Body," an extremely popular song at the time that commemorated the death of the abolitionist John Brown. Brown had been hanged—and in the eyes of his supporters martyred—for his role as leader of the famous raid on the federal arsenal at Harper's Ferry in 1859.

The words of "John Brown's Body" are simple and repetitive:

> John Brown's body lies a-mouldering in the grave,
> John Brown's body lies a-mouldering in the grave,
> John Brown's body lies a-mouldering in the grave,
>   But his soul goes marching on.

Howe's friend Reverend Clarke suggested that she set better words to this stirring tune, and Howe acknowledged that she had often thought of doing just that. The following morning, as Howe described it, "I awoke in the gray of the early dawn, and to my astonishment found that the wished-for lines were arranging themselves in my brain. I lay quite still until the last verse had completed itself in my thoughts, then hastily arose, saying to myself, 'I shall lose this if I don't write it down immediately.'" After hastily scrawling the words with the stub of a pen, in the dim light so as not to wake her sleeping infant, she returned to her bed in her Washington hotel room, saying to herself, "I like this better than most things that I have written."

So did the nation. Published in *The Atlantic Monthly*, Howe's "Battle Hymn of the Republic" became, almost overnight, the anthem of the Northern cause.

As a song that has been heard and memorized more often than read, the "Battle Hymn" has become almost too familiar, and too historic, to be appreciated for its literary merit. Yet it remains a poem of genuine grandeur, steeped in a high-flown, quasi-biblical language that supports a series of sweeping metaphors that, stanza by stanza, assert and amplify upon a righteous and widely shared commitment to a sacred cause: ending slavery. In her "Battle Hymn," Howe consistently develops and elevates the simple words of "John Brown's Body" and at the same time alters the poem's central figure from Brown the martyr to Jesus the redeemer, all the while developing the theme of transfiguration through sacrifice. The penultimate stanza of the original tribute to Brown, which simply repeats, three times, "John Brown died that the slaves might be free," is characteristically transformed in Howe's remarkable final stanza.

Though Howe never wrote another poem that approaches the level of her "Battle Hymn," either for artistic merit or for lasting popular appeal, she has earned a permanent place in American history and culture thanks to this single remarkable achievement.

FURTHER READING

Julia Ward Howe. *Reminiscences, 1819–1899*. Boston: Houghton Mifflin & Co., 1900.
Gary Williams. *Hungry Heart: The Literary Emergence of Julia Ward Howe*. Amherst: University of Massachusetts Press, 1999.

Battle Hymn of the Republic

Mine eyes have seen the glory of the coming of the Lord:
He is trampling out the vintage where the grapes of wrath are stored;
He hath loosed the fateful lightning of his terrible swift sword:
    His truth is marching on.

I have seen Him in the watch-fires of a hundred circling camps;
They have builded Him an altar in the evening dews and damps;
I can read His righteous sentence by the dim and flaring lamps:
    His day is marching on.

I have read a fiery gospel, writ in burnished rows of steel:
"As ye deal with my contemners, so with you my grace shall deal;
Let the Hero, born of woman, crush the serpent with his heel,
    Since God is marching on."

He has sounded forth the trumpet that shall never call retreat;
He is sifting out the hearts of men before his judgment-seat:
Oh, be swift, my soul, to answer Him! be jubilant, my feet!
    Our God is marching on.

*   *   *

In the beauty of the lilies Christ was born across the sea,
With a glory in his bosom that transfigures you and me:
As he died to make men holy, let us die to make men free,
    While God is marching on.

1862

The text of the "Battle Hymn" is taken from the poem's first (anonymous) publication in the February 1862 edition of *The Atlantic Monthly*, where it appeared exactly as printed here. Significantly, this printing did not mention the poem's having been designed to be sung to the tune of "John Brown's Body," but readers quickly made the connection. The often-sung chorus "Glory, glory, Hallelujah" is a later interpolation.

HERMAN MELVILLE
1819–1891

HERMAN MELVILLE WAS not only one of the most powerful American novelists of the nineteenth century but also a poet of originality and distinction who turned to verse when his later novels failed to win public approval. Melville was born into a position of wealth and privilege, the descendant of successful merchants and Revolutionary War patriots on both sides of his family, and yet he lived out the reverse of the archetypal American story, going abruptly from riches to rags with the collapse of his father's textile import business. His father, Allan Melvill, moved from New York City to Albany to escape creditors, and he there changed his name to Melville as a further disguise. A broken man financially and physically, and showing signs of mental collapse, Allan Melville died in 1832, leaving a widow and eight children. Melville's mother, Maria, withdrew into a dignified and genteel poverty. As a result, Herman was forced to shift for himself—and learn to think for himself—at an early age. After completing a voyage on a merchant ship to Liverpool, Melville shipped from New Bedford in 1841 aboard the whaler *Acushnet*, bound for the South Seas. He would not return to Boston Harbor until 1844, after a series of colorful adventures on many ships and on various Pacific islands that became grist for his later books. Lacking the formal education that he had earlier been led to expect from his prominent birth, Melville could aptly claim with Ishmael, his narrator in *Moby-Dick*, that "a whale-ship was my Yale College and my Harvard."

Melville's personal history as a writer was also marked by early success, followed by the declining popular fortunes that caused him to turn to poetry. Melville achieved contemporary acclaim with the fictional works he produced in the years immediately following his long voyage, *Typee: A Peep at Polynesian Life* (1846) and its sequel *Omoo: A Narrative of Adventure in the South Seas* (1847). These colorful and fast-selling treatments presented his mostly sympathetic observations of traditional Polynesian culture and the threats to that culture imposed by Western colonialism. His fiction took a more philosophical and less popular turn in *Mardi* (1849), after which Melville rapidly turned out two novels aimed at more success, *Redburn* (1849) and *White-Jacket* (1850). Then, under the combined influence of his recent reading of Shakespeare's great tragedies and his personal encounters with the novelist Nathaniel Hawthorne, whose masterpiece *The Scarlet Letter* had just been published in 1850 and who owned a farm near Melville's in the Berkshire Mountains of Massachusetts, Melville produced his own masterpiece, *Moby-Dick* (1851). But *Moby-Dick*, which received mixed and partially comprehending reviews, was not a popular success, and his subsequent novels, *Pierre: or, The Ambiguities* (1852) and the brilliantly sardonic *The Confidence Man* (1857), were even less well received. His *Piazza Tales* (1856)—now justly celebrated for such masterly writings as the short story "Bartleby, the Scrivener," the novella "Benito Cereno," and that extraordinary travelogue, "The Encantadas, or Enchanted Isles"— also found only a limited audience. These works were the last fiction Melville would publish in his lifetime. Thus, after an extraordinarily productive period of just over a decade, during which he had produced eight novels and numerous shorter pieces of lasting importance, Melville fell mute as a fiction writer, leaving only the brilliant novella *Billy Budd* (posthumously published in 1924) to be discovered long after his death in 1891.

Feeling thwarted as a novelist, Melville turned to poetry, producing three books of lyrics, *Battle-Pieces and Aspects of the War* (1866), *John Marr and Other Sailors* (1888), and *Timoleon* (1891), as well as the lengthy and philosophical *Clarel: A Poem and Pilgrimage in the Holy Land* (1876).

Melville's poems seem less spontaneously lyrical than his prose. One scans his verse in vain for the sheer adventurous flow, the emotional and intellectual bedazzlement of the best passages in *Moby-Dick*, but his poems persistently display the Melvillian eye for unusual and telling ironies, the probing inquiry into life's underlying ambiguities that pervades *Moby-Dick* and that is given a still sharper turn in *The Confidence Man*. Robert Lowell suggested that "poetry was not his medium, yet no other American poet has allowed such glimmers of genius to escape darkness," an observation that points particularly to *Battle-Pieces*, which Stanton Garner aptly terms "one of the most underestimated of [Melville's] works." Melville's reflection on a sequence of dramatic events of the Civil War, which reads like a diary written in verse, rivals Whitman's *Drum Taps* (1865) as the most lasting book of poems on that war. Far more than Whitman's, Melville's meditations anticipate key themes of Randall Jarrell's poignant and desolate poems of World War II, particularly the depersonalization of the soldier in wars fought increasingly with "plain mechanic power," the painful epiphanies forced on the individual by the stark challenge of combat, and the guilt and moral ambivalence forced on the victors of even a "just" war. In later poems such as "The Maldive Shark," "Art," and "Monody," Melville remains the alternately brooding and wistful ironist, troubled and uncertain yet ever willing "to wrestle with the angel — Art."

FURTHER READING

Stanton Garner. *The Civil War World of Herman Melville*. Lawrence, Kan.: University Press of Kansas, 1993.

Robert Lowell. "New England and Further," in *Collected Prose*. New York: Farrar, Straus & Giroux, 1983.

Herman Melville. *Poems*. New York: Russell & Russell, 1963.

FROM Battle-Pieces and Aspects of the War

The Portent

(1859)

Hanging from the beam,
    Slowly swaying (such the law),
Gaunt the shadow on your green,
    Shenandoah![1]
The cut is on the crown[2]
(Lo, John Brown),
And the stabs shall heal no more.

Hidden in the cap
    Is the anguish none can draw;
So your future veils its face,
    Shenandoah!
But the streaming beard is shown
(Weird John Brown),
The meteor[3] of the war.

1866

In Melville's opinion, the execution-by-hanging of the radical abolitionist John Brown in 1859 for his leadership role in the raid on the federal arsenal at Harper's Ferry, Maryland, was a portent or omen of the onset of the Civil War two years later. Brown aimed to capture guns for distribution to slaves as encouragement to a general antislavery insurrection.

1. Harper's Ferry, scene of Brown's execution, stands at the northern tip of the fertile Shenandoah Valley, which would serve as the scene of several of the most violent campaigns of the war.

2. On the scaffold, Brown's head was bandaged from still-recent wounds, and his head was covered.

3. Traditionally, an omen of an important event.

The March into Virginia,

ENDING IN THE FIRST MANASSAS.

(July, 1861.)

Did all the lets[1] and bars appear
　　To every just or larger end,
Whence should come the trust and cheer?
　　Youth must its ignorant impulse lend—
Age finds place in the rear.
　　All wars are boyish, and are fought by boys,[2]
The champions and enthusiasts of the state:
　　Turbid ardors and vain joys
　　　　Not barrenly abate—
Stimulants to the power mature,
　　　　Preparatives of fate.

Who here forecasteth the event?
What heart but spurns at precedent
And warnings of the wise,
Contemned foreclosures of surprise?
The banners play, the bugles call,
The air is blue and prodigal.
　　No berrying party, pleasure-wooed,
No picnic party in the May,
Ever went less loth than they
　　Into that leafy neighborhood.
In Bacchic glee they file toward Fate,
Moloch's uninitiate;[3]
Expectancy, and glad surmise
Of battle's unknown mysteries.
All they feel is this: 'tis glory,
A rapture sharp, though transitory,
Yet lasting in belaureled story.
So they gaily go to fight,
Chatting left and laughing right.

But some who this blithe mood present,
　　As on in lightsome files they fare,
Shall die experienced ere three days are spent—

---

1. Legal term for a hindrance or obstacle.
2. Robert Lowell cites this line in the 1946 poem "Christmas Eve Under Hooker's Statue."
3. Moloch was a deity whose worship required the sacrifice of children by their parents; thus, any enterprise requiring appalling sacrifice.

Perish, enlightened by the vollied glare;
Or shame survive, and, like to adamant,[4]
The throe of Second Manassas share.

1866

As Melville's poem indicates, the largely amateur Union and Confederate forces in northern Virginia marched cheerfully off to the first major battle of the Civil War, accompanied by holidaying companies of politicians and socialites. The subsequent battle, known as the First Manassas (or, in the Union style, First Bull Run), was a shocking Union defeat that sent both Northern soldiers and congressional sightseers scrambling back to Washington in disorderly flight.

Shiloh

A REQUIEM.

(April, 1862.)

Skimming lightly, wheeling still,
    The swallows fly low
Over the field in clouded days,
    The forest-field of Shiloh—
Over the field where April rain
Solaced the parched ones stretched in pain
Through the pause of night
That followed the Sunday fight
    Around the church of Shiloh—
The church so lone, the log-built one,
That echoed to many a parting groan
        And natural prayer
    Of dying foemen mingled there—
Foemen at morn, but friends at eve—
    Fame or country least their care:
(What like a bullet can undeceive!)
    But now they lie low,
While over them the swallows skim,
    And all is hushed at Shiloh.

1866

Melville recalls the epic early Civil War battle of Shiloh, a Confederate defeat fought over two violent days, April 6 and 7, 1862, in densely forested terrain in southwest Tennessee

4. A legendary stone of impenetrable hardness; hence, any impenetrable or unyielding substance or attitude.

around the one-room, log Shiloh Church. The unprecedented casualty figures—13,000 Union troops and 10,700 Confederates killed, wounded, and captured—shocked the nation.

A Utilitarian View of the Monitor's Fight

Plain be the phrase, yet apt the verse,
　　More ponderous than nimble;
For since grimed War here laid aside
His painted pomp, 'twould ill befit
　　　Overmuch to ply
　　The rhyme's barbaric symbol.

Hail to victory without the gaud
　　Of glory; zeal that needs no fans
Of banners; plain mechanic power
Plied cogently in War now placed—
　　　Where War belongs—
　　Among the trades and artisans.

Yet this was battle, and intense—
　　Beyond the strife of fleets heroic;
Deadlier, closer, calm 'mid storm;
No passion; all went on by crank.
　　　Pivot, and screw,
　　And calculations of caloric.

Needless to dwell; the story's known.
　　The ringing of those plates on plates
Still ringeth round the world—
The clangor of the blacksmiths' fray.
　　　The anvil-din
　　Resounds this message from the Fates:

War shall yet be, and to the end;
　　But war-paint shows the streaks of weather;
War yet shall be, but the warriors
Are now but operatives; War's made
　　　Less grand than Peace,
　　And a singe runs through lace and feather.
　　　　　　　1866

Melville believes that the first clash of steam-powered naval ironclads, between the Union's *Monitor* and the Confederate's *Merrimac* (or *Virginia*, in Southern parlance) on March 9, 1862, in Hampton Roads, Virginia, which ended in stalemate, foreshadows the end of the comparatively "romantic" battles between wooden men-of-war under full sail.

The House-Top.

A NIGHT PIECE.

(*July, 1863.*)

No sleep. The sultriness pervades the air
And binds the brain—a dense oppression, such
As tawny tigers feel in matted shades,
Vexing their blood and making apt for ravage.
Beneath the stars the roofy desert spreads
Vacant as Libya. All is hushed near by.
Yet fitfully from far breaks a mixed surf
Of muffled sound, the Atheist roar of riot.
Yonder, where parching Sirius set in drought,
Balefully glares red Arson—there—and there.
The Town is taken by its rats—ship-rats
And rats of the wharves. All civil charms
And priestly spells which late held hearts in awe—
Fear-bound, subjected to a better sway
Than sway of self; these like a dream dissolve,
And man rebounds whole aeons back in nature.
Hail to the low dull rumble, dull and dead,
And ponderous drag that shakes the wall.
Wise Draco comes, deep in the midnight roll
Of black artillery; he comes, though late;
In code corroborating Calvin's creed
And cynic tyrannies of honest kings;
He comes, nor parlies; and the Town, redeemed,
Gives thanks devout; nor, being thankful, heeds
The grimy slur on the Republic's faith implied,
Which holds that Man is naturally good,
And—more—is Nature's Roman, never to be scourged.

1866

Unlike the speaker of this poem, Melville was not present in New York City in July 1863 during the violent riots that occurred to protest inequalities in the draft. Melville's recorded comments and letters display some sympathy toward the rioters' grievances. Thus Stanton Garner suggests reading "The House-Top" as a dramatic monologue, portraying the impulsive hostility that the riots engendered in many, though not necessarily in Melville.

The College Colonel

He rides at their head;
    A crutch by his saddle just slants in view,
One slung arm is in splints, you see,
    Yet he guides his strong steed—how coldly too.

He brings his regiment home—
    Not as they filed two years before,
But a remnant half-tattered, and battered, and worn,
Like castaway sailors, who—stunned
    By the surf's loud roar,
    Their mates dragged back and seen no more—
Again and again breast the surge,
    And at last crawl, spent, to shore.

A still rigidity and pale—
    An Indian aloofness lones his brow;
He has lived a thousand years
Compressed in battle's pains and prayers,
    Marches and watches slow.

There are welcoming shouts, and flags;
    Old men off hat to the Boy,[1]
Wreaths from gay balconies fall at his feet,
    But to *him*—there comes alloy.

It is not that a leg is lost,
    It is not that an arm is maimed,
It is not that the fever has racked—
    Self he has long disclaimed.

But all through the Seven Days' Fight,[2]
    And deep in the Wilderness grim,[3]

1. Bartlett was just twenty-three when his regiment returned to Pittsfield in 1863.
2. Union defeat in the Peninsular Campaign, June 25 to July 1, 1862.
3. Bloody campaign in May and June 1864.

And in the field-hospital tent,
  And Petersburg crater,[4] and dim
Lean brooding in Libby,[5] there came—
  Ah heaven!—what *truth* to him.

                    1866

Melville's young friend William Francis Bartlett left his studies at Harvard College to enlist in the Union army at the war's outset. Several times wounded and once captured, he rose to the rank of colonel. Melville's poem, which slightly alters the actual chronology, depicts a moment when the much-battered Bartlett returned to his native Pittsfield, Massachusetts, leading the tattered remnants of his regiment. He would later return to combat, rising to the rank of general and commanding a division.

The Apparition

A RETROSPECT

Convulsions came; and, where the field
  Long slept in pastoral green,
A goblin-mountain was upheaved
(Sure the scared sense was all deceived),
  Marl-glen and slag-ravine.

The unreserve of Ill was there,
  The clinkers in her last retreat;
But, ere the eye could take it in,
Or mind could comprehension win,
  It sunk!—and at our feet.

So, then, Solidity's a crust—
  The core of fire below;
All may go well for many a year,
But who can think without a fear
  Of horrors that happen so?

                    1866

Melville's poem reconsiders an event in the Union's lengthy siege of Richmond and St. Petersburg, Virginia. Northern forces tunneled under the Confederate lines and set off a massive explosion, creating a huge crater and a temporary hole in the Confederate defenses.

---

4. See note to the following poem, "The Apparition."
5. Infamous Confederate prison in Richmond, Virginia, where Bartlett was, for a time, imprisoned. He was eventually released in a prisoner exchange.

The Union attack, after early progress, was eventually repulsed. Melville's poem ignores the battle as such to contemplate the revelation that the earth's solid and permanent surface is really just an "apparition" or crust, which can be rent apart by the application of sufficient force.

OTHER POEMS

The Maldive Shark

About the Shark, phlegmatical one,
Pale sot[1] of the Maldive sea,
The sleek little pilot-fish, azure and slim,
How alert in attendance be.
From his saw-pit of mouth, from his charnel of maw,
They have nothing of harm to dread,
But liquidly glide on his ghastly flank
Or before his Gorgonian[2] head;
Or lurk in the port of serrated teeth
In white triple tiers of glittering gates,
And there find a haven when peril's abroad,
An asylum in jaws of the Fates!
They are friends; and friendly they guide him to prey,
Yet never partake of the treat—
Eyes and brains to the dotard lethargic and dull,
Pale ravener of horrible meat.

1888

Melville wrote in *Mardi*, "There is a fish in the sea that ever more, like a surly lord, only goes abroad attended by his suite. It is the shovel-nosed shark." This shark's "suite" is his retinue of pilot fish. The Maldive Sea surrounds the Maldive Islands, off the southwest coast of India.

Art

In placid hours well pleased we dream
Of many a brave unbodied scheme.
But form to lend, pulsed life create,

1. Scourge or whip (obsolete).
2. Hideous, deadly. In Greek mythology, the Gorgons were frightful women with snakes for hair whose glance could turn men to stone.

What unlike things must meet and mate:
A flame to melt—a wind to freeze;
Sad patience—joyous energies;
Humility—yet pride and scorn;
Instinct and study; love and hate;
Audacity—reverence. These must mate
And fuse with Jacob's[1] mystic heart,
To wrestle with the angel—Art.

1891

Monody

To have known him, to have loved him
    After loneness long;
And then to be estranged in life,
    And neither in the wrong;
And now for death to set his seal—
    Ease me, a little ease, my song!

By wintry hills his hermit-mound
    The sheeted snow-drifts drape,
And houseless there the snow-bird flits
    Beneath the fir-trees' crape:
Glazed now with ice the cloistral vine[1]
    That hid the shyest grape.

1891

A monody is a Greek pastoral poem expressing grief at another's death, often a fellow poet-shepherd. This poem laments the death of Nathaniel Hawthorne, who died in 1864.

1. See Genesis 32:24–30: after wrestling with an angel, Jacob was blessed by God.

1. "Vine" was Melville's name for the introverted Hawthorne in the long poem *Clarel*.

JAMES RUSSELL LOWELL
1819–1891

DURING JAMES RUSSELL LOWELL'S lifetime, the United States grew from a largely rural young country to an increasingly urbanized and socially diversified industrial giant, a transition marked by a bloody and traumatic Civil War. Lowell's best and most popular works date from the earlier part of his life, and they reflect the simpler cultural values and social institutions that history would soon sweep away. For a brief period, he was one of the most popular poets of his time, the inheritor of Longfellow's crown. By the time of his death, however, this once-beloved "fireside poet" had already lost favor. He was "pedestalled for oblivion," as his great-grandnephew, the poet Robert Lowell, once acerbically observed.

Lowell's humorous poems remain his most enduring poetic accomplishments. *The Biglow Papers*, written in comic dialect, reflects both his opposition to the U.S.-Mexican War of 1846–48 and his antislavery beliefs. A *Fable for Critics* satirizes America's nascent literary establishment by making gentle—and not-so-gentle—fun of the leading writers of the pre–Civil War era. Rowdy and learned at the same time, this poem skewers and praises its chosen writers with a keen wit that still seems pointed today. Lowell's other, more serious poems have come to seem too hackneyed in their images and too slack in their ideas and emotions for a public taste educated by the likes of Emily Dickinson and Walt Whitman. Only the humorous poems retain enough bite to attract and hold most readers.

Lowell was born and lived most of his life in Cambridge, Massachusetts. After graduating with a law degree from Harvard University and marrying fellow poet Maria White (also included in this anthology), he began to make his way as a literary craftsman and public intellectual. He published volumes of poems, collections of critical essays, and articles in abolitionist journals. *The Biglow Papers* (first series) and A *Fable for Critics* both appeared in 1848, as the U.S.-Mexican War was concluding and the Civil War was looming. That year, Lowell's twenty-ninth, proved the high point of his creative life.

In the 1850s, Lowell's wife and three of his four children died. He remarried, helped to found and edit *The Atlantic Monthly*, and took a professorship of modern languages at Harvard, a post he held for the next twenty years. But his inspiration flagged as he increasingly played the role of worthy public figure. His poems and essays seemed to have less and less relevance to the developing nation. After serving as American ambassador to Spain (1877–80) and to Great Britain (1880–85), and after the death of his second wife, Frances, in 1885, Lowell retired from both public and literary life, publishing only one additional book, a collection of his speeches. He died where he was born, in Cambridge, but that city, like the nation, by then bore few resemblances to the world Lowell knew as a young man.

FURTHER READING

Dorothy Broaddus. *Genteel Rhetoric: Writing High Culture in Nineteenth-Century Boston*. Columbia: University of South Carolina Press, 1999.
Martin Duberman. *James Russell Lowell*. Boston: Houghton Mifflin, 1966.
James Russell Lowell. *Complete Poetical Works*. Ed. H. E. Scudder. Boston: Houghton Mifflin, 1897.
Claire McGlinchee. *James Russell Lowell*. New York: Twayne, 1967.

FROM *A Fable for Critics*

Ralph Waldo Emerson

"There comes Emerson first, whose rich words, every one,
Are like gold nails in temples to hang trophies on,[1]
Whose prose is grand verse, while his verse, the Lord knows,
Is some of it pr — No, 'tis not even prose;
I'm speaking of meters; some poems have welled
From those rare depths of soul that have ne'er been excelled;
They're not epics, but that doesn't matter a pin,
In creating, the only hard thing's to begin;
A grass blade's no easier to make than an oak;
If you've once found the way, you've achieved the grand stroke;
In the worst of his poems are mines of rich matter,
But thrown in a heap with a crush and a clatter;
Now it is not one thing nor another alone
Makes a poem, but rather the general tone,
The something pervading, uniting the whole,
The before unconceived, unconceivable soul,
So that just in removing this trifle or that, you
Take away, as it were, a chief limb of the statue;
Roots, wood, bark, and leaves singly perfect may be,
But, clapt hodge-podge together, they don't make a tree.

"But to come back to Emerson (whom, by the way,
I believe we left waiting) — his is, we may say,
A Greek head on right Yankee shoulders, whose range
Has Olympus[2] for one pole, for t'other the Exchange;
He seems, to my thinking (although I'm afraid
The comparison must, long ere this, have been made)

1. Possibly an allusion to Ecclesiastes 12:11: "The words of the wise are as goads, and as nails fastened by the masters of assemblies. . . ."

2. According to Greek myth, Mount Olympus was the home of the gods. The Exchange is the stock market.

A Plotinus-Montaigne,[3] where the Egyptian's gold mist
And the Gascon's shrewd wit cheek-by-jowl coexist;
All admire, and yet scarcely six converts he's got
To I don't (nor they either) exactly know what;
For though he builds glorious temples 'tis odd
He leaves never a doorway to get in a god,
'Tis refreshing to old fashioned people like me
To meet such a primitive Pagan as he,
In whose mind all creation is duly respected
As parts of himself—just a little projected;
And who's willing to worship the stars and the sun,
A convert to nothing but Emerson.
So perfect a balance there is in his head,
That he talks of things sometimes as if they were dead;
Life, nature, love, God, and affairs of that sort,
He looks at as merely ideas; in short,
As if they were fossils stuck round in a cabinet,
Of such vast extent that our earth's a mere dab in it;
Composed just as he is inclined to conjecture her,
Namely, one part pure earth, ninety-nine parts pure lecturer;
You are filled with delight at his clear demonstration,
Each figure, word, gesture, just fits the occasion,
With the quiet precision of science he'll sort 'em
But you can't help suspecting the whole a *post mortem.*

"There are persons, mole-blind to the soul's make and style,
Who insist on a likeness 'twixt him and Carlyle;[4]
To compare him with Plato would be vastly fairer,
Carlyle's the more burly, but E. is the rarer;
He sees fewer objects, but clearlier, trulier,
If C's as original, E's more peculiar;
That he's more of a man you might say of the one,
Of the other he's more of an Emerson. . . ."

---

3. The Egyptian-born philosopher Plotinus (205–270) revived the idealism of Plato, whereas Michel de Montaigne (1533–1592), born in the French province of Gascony, relied on rationalism and skepticism in his writing. Lowell suggests that Emerson blends the two kinds of thinking.

4. Thomas Carlyle (1795–1871), the author of *Sartor Resartus*, was a Scottish writer whose ideas overlapped with those of his acquaintance and correspondent, Emerson.

Edgar Allan Poe

"There comes Poe, with his raven, like Barnaby Rudge,[5]
Three fifths of him genius and two fifths sheer fudge,
Who talks like a book of iambs and pentameters,
In a way to make people of common sense damn meters,
Who has written some things quite the best of their kind,
But the heart somehow seems all squeezed out by the mind."

James Russell Lowell

"There is Lowell, who's striving Parnassus[6] to climb
With a whole bale of *isms* tied together with rhyme;
He might get on alone, spite of brambles and boulders,
But he can't with that bundle he has on his shoulders;
The top of the hill he will ne'er come nigh reaching
Till he learns the distinction 'twixt singing and preaching;
His lyre has some chords that would ring pretty well,
But he'd rather by half make a drum of the shell,
And rattle away till he's old as Methusalem,[7]
At the head of a march to the last new Jerusalem."[8]

1848

This book-length poem uses comic rhymes, erudite allusions, and a boisterous tone to survey the contemporary scene of American writing. It includes some memorably sharp comments about writers such as Emerson, Poe—and Lowell himself. The poem's speaker is a critic who is explaining American writers to the Greek god Apollo.

5. This line alludes to Poe's most famous poem, "The Raven" (included in this anthology), and to the title character of Charles Dickens's novel *Barnaby Rudge*, who lives with a raven.
6. In classical myth, Mount Parnassus was sacred to Apollo (the god of poetry) and the home of the Muses (nine goddesses who rule over the arts).

7. According to Genesis 5:27, Methuselah lived 969 years.
8. That is, Lowell will lead every new reform effort that arises.

WALT WHITMAN
1819–1892

Walt whitman transformed poetry by his revolutionary experiments with language and form and by re-imagining how a self and a people could be depicted. A poet of liberation, he modernized and in various ways radicalized verse in the United States and throughout the world. Like his contemporary, Emily Dickinson, who fostered different but equally imaginative poetic changes, Whitman reconceived how subjectivity might be evoked, explored, and expanded. At the same time, his acute social sense encouraged him to portray the rich diversity of human relationships and cultural influences that coursed through the developing nation.

Whitman's representations of the interior life run the gamut from pride, concern, desire, and ecstasy to loneliness, shame, fear, and anguish. Nevertheless, several key assumptions underlie the great emotional and linguistic variety of his poetry. He insisted on the equality of all human beings. "By God! I will accept nothing which all cannot have their counterpart of on the same terms," he wrote in "Song of Myself." He also believed that the phrase "life, liberty, and the pursuit of happiness" was not simply a political promise contained in the Declaration of Independence but a spiritual promise inherent in the human condition. "Do you see O my brothers and sisters?" he implored in "Song of Myself." "It is not chaos or death—it is form, union, plan—it is eternal life—it is Happiness."

Whitman was born in 1819 in West Hills, Long Island, to a struggling Quaker and deist farm family, of Dutch ancestry on his mother's side and of English on his father's. When Whitman was four, the family was forced to sell the farm and move to Brooklyn, where Whitman's father took a job as a carpenter. Whitman grew up in Brooklyn, along with eight brothers and sisters. Nevertheless, he continued to spend summers with his grandparents in rural Long Island, romping in fields and along the seashore, and reading books, including Homer's *Iliad* and Virgil's *Aeneid*. He left public school in his early teenage years to earn a living in the printing trade. After a series of jobs as printer, handyman, teacher, and journalist, he landed a job, while still in his mid-twenties, editing the *Brooklyn Eagle*, a prominent newspaper of the time. During this period he also wrote short stories attacking corporal punishment and a novel called *Franklin Evans*, which portrayed the evils of alcohol. But after two years at the *Eagle*, he was fired because of his antislavery editorials.

Between 1848 and 1855 Whitman drifted from job to job in journalism, printing, carpentry, and home building. He later told a friend that he was "simmering, simmering." Ralph Waldo Emerson, he said, brought him "to a boil." In 1842 Whitman had heard Emerson deliver a lecture that would eventually become his visionary essay "The Poet" (reprinted in this anthology). By the early 1850s Whitman apparently was thinking back to that lecture, or perhaps he read the published essay. Emerson had written, "Our logrolling, our stumps and their politics, our fisheries, our Negroes, and Indians, our boasts, and our repudiations, the wrath of rogues, and the pusillanimity of honest men, the northern trade, the southern planting, the western clearing, Oregon, and Texas, are yet unsung. Yet America is a poem in our eyes; its ample geography dazzles the imagination, and it will not wait long for metres." Whitman found in Emerson the inspiration he needed. Reflecting Emerson's call for "a metre-making argument," Whitman established free verse as a central mode of poetic expression. Just as Emerson had recommended that the poet provide a new and unique "confession," so Whitman took the individual as his central frame of reference. Responding to Emerson's argument that the poet should become a "liberating god," Whitman wrote in uplifting terms about both the soul and the body, though giving the body more attention than Emerson might have liked. Indeed, Whitman characteristically celebrated both sides of every binary Western civilization employed to sort and judge: body/soul, self/ other, male/female, white/black, and so on. Whitman would characteristically pronounce, "I give them the same, receive them the same." Whereas Emerson had asserted that "America is a poem in our eyes," Whitman sought to encompass the whole American experience in a vocabulary that was both "American" and multiplicitous.

Poems such as "Song of Myself" attempted for the first time "to put a human being, freely, fully, and truly on record," as he later remarked in his memoir "A Backward Glance o'er Travel'd Roads." That description, however, exaggerated the case. Whitman carefully gauged what he would reveal and conceal in his poems. The self that he put "on record" was at least partly an invention. But it provided a powerful and enduring myth of an independent self, filled with hopes, loves, doubts, and reassurances. Constructed out of a combination of the actual and the dreamed, this endlessly mobile, contradictory, and charismatic self became a prototype of modern personhood and the source of innumerable subsequent imaginings.

Whitman had the first version of *Leaves of Grass* ready for publication early in 1855. He intended the book, which included "Song of Myself," to be his "epic of democracy" ("Preface," 1872). Unable to find a publisher willing to take a risk on it, he finally sold his house and used the proceeds to publish the volume himself on July 4, 1855. The book was widely ignored. Nevertheless, it did receive a surprising endorsement from the one reader Whitman wished most to please: Ralph Waldo Emerson. Whitman sent Emerson a copy of the volume, and the elder writer, who had never even heard of Whitman, wrote back words of ringing praise, ending, "I greet you at the beginning of a great career." (The entire letter is reprinted in the Emerson section of this anthology.) Whitman was overjoyed.

Without permission, he published Emerson's letter in the *New York Tribune*, and then he quoted from it and replied to it in the second edition of *Leaves of Grass*, which he rushed out the very next year. Emerson's endorsement did not make *Leaves of Grass* a popular success, however. Nothing in Whitman's lifetime could accomplish that goal. But Emerson's letter did help to establish Whitman as a favorite among a small cultural avant-garde. After the poet's death, such limited but passionate approval would grow to global acclaim. Whitman's posterity would come to view him as one of the great and enduring creators in the history of poetry.

Following the second edition of *Leaves of Grass* in 1856, Whitman fell into a period of depression and creative silence. He supported himself for a while as editor of the *Brooklyn Times*, though again he was eventually fired, this time for writing in support of prostitutes and premarital sex. In the year following his dismissal, he wrote nothing. There were multiple causes for this poetic inactivity. Most obviously, *Leaves of Grass* had failed to find a large audience. Although Whitman had intended it to be America's epic, America seemed not to want it. Moreover, Whitman may have felt that he was growing older (he turned forty in 1859), that he had accomplished little, and that his talent had begun to wane. He also faced the obvious difficulty of earning a living. Some biographers have speculated that Whitman had a same-sex romantic relationship that ended badly, leaving him stunned by loneliness, regret, and loss. Despite the occasionally aggressive heterosexual pose in his self-representations, his actual love life was far more complex and seemed to center on men. Finally, public events were daily going from bad to worse: President Buchanan was failing as a leader, Southern slavery seemed more entrenched than ever, and an incredibly bloody fratricidal war loomed on the near horizon. The poet who wrote in the 1855 "Preface" to *Leaves of Grass* that "the United States themselves are essentially the greatest poem" watched in mute horror as the nation slowly fell apart.

Whitman broke his poetic silence at the end of the 1850s by writing "Out of the Cradle Endlessly Rocking," "As I Ebb'd with the Ocean of Life," and "I Sit and Look Out," poems that fully recognize loneliness and suffering. If the climactic words in "Song of Myself" are "eternal life" and "Happiness," the key word in "Out of the Cradle Endlessly Rocking" is "death." Whitman had traveled a great emotional distance in a few years. He published a new edition of *Leaves of Grass* in 1860, filled with new poems that spoke not of "form, union, plan" but of solitude, chaos, and loss. The doubt and despair that had appeared as a subtext in the earlier poems (for example, in sections 36–38 of "Song of Myself") now became the main text. The failures of intimacy, the frustrations of desire, and the anxieties about the public sphere, which had been hidden in the earlier poems, now came to light. Whitman overcame his silence by facing his demons.

After the Civil War began in 1861, Whitman moved from New York to Washington, D.C., where he tended wounded and dying soldiers in local hospitals. To support himself he held a series of government jobs. In June 1865 he was again fired from a job, this time because the secretary of the interior discovered he was the author of *Leaves of Grass*, which this cabinet member considered obscene. The preceding month Whitman's collection of Civil War poems appeared, entitled *Drum-Taps*. These poems moved from initial fervor for the Union cause to a profound sense of the great suffering the war had caused among both Union and Confederate soldiers. A sequel published later that same year included Whitman's great elegy for Abraham Lincoln, "When Lilacs Last in the Dooryard Bloom'd." The best of these poems express the pity of war and the agony of death in ways that are utterly unforgettable.

A fourth edition of *Leaves of Grass* appeared in 1867, containing the poems of *Drum-Taps* as well as several other new poems. As in the second and third editions, familiar poems such as "Song of Myself" were altered and expanded—a habit of revision that ceased only with the tenth or "deathbed" edition of the volume in 1891–92. Although his poetry was never popular in his lifetime, Whitman developed a band of loyal followers that included the journalist William O'Connor (who wrote a defense of the poet curiously called *The Good Gray Poet*), the naturalist John Burroughs (who wrote a memoir of Whitman), Richard Bucke (who wrote the first Whitman biography), William Michael Rossetti (who introduced Whitman's work to Great Britain), Horace Traubel (who reproduced some of Whitman's conversations), and such American poets as Adah Menken, William Vaughn Moody, and Sadakichi Hartmann (all included in this anthology). In 1873 Whitman suffered a paralyzing stroke. He moved from Washington to his brother's home in Camden, New Jersey, where his mother lay dying. After her death, he continued to live in Camden. He entertained his admirers when they visited, made one trip to the West in 1879, bought a modest home in 1884, and continued to write new poems for *Leaves of Grass*. He died on March 26, 1892, at the age of seventy-three at home in Camden.

Whitman broadened the cultural work of the nation's founders to include more kinds of people. He sympathized with individuals who were native-born and immigrant, female and male, agricultural and urban, of various races and classes and creeds—though he occasionally turned them into stereotypes or spectacles as well. Although he had a definite but limited effect on his own era, he subsequently became a tremendous force in global culture, helping to shape poetry in Asia, Africa, Latin America, and Europe as well as his homeland. His influence is evident in the work of poets as disparate as William Carlos Williams, Hart Crane, Langston Hughes, Federico García Lorca, Pablo Neruda, Muriel Rukeyser, Robert Lowell, Allen Ginsberg, Carlos Drummond de Andrade, and Cherríe Moraga. His poems evoke desire in ways that liberate romantic and erotic fantasies in readers of very different orientations. His verse breaks rules, forging a rebellious, individualistic, and varied style that mixes high discourse with low—the *Bhagavad*

Gita with the *New York Tribune*, as Emerson observed. The poems are alternately natural and urban, fleshly and spiritual, personal and public, loquacious and terse, extroverted and introspective, up-to-the-minute and timeless. "Do I contradict myself?" he asks in "Song of Myself." "Very well then, I contradict myself." Above all, Whitman incorporates a driving verbal inventiveness with a resonant and consoling humanity. Readers of many generations and places have found his final words in "Song of Myself" to ring true: "I stop somewhere waiting for you."

FURTHER READING

Betsy Erkkila. *Whitman: The Political Poet*. New York: Oxford University Press, 1989.

Ed Folsom. *Walt Whitman's Native Representations*. Cambridge, Eng.: Cambridge University Press, 1994.

Ezra Greenspan, ed. *The Cambridge Companion to Walt Whitman*. Cambridge, Eng.: Cambridge University Press, 1995.

Jerome Loving. *Emerson, Whitman, and the American Muse*. Chapel Hill: University of North Carolina Press, 1982.

James E. Miller, Jr. *A Critical Guide to Leaves of Grass*. Chicago: University of Chicago Press, 1957.

Michael Moon. *Disseminating Whitman*. Cambridge, Mass.: Harvard University Press, 1991.

Vivian R. Pollak. *The Erotic Whitman*. Berkeley: University of California Press, 2000.

Kenneth Price. *Whitman and Tradition: The Poet in His Century*. New Haven, Conn.: Yale University Press, 1990.

David S. Reynolds. *Walt Whitman's America: A Cultural Biography*. New York: Random House, 1995.

Horace Traubel. *With Walt Whitman in Camden*. Boston: Small, Maynard, 1906.

Walt Whitman. *Leaves of Grass*. Ed. Harold W. Blodgett and Sculley Bradley. New York: Norton, 1965.

Song of Myself

1

I celebrate myself, and sing myself,
And what I assume you shall assume,
For every atom belonging to me as good belongs to you.

I loafe and invite my soul,
I lean and loafe at my ease observing a spear of summer grass.

My tongue, every atom of my blood, form'd from this soil, this air,
Born here of parents born here from parents the same, and their parents the same,
I, now thirty-seven years old in perfect health begin,[1]
Hoping to cease not till death.

*   *   *

1. Whitman was in fact only thirty-five or thirty-six when he began the poem.

Creeds and schools in abeyance,
Retiring back a while sufficed at what they are, but never forgotten,
I harbor for good or bad, I permit to speak at every hazard,
Nature without check with original energy.

2

Houses and rooms are full of perfumes, the shelves are crowded with perfumes,
I breathe the fragrance myself and know it and like it,
The distillation would intoxicate me also, but I shall not let it.

The atmosphere is not a perfume, it has no taste of the distillation, it is odorless,
It is for my mouth forever, I am in love with it,
I will go to the bank by the wood and become undisguised and naked,
I am mad for it to be in contact with me.

The smoke of my own breath,
Echoes, ripples, buzz'd whispers, love-root, silk-thread, crotch and vine,
My respiration and inspiration, the beating of my heart, the passing of blood and air
     through my lungs,
The sniff of green leaves and dry leaves, and of the shore and dark-color'd sea-rocks, and
     of hay in the barn,
The sound of the belch'd words of my voice loos'd to the eddies of the wind,
A few light kisses, a few embraces, a reaching around of arms,
The play of shine and shade on the trees as the supple boughs wag,
The delight alone or in the rush of the streets, or along the fields and hill-sides,
The feeling of health, the full-noon trill, the song of me rising from bed and meeting
     the sun.

Have you reckon'd a thousand acres much? have you reckon'd the earth much?
Have you practis'd so long to learn to read?
Have you felt so proud to get at the meaning of poems?

Stop this day and night with me and you shall possess the origin of all poems,
You shall possess the good of the earth and sun, (there are millions of suns left,)
You shall no longer take things at second or third hand, nor look through the eyes of the
     dead, nor feed on the spectres in books,
You shall not look through my eyes either, nor take things from me,
You shall listen to all sides and filter them from your self.

3

I have heard what the talkers were talking, the talk of the beginning and the end,
But I do not talk of the beginning or the end.

✻   ✻   ✻

There was never any more inception than there is now,
Nor any more youth or age than there is now,
And will never be any more perfection than there is now,
Nor any more heaven or hell than there is now.

Urge and urge and urge,
Always the procreant urge of the world.

Out of the dimness opposite equals advance, always substance and increase, always sex,
Always a knit of identity, always distinction, always a breed of life.

To elaborate is no avail, learn'd and unlearn'd feel that it is so.

Sure as the most certain sure, plumb in the uprights,[2] well entretied, braced in the
    beams,
Stout as a horse, affectionate, haughty, electrical,
I and this mystery here we stand.

Clear and sweet is my soul, and clear and sweet is all that is not my soul.

Lack one lacks both, and the unseen is proved by the seen,
Till that becomes unseen and receives proof in its turn.

Showing the best and dividing it from the worst, age vexes age,
Knowing the perfect fitness and equanimity[3] of things, while they discuss I am silent,
    and go bathe and admire myself.

Welcome is every organ and attribute of me, and of any man hearty and clean,
Not an inch nor a particle of an inch is vile, and none shall be less familiar than the rest.

I am satisfied—I see, dance, laugh, sing;
As the hugging and loving bed-fellow[4] sleeps at my side through the night, and
    withdraws at the peep of the day with stealthy tread,
Leaving me baskets cover'd with white towels swelling the house with their plenty,
Shall I postpone my acceptation and realization and scream at my eyes,
That they turn from gazing after and down the road,
And forthwith cipher[5] and show me to a cent,
Exactly the value of one and exactly the value of two, and which is ahead?

2. That is, with vertical or erect posture. Well en-   4. In the 1855 version, the bed-fellow is identified
tretied: strongly cross-braced.   as God.
3. Calmness or equality.   5. Calculate.

4

Trippers and askers surround me,

People I meet, the effect upon me of my early life or the ward and city I live in, or the
nation,

The latest dates, discoveries, inventions, societies, authors old and new,

My dinner, dress, associates, looks, compliments, dues,

The real or fancied indifference of some man or woman I love,

The sickness of one of my folks or of myself, or ill-doing or loss or lack of money, or
depressions or exaltations,

Battles, the horrors of fratricidal war, the fever of doubtful news, the fitful events;

These come to me days and nights and go from me again,

But they are not the Me myself.

Apart from the pulling and hauling stands what I am,

Stands amused, complacent, compassionating, idle, unitary,

Looks down, is erect, or bends an arm on an impalpable certain rest,

Looking with side-curved head curious what will come next,

Both in and out of the game and watching and wondering at it.

Backward I see in my own days where I sweated through fog with linguists and
contenders,

I have no mockings or arguments, I witness and wait.

5

I believe in you my soul, the other I am must not abase itself to you,

And you must not be abased to the other.

Loafe with me on the grass, loose the stop from your throat,

Not words, not music or rhyme I want, not custom or lecture, not even the best,

Only the lull I like, the hum of your valvèd voice.

I mind[6] how once we lay such a transparent summer morning,

How you settled your head athwart my hips and gently turn'd over upon me,

And parted the shirt from my bosom-bone, and plunged your tongue to my bare-stript
heart,

And reach'd till you felt my beard, and reach'd till you held my feet.

Swiftly arose and spread around me the peace and knowledge that pass all the argument
of the earth,[7]

6. Recall.
7. Perhaps an allusion to or a revision of St. Paul's
assurance in the New Testament: "And the peace
of God, which passeth all understanding, shall
keep your hearts and minds through Christ Jesus"
(Philippians 4:7).

And I know that the hand of God is the promise of my own,
And I know that the spirit of God is the brother of my own,
And that all the men ever born are also my brothers, and the women my sisters and
      lovers,
And that a kelson[8] of the creation is love,
And limitless are leaves stiff or drooping in the fields,
And brown ants in the little wells beneath them,
And mossy scabs[9] of the worm fence, heap'd stones, elder, mullein and poke-weed.

6

A child said *What is the grass?* fetching it to me with full hands;
How could I answer the child? I do not know what it is any more than he.

I guess it must be the flag of my disposition, out of hopeful green stuff woven.

Or I guess it is the handkerchief of the Lord,
A scented gift and remembrancer designedly dropt,
Bearing the owner's name someway in the corners, that we may see and remark, and say
      Whose?

Or I guess the grass is itself a child, the produced babe of the vegetation.

Or I guess it is a uniform hieroglyphic,
And it means, Sprouting alike in broad zones and narrow zones,
Growing among black folks as among white,
Kanuck,[10] Tuckahoe, Congressman, Cuff, I give them the same, I receive them the same.

And now it seems to me the beautiful uncut hair of graves.

Tenderly will I use you curling grass,
It may be you transpire from the breasts of young men,
It may be if I had known them I would have loved them,
It may be you are from old people, or from offspring taken soon out of their mothers'
      laps,
And here you are the mothers' laps.

This grass is very dark to be from the white heads of old mothers,
Darker than the colorless beards of old men,
Dark to come from under the faint red roofs of mouths.

      ✳   ✳   ✳

8. Joined and bolted timbers bracing a ship's keel.
9. Fungi. Worm fence: fence of crossed logs.
Mullein: fig-wort herb.
10. Colloquial term for a French Canadian. The following terms indicate a native of Virginia, a member of the House of Representatives, and an African American.

O I perceive after all so many uttering tongues,
And I perceive they do not come from the roofs of mouths for nothing.

I wish I could translate the hints about the dead young men and women,
And the hints about old men and mothers, and the offspring taken soon out of their laps.

What do you think has become of the young and old men?
And what do you think has become of the women and children?

They are alive and well somewhere,
The smallest sprout shows there is really no death,
And if ever there was it led forward life, and does not wait at the end to arrest it,
And ceas'd the moment life appear'd.

All goes onward and outward, nothing collapses,
And to die is different from what any one supposed, and luckier.

7

Has any one supposed it lucky to be born?
I hasten to inform him or her it is just as lucky to die, and I know it.

I pass death with the dying and birth with the new-wash'd babe, and am not contain'd
     between my hat and boots,
And peruse manifold objects, no two alike and every one good,
The earth good and the stars good, and their adjuncts all good.

I am not an earth nor an adjunct of an earth,
I am the mate and companion of people, all just as immortal and fathomless as myself,
(They do not know how immortal, but I know.)

Every kind for itself and its own, for me mine male and female,
For me those that have been boys and that love women,
For me the man that is proud and feels how it stings to be slighted,
For me the sweet-heart and the old maid, for me mothers and the mothers of mothers,
For me lips that have smiled, eyes that have shed tears,
For me children and the begetters of children.

Undrape! you are not guilty to me, nor stale nor discarded,
I see through the broadcloth and gingham whether or no,
And am around, tenacious, acquisitive, tireless, and cannot be shaken away.

8

The little one sleeps in its cradle,
I lift the gauze and look a long time, and silently brush away flies with my hand.

*   *   *

The youngster and the red-faced girl turn aside up the bushy hill,
I peeringly view them from the top.

The suicide sprawls on the bloody floor of the bedroom,
I witness the corpse with its dabbled hair, I note where the pistol has fallen.

The blab of the pave,[11] tires of carts, sluff of boot-soles, talk of the promenaders,
The heavy omnibus, the driver with his interrogating thumb, the clank of the shod
    horses on the granite floor,
The snow-sleighs, clinking, shouted jokes, pelts of snow-balls,
The hurrahs for popular favorites, the fury of rous'd mobs,
The flap of the curtain'd litter, a sick man inside borne to the hospital,
The meeting of enemies, the sudden oath, the blows and fall,
The excited crowd, the policeman with his star quickly working his passage to the centre
    of the crowd,
The impassive stones that receive and return so many echoes,
What groans of overfed or half-starv'd who fall sunstruck or in fits,
What exclamations of women taken suddenly who hurry home and give birth to babes,
What living and buried speech is always vibrating here, what howls restrain'd by
    decorum,
Arrests of criminals, slights, adulterous offers made, acceptances, rejections with convex
    lips.
I mind them or the show or resonance of them — I come and I depart.

9
The big doors of the country barn stand open and ready,
The dried grass of the harvest-time loads the slow-drawn wagon,
The clear light plays on the brown gray and green intertinged,
The armfuls are pack'd to the sagging mow.

I am there, I help, I came stretch'd atop of the load,
I felt its soft jolts, one leg reclined on the other,
I jump from the cross-beams and seize the clover and timothy,
And roll head over heels and tangle my hair full of wisps.

10
Alone far in the wilds and mountains I hunt,
Wandering amazed at my own lightness and glee,

---

11. Conversation in the street.

In the late afternoon choosing a safe spot to pass the night,
Kindling a fire and broiling the fresh-kill'd game,
Falling asleep on the gather'd leaves with my dog and gun by my side.

The Yankee clipper is under her sky-sails,[12] she cuts the sparkle and scud,
My eyes settle the land, I bend at her prow or shout joyously from the deck.

The boatmen and clam-diggers arose early and stopt for me,
I tuck'd my trowser-ends in my boots and went and had a good time;
You should have been with us that day round the chowder-kettle.

I saw the marriage of the trapper in the open air in the far west, the bride was a red girl,
Her father and his friends sat near cross-legged and dumbly smoking, they had
     moccasins to their feet and large thick blankets hanging from their shoulders,
On a bank lounged the trapper, he was drest mostly in skins, his luxuriant beard and
     curls protected his neck, he held his bride by the hand,
She had long eyelashes, her head was bare, her coarse straight locks descended upon her
     voluptuous limbs and reach'd to her feet.[13]

The runaway slave came to my house and stopt outside,
I heard his motions crackling the twigs of the woodpile,
Through the swung half-door of the kitchen I saw him limpsy and weak,
And went where he sat on a log and led him in and assured him,
And brought water and fill'd a tub for his sweated body and bruis'd feet,
And gave him a room that enter'd from my own, and gave him some coarse clean clothes,
And remember perfectly well his revolving eyes and his awkwardness,
And remember putting plasters on the galls of his neck and ankles;
He staid with me a week before he was recuperated and pass'd north,
I had him sit next me at table, my fire-lock[14] lean'd in the corner.

11

Twenty-eight young men bathe by the shore,
Twenty-eight young men and all so friendly;
Twenty-eight years of womanly life and all so lonesome.

She owns the fine house by the rise of the bank,
She hides handsome and richly drest aft the blinds of the window.

Which of the young men does she like the best?
Ah the homeliest of them is beautiful to her.

12. Topsails. Scud: sea foam.
13. According to Edgeley W. Todd, Whitman based this verse-paragraph on Alfred Jacob Mill-er's mid-nineteenth-century painting *The Trapper's Bride*.
14. Gun.

*   *   *

Where are you off to, lady? for I see you,
You splash in the water there, yet stay stock still in your room.

Dancing and laughing along the beach came the twenty-ninth bather,
The rest did not see her, but she saw them and loved them.

The beards of the young men glisten'd with wet, it ran from their long hair,
Little streams pass'd all over their bodies.

An unseen hand also pass'd over their bodies,
It descended tremblingly from their temples and ribs.

The young men float on their backs, their white bellies bulge to the sun, they do not ask
    who seizes fast to them,
They do not know who puffs and declines with pendant and bending arch,
They do not think whom they souse with spray.

12

The butcher-boy puts off his killing-clothes, or sharpens his knife at the stall in the
    market,
I loiter enjoying his repartee and his shuffle and break-down.[15]

Blacksmiths with grimed and hairy chests environ the anvil,
Each has his main-sledge, they are all out, there is a great heat in the fire.

From the cinder-strew'd threshold I follow their movements,
The lithe sheer of their waists plays even with their massive arms,
Overhand the hammers swing, overhand so slow, overhand so sure,
They do not hasten, each man hits in his place.

13

The negro[16] holds firmly the reins of his four horses, the block swags underneath on its
    tied-over chain,
The negro that drives the long dray[17] of the stone-yard, steady and tall he stands pois'd
    on one leg on the string-piece,[18]
His blue shirt exposes his ample neck and breast and loosens over his hip-band,

---

15. The shuffle and the break-down were two dance steps common in minstrel shows.
16. It was common practice in the nineteenth century not to capitalize the word "Negro."
17. A cart used for hauling heavy material.
18. A heavy timber used to brace a load.

His glance is calm and commanding, he tosses the slouch of his hat away from his
    forehead,
The sun falls on his crispy hair and mustache, falls on the black of his polish'd and
    perfect limbs.

I behold the picturesque giant and love him, and I do not stop there,
I go with the team also.

In me the caresser of life wherever moving, backward as well as forward sluing,[19]
To niches aside and junior bending, not a person or object missing,
Absorbing all to myself and for this song.

Oxen that rattle the yoke and chain or halt in the leafy shade, what is that you express in
    your eyes?
It seems to me more than all the print I have read in my life.

My tread scares the wood-drake and wood-duck on my distant and day-long ramble,
They rise together, they slowly circle around.

I believe in those wing'd purposes,
And acknowledge red, yellow, white, playing within me,
And consider green and violet and the tufted crown intentional,
And do not call the tortoise unworthy because she is not something else,
And the jay in the woods never studied the gamut,[20] yet trills pretty well to me,
And the look of the bay mare shames silliness out of me.

14

The wild gander leads his flock through the cool night,
Ya-honk he says, and sounds it down to me like an invitation,
The pert[21] may suppose it meaningless, but I listening close,
Find its purpose and place up there toward the wintry sky.

The sharp-hoof'd moose of the north, the cat on the house-sill, the chickadee, the
    prairie-dog,
The litter of the grunting sow as they tug at her teats,
The brood of the turkey-hen and she with her half-spread wings,
I see in them and myself the same old law.

The press of my foot to the earth springs a hundred affections,
They scorn the best I can do to relate them.

19. Turning.   21. The bold or impertinent.
20. The whole musical scale.

*　　*　　*

I am enamour'd of growing out-doors,
Of men that live among cattle or taste of the ocean or woods,
Of the builders and steerers of ships and the wielders of axes and mauls, and the drivers
　　of horses,
I can eat and sleep with them week in and week out.

What is commonest, cheapest, nearest, easiest, is Me,
Me going in for my chances, spending for vast returns,
Adorning myself to bestow myself on the first that will take me,
Not asking the sky to come down to my good will,
Scattering it freely forever.

15

The pure contralto sings in the organ loft,
The carpenter dresses his plank, the tongue of his foreplane whistles its wild ascending
　　lisp,
The married and unmarried children ride home to their Thanksgiving dinner,
The pilot seizes the king-pin,[22] he heaves down with a strong arm,
The mate stands braced in the whale-boat, lance and harpoon are ready,
The duck-shooter walks by silent and cautious stretches,
The deacons are ordain'd with cross'd hands at the altar,
The spinning-girl retreats and advances to the hum of the big wheel,
The farmer stops by the bars[23] as he walks on a First-day[24] loafe and looks at the oats and
　　rye,
The lunatic is carried at last to the asylum a confirm'd case,[25]
(He will never sleep any more as he did in the cot in his mother's bed-room;)
The jour printer[26] with gray head and gaunt jaws works at his case,
He turns his quid of tobacco while his eyes blurr with the manuscript;
The malform'd limbs are tied to the surgeon's table,
What is removed drops horribly in a pail;
The quadroon girl[27] is sold at the auction-stand, the drunkard nods by the bar-room
　　stove,
The machinist rolls up his sleeves, the policeman travels his beat, the gate-keeper marks
　　who pass,
The young fellow drives the express-wagon, (I love him, though I do not know him;)
The half-breed straps on his light boots to compete in the race,

22. The spoke of the steering wheel.
23. Fence rails.
24. A Quaker term for Sunday.
25. Perhaps an allusion to Whitman's brother Jesse.
26. A journeyman printer who works for day wages.
27. A girl with one black grandparent and three white grandparents.

The western turkey-shooting draws old and young, some lean on their rifles, some sit on
    logs,
Out from the crowd steps the marksman, takes his position, levels his piece;
The groups of newly-come immigrants cover the wharf or levee,
As the woolly-pates[28] hoe in the sugar-field, the overseer views them from his saddle,
The bugle calls in the ball-room, the gentlemen run for their partners, the dancers bow
    to each other,
The youth lies awake in the cedar-roof'd garret and harks to the musical rain,
The Wolverine[29] sets traps on the creek that helps fill the Huron,
The squaw wrapt in her yellow-hemm'd cloth is offering moccasins and bead-bags for
    sale,
The connoisseur peers along the exhibition-gallery with half-shut eyes bent sideways,
As the deck-hands make fast the steamboat the plank is thrown for the shore-going
    passengers,
The young sister holds out the skein[30] while the elder sister winds it off in a ball, and stops
    now and then for the knots,
The one-year wife is recovering and happy having a week ago borne her first child,
The clean-hair'd Yankee girl works with her sewing-machine or in the factory or mill,
The paving-man leans on his two-handed rammer, the reporter's lead flies swiftly over the
    note-book, the sign-painter is lettering with blue and gold,
The canal boy trots on the tow-path, the book-keeper counts at his desk, the shoemaker
    waxes his thread,
The conductor beats time for the band and all the performers follow him,
The child is baptized, the convert is making his first professions,
The regatta is spread on the bay, the race is begun, (how the white sails sparkle!)
The drover watching his drove sings out to them that would stray,
The pedler sweats with his pack on his back, (the purchaser higgling about the odd cent;)
The bride unrumples her white dress, the minute-hand of the clock moves slowly,
The opium-eater reclines with rigid head and just-open'd lips,
The prostitute draggles her shawl, her bonnet bobs on her tipsy and pimpled neck,
The crowd laugh at her blackguard oaths, the men jeer and wink to each other,
(Miserable! I do not laugh at your oaths nor jeer you;)
The President holding a cabinet council is surrounded by the great Secretaries,
On the piazza walk three matrons stately and friendly with twined arms,
The crew of the fish-smack pack repeated layers of halibut in the hold,
The Missourian crosses the plains toting his wares and his cattle,
As the fare-collector goes through the train he gives notice by the jingling of loose
    change,

---

28. African-American slaves.   30. Coiled length of yarn.
29. Michigan resident.

The floor-men are laying the floor, the tinners are tinning the roof, the masons are calling for mortar,

In single file each shouldering his hod pass onward the laborers;

Seasons pursuing each other the indescribable crowd is gather'd, it is the fourth of Seventh-month,[31] (what salutes of cannon and small arms!)

Seasons pursuing each other the plougher ploughs, the mower mows, and the winter-grain falls in the ground;

Off on the lakes the pike-fisher watches and waits by the hole in the frozen surface,

The stumps stand thick round the clearing, the squatter strikes deep with his axe,

Flatboatmen make fast towards dusk near the cotton-wood or pecan-trees,

Coon-seekers[32] go through the regions of the Red river or through those drain'd by the Tennessee, or through those of the Arkansas,

Torches shine in the dark that hangs on the Chattahooche or Altamahaw,[33]

Patriarchs sit at supper with sons and grandsons and great-grandsons around them,

In walls of adobie, in canvas tents, rest hunters and trappers after their day's sport,

The city sleeps and the country sleeps,

The living sleep for their time, the dead sleep for their time,

The old husband sleeps by his wife and the young husband sleeps by his wife;

And these tend inward to me, and I tend outward to them,

And such as it is to be of these more or less I am,

And of these one and all I weave the song of myself.

16

I am of old and young, of the foolish as much as the wise,

Regardless of others, ever regardful of others,

Maternal as well as paternal, a child as well as a man,

Stuff'd with the stuff that is coarse and stuff'd with the stuff that is fine,

One of the Nation of many nations, the smallest the same and the largest the same,

A Southerner soon as a Northerner, a planter nonchalant and hospitable down by the Oconee[34] I live,

A Yankee bound my own way ready for trade, my joints the limberest joints on earth and the sternest joints on earth,

A Kentuckian walking the vale of the Elkhorn in my deer-skin leggings, a Louisianian or Georgian,

A boatman over lakes or bays or along coasts, a Hoosier, Badger, Buckeye;[35]

At home on Kanadian snow-shoes or up in the bush, or with fishermen off Newfoundland,

31. The Quaker term for July. In the 1855 version, Whitman wrote "July."
32. Raccoon hunters.
33. Rivers in Alabama and Louisiana.
34. A river in Georgia.
35. That is, a resident of Indiana, Wisconsin, Ohio.

At home in the fleet of ice-boats, sailing with the rest and tacking,
At home on the hills of Vermont or in the woods of Maine, or the Texan ranch,
Comrade of Californians, comrade of free North-Westerners, (loving their big
    proportions,)
Comrade of raftsmen and coalmen, comrade of all who shake hands and welcome to
    drink and meat,
A learner with the simplest, a teacher of the thoughtfullest,
A novice beginning yet experient of myriads of seasons,
Of every hue and caste am I, of every rank and religion,
A farmer, mechanic, artist, gentleman, sailor, quaker,
Prisoner, fancy-man,[36] rowdy, lawyer, physician, priest.

I resist any thing better than my own diversity,
Breathe the air but leave plenty after me,
And am not stuck up, and am in my place.

(The moth and the fish-eggs are in their place,
The bright suns I see and the dark suns I cannot see are in their place,
The palpable is in its place and the impalpable is in its place.)

    17
These are really the thoughts of all men in all ages and lands, they are not original with
    me,
If they are not yours as much as mine they are nothing, or next to nothing,
If they are not the riddle and the untying of the riddle they are nothing,
If they are not just as close as they are distant they are nothing.

This is the grass that grows wherever the land is and the water is,
This the common air that bathes the globe.

    18
With music strong I come, with my comets and my drums,
I play not marches for accepted victors only, I play marches for conquer'd and slain
    persons.

Have you heard that it was good to gain the day?
I also say it is good to fall, battles are lost in the same spirit in which they are won.

    *   *   *

36. A gigolo or pimp.

I beat and pound for the dead,
I blow through my embouchures[37] my loudest and gayest for them.

Vivas to those who have fail'd!
And to those whose war-vessels sank in the sea!
And to those themselves who sank in the sea!
And to all generals that lost engagements, and all overcome heroes!
And the numberless unknown heroes equal to the greatest heroes known!

   19

This is the meal equally set, this the meat for natural hunger,
It is for the wicked just the same as the righteous, I make appointments with all,
I will not have a single person slighted or left away,
The kept-woman, sponger, thief, are hereby invited,
The heavy-lipp'd slave is invited, the venerealee is invited;
There shall be no difference between them and the rest.

This is the press of a bashful hand, this the float and odor of hair,
This the touch of my lips to yours, this the murmur of yearning,
This the far-off depth and height reflecting my own face,
This the thoughtful merge of myself, and the outlet again.

Do you guess I have some intricate purpose?
Well I have, for the Fourth-month showers have, and the mica on the side of a rock has.

Do you take it I would astonish?
Does the daylight astonish? does the early redstart twittering through the woods?
Do I astonish more than they?

This hour I tell things in confidence,
I might not tell everybody, but I will tell you.

   20

Who goes there? hankering, gross, mystical, nude;
How is it I extract strength from the beef I eat?

What is a man anyhow? what am I? what are you?

All I mark as my own you shall offset it with your own,
Else it were time lost listening to me.

       *   *   *

37. A French term meaning the mouthpieces of musical instruments (such as trumpets or flutes).

I do not snivel that snivel the world over,
That months are vacuums and the ground but wallow and filth.

Whimpering and truckling fold with powders for invalids,[38] conformity, goes to the
    fourth-remov'd,
I wear my hat as I please indoors or out.

Why should I pray? why should I venerate and be ceremonious?

Having pried through the strata, analyzed to a hair, counsel'd with doctors and
    calculated close,
I find no sweeter fat than sticks to my own bones.

In all people I see myself, none more and not one a barley-corn less,
And the good or bad I say of myself I say of them.

I know I am solid and sound,
To me the converging objects of the universe perpetually flow,
All are written to me, and I must get what the writing means.

I know I am deathless,
I know this orbit of mine cannot be swept by a carpenter's compass,
I know I shall not pass like a child's carlacue[39] cut with a burnt stick at night.

I know I am august,
I do not trouble my spirit to vindicate itself or be understood,
I see that the elementary laws never apologize,
(I reckon I behave no prouder than the level I plant my house by, after all.)

I exist as I am, that is enough,
If no other in the world be aware I sit content,
And if each and all be aware I sit content.

One world is aware and by far the largest to me, and that is myself,
And whether I come to my own to-day or in ten thousand or ten million years,
I can cheerfully take it now, or with equal cheerfulness I can wait.

My foothold is tenon'd and mortis'd[40] in granite,
I laugh at what you call dissolution,
And I know the amplitude of time.

---

38. Whimpering and sleeping or submitting com-
bine with medicinal powders administered to the
ill.

39. Curlicue.
40. Joined securely.

21

I am the poet of the Body and I am the poet of the Soul,
The pleasures of heaven are with me and the pains of hell are with me,
The first I graft and increase upon myself, the latter I translate into a new tongue.

I am the poet of the woman the same as the man,
And I say it is as great to be a woman as to be a man,
And I say there is nothing greater than the mother of men.

I chant the chant of dilation or pride,
We have had ducking and deprecating about enough,
I show that size is only development.

Have you outstript the rest? are you the President?
It is a trifle, they will more than arrive there every one, and still pass on.

I am he that walks with the tender and growing night,
I call to the earth and sea half-held by the night.

Press close bare-bosom'd night—press close magnetic nourishing night!
Night of south winds—night of the large few stars!
Still nodding night—mad naked summer night.

Smile O voluptuous cool-breath'd earth!
Earth of the slumbering and liquid trees!
Earth of departed sunset—earth of the mountains misty-topt!
Earth of the vitreous[41] pour of the full moon just tinged with blue!
Earth of shine and dark mottling the tide of the river!
Earth of the limpid gray of clouds brighter and clearer for my sake!
Far-swooping elbow'd earth—rich apple-blossom'd earth!
Smile, for your lover comes.

Prodigal, you have given me love—therefore I to you give love!
O unspeakable passionate love.

22

You sea! I resign myself to you also—I guess what you mean,
I behold from the beach your crooked inviting fingers,
I believe you refuse to go back without feeling of me,
We must have a turn together, I undress, hurry me out of sight of the land,
Cushion me soft, rock me in billowy drowse,
Dash me with amorous wet, I can repay you.

41. Glassy.

*   *   *

Sea of stretch'd ground-swells,
Sea breathing broad and convulsive breaths,
Sea of the brine of life and of unshovell'd yet always-ready graves,
Howler and scooper of storms, capricious and dainty sea,
I am integral with you, I too am of one phase and of all phases.

Partaker of influx and efflux I, extoller of hate and conciliation,
Extoller of amies[42] and those that sleep in each others' arms.

I am he attesting sympathy,
(Shall I make my list of things in the house and skip the house that supports them?)

I am not the poet of goodness only, I do not decline to be the poet of wickedness also.

What blurt is this about virtue and about vice?
Evil propels me and reform of evil propels me, I stand indifferent,
My gait is no fault-finder's or rejecter's gait, I moisten the roots of all that has grown.

Did you fear some scrofula[43] out of the unflagging pregnancy?
Did you guess the celestial laws are yet to be work'd over and rectified?

I find one side a balance and the antipodal side a balance,
Soft doctrine as steady help as stable doctrine,
Thoughts and deeds of the present our rouse and early start.

This minute that comes to me over the past decillions,
There is no better than it and now.

What behaved well in the past or behaves well to-day is not such a wonder,
The wonder is always and always how there can be a mean man or an infidel.

23

Endless unfolding of words of ages!
And mine a word of the modern, the word En-Masse.[44]

A word of the faith that never balks,
Here or henceforward it is all the same to me, I accept Time absolutely.

It alone is without flaw, it alone rounds and completes all,
That mystic baffling wonder alone completes all.

---

42. French term meaning friends or lovers. Intentionally or not, Whitman uses the feminine form of the word.
43. Literally a form of tuberculosis, but metaphorically a moral taint.
44. Another of Whitman's French terms, meaning in general or in a body. Adding capitalization and hyphen, Whitman seems to suggest an additional meaning: humanity as a whole.

*   *   *

I accept Reality and dare not question it,
Materialism first and last imbuing.

Hurrah for positive science! long live exact demonstration!
Fetch stonecrop[45] mixt with cedar and branches of lilac,
This is the lexicographer, this the chemist, this made a grammar of the old cartouches,[46]
These mariners put the ship through dangerous unknown seas,
This is the geologist, this works with the scalpel, and this is a mathematician.

Gentlemen, to you the first honors always!
Your facts are useful, and yet they are not my dwelling,
I but enter by them to an area of my dwelling.

Less the reminders of properties told my words,
And more the reminders they of life untold, and of freedom and extrication,
And make short account of neuters and geldings, and favor men and women fully equipt,
And beat the gong of revolt, and stop with fugitives and them that plot and conspire.

24

Walt Whitman, a kosmos,[47] of Manhattan the son,
Turbulent, fleshy, sensual, eating, drinking and breeding,
No sentimentalist, no stander above men and women or apart from them,
No more modest than immodest.

Unscrew the locks from the doors!
Unscrew the doors themselves from their jambs!

Whoever degrades another degrades me,
And whatever is done or said returns at last to me.

Through me the afflatus[48] surging and surging, through me the current and index.

I speak the pass-word primeval, I give the sign of democracy,
By God! I will accept nothing which all cannot have their counterpart of on the same
    terms.

Through me many long dumb voices,
Voices of the interminable generations of prisoners and slaves,
Voices of the diseas'd and despairing and of thieves and dwarfs,

45. A medicinal herb.
46. That is, this person deciphered the Egyptian hieroglyphics.
47. A Greek-derived word meaning an orderly world within the self.
48. Poetic inspiration or divine wind imparting knowledge.

Voices of cycles of preparation and accretion,
And of the threads that connect the stars, and of wombs and of the father-stuff,
And of the rights of them the others are down upon,
Of the deform'd, trivial, flat, foolish, despised,
Fog in the air, beetles rolling balls of dung.

Through me forbidden voices,
Voices of sexes and lusts, voices veil'd and I remove the veil,
Voices indecent by me clarified and transfigur'd.

I do not press my fingers across my mouth,
I keep as delicate around the bowels as around the head and heart,
Copulation is no more rank to me than death is.

I believe in the flesh and the appetites,
Seeing, hearing, feeling, are miracles, and each part and tag of me is a miracle.

Divine am I inside and out, and I make holy whatever I touch or am touch'd from,
The scent of these arm-pits aroma finer than prayer,
This head more than churches, bibles, and all the creeds.

If I worship one thing more than another it shall be the spread of my own body, or any
     part of it,
Translucent mould of me it shall be you!
Shaded ledges and rests it shall be you!
Firm masculine colter[49] it shall be you!
Whatever goes to the tilth[50] of me it shall be you!
You my rich blood! your milky stream pale strippings of my life!
Breast that presses against other breasts it shall be you!
My brain it shall be your occult convolutions!
Root of wash'd sweet-flag![51] timorous pond-snipe! nest of guarded duplicate eggs! it shall
     be you!
Mix'd tussled hay of head, beard, brawn, it shall be you!
Trickling sap of maple, fibre of manly wheat, it shall be you!
Sun so generous it shall be you!
Vapors lighting and shading my face it shall be you!
You sweaty brooks and dews it shall be you!
Winds whose soft-tickling genitals rub against me it shall be you!
Broad muscular fields, branches of live oak, loving lounger in my winding paths, it shall
     be you!
Hands I have taken, face I have kiss'd, mortal I have ever touch'd, it shall be you.

49. Sharp blade of a plowshare.   51. Calamus plant.
50. Tillage.

* * *

I dote on myself, there is that lot of me and all so luscious,
Each moment and whatever happens thrills me with joy,
I cannot tell how my ankles bend, nor whence the cause of my faintest wish,
Nor the cause of the friendship I emit, nor the cause of the friendship I take again.

That I walk up my stoop, I pause to consider if it really be,
A morning-glory at my window satisfies me more than the metaphysics of books.

To behold the day-break!
The little light fades the immense and diaphanous shadows,
The air tastes good to my palate.

Hefts of the moving world at innocent gambols silently rising, freshly exuding,
Scooting obliquely high and low.

Something I cannot see puts upward libidinous prongs,
Seas of bright juice suffuse heaven.

The earth by the sky staid with, the daily close of their junction,
The heav'd challenge from the east that moment over my head,
The mocking taunt, See then whether you shall be master!

25

Dazzling and tremendous how quick the sun-rise would kill me,
If I could not now and always send sun-rise out of me.

We also ascend dazzling and tremendous as the sun,
We found our own O my soul in the calm and cool of the day-break.

My voice goes after what my eyes cannot reach,
With the twirl of my tongue I encompass worlds and volumes of worlds.

Speech is the twin of my vision, it is unequal to measure itself,
It provokes me forever, it says sarcastically,
Walt you contain enough, why don't you let it out then?

Come now I will not be tantalized, you conceive too much of articulation,
Do you not know O speech how the buds beneath you are folded?
Waiting in gloom, protected by frost,
The dirt receding before my prophetical screams,
I underlying causes to balance them at last,
My knowledge my live parts, it keeping tally with the meaning of all things,
Happiness, (which whoever hears me let him or her set out in search of this day.)

*   *   *

My final merit I refuse you, I refuse putting from me what I really am,
Encompass worlds, but never try to encompass me,
I crowd your sleekest and best by simply looking toward you.

Writing and talk do not prove me,
I carry the plenum[52] of proof and every thing else in my face,
With the hush of my lips I wholly confound the skeptic.

26

Now I will do nothing but listen,
To accrue what I hear into this song, to let sounds contribute toward it.

I hear bravuras of birds, bustle of growing wheat, gossip of flames, clack of sticks
    cooking my meals,
I hear the sound I love, the sound of the human voice,
I hear all sounds running together, combined, fused or following,
Sounds of the city and sounds out of the city, sounds of the day and night,
Talkative young ones to those that like them, the loud laugh of work-people at their
    meals,
The angry bass of disjointed friendship, the faint tones of the sick,
The judge with hands tight to the desk, his pallid lips pronouncing a death-sentence,
The heave'e'yo of stevedores unlading ships by the wharves, the refrain of the anchor-
    lifters,
The ring of alarm-bells, the cry of fire, the whirr of swift-streaking engines and hose-
    carts with premonitory tinkles and color'd lights,
The steam-whistle, the solid roll of the train of approaching cars,
The slow march play'd at the head of the association marching two and two,
(They go to guard some corpse, the flag-tops are draped with black muslin.)

I hear the violoncello, ('tis the young man's heart's complaint,)
I hear the key'd cornet, it glides quickly in through my ears,
It shakes mad-sweet pangs through my belly and breast.

I hear the chorus, it is a grand opera,
Ah this indeed is music — this suits me.

A tenor large and fresh as the creation fills me,
The orbic flex of his mouth is pouring and filling me full.

*   *   *

52. Fullness.

I hear the train'd soprano (what work with hers is this?)
The orchestra whirls me wider than Uranus[53] flies,
It wrenches such ardors from me I did not know I possess'd them,
It sails me, I dab with bare feet, they are lick'd by the indolent waves,
I am cut by bitter and angry hail, I lose my breath,
Steep'd amid honey'd morphine, my windpipe throttled in fakes[54] of death,
At length let up again to feel the puzzle of puzzles,
And that we call Being.

27

To be in any form, what is that?
(Round and round we go, all of us, and ever come back thither,)
If nothing lay more develop'd the quahaug[55] in its callous shell were enough.

Mine is no callous shell,
I have instant conductors all over me whether I pass or stop,
They seize every object and lead it harmlessly through me.

I merely stir, press, feel with my fingers, and am happy,
To touch my person to some one else's is about as much as I can stand.

28

Is this then a touch? quivering me to a new identity,
Flames and ether[56] making a rush for my veins,
Treacherous tip of me reaching and crowding to help them,
My flesh and blood playing out lightning to strike what is hardly different from myself,
On all sides prurient provokers stiffening my limbs,
Straining the udder of my heart for its withheld drip,
Behaving licentious toward me, taking no denial,
Depriving me of my best as for a purpose,
Unbuttoning my clothes, holding me by the bare waist,
Deluding my confusion with the calm of the sunlight and pasture-fields,
Immodestly sliding the fellow-senses away,
They bribed to swap off with touch and go and graze at the edges of me,
No consideration, no regard for my draining strength or my anger,
Fetching the rest of the herd around to enjoy them a while,
Then all uniting to stand on a headland and worry me.

53. The planet then thought to be the most re-
mote from the sun.
54. Rope coils.
55. Quahog, an Atlantic clam.

56. Possible meanings include an oxygen com-
pound, a flammable liquid, an anesthetic, space,
sky, air, and the heavens.

*   *   *

The sentries desert every other part of me,
They have left me helpless to a red marauder,
They all come to the headland to witness and assist against me.

I am given up by traitors,
I talk wildly, I have lost my wits, I and nobody else am the greatest traitor,
I went myself first to the headland, my own hands carried me there.

You villain touch! what are you doing? my breath is tight in its throat,
Unclench your floodgates, you are too much for me.

29

Blind loving wrestling touch, sheath'd hooded sharp-tooth'd touch!
Did it make you ache so, leaving me?

Parting track'd by arriving, perpetual payment of perpetual loan,
Rich showering rain, and recompense richer afterward.

Sprouts take and accumulate, stand by the curb prolific and vital,
Landscapes projected masculine, full-sized and golden.

30

All truths wait in all things,
They neither hasten their own delivery nor resist it,
They do not need the obstetric forceps of the surgeon,
The insignificant is as big to me as any,
(What is less or more than a touch?)

Logic and sermons never convince,
The damp of the night drives deeper into my soul.

(Only what proves itself to every man and woman is so,
Only what nobody denies is so.)

A minute and a drop of me settle my brain,
I believe the soggy clods shall become lovers and lamps,
And a compend[57] of compends is the meat of a man or woman,
And a summit and flower there is the feeling they have for each other,
And they are to branch boundlessly out of that lesson until it becomes omnific,[58]
And until one and all shall delight us, and we them.

---

57. A compendium, inventory, or summary.   58. All-creating.

31

I believe a leaf of grass is no less than the journey-work of the stars,
And the pismire[59] is equally perfect, and a grain of sand, and the egg of the wren,
And the tree-toad is a chef-d'oeuvre[60] for the highest,
And the running blackberry would adorn the parlors of heaven,
And the narrowest hinge in my hand puts to scorn all machinery,
And the cow crunching with depress'd head surpasses any statue,
And a mouse is miracle enough to stagger sextillions of infidels.

I find I incorporate gneiss,[61] coal, long-threaded moss, fruits, grains, esculent roots,
And am stucco'd with quadrupeds and birds all over,
And have distanced what is behind me for good reasons,
But call any thing back again when I desire it.

In vain the speeding or shyness,
In vain the plutonic rocks[62] send their old heat against my approach,
In vain the mastodon retreats beneath its own powder'd bones,
In vain objects stand leagues off and assume manifold shapes,
In vain the ocean settling in hollows and the great monsters lying low,
In vain the buzzard houses herself with the sky,
In vain the snake slides through the creepers and logs,
In vain the elk takes to the inner passes of the woods,
In vain the razor-bill'd auk sails far north to Labrador,
I follow quickly, I ascend to the nest in the fissure of the cliff.

32

I think I could turn and live with animals, they are so placid and self-contain'd,
I stand and look at them long and long.

They do not sweat and whine about their condition,
They do not lie awake in the dark and weep for their sins,
They do not make me sick discussing their duty to God,
Not one is dissatisfied, not one is demented with the mania of owning things,
Not one kneels to another, nor to his kind that lived thousands of years ago,
Not one is respectable or unhappy over the whole earth.

So they show their relations to me and I accept them,
They bring me tokens of myself, they evince them plainly in their possession.

*   *   *

59. Ant.
60. Masterpiece (French).
61. A metamorphic rock.

62. Rocks formed from molten material within the earth.

I wonder where they get those tokens,
Did I pass that way huge times ago and negligently drop them?

Myself moving forward then and now and forever,
Gathering and showing more always and with velocity,
Infinite and omnigenous,[63] and the like of these among them,
Not too exclusive toward the reachers of my remembrancers,
Picking out here one that I love, and now go with him on brotherly terms.

A gigantic beauty of a stallion, fresh and responsive to my caresses,
Head high in the forehead, wide between the ears,
Limbs glossy and supple, tail dusting the ground,
Eyes full of sparkling wickedness, ears finely cut, flexibly moving.

His nostrils dilate as my heels embrace him,
His well-built limbs tremble with pleasure as we race around and return.

I but use you a minute, then I resign you, stallion,
Why do I need your paces when I myself out-gallop them?
Even as I stand or sit passing faster than you.

33

Space and Time! now I see it is true, what I guess'd at,
What I guess'd when I loaf'd on the grass,[64]
What I guess'd while I lay alone in my bed,
And again as I walk'd the beach under the paling stars of the morning.

My ties and ballasts leave me, my elbows rest in sea-gaps,[65]
I skirt sierras, my palms cover continents,
I am afoot with my vision.

By the city's quadrangular houses—in log huts, camping with lumbermen,
Along the ruts of the turnpike, along the dry gulch and rivulet bed,
Weeding my onion-patch or hoeing rows of carrots and parsnips, crossing savannas,
    trailing in forests,
Prospecting, gold-digging, girdling the trees of a new purchase,
Scorch'd ankle-deep by the hot sand, hauling my boat down the shallow river,
Where the panther walks to and fro on a limb overhead, where the buck turns furiously
    at the hunter,
Where the rattlesnake suns his flabby length on a rock, where the otter is feeding on
    fish,

63. Of all forms. 65. Inlets.
64. A reference back to section 1 of the poem.

Where the alligator in his tough pimples sleeps by the bayou,

Where the black bear is searching for roots or honey, where the beaver pats the mud
    with his paddle-shaped tail;

Over the growing sugar, over the yellow-flower'd cotton plant, over the rice in its low
    moist field,

Over the sharp-peak'd farm house, with its scallop'd scum[66] and slender shoots from the
    gutters,

Over the western persimmon, over the long-leav'd corn, over the delicate blue-flower
    flax,

Over the white and brown buckwheat, a hummer and buzzer[67] there with the rest,

Over the dusky green of the rye as it ripples and shades in the breeze;

Scaling mountains, pulling myself cautiously up, holding on by low scragged[68] limbs,

Walking the path worn in the grass and beat through the leaves of the brush,

Where the quail is whistling betwixt the woods and the wheat-lot,

Where the bat flies in the Seventh-month eve, where the great gold-bug[69] drops through
    the dark,

Where the brook puts out of the roots of the old tree and flows to the meadow,

Where cattle stand and shake away flies with the tremulous shuddering of their hides,

Where the cheese-cloth hangs in the kitchen, where andirons straddle the hearth-slab,
    where cobwebs fall in festoons from the rafters;

Where trip-hammers crash, where the press is whirling its cylinders,

Wherever the human heart beats with terrible throes under its ribs,

Where the pear-shaped balloon is floating aloft, (floating in it myself and looking
    composedly down,)

Where the life-car[70] is drawn on the slip-noose, where the heat hatches pale-green eggs
    in the dented sand,

Where the she-whale swims with her calf and never forsakes it,

Where the steam-ship trails hind-ways its long pennant of smoke,

Where the fin of the shark cuts like a black chip out of the water,

Where the half-burn'd brig is riding on unknown currents,

Where shells grow to her slimy deck, where the dead are corrupting below;

Where the dense-starr'd flag is borne at the head of the regiments,

Approaching Manhattan up by the long-stretching island,

Under Niagara, the cataract falling like a veil over my countenance,

Upon a door-step, upon the horse-block[71] of hard wood outside,

Upon the race-course, or enjoying picnics or jigs or a good game of base-ball,

At he-festivals, with blackguard gibes, ironical license, bull-dances,[72] drinking, laughter,

---

66. Film of sediment or refuse washed down from
the roof.
67. That is, a hummingbird and a bee.
68. Perhaps scraggly, irregular, jagged.
69. Beetle.

70. A watertight vehicle used to evacuate ships.
71. A step used in mounting horses.
72. Country dances where men danced with
other men because of a shortage of women.

At the cider-mill tasting the sweets of the brown mash, sucking the juice through a
    straw,
At apple-peelings wanting kisses for all the red fruit I find,
At musters,[73] beach-parties, friendly bees, huskings, house-raisings;
Where the mocking-bird sounds his delicious gurgles, cackles, screams, weeps,
Where the hay-rick[74] stands in the barn-yard, where the dry-stalks are scatter'd, where
    the brood-cow waits in the hovel,
Where the bull advances to do his masculine work, where the stud to the mare, where
    the cock is treading the hen,
Where the heifers browse, where geese nip their food with short jerks,
Where sun-down shadows lengthen over the limitless and lonesome prairie,
Where herds of buffalo make a crawling spread of the square miles far and near,
Where the humming-bird shimmers, where the neck of the long-lived swan is curving
    and winding,
Where the laughing-gull scoots by the shore, where she laughs her near-human laugh,
Where bee-hives range on a gray bench in the garden half hid by the high weeds,
Where band-neck'd partridges roost in a ring on the ground with their heads out,
Where burial coaches enter the arch'd gates of a cemetery,
Where winter wolves bark amid wastes of snow and icicled trees,
Where the yellow-crown'd heron comes to the edge of the marsh at night and feeds
    upon small crabs,
Where the splash of swimmers and divers cools the warm noon,
Where the katy-did works her chromatic reed[75] on the walnut-tree over the well,
Through patches of citrons[76] and cucumbers with silver-wired leaves,
Through the salt-lick or orange glade, or under conical firs,
Through the gymnasium, through the curtain'd saloon, through the office or public
    hail;
Pleas'd with the native and pleas'd with the foreign, pleas'd with the new and old,
Pleas'd with the homely woman as well as the handsome,
Pleas'd with the quakeress as she puts off her bonnet and talks melodiously,
Pleas'd with the tune of the choir of the whitewash'd church,
Pleas'd with the earnest words of the sweating Methodist preacher, impress'd seriously at
    the camp-meeting;
Looking in at the shop-windows of Broadway the whole forenoon, flatting the flesh of
    my nose on the thick plate glass,
Wandering the same afternoon with my face turn'd up to the clouds, or down a lane or
    along the beach,
My right and left arms round the sides of two friends, and I in the middle;

73. Military or community assemblies.
74. Haystack (British).
75. Musical instrument, probably a harmonica.
76. Melons.

Coming home with the silent and dark-cheek'd bush-boy, (behind me he rides at the
    drape[77] of the day,)
Far from the settlements studying the print of animals' feet, or the moccasin print,
By the cot in the hospital reaching lemonade to a feverish patient,
Nigh the coffin'd corpse when all is still, examining with a candle;
Voyaging to every port to dicker and adventure,
Hurrying with the modern crowd as eager and fickle as any,
Hot toward one I hate, ready in my madness to knife him,
Solitary at midnight in my back yard, my thoughts gone from me a long while,
Walking the old hills of Judea with the beautiful gentle God by my side,
Speeding through space, speeding through heaven and the stars,
Speeding amid the seven satellites and the broad ring,[78] and the diameter of eighty
    thousand miles,
Speeding with tail'd meteors, throwing fire-balls like the rest,
Carrying the crescent child that carries its own full mother in its belly,[79]
Storming, enjoying, planning, loving, cautioning,
Backing and filling, appearing and disappearing,
I tread day and night such roads.

I visit the orchards of spheres and look at the product,
And look at quintillions ripen'd and look at quintillions green.

I fly those flights of a fluid and swallowing soul,
My course runs below the soundings of plummets.

I help myself to material and immaterial,
No guard can shut me off, no law prevent me.

I anchor my ship for a little while only,
My messengers continually cruise away or bring their returns to me.

I go hunting polar furs and the seal, leaping chasms with a pike-pointed staff, clinging to
    topples[80] of brittle and blue.

I ascend to the foretruck,[81]
I take my place late at night in the crow's-nest,
We sail the arctic sea, it is plenty light enough,
Through the clear atmosphere I stretch around on the wonderful beauty,

77. End.
78. The seven planets then known and perhaps
the rings of Saturn.
79. That is, a crescent moon with the image of the
full moon barely visible.
80. Toppled crags of ice.
81. The platform of a sailing ship's foremast.

The enormous masses of ice pass me and I pass them, the scenery is plain in all
    directions,
The white-topt mountains show in the distance, I fling out my fancies toward them,
We are approaching some great battle-field in which we are soon to be engaged,
We pass the colossal outposts of the encampment, we pass with still feet and caution,
Or we are entering by the suburbs some vast and ruin'd city,
The blocks and fallen architecture more than all the living cities of the globe.

I am a free companion, I bivouac by invading watchfires,
I turn the bridegroom out of bed and stay with the bride myself,
I tighten her all night to my thighs and lips.

My voice is the wife's voice, the screech by the rail of the stairs,
They fetch my man's body up dripping and drown'd.

I understand the large hearts of heroes,
The courage of present times and all times,
How the skipper saw the crowded and rudderless wreck of the steam-ship,[82] and Death
    chasing it up and down the storm,
How he knuckled tight and gave not back an inch, and was faithful of days and faithful
    of nights,
And chalk'd in large letters on a board, *Be of good cheer, we will not desert you*;
How he follow'd with them and tack'd with them three days and would not give it up,
How he saved the drifting company at last,
How the lank loose-gown'd women look'd when boated from the side of their prepared
    graves,
How the silent old-faced infants and the lifted sick, and the sharp-lipp'd unshaved men;
All this I swallow, it tastes good, I like it well, it becomes mine,
I am the man, I suffer'd, I was there.

The disdain and calmness of martyrs,
The mother of old, condemn'd for a witch, burnt with dry wood, her children gazing on,
The hounded slave that flags in the race, leans by the fence, blowing, cover'd with
    sweat,
The twinges that sting like needles his legs and neck, the murderous buckshot and the
    bullets,
All these I feel or am.

I am the hounded slave, I wince at the bite of the dogs,
Hell and despair are upon me, crack and again crack the marksmen,

---

82. This passage is based on the wreck of the *San Francisco*, which got caught in a storm one day out
from New York in December 1853 and drifted for two weeks.

I clutch the rails of the fence, my gore dribs,[83] thinn'd with the ooze of my skin,
I fall on the weeds and stones,
The riders spur their unwilling horses, haul close,
Taunt my dizzy ears and beat me violently over the head with whip-stocks.

Agonies are one of my changes of garments,
I do not ask the wounded person how he feels, I myself become the wounded person,
My hurts turn livid upon me as I lean on a cane and observe.

I am the mash'd fireman with breast-bone broken,
Tumbling walls buried me in their debris,
Heat and smoke I inspired,[84] I heard the yelling shouts of my comrades,
I heard the distant click of their picks and shovels,
They have clear'd the beams away, they tenderly lift me forth.

I lie in the night air in my red shirt, the pervading hush is for my sake,
Painless after all I lie exhausted but not so unhappy,
White and beautiful are the faces around me, the heads are bared of their fire-caps,
The kneeling crowd fades with the light of the torches.

Distant and dead resuscitate,
They show as the dial or move as the hands of me, I am the clock myself.

I am an old artillerist, I tell of my fort's bombardment,
I am there again.

Again the long roll of the drummers,
Again the attacking cannon, mortars,
Again to my listening ears the cannon responsive.

I take part, I see and hear the whole,
The cries, curses, roar, the plaudits for well-aim'd shots,
The ambulanza slowly passing trailing its red drip,
Workmen searching after damages, making indispensable repairs,
The fall of grenades through the rent roof, the fan-shaped explosion,
The whizz of limbs, heads, stone, wood, iron, high in the air.

Again gurgles the mouth of my dying general, he furiously waves with his hand,
He gasps through the clot *Mind not me—mind—the entrenchments.*

34
Now I tell what I knew in Texas in my early youth,
(I tell not the fall of Alamo,

83. Dribbles.   84. Inhaled.

Not one escaped to tell the fall of Alamo,
The hundred and fifty are dumb yet at Alamo,)
'Tis the tale of the murder in cold blood of four hundred and twelve young men.[85]

Retreating they had form'd in a hollow square with their baggage for breastworks,
Nine hundred lives out of the surrounding enemy's, nine times their number, was the
    price they took in advance,
Their colonel was wounded and their ammunition gone,
They treated for an honorable capitulation, receiv'd writing and seal, gave up their arms
    and march'd back prisoners of war.

They were the glory of the race of rangers,
Matchless with horse, rifle, song, supper, courtship,
Large, turbulent, generous, handsome, proud, and affectionate,
Bearded, sunburnt, drest in the free costume of hunters,
Not a single one over thirty years of age.

The second First-day morning they were brought out in squads and massacred, it was
    beautiful early summer,
The work commenced about five o'clock and was over by eight.

None obey'd the command to kneel,
Some made a mad and helpless rush, some stood stark and straight,
A few fell at once, shot in the temple or heart, the living and dead lay together,
The maim'd and mangled dug in the dirt, the new-comers saw them there,
Some half-kill'd attempted to crawl away,
These were despatch'd with bayonets or batter'd with the blunts of muskets,
A youth not seventeen years old seiz'd his assassin till two more came to release him,
The three were all torn and cover'd with the boy's blood.

At eleven o'clock began the burning of the bodies;
That is the tale of the murder of the four hundred and twelve young men.

35

Would you hear of an old-time sea-fight?[86]
Would you learn who won by the light of the moon and stars?
List to the yarn, as my grandmother's father the sailor told it to me.

    *   *   *

85. The shooting of several hundred American prisoners of war by order of the Mexican general Santa Anna near Goliad, Texas, in March 1836. Although the speaker claims to have been "in Texas in my early youth," Whitman had never been to Texas.

86. This section recounts the Revolutionary War battle between the American ship *Bonhomme Richard* and the British ship *Serapis* on September 23, 1779.

Our foe was no skulk in his ship I tell you, (said he,)
His was the surly English pluck, and there is no tougher or truer, and never was, and
    never will be;
Along the lower'd eve he came horribly raking us.[87]

We closed with him, the yards entangled, the cannon touch'd,
My captain lash'd fast with his own hands.[88]

We had receiv'd some eighteen pound shots under the water,
On our lower-gun-deck two large pieces had burst at the first fire, killing all around and
    blowing up overhead.

Fighting at sun-down, fighting at dark,
Ten o'clock at night, the full moon well up, our leaks on the gain, and five feet of water
    reported,
The master-at-arms loosing the prisoners confined in the after-hold to give them a
    chance for themselves.

The transit to and from the magazine[89] is now stopt by the sentinels,
They see so many strange faces they do not know whom to trust.

Our frigate takes fire,
The other asks if we demand quarter?[90]
If our colors are struck and the fighting done?

Now I laugh content, for I hear the voice of my little captain,
We have not struck, he composedly cries, *we have just begun our part of the fighting*.[91]

Only three guns are in use,
One is directed by the captain himself against the enemy's main-mast,
Two well serv'd with grape and canister[92] silence his musketry and clear his decks.

The tops[93] alone second the fire of this little battery, especially the main-top,
They hold out bravely during the whole of the action.

Not a moment's cease,
The leaks gain fast on the pumps, the fire eats toward the powder-magazine.

One of the pumps has been shot away, it is generally thought we are sinking.

*   *   *

87. That is, raking us with gunfire.
88. He lashed the two ships together.
89. Ammunition storeroom.
90. Mercy.
91. The American captain was John Paul Jones.

This quote is a version of the defiant words he was said to have uttered, often remembered as "We have not yet begun to fight."
92. That is, grapeshot and canister shot.
93. Marksmen firing from the ship's masts.

Serene stands the little captain,
He is not hurried, his voice is neither high nor low,
His eyes give more light to us than our battle-lanterns.

Toward twelve there in the beams of the moon they surrender to us.

36

Stretch'd and still lies the midnight,
Two great hulls motionless on the breast of the darkness,
Our vessel riddled and slowly sinking, preparations to pass to the one we have
    conquer'd,
The captain on the quarter-deck coldly giving his orders through a countenance white
    as a sheet,
Near by the corpse of the child that serv'd in the cabin,
The dead face of an old salt with long white hair and carefully curl'd whiskers,
The flames spite of all that can be done flickering aloft and below,
The husky voices of the two or three officers yet fit for duty,
Formless stacks of bodies and bodies by themselves, dabs of flesh upon the masts and
    spars,[94]
Cut of cordage,[95] dangle of rigging, slight shock of the soothe of waves,
Black and impassive guns, litter of powder-parcels, strong scent,
A few large stars overhead, silent and mournful shining,
Delicate sniffs of sea-breeze, smells of sedgy grass and fields by the shore, death-
    messages given in charge to survivors,
The hiss of the surgeon's knife, the gnawing teeth of his saw,
Wheeze, cluck, swash of falling blood, short wild scream, and long, dull, tapering
    groan,
These so, these irretrievable.

37

You laggards there on guard! look to your arms!
In at the conquer'd doors they crowd! I am possess'd!
Embody all presences outlaw'd or suffering,
See myself in prison shaped like another man,
And feel the dull unintermitted pain.

For me the keepers of convicts shoulder their carbines and keep watch,
It is I let out in the morning and barr'd at night.

    ✻   ✻   ✻

---

94. Poles.   95. Rope.

Not a mutineer walks handcuff'd to jail but I am handcuff'd to him and walk by his side,
(I am less the jolly one there, and more the silent one with sweat on my twitching lips.)

Not a youngster is taken for larceny but I go up too, and am tried and sentenced.

Not a cholera patient lies at the last gasp but I also lie at the last gasp,
My face is ash-color'd, my sinews gnarl, away from me people retreat.

Askers[96] embody themselves in me and I am embodied in them,
I project my hat, sit shame-faced, and beg.

38

Enough! enough! enough!
Somehow I have been stunn'd. Stand back!
Give me a little time beyond my cuff'd head, slumbers, dreams, gaping,
I discover myself on the verge of a usual mistake.

That I could forget the mockers and insults!
That I could forget the trickling tears and the blows of the bludgeons and hammers!
That I could look with a separate look on my own crucifixion and bloody crowning.

I remember now,
I resume the overstaid fraction,
The grave of rock multiplies what has been confided to it, or to any graves,
Corpses rise, gashes heal, fastenings roll from me.

I troop forth replenish'd with supreme power, one of an average unending procession,
Inland and sea-coast we go, and pass all boundary lines,
Our swift ordinances on their way over the whole earth,
The blossoms we wear in our hats the growth of thousands of years.

Eleves,[97] I salute you! come forward!
Continue your annotations, continue your questionings.

39

The friendly and flowing savage, who is he?
Is he waiting for civilization, or past it and mastering it?

Is he some Southwesterner rais'd out-doors? is he Kanadian?
Is he from the Mississippi country? Iowa, Oregon, California?
The mountains? prairie-life, bush-life? or sailor from the sea?

96. Beggars.
97. Based on the French word *élèves*, meaning pupils; here, probably disciples.

* * *

Wherever he goes men and women accept and desire him,
They desire he should like them, touch them, speak to them, stay with them.

Behavior lawless as snow-flakes, words simple as grass, uncomb'd head, laughter, and
    naiveté,
Slow-stepping feet, common features, common modes and emanations,
They descend in new forms from the tips of his fingers,
They are wafted with the odor of his body or breath, they fly out of the glance of his eyes.

40

Flaunt of the sunshine I need not your bask—lie over!
You light surfaces only, I force surfaces and depths also.

Earth! you seem to look for something at my hands,
Say, old top-knot,[98] what do you want?

Man or woman, I might tell how I like you, but cannot,
And might tell what it is in me and what it is in you, but cannot,
And might tell that pining I have, that pulse of my nights and days.

Behold, I do not give lectures or a little charity,
When I give I give myself.

You there, impotent, loose in the knees,
Open your scarf'd chops[99] till I blow grit within you,
Spread your palms and lift the flaps of your pockets,
I am not to be denied, I compel, I have stores plenty and to spare,
And any thing I have I bestow.

I do not ask who you are, that is not important to me,
You can do nothing and be nothing but what I will infold you.

To cotton-field drudge or cleaner of privies I lean,
On his right cheek I put the family kiss,
And in my soul I swear I never will deny him.

On women fit for conception I start bigger and nimbler babes,
(This day I am jetting the stuff of far more arrogant republics.)

To any one dying, thither I speed and twist the knob of the door,
Turn the bed-clothes toward the foot of the bed,
Let the physician and the priest go home.

98. Colloquial term for Native American.   99. Lined jaws.

*   *   *

I seize the descending man and raise him with resistless will,
O despairer, here is my neck,
By God, you shall not go down! hang your whole weight upon me.

I dilate you with tremendous breath, I buoy you up,
Every room of the house do I fill with an arm'd force,
Lovers of me, bafflers of graves.

Sleep—I and they keep guard all night,
Not doubt, not decease shall dare to lay finger upon you,
I have embraced you, and henceforth possess you to myself,
And when you rise in the morning you will find what I tell you is so.

41

I am he bringing help for the sick as they pant on their backs,
And for strong upright men I bring yet more needed help.

I heard what was said of the universe,
Heard it and heard it of several thousand years;
It is middling well as far as it goes—but is that all?

Magnifying and applying come I,
Outbidding at the start the old cautious hucksters,
Taking myself the exact dimensions of Jehovah,[100]
Lithographing Kronos, Zeus his son, and Hercules his grandson,
Buying drafts of Osiris, Isis, Belus, Brahma, Buddha,
In my portfolio placing Manito loose, Allah on a leaf, the crucifix engraved,
With Odin and the hideous-faced Mexitli and every idol and image,
Taking them all for what they are worth and not a cent more,
Admitting they were alive and did the work of their days,
(They bore mites as for unfledg'd birds who have now to rise and fly and sing for
     themselves,)
Accepting the rough deific sketches to fill out better in myself, bestowing them freely on
     each man and woman I see,
Discovering as much or more in a framer framing a house,
Putting higher claims for him there with his roll'd-up sleeves driving the mallet and
     chisel,

100. Jehovah is the Jewish and Christian God. In succeeding lines, Kronos was a Greek and Roman god; Hercules, his grandson, was a hero who performed great deeds; Osiris and Isis were an Egyptian god and goddess of fertility; Belus was an Assyrian god-king; Brahma is "the Creator" in the Hindu religion; Buddha is the founder of Buddhism; Manito is the Algonquin god of nature; Allah is the Supreme Being in Islam; Odin was the god of war and poetry in Scandinavian myth; and Mexitli was an Aztec war god.

Not objecting to special revelations, considering a curl of smoke or a hair on the back of
    my hand just as curious as any revelation,
Lads ahold of fire-engines and hook-and-ladder ropes no less to me than the gods of the
    antique wars,
Minding their voices peal through the crash of destruction,
Their brawny limbs passing safe over charr'd laths, their white foreheads whole and
    unhurt out of the flames;
By the mechanic's wife with her babe at her nipple interceding for every person born,
Three scythes at harvest whizzing in a row from three lusty angels with shirts bagg'd out
    at their waists,
The snag-tooth'd hostler[101] with red hair redeeming sins past and to come,
Selling all he possesses, traveling on foot to fee lawyers for his brother and sit by him
    while he is tried for forgery;
What was strewn in the amplest strewing the square rod about me, and not filling the
    square rod then,
The bull and the bug never worshipp'd half enough,
Dung and dirt more admirable than was dream'd,
The supernatural of no account, myself waiting my time to be one of the supremes,
The day getting ready for me when I shall do as much good as the best, and be as
    prodigious;
By my life-lumps![102] becoming already a creator,
Putting myself here and now to the ambush'd womb of the shadows.

42

A call in the midst of the crowd,
My own voice, orotund sweeping and final.

Come my children,
Come my boys and girls, my women, household and intimates,
Now the performer launches his nerve, he has pass'd his prelude on the reeds within.

Easily written loose-finger'd chords—I feel the thrum of your climax and close.

My head slues round on my neck,
Music rolls, but not from the organ,
Folks are around me, but they are no household of mine.

Ever the hard unsunk ground,
Ever the eaters and drinkers, ever the upward and downward sun, ever the air and the
    ceaseless tides,

---

101. Person who takes care of horses.   102. Testicles.

Ever myself and my neighbors, refreshing, wicked, real,
Ever the old inexplicable query, ever that thorn'd thumb, that breath of itches and
thirsts,
Ever the vexer's *hoot! hoot!* till we find where the sly one hides and bring him forth,
Ever love, ever the sobbing liquid of life,
Ever the bandage under the chin, ever the trestles of death.[103]

Here and there with dimes on the eyes walking,[104]
To feed the greed of the belly the brains liberally spooning,
Tickets buying, taking, selling, but in to the feast never once going,
Many sweating, ploughing, thrashing, and then the chaff for payment receiving,
A few idly owning, and they the wheat continually claiming.

This is the city and I am one of the citizens,
Whatever interests the rest interests me, politics, wars, markets, newspapers, schools,
The mayor and councils, banks, tariffs, steamships, factories, stocks, stores, real estate
and personal estate.

The little plentiful manikins skipping around in collars and tail'd coats,
I am aware who they are, (they are positively not worms or fleas,)
I acknowledge the duplicates of myself, the weakest and shallowest is deathless with me,
What I do and say the same waits for them,
Every thought that flounders in me the same flounders in them.

I know perfectly well my own egotism,
Know my omnivorous lines and must not write any less,
And would fetch you whoever you are flush with myself.

Not words of routine this song of mine,
But abruptly to question, to leap beyond yet nearer bring;
This printed and bound book—but the printer and the printing-office boy?
The well-taken photographs—but your wife or friend close and solid in your arms?
The black ship mail'd with iron, her mighty guns in her turrets—but the pluck of the
captain and engineers?
In the houses the dishes and fare and furniture—but the host and hostess, and the look
out of their eyes?
The sky up there—yet here or next door, or across the way?
The saints and sages in history—but you yourself?
Sermons, creeds, theology—but the fathomless human brain,
And what is reason? and what is love? and what is life?

103. Wooden supports for a coffin.
104. Coins were placed on the eyes of the dead; here, an image of those who live a greedy death-in-life.

43

I do not despise you priests, all time, the world over,
My faith is the greatest of faiths and the least of faiths,
Enclosing worship ancient and modern and all between ancient and modern,
Believing I shall come again upon the earth after five thousand years,
Waiting responses from oracles, honoring the gods, saluting the sun,
Making a fetich[105] of the first rock or stump, powowing with sticks in the circle of obis,
Helping the llama[106] or brahmin as he trims the lamps of the idols,
Dancing yet through the streets in a phallic procession, rapt and austere in the woods a
     gymnosophist,[107]
Drinking mead from the skull-cup, to Shastas[108] and Vedas admirant, minding the Koran,
Walking the teokallis,[109] spotted with gore from the stone and knife, beating the serpent-
     skin drum,
Accepting the Gospels, accepting him that was crucified, knowing assuredly that he is
     divine,
To the mass kneeling or the puritan's prayer rising, or sitting patiently in a pew,
Ranting and frothing in my insane crisis, or waiting dead-like till my spirit arouses me,
Looking forth on pavement and land, or outside of pavement and land,
Belonging to the winders of the circuit of circuits.

One of that centripetal and centrifugal gang I turn and talk like a man leaving charges
     before a journey.

Down-hearted doubters dull and excluded,
Frivolous, sullen, moping, angry, affected, dishearten'd, atheistical,
I know every one of you, I know the sea of torment, doubt, despair and unbelief.

How the flukes[110] splash!
How they contort rapid as lightning, with spasms and spouts of blood!

Be at peace bloody flukes of doubters and sullen mopers,
I take my place among you as much as among any,
The past is the push of you, me, all, precisely the same,
And what is yet untried and afterward is for you, me, all, precisely the same.

I do not know what is untried and afterward,
But I know it will in its turn prove sufficient, and cannot fail.

Each who passes is consider'd, each who stops is consider'd, not a single one can it fail.

105. Fetish. Obis: African and West Indian magi-cal charms.
106. A lama is a high priest in Tibetan Buddhism. A Brahmin is a member of the priestly caste among Hindus.
107. Hindu mystic.
108. Shastras (not Shastas) are books of Hindu law. Vedas are Hindu sacred writings.
109. Aztec temples.
110. Tail fins of whales.

*　*　*

It cannot fail the young man who died and was buried,
Nor the young woman who died and was put by his side,
Nor the little child that peep'd in at the door, and then drew back and was never seen
　　again,
Nor the old man who has lived without purpose, and feels it with bitterness worse than
　　gall,
Nor him in the poor house tubercled by rum and the bad disorder,[111]
Nor the numberless slaughter'd and wreck'd, nor the brutish koboo[112] call'd the ordure
　　of humanity,
Nor the sacs merely floating with open mouths for food to slip in,
Nor any thing in the earth, or down in the oldest graves of the earth,
Nor any thing in the myriads of spheres, nor the myriads of myriads that inhabit them,
Nor the present, nor the least wisp that is known.

44

It is time to explain myself—let us stand up.

What is known I strip away,
I launch all men and women forward with me into the Unknown.

The clock indicates the moment—but what does eternity indicate?

We have thus far exhausted trillions of winters and summers,
There are trillions ahead, and trillions ahead of them.

Births have brought us richness and variety,
And other births will bring us richness and variety.

I do not call one greater and one smaller,
That which fills its period and place is equal to any.

Were mankind murderous or jealous upon you, my brother, my sister?
I am sorry for you, they are not murderous or jealous upon me,
All has been gentle with me, I keep no account with lamentation,
(What have I to do with lamentation?)

I am an acme of things accomplish'd, and I an encloser of things to be.

My feet strike an apex of the apices of the stairs,
On every step bunches of ages, and larger bunches between the steps,
All below duly travel'd, and still I mount and mount.

*　*　*

111. That is, syphilis.　　　　　　　　　　112. Mythic wild men.

Rise after rise bow the phantoms behind me,
Afar down I see the huge first Nothing, I know I was even there,
I waited unseen and always, and slept through the lethargic mist,
And took my time, and took no hurt from the fetid carbon.

Long I was hugg'd close—long and long.

Immense have been the preparations for me,
Faithful and friendly the arms that have help'd me.

Cycles ferried my cradle, rowing and rowing like cheerful boatmen,
For room to me stars kept aside in their own rings,
They sent influences to look after what was to hold me.

Before I was born out of my mother generations guided me,
My embryo has never been torpid, nothing could overlay it.

For it the nebula cohered to an orb,
The long slow strata piled to rest it on,
Vast vegetables gave it sustenance,
Monstrous sauroids[113] transported it in their mouths and deposited it with care.

All forces have been steadily employ'd to complete and delight me,
Now on this spot I stand with my robust soul.

45

O span of youth! ever-push'd elasticity!
O manhood, balanced, florid and full.

My lovers suffocate me,
Crowding my lips, thick in the pores of my skin,
Jostling me through streets and public halls, coming naked to me at night,
Crying by day *Ahoy!* from the rocks of the river, swinging and chirping over my head,
Calling my name from flower-beds, vines, tangled underbrush,
Lighting on every moment of my life,
Bussing[114] my body with soft balsamic busses,
Noiselessly passing handfuls out of their hearts and giving them to be mine.

Old age superbly rising! O welcome, ineffable grace of dying days!

Every condition promulges[115] not only itself, it promulges what grows after and out of
    itself,
And the dark hush promulges as much as any.

---

113. Lizards or dinosaurs.
114. Kissing.

115. Archaic word meaning to promulgate or put
into operation.

*   *   *

I open my scuttle[116] at night and see the far-sprinkled systems,
And all I see multiplied as high as I can cipher edge but the rim of the farther systems.

Wider and wider they spread, expanding, always expanding,
Outward and outward and forever outward.

My sun has his sun and round him obediently wheels,
He joins with his partners a group of superior circuit,
And greater sets follow, making specks of the greatest inside them.

There is no stoppage and never can be stoppage,
If I, you, and the worlds, and all beneath or upon their surfaces, were this moment
    reduced back to a pallid float, it would not avail in the long run,
We should surely bring up again where we now stand,
And surely go as much farther, and then farther and farther.

A few quadrillions of eras, a few octillions of cubic leagues, do not hazard the span or
    make it impatient,
They are but parts, any thing is but a part.

See ever so far, there is limitless space outside of that,
Count ever so much, there is limitless time around that.

My rendezvous is appointed, it is certain,
The Lord will be there and wait till I come on perfect terms,
The great Camerado,[117] the lover true for whom I pine will be there.

46

I know I have the best of time and space, and was never measured and never will be
    measured.

I tramp a perpetual journey, (come listen all!)
My signs are a rain-proof coat, good shoes, and a staff cut from the woods,
No friend of mine takes his ease in my chair,
I have no chair, no church, no philosophy,
I lead no man to a dinner-table, library, exchange,
But each man and each woman of you I lead upon a knoll,
My left hand hooking you round the waist,
My right hand pointing to landscapes of continents and the public road.

*   *   *

116. Roof hatch.
117. God conceived as a comrade, chum, or ro-   mantic friend; perhaps based on the Spanish
    word *camarada*.

Not I, not any one else can travel that road for you,
You must travel it for yourself.

It is not far, it is within reach,
Perhaps you have been on it since you were born and did not know,
Perhaps it is everywhere on water and on land.

Shoulder your duds dear son, and I will mine, and let us hasten forth,
Wonderful cities and free nations we shall fetch[118] as we go.

If you tire, give me both burdens, and rest the chuff[119] of your hand on my hip,
And in due time you shall repay the same service to me,
For after we start we never lie by again.

This day before dawn I ascended a hill and look'd at the crowded heaven,
And I said to my spirit *When we become the enfolders of those orbs, and the pleasure and knowledge of every thing in them, shall we be fill'd and satisfied then?*
And my spirit said *No, we but level that lift to pass and continue beyond.*

You are also asking me questions and I hear you,
I answer that I cannot answer, you must find out for yourself.

Sit a while dear son,
Here are biscuits to eat and here is milk to drink,
But as soon as you sleep and renew yourself in sweet clothes, I kiss you with a good-by kiss and open the gate for your egress hence.

Long enough have you dream'd contemptible dreams,
Now I wash the gum from your eyes,
You must habit yourself to the dazzle of the light and of every moment of your life.

Long have you timidly waded holding a plank by the shore,
Now I will you to be a bold swimmer,
To jump off in the midst of the sea, rise again, nod to me, shout, and laughingly dash with your hair.

47

I am the teacher of athletes,
He that by me spreads a wider breast than my own proves the width of my own,
He most honors my style who learns under it to destroy the teacher.

The boy I love, the same becomes a man not through derived power, but in his own right,

118. Reach.   119. Fat.

Wicked rather than virtuous out of conformity or fear,
Fond of his sweetheart, relishing well his steak,
Unrequited love or a slight cutting him worse than sharp steel cuts,
First-rate to ride, to fight, to hit the bull's eye, to sail a skiff, to sing a song or play on the
    banjo,
Preferring scars and the beard and faces pitted with small-pox over all latherers,
And those well-tann'd to those that keep out of the sun.

I teach straying from me, yet who can stray from me?
I follow you whoever you are from the present hour,
My words itch at your ears till you understand them.

I do not say these things for a dollar or to fill up the time while I wait for a boat,
(It is you talking just as much as myself, I act as the tongue of you,
Tied in your mouth, in mine it begins to be loosen'd.)

I swear I will never again mention love or death inside a house,
And I swear I will never translate myself at all, only to him or her who privately stays
    with me in the open air.

If you would understand me go to the heights or water-shore,
The nearest gnat is an explanation, and a drop or motion of waves a key,
The maul, the oar, the hand-saw, second my words.

No shutter'd room or school can commune with me,
But roughs and little children better than they.

The young mechanic is closest to me, he knows me well,
The woodman that takes his axe and jug with him shall take me with him all day,
The farm-boy ploughing in the field feels good at the sound of my voice,
In vessels that sail my words sail, I go with fishermen and seamen and love them.

The soldier camp'd or upon the march is mine,
On the night ere the pending battle many seek me, and I do not fail them,
On that solemn night (it may be their last) those that know me seek me.

My face rubs to the hunter's face when he lies down alone in his blanket,
The driver thinking of me does not mind the jolt of his wagon,
The young mother and old mother comprehend me,
The girl and the wife rest the needle a moment and forget where they are,
They and all would resume what I have told them.

48

I have said that the soul is not more than the body,
And I have said that the body is not more than the soul,
And nothing, not God, is greater to one than one's self is,
And whoever walks a furlong without sympathy walks to his own funeral drest in his
    shroud,
And I or you pocketless of a dime may purchase the pick of the earth,
And to glance with an eye or show a bean in its pod confounds the learning of all times,
And there is no trade or employment but the young man following it may become a
    hero,
And there is no object so soft but it makes a hub for the wheel'd universe,
And I say to any man or woman, Let your soul stand cool and composed before a million
    universes.

And I say to mankind, Be not curious about God,
For I who am curious about each am not curious about God,
(No array of terms can say how much I am at peace about God and about death.)

I hear and behold God in every object, yet understand God not in the least,
Nor do I understand who there can be more wonderful than myself.

Why should I wish to see God better than this day?
I see something of God each hour of the twenty-four, and each moment then,
In the faces of men and women I see God, and in my own face in the glass,
I find letters from God dropt in the street, and every one is sign'd by God's name,
And I leave them where they are, for I know that wheresoe'er I go,
Others will punctually come for ever and ever.

49

And as to you Death, and you bitter hug of mortality, it is idle to try to alarm me.

To his work without flinching the accoucheur[120] comes,
I see the elder-hand pressing receiving supporting,
I recline by the sills of the exquisite flexible doors,
And mark the outlet, and mark the relief and escape.

And as to you Corpse I think you are good manure, but that does not offend me,
I smell the white roses sweet-scented and growing,
I reach to the leafy lips, I reach to the polish'd breasts of melons.

And as to you Life I reckon you are the leavings of many deaths,
(No doubt I have died myself ten thousand times before.)

120. A person who assists at childbirth (French).

* * *

I hear you whispering there O stars of heaven,
O suns—O grass of graves—O perpetual transfers and promotions,
If you do not say any thing how can I say any thing?

Of the turbid[121] pool that lies in the autumn forest,
Of the moon that descends the steeps of the soughing[122] twilight,
Toss, sparkles of day and dusk—toss on the black stems that decay in the muck,
Toss to the moaning gibberish of the dry limbs.

I ascend from the moon, I ascend from the night,
I perceive that the ghastly glimmer is noonday sunbeams reflected,
And debouch[123] to the steady and central from the offspring great or small.

50

There is that in me—I do not know what it is—but I know it is in me.

Wrench'd and sweaty—calm and cool then my body becomes,
I sleep—I sleep long.

I do not know it—it is without name—it is a word unsaid,
It is not in any dictionary, utterance, symbol.

Something it swings on more than the earth I swing on,
To it the creation is the friend whose embracing awakes me.

Perhaps I might tell more. Outlines! I plead for my brothers and sisters.

Do you see O my brothers and sisters?
It is not chaos or death—it is form, union, plan—it is eternal life—it is Happiness.

51

The past and present wilt—I have fill'd them, emptied them,
And proceed to fill my next fold of the future.

Listener up there! what have you to confide to me?
Look in my face while I snuff the sidle[124] of evening,
(Talk honestly, no one else hears you, and I stay only a minute longer.)

* * *

121. Muddy.
122. Sighing or rustling.
123. Military term meaning to emerge from a confined place.

124. Edging along; that is, the coming of evening.

Do I contradict myself?
Very well then I contradict myself,
(I am large, I contain multitudes.)

I concentrate toward them that are nigh, I wait on the door-slab.

Who has done his day's work? who will soonest be through with his supper?
Who wishes to walk with me?

Will you speak before I am gone? will you prove already too late?

52

The spotted hawk swoops by and accuses me, he complains of my gab and my loitering.

I too am not a bit tamed, I too am untranslatable,
I sound my barbaric yawp over the roofs of the world.

The last scud[125] of day holds back for me,
It flings my likeness after the rest and true as any on the shadow'd wilds,
It coaxes me to the vapor and the dusk.

I depart as air, I shake my white locks at the runaway sun,
I effuse[126] my flesh in eddies, and drift it in lacy jags.

I bequeath myself to the dirt to grow from the grass I love,
If you want me again look for me under your boot-soles.

You will hardly know who I am or what I mean,
But I shall be good health to you nevertheless,
And filter[127] and fibre your blood.

Failing to fetch me at first keep encouraged,
Missing me one place search another,
I stop somewhere waiting for you.

1855

"Song of Myself" appeared as the first poem in the first edition of *Leaves of Grass*. In this 1855 edition the poem had no title, the sections were unnumbered, and the text itself was considerably shorter than it eventually became. For example, the first line read simply "I celebrate myself." In subsequent editions, the poem expanded and changed. It was called "Poem of Walt Whitman, an American," and stanzas were numbered as in the Bible. In the

125. Rush of clouds.
126. Pour forth or diffuse. Eddies: air currents. Jags: barbs of cloud.
127. Cleanse. Fibre: toughen.

final edition, the poem gained its present title and length, and the stanzas were arranged in fifty-two sections. The fifty-two sections may be meant to suggest the weeks of the year, just as the poems in *Leaves of Grass* are metaphorically blades of grass.

"Song of Myself" might be seen as an internal epic—a poem about the interior drama of an individual confronting the diverse features of his nation as opposed to the exterior dramas of historical or mythic events narrated in traditional epics by Homer, Virgil, Spenser, and Milton. Although the structure appears at times to resemble free association, many readers have found a progression in it. Cleanth Brooks, R. W. B. Lewis, and Robert Penn Warren, for example, propose a tripartite division: the speaker becomes a poet (sections 1–17); the poet exhibits his human aspects (18–32); and the poet reveals his godlike capacities (33–52). Stephen Black suggests a radically different tripartite structure, in which the speaker journeys from isolation through a concern with others to autonomy, a sequence interrupted by moments of catharsis (in sections 5, 21, and 28). Other readers have detected a simpler two-part progression: the speaker defines himself, thereby becoming a poet (sections 1–25); then the poet defines the world and its people, thereby becoming a prophet (26–52). Whatever structure one may perceive, the "self" of the poem does indeed "contain multitudes." He is at once individual and representative, modest and grandiose, a poet of nature and of society, a sexual and spiritual visionary.

There Was a Child Went Forth

There was a child went forth every day,
And the first object he look'd upon, that object he became,
And that object became part of him for the day or a certain part of the day,
Or for many years or stretching cycles of years.

The early lilacs became part of this child,
And grass and white and red morning-glories, and white and red clover, and the song of
　　the phoebe-bird,
And the Third-month[1] lambs and the sow's pink-faint litter, and the mare's foal and the
　　cow's calf,
And the noisy brood of the barnyard or by the mire of the pond-side,
And the fish suspending themselves so curiously below there, and the beautiful curious
　　liquid,
And the water-plants with their graceful flat heads, all became part of him.

The field-sprouts of Fourth-month and Fifth-month became part of him,
Winter-grain sprouts and those of the light-yellow corn, and the esculent[2] roots of the
　　garden,
And the apple-trees cover'd with blossoms and the fruit afterward, and wood-berries,
　　and the commonest weeds by the road,

1. The Quaker designation for March.　　　2. Edible.

And the old drunkard staggering home from the outhouse of the tavern whence he had
lately risen,
And the schoolmistress that pass'd on her way to the school,
And the friendly boys that pass'd, and the quarrelsome boys,
And the tidy and fresh-cheek'd girls, and the barefoot negro boy and girl,
And all the changes of city and country wherever he went.

His own parents, he that had father'd him and she that had conceiv'd him in her womb
and birth'd him,
They gave this child more of themselves than that,
They gave him afterward every day, they became part of him.

The mother at home quietly placing the dishes on the supper-table,
The mother with mild words, clean her cap and gown, a wholesome odor falling off her
person and clothes as she walks by,
The father,[3] strong, self-sufficient, manly, mean, anger'd, unjust,
The blow, the quick loud word, the tight bargain, the crafty lure,
The family usages, the language, the company, the furniture, the yearning and swelling
heart,
Affection that will not be gainsay'd, the sense of what is real, the thought if after all it
should prove unreal,
The doubts of day-time and the doubts of night-time, the curious whether and how,
Whether that which appears so is so, or is it all flashes and specks?
Men and women crowding fast in the streets, if they are not flashes and specks what are
they?
The streets themselves and the façades of houses, and goods in the windows,
Vehicles, teams, the heavy-plank'd wharves, the huge crossing at the ferries,
The village on the highland seen from afar at sunset, the river between,
Shadow, aureola and mist, the light falling on roofs and gables of white or brown two
miles off,
The schooner near by sleepily dropping down the tide, the little boat slack-tow'd astern,
The hurrying rumbling waves, quick-broken crests, slapping,
The strata of color'd clouds, the tong bar of maroon-tint away solitary by itself, the
spread of purity it lies motionless in,
The horizon's edge, the flying sea-crow, the fragrance of salt marsh and short mud,
These became part of that child who went forth every day, and who now goes, and will
always go forth every day.

1855

3. The attention given to the father's negative
qualities may come as a surprise, given the tran-
quil quality of the poem's other images, but Whit-
man may be recalling his own father's "gruff"
temperament (as David Reynolds terms it).

Out of the Cradle Endlessly Rocking

Out of the cradle endlessly rocking,
Out of the mocking-bird's throat, the musical shuttle,
Out of the Ninth-month[1] midnight,
Over the sterile sands and the fields beyond, where the child leaving his bed wander'd
    alone, bareheaded, barefoot,
Down from the shower'd halo,
Up from the mystic play of shadows twining and twisting as if they were alive,
Out from the patches of briers and blackberries,
From the memories of the bird that chanted to me,
From your memories sad brother,[2] from the fitful risings and fallings I heard,
From under that yellow half-moon late-risen and swollen as if with tears,
From those beginning notes of yearning and love there in the mist,
From the thousand responses of my heart never to cease,
From the myriad thence-arous'd words,
From the word stronger and more delicious than any,
From such as now they start the scene revisiting,
As a flock, twittering, rising, or overhead passing,
Borne hither, ere all eludes me, hurriedly,
A man, yet by these tears a little boy again,
Throwing myself on the sand, confronting the waves,
I, chanter of pains and joys, uniter of here and hereafter,
Taking all hints to use them, but swiftly leaping beyond them,
A reminiscence sing.

Once Paumanok,[3]
When the lilac-scent was in the air and Fifth-month grass was growing,
Up this seashore in some briers,
Two feather'd guests from Alabama, two together,
And their nest, and four light-green eggs spotted with brown,
And every day the he-bird to and fro near at hand,
And every day the she-bird crouch'd on her nest, silent, with bright eyes,
And every day I, a curious boy, never too close, never disturbing them,
Cautiously peering, absorbing, translating.

Shine! shine! shine![4]
Pour down your warmth, great sun!
While we bask, we two together.

---

1. The Quaker designation for September, but also possibly an image of pregnancy.
2. That is, the bird that chanted to him.
3. Native-American name for Long Island.
4. Italicized passages represent the speaker's translations of the bird's song.

   ✻   ✻   ✻

Two together!
Winds blow south, or winds blow north,
Day come white, or night come black,
Home, or rivers and mountains from home,
Singing all time, minding no time,
While we two keep together.

Till of a sudden,
May-be kill'd, unknown to her mate,
One forenoon the she-bird crouch'd not on the nest,
Nor return'd that afternoon, nor the next,
Nor ever appear'd again.

And thenceforward all summer in the sound of the sea,
And at night under the full of the moon in calmer weather,
Over the hoarse surging of the sea,
Or flitting from brier to brier by day,
I saw, I heard at intervals the remaining one, the he-bird,
The solitary guest from Alabama.

Blow! blow! blow!
Blow up sea-winds along Paumanok's shore;
I wait and I wait till you blow my mate to me.

Yes, when the stars glisten'd,
All night long on the prong of a moss-scallop'd stake,
Down almost amid the slapping waves,
Sat the lone singer wonderful causing tears.

He call'd on his mate,
He pour'd forth the meanings which I of all men know.

Yes my brother I know,
The rest might not, but I have treasur'd every note,
For more than once dimly down to the beach gliding,
Silent, avoiding the moonbeams, blending myself with the shadows,
Recalling now the obscure shapes, the echoes, the sounds and sights after their sorts,
The white arms out in the breakers tirelessly tossing,
I, with bare feet, a child, the wind wafting my hair,
Listen'd long and long.

Listen'd to keep, to sing, now translating the notes,
Following you my brother.

* * *

Soothe! soothe! soothe!
Close on its wave soothes the wave behind,
And again another behind embracing and lapping, every one close,
But my love soothes not me, not me.

Low hangs the moon, it rose late,
It is lagging — O I think it is heavy with love, with love.

O madly the sea pushes upon the land,
With love, with love.

O night! do I not see my love fluttering out among the breakers?
What is that little black thing I see there in the white?

Loud! loud! loud!
Loud I call to you, my love!
High and clear I shoot my voice over the waves,
Surely you must know who is here, is here,
You must know who I am, my love.

Low-hanging moon!
What is that dusky spot in your brown yellow?
O it is the shape, the shape of my mate!
O moon do not keep her from me any longer.

Land! land! O land!
Whichever way I turn, O I think you could give me my mate back again if you only would,
For I am almost sure I see her dimly whichever way I look.

O rising stars!
Perhaps the one I want so much will rise, will rise with some of you.

O throat! O trembling throat!
Sound clearer through the atmosphere!
Pierce the woods, the earth,
Somewhere listening to catch you must be the one I want.

Shake out carols!
Solitary here, the night's carols!
Carols of lonesome love! death's carols!
Carols under that lagging, yellow, waning moon!
O under that moon where she droops almost down into the sea!
O reckless despairing carols.

✳   ✳   ✳

But soft! sink low!
Soft! let me just murmur,
And do you wait a moment you husky-nois'd sea,
For somewhere I believe I heard my mate responding to me,
So faint, I must be still, be still to listen,
But not altogether still, for then she might not come immediately to me.

Hither my love!
Here I am! here!
With this just-sustain'd note I announce myself to you,
This gentle call is for you my love, for you.

Do not be decoy'd elsewhere,
That is the whistle of the wind, it is not my voice,
That is the fluttering, the fluttering of the spray,
Those are the shadows of leaves.

O darkness! O in vain!
O I am very sick and sorrowful.

O brown halo in the sky near the moon, drooping upon the sea!
O troubled reflection in the sea!
O throat! O throbbing heart!
And I singing uselessly, uselessly all the night.

O past! O happy life! O songs of Joy!
In the air, in the woods, over fields,
Loved! loved! loved! loved! loved!
But my mate no more, no more with me!
We two together no more.

The aria sinking,
All else continuing, the stars shining,
The winds blowing, the notes of the bird continuous echoing,
With angry moans the fierce old mother incessantly moaning,
On the sands of Paumanok's shore gray and rustling,
The yellow half-moon enlarged, sagging down, drooping, the face of the sea almost
    touching,
The boy ecstatic, with his bare feet the waves, with his hair the atmosphere dallying,
The love in the heart long pent, now loose, now at last tumultuously bursting,
The aria's meaning, the ears, the soul, swiftly depositing,
The strange tears down the cheeks coursing,

The colloquy there, the trio, each uttering,
The undertone, the savage old mother[5] incessantly crying,
To the boy's soul's questions sullenly timing, some drown'd secret hissing,
To the outsetting bard.

Demon or bird! (said the boy's soul,)[6]
Is it indeed toward your mate you sing? or is it really to me?
For I, that was a child, my tongue's use sleeping, now I have heard you,
Now in a moment I know what I am for, I awake,
And already a thousand singers, a thousand songs, clearer, louder and more sorrowful
        than yours,
A thousand warbling echoes have started to life within me, never to die.

O you singer solitary, singing by yourself, projecting me,
O solitary me listening, never more shall I cease perpetuating you,
Never more shall I escape, never more the reverberations,
Never more the cries of unsatisfied love be absent from me,
Never again leave me to be the peaceful child I was before what there in the night,
By the sea under the yellow and sagging moon,
The messenger there arous'd, the fire, the sweet hell within,
The unknown want, the destiny of me.

O give me the clew! (it lurks in the night here somewhere,)
O if I am to have so much, let me have more!

A word then, (for I will conquer it,)
The word final, superior to all,
Subtle, sent up—what is it?—I listen;
Are you whispering it, and have been all the time, you sea-waves?
Is that it from your liquid rims and wet sands?

Whereto answering, the sea,
Delaying not, hurrying not,
Whisper'd me through the night, and very plainly before daybreak,
Lisp'd to me the low and delicious word death,
And again death, death, death, death,
Hissing melodious, neither like the bird nor like my arous'd child's heart,
But edging near as privately for me rustling at my feet,
Creeping thence steadily up to my ears and laying me softly all over,
Death, death, death, death, death.

5. An image of the sea.
6. Compare Poe's phrases in "The Raven" (included in this volume): "bird or devil" and "his eyes have all the seeming of a demon's that is dreaming" (lines 85, 105).

    ✻   ✻   ✻

Which I do not forget,
But fuse the song of my dusky demon and brother,
That he sang to me in the moonlight on Paumanok's gray beach,
With the thousand responsive songs at random,
My own songs awaked from that hour,
And with them the key, the word up from the waves,
The word of the sweetest song and all songs,
That strong and delicious word which, creeping to my feet,
(Or like some old crone rocking the cradle, swathed in sweet garments, bending aside,)
The sea whisper'd me.

1860

As I Ebb'd with the Ocean of Life

1

As I ebb'd with the ocean of life,
As I wended the shores I know,
As I walk'd where the ripples continually wash you Paumanok,[1]
Where they rustle up hoarse and sibilant,
Where the fierce old mother[2] endlessly cries for her castaways,
I musing late in the autumn day, gazing off southward,
Held by this electric self out of the pride of which I utter poems,
Was seiz'd by the spirit that trails in the lines underfoot,
The rim, the sediment that stands for all the water and all the land of the globe.

Fascinated, my eyes reverting from the south, dropt, to follow those slender windrows,[3]
Chaff, straw, splinters of wood, weeds, and the sea-gluten,
Scum, scales from shining rocks, leaves of salt-lettuce, left by the tide,
Miles walking, the sound of breaking waves the other side of me,
Paumanok there and then as I thought the old thought of likenesses,[4]
These you presented to me you fish-shaped island,
As I wended the shores I know,
As I walk'd with that electric self seeking types.[5]

1. Native-American name for Long Island.
2. That is, the sea.
3. Wind-driven rows of waves.
4. The Transcendentalist notion of correspondences between nature and the self, in this case between the sea drift and the poet.
5. Symbols.

2

As I wend to the shores I know not,
As I list[6] to the dirge, the voices of men and women wreck'd,
As I inhale the impalpable breezes that set in upon me,
As the ocean so mysterious rolls toward me closer and closer,
I too but signify at the utmost a little wash'd-up drift,
A few sands and dead leaves to gather,
Gather, and merge myself as part of the sands and drift.

O baffled, balk'd, bent to the very earth,
Oppress'd with myself that I have dared to open my mouth,
Aware now that amid all that blab whose echoes recoil upon me I have not once had the
    least idea who or what I am,
But that before all my arrogant poems the real Me stands yet untouch'd, untold,
    altogether unreach'd,
Withdrawn far, mocking me with mock-congratulatory signs and bows,
With peals of distant ironical laughter at every word I have written,
Pointing in silence to these songs, and then to the sand beneath.

I perceive I have not really understood any thing, not a single object, and that no man
    ever can,
Nature here in sight of the sea taking advantage of me to dart upon me and sting me,
Because I have dared to open my mouth to sing at all.

3

You oceans both, I close with you,
We murmur alike reproachfully rolling sands and drift, knowing not why,
These little shreds indeed standing for you and me and all.

You friable[7] shore with trails of debris,
You fish-shaped island, I take what is underfoot,
What is yours is mine my father.[8]

I too Paumanok,
I too have bubbled up, floated the measureless float, and been wash'd on your shores,
I too am but a trail of drift and debris,
I too leave little wrecks upon you, you fish-shaped island.

I throw myself upon your breast my father,
I cling to you so that you cannot unloose me,
I hold you so firm till you answer me something.

6. Listen. Dirge: a song of mourning.
7. Crumbly.

8. The speaker figures the island as his father, as
he figures the sea as his mother.

*   *   *

Kiss me my father,
Touch me with your lips as I touch those I love,
Breathe to me while I hold you close the secret of the murmuring I envy.

4

Ebb, ocean of life, (the flow will return,)
Cease not your moaning you fierce old mother,
Endlessly cry for your castaways, but fear not, deny not me,
Rustle not up so hoarse and angry against my feet as I touch you or gather from you.

I mean tenderly by you and all,
I gather for myself and for this phantom looking down where we lead, and following me
     and mine.

Me and mine, loose windrows, little corpses,
Froth, snowy white, and bubbles,
(See, from my dead lips the ooze exuding at last,
See, the prismatic colors glistening and rolling,)
Tufts of straw, sands, fragments,
Buoy'd hither from many moods, one contradicting another,
From the storm, the long calm, the darkness, the swell,
Musing, pondering, a breath, a briny tear, a dab of liquid or soil,
Up just as much out of fathomless workings fermented and thrown,
A limp blossom or two, torn, just as much over waves floating, drifted at random,
Just as much for us that sobbing dirge of Nature,
Just as much whence we come that blare of the cloud-trumpets,
We, capricious, brought hither we know not whence, spread out before you,
You up there walking or sitting,
Whoever you are, we too lie in drifts at your feet.

                                                                1860

I Sit and Look Out

I sit and look out upon all the sorrows of the world, and upon all oppression and shame,
I hear secret convulsive sobs from young men at anguish with themselves, remorseful
     after deeds done,
I see in low life the mother misused by her children, dying, neglected, gaunt, desperate,
I see the wife misused by her husband, I see the treacherous seducer of young women,
I mark the ranklings of jealousy and unrequited love attempted to be hid, I see these
     sights on the earth,
I see the workings of battle, pestilence, tyranny, I see martyrs and prisoners,

I observe a famine at sea, I observe the sailors casting lots who shall be kill'd to preserve
    the lives of the rest,
I observe the slights and degradations cast by arrogant persons upon laborers, the poor,
    and upon negroes, and the like;
All these—all the meanness and agony without end I sitting look out upon,
See, hear, and am silent.

1860

Native Moments

Native moments—when you come upon me—ah you here now,
Give me now libidinous joys only,
Give me the drench of my passions, give me life coarse and rank,
Today I go consort with nature's darlings, tonight too,
I am for those who believe in loose delights, I share the midnight orgies of young men,
I dance with the dancers and drink with the drinkers,
The echoes ring with our indecent calls, I pick out some low person for my dearest
    friend,
He shall be lawless, rude, illiterate, he shall be one condemn'd by others for deeds done,
I will play a part no longer, why should I exile myself from my companions?
O you shunn'd persons, I at least do not shun you,
I come forthwith in your midst, I will be your poet,
I will be more to you than to any of the rest.

1860

Once I Pass'd through a Populous City

Once I pass'd through a populous city imprinting my brain for future use with its shows,
    architecture, customs, traditions,
Yet now of all that city I remember only a woman I casually met there who detain'd me
    for love of me,
Day by day and night by night we were together—all else has long been forgotten by me,
I remember I say only that woman who passionately clung to me,
Again we wander, we love, we separate again,
Again she holds me by the hand, I must not go,
I see her close beside me with silent lips sad and tremulous.

1860

Facing West from California's Shores

Facing west from California's shores,
Inquiring, tireless, seeking what is yet unfound,
I, a child, very old, over waves, towards the house of maternity,[1] the
    land of migrations, look afar,
Look off the shores of my Western sea, the circle almost circled;
For starting westward from Hindustan,[2] from the vales of Kashmere,
From Asia, from the north, from the God, the sage, and the hero,
From the south, from the flowery peninsulas and the spice islands,[3]
Long having wander'd since, round the earth having wander'd,
Now I face home again, very pleas'd and joyous,
(But where is what I started for so long ago?
And why is it yet unfound?)

                                   1860

As Adam Early in the Morning

As Adam early in the morning,
Walking forth from the bower refresh'd with sleep,
Behold me where I pass, hear my voice, approach,
Touch me, touch the palm of your hand to my body as I pass,
Be not afraid of my body.

                                   1860

In Paths Untrodden

In paths untrodden,
In the growth by margins of pond-waters,
Escaped from the life that exhibits itself,
From all the standards hitherto publish'd, from the pleasure, profits, conformities,
Which too long I was offering to feed my soul,
Clear to me now standards not yet publish'd, clear to me that my soul,
That the soul of the man I speak for rejoices in comrades,
Here by myself away from the clank of the world,
Tallying and talk'd to here by tongues aromatic,

---

1. Asia, thought to be a birthplace of civilization.
2. India. Kashmir: a mountainous region now claimed by both India and Pakistan.
3. Indonesia.

No longer abash'd, (for in this secluded spot I can respond as I would not
     dare elsewhere,)
Strong upon me the life that does not exhibit itself, yet contains all the rest,
Resolv'd to sing no songs today but those of manly attachment,
Projecting them along that substantial life,
Bequeathing hence types of athletic love,
Afternoon this delicious Ninth-month in my forty-first year,
I proceed for all who are or have been young men,
To tell the secret of my nights and days,
To celebrate the need of comrades.

                                                                    1860

"In Paths Untrodden" is the first of the "Calamus" poems that were added to *Leaves of Grass* in the 1860 edition. Whitman explained to an editor that "calamus" is "the very large & aromatic grass, or rush, growing about water-ponds in the valleys—spears about three feet high—often called 'sweet flag.'" Prominent in these poems is the importance of "manly attachment." Some of the poems "celebrate the need of comrades"; others confront intense depression and loneliness that occur when such comradeship is absent. The six poems that follow in this anthology, concluding with "Here the Frailest Leaves of Me," are all from the "Calamus" section.

Hours Continuing Long

Hours continuing long, sore and heavy-hearted,
Hours of the dusk, when I withdraw to a lonesome and unfrequented spot, seating
     myself, leaning my face in my hands;
Hours sleepless, deep in the night, when I go forth, speeding swiftly the country roads,
     or through the city streets, or pacing miles and miles, stifling plaintive cries;
Hours discouraged, distracted—for the one I cannot content myself without, soon I saw
     him content himself without me;
Hours when I am forgotten, (O weeks and months are passing, but I believe I am never
     to forget!)
Sullen and suffering hours! (I am ashamed—but it is useless—I am what I am;)
Hours of my torment—I wonder if other men ever have the like, out of the like feelings?
Is there even one other like me—distracted—his friend, his lover, lost to him?
Is he too as I am now? Does he still rise in the morning, dejected, thinking who is lost to
     him? and at night, awaking, think who is lost?
Does he too harbor his friendship silent and endless? harbor his anguish and passion?
Does some stray reminder, or the casual mention of a name, bring the fit back upon
     him, taciturn and deprest?
Does he see himself reflected in me? In these hours, does he see the face of his hours
     reflected?

                                                                    1860

Trickle Drops

Trickle drops! my blue veins leaving!
O drops of me! trickle, slow drops,
Candid from me falling, drip, bleeding drops,
From wounds made to free you whence you were prison'd,
From my face, from my forehead and lips,
From my breast, from within where I was conceal'd, press forth red
    drops, confession drops,
Stain every page, stain every song I sing, every word I say, bloody drops,
Let them know your scarlet heat, let them glisten,
Saturate them with yourself all ashamed and wet,
Glow upon all I have written or shall write, bleeding drops,
Let it all be seen in your light, blushing drops.

            1860

City of Orgies

City of orgies, walks and joys,
City whom that I have lived and sung in your midst will one day make you illustrious,
Not the pageants of you, not your shifting tableaus, your spectacles, repay me,
Not the interminable rows of your houses, nor the ships at the wharves,
Nor the processions in the streets, nor the bright windows with goods in them,
Nor to converse with learn'd persons, or bear my share in the soiree or feast;
Not those, but as I pass O Manhattan, your frequent and swift flash of eyes offering
    me love,
Offering response to my own—these repay me,
Lovers, continual lovers, only repay me.

            1860

Behold This Swarthy Face

Behold this swarthy face, these gray eyes,
This beard, the white wool unclipt upon my neck,
My brown hands and the silent manner of me without charm;
Yet comes one a Manhattanese and ever at parting kisses me lightly on the
    lips with robust love,
And I on the crossing of the street or on the ship's deck give a kiss in return,
We observe that salute of American comrades land and sea,
We are those two natural and nonchalant persons.

            1860

I Saw in Louisiana a Live-Oak Growing

I saw in Louisiana a live-oak[1] growing,
All alone stood it and the moss hung down from the branches,
Without any companion it grew there uttering joyous leaves of dark green,
And its look, rude, unbending, lusty, made me think of myself,
But I wonder'd how it could utter joyous leaves standing alone there
    without its friend near, for I knew I could not,
And I broke off a twig with a certain number of leaves upon it, and twined
    around it a little moss,
And brought it away, and I have placed it in sight in my room,
It is not needed to remind me as of my own dear friends,
(For I believe lately I think of little else than of them,)
Yet it remains to me a curious token, it makes me think of manly love;
For all that, and though the live-oak glistens there in Louisiana solitary in
    a wide flat space,
Uttering joyous leaves all its life without a friend a lover near,
I know very well I could not.

1860

Here the Frailest Leaves of Me

Here the frailest leaves of me and yet my strongest lasting,
Here I shade and hide my thoughts, I myself do not expose them,
And yet they expose me more than all my other poems.

1860

A Hand-Mirror

Hold it up sternly—see this it sends back, (who is it? is it you?)
Outside fair costume, within ashes and filth,
No more a flashing eye, no more a sonorous voice or springy step,
Now some slave's eye, voice, hands, step,
A drunkard's breath, unwholesome eater's face, venerealee's flesh,
Lungs rotting away piecemeal, stomach sour and cankerous,
Joints rheumatic, bowels clogged with abomination,
Blood circulating dark and poisonous streams,
Words babble, hearing and touch callous,

---

1. Evergreen oak.

No brain, no heart left, no magnetism of sex;
Such from one look in this looking-glass ere you go hence,
Such a result so soon—and from such a beginning!

1860

When I Heard the Learn'd Astronomer

When I heard the learn'd astronomer,
When the proofs, the figures, were ranged in columns before me,
When I was shown the charts and diagrams, to add, divide, and measure them,
When I sitting heard the astronomer where he lectured with much applause
    in the lecture-room,
How soon unaccountable I became tired and sick,
Till rising and gliding out I wander'd off by myself,
In the mystical moist night-air, and from time to time,
Look'd up in perfect silence at the stars.

1865

"When I Heard the Learn'd Astronomer" originally appeared in *Drum-Taps*, a volume occasioned by the Civil War. Probably because this poem says nothing explicit about the war, Whitman later moved it to the "By the Roadside" section of *Leaves of Grass*.

Cavalry Crossing a Ford

A line in long array where they wind betwixt green islands,
They take a serpentine course, their arms flash in the sun—hark to the musical clank,
Behold the silvery river, in it the splashing horses loitering stop to drink,
Behold the brown-faced men, each group, each person a picture, the negligent rest
    on the saddles,
Some emerge on the opposite bank, others are just entering the ford—while,
Scarlet and blue and snowy white,
The guidon flags[1] flutter gayly in the wind.

1865

"Cavalry Crossing a Ford" derives from *Drum-Taps*, the book of Civil War poems that Whitman published in 1865. He said that the book was "put together by fits and starts, on the field, in the hospitals, as I worked with the soldier boys" (Horace Traubel, *With Walt Whitman in Camden*). Upon the death of Lincoln, Whitman wrote additional poems,

---

1. Small flags or streamers carried by soldiers for marking or signaling.

including "When Lilacs Last in the Dooryard Bloom'd," and included them in an expanded version of the book. "Cavalry Crossing a Ford" and the five poems that follow in this anthology, ending with "Reconciliation," were eventually included in sections of *Leaves of Grass* entitled "Drum-Taps" and "Memories of President Lincoln."

The Wound-Dresser

1

An old man bending I come among new faces,
Years looking backward resuming in answer to children,
Come tell us old man, as from young men and maidens that love me,
(Arous'd and angry, I'd thought to beat the alarum, and urge relentless war,
But soon my fingers fail'd me, my face droop'd and I resign'd myself,
To sit by the wounded and soothe them, or silently watch the dead;)
Years hence of these scenes, of these furious passions, these chances,
Of unsurpass'd heroes, (was one side so brave? the other was equally brave;)
Now be witness again, paint the mightiest armies of earth,
Of those armies so rapid so wondrous what saw you to tell us?
What stays with you latest and deepest? of curious panics,
Of hard-fought engagements or sieges tremendous what deepest remains?

2

O maidens and young men I love and that love me,
What you ask of my days those the strangest and sudden your talking recalls,
Soldier alert I arrive after a long march cover'd with sweat and dust,
In the nick of time I come, plunge in the fight, loudly shout in the rush of
    successful charge,
Enter the captur'd works—yet lo, like a swift-running river they fade,
Pass and are gone they fade—I dwell not on soldiers' perils or soldiers' joys,
(Both I remember well—many the hardships, few the joys, yet I was content.)

But in silence, in dreams' projections,
While the world of gain and appearance and mirth goes on,
So soon what is over forgotten, and waves wash the imprints off the sand,
With hinged knees returning I enter the doors, (while for you up there,
Whoever you are, follow without noise and be of strong heart.)

Bearing the bandages, water and sponge,
Straight and swift to my wounded I go,
Where they lie on the ground after the battle brought in,

Where their priceless blood reddens the grass the ground,
Or to the rows of the hospital tent, or under the roof'd hospital,
To the long rows of cots up and down each side I return,
To each and all one after another I draw near, not one do I miss,
An attendant follows holding a tray, he carries a refuse pail,
Soon to be fill'd with clotted rags and blood, emptied, and fill'd again.

I onward go, I stop,
With hinged knees and steady hand to dress wounds,
I am firm with each, the pangs are sharp yet unavoidable,
One turns to me his appealing eyes—poor boy! I never knew you,
Yet I think I could not refuse this moment to die for you, if that would save you.

   3
On, on I go, (open doors of time! open hospital doors!)
The crush'd head I dress, (poor crazed hand tear not the bandage away,)
The neck of the cavalry-man with the bullet through and through I examine,
Hard the breathing rattles, quite glazed already the eye, yet life struggles hard,
(Come sweet death! be persuaded O beautiful death!
In mercy come quickly.)

From the stump of the arm, the amputated hand,
I undo the clotted lint, remove the slough, wash off the matter and blood,
Back on his pillow the soldier bends with curv'd neck and side-falling head,
His eyes are closed, his face is pale, he dares not look on the bloody stump,
And has not yet look'd on it.

I dress a wound in the side, deep, deep,
But a day or two more, for see the frame all wasted and sinking,
And the yellow-blue countenance see.

I dress the perforated shoulder, the foot with the bullet-wound,
Cleanse the one with a gnawing and putrid gangrene, so sickening, so offensive,
While the attendant stands behind aside me holding the tray and pail.

I am faithful, I do not give out,
The fractur'd thigh, the knee, the wound in the abdomen,
These and more I dress with impassive hand, (yet deep in my breast a fire, a
      burning flame.)

4

Thus in silence in dreams' projections,
Returning, resuming, I thread my way through the hospitals,
The hurt and wounded I pacify with soothing hand,
I sit by the restless all the dark night, some are so young,
Some suffer so much, I recall the experience sweet and sad,
(Many a soldier's loving arms about this neck have cross'd and rested,
Many a soldier's kiss dwells on these bearded lips.)

                                                                        1865

Vigil Strange I Kept on the Field One Night

Vigil strange I kept on the field one night;
When you my son and my comrade dropt at my side that day,
One look I but gave which your dear eyes return'd with a look I shall never forget,
One touch of your hand to mine O boy, reach'd up as you lay on the ground,
Then onward I sped in the battle, the even-contested battle,
Till late in the night reliev'd to the place at last again I made my way,
Found you in death so cold dear comrade, found your body son of responding kisses,
    (never again on earth responding,)
Bared your face in the starlight, curious the scene, cool blew the moderate night-wind,
Long there and then in vigil I stood, dimly around me the battle-field spreading,
Vigil wondrous and vigil sweet there in the fragrant silent night,
But not a tear fell, not even a long-drawn sigh, long, long I gazed,
Then on the earth partially reclining sat by your side leaning my chin in my hands,
Passing sweet hours, immortal and mystic hours with you dearest comrade — not a
    tear, not a word,
Vigil of silence, love and death, vigil for you my son and my soldier,
As onward silently stars aloft, eastward new ones upward stole,
Vigil final for you brave boy, (I could not save you, swift was your death,
I faithfully loved you and cared for you living, I think we shall surely meet again,)
Till at latest lingering of the night, indeed just as the dawn appear'd,
My comrade I wrapt in his blanket, envelop'd well his form,
Folded the blanket well, tucking it carefully over head and carefully under feet,
And there and then and bathed by the rising sun, my son in his grave, in his rude-dug
    grave I deposited,
Ending my vigil strange with that, vigil of night and battle-field dim,
Vigil for boy of responding kisses, (never again on earth responding,)

Vigil for comrade swiftly slain, vigil I never forget, how as day brighten'd,
I rose from the chill ground and folded my soldier well in his blanket,
And buried him where he fell.

1865

Bivouac on a Mountain Side

I see before me now a traveling army halting,
Below a fertile valley spread, with barns and the orchards of summer,
Behind, the terraced sides of a mountain, abrupt, in places rising high,
Broken, with rocks, with clinging cedars, with tall shapes dingily seen,
The numerous camp-fires scatter'd near and far, some away up on the mountain,
The shadowy forms of men and horses, looming, large-sized, flickering,
And over all the sky—the sky! far, far out of reach, studded, breaking out, the
    eternal stars.

1865

When Lilacs Last in the Dooryard Bloom'd

1

When lilacs last in the dooryard bloom'd,
And the great star[1] early droop'd in the western sky in the night,
I mourn'd, and yet shall mourn with ever-returning spring.

Ever-returning spring, trinity sure to me you bring,
Lilac blooming perennial and drooping star in the west,
And thought of him I love.

2

O powerful western fallen star!
O shades of night—O moody, tearful night!
O great star disappear'd—O the black murk that hides the star!
O cruel hands that hold me powerless—O helpless soul of me!
O harsh surrounding cloud that will not free my soul.

3

In the dooryard fronting an old farm-house near the white-wash'd palings,
Stands the lilac-bush tall-growing with heart-shaped leaves of rich green,

1. Venus.

With many a pointed blossom rising delicate, with the perfume strong I love,
With every leaf a miracle—and from this bush in the dooryard,
With delicate-color'd blossoms and heart-shaped leaves of rich green,
A sprig with its flower I break.

4

In the swamp in secluded recesses,
A shy and hidden bird is warbling a song.

Solitary the thrush,
The hermit withdrawn to himself, avoiding the settlements,
Sings by himself a song.

Song of the bleeding throat,
Death's outlet song of life, (for well dear brother I know,
If thou wast not granted to sing thou would'st surely die.)

5

Over the breast of the spring, the land, amid cities,
Amid lanes and through old woods, where lately the violets peep'd from the ground,
    spotting the gray debris,
Amid the grass in the fields each side of the lanes, passing the endless grass,
Passing the yellow-spear'd wheat, every grain from its shroud in the dark-brown fields
    uprisen,
Passing the apple-tree blows of white and pink in the orchards,
Carrying a corpse to where it shall rest in the grave,
Night and day journeys a coffin.

6

Coffin that passes through lanes and streets,
Through day and night with the great cloud darkening the land,
With the pomp of the inloop'd flags with the cities draped in black,
With the show of the States themselves as of crape-veil'd women standing,
With processions long and winding and the flambeaus of the night,
With the countless torches lit, with the silent sea of faces and the unbared heads,
With the waiting depot, the arriving coffin, and the sombre faces,
With dirges through the night, with the thousand voices rising strong and solemn,
With all the mournful voices of the dirges pour'd around the coffin,
The dim-lit churches and the shuddering organs—where amid these you journey,
With the tolling tolling bells' perpetual clang,
Here, coffin that slowly passes,
I give you my sprig of lilac.

7

(Nor for you, for one alone,
Blossoms and branches green to coffins all I bring,
For fresh as the morning, thus would I chant a song for you O sane and sacred death.

All over bouquets of roses,
O death, I cover you over with roses and early lilies,
But mostly and now the lilac that blooms the first,
Copious I break, I break the sprigs from the bushes,
With loaded arms I come, pouring for you,
For you and the coffins all of you O death.)

8

O western orb sailing the heaven,
Now I know what you must have meant as a month since I walk'd,
As I walk'd in silence the transparent shadowy night,
As I saw you had something to tell as you bent to me night after night,
As you droop'd from the sky low down as if to my side, (while the other stars all look'd
    on,)
As we wander'd together the solemn night, (for something I know not what kept me
    from sleep,)
As the night advanced, and I saw on the rim of the west how full you were of woe,
As I stood on the rising ground in the breeze in the cool transparent night,
As I watch'd where you pass'd and was lost in the netherward black of the night,
As my soul in its trouble dissatisfied sank, as where you sad orb,
Concluded, dropt in the night, and was gone.

9

Sing on there in the swamp,
O singer bashful and tender, I hear your notes, I hear your call,
I hear, I come presently, I understand you,
But a moment I linger, for the lustrous star has detain'd me,
The star my departing comrade holds and detains me.

10

O how shall I warble myself for the dead one there I loved?
And how shall I deck my song for the large sweet soul that has gone?
And what shall my perfume be for the grave of him I love?

*   *   *

Sea-winds blown from east and west,
Blown from the Eastern sea and blown from the Western sea, till there on the prairies
    meeting,
These and with these and the breath of my chant,
I'll perfume the grave of him I love.

11

O what shall I hang on the chamber walls?
And what shall the pictures be that I hang on the walls,
To adorn the burial-house of him I love?

Pictures of growing spring and farms and homes,
With the Fourth-month² eve at sundown, and the gray smoke lucid and bright,
With floods of the yellow gold of the gorgeous, indolent, sinking sun, burning,
    expanding the air,
With the fresh sweet herbage under foot, and the pale green leaves of the trees prolific,
In the distance the flowing glaze, the breast of the river, with a wind-dapple here and
    there,
With ranging hills on the banks, with many a line against the sky, and shadows,
And the city at hand with dwellings so dense, and stacks of chimneys,
And all the scenes of life and the workshops, and the workmen homeward returning.

12

Lo, body and soul—this land,
My own Manhattan with spires, and the sparkling and hurrying tides, and the ships,
The varied and ample land, the South and the North in the light, Ohio's shores and
    flashing Missouri,
And ever the far-spreading prairies cover'd with grass and corn.

Lo, the most excellent sun so calm and haughty,
The violet and purple morn with just-felt breezes,
The gentle soft-born measureless light,
The miracle spreading bathing all, the fulfill'd noon,
The coming eve delicious, the welcome night and the stars,
Over my cities shining all, enveloping man and land.

13

Sing on, sing on you gray-brown bird,
Sing from the swamps, the recesses, pour your chant from the bushes,
Limitless out of the dusk, out of the cedars and pines.

2. The Quaker designation for April.

* * *

Sing on dearest brother, warble your reedy song,
Loud human song, with voice of uttermost woe.

O liquid and free and tender!
O wild and loose to my soul—O wondrous singer!
You only I hear—yet the star holds me, (but will soon depart,)
Yet the lilac with mastering odor holds me.

14

Now while I sat in the day and look'd forth,
In the close of the day with its light and the fields of spring, and the farmers preparing
    their crops,
In the large unconscious scenery of my land with its lakes and forests,
In the heavenly aerial beauty, (after the perturb'd winds and the storms,)
Under the arching heavens of the afternoon swift passing, and the voices of children
    and women,
The many-moving sea-tides, and I saw the ships how they sail'd,
And the summer approaching with richness, and the fields all busy with labor,
And the infinite separate houses, how they all went on, each with its meals and minutia
    of daily usages,
And the streets how their throbbings throbb'd, and the cities pent[3]—lo, then and there,
Falling upon them all and among them all, enveloping me with the rest,
Appear'd the cloud, appear'd the long black trail,
And I knew death, its thought, and the sacred knowledge of death.

Then with the knowledge of death as walking one side of me,
And the thought of death close-walking the other side of me,
And I in the middle as with companions, and as holding the hands of companions,
I fled forth to the hiding receiving night that talks not,
Down to the shores of the water, the path by the swamp in the dimness,
To the solemn shadowy cedars and ghostly pines so still.

And the singer so shy to the rest receiv'd me,
The gray-brown bird I know receiv'd us comrades three,
And he sang the carol of death, and a verse for him I love.

From deep secluded recesses,
From the fragrant cedars and the ghostly pines so still,
Came the carol of the bird.

* * *

3. Confined or penned in.

And the charm of the carol rapt[4] me,
As I held as if by their hands my comrades in the night,
And the voice of my spirit tallied[5] the song of the bird.

Come lovely and soothing death,[6]
Undulate round the world, serenely arriving, arriving,
In the day, in the night, to all, to each,
Sooner or later delicate death.

Prais'd be the fathomless universe,
For life and joy, and for objects and knowledge curious,
And for love, sweet love—but praise! praise! praise!
For the sure-enwinding arms of cool-enfolding death.

Dark mother always gliding near with soft feet,
Have none chanted for thee a chant of fullest welcome?
I chant it for thee, I glorify thee above all,
I bring thee a song that when thou must indeed come, come unfalteringly.

Approach strong deliveress,
When it is so, when thou hast taken them I joyously sing the dead,
Lost in the loving floating ocean of thee,
Laved in the flood of thy bliss O death.

From me to thee glad serenades,
Dances for thee I propose saluting thee, adornments and feastings for thee,
And the sights of the open landscape and the high-spread sky are fitting,
And life and the fields, and the huge and thoughtful night.

The night in silence under many a star,
The ocean shore and the husky whispering wave whose voice I know,
And the soul turning to thee O vast and well-veil'd death,
And the body gratefully nestling close to thee.

Over the tree-tops I float thee a song,
Over the rising and sinking waves, over the myriad fields and the prairies wide,
Over the dense-pack'd cities all and the teeming wharves and ways,
I float this carol with joy, with joy to thee O death.

4. Both wrapped and enraptured.
5. Corresponded with, registered, identified, or counted up.

6. The italicized passage represents the bird's song.

15

To the tally of my soul,
Loud and strong kept up the gray-brown bird,
With pure deliberate notes spreading filling the night.

Loud in the pines and cedars dim,
Clear in the freshness moist and the swamp-perfume,
And I with my comrades there in the night.

While my sight that was bound in my eyes unclosed,
As to long panoramas of visions.

And I saw askant[7] the armies,
I saw as in noiseless dreams hundreds of battle-flags,
Borne through the smoke of the battles and pierc'd with missiles I saw them,
And carried hither and yon through the smoke, and torn and bloody,
And at last but a few shreds left on the staffs, (and all in silence,)
And the staffs all splinter'd and broken.

I saw battle-corpses, myriads of them,
And the white skeletons of young men, I saw them,
I saw the debris and debris of all the slain soldiers of the war,
But I saw they were not as was thought,
They themselves were fully at rest, they suffer'd not,
The living remain'd and suffer'd, the mother suffer'd,
And the wife and the child and the musing comrade suffer'd,
And the armies that remain'd suffer'd.

16

Passing the visions, passing the night,
Passing, unloosing the hold of my comrades' hands,
Passing the song of the hermit bird and the tallying song of my soul,
Victorious song, death's outlet song, yet varying ever-altering song,
As low and wailing, yet clear the notes, rising and falling, flooding the night,
Sadly sinking and fainting, as warning and warning, and yet again bursting with joy,
Covering the earth and filling the spread of the heaven,
As that powerful psalm in the night I heard from recesses,
Passing, I leave thee lilac with heart-shaped leaves,
I leave thee there in the door-yard, blooming, returning with spring.

*   *   *

7. With suspicion or mistrust.

I cease from my song for thee,
From my gaze on thee in the west, fronting the west, communing with thee,
O comrade lustrous with silver face in the night.

Yet each to keep and all, retrievements out of the night,
The song, the wondrous chant of the gray-brown bird,
And the tallying chant, the echo arous'd in my soul,
With the lustrous and drooping star with the countenance full of woe,
With the holders holding my hand nearing the call of the bird,
Comrades mine and I in the midst, and their memory ever to keep, for the dead I loved
    so well,
For the sweetest, wisest soul of all my days and lands—and this for his dear sake,
Lilac and star and bird twined with the chant of my soul,
There in the fragrant pines and the cedars dusk and dim.

1865–66

Whitman composed this elegy in the weeks following Abraham Lincoln's assassination on April 14, 1865. He published it first in the expanded version of *Drum-Taps* and later in the "Memories of President Lincoln" section of *Leaves of Grass*. Whitman's editors Harold Blodgett and Sculley Bradley note "the subtle counterpoint of the three basic symbols—the lilacs of perennial spring (the poet's love), the fallen western star (Lincoln), the song of the hermit thrush (the chant of death)."

Reconciliation

Word over all, beautiful as the sky,
Beautiful that war and all its deeds of carnage must in time be utterly lost,
That the hands of the sisters Death and Night incessantly softly wash
    again, and ever again, this soil'd world;
For my enemy is dead, a man divine as myself is dead,
I look where he lies white-faced and still in the coffin—I draw near,
Bend down and touch lightly with my lips the white face in the coffin.

1865–66

One's-Self I Sing

One's-Self I sing, a simple separate person,
Yet utter the word Democratic, the word En-Masse.[1]

*   *   *

1. Earlier used in section 23 of "Song of Myself," this term, derived from French, means humanity as a whole.

Of physiology from top to toe I sing,
Not physiognomy alone nor brain alone is worthy for
　　　the Muse, I say the Form complete is worthier far,
The Female equally with the Male I sing.

Of Life immense in passion, pulse, and power,
Cheerful, for freest action form'd under the laws divine,
The Modern Man I sing.

　　　　　　　　　　　　　　　1867

Whitman used "One's-Self I Sing" as the initial "inscription" in his final editions of *Leaves of Grass*.

A Noiseless Patient Spider

A noiseless patient spider,
I mark'd where on a little promontory it stood isolated,
Mark'd how to explore the vacant vast surrounding,
It launch'd forth filament, filament, filament, out of itself,
Ever unreeling them, ever tirelessly speeding them.

And you O my soul where you stand,
Surrounded, detached, in measureless oceans of space,
Ceaselessly musing, venturing, throwing, seeking the spheres to connect them,
Till the bridge you will need be form'd, till the ductile anchor hold,
Till the gossamer thread you fling catch somewhere, O my soul.

　　　　　　　　　　　　　　　1868

Passage to India

1

Singing my days,
Singing the great achievements of the present,
Singing the strong light works of engineers,
Our modern wonders, (the antique ponderous Seven[1] outvied,)
In the Old World the east the Suez canal,[2]

1. The ancient Seven Wonders of the World.
2. This line and the succeeding two evoke recent technological triumphs that would potentially bring human beings closer to each other: the opening of the Suez Canal in 1869, the comple- tion of the first transcontinental rail line by the Union Pacific and Central Pacific Railroads in 1869, and the laying of the first Atlantic cable in 1866.

The New by its mighty railroad spann'd,
The seas inlaid with eloquent gentle wires;
Yet first to sound, and ever sound, the cry with thee O soul,
The Past! the Past! the Past!

The Past—the dark unfathom'd retrospect!
The teeming gulf—the sleepers and the shadows!
The past—the infinite greatness of the past!
For what is the present after all but a growth out of the past?
(As a projectile form'd, impell'd, passing a certain line, still keeps on,
So the present, utterly form'd, impell'd by the past.)

   2

Passage O soul to India![3]
Eclaircise[4] the myths Asiatic, the primitive fables.

Not you alone proud truths of the world,
Nor you alone ye facts of modern science,
But myths and fables of eld,[5] Asia's, Africa's fables,
The far-darting beams of the spirit, the unloos'd dreams,
The deep diving bibles and legends,
The daring plots of the poets, the elder religions;
O you temples fairer than lilies pour'd over by the rising sun!
O you fables spurning the known, eluding the hold of the known, mounting to heaven!
You lofty and dazzling towers, pinnacled, red as roses, burnish'd with gold!
Towers of fables immortal fashion'd from mortal dreams!
You too I welcome and fully the same as the rest!
You too with joy I sing.

Passage to India!
Lo, soul, seest thou not God's purpose from the first?
The earth to be spann'd, connected by network,
The races, neighbors, to marry and be given in marriage,
The oceans to be cross'd, the distant brought near,
The lands to be welded together.

A worship new I sing,
You captains, voyagers, explorers, yours,

---

3. Spiritual passage paralleling the physical jour-
ney facilitated by the Suez Canal.
4. Whitman's term, derived from French, mean-
ing clarify, explain, or illuminate.

5. Old.

You engineers, you architects, machinists, yours,
You, not for trade or transportation only,
But in God's name, and for thy sake O soul.

3

Passage to India!
Lo soul for thee of tableaus twain,
I see in one the Suez canal initiated, open'd;
I see the procession of steamships, the Empress Eugenie's leading the van,[6]
I mark from on deck the strange landscape, the pure sky, the level sand in the distance,
I pass swiftly the picturesque groups, the workmen gather'd,
The gigantic dredging machines.

In one again, different, (yet thine, all thine, O soul, the same.)
I see over my own continent the Pacific railroad surmounting every barrier,[7]
I see continual trains of cars winding along the Platte carrying freight and passengers,
I hear the locomotives rushing and roaring, and the shrill steam-whistle,
I hear the echoes reverberate through the grandest scenery in the world,
I cross the Laramie plains, I note the rocks in grotesque shapes, the buttes,
I see the plentiful larkspur and wild onions, the barren, colorless, sage-deserts,
I see in glimpses afar or towering immediately above me the great mountains, I see the
    Wind river and the Wahsatch mountains,
I see the Monument mountain and the Eagle's Nest, I pass the Promontory,[8] I ascend
    the Nevadas,
I scan the noble Elk mountain and wind around its base,
I see the Humboldt range, I thread the valley and cross the river,
I see the clear waters of lake Tahoe, I see forests of majestic pines,
Or crossing the great desert, the alkaline plains, I behold enchanting mirages of waters
    and meadows,
Marking through these and after all, in duplicate slender lines,
Bridging the three or four thousand miles of land travel,
Tying the Eastern to the Western sea,
The road between Europe and Asia.

(Ah Genoese[9] thy dream! thy dream!
Centuries after thou art laid in thy grave,
The shore thou foundest verifies thy dream.)

6. The Empress Eugénie of France was on the ship that led the procession in the ceremonies opening the Suez Canal.
7. The succeeding lines describe the train route from Omaha to San Francisco.
8. The Union Pacific and Central Pacific Railroad tracks met in Promontory, Utah.
9. Christopher Columbus, who was born in Genoa, Italy.

4

Passage to India!
Struggles of many a captain, tales of many a sailor dead,
Over my mood stealing and spreading they come,
Like clouds and cloudlets in the unreach'd sky.

Along all history, down the slopes,
As a rivulet running, sinking now, and now again to the surface rising,
A ceaseless thought, a varied train—lo, soul, to thee, thy sight, they rise,
The plans, the voyages again, the expeditions;
Again Vasco de Gama[10] sails forth,
Again the knowledge gain'd, the mariner's compass,
Lands found and nations born, thou born America,
For purpose vast, man's long probation fill'd,
Thou rondure of the world at last accomplish'd.

5

O vast Rondure, swimming in space,
Cover'd all over with visible power and beauty,
Alternate light and day and the teeming spiritual darkness,
Unspeakable high processions of sun and moon and countless stars above,
Below, the manifold grass and waters, animals, mountains, trees,
With inscrutable purpose, some hidden prophetic intention,
Now first it seems my thought begins to span thee.

Down from the gardens of Asia descending radiating,
Adam and Eve appear, then their myriad progeny after them,
Wandering, yearning, curious, with restless explorations,
With questionings, baffled, formless, feverish, with never-happy hearts,
With that sad incessant refrain, *Wherefore unsatisfied soul?* and *Whither O mocking life?*

Ah who shall soothe these feverish children?
Who justify these restless explorations?
Who speak the secret of impassive earth?
Who bind it to us? what is this separate Nature so unnatural?
What is this earth to our affections? (unloving earth, without a throb to answer ours,
Cold earth, the place of graves.)

Yet soul be sure the first intent remains, and shall be carried out,
Perhaps even now the time has arrived.

10. Vasco da Gama, a Portuguese navigator, sailed around the Cape of Africa to India in 1497–98. He was the first European to do so.

*   *   *

After the seas are all cross'd, (as they seem already cross'd,)
After the great captains and engineers have accomplish'd their work,
After the noble inventors, after the scientists, the chemist, the geologist, ethnologist,
Finally shall come the poet worthy that name,
The true son of God shall come singing his songs.

Then not your deeds only O voyagers, O scientists and inventors, shall be justified,
All these hearts as of fretted children shall be sooth'd,
All affection shall be fully responded to, the secret shall be told,
All these separations and gaps shall be taken up and hook'd and link'd together,
The whole earth, this cold, impassive, voiceless earth, shall be completely justified,
Trinitas[11] divine shall be gloriously accomplish'd and compacted by the true son of God,
    the poet,
(He shall indeed pass the straits and conquer the mountains,
He shall double the cape of Good Hope to some purpose,)
Nature and Man shall be disjoin'd and diffused no more,
The true son of God shall absolutely fuse them.

6

Year at whose wide-flung door I sing!
Year of the purpose accomplish'd!
Year of the marriage of continents, climates and oceans!
(No mere doge[12] of Venice now wedding the Adriatic,)
I see O year in you the vast terraqueous globe given and giving all,
Europe to Asia, Africa join'd, and they to the New World,
The lands, geographies, dancing before you, holding a festival garland,
As brides and bridegrooms hand in hand.

Passage to India!
Cooling airs from Caucasus[13] far, soothing cradle of man,
The river Euphrates[14] flowing, the past lit up again.

Lo soul, the retrospect brought forward,
The old, most populous, wealthiest of earth's lands,
The streams of the Indus and the Ganges[15] and their many affluents,

---

11. A word, based on Spanish, suggesting Chris-
tianity's Holy Trinity.
12. The chief magistrate who, in times past, sym-
bolized the marriage of Venice to the Adriatic Sea
by casting a ring into the sea.
13. Mountain range in Russia that divides Europe
from Asia.

14. River in Turkey, Syria, and Iraq. The Euphra-
tes Valley was traditionally thought to be the cra-
dle of Western civilization.
15. Two great rivers of India.

(I my shores of America walking to-day behold, resuming all,)
The tale of Alexander[16] on his warlike marches suddenly dying,
On one side China and on the other side Persia and Arabia,
To the south the great seas and the bay of Bengal,
The flowing literatures, tremendous epics, religions, castes,
Old occult Brahma[17] interminably far back, the tender and junior Buddha,
Central and southern empires and all their belongings, possessors,
The wars of Tamerlane,[18] the reign of Aurungzebe,
The traders, rulers, explorers, Moslems, Venetians, Byzantium, the Arabs, Portuguese,
The first travelers famous yet, Marco Polo,[19] Batouta the Moor,
Doubts to be solv'd, the map incognita, blanks to be fill'd,
The foot of man unstay'd, the hands never at rest,
Thyself O soul that will not brook a challenge.

The mediaeval navigators rise before me,
The world of 1492, with its awaken'd enterprise,
Something swelling in humanity now like the sap of the earth in spring,
The sunset splendor of chivalry declining.

And who art thou sad shade?
Gigantic, visionary, thyself a visionary,
With majestic limbs and pious beaming eyes,
Spreading around with every look of thine a golden world,
Enhuing it with gorgeous hues.

As the chief histrion,[20]
Down to the footlights walks in some great scena,
Dominating the rest I see the Admiral[21] himself,
(History's type of courage, action, faith,)
Behold him sail from Palos[22] leading his little fleet,
His voyage behold, his return, his great fame,
His misfortunes, calumniators, behold him a prisoner, chain'd,
Behold his dejection, poverty, death.

(Curious in time I stand, noting the efforts of heroes,
Is the deferment long? bitter the slander, poverty, death?

16. Alexander the Great (356–323 B.C.E.) extended the Macedonian empire to India and died on his return journey.
17. Brahma, "the Creator," is one of three great Hindu gods. Buddha is the founder of Buddhism.
18. Tamerlane (1336–1405) was the Mongol conqueror of much of central Asia. Aurangzeb (1618–1707), emperor of Hindustan, called himself "Conqueror of the World."
19. Polo (1254–1324) traveled from Venice to China. Batouta (1303–1377) explored Asia and Africa.
20. Actor.
21. Christopher Columbus.
22. The Spanish port from which Columbus sailed on August 3, 1492.

Lies the seed unreck'd[23] for centuries in the ground? lo, to God's due occasion,
Uprising in the night, it sprouts, blooms,
And fills the earth with use and beauty.)

7

Passage indeed O soul to primal thought,
Not lands and seas alone, thy own clear freshness,
The young maturity of brood and bloom,
To realms of budding bibles.

O soul, repressless, I with thee and thou with me,
Thy circumnavigation of the world begin,
Of man, the voyage of his mind's return,
To reason's early paradise,
Back, back to wisdom's birth, to innocent intuitions,
Again with fair creation.

8

O we can wait no longer,
We too take ship O soul,
Joyous we too launch out on trackless seas,
Fearless for unknown shores on waves of ecstasy to sail,
Amid the wafting winds, (thou pressing me to thee, I thee to me, O soul,)
Caroling free, singing our song of God,
Chanting our chant of pleasant exploration.

With laugh and many a kiss,
(Let others deprecate, let others weep for sin, remorse, humiliation,)
O soul thou pleasest me, I thee.

Ah more than any priest O soul we too believe in God,
But with the mystery of God we dare not dally.

O soul thou pleasest me, I thee,
Sailing these seas or on the hills, or waking in the night,
Thoughts, silent thoughts, of Time and Space and Death, like waters flowing,
Bear me indeed as through the regions infinite,
Whose air I breathe, whose ripples hear, lave me all over,
Bathe me O God in thee, mounting to thee, I and my soul to range in range of thee.

O Thou transcendent,
Nameless, the fibre and the breath,

23. Unheeded.

Light of the light, shedding forth universes, thou centre of them,
Thou mightier centre of the true, the good, the loving,
Thou moral, spiritual fountain—affection's source—thou reservoir,
(O pensive soul of me—O thirst unsatisfied—waitest not there?
Waitest not haply for us somewhere there the Comrade perfect?)
Thou pulse—thou motive of the stars, suns, systems,
That, circling, move in order, safe, harmonious,
Athwart[24] the shapeless vastnesses of space,
How should I think, how breathe a single breath, how speak, if, out of myself,
I could not launch, to those, superior universes?

Swiftly I shrivel at the thought of God,
At Nature and its wonders, Time and Space and Death,
But that I, turning, call to thee O soul, thou actual Me,
And lo, thou gently masterest the orbs,
Thou matest Time, smilest content at Death,
And fillest, swellest full the vastnesses of Space.

Greater than stars or suns,
Bounding O soul thou journeyest forth;
What love than thine and ours could wider amplify?
What aspirations, wishes, outvie thine and ours O soul?
What dreams of the ideal? what plans of purity, perfection, strength?
What cheerful willingness for others' sake to give up all?
For others' sake to suffer all?

Reckoning ahead O soul, when thou, the time achiev'd,
The seas all cross'd, weather'd the capes, the voyage done,
Surrounded, copest, frontest God, yieldest, the aim attain'd,
As fill'd with friendship, love complete, the Elder Brother found,
The Younger melts in fondness in his arms.

        9
Passage to more than India!
Are thy wings plumed indeed for such far flights?
O soul, voyagest thou indeed on voyages like those?
Disportest thou on waters such as those?
Soundest below the Sanscrit and the Vedas?[25]
Then have thy bent unleash'd.

    24. Across.
    25. Hindu holy books, written in the Sanskrit language.

* * *

Passage to you, your shores, ye aged fierce enigmas!
Passage to you, to mastership of you, ye strangling problems!
You, strew'd with the wrecks of skeletons, that, living, never reach'd you.

Passage to more than India!
O secret of the earth and sky!
Of you O waters of the sea! O winding creeks and rivers!
Of you O woods and fields! of you strong mountains of my land!
Of you O prairies! of you gray rocks!
O morning red! O clouds! O rain and snows!
O day and night, passage to you!

O sun and moon and all you stars! Sirius and Jupiter!
Passage to you!

Passage, immediate passage! the blood burns in my veins!
Away O soul! hoist instantly the anchor!
Cut the hawsers—haul out—shake out every sail!
Have we not stood here like trees in the ground long enough?
Have we not grovel'd here long enough, eating and drinking like mere brutes?
Have we not darken'd and dazed ourselves with books long enough?

Sail forth—steer for the deep waters only,
Reckless O soul, exploring, I with thee, and thou with me,
For we are bound where mariner has not yet dared to go,
And we will risk the ship, ourselves and all.

O my brave soul!
O farther farther sail!
O daring joy, but safe! are they not all the seas of God?
O farther, farther, farther sail!

1871

Whitman observed of "Passage to India," his last long poem, "There's more of me, the essential ultimate me, in that than in any of the poems. There is no philosophy, consistent or inconsistent, in that poem . . . but the burden of it is evolution—the one thing escaping the other—the unfolding of cosmic purposes" (Traubel, *With Walt Whitman in Camden*). James Miller has suggested that the first three sections establish spacial connections, the second three establish temporal connections, and the last three transcend space and time.

The Dalliance of the Eagles

Skirting the river road, (my forenoon walk, my rest,)
Skyward in air a sudden muffled sound, the dalliance of the eagles,
The rushing amorous contact high in space together,
The clinching interlocking claws, a living, fierce, gyrating wheel,
Four beating wings, two beaks, a swirling mass tight grappling,
In tumbling turning clustering loops, straight downward falling,
Till o'er the river pois'd, the twain yet one, a moment's lull,
A motionless still balance in the air, then parting, talons loosing,
Upward again on slow-firm pinions slanting, their separate diverse flight,
She hers, he his, pursuing.

                                                            1880

Good-Bye My Fancy!

Good-bye my Fancy!
Farewell dear mate, dear love!
I'm going away, I know not where,
Or to what fortune, or whether I may ever see you again,
So Good-bye my Fancy.

Now for my last—let me look back a moment;
The slower fainter ticking of the clock is in me,
Exit, nightfall, and soon the heart-thud stopping.

Long have we lived, joy'd, caress'd together;
Delightful!—now separation—Good-bye my Fancy.

Yet let me not be too hasty,
Long indeed have we lived, slept, filter'd, become really blended into one;
Then if we die we die together, (yes, we'll remain one,)
If we go anywhere we'll go together to meet what happens,
May-be we'll be better off and blither, and learn something,
May-be it is yourself now really ushering me to the true songs, (who knows?)
May-be it is you the mortal knob really undoing, turning—so now finally,
Good-bye—and hail! my Fancy.

                                                            1891

ALICE CARY
1820–1871

ALICE CARY, POPULAR IN her own day for her sympathetic portraits of common people and her sentimental elegies, also wrote poems exploring anger, frustration, and catastrophe. These latter poems, such as "The Sea-Side Cave," express what Paula Bennett has called a "dark, almost pagan vein inside herself."

Alice Cary and her younger sister Phoebe Cary (also included in this anthology) were born on a farm near Cincinnati, Ohio. Their mother died when Alice was fifteen, leaving her to care for her sister in a household managed by an unaffectionate stepmother. Alice published her first poem in a local newspaper when she was eighteen. For ten years afterwards, both sisters published their poetry in newspapers and magazines. In 1849, their work appeared in Rufus Griswold's anthology, *The Female Poets of America,* introducing them to a wider audience. Soon thereafter, they moved to New York, where they wrote for *Harper's* and *The Atlantic Monthly* and published volumes of poetry. Alice Cary also published novels and reminiscences. The sisters lived together on 20th Street in Manhattan, where they became famous for their literary receptions.

Both Alice and Phoebe Cary were productive and highly popular writers. Alice once wrote to her mentor Griswold, "We write with much facility, often producing two or three poems in a day, and never elaborate." Whereas her sister's poems are often witty and satirical, Alice Cary's poems (such as "Contradiction") tend to investigate sadness and loss. Whatever their temperamental differences, the two poets were united in their Universalist faith, which posited that all human beings were children of God and therefore redeemed. This spiritual foundation led them to oppose slavery and to support women's rights. Alice Cary, a friend of suffragists Susan B. Anthony and Elizabeth Cady Stanton, served as the first president of Sorosis, a pioneering women's club in New York. The two sisters died within six months of each other in 1871, Alice of tuberculosis and her sister of hepatitis.

FURTHER READING

Paula Bernat Bennett. "Alice Cary," in *Nineteenth-Century American Women Poets: An Anthology.* Pp. 89–94. Malden, Mass.: Blackwell, 1998.
Alice Cary and Phoebe Cary. *The Poetical Works.* 1876; reprint, Boston: Houghton Mifflin, 1898.
Jonathan Hall. "Alice and Phoebe Cary," in *Encyclopedia of American Poetry: The Nineteenth Century.* Ed. Eric L. Haralson. Pp. 65–70. Chicago: Fitzroy Dearborn, 1998.
Annette Kolodny. *The Land Before Her.* Chapel Hill: University of North Carolina Press, 1984.
Laura Long. *Singing Sisters.* New York: Longmans, 1941.

The Sea-Side Cave

A bird of the air shall carry the voice,
and that which hath wings tell the matter.[1]

At the dead of night by the side of the Sea
I met my gray-haired enemy—
The glittering light of his serpent eye
Was all I had to see him by.

At the dead of night, and stormy weather,
We went into a cave together—
Into a cave by the side of the Sea,
And—he never came out with me!

The flower that up through the April mould
Comes like a miser dragging his gold
Never made spot of earth so bright
As was the ground in the cave that night.

Dead of night and stormy weather!
Who should see us going together
Under the black and dripping stone
Of the cave from whence I came alone?

Next day as my boy sat on my knee
He picked the gray hairs off from me
And told with eyes brimful of fear
How a bird in the meadow near

Over her clay-built nest had spread
Sticks and leaves all bloody red,
Brought from a cave by the side of the Sea
Where some murdered man must be.

1850

This allegory of a cave reveals a vengeful and unassuaged aspect to Cary's work that is more typically kept well hidden. Both the sea and the cave may serve as symbolic repositories for unconscious or semiconscious desire.

1. From Ecclesiastes 10:20.

Contradiction

I love the deep quiet—all buried in leaves,
    To sit the day long just as idle as air,
Till the spider grows tame at my elbow and weaves,
    And toadstools come up in a row round my chair.

I love the new furrows—the cones of the pine,
    The grasshopper's chirp, and the hum of the mote;
And short pasture-grass where the clover-blooms shine
    Like red buttons set on a holiday coat.

Flocks packed in the hollows—the droning of bees,
    The stubble[1] so brittle—the damp and flat fen;
Old homesteads I love, in the clusters of trees,
    And children and books, but not women nor men.

Yet strange contradiction! I live in the sound
    Of a sea-girdled city[2]—'tis thus that it fell,
And years, oh how many! have gone since I bound
    A sheaf for the harvest, or drank at a well.

And if, kindly reader, one moment you wait
    To measure the poor little niche that you fill,
I think you will own it is custom or fate
    That has made you the creature you are, not your will.

1866

FREDERICK GODDARD TUCKERMAN
1821–1873

FREDERICK GODDARD TUCKERMAN was born to an accomplished Boston family. His father was a wealthy merchant, his uncle was a noted Unitarian minister, and his older brother became a well-known botanist. Tuckerman himself received a law degree from Harvard, married, and settled in the small town of Greenfield, Massachusetts, where he and his wife had three children. Tiring of the law, he began to write poetry and to study botany and astronomy. He eventually devoted

1. Stumps or cut stalks of plants. Fen: a marsh or bog.   2. That is, Manhattan.

himself entirely to his literary and scientific writing. When his wife died shortly af-
ter the birth of their third child in 1857, Tuckerman's poetry, like his life, took on a
mournful cast. His experimental "Sonnets" study nature with interest, sympathy,
and precision, but they cannot understand it completely. This inability, however,
seems to strengthen rather than weaken his faith. "The Cricket," which has been
called one of the great poems of the nineteenth century, counters grief with a
quest for spiritual transcendence. The poem ultimately fades into silence, as Tuck-
erman himself did in his final years.

FURTHER READING

Samuel A. Golden. *Frederick Goddard Tuckerman: An American Sonneteer*. New York: Twayne,
    1966.
Robert Regan. "Frederick Goddard Tuckerman," in *Encyclopedia of American Poetry: The Nine-
    teenth Century*. Ed. Eric L. Haralson. Pp. 440–45. Chicago: Fitzroy Dearborn, 1998.

Sonnets

1

The starry flower, the flowerlike stars that fade
And brighten with the daylight and the dark—
The bluet in the green I faintly mark,
Or glimmering crags with laurel overlaid,
Even to the Lord of Light, the Lamp of shade,
Seem one to me—nor less divinely made
Than the crowned moon or heaven's great hierarch.[1]
And so, dim grassy flower and night-lit spark
Still move me on and upward for the True;
Seeking through change, growth, death, in new and old,
The full in few, the statelier in the less,
With patient pain; always remembering this:
His Hand, who touched the sod with showers of gold,
Stippled[2] Orion on the midnight blue.

2

And so, as this great sphere (now turning slow
Up to the light from that abyss of stars,
Now wheeling into the gloom through sunset bars)—
With all its elements of form and flow,

1. That is, the sun.
2. Painted by means of dots. Orion, in classical
myth a hunter slain by Artemis, is a constellation
containing some notably bright stars.

And life in life; where crowned, yet blind, must go
The sensible king—is but an Unity
Compressed of motes³ impossible to know;
Which worldlike yet in deep analogy
Have distance, march, dimension, and degree:
So the round earth—which we the world do call—
Is but a grain in that that mightiest swells,
Whereof the stars of light are particles,
As ultimate atoms of one infinite Ball,
On which God moves, and treads beneath his feet the All!

1860

This is a freestanding pair of sonnets. Tuckerman was later to write numerous long series of sonnets. Robert Regan has observed that Tuckerman's sonnets are "invariably unorthodox" in structure. This pair exemplifies that assertion, manifesting a difficult syntax and obeying neither a Petrarchan rhyme scheme (ABBA ABBA CDE CDE) nor a Shakespearean one (ABAB CDCD EFEF GG). Although these two sonnets generally employ a standard iambic pentameter, the second ends with a surprising alexandrine (with six rather than five iambic feet). In "Sonnets," the speaker looks intently at stars, planets, and flowers. He locates God's intention and unity even in their smallness, dispersion, and mutability.

The Cricket

1

The humming bee purrs softly o'er his flower;
  From lawn and thicket
The dogday locust singeth in the sun
  From hour to hour:
Each has his bard, and thou, ere day be done,
  Shalt have no wrong.¹
So bright that murmur mid the insect crowd,
Muffled and lost in the bottom-grass, or loud
  By pale and picket:
Shall I not take to help me in my song
  A little cooing cricket?

2

The afternoon is sleepy; let us lie
Beneath these branches whilst the burdened brook,

3. Specks, or here perhaps atoms.
1. That is, the poet will sing the praises of the cricket, as previous poets have celebrated the bee and locust.

Muttering and moaning to himself, goes by;
And mark our minstrel's carol whilst we look
Toward the faint horizon swooning blue.
    Or in a garden bower,
Trellised and trammeled with deep drapery
    Of hanging green,
    Light glimmering through—
There let the dull hop be,
Let bloom, with poppy's dark refreshing flower:
Let the dead fragrance round our temples beat,
Stunning the sense to slumber, whilst between
The falling water and fluttering wind
    Mingle and meet,
    Murmur and mix,
No few faint pipings from the glades behind,
    Or alder-thicks:
But louder as the day declines,
From tingling tassel, blade, and sheath,
Rising from nets of river vines,
    Winrows[2] and ricks,
    Above, beneath,
    At every breath,
At hand, around, illimitably
Rising and falling like the sea,
    Acres of cricks!

    3
Dear to the child who hears thy rustling voice
Cease at his footstep, though he hears thee still,
Cease and resume with vibrance crisp and shrill,
Thou sittest in the sunshine to rejoice.
Night lover too; bringer of all things dark
And rest and silence; yet thou bringest to me
Always that burthen of the unresting Sea,
The moaning cliffs, the low rocks blackly stark;
These upland inland fields no more I view,
But the long flat seaside beach, the wild seamew,
    And the overturning wave!

---

2. Rows of hay raked up to dry. Ricks: haystacks.

Thou bringest too, dim accents from the grave[3]
To him who walketh when the day is dim,
Dreaming of those who dream no more of him,
With edged remembrances of joy and pain;
And heyday looks and laughter come again:
Forms that in happy sunshine lie and leap,
With faces where but now a gap must be,
Renunciations, and partitions deep
And perfect tears, and crowning vacancy!
And to thy poet at the twilight's hush,
No chirping touch of lips with laugh and blush,
But wringing arms, hearts wild with love and woe,
Closed eyes, and kisses that would not let go!

4

So wert thou[4] loved in that old graceful time
     When Greece was fair,
While god and hero hearkened to thy chime;
     Softly astir
Where the long grasses fringed Caÿster's[5] lip;
Long-drawn, with glimmering sails of swan and ship,
     And ship and swan;
     Or where
     Reedy Eurotas[6] ran.
Did that low warble teach thy tender flute
     Xenaphyle?[7]
Its breathings mild? say! did the grasshopper
Sit golden in thy purple hair
     O Psammathe?[8]
     Or wert thou mute,
Grieving for Pan[9] amid the alders there?
That thirsty tinkle in the herbage still,
Though the lost forest wailed to horns of Arcady?[10]

---

3. Possibly a reference to Tuckerman's dead wife, Hannah.
4. Crickets.
5. A river in Turkey (now called Küçük Menderes), site of the ruins of Ephesus, an ancient Greek city.
6. A river in the department of Laconia in Greece.

7. Perhaps Xenophilos, an ancient Greek philosopher and musician.
8. In Greek myth, Psamathe was the mother of the poet-musician Linus.
9. In Greek myth, the god of forests and flocks.
10. A mountain region of Greece traditionally associated with rustic harmony.

5

Like the Enchanter[11] old —
Who sought mid the dead water's weeds and scum
For evil growths beneath the moonbeam cold,
 Or mandrake or dorcynium;
And touched the leaf that opened both his ears,
So that articulate voices now he hears
In cry of beast, or bird, or insect's hum —
Might I but find thy knowledge in thy song!
 That twittering tongue,
Ancient as light, returning like the years.
 So might I be,
Unwise to sing, thy true interpreter
Through denser stillness and in sounder dark,
Than ere thy notes have pierced to harrow me.
 So might I stir
 The world to hark
 To thee my lord and lawgiver,
 And cease my quest:
Content to bring thy wisdom to the world;
Content to gain at last some low applause,
 Now low, now lost
Like thine from mossy stone, amid the stems and straws,
 Or garden gravemound tricked and dressed —
 Powered and pearled
 By stealing frost —
In dusky rainbow beauty of euphorbias![12]
For larger would be less indeed, and like
The ceaseless simmer in the summer grass
To him who toileth in the windy field,
 Or where the sunbeams strike,
Naught in innumerable numerousness.
 So might I much possess,
 So much must yield;
But failing this, the dell and grassy dike,
The water and the waste shall still be dear,
And all the pleasant plots and places

11. In Greek myth, Tiresias, the blinded prophet.
12. Plants, including poinsettias, whose flowers have no petals or sepals.

Where thou hast sung, and I have hung
   To ignorantly hear.
Then Cricket, sing thy song! or answer mine!
Thine whispers blame, but mine has naught but praises.
It matters not. Behold! the autumn goes,
   The shadow grows,
The moments take hold of eternity;
Even while we stop to wrangle or repine
   Our lives are gone—
   Like thinnest mist,
Like yon escaping color in the tree;
Rejoice! rejoice! whilst yet the hours exist—
Rejoice or mourn, and let the world swing on
Unmoved by the cricket song of thee or me.

                1870

PHOEBE CARY
1824–1871

PHOEBE CARY WROTE witty dialogues and parodies that still gleam today. Although she was a less productive, popular, and financially successful poet than her sister Alice Cary (also included in this anthology), her high spirits and her biting depictions of relations between women and men still have the power to amuse and provoke us.

Phoebe Cary grew up on a farm outside of Cincinnati, Ohio. When her mother and two of her sisters died when she was a young girl, her care fell to her older sister, Alice. Both sisters had literary interests, and both began to publish their poetry early—Phoebe at the age of fourteen. In 1849, the work of both sisters appeared in Rufus Griswold's *The Female Poets of America*. Within two years, Phoebe and her older sister were living in Manhattan and making their way as professional writers.

In 1854, Phoebe Cary published a volume called *Poems and Parodies*. Some of these poems adhered to the sentimental conventions associated with women poets at mid-century. But other comic poems, the "parodies" of the book's title, undermined such conventions. They satirized gender relations (as in "Dorothy's Dower") and made fun of classic poems by male authors (as does "Samuel

Brown"). These poems were a little too sharp, sophisticated, and funny for their era. In future years, Phoebe Cary learned to curtail her satirical bent. Many of her parodies (including "Samuel Brown") were omitted from the Cary sisters' posthumously published *Poetical Works*. There was something faintly scandalous about them—something upsetting to a culture's carefully tailored set of gender presuppositions.

Although shy by nature, Phoebe Cary was actively involved in New York's literary scene, hosting receptions with her sister. She also participated in the struggles then being waged against slavery and for women's rights. For a period she served as an assistant editor of Susan B. Anthony's feminist paper, *The Revolution*. Phoebe Cary died of hepatitis soon after the death of her sister Alice, with whom she had lived devotedly her entire life.

FURTHER READING

Alice Cary and Phoebe Cary. *The Poetical Works*. 1876; reprint, Boston: Houghton Mifflin, 1898.
Jonathan Hall. "Alice and Phoebe Cary," in *Encyclopedia of American Poetry: The Nineteenth Century*. Ed. Eric L. Haralson. Pp. 65–70. Chicago: Fitzroy Dearborn, 1998.
Laura Long. *Singing Sisters*. New York: Longmans, 1941.

Dorothy's Dower

1

"My sweetest Dorothy," said John,
    Of course before the wedding,
As metaphorically he stood,
    His gold upon her shedding,
"Whatever thing you wish or want
    Shall be hereafter granted,
For all my worldly goods are yours."
    The fellow was enchanted!

"About that little dower you have,
    You thought might yet come handy,
Throw it away, do what you please,
    Spend it on sugar-candy!
I like your sweet, dependent ways,
    I love you when you tease me;
The more you ask, the more you spend,
    The better it will please me."

2

"Confound it, Dorothy!" said John,
　　"I haven't got it by me.
You haven't, have you, spent that sum,
　　The dower from Aunt Jemima?
No; well that's sensible for you;
　　This fix is most unpleasant;
But money's tight, so just take yours
　　And use it for the present.
Now I must go—to—meet a man!
　　By George! I'll have to borrow!
Lend me a twenty—that's all right!
　　I'll pay you back tomorrow."

3

"Madam," says John to Dorothy,
　　And past her rudely he pushes,
"You think a man is made of gold,
　　And money grows on bushes!
Tom's shoes! Your doctor! Can't you now
　　Get up some new disaster?
You and your children are enough
　　To break John Jacob Astor.

Where's what you had yourself, when I
　　Was fool enough to court you?
That little sum, till you got me,
　　'Twas what had to support you!"
"It's lent and gone, not very far;
　　Pray don't be apprehensive."
"*Lent!* I've had use enough for it:
　　My family is expensive.
I didn't, as a woman would,
　　Spend it on sugar-candy!"
"No John, I think the most of it
　　Went for cigars and brandy!"

1854

A dower or dowry is the money or property a woman brings to her husband in marriage.
This poem satirically subverts pompous paeans to wedded bliss by charting the husband's
shifting attitudes toward his wife's money.

Samuel Brown

It was many and many a year ago,
    In a dwelling down in town,
That a fellow there lived whom you may know,
    By the name of Samuel Brown;
And this fellow he lived with no other thought
    Than to our house to come down.

I was a child, and he was a child,
    In that dwelling down in town,
But we loved with a love that was more than love,
    I and my Samuel Brown—
With a love that the ladies coveted,
    Me and Samuel Brown.

And this was the reason that, long ago,
    To that dwelling down in town,
A girl came out of her carriage, courting
    My beautiful Samuel Brown;
So that her high-bred kinsman came
    And bore away Samuel Brown,
And shut him up in a dwelling-house,
    In a street quite up in town.

The ladies not half so happy up there,
    Went envying me and Brown;
Yes! That was the reason (as all men know,
    In this dwelling down in town)
That the girl came out of the carriage by night,
    Coquetting and getting my Samuel Brown.

But our love is more artful by far than the love
    Of those who are older than we—
    Of many far wiser than we—
And neither the girls that are living above,
    Nor the girls that are down in town,
Can ever dissever my soul from the soul
    Of the beautiful Samuel Brown.

For the morn never shines without bringing me lines
    From my beautiful Samuel Brown;
And the night's never dark, but I sit in the park
    With my beautiful Samuel Brown.

And often by day, I walk down in Broadway,
  With my darling, my darling, my life and my stay,
    To our dwelling down in town,
    To our house in the street down town.

1854

This poem parodies Edgar Allan Poe's "Annabel Lee" (also included in this anthology). Cary achieves her comic effects by shifting the speaker from male to female, changing the locale from an ethereal "kingdom by the sea" to a very real Manhattan, and turning Poe's impossibly idealized love into a common adulterous liaison. She lances Poe's romanticizing male perspective, but she also reveals urban America's gritty gender and class disparities.

FRANCES ELLEN WATKINS HARPER
1825–1911

FRANCES ELLEN WATKINS HARPER, perhaps the most prominent African-American woman writer of her time, devoted her life to social progress. In addition to writing poetry on public issues, she wrote novels (such as her 1892 best-seller, *Iola Leroy*), stories, journalistic articles, and intellectual essays. She was also a powerful orator and political activist. An "oral poet," as Maryemma Graham has called her, Harper merged elements of vernacular black culture with traditional European-American forms, pioneering a highly effective poetry of advocacy. She became the most popular African-American poet prior to Paul Laurence Dunbar (also included in this anthology). Before the Civil War, her poetry promoted the abolition of slavery. After the war, it explored a wide range of public issues, including equal rights and opportunities for African Americans, women's rights and suffrage, the primacy of education, the dangers of alcohol, and the remediable sufferings of the underprivileged. She once said of her own unwavering identity as an African American, "I belong to this race, and when it is down, I belong to a down race; when it is up, I belong to a risen race." Involved in most of the great social movements of her century, she particularly fostered the advance of blacks and women. Like her fictional character Iola Leroy, she wrote in order "to inspire men and women with a deeper sense of justice and humanity."

    Frances Ellen Watkins was born in 1825 to a free black family in Baltimore, in the slave state of Maryland. After the death of her mother when she was three, the young girl was raised by her abolitionist aunt and uncle. Her experiences as an orphan and a foster child may have contributed to her later heartbreaking images of mother-child separation. Frances Watkins attended a school founded by her uncle, who was an educator, orator, and minister well respected in the African-American community. At the William Watkins Academy for Negro Youth, she studied Greek, Latin, the Bible, and public oratory. At the age of fourteen, she left school to become a domestic worker for a white family. She continued, however, to read voraciously, and she began to write poems and articles for publication.

As conditions for blacks worsened as a result of the Fugitive Slave Act of 1850, Watkins's aunt and uncle were forced to sell their house and school. Although they migrated for a time to Canada, she herself moved to the free state of Ohio, where she took a position teaching domestic science—sewing and embroidery—at the Union Seminary, a school affiliated with the African Methodist Episcopal church. A year later, in 1852, she took a position teaching black children to read and write in Little York, Pennsylvania. By 1854 she was living in Philadelphia. In danger of becoming enslaved if she were to return to Baltimore, she began to devote her life to the antislavery cause, living in an Underground Railroad Station and writing for abolitionist publications such as *Frederick Douglass' Paper* and William Lloyd Garrison's *Liberator*.

During this period, she wrote and published the antislavery poems that would make her famous. Such poems as "The Slave Mother" and "The Slave Auction" emphasized the painful family rendings enforced by the slave system. These works were among the first examples of a revivified African-American protest poetry following the much more veiled protests of Phillis Wheatley in the previous century. Relying on the nineteenth century's veneration of sentimental domesticity as well as personal freedom, Harper's poems encouraged whites to feel empathy for slave families and deepened the bonds free Northern blacks felt for the enslaved blacks. Moreover, these plainly stated and highly rhythmic texts addressed power issues in a remarkably direct and moving way. The poems thus mobilized Northern public opinion, contributed to the growing regional polarization, and set the stage for both the Civil War and emancipation. Moreover, they introduced themes of racial and gender equality that have reappeared in the work of many American poets, and particularly African-American poets, ever since.

Moving to New England in 1854, Frances Watkins (not yet Harper) became a lecturer for the Maine Anti-Slavery Society, speaking to white, black, and racially mixed audiences across the Northeast. Physically delicate yet graced by a strong voice and personality, she lectured on such topics as "Education and the Elevation of the Colored Race." That same year saw the publication of her first book, *Poems on Miscellaneous Subjects*, with an introduction by the white abolitionist Garrison. The volume, which contained all of the poems she had written up to that time, was an instant success, ultimately selling fifty thousand copies in multiple editions, an unheard-of figure. The book was popular among readers of all races and economic stations. Watkins was soon one of the best-known antislavery poets and orators in the country.

In 1860 Frances Watkins married Fenton Harper and moved back to Ohio. As the Civil War raged, she gave birth to her only child, a daughter named Mary, and she reduced her writing and speaking commitments in order to concentrate on her family. In 1864, however, her husband died. Over the next years, she returned to her public pursuits, writing more poetry and lecturing to racially mixed audiences on black rights, women's rights, Christian morality, temperance, religious tolerance toward Jews, and the welfare of freed slaves. She told audiences that "between the white people and the colored there is a community of interest, and the sooner they find it out, the better it will be for both parties; but that community of interests does not consist in increasing the privileges of one class and curtailing the rights of the other."

By the 1870s Harper was back living in Philadelphia, lecturing on "Enlightened Motherhood" and "The Colored Man as a Social and Political Force," and publishing new volumes of poems. Two tours of the Reconstruction-era South resulted in a volume of poems called *Sketches of Southern Life* (1872), which included vernacular poems spoken by a central character named Aunt Chloe. These poems, such as "Aunt Chloe's Politics" and "Learning to Read," make serious points about the importance of education and economic advancement for African Americans. At the same time they forge a new poetic language and a new humor out of the language and everyday culture of working-class blacks.

In the last decades of her life, Harper continued to write about racial equality (in poems and in her novel *Iola Leroy*) and about gender issues (in such poems as "A Double Standard"). She was an officer of both the National Association of Colored Women and the predominantly white National Council of Women of the United States. In 1893 she addressed the World Congress of Representative Women in Chicago, eloquently arguing that women belonged in the political sphere, that white women should oppose racism as well as sexism, and that feminism should go beyond suffrage to address a wide range of racial, economic, and social issues. She died in Philadelphia of heart disease at the age of eighty-five, several years after the death of her daughter.

FURTHER READING

Melva Joyce Boyd. *Discarded Legacy: Politics and Poetics in the Life of Frances E. W. Harper, 1825–1911*. Detroit. Wayne State University Press, 1994.

Paula Giddings. *When and Where I Enter: The Impact of Black Women on Race and Sex in America*. New York: William Morrow, 1984.

Frances E. W. Harper. *A Brighter Coming Day: A Frances Watkins Harper Reader*. Ed. Frances Smith Foster. New York: Feminist Press, 1990.

——. *Complete Poems*. Ed. Maryemma Graham. New York: Oxford University Press, 1988.

Joan R. Sherman. *Invisible Poets: Afro-Americans of the Nineteenth Century*. 2nd ed. Urbana: University of Illinois Press, 1989.

William Still. *The Underground Railroad*. Philadelphia: Porter & Coates, 1872.

The Slave Mother

Heard you that shriek? It rose
    So wildly on the air,
It seemed as if a burden'd heart
    Was breaking in despair.

Saw you those hands so sadly clasped—
    The bowed and feeble hand—
The shuddering of that fragile form—
    That look of grief and dread?

Saw you the sad, imploring eye?
    Its every glance was pain,
As if a storm of agony
    Were sweeping through the brain.

She is a mother, pale with fear,
    Her boy clings to her side,
And in her kirtle[1] vainly tries
    His trembling form to hide.

He is not hers, although she bore
    For him a mother's pains;
He is not hers, although her blood
    Is coursing through his veins!

He is not hers, for cruel hands
    May rudely tear apart
The only wreath of household love
    That binds her breaking heart.

His love has been a joyous light
    That o'er her pathway smiled,
A fountain gushing ever new,
    Amid life's desert wild.

His lightest word has been a tone
    Of music round her heart,
Their lives a streamlet blent in one—
    Oh, Father! must they part?

        *   *   *

---

1. A medieval English term meaning dress or gown.

They tear him from her circling arms,
    Her last and fond embrace.
Oh! never more may her sad eyes
    Gaze on his mournful face.

No marvel, then, these bitter shrieks
    Disturb the listening air;
She is a mother, and her heart
    Is breaking in despair.

            1854

This poem, written in traditional ballad-stanza form, tells a paradigmatic story of a slave mother's grief at losing her son at a slave auction. Note the poem's recurrent contrasts between breaking apart and blending together.

Bible Defence of Slavery

Take sackcloth[1] of the darkest dye,
    And shroud the pulpits round!
Servants of Him that cannot lie,
    Sit mourning on the ground.

Let holy horror blanch each cheek,
    Pale every brow with fears:
And rocks and stones, if ye could speak,
    Ye well might melt to tears!

Let sorrow breathe in every tone,
    In every strain ye raise;
Insult not God's majestic throne
    With th' mockery of praise.

A reverend man, whose light should be
    The guide of age and youth,
Brings to the shrine of slavery
    The sacrifice of truth!

For the direst wrong of man imposed,
    Since Sodom's fearful cry,
The word of life has been enclosed,
    To give your God the lie.

      *   *   *

1. A coarse garment worn as a sign of mourning or penitence in medieval Europe.

Oh! when we pray for the heathen lands,
    And plead for their dark shores,
Remember Slavery's cruel hands
    Make heathens at your doors!

1854

This poem provides a counterattack to defenses of slavery based on the Bible, a common form of argument at the time.

The Slave Auction

The sale began—young girls were there,
    Defenceless in their wretchedness,
Whose stifled sobs of deep despair
    Revealed their anguish and distress.

And mothers stood with streaming eyes,
    And saw their dearest children sold;
Unheeded rose their bitter cries,
    While tyrants bartered them for gold.

And woman, with her love and truth—
    For these in sable forms may dwell—
Gaz'd on the husband of her youth,
    With anguish none may paint or tell.

And men, whose sole crime was their hue,
    The impress of their Maker's hand,
And frail and shrinking children, too,
    Were gathered in that mournful band.

Ye who have laid your love to rest,
    And wept above their lifeless clay,
Know not the anguish of that breast,
    Whose lov'd are rudely torn away.

Ye may not know how desolate
    Are bosoms rudely forced to part,
And how a dull and heavy weight
    Will press the life-drops from the heart.

1854

This rhetorical and historically specific poem invokes both family values and religious piety in order to impel readers to take action against slavery.

Lines

At the Portals of the Future
    Full of madness, guilt and gloom,
Stood the hateful form of Slavery,
    Crying, "Give, Oh! give me room—

"Room to smite the earth with cursing,
    Room to scatter, rend and slay,
From the trembling mother's bosom
    Room to tear her child away;

"Room to trample on the manhood
    Of the country far and wide;
Room to spread o'er every Eden
    Slavery's scorching lava-tide."

Pale and trembling stood the Future,
    Quailing 'neath his frown of hate,
As he grasped with bloody clutches
    The great keys of Doom and Fate.

In his hand he held a banner
    All festooned with blood and tears:
'Twas a fearful ensign, woven
    With the grief and wrong of years.

On his brow he wore a helmet
    Decked with strange and cruel art;
Every jewel was a life-drop
    Wrung from some poor broken heart.

Though her cheek was pale and anxious,
    Wet, with look and brow sublime,
By the pale and trembling Future
    Stood the Crisis of our time.

And from many a throbbing bosom
    Came the words in fear and gloom,
"Tell us, oh! thou coming Crisis,
    What shall be our country's doom?

       *   *   *

"Shall the wings of dark destruction
 Brood and hover o'er our land,
Till we trace the steps of ruin
 By their blight, from strand to strand?"

With a look and voice prophetic
 Spake the solemn Crisis then:
"I have only mapped the future
 For the erring sons of men.

"If ye strive for Truth and Justice,
 If ye battle for the Right,
Ye shall lay your hands all strengthened
 On God's robe of love and light;

"But if ye trample on His children,
 To his ear will float each groan,
Jar the cords that bind them to Him,
 And they'll vibrate at his throne.

"And the land that forges fetters,
 Binds the weak and poor in chains,
Must in blood or tears of sorrow
 Wash away her guilty stains."

                                        1856

This biblical allegory, written five years before the Civil War, includes three personified abstractions as its main characters: Slavery (depicted as male and militaristic), Future (depicted as female and anxious), and Crisis (the judgment giver).

The Slave Mother, a Tale of the Ohio

I have but four,[1] the treasures of my soul,
 They lay like doves around my heart;
I tremble lest some cruel hand
 Should tear my household wreaths apart.

My baby girl, with childish glance,
 Looks curious in my anxious eye,
She little knows that for her sake
 Deep shadows round my spirit lie.

---

1. That is, children.

*   *   *

My playful boys could I forget,
    My home might seem a joyous spot,
But with their sunshine mirth I blend
    The darkness of their future lot.

And thou my babe, my darling one,
    My last, my loved, my precious child,
Oh! when I think upon thy doom
    My heart grows faint and then throbs wild.

The Ohio's bridged and spanned with ice,
    The northern star is shining bright,
I'll take the nestlings of my heart
    And search for freedom by its light.[2]

Winter and night were on the earth,
    And feebly moaned the shivering trees,
A sigh of winter seemed to run
    Through every murmur of the breeze.

She fled, and with her children all,
    She reached the stream and crossed it o'er,
Bright visions of deliverance came
    Like dreams of plenty to the poor.

Dreams! vain dreams, heroic mother,
    Give all thy hopes and struggles o'er,
The pursuer is on thy track,
    And the hunter at thy door.

Judea's refuge cities had power
    To shelter, shield and save,
E'en Rome had altars, 'neath whose shade
    Might crouch the wan and weary slave.

But Ohio had no sacred fane,
    To human rights so consecrated,
Where thou may'st shield thy hapless ones
    From their darkly gathering fate.

*   *   *

2. Here ends the mother's dramatic monologue. Beginning in the next stanza, an omniscient and sympathetic narrator takes over, speaking in the past tense. The narrator does quote the mother once more, in stanzas 11 and 12 below.

Then, said the mournful mother,
    If Ohio cannot save,
I will do a deed for freedom,
    Shalt find each child a grave.

I will save my precious children
    From their darkly threatened doom,
I will hew their path to freedom
    Through the portals of the tomb.

A moment in the sunlight,
    She held a glimmering knife,
The next moment she had bathed it
    In the crimson fount of life.

They snatched away the fatal knife,
    Her boys shrieked wild with dread;
The baby girl was pale and cold,
    They raised it up, the child was dead.

Sends this deed of fearful daring
    Through my country's heart no thrill,
Do the icy hands of slavery
    Every pure emotion chill?

Oh! if there is any honor,
    Truth or justice in the land,
Will ye not, as men and Christians,
    On the side of freedom stand?

                                    1857

This psychologically complex and disturbing poem was based on the 1856 case of Margaret Garner. It is set in Kentucky, on the banks of the Ohio River. Unlike some of Harper's earlier female protagonists, this character is fully individualized and not simply a type. The poem's plot anticipates that of Toni Morrison's novel *Beloved*, published in 1987.

Bury Me in a Free Land

Make me a grave where'er you will,
In a lowly plain, or a lofty hill,
Make it among earth's humblest graves,
But not in a land where men are slaves.

*   *   *

I could not rest if around my grave
I heard the steps of a trembling slave:
His shadow above my silent tomb
Would make it a place of fearful gloom.

I could not rest if I heard the tread
Of a coffle gang[1] to the shambles led,
And the mother's shriek of wild despair
Rise like a curse on the trembling air.

I could not sleep if I saw the lash
Drinking her blood at each fearful gash,
And I saw her babes torn from her breast,
Like trembling doves from their parent nest.

I'd shudder and start if I heard the bay
Of blood-hounds seizing their human prey,
And I heard the captive plead in vain
As they bound afresh his galling chain.

If I saw young girls from their mother's arms
Bartered and sold for their youthful charms,
My eye would flash with a mournful flame,
My death-paled cheek grow red with shame.

I would sleep, dear friends, where bloated might
Can rob no man of his dearest right;
My rest shall be calm in any grave
Where none can call his brother a slave.

I ask no monument, proud and high
To arrest the gaze of the passers-by;
All that my yearning spirit craves,
Is bury me not in a land of slaves.

1864

Written during a bout of illness, this poem utilizes a more autobiographical voice than is usual in Harper's work. Graham suggests that the poem portrays "slavery as living death."

1. A line of slaves. Shambles: a slaughterhouse.

Aunt Chloe's Politics

Of course, I don't know very much
　About these politics,
But I think that some who run 'em,
　Do mighty ugly tricks.

I've seen 'em honey-fugle round,
　And talk so awful sweet,
That you'd think them full of kindness
　As an egg is full of meat.

Now I don't believe in looking
　Honest people in the face,
And saying when you're doing wrong,
　That "I haven't sold my race."

When we want to school our children,
　If the money isn't there,
Whether black or white have took it,
　The loss we all must share.

And this buying up each other
　Is something worse than mean,
Though I thinks a heap of voting,
　I go for voting clean.

1872

This poem and the two that follow are from a series of five poems entitled "Aunt Chloe." Based on Harper's visits to the South after the Civil War, the poems use humor, a poeticized version of Southern black dialect, and down-home characters to spotlight political and social issues of the time. Graham writes that Aunt Chloe, the poems' speaker, implicitly "celebrates the cultural life of black people."

Learning to Read

Very soon the Yankee teachers
　Came down and set up school;
But, oh! how the Rebs[1] did hate it,
　It was agin' their rule.

1. White sympathizers with the now-defeated Confederate rebellion.

*   *   *

Our masters always tried to hide
  Book learning from our eyes;
Knowledge didn't agree with slavery—
  'Twould make us all too wise.

But some of us would try to steal
  A little from the book,
And put the words together,
  And learn by hook or crook.

I remember Uncle Caldwell,
  Who took pot liquor fat
And greased the pages of his book,
  And hid it in his hat.

And had his master ever seen
  The leaves upon his head,
He'd have thought them greasy papers,
  But nothing to be read.

And there was Mr. Turner's Ben,
  Who heard the children spell,
And picked the words right up by heart,
  And learned to read 'em well.

Well, the Northern folks kept sending
  The Yankee teachers down;
And they stood right up and helped us,
  Though Rebs did sneer and frown.

And I longed to read my Bible,
  For precious words it said;
But when I begun to learn it,
  Folks just shook their heads,

And said there is no use trying,
  Oh! Chloe, you're too late;
But as I was rising sixty,
  I had no time to wait.

*   *   *

So I got a pair of glasses,
    And straight to work I went,
And never stopped till I could read
    The hymns and Testament.

Then I got a little cabin
    A place to call my own
And I felt as independent
    As the queen upon her throne.

1872

Church Building

Uncle Jacob often told us,
    Since freedom blessed our race
We ought all to come together
    And build a meeting place.

So we pinched, and scraped, and spared,
    A little here and there:
Though our wages was but scanty,
    The church did get a share.

And, when the house was finished,
    Uncle Jacob came to pray;
He was looking mighty feeble,
    And his head was awful gray.

But his voice rang like a trumpet;
    His eyes looked bright and young;
And it seemed a mighty power
    Was resting on his tongue.

And he gave us all his blessing
    'Twas parting words he said,
For soon we got the message
    The dear old man was dead.

But I believe he's in the kingdom,
    For when we shook his hand
He said, "Children, you must meet me
    Right in the promised land;

*　　*　　*

"For when I done a moiling[1]
  And toiling here below,
Through the gate into the city
  Straightway I hope to go."

1872

A Double Standard

Do you blame me that I loved him?
  If when standing all alone
I cried for bread a careless world
  Pressed to my lips a stone.

Do you blame me that I loved him,
  That my heart beat glad and free,
When he told me in the sweetest tones
  He loved but only me?

Can you blame me that I did not see
  Beneath his burning kiss
The serpent's wiles, nor even hear
  The deadly adder hiss?

Can you blame me that my heart grew cold
  That the tempted, tempter turned;
When he was feted and caressed
  And I was coldly spurned?

Would you blame him, when you draw from me
  Your dainty robes aside,
If he with gilded baits should claim
  Your fairest as his bride?

Would you blame the world if it should press
  On him a civic crown;
And see me struggling in the depth
  Then harshly press me down?

Crime has no sex and yet to-day
  I wear the brand of shame;
Whilst he amid the gay and proud
  Still bears an honored name.

1. Working hard, doing drudgery.

*   *   *

Can you blame me if I've learned to think
   Your hate of vice a sham,
When you so coldly crushed me down
   And then excused the man?

Would you blame me if to-morrow
   The coroner should say,
A wretched girl, outcast, forlorn,
   Has thrown her life away?

Yes, blame me for my downward course,
   But oh! remember well,
Within your homes you press the hand
   That led me down to hell.

I'm glad God's ways are not our ways,
   He does not see as man,
Within His love I know there's room
   For those whom others ban.

I think before His great white throne,
   His throne of spotless light,
That whited sepulchres[1] shall wear
   The hue of endless night.

That I who fell, and he who sinned,
   Shall reap as we have sown;
That each the burden of his loss
   Must bear and bear alone.

No golden weights can turn the scale
   Of justice in His sight;
And what is wrong in woman's life
   In man's cannot be right.

1895

This dramatic monologue critiques the sexual double standard, revealing a complex combination of conformity and resistance to the gender norms of the time. The racial milieu of the poem remains unspecified.

1. An allusion to Matthew 23:27: "Woe unto you, scribes and Pharisees, hypocrites! for ye are like unto whited sepulchres, which indeed appear beautiful outward, but are within full of dead men's bones, and of all uncleanness."

MARIA WHITE LOWELL

1827–1853

BORN INTO A well-established and prosperous New England family, Maria White as a young woman was noted for her delicacy, beauty, and passionate devotion to social causes. She read avidly in her youth and participated, from age twelve to seventeen, in Margaret Fuller's famous "Conversations" on the rights of women. She began to publish her own poetry in 1843, when she was sixteen. The following year, she married the poet James Russell Lowell. The Lowells were linked by a shared commitment to literature and to the antislavery cause, as is suggested by her poetic lament "Africa," which personifies that continent as a massive maternal figure passively mourning the abduction of her children. Yet Maria Lowell, a moderate, remained troubled by the aggressively righteous tone of the more radical abolitionists. Close family friend and fellow poet Henry Wadsworth Longfellow noted in his diary in 1846, "We walked to Lowell's . . . saw his gentle wife, who, I fear, is not long of this world. Speaking of the Abolitionists, she said, 'They do not modulate their words and voices. They are like people who live with the deaf, or hear water-falls, and whose voices become high and harsh.'"

Though Maria Lowell, then just nineteen, would live seven more years, bearing four children and losing three in infancy, her health was never robust. Her frequent illnesses are reflected in two poems notable for their "original imagery and fervency," in Cheryl Walker's words, "The Sick-Room" and "An Opium Fantasy." The latter anticipates concerns that Sylvia Plath, Anne Sexton, and others would explore in the mid-twentieth century: body image, sickness, unrealistic gender norms, and the highly problematical means of escape through prescribed narcotic medications.

Maria Lowell died in 1853, after falling ill during a tour of Italy with her husband, James. James acknowledged that after her early death, "Something broke my life in two and I cannot piece it together again." He arranged for the private publication of her poems in 1855. In 1870, Thomas Wentworth Higginson advised Emily Dickinson to read Maria Lowell's poems, and they were later championed by the poet Amy Lowell.

FURTHER READING

Maria White Lowell. *The Poems of Maria Lowell, with Unpublished Letters and a Biography*. Ed. Hope Jillson Vernon. Providence: Brown University Press, 1936.

Cheryl Walker. "Maria White Lowell," in *American Women Poets of the Nineteenth Century: An Anthology*. Pp. 186–97. New Brunswick: Rutgers University Press, 1992.

Africa

She sat where the level sands
Sent back the sky's fierce glare;
She folded her mighty hands,
And waited with calm despair,
While the red sun dropped down the streaming air.

Her throne was broad and low,
Builded of cinnamon;—
Huge ivory, row on row,
Varying its columns dun,
Barred with the copper of the setting sun.

Up from the river came
The low and sullen roar
Of lions, with eyes of flame,
That haunted its reedy shore,
And the neigh of the hippopotamus trampling the watery floor.

Her great dusk face no light
From the sunset-glow could take;
Dark as the primal night
Ere over the earth God spake:
It seemed for her a dawn could never break.

She opened her massy lips,
And sighed with a dreary sound,
As when by the sand's eclipse
Bewildered men are bound,
And like a train of mourners the columned winds sweep round.

She said: "My torch at fount of day
I lit, now smouldering in decay;
Through futures vast I grope my way.

"I was sole Queen the broad earth through:
My children round my knees upgrew,
And from my breast sucked Wisdom's dew.

"Day after day to them I hymned;
Fresh knowledge still my song o'erbrimmed,
Fresh knowledge, which no time had dimmed.

*   *   *

"I sang of Numbers; soon they knew
The spell they wrought, and on the blue
Foretold the stars in order due;—

"Of Music; and they fain would rear,
Something to tell its influence clear;
Uprose my Memmon, with nice ear,

"To wait upon the morning air,
Until the sun rose from his lair
Swifter, at greet of lutings rare.

"I sang of Forces whose great bands
Could knit together feeble hands
To uprear Thought's supreme commands;

"Then, like broad tents, beside the Nile
They pitched the Pyramids' great pile;
Where light and shade divided smile;

"And on white walls, in stately show,
Did Painting with fair movement go,
Leading the long processions slow.

"All laws that wondrous Nature taught,
To serve my children's skill I brought,
And still for fresh devices sought.

"What need to tell? they lapsed away,
Their great light quenched in twilight gray,
Within their winding tombs they lay,

"And centuries went slowly by,
And looked into my sleepless eye,
Which only turned to see them die.

"The winds like mighty spirits came,
Alive and pure and strong as flame,
At last to lift me from my shame;

"For oft I heard them onward go,
Felt in the air their great wings row,
As down they dipped in journeying slow.

*   *   *

"Their course they steered above my head,
One strong voice to another said,—
'Why sits she here so drear and dead?

"'Her kingdom stretches far away;
Beyond the utmost verge of day,
Her myriad children dance and play.'

"Then throbbed my mother's heart again,
Then knew my pulse's finer pain,
Which wrought like fire within my brain.

"I sought my young barbarians, where
A mellower light broods on the air,
And heavier blooms swing incense rare.

"Swart-skinned, crisp-haired, they did not shun
The burning arrows of the sun;
Erect as palms stood every one.

"I said,—These shall live out their day
In song and dance and endless play;
The children of the world are they.

"Nor need they delve with heavy spade;
Their bread, on emerald dishes laid,
Sets forth a banquet in each shade.

"Only the thoughtful bees shall store
Their honey for them evermore;
They shall not learn such toilsome lore;

"Their finest skill shall be to snare
The birds that flaunt along the air,
And deck them in their feathers rare.

"So centuries went on their way,
And brought fresh generations gay
On my savannahs green to play.

"There came a change. They took my free,
My careless ones, and the great sea
Blew back their endless sighs to me:

*   *   *

"With earthquake shudderings oft the mould
Would gape; I saw keen spears of gold
Thrusting red hearts down, not yet cold,

"But throbbing wildly; dreadful groans
Stole upward through Earth's ribbed stones,
And crept along through all my zones.

"I sought again my desert bare,
But still they followed on the air,
And still I hear them everywhere.

"So sit I dreary, desolate,
Till the slow-moving hand of Fate
Shall lift me from my sunken state."

Her great lips closed upon her moan;
Silently sate she on her throne,
Rigid and black, carved in stone.

1855

The Sick-Room

A spirit is treading the earth,
    As wind treads the vibrating string;
I know thy feet so beautiful,
    Thy punctual feet, O Spring!

They slide from far-off mountains,
    As slides the untouched snow;
They move over deepening meadows,
    As vague cloud-shadows blow.

Thou wilt not enter the chamber,
    The door stands open in vain;
Thou art pluming the wands of cherry
    To lattice the window pane.

Thou flushest the sunken orchard
    With the lift of thy rosy wing;
The peach will not part with her sunrise
    Though great noon-bells should ring.

*   *   *

O life, and light, and gladness,
  Tumultuous everywhere!
O pain and benumbing sadness,
  That brood in the heavy air!

Here the fire alone is busy,
  And wastes, like the fever's heat,
The wood that enshrined past summers,
  Past summers, as bounteous as fleet.

The beautiful hanging gardens
  That rocked in the morning wind,
And sheltered a dream of Faery,
  And life so timid and kind,

The shady choir of the bobolink,
  The race-course of squirrels gay, —
They are changed into trembling smoke-wreaths,
  And a heap of ashes gray.

                                   1855

An Opium Fantasy

Soft hangs the opiate in the brain,
And lulling soothes the edge of pain,
Till harshest sound, far off or near,
Sings floating in its mellow sphere.

What wakes me from my heavy dream?
  Or am I still asleep?
Those long and soft vibrations seem
  A slumberous charm to keep.

The graceful play, a moment stopped,
  Distance again unrolls,
Like silver balls, that, softly dropped,
  Ring into golden bowls.

I question of the poppies red,
  The fairy flaunting band,
While I weed, with drooping head,
  Within their phalanx stand.

*   *   *

"Some airy one, with scarlet cap,
   The name unfold to me
Of this new minstrel, who can lap
   Sleep in his melody?"

Bright grew their scarlet-kerchiefed heads,
   As freshening winds had blown,
And from their gently swaying beds
   They sang in undertone,

"Oh, he is but a little owl,
   The smallest of his kin,
Who sits beneath the midnight's cowl,
   And makes this airy din.

"Deceitful tongues, of fiery tints,
   Far more than this you know,—
That he is your enchanted prince,
   Doomed as an owl to go;

"Nor his fond play for years hath stopped,
   But nightly he unrolls
His silver balls, that, softly dropped,
   Ring into golden bowls."

1855

Opium was a commonly prescribed medication in the early nineteenth century, used particularly as a painkiller.

ROSE TERRY COOKE
1827–1892

DURING THE COURSE of a forty-year career that spanned the latter half of the nineteenth century, Rose Terry Cooke was recognized as one of the leading poets and short-story writers in America. Her vigorous and imaginatively charged writings in both prose and verse appeared regularly in the leading literary journals. They were reviewed and praised by the nation's most prominent critics, and they were regularly featured in important anthologies. Yet in the early and middle years of the twentieth century, Cooke's body of work, like that of many prominent women writers of her time, faded from popular consciousness and was similarly effaced from the literary canon. In recent years, Cooke's short stories have attracted increasing attention and have reappeared in a substantial modern selection. On the other hand, her poems—which at their best are extraordinarily forceful, elegant, learned, and vividly imagined—have long been out of print and remain surprisingly little known.

Rose Terry, born on a farm near Hartford, Connecticut, was, like Emily Dickinson, the daughter of a banker and congressman. An early reader, she studied at the Hartford Female Seminary and then, following serious financial reverses suffered by her family, began working as a governess in 1844. An inheritance from an uncle in 1847 allowed her to give up teaching and return to Hartford, where she took on the care of a deceased sister's children and devoted her remaining time to writing. Starting in 1851, she published a steady stream of poems and short stories in leading journals such as *Harper's*, *Scribner's Monthly*, and *The Atlantic Monthly*. In 1873 Terry married a widower fifteen years her junior, Rollin Hillyer Cooke.

Her first volume of poetry, *Poems*, appeared in 1861, followed by a final collection, also titled *Poems*, in 1888. She also published four short-story collections and a novel. One of Cooke's earliest poems, "Captive," dramatizes several interlinked themes that would recur throughout her work: enclosing domesticity, the yearning for freedom, and the devouring force of passion, often struggling against constraint. These themes are echoed and amplified in such poems as "'Che Sara Sara,'" "Semele," "Arachne," and the uncannily unsettling "Blue-Beard's Closet," which establishes yet another important theme, the allures and dangers of what lies hidden. "A Hospital Soliloquy" displays Cooke's piquant reflections on contemporary politics and her mastery of New England dialect (a staple element of her fiction that was praised by Whittier and Howells) as well as her skillful exploitation of an emerging literary form: the dramatic monologue. In "Schemhammphorasch," a poem of almost overwhelming religious intensity, Cooke's lyric virtuosity and also her yearning for a potentially self-destructive knowledge and scope are on full display. Though Cooke's poetry is inconsistent, she remains a poet of great singularity and power.

FURTHER READING

Rose Terry Cooke. *Poems*. New York: Gottsberger, 1888.
Cheryl Walker. "Rose Terry Cooke," in *American Women Poets of the Nineteenth Century: An Anthology*. New Brunswick: Rutgers University Press, 1992.
www.gonzaga.edu/faculty/campbell/engl462/cooke.htm

Captive

The Summer comes, the Summer dies,
  Red leaves whirl idly from the tree,
But no more cleaving of the skies,
  No southward sunshine waits for me!

You shut me in a gilded cage,
  You deck the bars with tropic flowers,
Nor know that freedom's living rage
  Defies you through the listless hours.

What passion fierce, what service true,
  Could ever such a wrong requite?
What gift, or clasp, or kiss from you
  Were worth an hour of soaring flight?

I beat my wings against the wire,
  I pant my trammelled heart away;
The fever of one mad desire
  Burns and consumes me all the day.

What care I for your tedious love,
  For tender word or fond caress?
I die for one free flight above,
  One rapture of the wilderness!

1851

Blue-Beard's Closet

Fasten the chamber!
Hide the red key;[1]
Cover the portal,
That eyes may not see.
Get thee to market,
To wedding and prayer;
Labor or revel,
The chamber is there!

In comes a stranger
"Thy pictures how fine,
Titian or Guido,[2]
Whose is the sign?"
Looks he behind them?
Ah! have a care!
"Here is a finer."
The chamber is there!

Fair spreads the banquet,
Rich the array;
See the bright torches
Mimicking day;
When harp and viol
Thrill the soft air,
Comes a light whisper:
The chamber is there!

Marble and painting,
Jasper and gold,
Purple from Tyrus,[3]
Fold upon fold,
Blossoms and jewels,
Thy palace prepare:
Pale grows the monarch;
The chamber is there!

Once it was open
As shore to the sea;

1. The key to Bluebeard's chamber magically begins to bleed the moment his wife opens the lock. This bleeding, which cannot be stopped, alerts Bluebeard that the fateful door has been opened.

2. Noted painters of the Italian Renaissance.
3. Capital of ancient Phoenicia, famous for its purple-dyed cloth.

White were the turrets,
Goodly to see;
All through the casements
Flowed the sweet air;
Now it is darkness;
The chamber is there!

Silence and horror
Brood on the walls;
Through every crevice
A little voice calls:
"Quicken, mad footsteps,
On pavement and stair;
Look not behind thee,
The chamber is there!"

Out of the gateway,
Through the wide world,
Into the tempest
Beaten and hurled,
Vain is thy wandering,
Sure thy despair,
Flying or staying,
The chamber is there!
                    1856

Cooke's apparent source for the legend of Bluebeard, told in many versions, is Charles Per-rault's famous collection of fairy tales. There Bluebeard is a wealthy and powerful noble-man who has married and subsequently murdered a succession of wives. Bluebeard departs on a journey, leaving his latest wife in possession of all of his keys. But he warns her not to use one particular key on pain of severe punishment—the key to the chamber in which his dead wives' mangled bodies are locked. When her curiosity gets the best of her, the new wife opens the fateful chamber and recoils in horror. Soon after, Bluebeard arrives and pre-pares to kill his wife. She is saved only by the timely arrival of her three brothers, who kill Bluebeard and rescue their sister.

"Che Sara Sara"

She walked in the garden
    And a rose hung on a tree,
Red as heart's blood,
    Fair to see.
"Ah, kind south-wind,

Bend it to me!"
But the wind laughed softly,
And blew to the sea.

High on the branches,
Far above her head,
Like a king's cup
Round, and red.
"I am comely,"
The maiden said,
"I have gold like shore-sand,
I wish I were dead!

"Blushes and rubies
Are not like a rose,
Through its deep heart
Love-life flows.
Ah, what splendors
Can give me repose!
What is all the world worth?
I cannot reach my rose."

1861

The poem's title is Italian for "What will be will be."

Semele

*For there bee none of those pagan fables in whichle
there lyeth not a more subtle meanynge than the extern
expression thereof should att once signifye.*
MARRIAGES OF YE DEADE

Spirit of light divine!
Quick breath of power,
Breathe on these lips of mine,
Persuade the bud to flower;
Cleave thy dull swathe of cloud! No longer waits the hour.

Exulting, rapturous flame,
Dispel the night!
I dare not breathe thy name,
I tremble at thy light,
Yet come! in fatal strength, — come, in all matchless might.

   ❊   ❊   ❊

Burn, as the leaping fire
    A martyr's shroud;
Burn, like an Indian pyre,
    With music fierce and loud.
Come, Power! Love calls thee, — come, with all the god endowed!

Immortal life in death,
    On these rapt eyes,
On this quick, failing breath,
    In dread and glory rise.
The altar waits thy torch, — come, touch the sacrifice!

Come! not with gifts of life,
    Not for my good;
My soul hath kept her strife
    In fear and solitude;
More blest the inverted torch,[1] the horror-curdled blood.

Better in light to die
    Than silent live;
Rend from these lips one cry,
    One death-born utterance give,
Then, clay, in fire depart! then, soul in heaven survive!

1861

In Greek myth, Semele was a princess, beloved by Zeus, who gave birth to his son Dionysus, the god of wine. She was tricked by Zeus's jealous wife, Juno, into making Zeus swear an oath to come to her bedchamber not in the moderated form in which he usually approached her, but in his full glory. Despite Zeus's reluctance, she was insistent, and thus Semele was destroyed by the force of the god's overpowering presence.

A Hospital Soliloquy

April 10, 1865[1]

I swan![2] it's pleasant now we've beaten
    To think I staid an' seen it through.
I haint gin' in to no retreatin',
    And I've seen battles more'n two.

---

1. In classical iconography, the symbol of a doomed marriage.
1. The day following General Robert E. Lee's surrender of his Confederate army, marking the defeat of the Southern cause in the Civil War. President Lincoln was assassinated on April 14.
2. "I swear," in New England dialect.

＊　＊　＊

So now I'm finished and knocked under,
　　For one leg's gone, an' t'other's lame;
I like to hear them cannon thunder,
　　To tell the world we've got the game.

But better'n all the fire an flashin'
　　Down on the Shenandoah route,
Where Phil's a swearin' and a dashin',[3]
　　Is see'n' them English folks back out.[4]

I would ha gi'n a mint o'dollars
　　Two years ago, to see 'em try
With Abr'am's[5] hand gripped in their collars,
　　How they liked eatin' humble-pie.

An' there they set, while we're a grinnin',
　　And say 'twas all a darned mistake;
That old secesh[6] done all the sinnin',
　　And they have allers baked our cake.

I sot last night an' heerd the firin'
　　An' see the rockets shoot the dark,
And heerd the others all inquirin' —
　　'What's happened?' 'Who has hit the mark?'

The sick, and lame, and sore, an' sleepy,
　　They gin a cheer! — 'twa'n't loud I know,
But then it made me kind o' creepy
　　To hear their voices quaver so.

Thinks I, you're shot with English powder,
　　An' hacked with English swords and guns;[7]
They'll have to lie a little louder
　　Afore they cheat us knowin' ones.

3. Major General Philip Sheridan, a fiery and effective Union leader who capped his Civil War career with a successful campaign to clear Virginia's Shenandoah Valley of Confederate forces. 4. The Confederate cause received considerable support in England in the early years of the Civil War, particularly from the powerful landed aristocracy. Lord Palmerston's government considered granting diplomatic recognition of the Confederacy as a sovereign nation and toyed with the idea of military intervention. But ultimately England "backed out" of any such intervention, particularly after Lincoln's Emancipation Proclamation defined the conflict as a war against slavery and after major Union victories at Vicksburg and Gettysburg, both on July 4, 1863, turned the tide of the war against the Confederacy. 5. Abraham Lincoln. 6. Secessionists, i.e., Confederates. 7. Many Southern weapons were supplied by English blockade runners.

*   *   *

An' now the war's as good as over,
    And dead, and lame, an' mourners tell,
It wasn't livin' quite in clover,
    For them that lived or them that fell.

I kinder guess next time we do it,
    Them sassy English folks will find
When we get riled, an' buckle to it,
    They won't have time to change their mind!

1865

Schemhammmphorasch

This is the key which was given by the angel Michael to Pali, and
by Pali to Moses. If "thou canst read it, then shalt thou understand
the words of men, . . . the whistling of birds, the language of date-trees,
the unity of hearts, . . . nay, even the thoughts of the rains."
    GLEANINGS AFTER THE TALMUD[1]

Ah! could I read Schemhammphorasch,
The wondrous keynote of the world,
What voices could I always hear
From tempests, with their black wings furled,
That on the sudden west winds steer,
And, muttering low their awful song,
Or pealing through the mountains strong,
Robe all the skies with sheeted fire;
That pour from heaven a rushing river,
That bid the hill-tops bow and quiver,
Mad with some fierce and wild desire.

The dreadful anthem of the wind,
That sweeps through forests as a plow,
That lays the greensward heaped below,
Would chant its meaning to my mind,
And I could tell the tale to man
In words that burn and glow with splendor;
Then should the whole wide sky surrender
Its hidden voice, its wondrous plan,

---

1. Cooke's source is Hyam Isaacs's *Ceremonies, Customs, Rites and Traditions of the Jews, Interspersed with Gleanings from the Jerusalem and Babylonish Talmud* (W. Buck: London, 1836).

Asleep since earliest time began;
All my soul, most like a blaze
That burns the branches whence it springeth,
Should flame to heaven in mightier lays
Than any mortal poet singeth,
If I could read Schemhammphorasch.

If I could read Schemhammphorasch,
When little birds are softly singing,
Or twitter from their greenwood nests,
Where safe and still the mother rests;
Or else, upon the glad wind springing,
Send up their tender morning song;
Then should I know their secret blisses,
The thrill of life and love they feel
When summer's sun their bright heads kisses,
Or summer's winds about them steal.
Or, listening to the early blossoms
That are so fleeting and so fair,
With perfume sighing from their bosoms
Its incense on the gracious air,
I think that I should hear a prayer
So sweet, so patient, and so lowly,
That mortal words most pure and rare
Would scarce unveil its meaning holy.
From forests whence the murmurous leaves
Breathe their content in rustling quiver,
Or droop when any rain-wind grieves,
Or where some broad and brimming river
O'erflowing to the mighty sea,
Sings the proud joy of destiny,
The glad acclaim of life and breath;
The courage of confronted death;
Ah! what a rapturous, glorious song
Should seize with bliss this earthly throng,
If I could read Schemhammphorasch!

If I could read Schemhammphorasch,
Then should I know the souls of men,
Too deep for any other ken;
I could translate the silent speech
Of glittering eye and knotted brow,

Though still the wily tongue might teach
A different script with voice and vow.
The blood that runs in traitorous veins;
The breath that gasps with hope or fear;
The stifled sigh, the hidden tear;
The death-pang of immortal pains,
That hide their mortal agony,
Would have their own low voice for me;
Their tale of hate and misery,
Their sob of passion and despair,
Their sacred love, their frantic prayer.
My soul would be the listening priest
To hear confession far and near,
And woe and want from first to least
Would shriek its utterance in my ear.
Ah, could I bear to live and hear
These cries that heaven itself might flee,
These terrors heaven alone may see,
If I could read Schemhammphorasch?

If I could read Schemhammphorasch,
My brain would burn with such a fire
As lights the awful cherubim;[2]
My heart would burst with woe and ire,
My flesh would shrivel and expire;
Yea! God himself grow far and dim.
I cannot hold the boundless sea
In one small chalice lent to me;
I cannot grasp the starry sky
In one weak hand, and bid it lie
Where I would have a canopy;
I cannot hate and love together;
I cannot poise the heavy world,
Or hear its hiss through chaos hurled,
Or stay the falling of a feather.
No, not if Michael came once more,
Standing upon the sea and shore,
And held his right hand down to me,
That I that awful word might see,

---

2. Angelic beings, close servants of God, mentioned frequently in the Hebrew Scriptures.

And learn to read its lesson dread.
My soul in dust would bow her head,
Mine eyes would close, my lips would say,
'Oh, Master! take thy gift away:
Leave me to live my little day
In peace and trust while yet I may.
For could I live, or love, or pray,
If I could read Schemhammphorasch?'

                                        1873

In mystical Hebraic lore, Schemhammphorasch stands for the "Ineffable Name" of God that cannot be spoken because its true spelling and pronunciation have been lost or forgotten. A mortal who could read or pronounce this name would have miraculous powers.

Arachne

I watch her in the corner there,
As, restless, bold, and unafraid,
She slips and floats along the air
Till all her subtile house is made.

Her home, her bed, her daily food
All from that hidden store she draws;
She fashions it and knows it good,
By instinct's strong and sacred laws.

No tenuous threads to weave her nest,
She seeks and gathers there or here;
But spins it from her faithful breast,
Renewing still, till leaves are sere.

Then, worn with toil, and tired of life,
In vain her shining traps are set.
Her frost hath hushed the insect strife
And gilded flies her charm forget.

But swinging in the snares she spun.
She sways to every wintry wind:
Her joy, her toil, her errand done,
Her corse[1] the sport of storms unkind.

                    *   *   *

1. Corpse.

Poor sister of the spinster clan!
I too from out my store within
My daily life and living plan,
My home, my rest, my pleasure spin.

I know thy heart when heartless hands
Sweep all that hard-earned web away:
Destroy its pearled and glittering bands,
And leave thee homeless by the way.

I know thy peace when all is done.
Each anchored thread, each tiny knot,
Soft shining in the autumn sun;
A sheltered, silent, tranquil lot.

1881

In Greek mythology, Arachne, a mortal woman, was a brilliant spinner and weaver who dared to compete with the goddess Athena in these arts. She was transformed by Athena into a spider as a punishment for weaving a magnificent tapestry that depicted the scandals and foibles of the gods—hence the spider's biological name, arachnid.

R. W. Emerson

There is a tall grey cliff before mine eyes,
    The haughty trees, wind-swept, bow down to it;
    Its crest is with the coming day-time lit;
But at its foot the nestling wild-flower lies;
All forest breaths below like incense rise,
    And the shy birds around it sing and flit.
So standeth he 'mid men, supremely wise,
    Strong, and uplifted, yet aware of all
That Nature hides from common mortal eyes:
    The chariest bloom, the moss most fair and small,
    The sun-born insect that with night must fall,
The majesty of days that set and rise,
And that deep thought that in the human breast
Holds him for lifelong friend who knows and brings it rest.

1888

Ralph Waldo Emerson (also included in this anthology), who often wrote about the spiritual qualities of nature, died in 1882.

JOHN ROLLIN RIDGE
1827–1867

THE MIXED-RACE CHEROKEE writer John Rollin Ridge is best known for his 1854 romance fiction penned under the name "Yellow Bird"—*Life and Adventures of Joaquin Murieta, the Celebrated California Bandit*—because of its heroic portrayal of the Chicano outlaw. Nevertheless, he also was a widely published poet and the editor and owner of several California newspapers, including the *San Francisco Herald* and the *Sacramento Bee*. His combined literary talents and political acumen allowed him to pioneer in Native-American poetry and to contribute to Chicano literature as well. Ridge appropriated European-American poetic traditions for Native-American cultural goals, a strategy that continues to influence contemporary Native-American poets. His romance of Murieta was his response to the growing tensions among Mexicans, Chicanos, and European Americans along the Mexican border, hostilities that were depicted in the corridos (Mexican and Mexican-American ballads, also included in this anthology) in the 1850s in the Southwest.

Ridge moved to California from Arkansas and the Cherokee nation in Oklahoma when several Cherokees joined the gold rush in the mid-century. But he also needed to flee from his home. During a political argument he had killed someone from the John Ross Party of Cherokees, members of which earlier had assassinated his father and grandfather for signing the Treaty of New Echota (1835). This treaty had led to the forced death march of the Cherokees to Oklahoma in what is known as the "Trail of Tears." The Ridges had moved to the new area prior to removal, so they did not march with the rest of the people, who as a result felt betrayed by them. Ridge's father was killed in front of his European-American wife and all of his children, including Ridge himself. In spite of this history of conflict, Ridge remained an important political spokesman of the Cherokees and in his writing continued to advocate assimilation of the Cherokee nation into the United States—a policy that had dominated the two nations' relationship from the beginning. Undoubtedly his own mixed ancestry—he was part European American—contributed to his political viewpoint.

"The Stolen White Girl" reflects Ridge's assimilation politics both formally and thematically. Employing a highly sympathetic male perspective, he adapts the European-American poetics of sentimentality with its emphasis on affections to portray a greatly desired "stolen" romance between a European-American woman and a biracial Native-American/European-American man. This poem resists the U.S. coding of biracial males as Native American and the general popular condemnation of intermarriage between European Americans and Native Americans. It also positions itself in opposition to the growing view among many Native Americans that the Cherokee policy of assimilation would lead to eventual annihilation by portraying the biracial male as triumphant. The depiction of the poem's interracial romance offers a vexed gender politics in which the man speaks, but the woman is silent, suggesting that Ridge followed the era's most conservative gender conventions.

FURTHER READING

James W. Parins. *John Rollin Ridge: His Life and Works*. Lincoln: University of Nebraska Press, 1991.

The Stolen White Girl

The prairies are broad, and the woodlands are wide
And proud on his steed the wild half-breed may ride,
With the belt round his waist and the knife at his side.
And no white man may claim his beautiful bride.

Though he stole her away from the land of the whites,
Pursuit is in vain, for her bosom delights
In the love that she bears the dark-eyed, the proud,
Whose glance is like starlight beneath a night-cloud.

Far down in the depths of the forest they'll stray,
Where the shadows like the night are lingering all day;
Where the flowers are springing up wild at their feet,
And the voices of birds in the branches are sweet.

Together they'll roam by the streamlets that run,
O'ershadowed at times then meeting the sun —
The streamlets that soften their varying tune,
As up the blue heavens calm wanders the moon!

The contrast between them is pleasing and rare;
Her sweet eye of blue, and her soft silken hair,
Her beautiful waist, and her bosom of white
That heaves to the touch with a sense of delight;

His form more majestic and darker his brow,
Where the sun has imparted its liveliest glow —
An eye that grows brighter with passion's true fire,
As he looks on his loved one with earnest desire.

*   *   *

Oh, never let Sorrow's cloud darken their fate,
The girl of the "pale face," her Indian mate!
But deep in the forest of shadows and flowers,
Let Happiness smile, as she wings their sweet hours.

1868

HENRY TIMROD
1828–1867

Henry timrod was born in Charleston, South Carolina. His parents were of mixed English, Swiss, and German descent. After studying at what is now the University of Georgia, he worked as a private tutor and began writing and publishing poems. His early poems were love poems and idealized portraits of plantation life. During the Civil War he enlisted in the Confederate army but was discharged because of poor health. He wrote poems supporting the Confederate cause and, in the war's aftermath, poems mourning the Confederate dead, such as "Ode." In his final years he married, lost his only son in infancy, and lived in poverty and illness. He died of tuberculosis two years after the end of the Civil War.

FURTHER READING

Edd Winfield Parks. *Henry Timrod*. New York: Twayne, 1964.
Louis D. Rubin, Jr. *The Edge of the Swamp: A Study of the Literature of the Old South*. Baton Rouge: Louisiana State University Press, 1989.
David S. Shields. "Henry Timrod," in *Encyclopedia of American Poetry: The Nineteenth Century*. Ed. Eric L. Haralson. Pp. 428–33. Chicago: Fitzroy Dearborn, 1998.

Ode

*Sung on the occasion of decorating
the graves of the Confederate dead, at
Magnolia Cemetery, Charleston, S.C., 1867*

1

Sleep sweetly in your humble graves,
    Sleep, martyrs of a fallen cause;
Though yet no marble column craves
    The pilgrim here to pause.

2

In seeds of laurel in the earth
   The blossom of your fame is blown,
And somewhere, waiting for its birth,
   The shaft is in the stone!

3

Meanwhile, behalf the tardy years
   Which keep in trust your storied tombs,
Behold! Your sisters bring their tears,
   And these memorial blooms.

4

Small tributes! But your shades will smile
   More proudly on these wreaths to-day,
Than when some cannon-moulded pile
   Shall overlook this bay.

5

Stoop, angels, hither from the skies!
   There is no holier spot of ground
Than where defeated valor lies,
   By mourning beauty crowned!

1867

HAWAI'IAN PLANTATION WORK SONGS
1825–1930

Just as slavery and plantation culture were about to be dismantled by the federal government in the continental United States, a similar culture appeared in Hawai'i, which the U.S. government annexed as a territory in 1898. The work songs created by the laborers have held a place for some time in the Asian-American literary canon, and they merit an enduring position within the canon and history of American poetry. They offer overlooked perspectives on the culture of agricultural workers as well as an inspiring legacy to many contemporary poets, including Cathy Song and Garrett Hongo.

The first sugarcane and coffee plantations were established in 1825 shortly after New England ships began to arrive in search of whales in the prospering whale trade. In spite of slave-labor working conditions, these plantations, along with rapidly developing cattle ranches, attracted plantation workers, cowboys, and contract laborers from many nations experiencing economic hardship. Chinese sugarcane plantation masters and contract laborers arrived during the 1830s along with cowboys from South America, Mexico, and California. Japanese laborers began arriving in the 1860s, Portuguese workers in the 1870s, and Puerto Rican, Okinawan, Korean, and Filipino workers from 1900 on. Women were first admitted among the Japanese contract laborers in 1885 and worked alongside the men. These agricultural immigrants produced a multiracial, multicultural, and multilingual song culture that continued to expand and incorporate the languages and cultures of each arriving group.

The Hawai'ian work-song culture was both oral and written. In some cases a single composer/lyricist wrote a song, whereas in other cases many groups sang a lyric, changing it significantly over time. It is difficult to establish exact dates for the songs, but we can ascertain that the songs reflect the arrival of new immigrant groups and were developed sometime after 1825. Songs were written in the various languages of the laborers as well as in pidgin English, a mix of native Hawai'ian, Japanese, Portuguese, Chinese, Spanish, and other languages and dialects within a structure that is predominantly English. Such songs as the Okinawan "Uya Anma" by Nae Nakasone, translated by Mitsugu Sakihara as "My Mother Dear (A Dialogue)," reveal the homesickness and dreams of the immigrant laborers, regardless of nationality, who came in search of prosperity from countries suffering economic disaster. Sugarcane plantation workers in intolerable work conditions sang "Hana-hana: Working" and other similar songs. Work strikes and protests on the sugarcane plantations began almost immediately with their development. Chinese sugarcane workers, for example, struck in 1841 to protest their daily wage of twelve and a half cents. Songs such as "The Five O'Clock Whistle!" reveal a plantation-culture routine that could have been located in the antebellum South of the mainland United States. Some songs explain how work was divided. "Hole Hole Bushi," for instance, is sung by a wife who indicates that her husband cut the cane while she stripped the dry, withered leaves from the stalks.

FURTHER READING

Ronald Takaki. *Pau Hana: Plantation Life and Labor in Hawaii, 1835–1930*. Honolulu: University of Hawaii Press, 1984.

———. *Strangers from a Different Shore: A History of Asian Americans*. Boston: Back Bay Books, 1998.

Uya Anma

Nae Nakasone

Noji chabira Anma, mo kiti kuyonashigwa
Wamiyakuma wu toti, unigesukutu (kanusamayo)
Agato nu Uchina tu kugatonu Hawai tu
Jinkaninutamiya yinmusudi (kanusamayo)
Ni, san nin tumuti Hawaii watashi ga
Midorisashisuiti, nimutu yishiti (kanusamayo hari nagurisanu)

[TRANS.] My Mother Dear

(A DIALOGUE)

Let me take my leave, my mother.
Earn money and come home, my child.
As I stay home and pray to the gods.
To this Hawai'i from faraway Okinawa
We have come all the way for the sake of money.
Thinking it'd only be a few years we came.
But we have now grown our roots deep and with green leaves.

n.d.

The Okinawans hoped to escape poverty and starvation by emigrating as laborers. The sugarcane with its green leaves symbolized food and prosperity, in contrast to Okinawa's sago palm, which was seen as starvation food.

Hana-Hana: Working

Hana-hana[1]
Hawai'i, Hawai'i
Like a dream
So I came
But my tears
Are flowing now
In the canefields.

Hawai'i, Hawai'i
But when I came
What I saw
Was hell

1. Hana-hana is a repetition of hana, the Hawai'ian word for "work" and the pidgin term workers adopted to signify their plantation labor.

The boss was Satan
The lunas[2]
His helpers.

n.d.

The Five O'Clock Whistle!

"Awake! stir your bones! Rouse up!"
Shrieks the Five o'Clock Whistle.[1]
"Don't dream you can nestle
For one more sweet nap.
Or your ear-drums I'll rap
With my steam-hammer tap
Till they burst.
Br-r-row-aw-i-e-ur-ur-rup!
Wake up! wake up! wake up! w-a-k-e-u-u-u-up!

Filipino and Japanee;
Porto Rican and Portugee;
Korean, Kanaka[2] and Chinese;
Everybody whoever you be
On the whole plantation—
Wake up! wake up! wake up! w-a-k-e-u-u-u-up!
Br-r-row-aw-i-e-ur-ur-rup!

Luna and book-keeper
Sugar-boiler, store-keeper;
Time-keeper, chemist;
Clerk and machinist;
Boss and Boss' Missus;
I proclaim this is
The hour to get up,
And eat a rice cup;
For I boss the Boss,
Same as man, mule, and hoss,
And everything on the plantation,
I, the Sugar Mill Whistle!

---

2. The foremen overseeing the plantation workers.
1. Plantation whistles regulated the workers' hours, rousing them in the early morning and releasing them at 4:30 P.M., which was pau hana (quitting time, literally "finished working"). The evening whistle at 8:00 P.M. warned workers to head to bed. As one Filipino plantation worker recounted of his days at a sugarcane plantation, "Six days a week I worked from siren to siren" (Takaki, *Strangers from a Different Shore*).
2. A person of native Hawai'ian descent.

* * *

Br-r-row-aw-i-e-ur-ur-rup!
Get up! get up! get up! get up!
Mind the Five A.M. Whistle
The signal to hustle!"

n.d.

Hole Hole Bushi

Washa horehore yo
Ase to namida no
Kane wa Kachiken
Tomokasegi.

[TRANS.] Stripping Leaves from Sugarcane

I do the hole hole[1]
With sweat and tears we both work
My husband cuts the cane,
For our means.

n.d.

JINSHAN GE/SONGS OF GOLD MOUNTAIN
1838–1920

THE EMIGRATION OF primarily Cantonese men to the West Coast of the United States to work in farming, railroad construction, and mining—especially gold mining in the California gold rush of 1849—was accompanied by the development of new folk songs and rhymed narratives to relate their experiences. The anonymous popular song included here tells hyperbolically of one Cantonese native's emigration in 1852. Not only is this lyric, "Song of the Wife of a Gold Mountain Man," one of the earliest songs, but also it is considered highly valuable and quite rare because the story is told from the point of view of the male emigrant rather than of those, especially women, left behind in China.

---

1. The task of stripping the dry, withered leaves from the stalks of sugarcane.

Faced with marginal living and economic conditions in Canton, the men decided to work in the United States in order to better support their families. Their goal was to work hard and then return to Canton. While they waited to earn enough money to travel back to China, and to escape discrimination and violence, the men created communities of their own: the first "Chinatowns." San Francisco's "Chinatown," for instance, grew rapidly in the mid- and late 1800s. Folk songs such as the one included here evolved as the men organized poetry clubs, creating a flourishing poetry community by the early 1900s.

FURTHER READING

Marlon K. Hom. *Songs of Gold Mountain.* Berkeley: University of California Press, 1992.

[Jinshan Fu Xing]

咸豐二年造金山，
担起遙仙萬分難；
竹篙船，
撐過海，
離婦別姐去求財；
唔掛房中人女，
唔掛二高堂。

[TRANS.] Song of the Wife of a Gold Mountain Man

In the second reign year of Haamfung, a trip to Gold Mountain was made.[1]
With a pillow on my shoulder, I began my perilous journey:
Sailing a boat with bamboo poles across the sea,
Leaving behind wife and sisters in search of money,
No longer lingering with the woman in the bedroom,
No longer paying respect to parents at home.

n.d.

POPULAR EUROPEAN-AMERICAN SONGS

POPULAR EUROPEAN-AMERICAN SONGS in the mid-nineteenth century reflect the preoccupations of the dominant national culture: new settlements, cowboy life in the West, mining and periodic gold rushes such as the California gold rush, the expanding temperance movement, romance, and the loneliness of new immigrants. They also indicate that European Americans were spreading from coast to

1. Haamfung's second year of reign was 1852. The Cantonese called the United States "Gold Mountain" because of the 1849 California gold rush.

coast and from north to south so that the nation was no longer contained within the original colonies along the East Coast. Several of the songs boast of adventure, while others offer a popular-culture version of the poetics of sentimentality—for example, "Aura Lee" and Henry Clay Work's "Come Home, Father."

Equally, if not more, important to the public, however, were the songs of the Civil War. The selections included here offer not only the morale-boosting Union army song "The Battle Cry of Freedom" but also the more reflective, almost mournful "Tenting on the Old Camp Ground" and the hopeful homefront song "When Johnny Comes Marching Home."

Following the Civil War, European-American women also began to travel throughout the nation. Many at that time saw traveling as a form of education, spiritual growth, and recreation rather than as mere necessity, so it became very popular, especially among the elite and well educated. An 1893 trip to Pike's Peak in the Rocky Mountains with her lesbian companion inspired Wellesley College professor Katherine Lee Bates to compose "America, the Beautiful," now one of the nation's most popular patriotic hymns.

None of the lyrics included here are definitive, with the exception of those of Bates's national song. They have been sung for generations and are changing continually, a characteristic of any oral tradition.

FURTHER READING

Alan Lomax and John Lomax, eds. *American Ballads and Folk Songs*. New York: Dover, 1994.
Irwin Silber, ed. *Songs of the Civil War*. New York: Dover, 1995.

On Top of Old Smoky

On top of old Smoky[1]
All covered with snow,
Lost my true lover,
Come a courtin' too slow.

Well courting's a pleasure,
But parting is grief,
And a false-hearted lover
Is worse than a thief.

A thief he will rob you
And take all you save,
But a false-hearted lover
Will send you to your grave.

1. A reference to the Great Smoky Mountains in North Carolina and Tennessee.

*   *   *

He'll hug and kiss you
And tell you more lies
Than cross-ties on a railroad
Or the stars in the skies.

Early 1800s

Bury Me Not on the Lone Prairie

"O bury me not on the lone prairie."
   These words came low and mournfully
From the pallid lips of a youth who lay
   On his dying bed at the close of day.

He had wasted and pined till o'er his brow
   Death's shades were slowly gathering now.
He thought of home and loved ones nigh,
   As the cowboys gathered to see him die.

"O bury me not on the lone prairie.
   Where the coyotes howl and the wind blows free.
In a narrow grave just six by three—
   O bury me not on the lone prairie."

"It matters not, I've been told,
   Where the body lies when the heart grows cold.
Yet grant, o grant, this wish to me,
   O bury me not on the lone prairie."

I've always wished to be laid when I died
   In a little churchyard on the green hillside.
By my father's grave there let me be,
   O bury me not on the lone prairie."

"I wish to lie where a mother's prayer
   And a sister's tear will mingle there.
Where friends can come and weep o'er me.
   O bury me not on the lone prairie."

"For there's another whose tears will shed
   For the one who lies in a prairie bed.
It breaks my heart to think of her now,
   She has curled these locks, she has kissed this brow."

*   *   *

"O bury me not . . ." And his voice failed there.
    But they took no heed to his dying prayer.
In a narrow grave, just six by three,
    They buried him there on the lone prairie.

And the cowboys now as they roam the plain,
    For they marked the spot where his bones were lain,
Fling a handful of roses o'er his grave
    With a prayer to God, his soul to save.

Early 1800s

This song was originally sung at burials at sea and was adapted to fit the life of cowboys.

Clementine

In a cavern, in a canyon,
    Excavating for a mine,
Lived a miner, forty-niner,[1]
    And his daughter Clementine.
    Oh my darlin', oh my darlin', oh my darlin' Clementine
    You are lost and gone forever, dreadful sorry Clementine.

Light she was and like a fairy,
    And her shoes were number nine;
Herring boxes without topses,
    Sandals were for Clementine.
    Oh my darlin', &c.[2]

Drove she ducklings to the water,
    Every morning just at nine,
Hit her foot against a splinter,
    Fell into the foaming brine.
    Oh my darlin', &c.

Ruby lips above the water,
    Blowing bubbles soft and fine,
Alas for me, I was no swimmer,
    So I lost my Clementine.
    Oh my darlin', &c.

1. Refers to the 1849 gold rush in California.
2. Signal to repeat the last two lines of the first stanza at the end of each stanza of the song.

*   *   *

In a churchyard near the canyon,
    Where the myrtle doth etwine,
There grow roses and other posies,
    Fertilized by Clementine.
    Oh my darlin', &c.

In my dreams she oft doth haunt me,
    With her garments soaked in brine;
Though in life I used to hug her,
    Now she's dead I draw the line.
    Oh my darlin', &c.

Then the miner, forty-niner,
    Soon began to peak and pine;
Thought he oughter jin'e his daughter,
    Now he's with his Clementine.
    Oh my darlin', &c.

                                    1849

Aura Lee

As the blackbird in the spring, beneath the willow tree
Sat and pip'd, I heard him sing "Aura Lee."
Aura Lee, Aura Lee, maid of golden hair!
Sunshine came along with thee, and swallows in the air.

                                    1860

"Aura Lee" was a popular courtship and parlor song.

The Battle Cry of Freedom

Yes we'll rally round the flag boys, we'll rally once again,
Shouting the battle cry of Freedom,
We will rally from the hill-side, we'll gather from the plain,
Shouting the battle cry of Freedom.
The Union forever, Hurrah boys, hurrah!
Down with the Traitor, Up with the Star;
While we rally round the flag, boys,
Rally once again, Shouting the battle cry of Freedom.

*   *   *

We are springing to the call for Three Hundred Thousand more,
Shouting the battle cry of Freedom,
And we'll fill the vacant ranks of our brothers gone before,
Shouting the battle cry of Freedom.
The Union forever, &c.[1]

We will welcome to our numbers the loyal true and brave,
Shouting the battle cry of Freedom,
And altho' he may be poor he shall never be a slave,
Shouting the battle cry of Freedom.
The Union forever, &c.

So we're springing to the call from the East and from the West,
Shouting the battle cry of Freedom,
And we'll hurl the rebel crew from the land we love the best,
Shouting the battle cry of Freedom,
The Union forever, &c.

1862

Tenting on the Old Camp Ground

We're tenting tonight on the old Camp ground,
Give us a song to cheer
Our weary hearts, a song of home
And friends we love so dear.
Tenting tonight, Tenting tonight,
Tenting on the old Camp ground.

We've been tenting tonight on the old Camp ground,
Thinking of the days gone by,
Of the lov'd ones at home that gave us the hand,
And the tear that said, "Good-bye"!
Tenting tonight, &c.[1]

We are tired of war on the old Camp ground,
Many are dead and gone,
Of the brave and true who've left their homes,
Others been wounded long.
Tenting tonight, &c.

1. Signal to sing the last four lines of the first stanza at the end of each successive stanza.

1. Signal to sing the last two lines of the first stanza at the end of each successive stanza.

* * *

We've been fighting today on the old Camp ground,
Many are lying near;
Some are dead and some are dying,
Many are in tears.
Dying tonight, Dying tonight,
Dying on the old Camp ground.

1864

This song originated with the Union troops.

When Johnny Comes Marching Home

When Johnny comes marching home again, hurrah, hurrah!
We'll give him a hearty welcome then, hurrah, hurrah!
The men will cheer, and the boys will shout
And the ladies, they will all turn out
And we'll all feel gay, when Johnny comes marching home.

Get ready for the jubilee, hurrah, hurrah!
We'll give the hero three times three, hurrah, hurrah!
The laurel wreath is ready now
To place upon his loyal brow,
And we'll all feel gay, when Johnny comes marching home.

1863

Come Home, Father

Henry Clay Work

Father, dear father, come home with me now!
The clock in the steeple strikes one.
You said you were coming right home from the shop,
As soon as your day's work was done.
Our fire has gone out, our house is all dark,
And mother's been watching since tea,
With poor brother Benny so sick in her arms,
And no one to help her but me.
Come home! come home! come home!
Please, father, dear father, come home.

CHORUS

Hear the sweet voice of the child
Which the night winds repeat as they roam!
Oh, who could resist this most plaintive of prayers?
"Please, father, dear father, come home!"

Father, dear father, come home with me now!
The clock in the steeple strikes two.
The night has grown colder and Benny is worse,
But he has been calling for you.
Indeed he is worse, Ma says he will die,
Perhaps before morning shall dawn;
And this is the message she sent me to bring:
"Come quickly, or he will be gone."
Come home! come home! come home!
Please, father, dear father, come home.

Father, dear father, come home with me now!
The clock in the steeple strikes three.
The house is so lonely, the hours are so long,
For poor weeping mother and me.
Yes we are alone, poor Benny is dead,
And gone with the angels of light;
And these were the very last words that he said:
"I want to kiss Papa good night."
Come home! come home! come home!
Please, father, dear father, come home.

1864

This song was written specifically to focus public attention on the plight of families living in poverty because of husbands and fathers who spent most of their paychecks and time in saloons drinking liquor. The temperance movement used it to urge passage of prohibition laws.

I'll Take You Home Again, Kathleen

I'll take you home again, Kathleen,
Across the ocean wide and wide
To where your heart has ever been
Since first you were my bonny bride.
The roses all have left your cheek,

I've watched them fade a-way and die.
Your voice is sad whene'er you speak
And tears bedim your loving eyes.
Oh, I will take you back, Kathleen,
To where your heart will feel no pain,
And when the fields are fresh and green,
I'll take you to your home, Kathleen.

1876

This verse, another popular courtship song, suggests an immigrant couple's nostalgia for Ireland.

FROM *America, the Beautiful*

Katherine Lee Bates

O beautiful for spacious skies,
For amber waves of grain,
For purple mountain majesties
Above the fruited plain.
America! America!
God shed His grace on thee,
And crown thy good with brotherhood
From sea to shining sea.

1893

PART THREE

✦

Later
Nineteenth Century

INTRODUCTION

THE CIVIL WAR left the nation whole but certainly not homogenous. European immigrants flooded in from a wide variety of countries, as did immigrants from other corners of the globe. Their anthem, written by the poet Emma Lazarus (who was not an immigrant herself but who sympathized with their cause), appears on the Statue of Liberty, permanently associating the concept of freedom with that of diversity. Lazarus wrote:

> Give me your tired, your poor,
> Your huddled masses yearning to breathe free,
> The wretched refuse of your teeming shore.
> Send these, the homeless, tempest-tost to me,
> I lift my lamp beside the golden door!

And yet many had difficulty breathing free even in the United States. The social contradictions that had haunted the nation from its inception lingered. Moreover, this nation itself was "teeming" — with changing and often worsening social conditions, with people migrating within its borders in search of a better life. Industrialization, professionalization, and urbanization, as well as immigration, were all changing the way the nation lived, did business, and wrote and read poetry.

Emily Dickinson, the greatest poet of her generation and one of the greatest in history, seemed to sit alone and remote in rural Amherst, Massachusetts, watching the seasons change and studiously ignoring the factories sprouting up nearby. Yet her poems respond to social change as well — to the Civil War during which many of them were written, to the gender restrictions under which the poet lived and chafed, and to the growing interest in psychic realities that would soon produce the writings of William James and Sigmund Freud, neither of whom explored psychology in greater depth than did Dickinson herself. Dickinson's reshaping of the discourse of women was accompanied by complementary efforts by such poets as Helen Hunt Jackson, Adah Isaacs Menken, Sarah M. B. Piatt, Queen Lili'Uokalani of Hawai'i, Ina Coolbrith, and Lazarus herself.

Racial and ethnic differences continued to leave their mark on American poetry. The Zaragoza Clubs of California and the developing border genre of the corrido produced texts in Spanish that hybridized forms and concerns native to the

United States and Mexico. The poetry of José Martí, written in the Catskill Mountains of New York and influenced by Whitman, similarly brought the poetics of the United States and Cuba into contact. African-American culture produced such poets as Albery Allson Whitman, James Weldon Johnson, and the seminal figure Paul Laurence Dunbar, whose eloquent and melodious words of love and protest have reverberated through world literature ever since. Traditional Native-American texts were widely translated for the first time in the 1880s and 1890s, beginning their circulation through various other cultures of the United States and through cultures beyond its borders. New Native-American voices appeared as well, such as DeWitt Clinton Duncan and Owl Woman. European-American poets stretched their own poetic traditions in new and unexpected ways. Edwin Markham spoke eloquently for the exploited worker. The reserved and scholarly William Vaughn Moody roared like a lion in protesting the U.S. conquest of the Philippines. Writing from rural Maine, Edwin Arlington Robinson expressed a disconcerting fin de siècle melancholy that was at odds with official American optimism. And Stephen Crane expressed the horror and pity of war and the uncertainties of the human condition in words that echo to this day.

Finally, Ernest and Mary Fenollosa and Sadakichi Hartmann looked to Asia for clues about modernizing poetry in the West. Hartmann, a bohemian who was born in Japan and raised in Germany, made good use of his diverse exposures to nations, ethnicities, cultures, art forms, and localities. Gertrude Stein once remarked that the United States was the oldest country in the world because it had entered the twentieth century first. If that is so, Hartmann was the oldest poet in the United States, having been the first to step into the future.

Late-nineteenth-century poetry tells a variety of stories about change and contention. Frances Harper's earnest use of dialect transformed into Dunbar's ironized and popularized style. Whitman's Orphic volubility found a rival in Dickinson's gnomic utterance. Numerous American traditions persevered and altered, under pressure from various American rebellions. Free verse contested traditional meter. High and low vocabularies met, sometimes merging, sometimes sliding past each other untouched. Social and artistic change was in the air. Cultural and linguistic practices came into uneasy association, always within the continuing frame of economic, racial, and gender asymmetries. Sometimes the cultures recoiled from each other, but not always and never for ever. Cultures in contact eventually produce cultures that hybridize, regardless of the power dynamics shaping the encounter. Out of the tensions and differences as well as the common places and behaviors of a diverse people arose a vitally multicultural poetry, producing canons with roots in many distant pasts and manifesting a character that was always in motion.

CORRIDOS
1860s–1930s

CORRIDOS ARE MEXICAN and Mexican-American ballads written to be performed, either a cappella or with a guitar accompaniment. They usually tell stories about heroic figures or historical events. Those that have held the most importance for the Chicano community have been composed and performed in the service of social awareness, political intervention, and resistance to racism, oppression, colonization, and invasion. Because such struggles have been particularly acute along the borderlands between Mexico and the United States, corridos are also known as border ballads. The word corrido derives from the Spanish verb *correr* (which means to run) and thus could be described as a running account of a story—a narrative ballad about heroism and injustice. Some scholars believe that the roots of the corrido form can be traced to the narrative Andalusian romances of medieval Spain because the Spanish who invaded and colonized the Southwest brought their musical traditions along with them. Many scholars also link the narrative style of the corridos to the Nahuatl and native epic poetry of Pre-Columbian peoples. While the composition of corridos reached a peak in the period from about 1865 to 1915, they continue to remain relevant today, especially for many Chicano poets and readers and for those interested in a diversity of cultures. They therefore make a major contribution to American poetry.

The selection presented here is "Kiansis I," a section of "El corrido de Kiansis," which is the oldest corrido preserved in complete form. It was composed sometime in the 1860s by an unknown author, when cattle were being driven regularly from Texas to Kansas. As Américo Paredes has noted in the text that accompanies his English translation of this corrido, although the cattle drives to Kansas have been made famous by many film Westerns, few people realize that most of the herds driven north from Texas were owned by Mexicans and Texas-Mexicans. Moreover, many of the cowboys (or *vaqueros*) who drove the cattle were Mexican Americans. "Kiansis I" expresses the often heated antagonism between Mexican-American and European-American cowboys. Mexican Americans have often pointed out in their corridos that traditions such as ranching were first developed by Mexicans, only later to be claimed by European Americans as their own.

FURTHER READING

José E. Limón. *Mexican Ballads, Chicano Poems.* Berkeley: University of California Press, 1992.
Américo Paredes and Manuel Peña. *A Texas-Mexican Cancionero: Folksongs of the Lower Border.* Austin: University of Texas Press, 1995.

538   ◆   *Corridos*

Kiansis I

Cuando salimos pa' Kiansis
con una grande partida,
¡ah, qué camino tan largo!
no contaba con mi vida.

Nos decía el caporal,
como queriendo llorar:
—Allá va la novillada,
no me la dejen pasar.—

¡Ah, qué caballo tan bueno!
todo se le iba en correr,
¡y, ah, qué fuerte aguacerazo!
no contaba yo en volver.

Unos pedían cigarro,
otros pedían que comer,
y el caporal nos decía:
—Sea por Dios, qué hemos de hacer.—

En el charco de Palomas
se cortó un novillo bragado,
y el caporal lo lazó
en su caballo melado.

Avísenle al caporal
que un vaquero se le mató,
en las trancas del corral
nomás la cuera dejó.

Llegamos al Río Salado
y nos tiramos a nado,
decía un americano:
—Esos hombres ya se ahogaron.—

Pues qué pensaría ese hombre
que venimos a esp'rimentar,
si somos del Río Grande,
de los buenos pa'nadar.

            *   *   *

Y le dimos vista a Kiansis,
y nos dice el caporal:
—Ora sí somos de vida,
ya vamos a hacer corral.—

Y de vuelta en San Antonio
compramos buenos sombreros,
y aquí se acaban cantando
versos de los aventureros.

1860s

[TRANS.] Kansas 1

When we left for Kansas with a great herd of cattle,
ah, what a long trail it was! I was not sure I would survive.

The caporal would tell us, as if he were going to cry,
"Watch out for that bunch of steers; don't let them get past you."

Ah, what a good horse I had! He did nothing but gallop.
And, ah, what a violent cloudburst! I was not sure I would come back.

Some of us asked for cigarettes, others wanted something to eat;
and the caporal would tell us, "So be it, it can't be helped."

By the pond at Palomas a vicious steer left the herd,
and the caporal lassoed it on his honey-colored horse.

Go tell the caporal that a vaquero has been killed;
all he left was his leather jacket hanging on the rails of the corral.

We got to the Salado River, and we swam our horses across;
an American was saying, "Those men are as good as drowned."

I wonder what the man thought, that we came to learn, perhaps;
why, we're from the Rio Grande, where the good swimmers are from.

And then Kansas came in sight, and the caporal tells us,
"We have finally made it, we'll soon have them in the corral."

Back again in San Antonio, we all bought ourselves good hats,
and this is the end of the singing of the stanzas about the trail drivers.

This corrido is sung in a slow, reflective tempo, most often by one singer alone and frequently without guitar accompaniment. The rhythm here is not the one-two-three strum used for the standard corrido but rather a three-one-two-three-one rhythm similar to the *colombiana* or *yucateca* strum.

ZARAGOZA CLUBS
1860s

WHILE CHICANO COWBOYS in the Texas-Mexico borderlands were composing corridos, Chicanos in California were writing poems published in Spanish-language newspapers. Many of these poems, only recently recovered, display a strong political awareness as well as a devout loyalty to Mexico. In the 1860s, for example, women's poetry clubs in Los Angeles called the Zaragoza Clubs composed politically engaged poems that they published in the Spanish-language San Francisco newspaper *El Nuevo Mundo* (The New World). As Janet Gray has related, the poets of the Zaragoza Clubs wrote and published their poetry in solidarity with those who fought against France's invasion of Mexico. The clubs were named for General Ignacio Zaragoza, who led the Mexican forces to victory over the French in the Battle of Puebla on May 5, 1862, celebrated ever after as El Cinco de Mayo.

The two poems included here are relatively short in comparison with the longer balladic corridos (also included in this anthology). Nevertheless, they share the goal of sending a political message to the Chicano community through poetry. They also follow the same rhyme scheme, though not all the poetry written by the Zaragoza Clubs did so. Merced J. de Gonzáles's poem, "Méjico libre ha de ser," urges readers to support the leadership of Mexico's president Benito Juárez in the struggle against France. Filomeno Ibarra's poem, "En la antigua Roma había," invokes the Roman goddess Vesta, suggesting that the kind of faithfulness and devotion once shown to the goddess should be granted to Mexico.

FURTHER READING

Janet Gray, ed. *She Wields a Pen: American Women Poets of the Nineteenth Century.* Iowa City: University of Iowa Press, 1997.

Méjico libre ha de ser

Merced J. de Gonzáles

Méjico libre ha de ser
Pese al francés insolente.
Esto mi instinto presente
Si sabemos sostener
Nuestro digno presidente.
Con heroísmo defended
Donde quiera que te hallares

De nuestra patria los lores;
Y en su entusiasmo Merced
Brinda por Benito Juárez.

1865

[TRANS.] Mexico will be free

My heart tells me
Mexico will be free
Despite the arrogant French,
If we know how to assist
Our worthy president.
With heroism we should defend
The leaders of our country
Wherever we might be;
And Merced in her enthusiasm
Gives a Hail! to Benito Juárez.

En la antigua Roma había

Filomena Ibarra

En la antigua Roma había
De Vesta, templo formado,
Do por mujeres cuidado,
Perenne se mantenía
Constante el fuego sagrado.
Las socias de 'Zaragoza'
A las de Vesta imitando,
El fuego patrio atizando,
Con inquietud afanosa
La lámpara están cuidando.

1865

[TRANS.] In ancient Rome there stood

In ancient Rome there stood
A temple built to Vesta,
Tended all by women, and
Its constant sacred flame
Was kept perpetually burning.

Now the members of 'Zaragoza'
Following the rules of Vesta
Keep our country's fire bright
And with painstaking pride
Take constant care of our lamp.

DEWITT CLINTON DUNCAN
[TOO-QUA-STEE]
1829–1909

DEWITT CLINTON DUNCAN (Too-qua-stee) is anthologized here for the first time with his eulogy in English, "The Dead Nation," published in 1899. This poem, concerning the dissolution of the Cherokee nation with the Curtis Act of 1898, is the culmination point of Duncan's campaign of letters written under his Cherokee name critiquing the United States' attacks on the Cherokee nation's sovereignty. As a young child he had marched in 1839 with his tribe in the infamous forced death march, along the "Trail of Tears," from Georgia to Oklahoma, so he was in an excellent position to mourn the dissolution of his nation.

Duncan was born in the Cherokee nation in Georgia to John Ellis Redcloud Duncan and his European-American wife, Elizabeth Abercrombie, at a time when the Cherokee nation actively encouraged intermarriage between Cherokees and European-American settlers. Before he witnessed the suffering on the "Trail of Tears," he saw the violence leading up to the forced march. In 1834 the Georgia Guard began to intensify its surveillance of the Cherokee nation, destroying its press and burning the publishing building because the press had become too dissident in its criticism of U.S. policies toward Cherokees. Acts of violence and infringements on civil rights escalated during subsequent years. Finally, about five thousand unarmed Cherokees were imprisoned in rude stockades by U.S. troops until the march began, where they were subjected to rape, robbery, and murder. On the route from Georgia to Oklahoma, two thousand to four thousand Cherokees died.

Between 1846 and the Civil War, however, the Cherokee nation enjoyed relative prosperity. It built both a male and a female seminary, one hundred fifty day schools, a court, a mental health facility, an orphanage, and a high school for its African-American slaves. It also reestablished its printing press and resumed a newspaper published in both Cherokee and English. Duncan benefited as well from this strong recovery. He attended Dartmouth College and graduated in 1861; then he taught school in the North during the Civil War. This career path meant that he did not become involved in the Cherokee decision to ally itself with the Confederacy when the Confederacy invaded its territory and the U.S. government refused to honor its treaty agreement to protect the Cherokee nation from invasion. Already fractured by the earlier assassinations of its two major leaders who had signed a treaty leading to the "Trail of Tears," the Cherokees became further factionalized by its division into slaveholders (who held about four thousand African-American slaves) and abolitionists. After the Confederacy left Cherokee troops to starve following a battle, many Cherokees joined the Union army. But for the remainder of the war, the territory was invaded by troops on both sides who burned its buildings and lands and destroyed all the livestock. At the war's end more than four thousand Cherokees were widowed or orphaned; and the nation was bankrupt.

In 1866 Duncan settled in Iowa. Later he became superintendent of the reopened Cherokee national male seminary, and in 1906 he testified before a U.S. Senate committee on the reduction of the Cherokees from a prosperous farming and ranching nation to an impoverished minority on its own land.

"The Dead Nation" reflects Duncan's anger over what he considered the U.S. abandonment of morality, its denial of justice under the law and approximately twenty-two treaties, and its growing preoccupation with colonial expansion. By aiming the poem at a European-American educated audience, he hoped to arouse the support of readers and writers east of the Mississippi River, who already were addressing the Native-American plight just as they had supported the abolition of slavery. As early as 1878 he had become publicly critical of American historians who studiously avoided or touched only lightly upon the U.S. treatment of Native Americans, and he sought to write a poetic narrative of the wrongs sustained at the hands of the United States. As he states in the poem, however, "genius cannot paint a dying scream."

FURTHER READING

Rauna Kuokkaneu. "Alter-Native Nations and Narrations: The World of DeWitt Clinton Duncan, Charles A. Eastman, and E. Pauline Johnson," in *Indigenous Nations Studies Journal* 1, no. 2 (Winter 2001). 22–40.

Daniel F. Littlefield, Jr., and James W. Parins, eds. *Native American Writing in the Southeast: An Anthology, 1875–1935*. Jackson: University Press of Mississippi, 1995.

The Dead Nation

Alas! Poor luckless nation, thou art dead
    At last! And death ne'er came 'neath brighter bows
Of flattering hope; upon thine ancient head
    Hath late-time treason dealt its treacherous blows.

When out the watery chaos rose the land
    And built this continent thy venturous foe
Were first to tread the new-born world; a hand
    Divine had given it thee thy restful seat.

Here with thy God, without such wars as tore
    The entrails out of cultured Rome and Greece,
Thou didst abide ten thousand years or more,
    Thy wants by Him supplied, in halcyon peace.

But then came Art, in rouge and ribbons dressed,
    The scourge of woe, borne on the winged hours,
And squat upon thine own salubrious[1] west,
    Bred pestilence and rot within thy bowers.

Smit[2] by the blast of her contagious breath
    Thy children fell in armies at thy side;
And struggling in the grip of a strange death,
    Exclaimed, "O white man!" closed their eyes, and died.

Came also Might, the adjutant of Art,
    Wrenched off the hinges from the joints of truth,
And tore its system into shreds apart—
    Repealed, in short, the moral code, forsooth.

Then first it was, that on thy peaceful plains
    The roar of onset and the saber's gleam,
Began—but hold! humanity refrains,
    And genius cannot paint a dying scream.

Thus rotting Pestilence, and Art, and Might,
    In moonlight orgies o'er thy children's bones,
To honor civilization, hands unite
    And dance the music of their dying groans.

          *   *   *

---

1. Healthful.   2. Struck.

'Twas civ'lization, (said to be,) at work,
    To proselyte thy sons to ways of grace;
With savage means, the rifle, sword and drink,
    To slaughter night, that day might have a place.

And so, indeed, they made the day to shine
    Upon thy callow brood, and with the light
Awoke those works of greed that always twine
    In breasts exposed to suns too strangely bright.

Thy sons, touched by these strange transforming rays,
    Withdrew their love; to "end the strife,"
They said, they aped the white man's heartless ways,
    And tore the breast that nursed them into life.

Dear Cherokee nation, with the right to live,
    Art dead and gone; thy life was meanly priced;
Thy room to civilization hadst to give,
    And so did Socrates and Jesus Christ.

                                        1899

HELEN HUNT JACKSON
1830–1885

Rᴀɪsᴇᴅ ʙʏ ʜᴇʀ ᴀᴜɴᴛ ɪɴ Amherst, Massachusetts, Helen Hunt Jackson married in 1852 and had two sons. When her husband and sons tragically died, she overcame her grief by taking up writing both fiction and poetry. Ralph Waldo Emerson praised her poetry, and she was a friend and supporter of Emily Dickinson. Upon marrying her second husband in 1875, Jackson moved to Colorado. She ultimately became best known for *A Century of Dishonor* (1881), a protest of governmental mistreatment of Native Americans, and for her popular novel *Ramona* (1884), which sympathetically portrayed Native-American characters. Some of her poems present allegories of domestic despair and of friendship between women, as does the sonnet "Found Frozen." Others, such as "Danger," portray a cosmos dominated by chance and threat. Still other poems, like "Cheyenne Mountain," find solace in the beauty, history, and timelessness of the Western landscape that Jackson grew to love.

FURTHER READING

Evelyn I. Banning. *Helen Hunt Jackson*. New York: Random House, 1973.
Helen Hunt Jackson. *Poems*. Boston: Little, Brown, 1898.
Cheryl Walker. "Helen Hunt Jackson," in *Encyclopedia of American Poetry: The Nineteenth Century*. Ed. Eric L. Haralson. Pp. 233–36. Chicago: Fitzroy Dearborn, 1998.

Found Frozen

She died, as many travellers have died,
O'ertaken on an Alpine road by night;
Numbed and bewildered by the falling snow,
Striving, in spite of falling pulse, and limbs
Which faltered and grew feeble at each step,
To toil up the icy steep, and bear
Patient and faithful to the last, the load
Which, in the sunny morn, seemed light!
                    And yet
'Twas in the place she called her home, she died;
And they who loved her with the all of love
Their wintry natures had to give, stood by
And wept some tears, and wrote above her grave
Some common record which they thought was true;
But I, who loved her first, and last, and best, — I knew.

                        n.d.

Danger

With what a childish and short-sighted sense
Fear seeks for safety; reckons up the days
Of danger and escape, the hours and ways
Of death; it breathless flies the pestilence;
It walls itself in towers of defense;
By land, by sea, against the storm it lays
Down barriers; then, comforted, it says:
"This spot, this hour is safe." Oh, vain pretence!
Man born of man know nothing when he goes;
The winds blow where they list,[1] and will disclose
To no man which brings safety, which brings risk.

1. Like.

The mighty are brought low by many a thing
Too small to name. Beneath the daisy's disk
Lies hid the pebble for the fatal sling.[2]

n.d.

Cheryl Walker has praised the formal qualities of this sonnet by pointing to "the intricacy with which the poet has interwoven the short *i* and *e* sounds with the long *a* and *i* sounds and cross-laced them with the recurrent *s*."

Cheyenne Mountain

By easy slope to west as if it had
    No thought, when first its soaring was begun,
    Except to look devoutly to the sun,
It rises, and has risen, until, glad,
With light as with a garment, it is clad,
    Each dawn, before the tardy plains have won
    One ray; and after day has long been done
For us, the light doth cling reluctant, sad
To leave its brow. Beloved mountain, I
Thy worshiper, as thou the sun's, each morn,
    My dawn, before the dawn, receive from thee;
    And think, as thy rose-tinted peaks I see,
That thou wert great when Homer[1] was not born,
And ere thou change all human song shall die!

1879

This sonnet describes a mountain near Jackson's home in Colorado Springs, Colorado.

---

2. A reference to the story of David and Goliath in 1 Samuel 17 of the Jewish and Christian scriptures. The courageous Israelite David, armed only with a sling and pebbles, unexpectedly slew the Philistine giant Goliath.

1. Greek poet of the eighth century B.C.E., author of the *Iliad* and the *Odyssey*.

EMILY DICKINSON
1830–1886

Emily dickinson stands alongside Walt Whitman as one of the leading American poets of the nineteenth century—and arguably of all time. Even more remarkable, she is that rare poet who has been embraced by both literary "high" culture and popular culture. Perhaps Dickinson's most astonishing legacy is her poetry's ability to reach a broad range of readers regardless of temporal or cultural positioning. Some readers speak of Dickinson as if she were an intimate friend who has confided special secrets to them in such poems as *I'm nobody! Who are you?* Indeed, it is not unusual for a reader to speak about the poet as if she were "my" Dickinson. In other situations, Dickinson may be the voice for large numbers of people. A striking example of this phenomenon occurred immediately following the September 11, 2001, assaults on the World Trade Center in New York and the Pentagon in Washington, D.C. Such Dickinson poems as *Because I could not stop for death* appeared in cyberspace, in the national media, at funerals and memorial services, and in conversations and correspondence, as people turned to her writing for solace and strength.

It is not surprising that Dickinson's poems about grief, loss, dying, and death resonated at that historical moment. She lived during the Civil War and wrote about it in such poems as *Success is counted sweetest*. Her poetry depicts many different kinds of anguish during wartime. Interestingly, this renewed awareness of Dickinson's importance for a nation in crisis parallels some recent assessments of the poet in literary culture. Shira Wolosky, Alfred Habegger, and Cristanne Miller have argued that Dickinson should be recognized as a prominent Civil War poet, alongside Melville and Whitman.

Although twenty-first-century readers may be among the first to appreciate Dickinson fully as a poet of war and national emergency, readers have always found many Dickinsons in her various texts. For some, she is among the first European-American poets to rebel successfully against European poetic models and to create a compelling new lyric voice for the emerging postcolonial nation. For other readers, she is a great epistolary poet because she wrote so many poems in her letters. Readers also have learned that she offers a window into nineteenth-century bourgeois New England culture. Her poetry includes, for instance, many insights into art, music, quilting, needlework, and gardening; the dominant, if fading, Calvinism of religious culture; the complexity of Civil War–era life and the war's aftermath; the domestic world of women, men, children, relatives, servants, and pets; the stark contrasts between "wealth" and "poverty" that marked her industrializing world; and the treatment of such illnesses as Bright's disease, with which she lived and from which she died.

For still other readers, Dickinson is the feminist poet who refused her century's assigned gender role, creating instead a range of vulnerable but often surprisingly assertive feminist voices in such poems as *I was the slightest in the house* and *My life had stood a loaded gun*. She also wrote complexly about the pleasures and pains of close emotional attachments between women in such poems as *For largest woman's heart I knew*. More broadly, Dickinson achieved a formidable feat by constructing a new national poetic, a function traditionally reserved for male voices. This achievement is all the more remarkable because she accomplished it before women gained suffrage and many other legal rights. While prominent feminists such as Susan B. Anthony were mobilizing women as public leaders, Dickinson worked on behalf of women's culture and dignity with her pen.

Although Dickinson has been a canonical poet for many years, she has often been misrepresented. One myth was that she was too timid to seek publication, whereas in actuality she probably did not regard the literary marketplace very highly. She voiced her skepticism in poems such as *Publication is the auction*. Instead, she preserved her work in small, handwritten packets of sixteen to twenty-four pages of white, unlined stationery with an average of twenty poems per packet. These little self-made books are now known as fascicles. Discovered after her death, they included approximately 1,200 poems—her legacy to the world.

Even more astonishing is that Dickinson has been read as a poet with an intense intimate life only for the last twenty-five years. Her strong romantic attachments to both men and women now seem obvious in such varied lyrics as *Volcanoes be in Sicily*, *I cannot live with you*, *The daisy follows soft the sun*, and *Wild nights - Wild nights!* Moreover, the persistent image of Dickinson as a chaste and solitary dreamer is contradicted by the facts of her life, including her independent thinking and decision making and her many warm and at times tempestuous friendships.

Born into a prominent but financially unstable family in Amherst, Massachusetts, Dickinson grew up in a world of privilege. Her father, Edward, was a lawyer, congressman, treasurer of Amherst College, and, reputedly, a humorless autocrat. Her mother, Emily Norcross, was emotionally withdrawn. Her slightly older brother, Austin, and her younger sister, Lavinia (or Vinnie), were the initial mainstays of her emotional life. She studied at the Amherst Academy from the age of eleven to seventeen, and then she attended the prestigious Mount Holyoke Seminary for Women, leaving after one year, perhaps because she felt uncomfortable with the religiosity she encountered there or perhaps simply because she felt homesick. Although suitors courted her, Dickinson consciously decided to remain single and at home, pursuing her writing and cultivating her friendships and her close family life. She lived with her mother, father, and sister. When her brother married her close friend Susan Huntington Gilbert, the newlyweds lived next door. Emily and Susan Gilbert Dickinson maintained a remarkably intimate and intense friendship for many decades.

Emily Dickinson expressed many of her deepest emotions in her correspondence. Her letters of heartfelt affection—especially to Susan Gilbert Dickinson but also to various other friends and relatives, including Judge Otis Lord and an unidentified "Master"—as well as her more literary letters to Samuel Bowles, Helen Hunt Jackson, and Thomas Wentworth Higginson reveal her variously as lover, friend, and writer.

Dickinson began writing poetry in 1850 and assembling the fascicles in 1858. Her most productive years were between 1860 and 1865—as the Civil War loomed, raged, and waned. The psychoanalytic critic John Cody has suggested that Dickinson experienced a period of profound depression about this time. In one of her letters to her cousins, she referred to this psychic event as "a snarl in the brain which don't unravel yet." Such poems as *I felt a funeral in my brain, It was not death, for I stood up,* and *After great pain a formal feeling comes* also evoke a devastating psychological occurrence.

The poems of this period reveal an amazing dexterity with language, using cryptic plays of concealment and revelation, surprising and memorable images, slant rhymes and disrupted meters, and a feisty rebellion against any conventional form of syntax, punctuation, word choice, thought, or feeling. They address wide-ranging topics, from psychic pain, insecurity, and despair to wonder at nature, religious faith, and the passage of time—and from gender relations to social experiences of love, loss, and loneliness. In later years, Dickinson produced poems more slowly and tended increasingly to seclude herself in her house and garden. Neighbors began to refer to her as the "myth" of Amherst. After experiencing the deaths of her father, her mother, and many friends, Emily Dickinson herself died on May 15, 1886. Days before she died, she wrote to Thomas Wentworth Higginson, "Deity—does He live now? / My friend—does he breathe?" Her last known composition was a letter to two young cousins, consisting of five words: "Little Cousins. / Called back. Emily."

The misrepresentation of Dickinson began with her first editors, Higginson and Mabel Loomis Todd, who was the mistress of Dickinson's brother, Austin. Lavinia Dickinson asked Higginson and Todd to publish the poems after she found the fascicles. They edited volumes of selected poems in 1890 and 1891, and Todd edited a third volume alone in 1896. The first two volumes were received enthusiastically. Nevertheless, they had been severely edited. Moreover, Austin Dickinson and Mabel Loomis Todd had disfigured Dickinson's work by erasing the name of Austin's wife, Susan Gilbert Dickinson, on poems written to her, scratching out lines of poetry, and cutting out references to her with a pair of scissors. Later editions were similarly expurgated and overedited.

No accurate edition of Dickinson's poetry was available until Thomas Johnson published a complete and scrupulous edition of the poems in 1955. More recently, R. W. Franklin published a new variorum edition of the poems, with a more accurate chronology and occasional corrections to the texts themselves, as well as a reading edition. Because teachers and scholars of Dickinson are in transition between the Johnson variorum and the Franklin variorum edition, as well as Franklin's reading edition, this anthology includes both the Johnson and the Franklin variorum numbering schemes for the poems (in parentheses after the composition date). The dates and the texts themselves derive from Franklin's variorum edition, as do the poems' so-called titles assigned by Franklin. Dickinson often left many variant versions of the same poem, suggesting either that no poem could get the meaning quite right or that there were many varieties of rightness. We have indicated some of the significant variants in the footnotes.

Publication of Dickinson's letters did not occur until 1958, when Thomas Johnson and Theodora Ward published an edition. But the volume did not follow the poet's original manuscript or emphasize the importance of the letters between the poet and her sister-in-law, Susan Gilbert Dickinson. The only known poems and letters for Susan Gilbert Dickinson first appeared in 1913, when she permitted her daughter Martha Dickinson Bianchi to publish them. Given their private contents, it is possible that other such material may have been destroyed. In 1998 Ellen Louise Hart and Martha Nell Smith traced and interpreted fully for the first time the influence of this romantic friendship on Dickinson's work and life. The letters selected here offer readers the opportunity to consider the epistolary poem in wide-ranging examples of Dickinson's correspondence to Susan Gilbert Dickinson, as well as to an unnamed "Master," Judge Otis Lord, Samuel Bowles, and Thomas Wentworth Higginson.

FURTHER READING

Paula Bennett. *Emily Dickinson: Woman Poet.* Iowa City: University of Iowa Press, 1991.

Sharon Cameron. *Choosing, Not Choosing: Dickinson's Fascicles.* Chicago: University of Chicago Press, 1993.

John Cody. *After Great Pain: The Inner Life of Emily Dickinson.* Cambridge, Mass.: Harvard University Press, 1971.

Emily Dickinson. *Letters.* Ed. Thomas Johnson and Theodora Ward. Cambridge, Mass.: Harvard University Press, 1958.

———. *Poems.* 3 vols. Ed. Thomas Johnson. Cambridge, Mass.: Harvard University Press, 1955.

———. *The Poems of Emily Dickinson.* Reading edition. Ed. R. W. Franklin. Cambridge, Mass.: Harvard University Press, 1998.

———. *Poems: Variorum Edition.* 3 vols. Ed. R. W. Franklin. Cambridge, Mass.: Harvard University Press, 1998.

Emily Dickinson and Susan Huntington Dickinson. *Open Me Carefully: Emily Dickinson's Intimate Letters to Susan Huntington Dickinson.* Ed. Ellen Louise Hart and Martha Nell Smith. Ashfield, Mass.: Paris Press, 1998.

Jane Donahue Eberwein, ed. *An Emily Dickinson Encyclopedia.* Westport, Conn.: Greenwood Press, 1998.

Judith Farr. *The Passion of Emily Dickinson.* Cambridge, Mass.: Harvard University Press, 1992.

Gudrun Grabher, Roland Hagenbuchle, and Cristanne Miller, eds. *The Emily Dickinson Handbook.* Amherst: University of Massachusetts Press, 1999.

Alfred Habegger. *My Wars Are Laid Away in Books: The Life of Emily Dickinson.* New York: Random House, 2001.

Suzanne Juhasz, ed. *Feminist Critics Read Emily Dickinson.* Bloomington: Indiana University Press, 1983.

Vivian Pollak. *Dickinson: The Anxiety of Gender.* Ithaca, N.Y.: Cornell University Press, 1984.

Adrienne Rich, Barbara Gelpi, and Albert Gelpi, eds. *Adrienne Rich's Poetry and Prose.* New York: W. W. Norton, 1993.

Richard Sewall. *The Life of Emily Dickinson.* 2 vols. New York: Farrar, Straus & Giroux, 1974.

Martha Nell Smith, coordinator, Ellen Louise Hart and Marta Werner, eds. Dickinson Electronic Archives. Http: //Jefferson.village.Virginia.edu/dickinson.

Gary Lee Stonum. *The Dickinson Sublime.* Madison: University of Wisconsin Press, 1990.

Shira Wolosky. *Emily Dickinson: A Voice of War.* New Haven: Yale University Press, 1984.

I never lost as much but twice

I never lost as much but twice -
And that was in the sod.[1]
Twice have I stood a beggar
Before the door of God!

Angels - twice descending
Reimbursed my store -
Burglar! Banker - Father!
I am poor once more!

1858 (F 39, J 49)[2]

Success is counted sweetest

Success is counted sweetest
By those who ne'er succeed.
To comprehend a nectar[1]
Requires sorest need.

Not one of all the purple Host
Who took the Flag[2] today
Can tell the definition
So clear of Victory

＊　＊　＊

1. In the ground, buried.
2. For all of Dickinson's poems, the date provided indicates composition rather than publication, since most of the poems were not published until after her death. The date is followed by a parenthesis supplying the poem's number in both the Franklin (F) and the Johnson (J) variorum editions. For information about these two major editions, see the headnote and "Further Reading."
1. Drink of Greek and Roman gods.
2. Those seizing the flag of the enemy have won the battle.

As he defeated - dying -
On whose forbidden ear
The distant strains of triumph
Burst agonized and clear!
1859 (F 112, J 67)

These are the days when birds come back

These are the days when Birds come back -
A very few - a Bird or two -
To take a backward look.

These are the days when skies resume
The old - old sophistries[1] of June -
A blue and gold mistake.

Oh fraud that cannot cheat the Bee.
Almost thy plausibility
Induces my belief,

Till ranks of seeds their witness bear -
And softly thro' the altered air
Hurries a timid leaf.

Oh sacrament of summer days,
Oh Last Communion[2] in the Haze -
Permit a child to join -

Thy sacred emblems to partake -
Thy consecrated bread to take
And thine immortal wine!
1859 (F 122, J 130)

The daisy follows soft the sun

The Daisy follows soft the Sun -
And when his golden walk is done -
Sits shily at his feet -

1. Misleading or deceptive arguments.
2. A comparison of the last days of summer and the Last Supper of Christ according to the New Testament. The Last Supper is commemorated in some Christian denominations as the Sacrament of Communion, using bread and wine.

He - waking - finds the flower there -
Wherefore - Marauder - art thou here?
Because, Sir, love is sweet!

We are the Flower - Thou the Sun!
Forgive us, if as days decline -
We nearer steal to Thee!
Enamored of the parting West -
The peace - the flight - the amethyst -
Night's possibility!

　　　　　　　　　　　1860 (F 161, J 106)

This nature poem may also hint at power relations between the genders. The sun is repre-
sented as male, whereas "Daisy," in the "Master" letter also reprinted below, is another
name for Dickinson herself.

Title divine is mine!

Title divine - is mine!
The Wife - without the Sign!
Acute Degree - conferred on me -
Empress of Calvary![1]
Royal - all but the Crown!
Betrothed - without the swoon
God sends us Women -
When you - hold - Garnet to Garnet -
Gold - to Gold -
Born - Bridalled - Shrouded[2] -
In a Day -
"My Husband" - women say -
Stroking the Melody -
Is *this* - the way?

　　　　　　　　　　　1861 (F 194, J 1072)

"Faith" is a fine invention

"Faith" is a fine invention
For Gentlemen who *see!*
But Microscopes are prudent
In an Emergency!

　　　　　　　　　　　1861 (F 202, J 185)

---

1. The site of Christ's crucifixion.　　　　　　　2. To be completely covered.

I taste a liquor never brewed

I taste a liquor never brewed -
From Tankards scooped in Pearl -
Not all the Frankfort Berries[1]
Yield such an Alcohol!

Inebriate of Air - am I -
And Debauchee of Dew -
Reeling - thro' endless summer days -
From inns of molten Blue -

When "Landlords" turn the drunken Bee
Out of the Foxglove's door -
When Butterflies - renounce their "drams" -
I shall but drink the more!

Till Seraphs[2] swing their snowy Hats -
And Saints - to windows run -
To see the little Tippler
From Manzanilla come![3]

                    1861 (F 207, J 214)

This joyful poem employs hymn meter (4–3–4–3) but combines it with audacious slant rhymes (Pearl/Alcohol). In the 1890s, the popular poet Thomas Bailey Aldrich tried to straighten out the poem: "I taste a liquor never brewed / In vats upon the Rhine; / No tankard ever held a draught / Of alcohol like mine."

We dont cry - Tim and I

We dont cry - Tim[1] and I -
We are far too grand -
But we bolt the door tight
To prevent a friend -

            ⁂   ⁂   ⁂

1. Variant: Vats opon the Rhine. Dickinson spelled "upon" as "opon" in her poems.
2. Angels. Snowy Hats: perhaps halos.
3. Variant: Leaning against the - Sun! Franklin uses it in his reading edition. Manzanilla is both a Cuban city where rum is produced and a Spanish city where sherry is produced.

1. Perhaps the speaker's double or imaginary friend, possibly based on Charles Dickens's kindly and vulnerable character Tiny Tim in A Christmas Carol. Dickinson spelled "don't" as "dont."

Then we hide our brave face
Deep in our hand -
Not to cry - Tim and I -
We are far too grand -

Nor to dream - he and me -
Do we condescend -
We just shut our brown eye
To see to the end -

Tim - see Cottages -
But, Oh, so high!
Then - we shake - Tim and I -
And lest I - cry -

Tim - reads a little Hymn -
And we both pray,
Please, Sir, I and Tim -
Always lost the way!

We must die - by and by -
Clergymen say -
Tim - shall - if I - do -
I - too - if he -

How shall we arrange it -
Tim - was - so - shy?
Take us simultaneous - Lord -
I - "Tim" - and - me!

                    1861 (F 231, J 196)

I'm nobody! Who are you?

I'm Nobody! Who are you?
Are you - Nobody - too?
Then there's a pair of us!
Dont tell! they'd banish us[1] - you know!

          *   *   *

1. A manuscript variant for "banish us" is "advertise," which was used in some early editions and appears in Franklin's reading edition of the poetry. In Johnson's and Franklin's text, the poem's speaker fears exclusion (banishment) if the two of them are discovered, whereas in the variant text the speaker recoils from public disclosure and the dreariness of celebrity.

How dreary - to be - Somebody!
How public - like a Frog -
To tell your name[2] - the livelong June -
To an admiring Bog!

1861 *(F 260, J 288)*

Wild nights - Wild nights!

Wild nights - Wild nights!
Were I with thee
Wild nights should be
Our luxury!

Futile - the winds -
To a Heart in port -
Done with the Compass -
Done with the Chart!

Rowing in Eden -
Ah, the Sea!
Might I but moor - tonight -
In thee![1]

1861 *(F 269, J 249)*

There's a certain slant of light

There's a certain Slant of light,
Winter Afternoons -
That oppresses, like the Heft[1]
Of Cathedral Tunes -

Heavenly Hurt, it gives us -
We can find no scar,
But internal difference -
Where the Meanings, are -

*   *   *

2. Variant used in Franklin's reading edition: To tell one's name.
1. Dickinson compares the ports and moorings of the sea with the sheltering of a lover's body. The wild sea is seen as an Eden, or the paradisiacal garden in Genesis.

1. When Higginson and Todd published this poem in 1890, four years after Dickinson's death, they changed the New England term "heft" to its less remarkable synonym, "weight."

Emily Dickinson

None may teach it - Any[2] -
'Tis the Seal[3] Despair -
An imperial affliction
Sent us of the Air -

When it comes, the Landscape listens -
Shadows - hold their breath -
When it goes, 'tis like the Distance
On the look of Death -

1862 (F 320, J 258)

I felt a funeral in my brain

I felt a Funeral, in my Brain,
And Mourners to and fro
Kept treading - treading - till it seemed
That Sense was breaking through -

echo

And when they all were seated,
A Service, like a Drum -
Kept beating - beating till I thought
My mind was going numb -

And then I heard them lift a Box
And creak across my Soul
With those same Boots of Lead, again,
Then Space - began to toll,

As all the Heavens were a Bell,
And Being, but an Ear,
And I, and Silence, some strange Race
Wrecked, solitary, here -
And then a Plank in Reason, broke,
And I dropped down, and down -
And hit a World, at every plunge,
And Finished knowing - then -

1862 (F 340, J 280)

John Cody interprets this poem as a description of a gathering depression that leads to a severance from reality.

2. In their 1890 edition, Higginson and Todd changed "any" to the more easily comprehensible "anything."

3. Royal device or emblem.

I'm ceded - I've stopped being their's

I'm ceded - I've stopped being Their's -
The name They dropped opon[1] my face
With water, in the country church[2]
Is finished using, now,
And They can put it with my Dolls,
My childhood, and the string of spools,
I've finished threading - too -

Baptized, before, without the choice,
But this time, consciously, Of Grace[3] -
Unto supremest name -
Called to my Full - The Crescent dropped -
Existence's whole Arc, filled up,
With one - small Diadem -

My second Rank - too small the first -
Crowned - Crowing[4] - on my Father's breast -
A half unconscious Queen -
But this time - Adequate - Erect,
With Will to choose,
Or to reject,
And I choose, just a Crown -

                    1862 (F 353, J 508)

It was not death, for I stood up

It was not Death, for I stood up,
And all the Dead, lie down -
It was not Night, for all the Bells
Put out their Tongues, for Noon.

It was not Frost, for on my Flesh
I felt Siroccos - crawl -
Nor Fire - for just my marble feet
Could keep a Chancel, cool -

                *   *   *

---

1. Dickinson spelled "theirs" as "their's" and "upon" as "opon."
2. Refers to the Christian custom of infant or early childhood baptism.
3. This baptism is based on free will.
4. "Crowing" implies great satisfaction.

And yet, it tasted, like them all,
The Figures I have seen
Set orderly, for Burial,
Reminded me, of mine -

As if my life were shaven,
And fitted to a frame,
And could not breathe without a key,
And 'twas like Midnight, some -

When everything that ticked - has stopped -
And space stares - all around -
Or Grisly frosts - first Autumn morns,
Repeal the Beating Ground -

But, most, like Chaos - Stopless - cool -
Without a Chance, or spar -
Or even a Report of Land -
To justify - Despair.

1862 *(F 355, J 510)*

Gary Stonum observes that this "bleak" poem looks back "in retrospective bafflement at the moment when some catastrophic force has disrupted all normal modes of understanding."

A bird came down the walk

A Bird came down the Walk -
He did not know I saw -
He bit an Angle Worm in halves
And ate the fellow, raw,

And then, he drank a Dew
From a convenient Grass -
And then hopped sidewise to the Wall
To let a Beetle pass -

He glanced with rapid eyes
That hurried all around -
They looked like frightened Beads, I thought -
He stirred his Velvet Head

*   *   *

Like one in danger, Cautious,
I offered him a Crumb
And he unrolled his feathers
And rowed him softer Home -

Than Oars divide the Ocean,
Too silver for a seam -
Or Butterflies, off Banks of Noon,
Leap, plashless[1] as they swim.

              1862 (F 359, J 328)

The soul has bandaged moments

The Soul has Bandaged moments -
When too appalled to stir -
She feels some ghastly Fright come up
And stop to look at her -

Salute her, with long fingers -
Caress her freezing hair -
Sip, Goblin, from the very lips
The Lover - hovered - o'er -
Unworthy, that a thought so mean
Accost a Theme - so - fair -

The soul has moments of escape -
When bursting all the doors -
She dances like a Bomb, abroad,
And swings opon the Hours,

As do the Bee - delirious borne -
Long Dungeoned from his Rose -
Touch Liberty - then know no more,
But Noon, and Paradise -

The Soul's retaken moments -
When, Felon led along,
With shackles[1] on the plumed feet,
And staples, in the song,

---

1. Splashless.
1. Chained-together iron fastenings that bind a prisoner's ankles so that he or she has difficulty walking. Plumed: feathered.

*   *   *

The Horror welcomes her, again,
These, are not brayed of Tongue -
1862 (F 360, J 512)

After great pain a formal feeling comes

After great pain, a formal feeling comes -
The Nerves sit ceremonious, like Tombs -
The stiff Heart questions "was it He, that bore,"
And "Yesterday, or Centuries before?"

The Feet, mechanical, go round -
A Wooden way
Of Ground, or Air, or Ought[1] -
Regardless grown,[2]
A Quartz contentment, like a stone -

This is the Hour of Lead -
Remembered, if outlived,
As Freezing persons, recollect the Snow -
First - Chill - then Stupor - then the letting go -
1862 (F 372, J 341)

This poem uses vivid imagery of wood, stone, and snow as well as disconnected syntax to suggest emotional paralysis.

This world is not conclusion

This World is not conclusion.
A Species stands beyond -
Invisible, as Music -
But positive, as Sound -
It beckons, and it baffles -
Philosophy - dont know
And through a Riddle, at the last -

1. This may mean nought or nothing; or it may be Dickinson's spelling for aught, or anything whatever; or it may even suggest obligation, the feet doing what they are supposed to do.

2. Not noticed or not noticing.

Sagacity,[1] must go -
To guess it, puzzles scholars -
To gain it, Men have borne
Contempt of Generations
And Crucifixion, shown -
Faith slips - and laughs, and rallies -
Blushes, if any see -
Plucks at a twig of Evidence -
And asks a Vane,[2] the way -
Much Gesture, from the Pulpit -
Strong Hallelujahs roll -
Narcotics cannot still the Tooth
That nibbles at the soul -

                    1862 (F 373, J 501)

One need not be a chamber to be haunted

One need not be a Chamber - to be Haunted -
One need not be a House -
The Brain has Corridors - surpassing
Material Place - *can be haunted.*

Far safer, of a midnight meeting
External Ghost *a real" ghost*
Than it's[1] interior confronting -
That cooler Host.

Far safer, through an Abbey gallop,
The Stones a'chase - *through of rocks*
Than unarmed,[2] one's a'self encounter -
In lonesome Place - *self · ponde*

Ourself behind ourself, concealed -
Should startle most -
Assassin hid in our Apartment
Be Horror's least[3] -

              *   *   *

---

1. Keenness or wisdom.
2. Weather vane.
1. Dickinson spelled "its" as "it's."

2. Variant: moonless.
3. The least fearful of what we fear.

The Body - borrows a Revolver -
He bolts the Door -
O'erlooking a superior spectre[4] -
Or More[5] -

        1862 *(F 407, J 670)*

According to Vivian Pollak, this poem evokes the divided self or the "stranger within."

The soul selects her own society

The Soul selects her own Society -
Then - shuts the Door -
To her divine Majority -
Present no more -

Unmoved - she notes the Chariots - pausing -
At her low Gate -
Unmoved - an Emperor be kneeling
Opon her Mat -

I've known her - from an ample nation -
Choose One -
Then - close the Valves of her attention -
Like Stone -

        1862 *(F 409, J 303)*

I had been hungry all the years

I had been hungry, all the Years -
My Noon had Come - to dine -
I trembling drew the Table near -
And touched the Curious Wine -

'Twas this on Tables I had seen -
When turning, hungry, Home
I looked in Windows, for the Wealth
I could not hope - for Mine -

        *   *   *

---

4. Ghost.　　　　　　　　　　　5. Variant: More near.

I did not know the ample Bread -
'Twas so unlike the Crumb
The Birds and I, had often shared
In Nature's - Dining Room -

The Plenty hurt me - 'twas so new -
Myself felt ill - and odd -
As Berry - of a Mountain Bush -
Transplanted - to the Road -

Nor was I hungry - so I found
That Hunger - was a way
Of persons Outside Windows -
The entering - takes away -

1862 (F 439, J 579)

They shut me up in prose

They shut me up in Prose
As when a little Girl
They put me in the Closet -
Because they liked me "still" -

Still! Could themself have peeped -
And seen my Brain - go round -
They might as wise have lodged a Bird
For Treason - in the Pound[1] -

Himself has but to will
And easy as a Star
Look down opon Captivity -
And laugh - No more have I -

1862 (F 445, J 613)

This was a poet

This was a Poet -
It is That[1]
Distills amazing sense
From Ordinary Meanings -
And Attar[2] so immense

---

1. A place in which animals are caged.   2. Perfume or oil from crushed flower petals.
1. "It is that" can be read as "the one who."

*　*　*

From the familiar species
That perished by the Door -
We wonder it was not Ourselves
Arrested it - before -

Of Pictures, the Discloser -
The Poet - it is He -
Entitles Us - by Contrast -
To ceaseless Poverty -

Of Portion - so unconscious -
The Robbing - could not harm -
Himself - to Him - a Fortune -
Exterior - to Time -

    1862 (F 446, J 448)

I died for beauty but was scarce

I died for Beauty - but was scarce
Adjusted in the Tomb
When One who died for Truth, was lain
In an adjoining Room[1] -

He questioned softly "Why I failed?"[2]
"For Beauty", I replied -
"And I - for Truth - Themself are One -
We Bretheren, are," He said -

And so, as Kinsmen, met a Night -
We talked between the Rooms -
Until the Moss had reached our lips -
And covered up - Our names -

    1862 (F 448, J 449)

I dwell in possibility

I dwell in Possibility -
A fairer House than Prose -
More numerous of Windows -
Superior - for Doors -

---

1. Another tomb within a larger burial area.　　　2. Died.

*   *   *

Of Chambers as the Cedars -
Impregnable[1] of Eye -
And for an everlasting Roof
The Gambrels of the Sky -

Of Visitors - the fairest -
For Occupation - This -
The spreading wide my narrow Hands
To gather Paradise -

1862 (F 466, J 657)

I was the slightest in the house

I was the slightest in the House -
I took the smallest Room -
At night, my little Lamp, and Book -
And one Geranium -

So stationed I could catch the mint[1]
That never ceased to fall -
And just my Basket -
Let me think - I'm sure
That this was all -

I never spoke - unless addressed -
And then, 'twas brief and low -
I could not bear to live - aloud -
The Racket shamed me so -

And if it had not been so far -
And any one I knew
Were going - I had often thought
How noteless - I could die -

1862 (F 473, J 486)

Because I could not stop for death

Because I could not stop for Death -
He kindly stopped for me -
The Carriage held but just Ourselves -
And Immortality.

---

1. Too dense to see through.   1. An aromatic herb.

* * *

We slowly drove - He knew no haste
And I had put away
My labor and my leisure too,
For His Civility -

We passed the School, where Children strove
At Recess - in the Ring -
We passed the Fields of Gazing Grain -
We passed the Setting Sun -

Or rather - He passed Us -
The Dews drew quivering and Chill -
For only Gossamer,[1] my Gown -
My Tippet[2] - only Tulle -

We paused before a House that seemed
A Swelling of the Ground -
The Roof was scarcely visible -
The Cornice[3] - in the Ground -

Since then - 'tis Centuries - and yet
Feels shorter than the Day
I first surmised the Horses' Heads
Were toward Eternity -

1862 (F 479, J 712)

A still volcano life

A still - Volcano - Life -
That flickered in the night -
When it was dark enough to do
Without erasing sight -

A quiet - Earthquake style -
Too subtle to suspect
By natures this side Naples[1]
The North cannot detect

* * *

1. Very fine cloth.
2. Shoulder cape. Tulle: silk netting.
3. Decorative molding.

1. The volcanic Mount Vesuvius is near Naples, Italy.

The solemn - Torrid - Symbol -
The lips that never lie -
Whose hissing Corals part - and shut -
And Cities - ooze away[2] -
1863 (F 517, J 601)

This is my letter to the world

This is my letter to the World
That never wrote to Me -
The simple News that Nature told -
With tender Majesty

Her Message is committed
To Hands I cannot see -
For love of Her - Sweet - countrymen -
Judge tenderly - of Me
1863 (F 519, J 441)

For largest woman's heart I knew

For largest Woman's Heart I knew -
'Tis little I can do -
And yet the largest Woman's Heart
Could hold an Arrow, too,
And so, instructed by my own,
I tenderer - turn me to.
1863 (F 542, J 309)

This is one of the epistolary poems that Dickinson sent to her sister-in-law, Susan Gilbert Dickinson.

I heard a fly buzz when I died

I heard a Fly buzz - when I died -
The Stillness in the Room
Was like the Stillness in the Air -
Between the Heaves of Storm -

2. An eruption of Mount Vesuvius destroyed the cities of Pompeii and Herculaneum.

*   *   *

The Eyes around - had wrung them dry -
And Breaths were gathering firm
For that last Onset - when the King[1]
Be witnessed - in the Room -

I willed my Keepsakes - Signed away
What portion of me be
Assignable - and then it was
There interposed a Fly -

With Blue - uncertain stumbling Buzz -
Between the light - and me -
And then the Windows failed - and then
I could not see to see -

> 1863 *(F 591, J 465)*

The brain is wider than the sky

The Brain - is wider than the Sky -
For - put them side by side -
The one the other will contain
With ease - and You - beside -

The Brain is deeper than the sea -
For - hold them - Blue to Blue -
The one the other will absorb -
As Sponges - Buckets - do -

The Brain is just the weight of God -
For - Heft them - Pound for Pound -
And they will differ - if they do -
As Syllable from Sound -

> 1863 *(F 598, J 632)*

Much madness is divinest sense

Much Madness is divinest Sense -
To a discerning Eye -
Much Sense - the starkest Madness -

---

1. Possibly Jesus Christ.

'Tis the Majority
In this, as all, prevail -
Assent - and you are sane -
Demur - you're straightway dangerous -
And handled with a Chain -

        1863 (F 620, J 435)

I've seen a dying eye

I've seen a Dying Eye
Run round and round a Room -
In search of Something - as it seemed -
Then Cloudier become -
And then - obscure with Fog -
And then - be soldered down
Without disclosing what it be
'Twere blessed to have seen -

        1863 (F 648, J 547)

I started early - took my dog

I started Early - Took my Dog -
And visited the Sea -
The Mermaids in the Basement
Came out to look at me -

And Frigates - in the Upper Floor
Extended Hempen[1] Hands -
Presuming Me to be a Mouse -
Aground - opon the Sands -

But no Man moved Me - till the Tide
Went past my simple Shoe -
And past my Apron - and my Belt
And past my Boddice[2] - too -

---

1. Made of hemp rope.
2. "Boddice" is Dickinson's spelling of "bodice," a vest worn over a blouse, but laced up, or the upper part of a dress.

* * *

And made as He would eat me up -
As wholly as a Dew
Opon a Dandelion's Sleeve
And then - I started - too -

And He - He followed - close behind -
I felt His Silver Heel
Opon my Ancle[3] - Then my Shoes
Would overflow with Pearl -

Until We met the Solid Town -
No One He seemed to know -
And bowing - with a Mighty look -
At me - The Sea withdrew -

1863 (F 656, J 520)

I cannot live with you

I cannot live with You -
It would be Life -
And Life is over there -
Behind the Shelf

The Sexton[1] keeps the Key to -
Putting up
Our Life - His Porcelain -
Like a Cup -

Discarded of the Housewife -
Quaint - or Broke -
A new Sevres[2] pleases -
Old Ones crack -

I could not die - with You -
For One must wait
To shut the Other's Gaze down -
You - could not -

* * *

3. "Ancle" is Dickinson's spelling of "ankle."   2. Fine porcelain china from Sèvres, France.
1. Church custodian.

And I - Could I stand by
And see You - freeze -
Without my Right of Frost -
Death's privilege?

Nor could I rise - with You -
Because Your Face
Would put out Jesus' -
That New Grace

Glow plain - and foreign
On my homesick Eye -
Except that You than He
Shone closer by -

They'd judge Us - How -
For You - served Heaven[3] - You know,
Or sought to -
I could not -

Because You saturated sight -
And I had no more eyes
For sordid excellence
As Paradise

And were You lost, I would be -
Though my Name
Rang loudest
On the Heavenly fame -

And were You - saved -
And I - condemned to be
Where You were not -
That self - were Hell to Me -

So We must meet apart -
You there - I - here -
With just the Door ajar
That Oceans are - and Prayer -
And that White Sustenance -
Despair -

        1863 (F 706, J 640)

---

3. Implying that he is religious or perhaps even a clergyman.

Pain has an element of blank

Pain - has an Element of Blank -
It cannot recollect
When it begun - or if there were
A time when it was not -

It has no Future - but itself -
It's Infinite contain[1]
It's Past - enlightened to perceive
New Periods - of Pain.
          1863 (F 760, J 650)

My life had stood a loaded gun

My Life had stood - a Loaded Gun -
In Corners - till a Day
The Owner passed - identified -
And carried Me away -

And now We roam in Sovreign Woods -
And now We hunt the Doe -
And every time I speak for Him
The Mountains straight reply -

And do I smile, such cordial light
Opon the Valley glow -
It is as a Vesuvian[1] face
Had let it's pleasure through -

And when at Night - Our good Day done -
I guard My Master's Head -
'Tis better than the Eider-Duck's
Deep Pillow[2] - to have shared -

To foe of His - I'm deadly foe -
None stir the second time -
On whom I lay a Yellow Eye -
Or an emphatic Thumb -

*   *   *

1. In their effort to make Dickinson more acceptable and comprehensible, Higginson and Todd changed this line in their 1890 edition to "Its infinite realms contain."

1. Resembling the volcanic Mount Vesuvius; perhaps implying explosive anger.
2. A down pillow made from duck feathers.

Though I than He - may longer live
He longer must - than I -
For I have but the power[3] to kill,
Without - the power to die -
1863 (F 764, J 754)

Sharon Cameron interprets this enigmatic poem to be about the "denial of death," whereas Vivian Pollak sees it as a "fantasy of phallic womanhood" and Adrienne Rich as an expression of "ambivalence toward power."

Publication is the auction

Publication - is the Auction
Of the Mind of Man -
Poverty - be justifying
For so foul a thing.

Possibly - but We - would rather
From Our Garret go
White - unto the White Creator -
Than invest - Our Snow[1] -

Thought belong to Him who gave it -
Then - to Him Who bear
It's Corporeal illustration - sell
The Royal Air -

In the Parcel - Be the Merchant
Of the Heavenly Grace -
But reduce no Human Spirit
To Disgrace of Price -
1863 (F 788, J 709)

This consciousness that is aware

This Consciousness that is aware
Of Neighbors and the Sun
Will be the one aware of Death
And that itself alone

---

3. Variant: art.
1. That is, not even poverty would convince the speaker to publish.

*   *   *

Is traversing the interval
Experience between
And most profound experiment
Appointed unto Men -

How adequate unto itself
It's properties shall be
Itself unto itself and None
Shall make discovery -

Adventure most unto itself
The Soul condemned to be -
Attended by a single Hound
It's own identity.

1864 (F 817, J 822)

Color - caste - denomination

Color - Caste - Denomination[1] -
These - are Time's Affair -
Death's diviner Classifying
Does not know they are -

As in sleep - All Hue forgotten -
Tenets - put behind -
Death's large - Democratic fingers
Rub away the Brand -

If Circassian[2] - He is careless -
If He put away
Chrysalis of Blonde - or Umber[3] -
Equal Butterfly -

They emerge from His Obscuring -
What Death - knows so well -
Our minuter intuitions -
Deem unplausible

1864 (F 836, J 970)

1. Color refers to race. Caste: social or religious rank or status. Denomination: religious group.
2. Inhabitant of the land bordering the Black Sea in southeastern Europe.
3. Dusky brown.

She rose to his requirement - dropt

She rose to His Requirement - dropt
The Playthings of Her Life
To take the honorable Work
Of Woman, and of Wife -

If ought[1] She missed in Her new Day,
Of Amplitude, or Awe -
Or first Prospective - Or the Gold
In using, wear away,

It lay unmentioned - as the Sea
Develope[2] Pearl, and Weed,
But only to Himself - be known
The Fathoms[3] they abide -

1864 (F 857, J 732)

Under the light yet under

Under the Light, yet under,
Under the Grass and the Dirt,
Under the Beetle's Cellar
Under the Clover's Root,

Further than Arm could stretch
Were it Giant long,
Further than Sunshine could
Were the Day Year long,

Over the Light, yet over,
Over the Arc of the Bird -
Over the Comet's chimney -
Over the Cubit's Head,

Further than Guess can gallop
Further than Riddle ride -
Oh for a Disc[1] to the Distance
Between Ourselves and the Dead!

1865 (F 1068, J 949)

---

1. Anything.
2. "Develope" is Dickinson's spelling of "develop."

3. Measurement for depth of water.
1. A disk, which can be thrown very far.

A narrow fellow in the grass

A narrow Fellow in the Grass
Occasionally rides -
You may have met Him? Did you not
His notice instant is -

The Grass divides as with a Comb -
A spotted Shaft is seen -
And then it closes at your Feet
And opens further on -

He likes a Boggy Acre
A Floor too cool for Corn
Yet when a Boy[1] and Barefoot -
I more than once at Noon

Have passed, I thought, a Whip lash
Unbraiding in the Sun
When stooping to secure it
It wrinkled And was gone -

Several of Nature's People
I know, and they know me -
I feel for them a transport
Of Cordiality -

But never met this Fellow
Attended or alone
Without a tighter breathing
And Zero at the Bone.

1865 (F 1096, J 986)

One of the handful of poems to be published in Dickinson's lifetime, this poem appeared in the *Springfield Daily Republican* on February 14, 1866, under the title of "The Snake."

The bustle in a house

The Bustle in a House
The Morning after Death
Is solemnest of industries
Enacted opon Earth -

---

1. Sometimes Dickinson employs the voice of a boy.

* * *

The Sweeping up the Heart
And putting Love away
We shall not want to use again
Until Eternity -

    1865 *(F 1108, J 1078)*

Tell all the truth but tell it slant

Tell all the truth but tell it slant -
Success in Circuit lies
Too bright for our infirm Delight
The Truth's superb surprise
As Lightning to the Children eased
With explanation kind
The Truth must dazzle gradually
Or every man be blind -

    1872 *(F 1263, J 1129)*

What mystery pervades a well!

What mystery pervades a well!
The water lives so far -
A neighbor from another world
Residing in a jar

Whose limit none have ever seen,
But just his lid of glass -
Like looking every time you please
In an abyss's face!

The grass does not appear afraid,
I often wonder he
Can stand so close and look so bold
At what is awe to me.

Related somehow they may be,
The sedge stands next the sea
Where he is floorless
And does no timidity betray

* * *

But nature is a stranger yet;
The ones that cite her most
Have never passed her haunted house,
Nor simplified her ghost.

To pity those that know her not
Is helped by the regret
That those who know her, know her less
The nearer her they get.

1877 (F 1433, J 1400)

Volcanoes be in Sicily

Volcanoes be in Sicily
And South America
I judge from my Geography
Volcanoes nearer here
A Lava step at any time
Am I inclined to climb
A Crater I may contemplate
Vesuvius[1] at Home

n.d. (F 1691, J 1705)

My life closed twice before it's close

My life closed twice before it's close;
It yet remains to see
If Immortality unveil
A third event to me,

So huge, so hopeless to conceive
As these that twice befell.
Parting is all we know of heaven,
And all we need of hell.

n.d. (F 1773, J 1732)

---

1. Another of Dickinson's recurrent references to the active volcano Mount Vesuvius near Naples, Italy.

LETTERS

To Susan Gilbert (Dickinson)

June 27, 1852

. . . Susie, will you indeed come home next Saturday, and be my own again, and kiss me as you used to? Shall I indeed behold you, not "darkly, but face to face" or am I *fancying* so, and dreaming blessed dreams from which the day will wake me? I hope for you so much, and feel so eager for you, feel that I *cannot* wait, feel that *now* I must have you—that the expectation once more to see your face again, makes me feel hot and feverish, and my heart beats so fast—I go to sleep at night, and the first thing I know, I am sitting there wide awake, and clasping my hands tightly, and thinking of next Saturday, and "never a bit" of you.

Sometimes I must have Saturday before tomorrow comes, and I wonder if it w'd make any difference with God, to give it to me *today,* and I'd let him have Monday, to make him a Saturday; and then I feel so funnily, and wish the precious day wouldn't come quite so soon, till I could know how to feel, and get my thoughts ready for it.

Why, Susie, it seems to me as if my absent Lover was coming home so soon— and my heart must be so busy, making ready for him.

While the minister this morning was giving an account of the Roman Catholic system, and announcing several facts which were usually startling, I was trying to make up my mind wh' of the two was prettiest to go and welcome *you* in, my fawn colored dress, or my blue dress. Just as I had decided by all means to wear the blue, down came the minister's fist with a terrible rap on the counter, and Susie, it scared me so, I haven't got over it yet, but I'm glad I reached a conclusion! I walked home from meeting with Mattie, and *incidentally* quite, something was said of you, and I think one of us remarked that you would be here next Sunday; well—Susie—what it was I dont presume to know, but my gaiters seemed to leave me, and I seemed to move on wings—and I move on wings now, Susie, on wings as white as snow, and as bright as the summer sunshine —because I am with you, and so few short days, you are with me at home. Be patient then, my Sister, for the hours will haste away, and Oh *so* soon! Susie, I write most hastily, and very carelessly too, for it is time for me to get the supper, and my mother is gone and besides, my darling, so near I seem to you, that I *disdain* this pen, and wait for a *warmer* language. With Vinnie's love, and my love, I am once more

Your Emilie—

To Samuel Bowles

About February 1861

Dear friend.[1]

You remember the little "Meeting"—we held for you—last spring? We met again—Saturday—'Twas May—when we "adjourned"—but then Adjourns—are all—The meetings wore alike—Mr Bowles—The Topic—did not tire us—so we chose no new—We voted to remember you—so long as both should live— including Immortality. To count you as ourselves—except sometimes more tenderly—as now—when you are ill—and we—the haler of the two—and so I bring the Bond—we sign so many times—for you to read, when Chaos comes—or Treason—or Decay—still witnessing for Morning.

We hope—it is a tri-Hope—composed of Vinnie's—Sue's—and mine—that you took no more pain—riding in the sleigh.

We hope our joy to see you—gave of it's own degree—to you—We pray for your new health—the prayer that goes not down—when they shut the church— We offer you our cups—stintless—as to the Bee—the Lily, her new Liquors—

> Would you like summer? Taste of our's.
> Spices? Buy here!
> Ill! We have berries, for the parching!
> Weary! Furloughs of down!
> Perplexed! Estates of Violet trouble ne'er looked on!
> Captive! We bring reprieve of roses!
> Fainting! Flasks of air!
> Even for Death, a fairy medicine—
> But, which is it, sir?

Emily

To recipient unknown

About 1861

Master.[1]

If you saw a bullet hit a Bird—and he told you he was'nt[2] shot—you might weep at his courtesy, but you would certainly doubt his word.

---

1. Bowles was editor of the *Springfield Daily Republican*, the local daily newspaper published near Dickinson's home in Amherst. Under Bowles's editorship, it became a nationally influential liberal newspaper. Dickinson considered both Bowles and his wife to be lifelong friends. Several scholars have speculated that Dickinson may have been in love with him and addressed her "Master" letters to him (see example below);

but the identity of "Master" remains unknown and the question of Dickinson and Bowles's relationship unresolved.

1. Dickinson refers to herself as Daisy in this letter to the unknown "Master."

2. In contractions containing "not," Dickinson either transposed the "n" and apostrophe or did not use the apostrophe.

One drop more from the gash that stains your Daisy's bosom—then would you *believe?* Thomas'[3] faith in Anatomy, was stronger than his faith in faith. God made me—[Sir] Master—I did'nt be—myself. I dont know how it was done. He built the heart in me—Bye and bye it outgrew me—and like the little mother—with the big child—I got tired holding him. I heard of a thing called "Redemption"—which rested men and women. You remember I asked you for it—you gave me something else. I forgot the Redemption [in the Redeemed—I did'nt tell you for a long time, but I knew you had altered me—I] and was tired—no more—[so dear did this stranger become that were it, or my breath—the Alternative—I had tossed the fellow away with a smile.] I am older—tonight, Master—but love is the same—so are the moon and the crescent. If it had been God's will that I might breathe where you breathed—and find the place—myself—at night—if I (can) never forget that I am not with you—and that sorrow and frost are nearer than I—if I wish with a might I cannot repress—that mine were the Queen's place—the love of the Plantagenet[4] is my only apology—To come nearer than presbyteries[5]—and nearer than the new Coat—that the Tailor made—the prank of the Heart at play on the Heart—in holy Holiday—is forbidden me—You make me say it over—I fear you laugh—when I do not see—[but] "Chillon"[6] is not funny. Have you the Heart in your breast—Sir—is it set like mine—a little to the left—has it the misgiving—if it wake in the night—perchance—itself to it—timbrel is it—itself to it a tune?

These things are [reverent] holy, Sir, I touch them [reverently] hallowed, but persons who pray—dare remark [our] "Father"! You say I do not tell you all—Daisy confessed—and denied not.

Vesuvius dont talk—Etna—dont—[Thy] one of them—said a syllable—a thousand years ago, and Pompeii heard it, and hid forever—She could'nt look the world in the face, afterward—I suppose—Bashful Pompeii![7] "Tell you of the want"—you know what a leech is, dont you—and [remember that] Daisy's arm is small—and you have felt the horizon have'nt you—and did the sea—never come so close as to make you dance?

I dont know what you can do for it—thank you—Master—but if I had the Beard on my cheek—like you—and you—had Daisy's petals—and you cared so for me—what would I become of you? Could you forget me in fight, or flight—or the foreign land? Could'nt Carlo,[8] and you and I walk in the meadows an hour—and nobody care but the Bobolink—and *his*—a *silver* scruple? I used to

3. Thomas who doubted the resurrection of Christ in the Gospel of John 20:25.
4. Royal British line.
5. Church elders.
6. Castle prison in Byron's poem "The Prisoner of Chillon."
7. Mount Vesuvius and Mount Etna are located in Italy, the first near Naples and the second in Sicily. Pompeii was destroyed in the first century by a volcanic eruption from Vesuvius.
8. Dickinson's dog.

think when I died—I could see you—so I died as fast as I could—but the "Corpo-
ration"[9] are going Heaven too so [Eternity] wont be sequestered—now [at all]—
Say I may wait for you—say I need go with no stranger to the to me—untried
[country] fold—I waited a long time—Master—but I can wait more—wait till
my hazel hair is dappled—and you carry the cane—then I can look at my
watch—and if the Day is too far declined—we can take the chances [of] for
Heaven—What would you do with me if I came "in white?"[10] Have you the
little chest to put the Alive—in?

I want to see you more—Sir—than all I wish for in this world—and the
wish—altered a little—will be my only one—for the skies.

Could you come to New England—[this summer—could] would you come
to Amherst—Would you like to come—Master?

[Would it do harm—yet we both fear God—] Would Daisy disappoint you—
no—she would'nt—Sir—it were comfort forever—just to look in your face, while
you looked in mine—then I could play in the woods till Dark—till you take me
where Sundown cannot find us—and the true keep coming—till the town is full.
[Will you tell me if you will?]

I did'nt think to tell you, you did'nt come to me "in white," nor ever told me
why,

No Rose, yet felt myself a'bloom,
No Bird—yet rode in Ether.

To Thomas Wentworth Higginson

April 15, 1862

Mr. Higginson.[1]
Are you too deeply occupied to say if my Verse is alive?

The Mind is so near itself—it cannot see, distinctly—and I have none to ask—

Should you think it breathed—and had you the leisure to tell me, I should
feel quick gratitude—

If I make the mistake—that you dared to tell me—would give me sincerer
honor—toward you—

I enclose my name   asking you, if you please—Sir—to tell me what is true?

That you will not betray me—it is needless to ask—since Honor is *its* own
pawn—

9. Church elders.
10. Dickinson wore white in her later years; she as-
sociated it with immortality.
1. Higginson was a prominent editor and critic
who encouraged many writers to publish. In this
letter, Dickinson was seeking advice on four of
her poems. In place of a signature, Dickinson en-
closed a card on which she wrote her name.

To Thomas Wentworth Higginson

April 25, 1862

Mr. Higginson.

Your kindness claimed earlier gratitude—but I was ill—and write today, from my pillow.

Thank you for the surgery[1]—it was not so painful as I supposed. I bring you others—as you ask—though they might not differ—

While my thought is undressed—I can make the distinction, but when I put them in the Gown—they look alike, and numb.[2]

You asked how old I was? I made no verse—but one or two—until this winter—Sir—

I had a terror—since September—I could tell to none—and so I sing, as the Boy does by the Burying Ground—because I am afraid—You inquire my Books—For Poets—I have Keats—and Mr and Mrs Browning. For Prose—Mr Ruskin—Sir Thomas Browne—and the Revelations.[3] I went to school—but in your manner of the phrase—had no education. When a little Girl, I had a friend, who taught me Immortality—but venturing too near, himself—he never returned—Soon after, my Tutor, died—and for several years, my Lexicon—was my only companion—Then I found one more—but he was not contented I be his scholar—so he left the Land.[4]

You ask of my Companions Hills—Sir—and the Sundown—and a Dog—large as myself, that my Father bought me—They are better than Beings—because they know—but do not tell—and the noise in the Pool, at Noon—excels my Piano. I have a Brother and Sister—My Mother does not care for thought—and Father, too busy with his Briefs[5]—to notice what we do—He buys me many Books—but begs me not to read them—because he fears they joggle the Mind. They are religious—except me—and address an Eclipse, every morning—whom they call their "Father." But I fear my story fatigues you—I would like to learn—Could you tell me how to grow—or is it unconveyed—like Melody—or Witchcraft?

You speak of Mr Whitman—I never read his Book—but was told that he was disgraceful[6]—

I read Miss Prescott's "Circumstance,"[7] but it followed me, in the Dark—so I avoided her—

1. Cuts suggested in the poems that Dickinson had sent for his criticism.
2. Unclear, but Dickinson may be saying that once she writes out her thoughts on paper, all look the same.
3. The terror is unclear, perhaps an attack of anxiety or depression. She lists five English writers and includes the Book of Revelation from the New Testament.
4. None identified.
5. Legal arguments or documents.
6. Whitman's *Leaves of Grass*, published in 1855, was considered shocking because of his overt references to the body and sexuality.
7. Harriet Prescott Spofford's "Circumstance."

Two Editors of Journals came to my Father's House, this winter—and asked me for my Mind—and when I asked them "Why," they said I was penurious— and they, would use it for the World[8]—

I could not weigh myself—Myself—

My size felt small—to me—I read your Chapters in the Atlantic[9]—and experienced honor for you—I was sure you would not reject a confiding question—

Is this—Sir—what you asked me to tell you?

> Your friend,
> E—Dickinson

To Thomas Wentworth Higginson

June 7, 1862

Dear friend.

Your letter gave no Drunkenness, because I tasted Rum before—Domingo[1] comes but once—yet I have had few pleasures so deep as your opinion, and if I tried to thank you, my tears would block my tongue—

My dying Tutor told me that he would like to live till I had been a poet, but Death was much of Mob as I could master—then—and when far afterward—a sudden light on Orchards, or a new fashion in the wind troubled my attention— I felt a palsy, here—the Verses just relieve—

Your second letter surprised me, and for a moment, swung—I had not supposed it. Your first—gave no dishonor, because the True—are not ashamed—I thanked you for your justice—but could not drop the Bells whose jingling cooled my Tramp—Perhaps the Balm, seemed better, because you bled me first.

I smile when you suggest that I delay "to publish"—that being foreign to my thought, as Firmament to Fin—

If fame belonged to me, I could not escape her—if she did not, the longest day would pass me on the chase—and the approbation of my Dog, would forsake me—then—My Barefoot-Rank is better—

You think my gait "spasmodic"—I am in danger—Sir—

You think me "uncontrolled"—I have no Tribunal.

Would you have time to be the "friend" you should think I need? I have a little shape—it would not crowd your Desk—nor make much Racket as the Mouse, that dents your Galleries—

If I might bring you what I do—not so frequent to trouble you—and ask you if I told it clear—'twould be control, to me—

8. Both Bowles and another editor from the same newspaper sought to publish Dickinson's poems.
9. *The Atlantic Monthly*, one of the most prestigious journals of the time.

1. Highly regarded rum from the Dominican Republic.

The Sailor cannot see the North—but knows the Needle can[2]—

The "hand you stretch in the Dark," I put mine in, and turn away—I have no Saxon,[3] now—

> As if I asked a common Alms,
> And in my wondering hand
> A stranger pressed a Kingdom,
> And I, bewildered, stand—
> As if I asked the Orient
> Had it for me a Morn—
> And it should lift its purple Dikes,
> And shatter me with Dawn!

But, will you be my Preceptor, Mr Higginson?

Your friend,
E Dickinson—

To Thomas Wentworth Higginson

July 1862

Could you believe me—without? I had no portrait,[1] now, but am small, like the Wren, and my Hair is bold, like the Chestnut Bur—and my eyes, like the Sherry in the Glass, that the Guest leaves—Would this do just as well?

It often alarms Father—He says Death might occur, and he has Molds of all the rest—but has no Mold of me, but I noticed the Quick wore off those things, in a few days, and forestall the dishonor—You will think no caprice of me—

You said "Dark." I know the Butterfly—and the Lizard—and the Orchis—

Are not those *your* Countrymen?

I am happy to be your scholar, and will deserve the kindness, I cannot repay.

If you truly consent, I recite now—

Will you tell me my fault, frankly as to yourself, for I had rather wince, than die. Men do not call the surgeon, to commend—the Bone, but to set it, Sir, and fracture within, is more critical. And for this, Preceptor, I shall bring you—Obedience—the Blossom from my Garden, and every gratitude I know. Perhaps you smile at me. I could not stop for that—My Business is Circumference—An ignorance, not of Customs, but if caught with the Dawn—or the Sunset see me—Myself the only Kangaroo among the Beauty, Sir, if you please, it afflicts me, and I thought that instruction would take it away.

Because you have much business, beside the growth of me—you will appoint,

---

2. Compass needle.
3. No words in English.

1. Dickinson apparently had no photograph to offer Higginson.

588 ♦ *Emily Dickinson*

yourself, how often I shall come—without your inconvenience. And if at any time—you regret you received me, or I prove a different fabric to that you supposed—you must banish me—

When I state myself, as the Representative of the Verse—it does not mean—me—but a supposed person. . . .

To thank you, baffles me. Are you perfectly powerful? Had I a pleasure you had not, I could delight to bring it.

Your Scholar

To Otis P. Lord

[rough draft]
About 1878

My lovely Salem smiles at me I seek his Face so often—but I am past disguises (have dropped—) (have done with guises—)[1]

I confess that I love him—I rejoice that I love him—I thank the maker of Heaven and Earth that gave him me to love—the exultation floods me—I can not find my channel—The Creek turned Sea at thoughts of thee—will you punish it—[turn I] involuntarily Bankruptcy as the Debtors say. Could that be a Crime—How could that be a crime—Incarcerate me in yourself—that will punish me—Threading with you this lovely maze which is not Life or Death tho it has the intangibleness of one and the flush of the other waking for your sake on Day made magical with [before] you before I went to sleep—What pretty phrase—we went to sleep as if it were a country—let us make it one—we could (will) make it one, my native Land—my Darling come oh *be* a patriot now—Oh nation of the soul thou hast thy freedom now

To Susan Gilbert Dickinson

About 1884

Morning might come by Accident—Sister—
Night comes by Event—
To believe the final line of the Card[1] would foreclose Faith—

---

1. Judge Otis Lord was a friend of the Dickinson family. He lived in Salem, Massachusetts, from about 1878 until his death in 1884. Dickinson's letters reveal that they loved one another.

1. Unclear, but Dickinson may be referring to a calling card or greeting card.

Faith is *Doubt*—

Sister—

Show me Eternity,—and I will show you Memory—
Both in one package lain
And lifted back again—
Be Sue—while I am Emily—
Be next—what you have ever been—Infinity—

This version of the letter reveals Johnson's, rather than Dickinson's, editorial decisions on margins, line breaks, and stanzas.

ADAH ISAACS MENKEN
ca. 1835–1868

ALMOST NOTHING IS KNOWN for certain about Adah Isaacs Menken's background. Although she was one of the most celebrated stage actresses of her time, her race, ethnicity, sexuality, and religious affiliation remain in doubt as she crossed and recrossed seemingly fixed identity boundaries. In her signature stage role, she appeared outfitted as the male hero. Her poetry possesses this same chameleon-like quality. At times assertive and exaggerated, it can also be introspective and thoughtful. Sometimes written in free verse, reflecting Walt Whitman's influence, it also employs more conventional measures. In its range of moods and voices, it resembles little else in nineteenth-century American poetry.

Adah Menken was born perhaps in 1835, perhaps in New Orleans, and perhaps with the name Philomène Croi Théodore (or, alternatively, Adah Bertha Theodore, Dolores Adios Fuertes, or Ada McCord). She was of black, white, mulatto, Creole, Jewish, Spanish, French, Mexican, or Irish ancestry—or, perhaps, a combination of some of those races and ethnicities. Menken carefully created and maintained such uncertainties in order to give herself a maximum of freedom in an age when racial identity was destiny.

As a young performer and poet, she married Alexander Isaac Menken, a Jewish musician from a prominent Cincinnati family. The marriage was the first of several. She adopted the name Adah Isaacs Menken, which she used as a performer and a poet for the rest of her life, though in private dealings she sometimes used a later married name as well, Barclay (or Barkley). She also adopted Menken's Jewish faith, claiming that she had Jewish forebears herself. She initially gained fame as an extravagant and at times notorious actress. Playing the white, male hero of the Byronic melodrama *Mazeppa*, she appeared on horseback, in heavy white makeup, and seemingly in the nude (though she actually invented the body stocking for the occasion). Her appearance reputedly caused both male and female spectators to faint. She enacted this role, and others like it, throughout the United States and in foreign capitals such as Havana, London, Vienna, and Paris. Known as "The Naked Actress" or "La Belle Menken," she typically called herself simply "The Menken."

Although famous and at times well paid as an actress, Menken told friends that "writing . . . is my only salvation." She became a friend of Mark Twain in San Francisco, Walt Whitman in New York, Charles Dickens and Charles Swinburne in London, and George Sand in Paris. She wrote newspaper articles and poems throughout her adult life and above all longed for recognition as a poet. In the last year of her life—after the death of her only son, and as she herself was dying in Paris—she prepared her single book of poetry, called *Infelicia*. It appeared a week after her death in 1868, received savagely negative reviews, and was remarkably popular, especially with women readers, who carried it through twelve editions from 1868 through 1902.

This extraordinary poet, so adept at slipping the knots of identity and so addicted to celebrity, wrote in many different voices. In "Myself," for example, she writes in the voice of abjection, expressing betrayal, suffering, paralysis, and despair. Critic Joan Sherman writes that such poems are "remarkably dramatic, intensely self-aware and 'confessional,' and unsparing in [their] condemnation of a male-dominated world that restricts woman's freedom." This description is apt, though "Myself" is only ambiguously "confessional," given that its protagonist avows that "living is but to play a part." Another voice in Menken's poetry articulates female friendship or erotic love. The narrator of "A Memory," so different from the tortured speaker in "Myself," recalls a relationship with a "dark-eyed" woman that was equitable and mutually satisfying.

Yet another distinct voice speaks what may be Menken's last poem, "Infelix," in which the speaker faces imminent death. Complex and moving, "Infelix" candidly acknowledges its protagonist's weaknesses as well as her gifts. She has been limited not only by the "jeers" of others but by her own "errors" and "fears" as well. The poem's final self-images of a "houseless shadow" and an "exile" remind us of the enduring artistic potential of cultural margins. Living near the border of every category of feeling and social identity, Menken subversively crossed over at will. Her poems explore the haunted relations between poetry and subjectivity, body and identity, women and society, hope and anger, and love and pain.

FURTHER READING

Daphne A. Brooks. "Lady Menken's Secret," in *Legacy* 15 (1998): 68–77.

Wolf Mankowitz. *Mazeppa: The Life, Loves and Legends of Adah Isaacs Menken*. New York: Stein and Day, 1982.

Adah Isaacs Menken. *Infelicia*, in *Collected Black Women's Poetry*, vol. 1. Ed. Joan R. Sherman. New York: Oxford University Press, 1988.

Myself

La patience est amère; mais le fruit en est doux![1]

1

Away down into the shadowy depths of the Real I once lived.
I thought that to seem was to be.
But the waters of Marah[2] were beautiful, yet they were bitter.
I waited, and hoped, and prayed;
Counting the heart-throbs and the tears that answered them.
Through my earnest pleadings for the True, I learned that the mildest mercy of life was
    a smiling sneer;
And that the business of the world was to lash with vengeance all who dared to be what
    their God had made them.
Smother back tears to the red blood of the heart!
Crush out things called souls!
No room for them here!

2

Now I gloss my pale face with laughter, and sail my voice on with the tide.
Decked in jewels and lace, I laugh beneath the gas-light's glare, and quaff the purple
    wine.
But the minor-keyed soul is standing naked and hungry upon one of Heaven's high hills
    of light.
Standing and waiting for the blood of the feast!
Starving for one poor word!
Waiting for God to launch out some beacon on the boundless shores of this Night.
Shivering for the uprising of some soft wing under which it may creep, lizard-like, to
    warmth and rest.
Waiting! Starving and shivering!

1. Patience is bitter; but the fruit of it is sweet (French).
2. After the Israelites crossed the Red Sea, they traveled for three days without water. When they came to Marah, they could not drink the water there because it was bitter. But God showed Moses a piece of wood that, when thrown into the water, made it sweet (Exodus 15:22–25).

3

Still I trim my white bosom with crimson roses; for none shall see the thorns.
I bind my aching brow with a jeweled crown, that none shall see the iron one beneath.
My silver-sandaled feet keep impatient time to the music, because I cannot be calm.
I laugh at earth's passion-fever of Love; yet I know that God is near to the soul on the
    hill, and hears the ceaseless ebb and flow of a hopeless love, through all my
    laughter.
But if I can cheat my heart with the old comfort, that love can be forgotten, is it not
    better?
After all, living is but to play a part!
The poorest worm would be a jewel-beaded snake if she could!

4

All this grandeur of glare and glitter has its night-time.
The pallid eyelids must shut out smiles and daylight.
Then I fold my cold hands, and look down at the restless rivers of a love that rushes
    through my life.
Unseen and unknown they tide on over black rocks and chasms of Death.
Oh, for one sweet word to bridge their terrible depths!
O jealous soul! why wilt thou crave and yearn for what thou canst not have?
And life is so long—so long.

5

With the daylight comes the business of living.
The prayers that I sent trembling up the golden thread of hope all come back to me.
I lock them close in my bosom, far under the velvet and roses of the world.
For I know that stronger than these torrents of passion is the soul that hath lifted itself
    up to the hill.
What care I for his careless laugh?
I do not sigh; but I know that God hears the life-blood dripping as I, too, laugh.
I would not be thought a foolish rose, that flaunts her red heart out to the sun.
Loving is not living!

6

Yet through all this I know that night will roll back from the still, gray plain of heaven,
    and that my triumph shall rise sweet with the dawn!
When these mortal mists shall unclothe the world, then shall I be known as I am!
When I dare be dead and buried behind a wall of wings, then shall he know me![3]

3. Compare Psalms 139:1–2: "Lord, you have examined me and you know me. / You know me at rest and
in action; you discern my thoughts from afar."

When this world shall fall, like some old ghost, wrapped in the black skirts of the wind,
    down into the fathomless eternity of fire, then shall souls uprise!
When God shall lift the frozen seal from struggling voices, then shall we speak!
When the purple-and-gold of our inner natures shall be lighted up in the Eternity of
    Truth, then will love be mine!
I can wait.

1868

Although Menken's title "Myself" resembles that of Walt Whitman's "Song of Myself,"
Whitman did not adopt his title until 1881. Menken may have influenced him, rather than
vice versa.

A Memory

I see her yet, that dark-eyed one,
Whose bounding heart God folded up
In His, as shuts when day is done,
Upon the elf the blossom's cup.
On many an hour like this we met,
And as my lips did fondly greet her,
I blessed her as love's amulet:
Earth hath no treasure, dearer, sweeter.

The stars that look upon the hill,
And beckon from their homes at night,
Are soft and beautiful, yet still
Not equal to her eyes of light.
They have the liquid glow of earth,
The sweetness of a summer even,
As if some Angel at their birth
Had dipped them in the hues of Heaven.

They may not seem to others sweet,
Nor radiant with the beams above,
When first their soft, sad glances meet
The eyes of those not born for love;
Yet when on me their tender beams
Are turned, beneath love's wide control,
Each soft, sad orb of beauty seems
To look through mine into my soul.

I see her now that dark-eyed one,
Whose bounding heart God folded up

In His, as shuts when day is done,
Upon the elf the blossom's cup.
Too late we met, the burning brain,
The aching heart alone can tell,
How filled our souls of death and pain
When came the last, sad word, *Farewell!*

1868

Menken initially composed this poem as an elegy for a young Native-American woman named "Laulerack, the dark-eyed one." It is unclear whether this woman and the love commemorated in the poem are real, invented, or a combination of the two.

Infelix

Where is the promise of my years;
Once written on my brow?
Ere errors, agonies and fears
Brought with them all that speaks in tears,
Ere I had sunk beneath my peers;
Where sleeps that promise now?

Naught lingers to redeem those hours,
Still, still to memory sweet!
The flowers that bloomed in sunny bowers
Are withered all; and Evil towers
Supreme above her sister powers
Of Sorrow and Deceit.

I look along the columned years,
And see Life's riven fane,[1]
Just where it fell, amid the jeers
Of scornful lips, whose mocking sneers,
For ever hiss within mine ears
To break the sleep of pain.

I can but own my life is vain
A desert void of peace;
I missed the goal I sought to gain,

1. Broken temple.

I missed the measure of the strain[2]
That lulls Fame's fever in the brain,
And bids Earth's tumult cease.

Myself! alas for theme so poor
A theme but rich in Fear;
I stand a wreck on Error's shore,
A spectre not within the door,
A houseless shadow evermore,
An exile lingering here.

1868

Menken wrote this poem while enduring a fatal illness that might have been cancer, tuber-
culosis, or peritonitis.

SARAH M. B. PIATT
1836–1919

SARAH M. B. PIATT received attention and praise in her own day but then passed
from memory for many decades. Rediscovered in the 1990s by scholars such as
Paula Bennett and Jessica Roberts, her witty and astringent poems shine as
brightly today as they did when first composed. Focusing on the ironies and im-
posed limitations of female experience, the poems often imply balked desire and
abandoned hopes. Alternately bitter, sad, angry, and self-mocking, Piatt's texts are
psychologically complicated and verbally subtle. They suggest overpowering so-
cial and metaphysical dramas in an often understated and deceptively casual way.
As in poems by Emily Dickinson, much more goes on in these poems than initially
meets the eye.

Born Sarah Morgan Bryan in 1836, the poet grew up on a plantation outside
of Lexington, Kentucky. Her family was wealthy and well established, and it in-
cluded, on her father's side, descendants of Daniel Boone. But when Bryan was
seven, her mother died, ending Bryan's years of security. She lived first with her
grandmother, then with her father and her new stepmother, and finally with her
aunt, Annie Boone, in New Castle, Kentucky. During these isolated and unsettled

2. Passage of music or poetry.

years, she found her consolation and her escape from loneliness in English poetry, especially in the work of Romantics such as William Blake, Walter Scott, Samuel Taylor Coleridge, Byron, and Percy Shelley. After graduating from Henry Female College in 1855, she began to publish her own poetry in newspapers, initially in Kentucky and then across the country.

In 1861, Bryan married John J. Piatt, an editor and writer, and soon to be a civil servant. By this time she was already a well-known poet. The couple moved to Washington, D.C., where John Piatt took a job in the Treasury Department. Although she was from a slave state, she sympathized with the Union cause and therefore felt torn by the war that fractured the nation. Moreover, her marriage brought its own share of pain, including the infant deaths of three of her seven children. Over the next twenty years, while living in Washington, D.C., and North Bend, Ohio, Sarah M. B. Piatt published numerous volumes of poetry. Her work also appeared in such notable journals as *The Atlantic Monthly* and *Harper's*.

Piatt's poems are marked by pain, disillusionment, and deep emotion. Often framed as conversations, they employ ironies and ellipses to produce a powerfully enigmatic quality, portraying a self and a nation riven by internal conflicts and lost hopes. The poems refuse to gloss or to mollify, as the popular poetry of the day typically did. For example, poems such as "Giving Back the Flower," "Shapes of a Soul," and "A Hundred Years Ago" suggest an unbridgeable gulf between the way a woman sees and feels and the way her male companion does. In "The Palace-Burner" a female speaker confronts her anger at class and gender inequality and her inability to act on it. Even the intensely private poem "Giving Back the Flower" alludes to broader social problems and catastrophes: impoverished "children crying for bread and fire" and men dying on the "ghastly field" of war. Other poems, such as "Her Blindness in Grief" and "We Two," suggest religious doubt or at least a continuing struggle with belief. And all of the poems, including the late "The Witch in the Glass," strongly challenge sentimental stereotypes of women, subverting the era's norms for women's poetry by constructing a female sensibility and a social landscape that are remarkably complicated and dissonant.

In 1882 John Piatt was named a U.S. consul, and the couple moved to Cork, Ireland. During the next decade, Sarah Piatt published many additional books of poems. Some of these poems reflected Irish settings and themes, whereas others looked back on her childhood in Kentucky. She also published numerous poems for children. Returning to Ohio in the mid-1890s, she published one last volume of poetry and then settled into retirement. When her husband died in 1917, she moved to the home of one of her sons. By the time of her death in 1919, her poetry had already been forgotten.

FURTHER READING

Paula Bernat Bennett. "'The Descent of the Angel': Interrogating Domestic Ideology in American Women's Poetry, 1858–1890," in *American Literary History* 7 (1995): 591–610.
———, ed. *Nineteenth-Century American Women Poets: An Anthology.* Pp. 234–62. Oxford, Eng.: Blackwell, 1998.
Sarah M. B. Piatt. *Palace Burner: The Selected Poetry of Sarah Piatt.* Ed. Paula Bernat Bennett. Champaign-Urbana: University of Illinois Press, 2001.
William C. Spengemann with Jessica F. Roberts, eds. *Nineteenth-Century American Poetry.* Pp. 397–412. New York: Penguin, 1996.

Giving Back the Flower

So, because you[1] chose to follow me into the subtle sadness of night,
    And to stand in the half-set moon with the weird fall-light on your glimmering hair,
Till your presence hid all of the earth and all of the sky from my sight,
    And to give me a little scarlet bud, that was dying of frost, to wear,

Say, must you taunt me forever, forever? You looked at my hand and you knew
    That I was the slave of the Ring,[2] while you were as free as the wind is free.
When I saw your corpse in your coffin,[3] I flung back your flower to you;
    It was all of yours that I ever had; you may keep it, and—keep from me.

Ah? so God is your witness. Has God, then, no world to look after but ours?
    May He not have been searching for that wild star, with trailing plumage, that flew
Far over a part of our darkness while we were there by the freezing flowers,
    Or else brightening some planet's luminous rings, instead of thinking of you?

Or, if He was near us at all, do you think that He would sit listening there
    Because you sang "Hear me, Norma,"[4] to a woman in jewels and lace,
While, so close to us, down in another street, in the wet, unlighted air,
    There were children crying for bread and fire, and mothers who questioned His
      grace?

Or perhaps He had gone to the ghastly field where the fight had been that day,
    To number the bloody stabs that were there, to look at and judge the dead;
Or else to the place full of fever and moans where the wretched wounded lay,
    At least I do not believe that He cares to remember a word that you said.

1. A male lover or would-be lover from the speaker's past.
2. The speaker's wedding ring.
3. He may have died fighting in the Civil War.
4. Allusion to Vincenzo Bellini's tragic opera *Norma* (1831), in which the native heroine carries on an affair with a Roman overlord.

*   *   *

So take back your flower, I tell you of its sweetness I now have no need;
   Yes, take back your flower down into the stillness and mystery to keep;
When you wake I will take it, and God, then, perhaps will witness indeed,
   But go, now, and tell Death he must watch you, and not let you walk in your sleep.

1867

Shapes of a Soul

White with the starlight folded in its wings,
   And nestling timidly against your love,
At this soft time of hushed and glimmering things,
   You[1] call my soul a dove, a snowy dove.

If I shall ask you in some shining hour,
   When bees and odors through the clear air pass,
You'll say my soul buds as a small flush'd flower,
   Far off, half hiding, in the old home-grass.

Ah, pretty names for pretty moods; and you,
   Who love me, such sweet shapes as these can see;
But, take it from its sphere of bloom and dew,
   And where will then your bird or blossom be?

Could you but see it, by life's torrid light,
   Crouch in its sands and glare with fire-red wrath,
My soul would seem a tiger,[2] fierce and bright
   Among the trembling passions in its path.

And, could you sometimes watch it coil and slide,
   And drag its colors through the dust a while,
And hiss its poison under-foot, and hide,
   My soul would seem a snake—ah, do not smile!

*   *   *

1. The female speaker's husband or lover.
2. Whereas he conceives of her soul as a dove or a flower, she conceives of it as a tiger or, later, a snake. This line may allude to William Blake's "The Tyger," which begins, "Tyger! Tyger! Burning bright / In the forests of the night, / What immortal hand or eye / Could frame thy fearful symmetry?"

Yet fiercer forms and viler it can wear;[3]
　　No matter, though, when these are of the Past, *what she dies*
If as a lamb in the Good Shepherd's care
　　By the still waters it lie down at last.[4]

1867

A Hundred Years Ago

You[1] wrong that lovely time to smile and say
　　Sharp desolation shivered in the snow,
And bright sands nursed bright serpents, as to-day,
　　A hundred years ago.

The world was full of dew and very fair,
　　Before I saw it scarr'd and blacken'd so;
There was wide beauty and flush'd silence there,
　　A hundred years ago.

No child's sweet grave, with rose-buds torn away
　　By the most bitter winds the falls can blow,
Before my tears in freezing loneness lay
　　A hundred years ago.

No phantom stars, one night in every Spring,
　　Saw my faint hands, with pallor wavering slow,
Give back the glimmering fragment of a ring,
　　A hundred years ago.

I did not feel this dim far-trembling doubt
　　Of Christ's love in the sky, or man's below,
And hold my heart to keep one Terror out,
　　A hundred years ago.

*　*　*

3. That is, her soul can wear forms even fiercer and viler than that of the snake. The snake image undoubtedly derives from the figure of Satan in the form of a snake in John Milton's epic poem *Paradise Lost*.
4. An allusion to Psalm 23:1–2: "The Lord . . . leadeth me beside the still waters." Piatt's conclusion may imply that the speaker will ultimately re-vert to feminine stereotypes of passivity and frailty or, conversely, that she will only appear in that guise in her husband's distorted memory after her death. It is also worth recalling Blake's last question addressed to the "tyger": "Did he who made the Lamb make thee?"
1. The speaker's husband or a friend.

The shadow Life may wither from the grass,
 Back to God's hand the unresting seas may flow;
But what shall take me where I dream I was
 A hundred years ago?

Ah, would I care to look beyond the shine
 Of this weird-setting moon, if I could know
The peace that made my nothingness divine
 A hundred years ago?

1870

The Palace-Burner

A *Picture in a Newspaper*[1]

She has been burning palaces. "To see
 The sparks look pretty in the wind?"[2] Well, yes
And something more. But women brave as she
 Leave much for cowards, such as I, to guess.

But this is old,[3] so old that everything
 Is ashes here — the woman and the rest.
Two years are oh! so long. Now you[4] may bring
 Some newer pictures. You like this one best?

You wish that you had lived in Paris then?
 You would have loved to burn a palace, too?
But they had guns in France, and Christian men
 Shot wicked little Communists,[5] like you.

You would have burned the palace? Just because
 You did not live in it yourself! Oh! why?
Have I not taught you to respect the laws?
 You would have burned the palace. Would not *I*?

✳   ✳   ✳

---

1. The newspaper illustration shows the execution of a female member of the revolutionary Paris Commune. The Commune, composed of urban workers, staged an insurrection March 18 to May 28, 1871, against an iniquitous and pro-monarchical French regime. About twenty thousand men, women, and children were killed by government troops in the bloody week that ended the revolt.

2. The quoted question is posed by a child, presumably the speaker's son, who is looking at the picture with her.
3. That is, the newspaper is now a year out of date.
4. The "you" here and below is the child.
5. The Communards, sometimes referred to as communists, were actually various sorts of socialists and anarchists.

Would I? Go to your play.[6] Would I, indeed?
   I? Does the boy not know my soul to be
Languid and worldly, with a dainty need
   For light and music? Yet he questions me.

Can he have seen my soul more near than I?
   Ah! in the dusk and distance sweet she[7] seems,
With lips to kiss away a baby's cry,
   Hands fit for flowers, and eyes for tears and dreams.

Can he have seen my soul? And could she wear
   Such utter life upon a dying face,
Such unappealing, beautiful despair,
   Such garments — soon to be a shroud — with grace?

Has she a charm so calm that it could breathe
   In damp, low places till some frightened hour;
Then start, like a fair, subtle snake, and wreathe
   A stinging poison with a shadowy power?

Would *I* burn palaces? The child has seen
   In this fierce creature of the Commune here,
So bright with bitterness and so serene,
   A being finer than my soul, I fear.

                                  1872

Her Blindness in Grief

What if my soul is left to me?
Oh! sweeter than my soul was he.[1]
   Its breast broods on a coffin lid;
Its empty eyes stare at the dust,
   Tears follow tears, for treasure hid
Forevermore from moth and rust.[2]

The sky a shadow is; how much
I long for something I can touch!

6. At this point the child leaves, and the speaker is alone with her thoughts.
7. The "she" here and below is the speaker's soul.
1. The infant son who has just died.
2. That is, death has removed the infant from the world of decay and dissolution. Compare these lines from the Christian New Testament: "Lay not up for yourselves treasures upon earth, where moth and rust doth corrupt, and where thieves break through and steal; but lay up for yourselves treasures in heaven" (Matthew 6:19–20).

God is a silence: could I hear
Him whisper once, "Poor child," to me!
   God is a dream, a hope, a fear,
A vision—that the seraphs[3] see.

"Woman, why weepest thou?" One said,
To His own mother, from the dead.[4]
   If He should come to mock me now,
Here in my utter loneliness,
   And say to me, "Why weepest thou?"
I wonder would I weep the less.

Or, could I, through these endless tears,
Look high into the lovely spheres
   And see him there my little child—
Nursed tenderly at Mary's breast,
   Would not my sorrow be as wild?
Christ help me. Who shall say the rest?

There is no comfort anywhere.
My baby's clothes, my baby's hair,
   My baby's grave are all I know.
What could have hurt my baby? Why,
   Why did he come; why did he go?
And shall I have him by and by?

Poor grave of mine, so strange, so small,
You cover all, you cover all!
   The flush of every flower, the dew,
The bird's old song, the heart's old trust,
   The star's fair light, the darkness, too,
Are hidden in your heavy dust.

Oh! but to kiss his little feet,[5]
And say to them, "So sweet, so sweet,"
   I would give up whatever pain
(What else is there to give, I say?)
   This wide world holds. Again, again,
I yearn to follow him away.

---

3. Angels.
4. According to John 20:15, Christ said this to
Mary after his death and resurrection.

5. That is, the feet of her dead child.

＊　＊　＊

My cry is but a human cry.
Who grieves for angels? Do they die?
   Oh! precious hands, as still as snows,
How your white fingers hold my heart!
   Yet keep your buried buds of rose,
Though earth and Heaven are far apart.

The grief is bitter. Let me be.
He lies beneath that lonesome tree.
   I've heard the fierce rain beating there.
Night covers it with cold moonshine.
   Despair can only be despair.
God has his will. I have not mine.

            1873

This poem of mourning may evoke Piatt's anguished feelings following the death of one of her children.

We Two

God's will is—the bud of the rose for your hair,[1]
   The ring for your hand and the pearl for your breast;
God's will is—the mirror that makes you look fair.
   No wonder you whisper: "God's will is the best."

But what if God's will were the famine, the flood?
   And were God's will the coffin shut down in your face?
And were God's will the worm in the fold of the bud,
   Instead of the picture, the light, and the lace?

Were God's will the arrow that flieth by night,
   Were God's will the pestilence walking by day,[2]
The clod in the valley, the rock on the height[3]—
   I fancy "God's will" would be harder to say.

1. The first stanza addresses a privileged and fortunate female acquaintance, whereas the second evokes a subject in a very different position, the speaker's own.
2. An inversion of Psalm 91:5–6: "Thou shalt not be afraid for the terror by night; nor for the arrow that flieth by day; nor for the pestilence that walketh in darkness; nor for the destruction that wasteth at noonday."
3. This mysterious line may refer to "the clods" and "the rock" of the Book of Job (21:33, 18:4), both of which are associated with the wicked. Or it may evoke William Blake's "The Clod and the Pebble," in which both title characters have limited (and mutually exclusive) conceptions of love.

*   *   *

God's will is your own will. What honor have you
 For having your own will, awake or asleep?
Who praises the lily for keeping the dew,
 When the dew is so sweet for the lily to keep?

God's will unto me is not music or wine.
 With helpless reproaching, with desolate tears
God's will I resist, for God's will is divine;
 And I shall be dust to the end of my years.

God's will is not mine. Yet one night I shall lie
 Very still at his feet, where the stars may not shine.
"Lo! I am well pleased"[4] I shall hear from the sky;
 Because—it is God's will I do, and not mine.

1874

The Witch in the Glass

"My mother says I must not pass
Too near that glass;[1]
She is afraid that I will see
A little witch that looks like me,
With a red, red mouth to whisper low
The very thing I should not know!"

"Alack for all your mother's care!
A bird of the air,
A wistful wind, or (I suppose
Sent by some hapless boy) a rose,
With breath too sweet, will whisper low
The very thing you should not know!"

1889

---

4. In the Christian scripture, God says at Jesus'
baptism, "This is my beloved Son, in who I am
well pleased" (Matthew 3:17).

1. Mirror.

LYDIA KAMAKAEHA
[QUEEN LILI'UOKALANI]
1838–1917

Hawai'i's last queen, Lydia Kamakaeha (Queen Lili'Uokalani), holds an important position in Hawai'ian poetry and culture because she composed over 160 poetic melodies and chants, including one of the four Hawai'ian national anthems, and helped preserve indigenous history and culture through native chants known as meles. Several of her songs remain internationally popular today; and her work in native lyrics has influenced many later poets as well as songwriters from all cultures interested in preserving and revising native Hawai'ian poetry and music for contemporary audiences. She wrote songs in both her native Hawai'ian language and English in order to reach a very wide audience.

Hawai'i had been an independent kingdom since 1795 and an American protectorate since 1851. Queen Lili'Uokalani succeeded her brother King Kalakaua in 1891, taking over a throne already damaged by royal scandals and weakened by Western economic dominance of the islands. She was deposed in 1893 in a bloodless coup led by nine Americans and four Europeans and backed by the United States Marines. In 1894 Sanford Dole, owner of Dole pineapple company, became president of a Hawai'ian republic controlled by American business interests.

Many of Lydia Kamakaeha's poems were written before she became queen. The first and third lyrics included here reveal Kamakaeha's skill at interweaving songs of romance with tales of political intrigue. "Aloha `Oe," or "Farewell to Thee," is her most famous song today. She composed it during a visit in 1878 to the European-American Edwin Boyd's Oahu ranch, known as Maunawili, which is named in the song. According to legend, she wrote it after watching Colonel James Boyd receive a lei made of the Hawaiian state flower, the lehua, from a young native girl on the ranch just as her riding party prepared to leave on horseback to return to Honolulu. Some scholars believe that the references to rain and wetness here and in other Hawai'ian poems and songs symbolize love. In her lyrics, Kamakaeha suggests a poignant romance that crosses races and cultures as the lovers embrace fondly in their parting. The third lyric tells the story of a romance in the Hawai'ian royal court between one of the queen's attendants, Sanoe, and an unnamed man, relying again upon references to the lehua, rain, and wetness. Princess Likelike in the poem is Kamakaeha's sister.

The second selection, "Ku'u Pua I Paoa-ka-lani," or "My Flower at Paoa-ka-lani," was written after the coup that deposed her. Combining dramatic romance and high-powered politics, it tells the story of Kamakaeha's house arrest in 1895 when she was accused of plotting to regain her throne. During her detainment Kamakaeha was forbidden information from the outside world. However, a future mayor of Honolulu smuggled newspapers to Kamakaeha by wrapping them around flowers sent to her by her husband from their garden in Waikiki. Following release from house arrest in 1896, she took her plea for reinstatement personally to President Grover Cleveland. But in 1898, the United States formally annexed Hawai'i. The deposed queen continued to write poetry and subsequently published her own book about Hawai'i.

FURTHER READING

Helena G. Allen. *The Betrayal of Liliuokalani: The Last Queen of Hawaii, 1838–1917*. Honolulu: Mutual Publishing, 1982.

Samuel H. Elbert and Noelani Manhoe, eds. *Na Mele o Hawai'i Nei: 101 Hawaiian Songs*. Honolulu: University of Hawaii Press, 1970.

Aloha 'Oe

Ha`aheo ka ua i nä pali
Ke nihi a`e la i ka nahele
E hahai ana paha i ka liko
Pua `ähihi lehua o uka

HUI

Aloha `oe, aloha `oe
E ke onaona noho i ka lipo
One fond embrace, a ho`i a`e au
Until we meet again

`O ka hali`a aloha i hiki mai
Ke hone a`e nei i ku`u manawa
`O `oe nö ka`u ipo aloha
A loko e hana nei

Maopopo ku`u `ike i ka nani
Nä pua rose o Maunawili
I laila hia`ia nä manu
Miki`ala i ka nani o ka lipo

1878

[TRANS.] Farewell to Thee

Proudly swept the rain by the cliffs
As it glided through the trees
Still following ever the bud
The `ahihi lehua[1] of the vale

CHORUS

Farewell to you, farewell to you
The charming one who dwells in the shaded bowers
One fond embrace, 'ere I depart
Until we meet again

Sweet memories come back to me
Bringing fresh remembrances of the past
Dearest one, yes, you are mine own
From you, true love shall never depart

I have seen and watched your loveliness
The sweet rose of Maunawili
And 'tis there the birds of love dwell
And sip the honey from your lips

Ku`u Pua I Paoa-ka-lani

E ka gentle breeze e waft mai nei
Ho`oh.li`ali`a mai ana ia`u
`O ku`u sweet never fading flower
I bloom i ka uka o Paoa-ka-lani.

HUI

`Ike mau i ka nani o n_ pua
I uka o Ulu-hai-malama.
`A `ole na`e ho`i e like
Me ku`u pua la`i o Paoa-ka-lani.

I,ahilahi kona mau hi`ona
With softest eyes as black as jet,
Pink cheeks so delicate of hue
I ulu i ka uka o Paoa-ka-lani.

---

1. The `ahihi lehua is a kind of low-spreading bush once numerous on Oahu.

＊   ＊   ＊

Nanea `ia mai ana ku`u aloha.
E ka gentle breeze e waft mai nei,
O come to me ka`u mea li`a nei
I ulu i ka uka o Paoa-ka-lani.

ca. 1895

[TRANS.] My Flower at Paoa-ka-lani

O gentle breeze waft hither
And remind me
Of my sweet never fading flower
That has bloomed in the depths of Paoa-ka-lani.

CHORUS

See forever the beauty of the flowers
Inland at Ulu-hai-malama.
None the equal
Of my gentle flower of Paoa-ka-lani.

Dainty face
With softest eyes as black as jet,
Pink cheeks so delicate of hue
Growing in the depths of Paoa-ka-lani.

My love delights.
O gentle breeze, waft hither,
O come to me my beloved
Growing in the depths of Paoa-ka-lani.

Sanoe

'Auhea 'oe e Sanoe
Ho'opulu liko ka lehua
Eia ho'i au
Ke kali nei i ko leo

`O ka pane wale mai no
`Olu wau mehe wai 'ala
Honehone me he ipo ala
Paila i ka nui kino

* * *

E kala neia kino
I piliwi ai i laila
Pehea e hiki ai
E ko ai o ka mana'o

Ke hea mai nei water lily
Ke ao mai `oe ia kaua
Eia a'e no o pelo
Manu `aha'i 'olelo

Lohe aku nei na kuhina nui
A he 'ahahui ko Loma
Ke 'oni a'e la iluna
E like me Likelike

n.d.

[TRANS.] Sanoe

Where can you be, Sanoe?
Moistened by the lehua buds
Here I am
Waiting to hear your voice

For the answer only you can give
Refreshing with a sweet perfume
Appealing softly as a sweetheart
Stirring the whole body

It's been a while since this body
Believed all that was there
How is it possible
To fulfill thoughts of love?

The water lily warns us
Be careful
Here comes the carrier of tales
The bird who gossips

The titled persons have heard
Of a gathering in Rome
Moving now upward
Like the Princess Likelike

INA COOLBRITH
1841–1928

ALTHOUGH INA COOLBRITH was an intriguing and beloved literary figure in her own day, she has yet to receive much attention in ours. Because she lived and wrote in California at a time when most important writers lived in, or migrated to, the East Coast, she has often been thought of as merely a regional poet. Moreover, she wrote poems with a wide variety of moods and tones in a period when women writers were expected to be either uplifting or melancholic. But Coolbrith's poetry deserves new attention now. Her landscape and nature poems contain sensuous descriptions and imaginative comparisons foreshadowing such twentieth-century poets as Robert Frost and the imagist group. Her public poems demonstrate considerable complexity of thought and breadth of sympathy. And her signature poems about women break new ground in their expressions of love, yearning, pride, and celebration.

Ina Donna Coolbrith was born Josephine Donna Smith, the niece of Joseph Smith, who founded the Church of Jesus Christ of the Latter Day Saints. Coolbrith, however, chose to devote her life to poetry rather than religion. At the age of ten, she traveled by wagon train with her mother, stepfather, and three siblings to California, led over the Sierra Nevada by the famed African-American scout, James Beckwourth. After attending school in Los Angeles, she married at the age of seventeen, suffered abuse, and divorced within three years. She had already begun to publish poetry under the name of Ina Donna Coolbrith, adopting her mother's maiden name. She moved to San Francisco to ward off debilitating depression and soon became a member of a literary group that also included Ambrose Bierce, Bret Harte, Joaquin Miller, Mark Twain, and, for a brief time, Adah Menken (also included in this anthology).

From the 1870s through the 1890s, Ina Coolbrith worked as a librarian to support a family that included her mother, a niece and nephew, and a young half-Indian girl who was left on her doorstep. In 1873 she was named chief librarian of the Oakland Free Public Library, and she later served as head of the San Francisco Mercantile Library and the Bohemian Club Library. A major force in the Bay Area literary scene, she published her poetry in local, national, and international magazines. Her first major volume, *Songs from the Golden Gate*, appeared in 1895. It included "The Mariposa Lily," one of a series of poems evoking the beauty of the California environment. Also in the collection was "The Captive of the White City," which brings to light the cruelty and exploitation that Native Americans confronted at the turn of the century. Finally, the volume contained poems of love for women, such as "The Sea-Shell" and "Sailed," which are remarkable for their depth of feeling and their vivid physical imagery. Coolbrith's subsequent poetry—at least that portion of it not destroyed in the San Francisco earthquake and fire of 1906—appeared posthumously. California's first poet laureate, Ina Coolbrith played a formative role in the cultural history of her place and time.

FURTHER READING

Frances Laurence. *Maverick Women: 19th Century Women Who Kicked Over the Traces.* Carpinteria, Calif.: Manifest, 1998.
Josephine DeWitt Rhodehamel and Raymund Wood. *Ina Coolbrith: Librarian and Laureate of California.* Provo, Utah: Brigham Young University Press, 1973.

The Mariposa Lily

Insect or blossom?[1] Fragile, fairy thing,
Poised upon slender tip, and quivering
   To flight! A flower of the fields of air;
   A jeweled moth; a butterfly, with rare
And tender tints upon his downy wing
   A moment resting in our happy sight;
   A flower held captive by a thread so slight
Its petal-wings of broidered gossamer[2]
Are, light as the wind, with every wind astir—
   Wafting sweet odor, faint and exquisite.
O dainty nursling of the field and sky,
   What fairer thing looks up to heaven's blue
   And drinks the noontide sun, the dawning's dew?
Thou wingëd bloom! thou blossom-butterfly!

         1885

The mariposa lily (or *Calochortus*) has bowl-shaped flowers with red or pale pink patterns and blotches. This delicate California native, which blooms in late spring and summer, "grows in shaded, often rocky, places in woods and canyons" (Philip Munz, *California Spring Wildflowers*).

1. This opening question commences the poem's sustained comparison of the flower to beings apparently quite dissimilar—flying creatures. This poetic practice looks backward to seventeenth-century metaphysical poetry and forward to the imagism of Hilda Doolittle and William Carlos Williams.
2. Embroidered gauze or a fine, filmy cobweb.

The Sea-Shell

"And love will stay, a summer's day!"
    A long wave rippled up the strand,
She flashed a white hand through the spray
    And plucked a sea-shell from the sand;
And laughed—"O doubting heart, have peace!
    When faith of mine shall fail to thee
This fond, remembering shell will cease
    To sing its love, the sea."

Ah well, sweet summer's past and gone—
    And love, perchance, shuns wintry weather—
And so the pretty dears are flown
    On lightsome, careless wings together.
I smile: this little pearly-lined,
    Pink-veinëd shell she gave to me,
With foolish, faithful lips to find
    Still sing its love, the sea.[1]

          1895

The Captive of the White City

Flower of the foam of the waves
    Of the beautiful inland sea—
White as the foam that laves
    The ships of the Sea-kings past—
    Marvel of human hands,
    Wonderful, mystical, vast,
        The great White City[1] stands;
And the banners of all the lands
Are free on the western breeze,
    Free as the West is free.
And the throngs go up and down
In the streets of the wonderful town

1. That is, the lonely speaker ruefully smiles to find the seashell still singing of love, whereas the speaker's own beloved has abandoned her.

1. The "White City" was another name for the World's Columbian Exposition, held in Chicago in 1893. The name refers to the fair's white plaster facades and electrical lighting, but, as used in this poem, it also has a relevant racial significance. Despite its ambiguities, the poem reveals a surprising identification between its speaker and a Native-American man, and it expresses feelings of universal forgiveness that were unusual in an age marked by lingering hatreds.

In brotherly love and grace —
Children of every zone
The light of the sun has known:
  And there in the Midway Place,[2]
  In the House of the Unhewn Trees,
There in the surging crowd,
Silent, and stern, and proud,
  Sits Rain-in-the-Face![3]

Why is the captive here?
Is the hour of the Lord so near
When slayer and slain shall meet
In the place of the Judgment seat
  For the word of the last decree?
  Ah, what is that word to be?
For the beautiful City stands
On the Red Man's wrested lands,[4]
  The home of a fated race;
And a ghostly shadow falls
Over the trophied walls[5]
  Of the House of the Unhewn Tree,
  In the pleasant Midway Place.
There is blood on the broken door,
There is blood on the broken floor,
Blood on your bronzed hands,[6]
  O Rain-in-the-Face!

  Shut from the sunlit air,
Like a sun-god overthrown,
  The soldier, Custer, lies.
Dust is the sun-kissed hair,
  Dust are the dauntless eyes,
Dust and a name alone —

2. The Midway Plaisance was the crowded section of the fair dedicated to commercial and popular attractions.

3. The legendary Sioux warrior, who fought to preserve Indian lands under the command of Sitting Bull, appeared in defeat as one of the fair's exhibits. According to Coolbrith, this man who was "immortalized by the verse of Longfellow and whose name will go down in history as the slayer of General George A. Custer, in the fight on the Little Big Horn" was displayed "in the log cabin owned by Sitting Bull, and in which that chief and his son were killed." The poem terms the cabin "the House of the Unhewn Tree."

4. According to Coolbrith's note, "the Indians claim that the land upon which Chicago is built was never fully paid for."

5. According to Coolbrith, the walls of the cabin in which Rain-in-the-Face was confined "were hung with relics of the fight."

6. This line may be interpreted as accusation, lamentation, or both.

While the wife holds watch with grief
For the never-returning chief.
What if she walked today
In the City's pleasant way,
    The beautiful Midway Place,
    And there to her sudden gaze,
Dimmed with her widow's tears,
After the terrible years,
Stood Rain-in-the-Face!

Quench with a drop of dew
From the morning's cloudless blue
    The prairies' burning plains—
    The seas of seething flame;
Turn from its awful path
The tempest, in its wrath;
    Lure from his jungle-lair
    The tiger, crouching there
For the leap on his sighted prey:
    Then seek as well to tame
The hate in the Red Man's veins,
    His tiger-thirst to cool,
In the hour of the evil day
When his foe before him stands!
    From the wrongs of the White Man's rule
    Blood only may wash the trace.
    Alas, for the death-heaped plain!
    Alas, for slayer and slain!
    Alas for your blood-stained hands,
        O Rain-in-the-Face!

And the throngs go up, go down,
In the streets of the wonderful town;
And jests of the merry tongue,
And the dance, and the glad songs sung,
    Ring through the sunlit space.
And there, in the wild, free breeze,
In the House of the Unhewn Trees,
    In the beautiful Midway Place,
        The captive sits apart,
        Silent, and makes no sign.

But what is the word in your heart,
O man of a dying race?
What tale on your lips for mine,
   O Rain-in-the-Face?

                              1895

Sailed

O shining, sapphire sea!
From thy bosom put away
Every vexing thought today;
Smile through all thy dimpling spray:
   All that earth contains for me,
   Of love, and truth, and purity
      Trust I unto thee!

O foam-flecked azure sea!
Let thy calm, untroubled waves,
   By the softest gales caressed,
Rise and fall like love-beats in
   Her timid maiden breast;
Let thy dreamiest melodies
   Cradle her to rest.

O wild, white, mystic sea!
Let thy strong upholding arm
   Tender as a lover's be;
Let no breath of rude alarm
   Mar her heart's tranquillity;
Through the sunshine, past the storm,
Bear her safe from every harm,
   Once again to me!

                              1895

Woman

What were this human
World without woman?
Think—just a minute!—
Without one in it—

A Man-Eden only,
Wretched and lonely.
True, there's a story
Scarce to her glory
Therewith connected,
But 'tis suspected
Man, after all,
Was quite ready to fall!¹
If fault, he condoned it—
And through the years since,
Even has atoned it.

Woman! Be honor
Ever upon her,
Whether as maiden,
Shy, beauty-laden—
Daughter, wife, sister,
Who can resist her?
Or as that other
And great, the Mother,
Her babe—blossoms moulding
To perfect unfolding—
To home-temple guarding
To richest rewarding.

Though none be purer,
Sweeter and surer,
Avenues wider
Now open beside her.
Each day some new way!
God send the true way
She may seek ever
With earnest endeavor.
Here to the dark, a light!
Here to the wrong, the right!
There the truth sifting!
A soul, here, uplifting!
Patient, prevailing,
With purpose unfailing,

1. A reference to Adam and Eve's fall from grace and expulsion from the Garden of Eden. See Genesis 3 and John Milton's epic poem *Paradise Lost*.

Till at Life's portal
Through Love immortal,
Supremely she stands,
The *World* in her hands.

Woman! All honor
And blessing upon her!
Knowing her truly,
Knowing her fully,
All her completeness,
Tenderness, sweetness—
Though there be times, too,
Sweet hardly rhymes to,
All of the changes
Through which she ranges,
Moods, tenses, phases,
I sing her praises.

1929

SIDNEY LANIER
1842–1881

SIDNEY LANIER, a European-American poet, musician, critic, and novelist, experimented with writing poetry on the principles of music or the physics of sounds, including such elements as color, tone, and contrast. This work has proven to be his major contribution to nineteenth-century American poetry and to many later European-American poets. Born in Georgia, Lanier graduated from Oglethorpe College in 1860 and joined the Confederate army. He was captured and contracted tuberculosis in the poor living conditions of prison camp, an illness that ultimately led to his death at the age of thirty-nine. After the war, Lanier married Mary Day and fathered four children. He initially worked in his father's law office in Georgia, then moved to Texas and later to Baltimore, where he became the first flutist in the Peabody Orchestra and a professor at Johns Hopkins University. The following poem, "The Marshes of Glynn," which depicts a sea-marsh scene near Brunswick, Georgia, is based on Lanier's theory of poetry as the music of language.

FURTHER READING

Jack De Bellis. *Sidney Lanier*. New York: Twayne, 1972.
Sidney Lanier. *Poems of Sidney Lanier*. Ed. Mary Lanier. Athens: University of Georgia Press,
    1981.

The Marshes of Glynn

Glooms of the live-oaks, beautiful-braided and woven
With intricate shades of the vines that myriad-cloven
    Clamber the forks of the multiform boughs,—
        Emerald twilights,—
        Virginal shy lights,
Wrought of the leaves to allure to the whisper of vows,
When lovers pace timidly down through the green colonnades
    Of the dim sweet woods, of the dear dark woods,
        Of the heavenly woods and glades,
That run to the radiant marginal sand-beach within
    The wide sea-marshes of Glynn;—

Beautiful glooms, soft dusks in the noon-day fire,—
Wildwood privacies, closets of lone desire,
Chamber from chamber parted with wavering arras of leaves,—
Cells for the passionate pleasure of prayer to the soul that grieves,
    Pure with a sense of the passing of saints through the wood,
    Cool for the dutiful weighing of ill with good;—

O braided dusks of the oak and woven shades of the vine,
While the riotous noon-day sun of the June-day long did shine
Ye held me fast in your heart and I held you fast in mine;
    But now when the noon is no more, and riot is rest,
    And the sun is a-wait at the ponderous gate of the West,
        And the slant yellow beam down the wood-aisle doth seem
        Like a lane into heaven that leads from a dream,—
Ay, now, when my soul all day hath drunken the soul of the oak,
And my heart is at ease from men, and the wearisome sound of the stroke
    Of the scythe of time and the trowel of trade is low,
    And belief overmasters doubt, and I know that I know,
    And my spirit is grown to a lordly great compass within,
        That the length and the breadth and the sweep of the marshes of Glynn
        Will work me no fear like the fear they have wrought me of yore
            When length was fatigue, and when breadth was but bitterness sore,

And when terror and shrinking and dreary unnamable pain
Drew over me out of the merciless miles of the plain,—
    Oh, now, unafraid, I am fain to face
      The vast sweet visage of space.
   To the edge of the wood I am drawn, I am drawn,
Where the gray beach glimmering runs, as a belt of the dawn,
      For a mete and a mark
      To the forest-dark:—
        So:
    Affable live-oak, leaning low,—
Thus—with your favor—soft, with a reverent hand,
(Not lightly touching your person, Lord of the land!)
Bending your beauty aside, with a step I stand
      On the firm-packed sand,
        Free
   By a world of marsh that borders a world of sea.
  Sinuous southward and sinuous northward the shimmering band
 Of the sand-beach fastens the fringe of the marsh to the folds of the land.
Inward and outward to northward and southward the beach-lines linger and curl
As a silver-wrought garment that clings to and follows the firm sweet limbs of a girl.
  Vanishing, swerving, evermore curving again into sight,
  Softly the sand-beach wavers away to a dim gray looping of light.
  And what if behind me to westward the wall of the woods stands high?
  The world lies east: how ample, the marsh and the sea and the sky!
  A league and a league of marsh-grass, waist-high, broad in the blade,
  Green, and all of a height, and unflecked with a light or a shade,
     Stretch leisurely off, in a pleasant plain,
     To the terminal blue of the main.

   Oh, what is abroad in the marsh and the terminal sea?
     Somehow my soul seems suddenly free
  From the weighing of fate and the sad discussion of sin,
   By the length and the breadth and the sweep of the marshes of Glynn.
Ye marshes, how candid and simple and nothing-withholding and free
Ye publish yourselves to the sky and offer yourselves to the sea!
Tolerant plains, that suffer the sea and the rains and the sun,
Ye spread and span like the catholic man who hath mightily won
  God out of knowledge and good out of infinite pain
  And sight out of blindness and purity out of a stain.

As the marsh-hen secretly builds on the watery sod,
Behold I will build me a nest on the greatness of God:

I will fly in the greatness of God as the marsh-hen flies
In the freedom that fills all the space 'twixt the marsh and the skies:
By so many roots as the marsh-grass sends in the sod
I will heartily lay me a-hold on the greatness of God:
Oh, like to the greatness of God is the greatness within
The range of the marshes, the liberal marshes of Glynn.

And the sea lends large, as the marsh: lo, out of his plenty the sea
Pours fast: full soon the time of the flood-tide must be:
Look how the grace of the sea doth go
About and about through the intricate channels that flow
Here and there,
Everywhere,
Till his waters have flooded the uttermost creeks and the low-lying lanes,
And the marsh is meshed with a million veins,
That like as with rosy and silvery essences flow
In the rose-and-silver evening glow.
Farewell, my lord Sun!
The creeks overflow: a thousand rivulets run
'Twixt the roots of the sod; the blades of the marsh-grass stir;
Passeth a hurrying sound of wings that westward whirr;
Passeth, and all is still; and the currents cease to run;
And the sea and the marsh are one.

How still the plains of the waters be!
The tide is in his ecstasy.
The tide is at his highest height:
And it is night.

And now from the Vast of the Lord will the waters of sleep
Roll in on the souls of men,
But who will reveal to our waking ken
The forms that swim and the shapes that creep
Under the waters of sleep?
And I would I could know what swimmeth below when the tide comes in
On the length and the breadth of the marvellous marshes of Glynn.

1878

EMMA LAZARUS
1849–1887

IN EMMA LAZARUS'S OWN day, her poetry received wide recognition and high acclaim. Her poem "The New Colossus" was enshrined on the Statue of Liberty. But over the years, her work gradually slipped from its position of cultural prominence, and Lazarus is now primarily remembered for that one iconic poem. Nevertheless, she wrote a wide variety of poems, some taking up the cause of groups lacking social prestige, such as workers, Jews, women, and refugees, and others more private, meditating on the natural environment and the power of art and spirit.

Emma Lazarus was born in 1849 to a bourgeois Jewish family that had resided in the United States since the eighteenth century. Thus, the poet who would become identified with the perspectives of immigrants and the poor was neither an immigrant nor poor. She simply empathized with the less fortunate around her. Lazarus and her two sisters, daughters of a New York sugar merchant and his wife, grew up in sheltered and comfortable surroundings. The girls had little formal education or religious training, but they did have private tutors. In her teens, Lazarus learned German, French, and Italian. She read widely in Shakespeare and in such nineteenth-century poets as Keats, Shelley, Tennyson, Emerson, and Longfellow. A prodigy, she published her first volume of poems and translations at the age of eighteen. She sent a copy to the aging Emerson, who became a kind and encouraging friend and correspondent.

Lazarus, who never married, continued to write poetry, fiction, drama, and essays for the rest of her life. When she became aware of the genocidal attacks against Jews that commenced in Russia in 1879, she began to explore and assert her Jewish identity. She organized relief work for oppressed European Jews and advocated the establishment of Israel as their homeland. She wrote articles on Jewish topics for magazines, and she wrote poems on Jewish themes. Influenced by the British reformer William Morris, she also concerned herself with underprivileged groups in the United States, such as immigrants, laborers, and the urban poor. Yet there was a Romantic strain in her work as well. She wrote feelingly about the natural scene, the spiritual transcendence Emerson had invited her to experience in nature, the beauty of art and philosophy, and the importance of creativity. In 1884, when Lazarus was only thirty-five, she fell ill with cancer. The following year she took an extended tour of Europe, immersing herself in the music, theater, and art that she loved. She returned to the United States in 1887, where she died at the age of thirty-eight.

Lazarus originally wrote "The New Colossus" in 1883 to support the construction of a pedestal for the Statue of Liberty, a gift from France. In 1886 the poem was recited at the statue's dedication, and in 1903 it was inscribed on the pedestal, where it may still be read today. The poem single-handedly transformed the monument's significance from the intended commemoration of the American Revolution to a celebration of immigration. It helped reconfigure the United States as a "nation of immigrants," as John F. Kennedy was later to term it. Borrowing the theme of the promised land from Exodus, the poem installs a relatively new ideology, one that idealizes both immigrants and the nation to which they have come. The poem, viewed both aesthetically and in terms of its iconic status, evokes a complex response today. It transmits a long-standing notion of American exceptionalism but one stripped of nativist, racial, and class privilege. Repressing the economic difficulties and ethnic prejudice most poor immigrants actually faced, "The New Colossus" re-creates the United States as a multiethnic haven. The poem imposes this pleasing myth in hopes of ameliorating a rather troubled social reality and replacing a dysfunctional myth of social homogeneity. In addition, it highlights the gender difference between the male Colossus of Rhodes and the female Statue of Liberty, "mild" yet "mighty." The poem thus inscribes the United States as female and protective, in contrast to an implicitly male and aggressive Europe. Paradoxically, this radical social vision appears within a quite traditional European form: a Petrarchan sonnet employing iambic pentameter, elevated tone, and conventional syntactical inversions ("cries she"). One might say that this poem uses a traditional form to achieve new ends and thus articulates a fresh national and poetic identity.

Other poems by Lazarus make similar interventions in the public life of the country. "1492," written in a similarly oratorical style, also idealizes the New World as being devoid of racial, religious, and class barriers. "The South," though primarily a narrative of romantic loss and survival, pointedly makes its resilient protagonist a Creole, a woman with an ambiguous ethnic background. "In Exile" sympathetically evokes the relief experienced by Russian Jews newly arrived in Texas. Other, more personal poems concern the perception of nature and the value of the imagination. "Long Island Sound" and "Echoes" discover aesthetic potential in the natural scene and in a woman's poetic voice. "The Cranes of Ibycus" and "Venus of the Louvre" suggest the richness of art, while implying the suffering of the artist. Although Lazarus's public and personal poems differ in tone, they equally reflect a thoughtful and assertive woman poet consciously adapting a medium historically reserved for men.

Traditional in some ways and rebellious in others, Lazarus's poetry remains a paradox. It manifests a wish for social change and a disinclination to confront the "dismal here and now" ("City Visions"), a defense of difference and a commitment to assimilation, an eagerness to enter the public arena and a yearning for contemplative solitude. Vibrating with such contradictions, the poems speak eloquently of their time and pertinently to our own.

FURTHER READING

Jules Chametzky, John Felstiner, Hilene Flanzbaum, and Kathryn Hellerstein, eds. *Jewish American Literature: A Norton Anthology*. New York: Norton, 2001.
Emma Lazarus. *Poems*. 2 vols. New York: Houghton Mifflin, 1889.
Diane Lichtenstein. *Writing Their Nations: The Tradition of Nineteenth-Century American Jewish Women Writers*. Bloomington: Indiana University Press, 1992.
Ranen Omer-Sherman. *Diaspora and Zionism in Jewish American Literature: Lazarus, Syrkin, Reznikoff, and Roth*. Hanover, N.H.: University Press of New England, 2002.
Bette Roth Young, ed. *Emma Lazarus in Her World: Life and Letters*. New York: Jewish Publication Society, 1997.
Dan Vogel. *Emma Lazarus*. Boston: Twayne, 1980.

Long Island Sound

I see it as it looked one afternoon
In August — by a fresh soft breeze o'erblown.
The swiftness of the tide, the light thereon,
A far-off sail, white as a crescent moon.
The shining waters with pale currents strewn,
The quiet fishing-smacks,[1] the Eastern cove,
The semi-circle of its dark, green grove.
The luminous grasses, and the merry sun
In the grave sky; the sparkle far and wide,
Laughter of unseen children, cheerful chirp
Of crickets, and low lisp of rippling tide,
Light summer clouds fantastical as sleep
Changing unnoted while I gazed thereon.
All these fair sounds and sights I made my own.

1869

This poem may be Lazarus's poetic response to advice she received from Ralph Waldo Emerson (included in this anthology), who wrote to her, "The high success must ever be to penetrate unto and show the celestial element in the despised Present, & detect the deity that still challenges you under all the gross & vulgar masks."

---

1. Fishing vessels that have a well for keeping the catch alive.

The Cranes of Ibycus

There was a man who watched the river flow
Past the huge town, one gray November day.
Round him in narrow high-piled streets at play
The boys made merry as they saw him go,
Murmuring half-loud, with eyes upon the stream,
The immortal screed[1] he held within his hand.
For he was walking in an April land
With Faust and Helen. Shadowy as a dream
Was the prose-world, the river and the town.
Wild joy possessed him; through enchanted skies
He saw the cranes of Ibycus[2] swoop down.
He closed the page, he lifted up his eyes,
Lo — a black line of birds in wavering thread
Bore him the greetings of the deathless dead!

1877

The South

Night, and beneath star-blazoned summer skies
    Behold the Spirit of the musky South,
A Creole[1] with still-burning, languid eyes,
    Voluptuous limbs and incense-breathing mouth:
        Swathed in spun gauze is she,
From fibres of her own anana tree.

Within these sumptuous woods she lies at ease,
    By rich night-breezes, dewy cool, caressed:
'Twixt cypresses and slim palmetto trees,
    Like to the golden oriole's hanging nest,
        Her airy hammock swings,
And through the dark her mocking-bird yet sings.

1. Long discourse; here, apparently Johann von Goethe's verse drama *Faust* (1823).
2. In Greek legend, a poet named Ibycus was attacked by robbers near Corinth, and as he lay dying he called to a flock of cranes to avenge his murder. Later, when one of the robbers saw cranes flying overhead he exclaimed that they were Ibycus's avengers, thus unmasking himself and his friends as the murderers. In Lazarus's poem, the cranes become symbolic of poetic immortality.

1. This wealthy, beautiful, and grief-stricken Creole woman is of ambiguous ancestry. She might well be of French or Spanish descent. But the exoticized imagery ("like some half-savage, dusky Indian queen") suggests that she may possess some Native-American, African, or Jewish inheritance as well.

* * *

How beautiful she is! A tulip-wreath
   Twines round her shadowy, free-floating hair:
Young, weary, passionate, and sad as death,
   Dark visions haunt for her the vacant air,
     While movelessly she lies
With lithe, lax, folded hands and heavy eyes.

Full well knows she how wide and fair extend
   Her groves bright-flowered, her tangled everglades,
Majestic streams that indolently wend
   Through lush savanna or dense forest shades,
     Where the brown buzzard flies
To broad bayous 'neath hazy-golden skies.

Hers is the savage splendor of the swamp,
   With pomp of scarlet and of purple bloom,
Where blow warm, furtive breezes faint and damp,
   Strange insects whir, and stalking bitterns boom —
     Where from stale waters dead
Oft looms the great-jawed alligator's head.

Her wealth, her beauty, and the blight on these —
   Of all she is aware: luxuriant woods,
Fresh, living, sunlit, in her dream she sees;
   And ever midst those verdant solitudes
     The soldier's wooden cross,[2]
O'ergrown by creeping tendrils and rank moss.

Was hers a dream of empire? Was it sin?
   And is it well that all was borne in vain?
She knows no more than one who slow doth win,
   After fierce fever, conscious life again,
     Too tired, too weak, too sad,
By the new light to be or[3] stirred or glad.

From rich sea-islands fringing her green shore,
   From broad plantations where swart[4] freemen bend
Bronzed backs in willing labor, from her store

---

2. This soldier may have been her beloved, and his death the "blight" referred to above.

3. Either.

4. Swarthy, dark colored.

Of golden fruit, from stream, from town, ascend
    Life-currents of pure health:
Her aims shall be subserved with boundless wealth.

Yet now how listless and how still she lies,
    Like some half-savage, dusky Indian queen,
Rocked in her hammock 'neath her native skies,
    With the pathetic, passive, broken mien[5]
        Of one who, sorely proved,[6]
Great-souled, hath suffered much and much hath loved!

But look! Along the wide-branched, dewy glade
    Glimmers the dawn: the light palmetto-trees
And cypresses reissue from the shade,
    And she hath wakened. Through clear air she sees
        The pledge, the brightening ray,
And leaps from dreams to hail the coming day.

                            1878

Echoes

Late-born and woman-souled I dare not hope,
The freshness of the elder lays,[1] the might
Of manly, modern passion shall alight
Upon my Muse's lips, nor may I cope
(Who veiled and screened by womanhood must grope)
With the world's strong-armed warriors and recite
The dangers, wounds, and triumphs of the fight;
Twanging the full-stringed lyre through all its scope.
But if thou ever in some lake-floored cave
O'erbrowed by rocks, a wild voice wooed and heard,
Answering at once from heaven and earth and wave,
Lending elf-music to thy harshest word,
Misprize[2] thou not these echoes that belong
To one in love with solitude and song.

                            1880

5. Appearance.
6. Tested.

1. Older poems or songs.
2. Scorn.

City Visions

1

As the blind Milton's[1] memory of light,
The deaf Beethoven's[2] phantasy of tone,
Wrought joys for them surpassing all things known
In our restricted sphere of sound and sight—
So while the glaring streets of brick and stone
Vex with heat, noise, and dust from morn till night,
I will give rein to Fancy, taking flight
From dismal now and here, and dwell alone
With new-enfranchised senses. All day long,
Think ye 't is I, who sit 'twixt darkened walls,
While ye chase beauty over land and sea?
Uplift on wings of some rare poet's song,
Where the wide billow laughs and leaps and falls,
I soar cloud-high, free as the winds are free.

2

Who grasps the substance? Who 'mid shadows strays?
He who within some dark-bright wood reclines,
'Twixt sleep and waking, where the needled pines
Have cushioned all his couch with soft brown sprays?
He notes not how the living water shines,
Trembling along the cliff, a flickering haze,
Brimming a wine-bright pool, nor lifts his gaze
To read the ancient wonders and the signs.
Does he possess the actual, or do I,
Who paint on air more than his sense receives,
The glittering pine-tufts with closed eyes behold,
Breathe the strong resinous perfume, see the sky
Quiver like azure flame between the leaves,
And open unseen gates with key of gold?[3]

1881

1. Blind English poet John Milton (1608–1674), author of *Paradise Lost.*
2. German composer Ludwig van Beethoven (1770–1827) who became deaf in mid-career.
3. Lazarus here revives a trope of nature as imaginative resource for the city-bound poet that goes back at least to William Wordsworth and John Keats.

In Exile

Since that day till now our life is one unbroken paradise.
We live a true brotherly life. Every evening after supper
we take a seat under the mighty oak and sing our songs.

EXTRACT FROM A LETTER
OF A RUSSIAN REFUGEE IN TEXAS[1]

Twilight is here, soft breezes bow the grass,
  Day's sounds of various toil break slowly off,
The yoke-freed oxen low, the patient ass
  Dips his dry nostril in the cool, deep trough.
Up from the prairie the tanned herdsmen pass
  With frothy pails, guiding with voices rough
Their udder-lightened kine.[2] Fresh smells of earth,
The rich, black furrows of the glebe[3] send forth.

After the Southern day of heavy toil,
  How good to lie, with limbs relaxed, brows bare
To evening's fan, and watch the smoke-wreaths coil
  Up from one's pipe-stem through the rayless air.
So deem these unused tillers of the soil,
  Who stretched beneath the shadowing oak-tree, stare
Peacefully on the star-unfolding skies,
And name their life unbroken paradise.

The hounded stag that has escaped the pack,
  And pants at ease within a thick-leaved dell;
The unimprisoned bird that finds the track
  Through sun-bathed space, to where his fellows dwell;
The martyr, granted respite from the rack,
  The death-doomed victim pardoned from his cell,
Such only know the joy these exiles gain,
Life's sharpest rapture is surcease of pain.

Strange faces theirs, wherethrough the Orient[4] sun
  Gleams from the eyes and glows athwart the skin.

---

1. This letter appeared in the *Jewish Messenger* (April 28, 1882). Michael Heilprin (1823–1888), who was active in aiding Jewish refugees from the Russian pogroms, showed it to Lazarus.
2. Poetic term for cattle.
3. Field. Dan Vogel observes that the poem's opening section resembles Thomas Gray's "Elegy Written in a Country Churchyard" (1751), which begins: "The curfew tolls the knell of parting day, / The lowing herd wind slowly o'er the lea, / The ploughman homeward plods his weary way, / And leaves the world to darkness and to me."
4. Eastern; a reference to Jewish origins in the Middle East.

Grave lines of studious thought and purpose run
    From curl-crowned forehead to dark-bearded chin.
And over all the seal is stamped thereon
    Of anguish branded by a world of sin,
In fire and blood through ages on their name,
Their seal of glory and the Gentiles' shame.

Freedom to love the law that Moses brought,
    To sing the songs of David, and to think
The thoughts Gabirol[5] to Spinoza taught,
    Freedom to dig the common earth, to drink
The universal air—for this they sought
    Refuge o'er wave and continent, to link
Egypt with Texas in their mystic chain,
And truth's perpetual lamp forbid to wane.

Hark! through the quiet evening air, their song
    Floats forth with wild sweet rhythm and glad refrain.
They sing the conquest of the spirit strong,
    The soul that wrests the victory from pain;
The noble joys of manhood that belong
    To comrades and to brothers. In their strain[6]
Rustle of palms and Eastern streams one hears,
And the broad prairie melts in mist of tears.

                    1882

The New Colossus

Not like the brazen giant of Greek fame,
    With conquering limbs astride from land to land;[1]
Here at our sea-washed, sunset gates shall stand
    A mighty woman with a torch, whose flame
Is the imprisoned lightning, and her name
    Mother of Exiles. From her beacon-hand
Glows world-wide welcome; her mild eyes command

---

5. Solomon Ibn Gabirol (ca. 1022–1070) was a Jewish-Spanish philosopher and poet. Baruch Spinoza (1632–1677) was a Jewish-Dutch philosopher.
6. Song. "Strain" may also mean an ancestral line.
1. The Colossus of Rhodes was a gigantic statue of the Greek god Helios erected at the harbor of the island of Rhodes in 280 B.C.E. to celebrate a military victory. In contrast to the warlike colossus of old, the "new" colossus, the Statue of Liberty in New York Harbor, symbolizes American freedom and also, in Lazarus's reinterpretation, America's "open door" to the world's homeless.

The air-bridged harbor that twin cities[2] frame.
"Keep, ancient lands, your storied pomp!" cries she
With silent lips. "Give me your tired, your poor,
Your huddled masses yearning to breathe free,
The wretched refuse of your teeming shore.
Send these, the homeless, tempest-tost to me,
I lift my lamp beside the golden door!"

1883

Composed in 1883 to aid the Pedestal Fund, this sonnet was inscribed on the base of the Statue of Liberty in 1903. The statue, designed by the French sculptor Frédéric Bartholdi (1834–1904), was formally dedicated in 1886 and became a national monument in 1924.

1492

Thou two-faced year,[1] Mother of Change and Fate,
Didst weep when Spain cast forth with flaming sword,
The children of the prophets of the Lord,
Prince, priest, and people, spurned by zealot hate.
Hounded from sea to sea, from state to state,
The West refused them, and the East abhorred.
No anchorage the known world could afford,
Close-locked was every port, barred every gate.
Then smiling, thou unveil'dst, O two-faced year,
A virgin world where doors of sunset part,
Saying, "Ho, all who weary, enter here!
There falls each ancient barrier that the art
Of race or creed or rank devised, to rear
Grim bulwarked hatred between heart and heart!"

1883

Venus of the Louvre

Down the long hall she glistens like a star,
The foam-born mother of Love, transfixed to stone,
Yet none the less immortal, breathing on.

2. That is, New York City's boroughs of Manhattan and Brooklyn.
1. The year 1492 was "two-faced" in that it witnessed both the Inquisition's banishment of Jews from Spain and Christopher Columbus's discovery of the New World.

Time's brutal hand hath maimed but could not mar.
When first the enthralled enchantress from afar
Dazzled mine eyes, I saw not her alone,
Serenely poised on her world-worshipped throne,
As when she guided once her dove-drawn car—
But at her feet a pale, death-stricken Jew,[1]
Her life adorer, sobbed farewell to love.
Here *Heine* wept! Here still he weeps anew,
Nor ever shall his shadow lift or move,
While mourns one ardent heart, one poet-brain,
For vanished Hellas and Hebraic pain.

1884

The classical statue of Venus, the Roman goddess of love and beauty, is one of the most notable artworks on display in the Louvre Museum in Paris. Its arms have been lost over time (line 4), but the statue is otherwise preserved. Lazarus first saw the Venus during a visit to Paris in 1883. Dying of cancer in 1887, she made one last visit, as her sister later recalled, "to the feet of the Venus, 'the goddess without arms, who could not help.'"

SARAH ORNE JEWETT
1849–1909

SARAH ORNE JEWETT IS best known for fiction that offers subtle observations of nineteenth-century New England, but she also wrote poems throughout her life. Like her stories and her novel *The Country of the Pointed Firs*, Jewett's poems comment frequently on the enclosed domestic lives of women. Born in 1849 to a distinguished physician, Dr. Theodore Herman Jewett, and his wife, Caroline Frances (Perry) Jewett, Sarah Orne Jewett was a fragile and delicate child. She grew up in South Berwick, Maine—the basis for "Deephaven" in her stories—and as she was often ill and her schooling was disrupted, she educated herself through observing her father's medical practice and reading the volumes in his library.

She wrote her first story under the pseudonym "Alice C. Eliot" while in her late teens, and it was printed in the young persons' magazine, *Riverside*. In 1869,

1. Heinrich Heine (1797–1856), a German poet who, like Lazarus, asserted his Jewish identity in midlife. Dying of cancer, Heine—like Lazarus after him—made a final pilgrimage to view the Venus.

she began publishing a series of stories about her native locality in *The Atlantic Monthly*, later collected as *Deephaven* (1877).

In 1878, Jewett's father died. Though his death was a traumatic event in her life, Sarah kept writing. She never married, though she became a lifelong companion to Annie Adams Fields, and the two traveled frequently together as Jewett continued her career. In 1901, Jewett fell from a carriage and suffered spinal injuries from which she never recovered. She died in 1909 in her hometown of South Berwick, Maine.

FURTHER READING

Sarah Orne Jewett. *The Complete Poems*. Forest Hills, N.Y.: Ironweed Press, 1999.

A Caged Bird

High at the window in her cage
   The old canary flits and sings,
Nor sees across the curtain pass
   The shadow of a swallow's wings.

A poor deceit and copy, this,
   Of larger lives that mark their span,
Unreckoning of wider worlds
   Or gifts that Heaven keeps for man.

She gathers piteous bits and shreds,
   This solitary, mateless thing,
To patient build again the nest
   So rudely scattered spring by spring;

And sings her brief, unlistened songs,
   Her dreams of bird life wild and free,
Yet never beats her prison bars
   At sound of song from bush or tree.

But in my busiest hours I pause,
   Held by a sense of urgent speech,
Bewildered by that spark-like soul,
   Able my very soul to reach.

She will be heard; she chirps me loud,
   When I forget those gravest cares,
Her small provision to supply,
   Clear water or her seedsman's wares.

*   *   *

She begs me now for that chief joy
    The round great world is made to grow, —
Her wisp of greenness. Hear her chide,
    Because my answering thought is slow!

What can my life seem like to her?
    A dull, unpunctual service to mine;
Stupid before her eager call,
    Her flitting steps, her insight fine.

To open wide thy prison door,
    Poor friend, would give thee to thy foes;
And yet a plaintive note I hear,
    As if to tell how slowly goes

The time of thy long prisoning.
    Bird! does some promise keep thee sane?
Will there be better days for thee?
    Will thy soul too know life again?

Ah, none of us have more than this:
    If one true friend green leaves can reach
From out some fairer, wider place,
    And understand our wistful speech!

                n.d.

ALBERY ALLSON WHITMAN
1851–1901

ALBERY ALLSON WHITMAN devoted his work to proving that African-American poets could write a poetry of social protest in standard English employing such major European genres as the epic. He published *The Rape of Florida: Or Twasinta's Seminoles*, composed in four cantos, in 1884 and *An Idyl of the South*, an epic in two parts, in 1901. He gained his greatest popularity when he read his poem "World's Fair Poem" at the Chicago World's Fair in 1893. Although his poetic legacy has been acknowledged by African Americans, especially his appropriation and subversion of European-American literary traditions as a way of signifying his "double culture" as an African American, he has rarely been anthologized. His inclusion here, then, in the canon of American poetry retrieves a neglected but vital African-American poet who addressed his work and his life to the concerns of African Americans, European Americans, Native Americans (especially the Seminoles in Florida), Latino/as, and Asian Americans (especially Filipinos).

Born into slavery in Kentucky, Whitman was freed by the Emancipation Proclamation but faced life alone as an orphan because both parents died during his childhood. In 1870 he entered Wilberforce University and later became a teacher, a minister of the African Methodist Episcopal Church, and general financial agent of Wilberforce University. He published his first collection of poetry, *Not a Man; and Yet a Man*, in 1877 to raise money for the university, dedicating it to "the abolition fathers" and other persons interested in the plight of the newly freed African Americans. Shortly before his death, he signed an antiwar petition by the American Anti-Imperialist League addressed to President William McKinley that condemned the Spanish-American War against the Filipinos as a war of conquest and colonialism.

The abridged selection presented here, entitled "The Octoroon," is the first part of the epic poem *An Idyl of the South*, and it is generally regarded as some of his strongest work. It reveals not only Whitman's talents in the epic form but also his interest in using a poetics of sentimentality to reach as many readers as possible with his representation of slave life. Especially noteworthy is his creation of an African-American slave heroine in the European-American literary tradition of saintly maiden figures, like Beth March in *Little Women*. He thus introduces his readers to the idea that such heroines can be found in all races and classes. The poem tells the tragic love story of a slavemaster's young son, Sheldon Maury, and his mother's servant Lena. Sheldon's father sells Lena, in spite of agonized protests from his wife, because his son refuses to relinquish his love for her. This plot reveals Whitman's perception of the complex family dynamics of many slaveholding plantations. Lena learns immediately that her new owner is crude, cruel, and sexually abusive. Her daring escape from him is enabled by one of the new master's elderly slaves, Andy, who shows her how to reach freedom and then lies to his master about not being able to find her. Lena dies, but not before she and Sheldon are briefly reunited. Lena's death transforms the Maury plantation world into a more compassionate place, and she is remembered for her saintliness.

FURTHER READING

James Robert Payne. "Albery Allson Whitman," in *Encyclopedia of American Poetry: The Nineteenth Century*. Ed. Eric L. Haralson. Chicago: Fitzroy Dearborn, 1998.
Albery Allson Whitman. *An Idyl of the South*. Upper Saddle River, N.J.: Literature House, 1970.
www.hti.umich.edu/english/amverse (website of the American Verse Project, a University of Michigan Humanities Text Initiative).

FROM *The Octoroon*

1

Hail! land of the palmetto and the pine,
From Blue Ridge Mountain down to Mexic's sea:
Sweet with magnolia and cape jessamine,
And thrilled with song,—thou art the land for me!
I envy not the proud old Florentine
The classic beauties of his Italy;
Give me but here to have my glory dream,
'Mid fragrant woods and fields—by lake and stream.

8

And I must tell you of this Octoroon,
    This blue-eyed slave, what sounds like a romance:
Her master was a fair young man, and soon
    The proudest soul that Love, in seeming chance,
Had led beneath the full round Southern moon,
    To coax sweet eyes to give him glance for glance;
And with her happy speech and sparkling wit
His fair slave charmed his soul—and captured it.

10

Her name was Lena. She was but a child
    In all save beauty; but she was a slave.
In far Unyoro's wastes, Obokko's wild,
    Or by the blue N'yanza's boatless wave,[1]
Where hearts by worldly greed were undefiled,
    'Mid Afric's groves some sweet ancestress gave
The strain of life which now still rushed along,
To warm her soul and break in tides of song.

20

Young Maury loved his slave—she was his own;
    A gift, for all he questioned, from the skies.
No other fortune had he ever known,
    Like that which sparkled in her wild blue eyes.

---

1. References to geographical locations in Africa.

Her seal-brown locks and cheeks like roses blown,
   Were wealth to him that e'en the gods might prize.
And when her slender waist to him he drew,
The sum of every earthly bliss he knew.

21

They had grown up together,—he and she—
   A world unto themselves. All else was bare,—
A desert to them and an unknown sea.
   Their lives were like the birds' lives—free and fair,
And flowed together like a melody.
   They could not live apart, Ah! silly pair!
But since she was his slave, what need to say,
A swarm of troubles soon beset their way?

22

Just in the dawn of blushing womanhood;
   Her swan-neck glimpsed through shocks of wavy hair;
A hint of olives in her gentle blood,
   Suggesting passion in a rosy lair;
This shapely Venus of the cabins stood,
   In all but birth a princess, tall and fair;
And is it any wonder that this brave
And proud young master came to love his slave?

26

And Maury clasped her, waving like a spray;
   He stroked her locks; he tossed them—let them fall;
And saw the scattered moonbeams flash away,
   Like silver arrows from a golden wall.
And there were whispers then like elves at play,
   And through the leaves the winds began to crawl;
When Lena listening, heard her heart's quick beat,
And startled, thought she heard approaching feet.

30

As homeward with his maid young Maury went,
   His father shortly met him in the way,
And asked abruptly—what such conduct meant;
   But would not hear what Sheldon had to say.

His heart was fixed and on prompt action bent;
   He threatened in his ire to bring dismay
To son and slave — "to drive from home the pair;"
But Sheldon smiled to see him "beat the air."

   34

Infatuation. But it would not do.
   "A shame!" his father cried, and then looked grave.
"The girl was good and pretty, that he knew;
   But Sheldon must remember — was his slave."
Into a rage, the young man straightway flew;
   Against "Society" began to rave;
Withdrew and walked alone or stood morose,
As if the world for him held only foes.

   35

Refusing food, he scarcely spoke a word,
   But he would talk with Lena when he could;
And from his room upstairs, he seldom stirred.
   "The truth was clear," his mother understood.
"My boy will lose his mind," she oft was heard
   To whisper. "Nay, don't cross him in his mood."
And then she'd say to Lena: "You may go
And tell your dear young master" so and so.

   36

And Lena went, — to his dear arms she flew.
   A gust of joy, — a thousand nothings said;
Heard all he told her, — told him all she knew,
   And like a burst of sunshine round him played.
Ah! she was helpless, but her heart was true;
   And woman's heart when true, with earth arrayed
Against her, conquers all, and ever will.
The gods are with a loving woman still.

   46

But to our story let us now return:
   Young Maury grew more moody every day,
And his proud mother thought she could discern
   His mind "beginning, plainly, to give way."

But "Wait," his father urged; "I'll have him learn
    That I can check him in his childish play.
I'll sell the girl and straightway let her go;
But till she's gone, I will not let him know."

48

The mother shook her head and sadly smiled;
    And said, "I have not anything to say."
But vowed: "I never will be reconciled,
    Will not agree to send the girl away.
She is my slave and nothing but a child;
    And she has done no crime; say what we may."
And as she spoke, the mists came in her eyes
Like hints of rain which fill blue summer skies.

66

At early morn the old plantation stirred,
    And toil went humming in its usual way,
While heart-born shouts in all directions heard,
    Were earnest signals of a busy day.
Then Maury's father with a friend conferred;
    And calling up a house boy, turned to say,
With nimble speech and glibbest unconcern:
"Bring out the wagon. Quick! Let's see you turn."

76

But times were stormy on the old plantation.
    Ill news on eager wings had spread uproar:
The Negroes raised a mighty lamentation,
    And went about the outrage to deplore.
"Lena was sold!" Ah! now was tribulation,
    And Grief began a rain of tears to pour.
The master watched the storm that he had made;
But trusted that it soon would be allayed.

78

Of their "ole Massa," who had made the sale.
    Well, such is life. We oft lose sight of cause,
And o'er effect set up a noisy wail;
    Too oft oppose the gathering stream by laws;

When at the source wise actions should prevail.
    But Lena's master made of proud stuff was;
He vowed—the act if wrong, was his own doing,—
His way was his, and of his own pursuing.

81

With tears, his mother stayed him in the door;
    He kissed her, passed, and at a single bound,
Into his saddle sprang. "By Heaven," he swore,
    "I'll bring her back!" and wheeling short around,
His roweled heels against his horse he bore,
    That forward sprang, and, flying, spurned the ground.
And through the dark, these words, impassioned, clear,
"I'll bring her back," fell on the listener's ear.

82

And on, right onward toward the hills he shot;
    On, on, and on; till, miles and miles away,
He drew his reins upon an abrupt spot,
    Where rocks and fallen trees around him lay;
And o'er him rose a cliff,—an inky blot
    On outer darkness; when he heard the play
Of angry waters seething far below;
And, scorning danger, could no farther go.

85

And to his joy he found an open door;
    For man and beast the cotter soon found rest,—
And then he took his baby from the floor,
    And tossed him high and held him on his breast.
And said, "Now, stranger, we be mighty poor;
    But you are welcome to our little nest;"
And then there was no heed to outside din,—
For only peace and sunshine reigned within.

87

The morning came with not a cloud in view,
    And Maury was again upon his way.
The birds were everywhere in brilliant hue,
    And thrilled the forests through the livelong day

With hours of vain pursuit he weary grew,
    To chagrin and conflicting fears a prey.
But Hanks with Lena, as the sun went down,
Had reached the outskirts of a country town.

92

Embarrassing with exclamations strange
    And interjections meek, his gentle guest;
But Hanks withdrew his feelings from the range
    Of these sweet motives in the old man's breast;
And spurning e'en a kind word to exchange,
    The old spouse in the doorway thus addressed:
"This here's your master's niggah house-gal, aunty;
She'll stop till after supper in your shanty."

98

I shall not say how long and late she heard
    A fiddle snoring an old cabin tune;
A banjo's "plunk, plunk, plunk," unskilled and weird;
    And thumping heels that shuffled off "Zip Coon;"
But night crept by and tardy morn appeared,
    A brilliant dawning in a Southern June.
And that were better, for I could not bear
To tell of Lena's grief,—nor you to hear.

101

Word from the "great house" came—a master's call—
    He wanted Lena, and she must obey.
"He wanted to talk with her,—that was all,"
    The old slave said, and meekly led the way
Through wide grounds, up great steps and through a hall
    To where the master's wont was most to stay
At night; a room with sideboard, cups and—well
You know the rest, and so I need not tell.

102

He filled a glass, held it before his eyes,
    Then drank, and handed his old slave a drink;
Who took the glass and bowed beseechingly,
    But durst not once of a refusal think.

But Lena did refuse, and with a sigh
   Which showed her near revolt's abruptest brink.
And when her dark old friend had turned to go,
She, too, rose up. Then cried her master, "No."

103

"I have a word with you, and you're to wait;
   I must acquaint you with your proper station.
At Colonel Maury's, I right here may state,
   You had your own way; but on this plantation
I rule, and every nigger must walk straight
   Or I will bring him to the situation.
But, at the same time, you need have no fear,
If you will but obey me — do you hear?"

107

"A man could love a girl like you; in fact,
   I wouldn't hardly be ashamed to have
It said that I like you." And in the act
   Of patting now the fair cheek of his slave,
He moved, but she avoided him with tact
   As sweetly proper as 'twas truly brave;
And faced him straight, when he, half smiling, said:
"Tut, tut, you silly thing; are you afraid?"

108

She frowned. He was amazed — he could not speak.
   A storm was brewing in his baffled mind;
The blood-like liquid flame rushed to his cheek,
   And clouds of gath'ring wrath had made him blind.
He seized her hand and pressed, but he was weak,
   And in his desperation would be kind;
And so he paused and hesitating stood;
But, at the bottom, fury filled his blood.

109

But words were lost, now aimed at Lena's ear;
   Her master coaxed — she drew her hand away.
She heard him talking, yet she did not hear;
   Her soul was loathing all he had to say.

The object of his craven heart was clear;
 And, though she was his slave, she spurned him—yea!
She turned upon her heel as if to go;
But, with a husky growl, he muttered, "No."

111

She wheeled, then sprang, and threw the arm from her;
 And from her splendid shoulders tossed her hair.
She turned upon him, pointing, spoke out: "Sir,
 Begone from me." Superb in her despair,
She stood so firmly that he feared to stir.
 But now she reeled—she sank upon a chair—
And with her hands upon her downcast eyes,
With greatest effort she restrained her cries.

112

The "Major" moved to lift her from her seat;
 She felt his touch that half an appeal meant;
She threw his hands off, bounded to her feet,
 And through the doorway like an arrow went.
Ah! then her master's wrath was at "white heat."
 To her receding ears this threat he sent:
"I'll make you know!" and followed where she flew,
Declaring in his rage what he would do.

113

But on she went—on to the cabin sped.
 The aged inmates met her at the door;
She brushed them by. "Good Lawd!" the old man said,
 And followed her across the creaking floor
To where she threw herself upon a bed;
 When his old spouse began to thus deplore:
"I knowed it, Andy, I'se don' tole you so;
Ole Massa's drunk—ef dat ain't like him—sho!"

114

There Lena rested but a breathing spell;
 Upon her closely came pursuing fate;
Her master's footsteps on the threshold fell,
 And in his speech she heard hoarse anger grate.

The beast would seize his prey—she knew it well;
　The instant was supreme—she must not wait—
She rose, she sprang, she faced him as before;
Threw him aside and darted from the door.

118

"Here, Missy! dis way, Missy! come along."
　The speaker was old Andy, Lena's friend,
Who, like an apparition, there among
　The shadows rose. At first fright served to lend
Wings to her speed; but, like a thrush's song,
　The old man's words did with such coaxing blend,
That Lena's heart beat free—her fears were gone—
She grasped the offered hand and hurried on.

121

"Here we must stop." He breathed, and opening wide
　His patient eyes with satisfaction clear,
He stepped ashore with Lena at his side.
　They paused,—the old man turned a list'ning ear,
While his dark features Lena closely eyed.
　There was no sound of any danger near.
"He thinks I'se come to find and bring you back!"
Said Lena's guide, "but he's clean off de track."

126

And looking up devoutly as he went—
　(So the Apostles gazed from Judah's hill,
Whence their Redeemer had made His ascent
　To Heaven)—he prayed: "De Lawd be with her still!"
To him it all divine occurrence meant.
　And so, with secret joy, he ran on, till
He reached his cabin and his master met,
Who shouted: "Andy, haven't you found her yet?"

127

The old man grinned and bowed low with a groan,
　Which told the fruitlessness of his pursuit
And his deep chagrin in a single tone—
　Which meant: "My greatest efforts bore no fruit!"

He said: "I dunno whar she iz. I'se done!"
   And then he shook his head and stood as mute
As death and looked to see his master rave.
Ah! Who could read the thoughts of that old slave?

130

Earth hath one spot on which none may intrude,
   And not invite the certain frowns of Heaven;
There loving hearts with light divine imbued,
   Clasp erring ones, and there are sins forgiven.
That spot is home, however poor and rude —
   The holiest shrine at which one may be shriven —
And Lena came upon this sacred spot,
Where Maury erst found shelter in a cot.

131

She entered, sore and wan — she could not speak.
   The housewife took her hand and said: "How do?"
Long hours of ceaseless flight had made her weak;
   And in her eyes the mists now dimmed the blue.
She sadly smiled, she bowed divinely meek;
   And followed where her hostess tiptoed through
An inner doorway till she reached a bed,
Where Lena sank to rest her drooping head.

135

But now the stillness of this touching scene
   Was broken by the sounds of flying feet.
Young Maury had arrived, who late had been
   Urging his foam-flecked steed through dust and heat;
O'er barren hills and through the valleys green;
   Till here directed to this wild retreat,
Where he at night had once been tempest bound,
The tender object of his search he found.

136

He knew the wife, who quickly did admit:
   Then Lena's soul, that had already heard
The summons that would bid her spirit flit,
   The moment of departure now deferred;

And while a glow of recognition lit
    Her sad blue eyes, she rose, she gasped a word;
And as young Maury hastened to her side,
She clasped his hand, then sank back satisfied.

139

The day of reckoning came. With bearing fine
    O'er Lena's corpse stood Sheldon, now of age.
And to his father said: "Give me what's mine,
    And I'll get out, and for myself engage
In business; but I'll never beg nor whine,
    If I go empty handed. At no stage
In Life's uncertain game will I return;
I ask of Fortune naught but what I earn!"

140

"To Lena I've been partial. I have been
    No master merely, but I've been her friend.
God is my judge, I've known her not in sin,
    And I'm proud of her; proud that to the end
I've dared to stand, with all the power within
    My heart and arm, her honor to defend.
For her, my faithful playmate, pretty slave,
My love and friendship shall survive the grave!"

141

"In childhood once I saw a mouser spring
    Upon a poor canary in its cage.
I heard its tiny plea, saw desperate wing
    Resist in vain the monster's cruel rage;
And I were guilty of a meaner thing,
    Had harm befallen Lena's tender age —
And she my slave, I should, to say the least,
Now own myself a wretch — a human beast!"

142

His father answered: "Son, you are a Maury;
    We've suffered no dishonor at your hands.
I have not understood you, and I'm sorry;
    Hence, I shall not now yield to your demands.

You're brave and true, now don't be in a hurry;
   For there are other days, and he who stands
At parting of the ways, should calmly wait
Till Wisdom makes the path of duty straight."

148

No useless drapings of a funeral
   Like shadows hung round Lena's resting place;
There was no mourning — no loud grief, nor pall —
   But tender glories of day's ending race,
Did o'er earth like celestial curtains fall;
   And Heav'n was lovely as a maiden's face;
While humble negroes sang a low refrain —
A burst of hope, with undertones of pain.

1901

EDWIN MARKHAM
1852–1940

Edwin markham is best known as a poet and lecturer who protested the unjust conditions of workers at the turn of the twentieth century. His most noted poem, "The Man with the Hoe," inspired by Jean-François Millet's painting of the same name, made the depicted French peasant a universal symbol of exploited labor. After composing "The Man with the Hoe," Markham spent the rest of his life as a venerated public figure, writing poems marked by their mysticism and their social conscience.

Markham grew up in a central California valley, raised with his siblings by his rancher-mother. After graduating from college, he worked as a teacher and school administrator. After several failed marriages, he married Anna Murphy in 1898, with whom he had one child. In 1899 he published "The Man with the Hoe" in the *San Francisco Examiner*. The poem was reprinted thousands of times in his lifetime, in newspapers across the world. It made Markham famous among poetry readers and also among laborers, subsistence farmers, and those sympathetic to their plight. Although his traditional poetic forms and style soon began to seem dated in contrast to the innovative work of Gertrude Stein, Ezra Pound, and William Carlos Williams, Markham retained his position as an honored public figure. He suffered a debilitating stroke in 1936, his wife died in 1938, and Markham himself died at home in New York City early in 1940.

FURTHER READING

Paul J. Ferlazzo. "Edwin Markham," in *Encyclopedia of American Poetry: The Nineteenth Century.* Ed. Eric L. Haralson. Pp. 181–83. Chicago: Fitzroy Dearborn, 1998.
Edwin Markham. *Poems.* Ed. Charles L. Wallis. New York: Harper, 1950.
William R. Nash. "Edwin Markham," in *American National Biography*, vol. 14. New York: Oxford University Press, 1999.

The Man with the Hoe

Bowed by the weight of centuries he leans
Upon his hoe and gazes on the ground,
The emptiness of ages in his face,
And on his back the burden of the world.
Who made him dead to rapture and despair,
A thing that grieves not and that never hopes,
Stolid and stunned, a brother to the ox?
Who loosened and let down this brutal jaw?
Whose was the hand that slanted back this brow?
Whose breath blew out the light within this brain?

Is this the Thing the Lord God made and gave
To have dominion over sea and land;[1]
To trace the stars and search the heavens for power;
To feel the passion of Eternity?
Is this the dream He dreamed who shaped the suns
And marked their ways upon the ancient deep?
Down all the caverns of Hell to their last gulf
There is no shape more terrible than this—
More tongued with censure of the world's blind greed—
More filled with signs and portents for the soul—
More packed with danger to the universe.

1. This line alludes to Genesis 1:26: "And God said, Let us make man in our image, after our likeness: and let them have dominion over the fish of the sea, and over the fowl of the air, and over the cattle, and over all the earth." In the initial printing of the poem, Markham underlined the significance of this biblical passage by using a rephrased version as the poem's epigraph: "God made man in His own image, in the image of God made He him."

*   *   *

What gulfs between him and the seraphim![2]
Slave of the wheel of labor, what to him
Are Plato[3] and the swing of Pleiades?
What the long reaches of the peaks of song,
The rift of dawn, the reddening of the rose?
Through this dread shape the suffering ages look;
Time's tragedy is in that aching stoop;
Through this dread shape humanity betrayed,
Plundered, profaned, and disinherited,
Cries protest to the Judges of the World,
A protest that is also prophecy.

O masters, lords and rulers in all lands,
Is this the handiwork you give to God,
This monstrous thing distorted and soul-quenched?
How will you ever straighten up this shape;
Touch it again with immortality;
Give back the upward looking and the light;
Rebuild in it the music and the dream;
Make right the immemorial[4] infamies,
Perfidious wrongs, immedicable woes?

O masters, lords and rulers in all lands,
How will the Future reckon with this man?
How answer his brute question in that hour
When whirlwinds of rebellion shake all shores?
How will it be with kingdoms and with kings—
With those who shaped him to the thing he is—
When this dumb Terror shall rise to judge the world,[5]
After the silence of the centuries?

1899

Markham prefaced the poem by explaining that it was "written after seeing Millet's world-famous painting": Jean-François Millet's oil painting of 1862, also called "The Man with the Hoe." Millet's painting depicts an exhausted agricultural worker leaning on his hoe in a rocky landscape. The painting stirred controversy for its apparent sympathy with the work-

---

2. Angels.
3. The ancient Greek philosopher and ethicist (428–348 B.C.E.). In Greek myth, the Pleiades are the seven daughters of Atlas and Pleione. Zeus turned them into a constellation of stars.

4. Extending back beyond memory.
5. "Rise to judge the world" is Markham's later revision of his initial phrase, "reply to God."

ing class. Markham — influenced by his reading of Karl Marx, William Morris, and other social revolutionaries — used the painting as a starting point for his own, more explicit condemnation of capitalist exploitation.

Preparedness

For all your days prepare,
And meet them ever alike:
When you are the anvil, bear —
When you are the hammer, Strike.

1899

Outwitted

He drew a circle that shut me out —
Heretic, a rebel, a thing to flout.
But Love and I had the wit to win:
We drew a circle that took him in!

1899

JOSÉ MARTÍ
1853–1895

JOSÉ MARTÍ WAS a great hero of Cuba's struggle for independence. Born in Cuba, and killed there in the fight for liberation from Spain, he is deeply embedded in that nation's history and in the culture of all the Americas. Although never a citizen of the United States, Martí did reside in this country for fifteen years, from January 1880 to January 1895. Living primarily in New York City, though traveling to Washington, D.C., Florida, and elsewhere, he worked tirelessly to advance the cause of Cuba's liberation. He also supported the rights of Cuban immigrants in the United States, campaigned for the advancement of black Cuban workers in New York City, lamented the death of the Haymarket protesters in Chicago, argued for Native-American rights and racial equality, and warned against U.S. imperialist desires.

In addition to his political activity and advocacy, Martí engaged in many

cultural endeavors in the United States. He edited several magazines aimed at La-
tino/a readers. He gave speeches and wrote articles on the cultural unity of the
Americas and in praise of Ralph Waldo Emerson and Walt Whitman. And he
published poems, including the book-length *Versos sencillos* (or *Simple Verses*) in
1890. *Simple Verses* exhibits Martí's love of freedom and justice and his comple-
mentary commitment to introspection and the perception of beauty. Elegant,
self-reflexive, and surprising in its shifts of image and feeling, this autobiographi-
cal poem recalls the mid-nineteenth-century poetics of Emerson and Whitman
even as it looks forward to twentieth-century modernism and surrealism. It has in-
fluenced poetic developments throughout the Americas.

In 1892 the Partido Revolucionario Cubano (Cuban Revolutionary Party)
chose Martí as its leader. From his base in New York, he planned the liberation of
his homeland, one of Spain's last remaining colonies in the New World. In April
1895 Martí and a small band of revolutionaries landed in Cuba. A little over a
month later he was killed in battle at Dos Ríos, Oriente Province, Cuba.

FURTHER READING

Jeffrey Belnap and Raul Fernandez, eds. *José Martí's "Our America": From National to Hemi-
spheric Cultural Studies*. Durham, N.C.: Duke University Press, 1999.
Anne Fountain. *Versos Sencillos by José Martí: A Translation*. University, Miss.: Romance Mono-
graphs, University of Mississippi, 2000.
José Martí. *José Martí Reader: Writings on the Americas*. Ed. Deborah Shnookal and Mirta
Muñiz. Melbourne, Australia: Ocean Press, 1999.
———. *Versos sencillos / Simple Verses*. Translated by Manuel A. Tellechea. Houston: Arte Pú-
blico Press, 1999.
Julio Rodríguez-Luis, ed. *Re-reading José Martí: One Hundred Years Later*. New York: SUNY
Press, 1999.

FROM *Versos sencillos*

1

Yo soy un hombre sincero
De donde crece la palma,
Y antes de morirme quiero
Echar mis versos del alma.

Yo vengo de todas partes,
Y hacia todas partes voy:
Arte soy entre las artes,
En los montes, monte soy.

*   *   *

Yo sé los nombres extraños
De las yerbas y las flores,
Y de mortales engaños,
Y de sublimes dolores.

Yo he visto en la noche oscura
Llover sobre mi cabeza
Los rayos de lumbre pura
De la divina belleza.

Alas nacer vi en los hombros
De las mujeres hermosas:
Y salir de los escombros
Vilando las mariposas.

He visto vivir a un hombre
Con el puñal al costado,
Sin decir jamás el nombre
De aquella que lo ha matado.

Rápida, como un reflejo,
Dos veces vi el alma, dos:
Cuando murió el pobre viejo,
Cuando ella me adiós.

Temblé una vez, — en la reja,
A la entrada de la viña, —
Cuando la bárbara abeja
Picó en la frente a mi niña.

Gocé una vez, de tal suerte
Que gocé cual nunca: — cuando
La sentencia de mi muerte
Leyó el alcaide llorando.

Oígo un suspiro, a través
De las tierras y la mar,
Y no es un suspiro, — es
Que mi hijo va a despertar.

Si dicen que del joyero
Tome la joya mejor,
Tomo a un amigo sincero
Y pongo a un lado el amor.

✧ ✲ ✧

Yo he visto al águila herida
Volar al azul sereno,
Y morir en su guarida
La víbora del veneno.

Yo sé bien que cuando el mundo
Cene, lívido, al descanso,
Sobre el silencio profundo
Murmura el arroyo manso.

Yo he puesto la mano osada,
De horror y júbilo yerta,
Sobre la estrella apagada
Que cayó frente a mi puerta.

Oculto en mi pecho bravo
La pena que me lo hiere:
El hijo de un pueblo esclavo
Vive por él, calla, y muere.

Todo es hermoso y constante,
Todo es música y razón,
Y todo, como el diamante,
Antes que luz es carbón.

Yo sé que el necio se entierra
Con gran lujo y con gran llanto,—
Y que no hay fruta en la tierra
Como la del camposanto.

Callo, y entiendo, y me quito
La pompa del rimador:
Cuelgo de un árbol marchito
Mi muceta de doctor.

5

Si ves un monte de espumas
Es mi verso lo que ves:
Mi verso es un monte, y es
Un abanico de plumas.

✧ ✧ ✧

Mi verso es como un puñal
Que por el puño echa flor:
Mi verso es un surtidor
Que da un agua de coral.

Mi verso es de un verde claro
Y de un carmín encendido:
Mi verso es un ciervo herido
Que busca en el monte amparo.

Mi verso al valiente agrada:
Mi verso, breve y sincero,
Es del vigor del acero
Con que se funde la espada.

1890

[TRANS.] *From* Simple Verses

1

A sincere man am I,[1]
Born where the palm trees grow,
And I long before I die
My soul's verses to bestow.

No boundaries bind my heart,
I belong to every land:
I am art among the arts,
A peak among peaks I stand.

I know the exotic names
Of every flower and leaf;
I know of betrayal's claims,
And I know of exalted grief.

I've seen how beauteous streams
Flow through the dark of night,
And descend as radiant beams
In a luminous shower of light.

* * *

1. Section one of *Versos sencillos* became the basis for the song "Guantanamera," Cuba's most popular song and a song well known in the United States and throughout the Americas.

As if by wings set free,
I've seen women's shoulders rise,
And beauty emerge from debris
In a flight of butterflies.

I've seen a man live with pain
The dagger wounds at his side,
And never reveal the name
Of her[2] by whose hand he died.

Two times I've sensed inside
The soul's reflection go by,
Once when my father died
And once when she[3] bade me good-bye.

Once I trembled with fear
Close by the arbor's vine,
As an angry bee drew near
To sting a child of mine.[4]

That day of my death decree[5]
I felt both triumph and pride,
For the warden who read it to me
Pronounced the sentence and cried.

Beneath me I hear a sigh
From the slumber of earth and sea.
But in truth it's the morning cry
Of my son who awakens me.

The jewel esteemed the most?
The value I most revere?
I would of friendship boast
And hold not love so dear.

The wounded eagle, I know,
Can soar to the bluest skies
While the venomous viper below
Chokes on its poison and dies.

---

2. According to Anne Fountain, the allusion to "a woman who inflicts dagger wounds" is assumed by many to be "a reference to Carmen Zayas Bazán, Martí's wife."
3. Another likely reference to Carmen Zayas Bazán.
4. Fountain calls this "a likely reference to María Mantilla," who is presumed to be Martí's daughter.
5. At the the age of sixteen, Martí was condemned to death when imprisoned by Spanish authorities.

* * *

I know that when life must yield
And leave us to restful dreams
That alongside the silent field
Is the murmur of gentle streams.

To sorrows and joy, I reply
By placing a loyal hand
On the star that refused to die —
Proud symbol of my land.

My heart holds anguish and pains
From a wound that festers and cries:
The son of a people in chains
Lives for them, hushes, and dies.

All is lovely and right,
All is reason and song,
Before the diamond is bright,
Its night of carbon is long.

I know that the foolish may die
With burial pomp and tears
And that no land can supply
The fruit that the graveyard bears.

Silent, I quit the renown
And boast of a poet's rhyme
And rest my doctoral gown
On a tree withered with time.

5

When sea caps rush to shore
My verses find their voice,
With feathered fans they soar
And in the hills rejoice.

My verse cuts like a blade
But the hilt holds just a flower.
From a fountain's music made
My verse is a coral shower.

* * *

My verse is a gentle green
And is fiery red in part.
In the forest refuge seen,
My verse is the wounded hart.[6]

My poems the brave inspire,
My poems are brief, sincere.
They forge the sword with fire
And make the steel ring clear.

Sapped by ceaseless political activity and his fears that Cuba would remain a Spanish colony or be annexed by the United States, Martí was sent by his doctor to the Catskill Mountains of upstate New York in the summer of 1890. There he composed *Versos sencillos / Simple Verses*. As he explained in the poem's prologue, in the Catskills, "streams ran, clouds closed-in upon clouds, and I wrote poetry." The verses, he added, "came from my heart." He chose to experiment with imagery and to playfully repeat rhymes or dispense with them as suited the poem's mood. Although the poem modernized poetic practice throughout the Americas and remains influential today, Martí was modest about his aims and achievement. He said that he wrote the poem "because I love simplicity, and believe in the necessity of putting feelings in plain and sincere form." The translation here is by Anne Fountain.

ERNEST FRANCISCO FENOLLOSA
1853–1908

ERNEST FRANCISCO FENOLLOSA is generally viewed as an originator of "high" Anglo-American modernism because of his landmark essay, "The Chinese Written Character as a Medium for Poetry," drafted in about 1890, and his unfinished translation notes on the Chinese classical poet Li Po in *Cathay* (completed by Ezra Pound and published in 1915), both of which influenced Amy Lowell and others of that generation. In spite of Fenollosa's privileged status, however, his own poetry has been little noted. Nevertheless, it demands reevaluation now in the context of the emerging history of transnational and multicultural modernisms.

Fenollosa was well positioned historically, geographically, culturally, and socially to become an architect of literary modernism. He became the center of an

6. Male deer.

elite late-nineteenth-century circle sometimes known as "The Boston Oriental-ists," made up of such figures as Henry Adams, Arthur Dow, John La Farge, James McNeill Whistler, Bernard Berenson, William Bigelow, Charles Goddard Weld, and Percival Lowell. This circle dominated the "high" culture in which many modernist poets grew up. It encouraged them to view "the Orient" through what postcolonial critic Edward Said would call the "colonizing" eyes of the West and thus to embrace a Western invention of the East.

The son of a Spanish-American musician, Fenollosa was born in 1853 in Salem, Massachusetts, about the same time that Commodore William Perry reopened U.S. trade relations with Japan through military force. The city of Salem, interest-ingly, had been responsible for the initial trade relationship between the two countries. It sent two ships in 1800 to open up trade in Nagasaki and to return with Japanese art and other goods. When Fenollosa was seven years old, Japan sent its first diplomatic delegation to the United States, and Walt Whitman wrote "A Broadway Pageant" to mark the New York City parade down Broadway in their honor. American elites were equally enamored of China because of the Chinese trade and the British colony of Hong Kong. Children's books about China and the Chinese began appearing in 1837, and Confucius was translated at about this time. The cultural elite thus began a long courtship of "the Orient," as it patronized *The Mikado* and *Madame Butterfly*; collected Oriental art; incorporated Asian design into homes, public buildings, and books; and studied Eastern religions. Collectors particularly benefited from the Meiji Restoration in Japan in 1868, which forced many privileged families and temples to sell artwork at very low prices.

After Fenollosa graduated from Harvard, where he had become a follower of Ralph Waldo Emerson, he went to Tokyo at the age of twenty-five as a professor of philosophy at Tokyo University; his interest in east Asia had undoubtedly been stimulated when he saw Japanese arts and crafts for the first time at the 1876 U.S. Centennial International Exhibition in Philadelphia. He became curator of the Imperial Museum of Japan after urging Japanese artists to accommodate contem-porary interests while retaining their traditional themes—instead of abandoning them and learning Western art with Italian artists, which had been their practice when he arrived. He also served as the curator of Oriental art at the Boston Mu-seum of Fine Arts and exerted great influence nationally and internationally. In-deed, his own collection of Oriental art formed the basis of the museum's first holdings in this area. In addition, he sold part of his Asian collection to Charles Freer and advised him extensively on the acquisitions that formed the Freer Gal-lery of Art, part of the Smithsonian Institution, in Washington, D.C. His *Epochs of Chinese and Japanese Art Before 1800* (1912), compiled by his second wife, Mary McNeil Fenollosa, is regarded as a pathbreaking work in art history.

Fenollosa published his poetry in *East and West* (1893). When he died, he was still working on studies of Japanese Noh drama and on translations of Li Po.

Fenollosa produced English-language interlinear versions of the Chinese poems. These translations, however, were filtered through prior Japanese translations. Thus, Fenollosa viewed the Chinese poet's writing through the lens of Japanese culture, history, and language as well as through his own American perspective.

The selection here reveals Fenollosa's view of "the Orient" as a beloved to be gazed upon with pleasure and courted. The tender, intimate tones bear comparison with Pound's in the collection *Cathay*, indicating Fenollosa's influence on Pound's own invention of China as well as that of many other twentieth-century American poets.

FURTHER READING

Ernest Fenollosa. *East and West: The Discovery of America and Other Poems*. New York: Thomas Crowell, 1893.

Robert Kern. *Orientalism, Modernism, and the American Poem*. Cambridge, Eng.: Cambridge University Press, 1996.

Ezra Pound. *Cathay: For the Most Part from the Chinese of Rihaku, from the Notes of the Late Ernest Fenollosa, and the Decipherings of the Professors Mori and Ariga*. London: El Kins Mathews, 1915.

Edward Said. *Orientalism*. New York: Vintage, 1979.

The Wood Dove

Gentle purple-throated dove
Nesting in the bamboo grove,
  Cooing, cooing, cooing;
I've a secret for you, dear.
Let me whisper in your ear.
Let no other creature hear;
  'T would be my undoing.

Tenderly pressed, pressed, pressed
Soft in your nest, nest, nest,
Carefully list, list, list,[1]
If I be kissed, kissed, kissed,
If I be——

There, you know my secret now,
You, too, on the topmost bough
  Wooing, wooing, wooing.
Did you tremble when he came?

---

1. Listen.

Did you feel his lips a-flame?
But you shall not know his name;
   'T would be my undoing.

Tenderly pressed, pressed, pressed
Close to his breast, breast, breast,
Under your nest, nest, nest,
There shall I rest, rest, rest,
There shall I——

1893

Fuji at Sunrise

Startling the cool gray depths of morning air
   She throws aside her counterpane of clouds,
   And stands half folded in her silken shrouds
With calm white breast and snowy shoulder bare.
High o'er her head a flush all pink and rare
   Thrills her with foregleam of an unknown bliss,
   A virgin pure who waits the bridal kiss,
Faint with expectant joy she fears to share.
Lo, now he comes, the dazzling prince of day!
   Flings his full glory o'er her radiant breast;
   Enfolds her to the rapture of his rest,
Transfigured in the throbbing of his ray.
O fly, my soul, where love's warm transports are;
And seek eternal bliss in yon pink kindling star!

1893

LOUISE IMOGEN GUINEY
1861–1920

WHILE THE AGE OF THE European-American "new woman" poet is associated with the twentieth-century generation of Edna St. Vincent Millay, Louise Guiney's poetry reveals that she was a nineteenth-century precursor. Guiney rebelled against sentimentalism and puritanical decorum, offering an unexpectedly frank literary legacy.

Born in Boston, Guiney supported herself by working first as a postmistress in the suburb of Auburndale and then as a cataloguer at the Boston Public Library. During these same years, she developed a significant literary life. She began to publish her poetry, and she cultivated friendships with such important figures as Sarah Orne Jewett, Annie Fields, Alice Brown, and Lizette Reese. Brown eventually became her companion. She also helped discover and promote the Lebanese-American poet Kahlil Gibran and supported the publication of Canadian writers.

The selection "Tarpeia" illustrates Guiney's progressive treatment of sexual topics. Originally published in *Scribner's Magazine*, this ballad tells a haunting cautionary tale about a female Roman prostitute who agrees to accept Sabine soldiers as customers in exchange for jewels and then is not only cheated of her wages but murdered with their shields and the jewels they had promised her. The ballad's subject is unusual for a woman poet of the time, and Guiney's sympathetic view of the prostitute as a victim counters the dominant culture's conventional attitude.

FURTHER READING

Cheryl Walker. *American Women Poets of the Nineteenth Century: An Anthology.* New Brunswick: Rutgers University Press, 1992.
———. *The Nightingale's Burden.* Bloomington: Indiana University Press, 1982.

Tarpeia

Woe: lightly to part with one's soul as the sea with its foam!
Woe to Tarpeia, Tarpeia, daughter of Rome!

Lo, now it was night, with the moon looking chill as she went;
It was morn when the innocent stranger strayed into the tent.

The hostile Sabini[1] were pleased, as one meshing a bird;
She sang for them there in the ambush: they smiled as they heard.

Her sombre hair purpled in gleams as she leaned to the light;
All day she had idled and feasted, and now it was night.

The chief sat apart, heavy-browed, brooding, elbow on knee;
The armlets he wore were thrice royal, and wondrous to see —

Exquisite artifice, whorls of barbaric design,
Frost's fixed mimicry, orbic[2] imaginings fine

---

1. Ancient people of central Italy.   2. Round, like an orb.

*   *   *

In sevenfold coils: and in orient glimmer from them,
The variform, voluble swinging of gem upon gem.

And the glory thereof sent fever and fire to her eye:
"I had never such trinkets!" she sighed—like a lute was her sigh;

"Were they mine at the plea, were they mine for the token, all told,
Now the citadel sleeps, now my father the keeper is old,

"If I go by the way that I know, and thou followest hard,
If yet by the touch of Tarpeia the gates be unbarred?"

The chief trembled sharply for joy, then drew rein on his soul:
"Of all this arm beareth, I swear I will cede thee the whole."

And up from the nooks of the camp, with hoarse plaudit outdealt,
The bearded Sabini glanced hotly, and vowed, as they knelt,

Bare-stretching the wrists that bore also the glowing great boon:
"Yea! surely as over us shineth the lurid low moon,

"Not alone of our lord, but of each of us take what he hath!
Too poor is the guerdon,[3] if thou wilt but show us the path."

Her nostrils upraised, like a fawn's on the arrowy air,
She sped. In a serpentine gleam, to the precipice stair,

They climbed in her traces, they closed on their evil swift star:
She bent to the latches, and swung the huge portal ajar.

Repulsed where they passed her, half-tearful for wounded belief,
"The bracelets!" she pleaded. Then faced her the leonine chief,

And answered her: "Even as I promised, maid-merchant! I do."
Down from his dark shoulder the baubles he sullenly drew.

"This left arm shall nothing begrudge thee. Accept. Find it sweet!
Give, too, O my brothers!" The jewels he flung at her feet,

The jewels hard, heavy; she stooped to them, flushing with dread,
But the shield he flung after: it clanged on her beautiful head.

Like the Apennine[4] bells when the villagers' warnings begin,
Athwart the first lull broke the ominous din upon din:

---

3. Reward.   4. In the Apennine Mountains in Italy.

*   *   *

With a "Hail, benefactress!" upon her they heaped, in their zeal,
Death: agate[5] and iron; death: chrysoprase, beryl, and steel.

'Neath the outcry of scorn, 'neath the sinewy tension and hurl,
The moaning died slowly, and still they massed over the girl

A mountain of shields! and the gemmy bright tangle in links,
A torrent-like gush, pouring out on the grass from the chinks.

Pyramidal gold! the sumptuous monument won
By the deed they had loved her for, doing, and loathed her for, done.

Such was the wage that they paid her, such the acclaim:
All Rome was aroused with the thunder that buried her shame.

On surged the Sabini to battle. O you that aspire!
Tarpeia the traitor had fill of her woman's desire.

Woe: lightly to part with one's soul as the sea with its foam!
Woe to Tarpeia, Tarpeia, daughter of Rome!

1887

Planting the Poplar

Because thou'rt not an oak
To breast the thunder-stroke,
Or flamy-fruited yew
Darker than Time, how few
Of birds or men or kine[1]
Will love this throne of thine,
Scant Poplar, without shade
Inhospitably made!
Yet, branches never parted
From their straight secret bole,
Prosper as my soul.

In loneliness, in quaint
Perpetual constraint,

---

5. A kind of quartz with colored bands, capable   1. Cattle.
of being made into a weapon. Chrysoprase and
beryl are green, gemlike minerals.

In gallant poverty,
A girt and hooded tree,
See if against the gale
Our leafage can avail:
Lithe, equal, naked, true,
Rise up as spirits do,
And be a spirit crying
Before the folk that dream!
My slender early-dying
Poplar, by the stream.

1896

MARY MCNEIL FENOLLOSA
1865–1954

WHEN HISTORIANS OF THE "high" Anglo-American modernism of Ezra Pound and T. S. Eliot date its inception by the publication in 1915 of *Cathay*, which was Pound's completion of Ernest Fenollosa's unfinished translation of the Chinese classical poet Li Po, they overlook the poet who was actually responsible for this literary "moment"—Mary McNeil Fenollosa. Mary Fenollosa's story within this conventional history of modernism begins and ends with the acknowledgment that, when she read Pound's haiku-like "In a Station at the Metro" published in 1913, she realized that he might be able to complete the work that her late husband had started on Li Po and classic Japanese Noh theater. So she contacted Pound, and he became her husband's literary executor and translator. But Mary Fenollosa also had devoted her life and writing to acting as a cultural mediator between East and West in collaboration with her husband and their elite circle sometimes known as "The Boston Orientalists." Her inclusion in this anthology signals a need to rethink the relationship between nineteenth-century American poetry and modernism as well as Mary Fenollosa's particular role in inventing the "Orientalism" that eventually attracted not only Pound but also Amy Lowell, H.D., Marianne Moore, and many other poets. Mary Fenollosa, along with the Japanese-German-American poet and litterateur Sadakichi Hartmann (also included in this anthology), may be the underestimated source of twentieth-century modernism.

Born in Mobile, Alabama, Fenollosa found herself at the cultural center of U.S.

interests in Japan and China after she married Ernest, her third husband. Along with Ernest, she traveled in international cultural and society circles and attracted much attention. She is credited with introducing the Japanese empress to the renowned Worth evening gowns of Parisian high society, for example, because she owned and wore two of them while living in Japan. But Fenollosa refused to settle for the role of fashion style-setter. She used her privileged status to further her vision of East-West relations in her writing. She published *Out of the Nest: A Flight of Verses* in 1899 and *Blossoms from a Japanese Garden: A Book of Child-Verses* in 1915, which included illustrations by contemporary Japanese artists. In her poems, she constructs "the Orient" as a beloved mysterious other. Her tone is personal, nostalgic, and melancholic, through at the same time, as postcolonial theorist Edward Said would point out, she participates in the imperialistic production of the Orient for Western readers. Indeed, Pound's often-praised tenderness toward women characters in *Cathay* poems—as in the widely popular "The River Merchant's Wife: A Letter"—seems influenced by such Fenollosa poems as "Miyoko San" and "Yuki." After Ernest's death, Mary compiled the material for his landmark work in Japanese and Chinese art, *Epochs of Chinese and Japanese Art Before 1800* (1912). She also published a study of the Japanese artist Hiroshige in 1906.

Mary Fenollosa enjoyed a successful career as a fiction writer as well. *The Dragon Painter* (1906) was made into a Japanese silent film in 1919. She published several novels under the pen name Sidney McCall, including *Red Horse Hill*, which was made into the American silent film *The Eternal Mother*, starring Ethel Barrymore, in 1917.

FURTHER READING

Caldwell Delaney. "Mary McNeil Fenollosa," in *The Alabama Review* 16 (July 1963): 163–173.
Edmund Clarence Stedman, ed. *An American Anthology, 1787–1900*. Boston: Houghton Mifflin, 1900.
www.unl.edu/legacy

Miyoko San

Snare me the soul of a dragon-fly,
The jewelled heart of a dew-tipped spray,
A star's quick eye,
Or the scarlet cry
Of a lonely wing on a dawn-lit bay.
Then add the gleam of a golden fan,
And I will paint you Miyoko San.
Find me the thought of a rose, at sight
Of her own pale face in a fawning stream,

The polished night
Of a crow's slow flight,
And the long, sweet grace of a willow's dream.
Then add the droop of a golden fan,
And I will paint you Miyoko San.
Lure me a lay from a sunbeam's throat,
The chant of bees in a perfumed lair,
Or a single note
Gone mad to float
To its own sweet death in the upper air.
Then add the click of a golden fan,
And I have painted Miyoko San.

1899

Yuki

When cherry flowers begin to blow
With Yuki's face beneath them,
The richest petals lose their glow,
And small buds hast to sheath them.
When blue wisteria hangs its head
And Yuki leans above it,
The swallow flits discomforted, —
With none to see or love it.
When lotus blossoms open wide,
And beckon men to dreaming,
My Yuki smiles, — and all their pride
Is but a perfumed seeming.
When snow is white on moat and tree
And crusts each bamboo feather,
My Yuki lifts her eyes to me, —
'T is all I know of weather.

1899

OWL WOMAN
[JUANA MANWELL]
1867–1957

OWL WOMAN (JUANA MANWELL), a fifty-three-year-old Papago healer, was living on the San Xavier reserve in Arizona when she attracted the attention of the ethno-musicologist Frances Densmore, who was recording Native-American music on a visit in 1920. Densmore preserved Owl Woman's songs of spiritual healing by trans-lating them into English and rendering their complex evocation of nature and the spiritual world through an imagist poetics that is indebted to Asian poetry, espe-cially such forms as haiku. Owl Woman's oral poetry retains a vital place in the de-velopment of a written Native-American poetry as well as an influence on poets from all American cultures who invoke Native-American feminine spirituality.

Owl Woman is said to have received her songs from the dead and used them to attempt cures. Her treatment consisted of a full night of song and physical tech-niques divided into four parts, following the pattern of Native-American sacred numbers that correspond to the four compass points. Each part consisted of two sections—first she sang four songs, and then she stroked the patient with owl feath-ers that she had sprinkled with ashes. The selection here represents the songs in the first two parts of the treatment.

In reading the poetry, it is important to note that these printed versions of Owl Woman's poems have been mediated by Densmore, who arguably brought a Vic-torian colonial perspective to her understanding of the healer's spiritual practice. In addition, the language not only has undergone translation but also has been filtered through two cultural poetics outside of Native-American culture: European-American and Asian. The result is a distanced and partial retrieval of Owl Woman's poetry that highlights the difficulty of transforming oral ritual into transcribed lyrics—and the need for respecting cultural differences that cannot be bridged easily.

FURTHER READING

Frances Densmore. "Papagao Music," in *Bulletin* 90. Smithsonian Institution Bureau of Ameri-can Ethnology, 1929.
Karen Kilcup, ed. *Native American Women's Writing, c. 1800–1924: An Anthology*. Oxford, Eng.: Blackwell Publishers, 2000.

FROM *Songs for Treating Sickness,*
Sung during the Four Parts of the Night
PARTS ONE AND TWO: BEGINNING SONGS
AND SONGS SUNG BEFORE MIDNIGHT

No. 72. *Brown Owls*

Brown owls come here in the blue evening,
They are hooting about,
They are shaking their wings and hooting.

No. 73. *In the Blue Night*

How shall I begin my song
In the blue night that is settling?
I will sit here and begin my song.

No. 74. *The Owl Feather*

The owl feather is rolling in this direction and beginning to sing.
The people listen and come to hear the owl feather
Rolling in this direction and beginning to sing.

No. 75. *They Come Hooting*

Early in the evening they come hooting about,
Some have small voices and some have large voices,
Some have voices of medium strength, hooting about.

No. 76. *In the Dark I Enter*

I can not make out what I see.
In the dark I enter.
I can not make out what I see.

No. 77. *His Heart Is Almost Covered with Night*

Poor old sister, you have cared for this man and you want to see him again,
But now his heart is almost covered with night.
There is just a little left.

No. 78. I See Spirit-Tufts of White Feathers

Ahead of me some owl feathers are lying,
I hear someone running toward me,
They pass by me, and farther ahead
I see spirit-tufts of downy white feathers.

No. 79. Yonder Lies the Spirit Land

Yonder lies the spirit land.
Yonder the spirit land I see.
Farther ahead, in front of me,
I see a spirit stand.

[Untitled]

Sadly I was treated, sadly I was treated,
Through the night I was carried around,
Sadly I was treated.

No. 80. Song of a Spirit

A railroad running west,
He travels westward.
When he gets a certain distance
He flaps his wings four times and turns back.

No. 81. We Will Join Them

Yonder are spirits laughing and talking as though drunk.
They do the same things that we do.
Now we will join them.

No. 82. My Feathers

I pity you, my feathers,
I pity you, my feathers, that they make fun of,
They must mean what they say,
Or perhaps they are crazy in their hearts.

No. 83. The Women Are Singing

On the west side people are singing as though drunk.
The women are singing as though they were drunk.

[Untitled]

In the great night my heart will go out,
Toward me the darkness comes rattling,
In the great night my heart will go out.

[Untitled]

On the west side they are singing, the women hear it.

No. 84. *I Am Going to See the Land*

I am going far to see the land,
I am running far to see the land,
While back in my house the songs are intermingling.

No. 85. *I Run Toward Ashes Hill*

Ashes Hill Mountain, toward it I am running,
I see the Ashes Hill come out clearer.

No. 86. *The Waters of the Spirits*

They brought me to the waters of the spirits.
In these waters the songs seem to be stringing out.

1929

SADAKICHI HARTMANN
1867–1944

Sadakichi hartmann, a writer with a mixed-race background, actively resisted all attempts to pigeonhole him as he crossed numerous national, racial, cultural, religious, and aesthetic boundaries. Associating with many of the greatest writers and artists of his time, he achieved a pathbreaking career as a poet, dramatist, and art critic. He helped bring Asian, European, and Middle Eastern influences to bear on American art and literature. And he anticipated and participated in the artistically innovative enterprises that are now grouped under the label of twentieth-century "modernism." His friend, the modernist poet Ezra Pound, wrote in *Guide to Kulchur* that "if one hadn't been oneself, it wd. have been worthwhile to have been Sadakichi (not that my constitution wd. have weathered the strain)." Another great modernist writer, Gertrude Stein, commented that "Sadakichi is singular, never plural."

Carl Sadakichi Hartmann was born in 1867 in Nagasaki, Japan, the son of a German trader and a Japanese mother, who died in childbirth. After a rather circuitous journey, he was to become an American citizen in 1894. He later wrote, "I personally never think of myself as a German or Asiatic. Others do it for me." Soon after Hartmann's birth, his father placed him and his elder brother, Taru, in the care of relatives in Hamburg, Germany. When they enrolled him in a naval academy at the age of thirteen, he rebelled and escaped to Paris. Furious, his father disinherited him and sent him to live with relatives in Philadelphia. In the United States, Hartmann worked at a series of menial jobs while studying at night in a library. In 1884 he discovered Walt Whitman's poems and began to pay periodic visits to the aging poet as well as to other notable members of the "literati," such as John Greenleaf Whittier. Although Whitman and Hartmann eventually quarreled, Whitman at first praised his young disciple's "surprising differences of perspective" and asserted, "I have more hopes of him, more faith in him, than any of the boys."

Beginning at the age of nineteen, Hartmann made four trips to Paris and Germany to meet important artists and to study the arts. Back in New York in his mid-twenties, he became discouraged by his lack of success as a dramatist and attempted suicide. As he was recovering, he fell in love with his nurse, Elizabeth Walsh, and married her. The marriage brought him more than a decade of stability in an otherwise untethered life. Soon thereafter he succeeded in publishing his symbolist drama, *Christ* (1893), which despite its title promoted free love. Most copies of the play were burned, and Hartmann spent a brief time in jail. In subsequent years he wrote additional avant-garde dramas about Buddha, Confucius, Moses, and Mohammed, none of which found an audience. Nor did his poems receive positive notice. But he did begin to receive recognition as the author of revolutionary essays in art and photography theory and a series of textbooks on American and Japanese art. Hartmann's reputation as an art critic reached its zenith just before World War I.

After divorcing his wife in 1908, Hartmann assumed the role of "the King of Bohemia," as a friend labeled him. He lived by his own rules, forging an experimental alternative to mainstream culture. But after World War I, his trajectory pointed downward. By 1923, Hartmann was writing unproduced film scripts and living in Los Angeles. He could not find a publisher for a thousand-page book on aesthetics. By 1930 he was supporting himself by lecturing on art to small audiences across mid-America. In his last years he lived in seclusion in the small, dusty town of Banning, California, a way station on the road from Los Angeles to Palm Springs.

Hartmann's poetry includes bold and unusual images in the style of Ezra Pound and aphoristic language play similar to that of Gertrude Stein. Older than those writers, Hartmann was often ahead of them in such experiments. He composed haiku, for example, as early as 1898, about fifteen years before Pound's analogous imagist poems. Hartmann introduced French symbolist poetry, Japanese tanka and haiku, and medieval Persian lyric into American avant-garde poetic practice. By means of his poems and his essays, he put poetry into conversation with the latest developments in art, drama, music, photography, and cinema. Because Hartmann was noticed by his fellow artists, if not by poetry readers at large, he made a difference at a pivotal time. With his help, American poetry began to internationalize and modernize itself. Hartmann encouraged American poetry to embark on a journey of discovery.

FURTHER READING

Sadakichi Hartmann. *My Rubaiyat*. St. Louis: Mangan Printing, 1913.
———. *Tanka and Haikai: Japanese Rhythms*. San Francisco: Author's Edition, 1916.
———. *White Chrysanthemums: Literary Fragments and Pronouncements*. Ed. George Knox and Harry Lawton. New York: Herder & Herder, 1971.
George Knox and Harry Lawton, eds. *The Whitman-Hartmann Controversy*. Frankfurt, Germany: Peter Lang, 1976.
Marshall Van Deusen. "Sadakichi Hartmann," in *Dictionary of Literary Biography*, vol. 54. Detroit: Gale, 1987.

Cyanogen Seas Are Surging

Cyanogen[1] seas are surging
On fierce cinnabarine[2] strands,
Where white Amazons[3] are marching,
Through the radiance of the sands.

Oh, could only lambent love-flame
Be like the surging sea,
Deluge the red of the desert
And drown the white virgins in me!

1898

1. A colorless, poisonous, flammable gas that has an almondlike odor and turns pigment dark blue.
2. Bright red, like crystals of cinnabar, the principal ore of mercury.

3. A race of female warriors in Greek and Roman mythology.

FROM *My Rubaiyat*

12

Sex is a power all cherish,
We worship it on bended knees,
Like old wine it yields the magic
Of oblivion and ecstasies,
The moments drift on golden clouds
To regions of the white beyond.

37

Why do we live, why do we hope,
Why does this life exist at all!
How do we dare to love and mate
When every path is strewn with thorns,
When children share in our fate
And age is glad to greet the night!

42

But what sad use the world has made
Of nature's boundless plenitude.
The free and good, the fair and true
Is trodden down by foolish crowds.
Greed, barren, shameless, rules supreme,
There is no brotherhood 'mong men.

44

The sword shall break the sword they say,
And force shall strangle force some day.
Thus men march toward battles red,
Their mangled bodies strew the plains,
While o'er the corpse the mother wails,
Her firstborn slain, her pride in life.

46

If youth would refuse to obey
To die without cause or reason,
If youth would refuse to bear arms

Against brothers they do not know,
Then like the Chaldean[1] shepherds
We might greet a rosier dawn.

48

For certain things must need be changed,
Life cannot stay so dull and grey.
Men must live a freer windblown life,
Women no longer lose their bloom
In drudgery for bed and fare,
And children age before their time.

52

What can we do, how can we help!
The poor can never help the poor,
The rich but scatter alms derived
From what is due the common herd.
The weed plots are crowded thick,
Who cuts a path for weary feet!

58

How can I give right directions
When I am a wanderer myself!
Onward I stroll and ever on
In my own way courting the sun
And fashioning some paradise
Of passing winds and flying clouds.

1913

These verses comprise a selection from Hartmann's imitation of the *Rubáiyát of Omar Khayyám*, a twelfth-century Persian poem loosely translated into English by the British poet Edward FitzGerald in 1859. Hartmann renounced his predecessors' rhymes, substituted six-line stanzas for the original quatrains, and in other ways made the sequence completely his own. From his predecessors he retained only a tone of philosophical melancholy. He explained that "the meter is a combination of Whitman's free rhymeless rhythm, the *vers libre* [free verse] which changes with every subject and mood, and the

1. Chaldea is another name for Babylonia or present-day Iraq. Chaldean shepherds, who followed the movement of the stars in the night skies, became early astronomers, astrologers, and mystics.

vague alliteration of sound in quarter tones characteristic of Japanese poetry." Hartmann's sequence includes meditations on sexual passion (part 12), society and politics (parts 37 through 52), and one's own soul (part 58).

Tanka

1

Winter? Spring! Who knows!
    White buds from the plumtrees wing
And mingle with the snows.
No blue skies these flowers bring,
Yet their fragrance augurs Spring.

2

Oh, were the white waves,
    Far on the glimmering sea
That the moonshine laves,
Dream flowers drifting to me—
I would cull them, love, for thee.

3

Moon, somnolent, white,
    Mirrored in a waveless sea,
What fickle mood of night
Urged thee from heaven to flee
And live in the dawnlit sea?

4

Like mist on the lees,[1]
    Fall gently, oh rain of Spring
On the orange trees
That to Ume's casement[2] cling—
Perchance, she'll hear the love-bird sing.

5

Though love has grown cold
    The woods are bright with flowers,

---

1. Parts of a structure sheltered from the wind.   2. A kind of window.

Why not as of old
Go to the wildwood bowers
And dream of—bygone hours.

6

Tell, what name beseems
    These vain and wandering days!
Like the bark[3] of dreams
That from souls at daybreak strays
They are lost on trackless ways.

7

Oh, climb to my lips,
    Frail muse of the amber wine!
Joy to him who sips
Cups of fragrant sake wine
Flowing from some fount divine.

8

If pleasures be mine
    As aeons and aeons roll by,
Why should I repine[4]
That under some future sky
I may live as butterfly?

9

Were we able to tell
    When old age would come our way
We would muffle the bell,
Lock the door and go away—
Let him call some other day.

1915

Hartmann writes, "The Tanka (short poem) is the most popular and characteristic of the various forms of Japanese poetry. It consists of five lines of 5, 7, 5, 7, and 7 syllables—31 syllables in all. The addition of the rhyme is original with the author." The poems themselves, though they take the Japanese form, are also original with the author.

---

3. Sailing vessel.

4. Fret, complain.

FROM *Haikai*

1

White petals afloat
   On a winding woodland stream—
What else is life's dream!

2

Butterflies a-wing—
   Are you flowers returning
To your branch in Spring?

1915

These verses are the first two in a sequence of four haikai or haiku. As Hartmann explained, the haiku, a poetic form that flourished in sixteenth-century Japan, is a tanka minus the last two lines.

EDGAR LEE MASTERS
1868–1950

EDGAR LEE MASTERS, born in Kansas, was brought up in two small Illinois towns, Petersburg and Lewiston. These places set a permanent stamp on Masters's prolific career as a writer. By bringing to imaginative life the secret underside of a small Midwestern town—the fictional Spoon River—Masters, a prolific but until then largely overlooked writer, emerged from obscurity with his 1915 *Spoon River Anthology*, one of the best-selling volumes of poetry in the history of American letters. Arranged as a series of short, interlinked poems, in the form of succinct autobiographies spoken from the grave by deceased inhabitants of Spoon River, Masters's book tells a revealing series of connected stories about the townspeople and their private lives.

Masters was forty-seven when the publication of *Spoon River Anthology* brought him sudden fame and fortune. An opinionated and keenly ambitious man, he had led a life that to that point had been marked by frustration, bitterness, and disappointment. He yearned from early youth to devote himself to writing, but his father, a lawyer, insisted that he follow a legal career. Therefore Masters left Knox College after a year to read law in his father's law office. He passed the bar exams and entered the legal profession, both to please his father and because a writing career offered few immediate financial prospects, but he did so reluctantly. Then, in 1891, at the age of twenty-three, he severed ties with both his parents and moved to Chicago, where he continued to practice law. But he also wrote a series of volumes in prose and verse that show a gradual movement away from formal conventions toward a new style: the free-verse study in narrative from multiple perspectives embodied in his *Spoon River*.

Masters's move toward a more modern style was influenced by his growing involvement in the Chicago Renaissance. He worked with Harriet Monroe, editor of the influential *Poetry: A Magazine of Verse*, and gravitated toward such poets as Carl Sandburg. But, as with fellow *Poetry* contributors Ezra Pound and T. S. Eliot (younger poets who would emerge as two of the leading figures of modernism), a key part of Masters's inspiration derived from his assimilation of the ancient classics—in Masters's case, the specific inspiration was J. W. Makail's *Selected Epigrams from the Greek Anthology*, a volume sent to him by a literary friend. Here Masters found prose translations of several hundred short autobiographical poems from ancient Greece, with the speakers often commenting bluntly on both their own lives and their relationships with fellow speakers. One section, which took the form of fictional gravestone epitaphs, provides the direct model for Masters's *Spoon River Anthology*. Masters had at last found a form in which he could communicate his brooding vision of the interconnectedness of individual lives in a small, deeply interwoven Midwestern community, leading him to create what the poet May Swenson terms, in an introduction to a later reprinting, "this ingenious, multi-layered, dramatic, socio-historic, intuitive collection of lives-in-death." Masters lived until 1950 and continued to write prolifically, but he never again approached the popularity or critical acclaim won by his single outstanding success, the 1915 *Spoon River Anthology*.

FURTHER READING

Edgar Lee Masters. *Spoon River Anthology* (with a New Introduction by May Swenson). 1915; reprint, New York: Macmillan, 1962.
Herbert K. Russell. *Edgar Lee Masters: A Biography*. Urbana: University of Illinois Press, 2001.

FROM Spoon River Anthology

The Unknown

Ye aspiring ones, listen to the story of the unknown
Who lies here with no stone to mark the place.
As a boy reckless and wanton,

Wandering with gun in hand through the forest
Near the mansion of Aaron Hatfield,
I shot a hawk perched on the top
Of a dead tree.
He fell with guttural cry
At my feet, his wing broken.
Then I put him in a cage
Where he lived many days cawing angrily at me
When I offered him food.
Daily I search the realms of Hades
For the soul of the hawk,
That I may offer him the friendship
Of one whom life wounded and caged.

1915

Elsa Wertman

I was a peasant girl from Germany,
Blue-eyed, rosy, happy and strong.
And the first place I worked was at Thomas Greene's.
On a summer's day when she was away
He stole into the kitchen and took me
Right in his arms and kissed me on the throat,
I turning my head. Then neither of us
Seemed to know what happened.
And I cried for what would become of me.
And cried and cried as my secret began to show.
One day Mrs. Greene said she understood,
And would make no trouble for me,
And, being childless, would adopt it.
(He had given her a farm to be still.)
So she hid in the house and sent out rumors,
As if it were going to happen to her.
And all went well and the child was born—They were so kind to me.
Later I married Gus Wertman, and years passed.
But—at political rallies when sitters-by thought I was crying
At the eloquence of Hamilton Greene—
That was not it.
No! I wanted to say:
That's my son! That's my son!

1915

Hamilton Greene

I was the only child of Frances Harris of Virginia
And Thomas Greene of Kentucky,
Of valiant and honorable blood both.
To them I owe all that I became,
Judge, member of Congress, leader in the State.
From my mother, I inherited
Vivacity, fancy, language;
From my father will, judgment, logic.
All honor to them
For what service I was to the people!

1915

W. E. B. DU BOIS
1868–1963

THE LEGACY OF W. E. B. Du Bois, one of the nation's most influential African-American intellectuals, includes his famous statement in 1897 about the double identity of African Americans, which he then developed in *The Souls of Black Folk* (1903): "One feels a two-ness—an American, a Negro, two souls, two thoughts, two unreconciled strivings, two warring ideas in one dark body." But his legacy also encompasses poetry; twenty books in politics, sociology, and history; and his autobiography, which was written as he moved among European-American, African-American, African, and international communities. His life work contrasted sharply with Booker T. Washington's politics of accommodation and compromise.

Du Bois was born into a privileged African-American family that included French and Dutch ancestry as well as a great-grandfather who fought in the American Revolution in Great Barrington, Massachusetts. Du Bois learned to understand his double identity in American society when he was sent to Fisk University in Nashville instead of Harvard, his first choice, and encountered for the first time blatant sentiments of white supremacy and racial violence. Several years later he did indeed enter Harvard University and received the first Harvard Ph.D. granted to an African American. He pursued an outstanding career as a university professor, writer, editor of *The Crisis*, National Association for the Advancement of Colored People (NAACP) founder, peace and anticolonial activist, founding United

Nations delegate, and "father of Pan-Africanism." During the 1950s, Du Bois began to face harassment from the U.S. government just as his first wife died and he remarried. He was tried and acquitted for alleged membership in the Communist Party and subjected to passport difficulties on account of his politics, his later Communist Party membership, and a trip he made to the Soviet Union. He moved to Ghana, and when his expired passport was not renewed in 1963, he gave up his U.S. citizenship, becoming a citizen of Ghana several months before he died.

The poems included here express Du Bois's identification with the African-American community, his outrage at racial violence, and his commitment to social equality. The first selection, "A Litany of Atlanta," originally published in *The Independent* in New York, is his response to the news of a 1906 race riot in Atlanta as he traveled back there to his family from his work in Alabama. The last two selections reveal his strategy of political resistance and pay tribute to a multiracial woman.

FURTHER READING

W. E. B. Du Bois. *The Oxford W. E. B. Du Bois Reader*. Ed. Eric J. Sundquist. Oxford: Oxford University Press, 1996.
————. *The Souls of Black Folk*. Harmondsworth, Eng.: Penguin, 1996.
David Levering Lewis. *W. E. B. Du Bois: Biography of a Race, 1868–1919*. New York: Henry Holt, 1994.

A Litany of Atlanta

O Silent God, Thou whose voice afar in mist and mystery hath left our ears a-hungered in these fearful days —
> *Hear us, good Lord!*

Listen to us, Thy children: our faces dark with doubt, are made a mockery in Thy sanctuary. With uplifted hands we front Thy heaven, O God, crying:
> *We beseech Thee to hear us, good Lord!*

We are not better than our fellows, Lord; we are but weak and human men. When our devils do deviltry, curse Thou the doer and the deed: curse them as we curse them, do to them all and more that ever they have done to innocence and weakness, to womanhood and home.
> *Have mercy upon us, miserable sinners!*

And yet whose is the deeper guilt? Who made these devils? Who nursed them in crime and fed them on injustice? Who ravished and debauched their mothers and their grandmothers? Who bought and sold their crime, and waxed fat and rich on public iniquity?

> *Thou knowest, good God!*

Is this Thy justice, O Father, that guilt be easier than innocence, and the innocent crucified for the guilt of the untouched guilty?

> *Justice, O Judge of men!*

Wherefore do we pray? Is not the God of the fathers dead? Have not seers seen in Heaven's halls Thine hearsed and lifeless form stark amidst the black and rolling smoke of sin, where all along bow bitter forms of endless dead?

> *Awake, Thou that sleepest!*

Thou art not dead, but flown afar, up hills of endless light, thru blazing corridors of suns, where worlds do swing of good and gentle men, of women strong and free — far from the cozeage, black hypocrisy and chaste prostitution of this shameful speck of dust!

> *Turn again, O Lord, leave us not to perish in our sin!*

From lust of body and lust of blood

> *Great God deliver us!*

From lust of powers and lust of gold,

> *Great God deliver us!*

From the leagued lying of despot and of brute,

> *Great God deliver us!*

A city lay in travail, God our Lord, and from her loins sprang twin Murder and Black Hate. Red was the midnight; clang, crack and cry of death and fury filled the air and trembled underneath the stars when church spires pointed silently to Thee. And all this was to sate the greed of greedy men who hide behind the veil of vengeance!

> *Bend us Thine ear, O Lord!*

In the pale, still morning we looked upon the deed. We stopped our ears and held our leaping hands, but they — did they not wag their heads and leer and cry with bloody jaws: *Cease from crime!* The word was mockery, for thus they train a hundred crimes while we do cure one.

> *Turn again our captivity, O Lord!*

Behold this maimed and broken thing; dear God, it was an humble black man who toiled and sweat to save a bit from the pittance paid him. They told him: *Work and Rise.* He worked. Did this man sin? Nay, but some one told how some one said another did—one whom he had never seen nor known. Yet for that man's crime this man lieth maimed and murdered, his wife naked to shame, his children, to poverty and evil.

Hear us, O heavenly Father!

Doth not this justice of hell stink in Thy nostrils, O God? How long shall the mounting flood of innocent blood roar in Thine ears and pound in our hearts for vengeance? Pile the pale frenzy of blood-crazed brutes who do such deeds high on Thine altar, Jehovah Jireh, and burn it in hell forever and forever!

Forgive us, good Lord; we know not what we say!

Bewildered we are, and passion-tost, mad with the madness of a mobbed and mocked and murdered people; straining at the armposts of Thy Throne, we raise our shackled hands and charge Thee, God, by the bones of our stolen fathers, by the tears of our dead mothers by the very blood of Thy crucified Christ: *What meaneth this?* Tell us the Plan; give us the Sign!

Keep no thou silent, O God!

Sit no longer blind, Lord God, deaf to our prayer and dumb to our dumb suffering. Surely Thou too are not white, O Lord, a pale, bloodless, heartless thing?

Ah! Christ of all the Pities!

Forgive the thought! Forgive these wild, blasphemous words. Thou art still the God of our black fathers, and in Thy soul's soul sit some soft darkenings of the evening, some shadowings of the velvet night.

But whisper—speak—call, great God, for Thy silence is white terror to our hearts! The way, O God, show us the way and point us the path.

Whither? North is greed and South is blood; within, the coward, and without, the liar. Whither? To death?

Amen! Welcome dark sleep!

Whither? To life? But not this life, dear God, not this. Let the cup pass from us, tempt us not beyond our strength, for there is that clamoring and clawing within, to whose voice we would not listen, yet shudder lest we must, and it is red, Ah! God! It is a red and awful shape.

Selah!

In yonder East trembles a star.

Vengeance is mine; I will repay, saith the Lord!

Thy will, O Lord, be done!

Kyrie Eleison!

Lord, we have done these pleading, wavering words.
    We beseech Thee to hear us, good Lord!

We bow our heads and hearken soft to the sobbing of women and little children.
    We beseech Thee to hear us, good Lord!

Our voices sink in silence and in night.
    Hear us, good Lord!

In night, O God of a godless land!
    Amen!

In silence, O Silent God.
    Selah!

                    Done at Atlanta, in the Day of Death, 1906

                                                        1906

My Country 'Tis of Thee

   Of course you have faced the dilemma: it is announced, they all smirk and
rise. If they are ultra, they remove their hats and look ecstatic; then they look at
you. What shall you do? Noblesse oblige; you cannot be boorish, or ungracious;
and too, after all it is your country and you do love its ideals if not all of its reali-
ties. Now, then, I have thought of a way out: Arise, gracefully remove your hat,
and tilt your head. Then sing as follows, powerfully and with deep unction.
They'll hardly note the little changes and their feelings and your conscience
will thus be saved:

                    My country 'tis of thee,
                    Late land of slavery,
                        Of thee I sing.
                    Land where my father's pride
                    Slept where my mother died,
                    From every mountain side
                        Let freedom ring!

                    My native country thee
                    Land of the slave set free,
                        Thy fame I love.
                    I love thy rocks and rills
                    And o'er thy hate which chills,
                    My heart with purpose thrills,
                        To rise above.

❋   ❋   ❋

Let laments swell the breeze
And wring from all the trees
   Sweet freedom's song.
Let laggard tongues awake,
Let all who hear partake,
Let Southern silence quake,
   The sound prolong.

Our fathers' God to thee
Author of Liberty,
   To thee we sing
Soon may our land be bright,
With Freedom's happy light
Protect us by Thy might,
   Great God our King.

             1907

The Quadroon

Daughter of Twilight,
Mothered of Midnight,
Fathered of Daylight and Dawn;
Shadow of Sunlight,
Shimmering Starlight,
Sister of Forest and Fawn!

Maid of a Morrow,
Mistress of Sorrow,
Mingled of Mourning and Mirth;
Born of World Brotherhood,
Crowned of all Motherhood,
Beauty of Heaven and Earth!

             1911

A quadroon is a person who is one quarter black and three quarters white.

WILLIAM VAUGHN MOODY
1869–1910

As a poet, William Vaughn Moody specialized in quietly eloquent nature poems. "The Bracelet of Grass," for example, meditates on the natural scene, balked desire, love, and loss. This lyric demonstrates Moody's ability to refresh traditional poetic forms and to transform natural objects into evocative symbols. Moody's most notable poem, however, is quite different. "An Ode in Time of Hesitation" assertively entered the public arena to protest national policy at a time of war. Influenced by the work of John Milton, Walt Whitman, and John Greenleaf Whittier, the poem uses free verse and an impassioned rhetoric to make a moral statement. It warns Americans against converting the Spanish-American War into an unjust war of conquest. Although widely read, the poem went unheeded by policy makers. After defeating the Philippines' Spanish colonizers, the United States went on to vanquish the Filipino independence movement. It retained the Philippines as its own colony for the next fifty years.

Moody grew up in several small towns in Indiana. After his parents died when he was seventeen, he moved to Poughkeepsie, New York, where he supported himself as a tutor. He then worked his way through Harvard, receiving his B.A. in 1893 and his M.A. in 1894. Soon thereafter, he accepted a teaching job at the newly founded University of Chicago. Over the following years he collaborated on an edition of the English Puritan and revolutionary poet John Milton and on a college textbook entitled *History of English Literature*. But his heart was in his creative work. In addition to *Poems* (1901), he wrote a mystical play called *The Fire-Bringer* (1904) and a popular melodrama entitled *The Great Divide* (1906). Moody married his longtime lover, Harriet Brainard, at forty but soon afterward became ill. He died of cancer at the age of forty-one, while still in his creative prime.

FURTHER READING

Steven Gould Axelrod. "Colonel Shaw in American Poetry," in *American Quarterly* 24 (October 1972): 523–37.
Maurice Brown. *Estranging Dawn: The Life and Works of William Vaughn Moody.* Carbondale: Southern Illinois University Press, 1973.
Martin Halpern. *William Vaughn Moody.* New York: Twayne, 1964.
William Vaughn Moody. *Poems and Plays.* 1912. New York: AMS Press, 1969.

The Bracelet of Grass

The opal heart of afternoon
Was clouding on to throbs of storm,
Ashen within the ardent west

The lips of thunder muttered harm,
And as a bubble like to break
Hung heaven's trembling amethyst,
When with the sedge-grass by the lake
I braceleted her wrist.

And when the ribbon grass was tied,
Sad with the happiness we planned,
Palm linked in palm we stood awhile
And watched the raindrops dot the sand;
Until the anger of the breeze
Chid all the lake's bright breathing down,
And ravished all the radiancies
From her deep eyes of brown.

We gazed from shelter on the storm,
And through our hearts swept ghostly pain
To see the shards of day sweep past,
Broken, and none might mend again.
Broken, that none shall ever mend;
Loosened, that none shall ever tie.
O the wind and the wind, will it never end?
O the sweeping past of the ruined sky!

1899

An Ode in Time of Hesitation

1

Before the solemn bronze Saint Gaudens made
To thrill the heedless passer's heart with awe,[1]
And set here in the city's talk and trade
To the good memory of Robert Shaw,
This bright March morn I stand,
And hear the distant spring come up the land;
Knowing that what I hear is not unheard

---

1. Augustus St. Gaudens's sculpted, bronze bas-relief of Colonel Robert Gould Shaw and the Massachusetts 54th Regiment stands at a corner of the Boston Common. Although Colonel Shaw was white, the enlisted men of the 54th were black—the first regiment of free blacks in the Union army. After fighting heroically, Colonel Shaw and half his soldiers were killed in Charleston, South Carolina, in 1863. The St. Gaudens statue in their honor was erected in 1896. The poem oscillates between that memory of idealism and courage and what it considers the present moment of base imperialism.

Of this boy soldier and his negro band,
For all their gaze is fixed so stern ahead,
For all the fatal rhythm of their tread.
The land they died to save from death and shame
Trembles and waits, hearing the spring's great name,
And by her pangs these resolute ghosts are stirred.

2

Through street and mall the tides of people go
Heedless; the trees upon the Common show
No hint of green; but to my listening heart
The still earth doth impart
Assurance of her jubilant emprise,[2]
And it is clear to my long-searching eyes
That love at last has might upon the skies.
The ice is runneled[3] on the little pond;
A telltale patter drips from off the trees;
The air is touched with southland spiceries,
As if but yesterday it tossed the frond
Of pendant mosses where the live-oaks grow
Beyond Virginia and the Carolines,
Or had its will among the fruits and vines
Of aromatic isles asleep beyond
Florida and the Gulf of Mexico.

3

Soon shall the Cape Ann children shout in glee,
Spying the arbutus, spring's dear recluse;
Hill lads at dawn shall hearken the wild goose
Go honking northward over Tennessee;
West from Oswego to Sault Sainte-Marie,
And on to where the Pictured Rocks are hung,
And yonder where, gigantic, willful, young,
Chicago sitteth at the northwest gates,
With restless violent hands and casual tongue
Moulding her mighty fates,
The Lakes shall robe them in ethereal sheen;
And like a larger sea, the vital green

2. Adventurous enterprise.   3. Channeled, streaming with water.

Of springing wheat shall vastly be outflung
Over Dakota and the prairie states.
By desert people immemorial
On Arizonan mesas shall be done
Dim rites unto the thunder and the sun;
Nor shall the primal gods lack sacrifice
More splendid, when the white Sierras call
Unto the Rockies straightway to arise
And dance before the unveiled ark of the year,
Sounding their windy cedars as for shawms,[4]
Unrolling rivers clear
For flutter of broad phylacteries;[5]
While Shasta signals to Alaska seas
That watch old sluggish glaciers downward creep
To fling their icebergs thundering from the steep,
And Mariposa through the purple calms
Gazes at far Hawaii crowned with palms
Where East and West are met—
A rich real on the ocean's bosom set
To say that East and West are twain,
With different loss and gain:
The Lord hath sundered them; let them be sundered yet.

4

Alas! what sounds are these that come
Sullenly over the Pacific seas—
Sounds of ignoble battle,[6] striking dumb
The season's half-awakened ecstasies?
Must I be humble, then,
Now when my heart hath need of pride?
Wild love falls on me from these sculptured men;[7]
By loving much the land for which they died
I would be justified.

---

4. Early woodwind instruments that resemble oboes.

5. Amulets, charms, or safeguards. In orthodox Judaism, phylacteries are leather cubes that contain biblical verses and are held to the body by straps.

6. A reference to the war the United States was then waging against Filipino independence. The United States had defeated the Spanish forces at Manila Bay in May 1898. Despite earlier expressions of sympathy for Filipino independence, Admiral Dewey immediately turned his forces against the nationalist movement. The cession of the Philippines to the United States was completed by February 1899. Hostilities between American and rebellious Filipino forces, however, lasted until March 1901. Moody's poem opposes this colonialist war, which it terms "ignoble."

7. That is, the moral heroes depicted in St. Gaudens's bas-relief.

My spirit was away on pinions wide
To soothe in praise of her its passionate mood
And ease it of its ache of gratitude.
Too sorely heavy is the debt they lay
On me and the companions of my day.
I would remember now
My country's goodliness, make sweet her name.
Alas! what shade art thou
Of sorrow or of blame
Liftest the lyric leafage from her brow,
And pointest a slow finger at her shame?

5

Lies! lies! It cannot be! The wars we wage
Are noble, and our battles still are won
By justice for us, ere we lift the gage.
We have not sold our loftiest heritage.
The proud republic hath not stooped to cheat
And scramble in the market-place of war;
Her forehead weareth yet its solemn star.
Here is her witness; this, her perfect son,
This delicate and proud New England soul
Who leads despisèd men, with just-unshackled feet,
Up the large ways where death and glory meet,
To show all peoples that our shame is done,
That once more we are clean and spirit-whole.

6

Crouched in the sea fog on the moaning sand
All night he lay, speaking some simple word
From hour to hour to the slow minds that heard,
Holding each poor life gently in his hand
And breathing on the base rejected clay
Till each dark face shone mystical and grand
Against the breaking day;
And lo, the shard the potter cast away
Was grown a fiery chalice crystal-fine
Fulfilled of the divine
Great wine of battle wrath by God's ring-finger stirred.[8]

8. A fantasized reenactment of the heroism and death of Colonel Shaw and his regiment.

Then upward, where the shadowy bastion loomed
Huge on the mountain in the wet sea light,
Whence now, and now, infernal flowerage bloomed,
Bloomed, burst, and scattered down its deadly seed—
They swept, and died like freemen on the height,
Like freemen, and like men of noble breed;
And when the battle fell away at night
By hasty and contemptuous hands were thrust
Obscurely in a common grave with him
The fair-haired keeper of their love and trust.[9]
Now limb doth mingle with dissolvèd limb
In nature's busy old democracy
To flush the mountain laurel when she blows
Sweet by the southern sea,
And heart with crumbled heart climbs in the rose:
The untaught hearts with the high heart that knew
This mountain fortress for no earthly hold
Of temporal quarrel, but the bastion old
Of spiritual wrong,
Built by an unjust nation sheer and strong,
Expugnable[10] but by a nation's rue
And bowing down before that equal shrine
By all men held divine,
Whereof his band and he were the most holy sign.

7

O bitter, bitter shade![11]
Wilt thou not put the scorn
And instant tragic question from thine eye?
Do thy dark brows yet crave
That swift and angry stave—
Unmeet for this desirous morn—
That I have striven, striven to evade?
Gazing on him, must I not deem they err
Whose careless lips in street and shop aver
As common tidings, deeds to make his cheek
Flush from the bronze, and his dead throat to speak?
Surely some elder singer would arise,
Whose harp hath leave to threaten and to mourn

---

9. The white and the black soldiers of the 54th Regiment were thrown in a common grave.

10. Able to be defeated.

11. The figure of Shaw on the bronze sculpture.

Above this people when they go astray.
Is Whitman, the strong spirit, overworn?
Has Whittier put his yearning wrath away?
I will not and I dare not yet believe!
Though furtively the sunlight seems to grieve,
And the spring-laden breeze
Out of the gladdening west is sinister
With sounds of nameless battle overseas;
Though when we turn and question in suspense
If these things be indeed after these ways,
And what things are to follow after these,
Our fluent men of place and consequence
Fumble and fill their mouths with hollow phrase,
Or for the end-all of deep arguments
Intone their dull commercial liturgies—
I dare not yet believe! My ears are shut!
I will not hear the thin satiric praise
And muffled laughter of our enemies,
Bidding us never sheathe our valiant sword
Till we have changed our birthright for a gourd
Of wild pulse stolen from a barbarian's hut;
Showing how wise it is to cast away
The symbols of our spiritual sway,[12]
That so our hands with better ease
May wield the driver's whip and grasp the jailer's keys.

8

Was it for this our fathers kept the law?
This crown shall crown their struggle and their ruth?[13]
Are we the eagle nation Milton saw
Mewing its mighty youth,
Soon to possess the mountain winds of truth,
And be a swift familiar of the sun
Where aye before God's face his trumpets run?
Or have we but talons and the maw,
And for the abject likeness of our heart
Shall some less lordly bird be set apart?—
Some gross-billed wader where the swamps are fat?
Some gorger in the sun? Some prowler with the bat?

12. Spiritual power.   13. Kindness.

9

Ah no!
We have not fallen so.
We are our fathers' sons: let those who lead us know!
'Twas only yesterday sick Cuba's cry
Came up the tropic wind, "Now help us, for we die!"[14]
Then Alabama heard,
And rising, pale, to Maine and Idaho
Shouted a burning word.
Proud state with proud impassioned state conferred,
And at the lifting of a hand sprang forth,
East, west, and south, and north,
Beautiful armies. Oh, by the sweet blood and young
Shed on the awful hill slope at San Juan,[15]
By the unforgotten names of eager boys
Who might have tasted girls' love and been stung
With the old mystic joys
And starry griefs, now the spring nights come on,
But that the heart of youth is generous—
We charge you, ye who lead us,
Breathe on their chivalry no hint of stain!
Turn not their new-world victories to gain!
One least leaf plucked for chaffer from the bays
Of their dear praise,
One jot of their pure conquest put to hire,
The implacable republic will require;
With clamor, in the glare and gaze of noon,
Or subtly, coming as a thief at night,
But surely, very surely, slow or soon
That insult deep we deeply will requite.
Tempt not our weakness, our cupidity!
For save we let the island men go free,[16]
Those baffled and dislaureled ghosts
Will curse us from the lamentable coasts
Where walk the frustrate dead.
The cup of trembling shall be drainèd quite,

14. A reference to the idealistic arguments against Spanish colonialism in Cuba that accompanied the commencement of the Spanish-American War in 1898. Such arguments looked ironic by 1900, when the United States was in the pro-cess of taking over, rather than liberating, the Philippines.
15. The battle of San Juan Hill in Cuba.
16. That is, the people of the Philippines.

Eaten the sour bread of astonishment,
With ashes of the hearth shall be made white
Our hair, and wailing shall be in the tent;
Then on your guiltier head
Shall our intolerable self-disdain
Wreak suddenly its anger and its pain;
For manifest in that disastrous light
We shall discern the right
And do it, tardily. —O ye who lead,
Take heed!
Blindness we may forgive, but baseness we will smite.

1900

EDWIN ARLINGTON ROBINSON
1869–1935

Eᴅᴡɪɴ ᴀʀʟɪɴɢᴛᴏɴ ʀᴏʙɪɴsᴏɴ's best poems hold in balance an array of contradictory qualities that makes his work seem at once disarmingly straightforward and peculiarly elusive. A leading feature of such poems as "Richard Cory" and "Miniver Cheevy" is an unusual plainspokenness and candor. Yet, just as often, in haunting poems such as "The House on the Hill," "Luke Havergal," and "Eros Turannos," Robinson's style is deeply riddling and enigmatic. Each of these poems centers on an unsolved mystery that lingers in memory long after one has finished reading the poem. Even such frank poems as "Richard Cory" contain a profound riddle at their core.

One continues to face contradictions as one considers Robinson's handling of poetic form. For example, his versification, like his subject matter, has at times been praised or dismissed for its prosy plainness, yet he was a conspicuous master of craft who skillfully manipulated elaborate traditional forms (such as sonnets, villanelles, and a great variety of stanza patterns). Moreover, the most prosaic of his poems modulate at decisive moments into a haunted and haunting lyricism.

Robinson's work emerges, in large part, from a deep-seated loneliness and sense of loss. Robinson never married. However, his youthful sweetheart Emma Sheppard was courted and married by his elder brother Herman. Edwin could not attend the wedding because he found the event too painful. Yet Robinson, despite the lonely spirit that pervades his work, was keenly observant of his fellow human beings, and his many individual portraits are written, in the words of poet Louise Bogan, "with the sympathy of a brother in misfortune [who] notes their failures and degradations without losing sight of their peculiar courage." Thus, while Robinson's prevailing tone is darkly pessimistic, within this pessimism resides a deep core of toughness. In a poem like "The Children of the Night" — whose opening is agonizingly bleak — he is capable of closing on a note of tenacious affirmation. And for every Richard Cory or Miniver Cheevy who surrenders to his fate, one finds a man like Eben Flood or a woman like the unnamed protagonist of "Eros Turannos" — figures who persist in spite of devouring loneliness and daunting losses and uncertainties.

Robinson's life, too, was marked by a peculiar courage. Robinson's family history, which centered in Gardiner, Maine (the model for his Tilbury Town), laid out a pattern of early brilliant success followed by later failure and degradation. Robinson's father, Edward, was a prosperous Maine timber merchant and civic leader who later suffered financial reverses. Robinson's elder brother Dean was a promising doctor who succumbed to morphine addiction and eventually died as a consequence. His oldest brother, Herman, the family business manager, who stole away Edwin's childhood sweetheart, allowed the family business to sink slowly into bankruptcy while he himself sank into alcoholism. Though Robinson was the somewhat sickly and neglected younger son, his career reversed the family pattern, going from early obscurity and apparent failure to later widespread recognition and success. Edwin, despite family discouragement, persisted with his poetry. He suffered years of neglect and poverty as he privately published *The Torrent and the Night Before* (1896), *The Children of the Night* (1897), *Captain Craig* (1902), and *The Town Down the River* (1910) before finally being hailed as an American original for *The Man Against the Sky* (1916). This book hardly varied in style from his previous collections. But public taste — conditioned, perhaps, by the warm reception recently given to Robert Frost (a fellow New England poet, five years Robinson's junior, who had also suffered early neglect) and to Edgar Lee Masters — found Robinson's poems suddenly more attractive and accessible. Robinson's ruggedly and enigmatically "traditional" poetry also offered an alternative to the affronting newness and strangeness of still more radical and "modern" poets such as Ezra Pound, Amy Lowell, and T. S. Eliot. Robinson, about whom a friend had early observed "he was one of those persons whom you cannot influence ever, he went his own way," doggedly persisted in his unique manner until public recognition at last caught up with him.

Ironically, as his poetry became more popular and widely praised — his Arthurian romance *Tristram* (1927) was a best-seller, and when he died in 1935, he was the possessor of three Pulitzer Prizes — his later verse began to lose the austere concentration and haunting power that had marked his earlier lyrics. Moreover, the new poetics of Pound, Lowell, Eliot, and others began to suggest fresh directions for poetry that would ultimately define as "modern" a more radical aesthetic than Robinson's. Yet beginning with his earliest poems in 1890, and for a quarter century thereafter, when the state of American poetry was, arguably, at its lowest ebb, Robinson persisted in going his own way, writing poems that continue to strike home with their distinctively enigmatic clarity.

FURTHER READING

Ellsworth Barnard. *Edwin Arlington Robinson: A Critical Study.* New York: Octagon, 1969.
David Henry Burton. *Edwin Arlington Robinson: Stages in a New England Poet's Development.* Lewiston, N.Y.: E. Mellen, 1987.
Edwin Arlington Robinson. *Collected Poems.* New York: Macmillan, 1937.

The House on the Hill

They are all gone away,
    The House is shut and still,
There is nothing more to say.

Through broken walls and gray
    The winds blow bleak and shrill:
They are all gone away.

Nor is there one today
    To speak them good or ill:
There is nothing more to say.

Why is it then we stray
    Around the sunken sill?
They are all gone away.

And our poor fancy-play
    For them is wasted skill:
There is nothing more to say.

There is ruin and decay
    In the House on the Hill
They are all gone away,
There is nothing more to say.

1893

The Children of the Night

For those that never know the light,
    The darkness is a sullen thing;
And they, the Children of the Night,
    Seem lost in Fortune's winnowing.

But some are strong and some are weak, —
    And there's the story. House and home
Are shut from countless hearts that seek
    World-refuge that will never come.

And if there be no other life,
    And if there be no other chance
To weigh their sorrow and their strife
    Than in the scales of circumstance,

'T were better, ere the sun go down
    Upon the first day we embark,
In life's imbittered sea to drown,
    Than sail forever in the dark.

But if there be a soul on earth
    So blinded with its own misuse
Of man's revealed, incessant worth,
    Or worn with anguish, that it views

No light but for a mortal eye
    No rest but of a mortal sleep,
No God but in a prophet's lie,
    No faith for "honest doubt" to keep;

If there be nothing, good or bad,
    But chaos for a soul to trust, —
God counts it for a soul gone mad,
    And if God be God, He is just.

And if God be God, He is Love;
    And though the Dawn be still so dim,
It shows us we have played enough
    With creeds that make a fiend of Him.

       *   *   *

There is one creed, and only one,
    That glorifies God's excellence;
So cherish, that His will be done,
    The common creed of common sense.

It is the crimson, not the gray,
    That charms the twilight of all time;
It is the promise of the day
    That makes the starry sky sublime;

It is the faith within the fear
    That holds us to the life we curse;—
So let us in ourselves revere
    The Self which is the Universe!

Let us, the Children of the Night,
    Put off the cloak that hides the scar!
Let us be Children of the Light,
    And tell the ages what we are!

1897

John Evereldown

"Where are you going to-night, to-night,—
    Where are you going, John Evereldown?
There's never the sign of a star in sight,
    Nor a lamp that's nearer than Tilbury Town.
Why do you stare as a dead man might?
Where are you pointing away from the light?
And where are you going to-night, to-night,—
    Where are you going, John Evereldown?"

"Right through the forest, where none can see,
    There's where I'm going, to Tilbury Town.
The men are asleep,—or awake, may be,—
    But the women are calling John Evereldown.
Ever and ever they call for me,
And while they call can a man be free?
So right through the forest, where none can see,
    There's where I'm going, to Tilbury Town."

      *   *   *

"But why are you going so late, so late,—
 Why are you going, John Evereldown?
Though the road be smooth and the path be straight,
 There are two long leagues to Tilbury Town.
Come in by the fire, old man, and wait!
Why do you chatter out there by the gate?
And why are you going so late, so late,—
 Why are you going, John Evereldown?"

"I follow the women wherever they call,—
 That's why I'm going to Tilbury Town.
God knows if I pray to be done with it all,
 But God is no friend to John Evereldown.
So the clouds may come and the rain may fall,
The shadows may creep and the dead men crawl,—
But I follow the women wherever they call,
 And that's why I'm going to Tilbury Town."

                                        1897

Luke Havergal

Go to the western gate, Luke Havergal,—
There where the vines cling crimson on the wall,—
And in the twilight wait for what will come.
The wind will moan, the leaves will whisper some—
Whisper of her, and strike you as they fall;
But go, and if you trust her she will call.
Go to the western gate, Luke Havergal—
Luke Havergal.

No, there is not a dawn in eastern skies
To rift the fiery night that's in your eyes;
But there, where western glooms are gathering,
The dark will end the dark, if anything:
God slays Himself with every leaf that flies,
And hell is more than half of paradise.
No, there is not a dawn in eastern skies—
In eastern skies.

Out of a grave I come to tell you this,—
Out of a grave I come to quench this kiss

That flames upon your forehead with a glow
That blinds you to the way that you must go.
Yes, there is yet one way to where she is, —
Bitter, but one that faith can never miss.
Out of a grave I come to tell you this —
To tell you this.

There is the western gate, Luke Havergal,
There are the crimson leaves upon the wall.
Go, — for the winds are tearing them away, —
Nor think to riddle the dead words they say,
Nor any more to feel them as they fall;
But go! and if you trust her she will call.
There is the western gate, Luke Havergal —
Luke Havergal.

1897

Richard Cory

Whenever Richard Cory went down town,
We people on the pavement looked at him:
He was a gentleman from sole to crown,
Clean favored, and imperially slim.

And he was always quietly arrayed,
And he was always human when he talked;
But still he fluttered pulses when he said,
"Good-morning," and he glittered when he walked.

And he was rich, — yes, richer than a king, —
And admirably schooled in every grace:
In fine, we thought that he was everything
To make us wish that we were in his place.

So on we worked, and waited for the light,
And went without the meat, and cursed the bread;
And Richard Cory, one calm summer night,
Went home and put a bullet through his head.

1897

Calverly's

We go no more to Calverly's,
For there the lights are few and low;
And who are there to see by them,
Or what they see, we do not know.
Poor strangers of another tongue
May now creep in from anywhere,
And we, forgotten, be no more
Than twilight on a ruin there.

We two, the remnant. All the rest
Are cold and quiet. You nor I,
Nor fiddle now, nor flagon-lid,
May ring them back from where they lie.
No fame delays oblivion
For them, but something yet survives:
A record written fair, could we
But read the book of scattered lives.

There'll be a page for Leffingwell,
And one for Lingard, the Moon-calf;
And who knows what for Clavering,
Who died because he couldn't laugh?
Who knows or cares? No sign is here,
No face, no voice, no memory;
No Lingard with his eerie joy,
No Clavering, no Calverly.

We cannot have them here with us
To say where their light lives are gone,
Or if they be of other stuff
Than are the moons of Ilion.
So, be their place of one estate
With ashes, echoes, and old wars, —
Or ever we be of the night,
Or we be lost among the stars.

1910

Miniver Cheevy

Miniver Cheevy, child of scorn,
  Grew lean while he assailed the seasons;
He wept that he was ever born,
  And he had reasons.

Miniver loved the days of old
  When swords were bright and steeds were prancing;
The vision of a warrior bold
  Would set him dancing.

Miniver sighed for what was not,
  And dreamed, and rested from his labors;
He dreamed of Thebes and Camelot,[1]
  And Priam's neighbors.[2]

Miniver mourned the ripe renown
  That made so many a name so fragrant;
He mourned Romance, now on the town,
  And Art, a vagrant.

Miniver loved the Medici,[3]
  Albeit he had never seen one;
He would have sinned incessantly
  Could he have been one.

Miniver cursed the commonplace
  And eyed a khaki suit with loathing;
He missed the medieval grace
  Of iron clothing.

Miniver scorned the gold he sought,
  But sore annoyed was he without it;
Miniver thought, and thought, and thought,
  And thought about it.

1. Thebes: an ancient Greek city of mythic renown. Camelot: King Arthur's legendary capital and center for the Knights of the Round Table. Each was a locale both of glamorous undertakings and of tragic catastrophes.
2. Priam was king of Troy. His neighbors were, ironically, the ancient Greeks of Homer's *Iliad* who assailed and eventually destroyed the city after a ten-year siege.
3. A powerful family of wealthy merchants, civic leaders, and patrons of literature and art in Renaissance Florence, who were known both for their enlightened support of philosophy, painting, poetry, and music and for their ruthless business practices and violent suppression of their rivals.

＊   ＊   ＊

Miniver Cheevy, born too late,
    Scratched his head and kept on thinking;
Miniver coughed, and called it fate,
    And kept on drinking.

1910

Eros Turannos

She fears him, and will always ask
    What fated her to choose him;
She meets in his engaging mask
    All reasons to refuse him;
But what she meets and what she fears
Are less than are the downward years,
Drawn slowly to the foamless weirs
    Of age, were she to lose him.

Between a blurred sagacity
    That once had power to sound him,
And Love, that will not let him be
    The Judas that she found him,
Her pride assuages her almost,
As if it were alone the cost. —
He sees that he will not be lost,
    And waits and looks around him.

A sense of ocean and old trees
    Envelops and allures him;
Tradition, touching all he sees,
    Beguiles and reassures him;
And all her doubts of what he says
Are dimmed with what she knows of days —
Till even prejudice delays
    And fades, and she secures him.

The falling leaf inaugurates
    The reign of her confusion;
The pounding wave reverberates
    The dirge of her illusion;
And home, where passion lived and died,

Becomes a place where she can hide,
While all the town and harbor side
    Vibrate with her seclusion.

We tell you, tapping on our brows,
    The story as it should be,—
As if the story of a house
    Were told, or ever could be;
We'll have no kindly veil between
Her visions and those we have seen,—
As if we guessed what hers have been,
    Or what they are or would be.

Meanwhile we do no harm; for they
    That with a god have striven,
Not hearing much of what we say,
    Take what the god has given;
Though like waves breaking it may be,
Or like a changed familiar tree,
Or like a stairway to the sea
    Where down the blind are driven.

              1913

A literal translation of this title from the Greek would be "Love, the King," but the more evocative cognate "Love, the Tyrant" seems still more appropriate.

The Mill

The miller's wife had waited long,
    The tea was cold, the fire was dead;
And there might yet be nothing wrong
    In how he went and what he said:
"There are no millers any more,"
    Was all that she heard him say;
And he had lingered at the door
    So long that it seemed yesterday.

Sick with a fear that had no form
    She knew that she was there at last;
And in the mill there was a warm
    And mealy fragrance of the past.

What else there was would only seem
    To say again what he had meant;
And what was hanging from a beam
    Would not have heeded where she went.

And if she thought it followed her,
    She may have reasoned in the dark
That one way of the few there were
    Would hide her and would leave no mark:
Black water, smooth above the weir
    Like starry velvet in the night,
Though ruffled once, would soon appear
    The same as ever to the sight.

                                        1920

Mr. Flood's Party

Old Eben Flood, climbing alone one night
Over the hill between the town below
And the forsaken upland hermitage
That held as much as he should ever know
On earth again of home, paused warily.
The road was his with not a native near;
And Eben, having leisure, said aloud,
For no man else in Tilbury Town to hear:

"Well, Mr. Flood, we have the harvest moon
Again, and we may not have many more;
The bird is on the wing, the poet says,
And you and I have said it here before.
Drink to the bird." He raised up to the light
The jug that he had gone so far to fill,
And answered huskily: "Well, Mr. Flood,
Since you propose it, I believe I will."

Alone, as if enduring to the end
A valiant armor of scarred hopes outworn,
He stood there in the middle of the road
Like Roland's[1] ghost winding a silent horn.

1. Roland was a legendary knight who served King Charlemagne. Just before he died heroically in battle, he sounded his horn to call for help for his outnumbered band. His exploits are featured in *The Song of Roland* (ca. 1100).

Below him, in the town among the trees,
Where friends of other days had honored him,
A phantom salutation of the dead
Rang thinly till old Eben's eyes were dim.

Then, as a mother lays her sleeping child
Down tenderly, fearing it may awake,
He set the jug down slowly at his feet
With trembling care, knowing that most things break;
And only when assured that on firm earth
It stood, as the uncertain lives of men
Assuredly did not, he paced away,
And with his hand extended paused again:

"Well, Mr. Flood, we have not met like this
In a long time; and many a change has come
To both of us, I fear, since last it was
We had a drop together. Welcome home!"
Convivially returning with himself,
Again he raised the jug up to the light;
And with an acquiescent quaver said:
"Well, Mr. Flood, if you insist, I might.

"Only a very little, Mr. Flood—
For auld lang syne. No more, sir; that will do."
So, for the time, apparently it did,
And Eben evidently thought so too;
For soon amid the silver loneliness
Of night he lifted up his voice and sang,
Secure, with only two moons listening,
Until the whole harmonious landscape rang—

"For auld lang syne." The weary throat gave out,
The last word wavered, and the song was done.
He raised again the jug regretfully
And shook his head, and was again alone.
There was not much that was ahead of him,
And there was nothing in the town below—
Where strangers would have shut the many doors
That many friends had opened long ago.

1921

STEPHEN CRANE

1871–1900

THE CRITIC CARL VAN DOREN declared in 1924 that "modern American literature may be said, accurately enough, to have begun with Stephen Crane." Claims by Van Doren and others for Crane as an initiating force in the first phase of modern American letters rest primarily on his fiction, particularly that vividly realistic and psychologically probing re-creation of two days of Civil War combat, *The Red Badge of Courage* (1896). This short novel, arguably the most convincing dramatization of the trauma of war in American literature, brought Crane national and international fame when he was just twenty-five. His other important fictional works, which share such characteristics with *Red Badge* as conciseness, uniqueness, and a bleak and penetrating treatment of human psychology, include an early novella of the blighting effects of urban poverty, *Maggie: A Girl of the Streets*, as well as such arresting and original short stories as "The Open Boat," "The Blue Hotel," and "The Bride Comes to Yellow Sky." Yet Crane was not simply an innovative fiction writer. He was also a prolific and hard-hitting journalist, travel writer, and war correspondent. A modern edition of the writings he completed before his early death from tuberculosis at twenty-nine now fills ten very thick volumes. But Crane placed particular value on the two slim books of poetry published in his lifetime, *The Black Riders and Other Lines* (1895) and *War is Kind* (1899).

Crane is a distinctive and original poet, and his verse—which shares his fiction's characteristic terseness and psychological probing—anticipates many modernist tendencies. These include experimentation with free verse and the prose poem, an anti-Romantic hardness of surface, an attraction to symbolism, an exploration of the potentialities of the lyric sequence, and an edgily ironic sharpness of moral inquiry, all blended with that covert attraction to Romantic themes so typical of the early moderns. Yet as Crane's biographer and fellow poet John Berryman has acutely observed, his modernity is troubled and beset by contradictory impulses: "Part of the irony in Crane's poetry results from the imposition of his complex modern doubt upon a much stronger primeval set of his mind."

Crane's earliest book of poems, *The Black Riders and Other Lines*, appeared in 1895, when Crane was just twenty-four years old. It is a numbered sequence of sixty-eight brief, untitled poems that, through its short lines and probing introspection, shows a strong affinity with the work of Emily Dickinson, samples of whose work had begun to appear posthumously in two selected volumes in 1890 and 1891. But Crane's rhythm and tone, and his stark and unsettling little dramatic scenes, remain sharply his own. Moreover, despite his upbringing in a strictly religious household as the son of a Methodist minister, Crane utterly abandons the Christian and Transcendentalist elements native to Dickinson's cultural framework, replacing them with a desperate and embattled paganism whose gods rebuff humankind with either violence or indifference. Crane's second volume, *War is Kind*, which appeared one year before his death, continues to explore with bleak irony the plight of the human race in a hostile or apathetic universe. These poems, numbered and untitled like those in *The Black Riders*, are often slightly more extended, but they continue to be shocking in their directness. A final grouping of poems was published posthumously. Berryman has aptly suggested of Crane's peculiarly enigmatic candor, "His poetry has the inimitable sincerity of a frightened savage anxious to learn what his dream means."

FURTHER READING

John Berryman. *Stephen Crane*. New York: Sloane, 1950.
Stephen Crane. *Works*. Vol. 10, *Poems and Literary Remains*. Charlottesville: University of Virginia Press, 1969.
David Halliburton. *The Color of the Sky: A Study of Stephen Crane*. New York: Cambridge University Press, 1989.

FROM The Black Riders and Other Lines

1

Black riders came from the sea.
There was clang and clang of spear and shield,
And clash and clash of hoof and heel,
Wild shouts and the wave of hair
In the rush upon the wind:
Thus the ride of sin.

1895

3

In the desert
I saw a creature, naked, bestial,
Who, squatting upon the ground,
Held his heart in his hands,
And ate of it.
I said, "Is it good, friend?"
"It is bitter—bitter," he answered;

"But I like it
"Because it is bitter,
"And because it is my heart."[1]

1895

9

I stood upon a high place,
And saw, below, many devils
Running, leaping,
And carousing in sin.
One looked up, grinning,
And said, "Comrade! Brother!"

1895

19

A god in wrath
Was beating a man;
He cuffed him loudly
With thunderous blows
That rang and rolled over the earth.
All people came running.
The man screamed and struggled,
And bit madly at the feet of the god.
The people cried,
"Ah, what a wicked man!"
And—
"Ah, what a redoubtable god!"

1895

24

I saw a man pursuing the horizon;
Round and round they sped.

---

1. The last two lines of this poem became the title of one of contemporary fiction writer Joyce Carol Oates's most memorable novels.

I was disturbed at this;
I accosted the man.
"It is futile," I said,
"You can never—"

"You lie," he cried,
And ran on.

1895

27

A youth in apparel that glittered
Went to walk in a grim forest.
There he met an assassin
Attired all in garb of old days;
He, scowling through the thickets,
And dagger poised quivering,
Rushed upon the youth.
"Sir," said this latter,
"I am enchanted, believe me,
"To die, thus,
"In this medieval fashion,
"According to the best legends;
"Ah, what joy!"
Then took he the wound, smiling,
And died, content.

1895

46

Many red devils ran from my heart
And out upon the page,
They were so tiny
The pen could mash them.
And many struggled in the ink.
It was strange
To write in this red muck
Of things from my heart.

1895

56

A man feared that he might find an assassin;
Another that he might find a victim.
One was more wise than the other.

1895

FROM War is Kind

76

Do not weep, maiden, for war is kind.
Because your lover threw wild hands toward the sky
And the affrighted steed ran on alone,
Do not weep.
War is kind.

    Hoarse, booming drums of the regiment
    Little souls who thirst for fight,
    These men were born to drill and die
    The unexplained glory flies above them
    Great is the battle-god, great, and his kingdom—
    A field where a thousand corpses lie.

Do not weep, babe, for war is kind.
Because your father tumbled in the yellow trenches,
Raged at his breast, gulped and died,
Do not weep.
War is kind.

    Swift, blazing flag of the regiment
    Eagle with crest of red and gold,
    These men were born to drill and die
    Point for them the virtue of slaughter
    Make plain to them the excellence of killing
    And a field where a thousand corpses lie.

Mother whose heart hung humble as a button
On the bright splendid shroud of your son,
Do not weep.
War is kind.

1899

96

A man said to the universe:
"Sir, I exist!"
"However," replied the universe,
"The fact has not created in me
"A sense of obligation."

1899

POSTHUMOUSLY PUBLISHED POEMS

113

A man adrift on a slim spar
A horizon smaller than the rim of a bottle
Tented waves rearing lashy dark points
The near whine of froth in circles.

God is cold.

The incessant raise and swing of the sea
And growl after growl of crest
The sinkings, green, seething, endless
The upheaval half-completed.

God is cold.

The seas are in the hollow of The Hand;
Oceans may be turned to a spray
Raining down through the stars
Because of a gesture of pity toward a babe.
Oceans may become grey ashes,
Die with a long moan and a roar
Amid the tumult of the fishes
And the cries of the ships,
Because The Hand beckons the mice.

A horizon smaller than a doomed assassin's cap,
Inky, surging tumults
A reeling, drunken sky and no sky
A pale hand sliding from a polished spar.

God is cold.

　　✻　✻　✻

The puff of a coat imprisoning air.
A face kissing the water-death
A weary slow sway of a lost hand
And the sea, the moving sea, the sea.

God is cold.

1900

JAMES WELDON JOHNSON
1871–1938

THE SLOGAN "BLACK IS beautiful" could have been coined by James Weldon
Johnson. He built his poetry on what he saw as the noble and valorous character
and history of African-American folk culture, art, and music. His resulting legacy
was an ethos for future African-American poets that urged them to turn their social
marginality into revolutionary and transformational artistic power rather than di-
vided cultural consciousness.

Johnson was born in Jacksonville, Florida, and enjoyed a privileged childhood
and education. After graduating from Atlanta University with a bachelor's and
then a master's degree, he taught high school and became a high school principal.
Soon, however, he embarked upon a remarkable political and literary career. As
a journalist, he helped found the *Daily American*, the nation's first African-
American daily newspaper, and he wrote columns for *New York Age*. He also pub-
lished a novel entitled *The Autobiography of an Ex-Colored Man* in 1912, but he
did so anonymously. The book did not gain its deserved recognition until he pub-
lished it under his own name in 1927. From 1916 through 1930, Johnson served as
an official for the NAACP. He also lobbied for the Dyer Anti-Lynching Bill, be-
came a U.S. consul to Venezuela and Nicaragua, and served as a diplomat in Ja-
pan. Toward the end of his life, he held a series of academic professorships at Fisk
University and elsewhere that extended his reputation as a poet, novelist, literary
critic, biographer, cultural historian, and philosopher.

Johnson published three volumes of poetry and edited *The Book of American
Negro Poetry* (1922) and two books of American spirituals. In 1900 his lyric "Lift
Ev'ry Voice and Sing" became known as the "Black National Anthem." The two
selections presented here pay tribute to two major sources of African-American
poetic creativity: African-American ancestral bards and the city of Manhattan.

FURTHER READING

Dickson D. Bruce, Jr. *Black Writing from the Nadir: The Evolution of a Literary Tradition, 1877–1915*. Baton Rouge: Louisiana State University Press, 1989.
James Weldon Johnson. *Complete Poems*. Ed. Sondra Kathryn Wilson. Harmondsworth, Eng.: Penguin, 2000.
Kenneth Price and Lawrence Oliver, eds. *Critical Essays on James Weldon Johnson*. Boston: G. K. Hall, 1997.

O Black and Unknown Bards

O black and unknown bards of long ago,
How came your lips to touch the sacred fire?
How, in your darkness, did you come to know
The power and beauty of the minstrels' lyre?
Who first from midst his bonds lifted his eyes?
Who first from out the still watch, lone and long,
Feeling the ancient faith of prophets rise
Within his dark-kept soul, burst into song?

Heart of what slave poured out such melody
As "Steal away to Jesus"? On its strains
His spirit must have nightly floated free
Though still about his hands he felt his chains.
Who heard great "Jordan roll"? Whose starward eye
Saw chariot "swing low"? And who was he
That breathed that comforting, melodic sigh,
"Nobody knows de trouble I see"?

What merely living clod, what captive thing,
Could up toward God through all its darkness grope,
And find within its deadened heart to sing
These songs of sorrow, love and faith, and hope?
How did it catch that subtle undertone
That note in music heard not with the ears?
How sound the elusive reed so seldom blown,
Which stirs the soul or melts the heart to tears.

Not that great German master in his dream
Of harmonies that thundered amongst the stars
At the creation, ever heard a theme
Nobler than "Go down, Moses." Mark its bars
How like a mighty trumpet-call they stir

The blood. Such are the notes that men have sung
Going to valorous deeds; such tones there were
That helped make history when Time was young.

There is a wide, wide wonder in it all,
That from degraded rest and servile toil
The fiery spirit of the seer should call
These simple children of the sun and soil.
O black slave singers, gone, forgot, unfamed,
You—you alone, of all the long, long line
Of those who've sung untaught, unknown, unnamed,
Have stretched out upward, seeking the divine.

You sang not deeds of heroes or of kings;
No chant of bloody war, no exulting paean
No arms-won triumphs; but your humble strings
You touched in chord with music empyrean.
You sang far better than you knew; the songs
That for your listeners' hungry hearts sufficed
Still live—but more than this to you belongs:
You sang a race from wood and stone to Christ.

1908

My City

When I come down to sleep death's endless night,
   The threshold of the unknown dark to cross,
   What to me then will be the keenest loss,
When this bright world blurs on my fading sight?
Will it be that no more I shall see the trees
   Or smell the flowers or hear the singing birds
   Or watch the flashing streams or patient herds?
No, I am sure it will be none of these.
But, ah! Manhattan's sights and sounds, her smells,
   Her crowds, her throbbing force, the thrill that comes
From being of her a part, her subtle spells,
   Her shining towers, her avenues, her slums—
   O God! the stark, unutterable pity,
To be dead, and never again behold my city!

1923

PAUL LAURENCE DUNBAR
1872–1906

Paul laurence dunbar is one of the key writers in African-American literary tradition and the American canon of poetry. Henry Louis Gates has written that Dunbar initiated an enduring debate within black aesthetic theory concerning "the absence and presence of the black voice in the text." Joanne Braxton has called Dunbar an author "whose career transcends race and locality even while he makes use of racialized and regional cultural materials to create an African-American aesthetic and a unique black poetic diction." Dunbar was best known in his own day for his humorous and touching poems written in Southern black dialect. These very popular poems were subsequently condemned for reinforcing white stereotypes of blacks, though they may be seen today as containing resistant codes of meaning. Dunbar also wrote serious poems in standard English, which were less recognized in his time but are perhaps more powerful in ours. J. Saunders Redding once wrote of Dunbar that "no Negro of finer artistic spirit has been born in America, and none whose fierce, secret energies were more powerfully directed toward breaking down the vast wall of emotional and intellectual misunderstanding with which he, as a poet, was immured." Dunbar's serious poems were particularly effective in attacking "the vast wall of misunderstanding" that had been constructed around black culture, and they explored black subjectivity and sociality with eloquence and insight.

Paul Laurence Dunbar was born in Dayton, Ohio, to parents who had been slaves in Kentucky. His father had escaped from slavery and then served in the Union army. When Paul was four, his parents separated, and his father died soon thereafter. Paul was brought up by his mother, a laundry worker. The only African-American student in his public school class, he excelled in his studies and served as editor of his high school literary magazine. Too poor to afford college and unable to find a job in journalism because of racial prejudice, Dunbar took odd jobs, such as elevator operator, and began to write poetry, publishing his first books at his own expense. Soon his poetry was appearing in magazines and the *New York Times*.

Dunbar's second self-published book, *Majors and Minors* (1895), received a favorable review in *Harper's* from one of the country's leading men of letters, the white novelist William Dean Howells. Howells wrote that Dunbar was "the only man of pure African blood and of American civilization to feel the Negro life aesthetically and express it lyrically." The review made Dunbar famous—but at a price. Howells made clear his preference for Dunbar's entertaining dialect poems (which Dunbar called "minors") over his more serious poems (Dunbar's "majors"). The review initiated a taste for the dialect poems that Dunbar would have to deal with throughout the rest of his career. As the poet was later to lament to his friend James Weldon Johnson, "You know, of course, that I didn't start as a dialect poet. I simply came to the conclusion that I could write it as well, if not better, than anybody else I knew of, and that by doing so I could gain a hearing. I gained the hearing, and now they don't want me to write anything but dialect."

In 1896 Dunbar's *Lyrics of Lowly Life* appeared, published by a top-flight New York publishing house. A compendium of old and new poems, the volume met with great success, making its author a household name among readers of poetry. The volume's popularity resulted from its inclusion of many dialect poems, such as "Accountability" and "When Malindy Sings." Owing some of their familiarity to minstrelsy (in which white performers sang songs and made jokes in the guise of African Americans), these "plantation" poems seemed to reinforce a notion of black culture as enjoyable and unthreatening. Such an interpretation, however, overlooked the subversive elements of the poems. Although "Accountability," for example, is humorous, the humor disguises serious ideas. For one thing, its speaker—a slave or tenant farmer—defends what is ultimately a transgressive act. In doing so, he makes a plea for tolerance and diversity that, however facetious, may also be read as straightforward and thought-provoking. Moreover, his rationale for having stolen a chicken reveals, beneath the comic surface, some grim realities: the hunger, poverty, privation, and powerlessness in which plantation blacks were forced to live. Finally, the sophistication of the speaker's argument undermines any condescension the reader might be tempted to feel toward him. In a similar way, "Malindy" sentimentalizes the singing of a black woman but also emphasizes the cultural importance of music in binding African Americans together as a community. Although these dialect poems may have reflected patronizing white stereotypes about blacks, they also revised the stereotypes with layers of love, pride, and assertiveness. In effect, they were a deforming mimicry of white minstrelsy and a reappropriation of black culture and voice.

Majors and Minors and *Lyrics of Lowly Life* also contained many powerful poems written in standard poetic English. These poems meant the most to Dunbar himself. They reveal the influence both of black intellectuals and writers, such as Frederick Douglass, Frances Harper, and James Weldon Johnson (the latter two included in this anthology), and of white poets, such as Alfred, Lord Tennyson and John Greenleaf Whittier (the latter also included in this anthology). These poems reveal the daily realities of an African-American poet while showing at the same time his mastery of European-American poetic traditions. Some deal with racial issues, often by means of coded messages of the sort that Phillis Wheatley, writing in the eighteenth century, was forced to use but that Frances Harper, writing only a couple of decades before Dunbar, was not. "We Wear the Mask," for example, is about codes or "masks" and itself employs a mask: the "we" is never explicitly identified as black, though black readers and sympathetic others are meant to understand. The poem may thus be read as edgily depicting the hidden condition of American blacks or, more blandly, as invoking a universal human condition. "We Wear the Mask" suggests what W. E. B. Du Bois (also included in this anthology) was soon to identify as the "double-consciousness" of African-American life, a dichotomy between being black and existing in a white-dominated world. That "twoness" can be detected as well in the shape of Dunbar's career: in the difference between his serious poems, which expressed his honest feelings, and his dialect poems, which white readers found amusing. Other poems in these early volumes address issues that cross racial lines. "The Mystery," for example, meditates somberly on the meaning of existence, suspended between a wish to believe and a ceaseless doubt. "A Summer's Night" ponders the enchantments and the costs of desire.

The publication of these volumes made Dunbar a literary star among black and white audiences alike. He married Alice Dunbar (later Alice Dunbar-Nelson), a teacher and fellow poet, and the couple settled down in Washington, D.C. Publishing volumes of fiction as well as poetry, Dunbar was soon able to quit his job at the Library of Congress to live off his royalties. He published some of his best poetry in these later years. "Sympathy," perhaps his masterpiece, expresses a desire for political freedom and racial equality, at the same time revealing a core of personal anguish and a belief in the prayerlike qualities of poetry or song. This poem beautifully evokes the way history impinges on and shapes personal destiny. It exemplifies many of Dunbar's most striking qualities as a poet: lyricism, sadness, self-doubt, a sense of fair play, and a quiet goodness.

"The Haunted Oak," another late poem, addresses history as well. It tells the story of a mob lynching an innocent man who, again in a coded discourse, is implicitly black. The code, however, is easy to break, making the poem's political and social significance available to anyone who wishes to perceive it. Other late poems are more deeply personal. "The Debt" explores the anguish, guilt, and sorrow that are never far below the surface of Dunbar's discourse. "Compensation" gathers for a last time several of the threads that tie his poems together: the power of desire, the fragility of love, the beauty and difficulty of song, and the persistence of despair.

Dunbar spent his last years in pain. Separated from his wife, he was drinking heavily. In addition, like Henry David Thoreau and Stephen Crane, he had contracted tuberculosis, and his health began to fail. After spending time in New York and Chicago, he returned in 1903 to his birthplace of Dayton, Ohio. Three years later he died in his mother's house.

718 ◆ *Paul Laurence Dunbar*

Fahamisha Patricia Brown. *Performing the Word: African American Poetry as Vernacular Culture.* New Brunswick, N.J.: Rutgers University Press, 1999.

Dickson D. Bruce, Jr. *Black American Writing from the Nadir: The Evolution of a Literary Tradition, 1877–1915.* Baton Rouge: Louisiana State University Press, 1989.

Paul Laurence Dunbar. *Collected Poetry.* Edited and with an introduction by Joanne M. Braxton. Charlottesville: University of Virginia Press, 1993.

Henry Louis Gates, Jr. *The Signifying Monkey: A Theory of African-American Literary Criticism.* New York: Oxford University Press, 1988.

J. Saunders Redding. *To Make a Poet Black.* 1939. Ithaca, N.Y.: Cornell University Press, 1988.

Accountability

Folks ain't got no right to censuah[1] other folks about dey habits;
Him dat giv' de squir'ls de bushtails made de bobtails fu' de rabbits.
Him dat built de gread big mountains hollered out de little valleys,
Him dat made de streets an' driveways wasn't shamed to make de alleys.[2]

We is all constructed diff'ent, d'ain't no two of us de same;
We cain't he'p ouah likes an' dislikes, ef we'se bad we ain't to blame.
Ef we'se good, we needn't show off, case you bet it ain't ouah doin'
We gits into su'ttain channels dat we jes' cain't he'p pu'suin.

But we all fits into places dat no othah ones could fill,
An we does the things we has to, big er little, good er ill.
John cain't tek de place o' Henry, Su an' Sally ain't alike;
Bass ain't nuthin' like a suckah, chub ain't nuthin' like a pike.[3]

When you come to think about it, how it's all planned out it's splendid.
Nuthin's done er evah happens, 'dout hit's somefin' dat's intended;
Don't keer whut you does, you has to, an' hit sholy beats de dickens—
Viney,[4] go put on de kittle, I got one o' mastah's chickens.

1895

One of the dialect poems that made Dunbar famous, this dramatic monologue, in trochaic octameter, is spoken by a lovable and cunning rascal in a stylized language fashioned from, yet different from, actual speech.

1. Censure, reproach.
2. Note the way that the discourse parodies, or makes use of, Protestant moralizing sermons, Darwinian evolutionary theory, and philosophical debates about free will.
3. Different varieties of fish.
4. The speaker's wife.

The Mystery

I was not; now I am—a few days hence
I shall not be; I fain[1] would look before
And after, but can neither do; some Power
Or lack of power says "no" to all I would.
I stand upon a wide and sunless plain,
Nor chart nor steel to guide my steps aright.
Whene'er, o'ercoming fear, I dare to move,
I grope without direction and by chance.
Some feign to hear a voice and feel a hand
That draws them ever upward thro' the gloom.
But I—I hear no voice and touch no hand,
Tho' oft thro' silence infinite I list.[2]
And strain my hearing to supernal[3] sounds;
Tho' oft thro' fateful darkness do I reach,
And stretch my hand to find that other hand.
I question of th' eternal bending skies
That seem to neighbor with the novice earth;
But they roll on, and daily shut their eyes
On me, as I one day shall do on them,
And tell me not the secret that I ask.

1895

This spiritual confession employs the unrhymed pentameter of blank verse, an elevated poetic form traditionally used to probe complex philosophical, intellectual, and emotional issues.

A Summer's Night

The night is dewy as a maiden's mouth,
    The skies are bright as are a maiden's eyes,
    Soft as a maiden's breath, the wind that flies
Up from the perfumed bosom of the South.
Like sentinels, the pines stand in the park;
    And hither hastening like rakes[1] that roam,
    With lamps to light their wayward footsteps home,
The fire-flies come stagg'ring down the dark.

1895

1. Gladly, willingly.
2. Listen.

3. Heavenly, divine.
1. Rakehells, men who are sexually promiscuous.

We Wear the Mask

We wear the mask that grins and lies,
It hides our cheeks and shades our eyes—
This debt we pay to human guile;
With torn and bleeding hearts we smile,
And mouth with myriad subtleties.

Why should the world be over-wise,
In counting all our tears and sighs?
Nay, let them only see us, while
    We wear the mask.

We smile, but, O great Christ, our cries
To thee from tortured souls arise.
We sing, but oh the clay is vile
Beneath our feet, and long the mile;
But let the world dream otherwise,
    We wear the mask!

                1895

This poem, written in iambic tetrameter with intricately interwoven rhymes, makes a point about the lives of minorities—and specifically blacks—that has reverberated ever since. Eight years after the publication of this poem, Dunbar's friend W. E. B. Du Bois similarly described the "double-consciousness" of African Americans in *The Souls of Black Folk*: "This sense of always looking at one's self through the eyes of others, of measuring one's soul by the tape of a world that looks on in amused contempt and pity. One ever feels his twoness—an American, a Negro; two souls, two thoughts, two unreconciled strivings, two warring ideals in one dark body." This image of a masked or divided black self can also be observed in such later works as Langston Hughes's poem "Brass Spittoons," Richard Wright's story "The Man Who Lived Underground," and Ralph Ellison's novel *Invisible Man*.

When Malindy Sings

G'way an' quit dat noise, Miss Lucy[1]—
    Put dat music book away;
What's de use to keep on tryin'?

[1]. Joanne Braxton comments, "Using irony, caricature, and understatement, Dunbar here 'signifies' on the whites' assumption of biological and intellectual superiority as well as their ability to read books and music. With all these supposed assets, Miss Lucy can't sing 'right.' . . . The comic use of dialect in 'When Malindy Sings' cuts two ways, masking the speaker's critique of a white woman he is not free to criticize openly."

Ef you practice twell you're gray,
    You cain't sta't no notes a-flyin'
      Lak de ones dat rants and rings
    F'om de kitchen to de big woods
      When Malindy sings.

You ain't got de nachel o'gans
      Fu' to make de soun' come right,
You ain't got de tu'ns an' twistin's
      Fu' to make it sweet an' light.
Tell you one thing now, Miss Lucy,
      An' I'm tellin' you fu' true,
When hit comes to raal right singin',
      'Tain't no easy thing to do.

Easy 'nough fu' folks to hollah,
      Lookin' at de lines an' dots,
When dey ain't no one kin sense it,
      An' de chune[2] comes in, in spots;
But fu' real melojous music,
      Dat jes' strikes yo' hea't and clings,
Jes' you stan' an' listen wif me
      When Malindy sings.

Ain't you nevah hyeahd Malindy?
      Blessed soul, tek up de cross!
Look hyeah, ain't you jokin', honey?
      Well, you don't know whut you los'.
Y' ought to hyeah dat gal a-wa'blin',
      Robins, la'ks,[3] an' all dem things,
Heish dey moufs an' hides dey faces,
      When Malindy sings.

Fiddlin' man jes' stop his fiddlin',
      Lay his fiddle on de she'f;
Mockin'-bird quit tryin' to whistle,
      'Cause he jes' so shamed hisse'f
Folks a-playin' on de banjo
      Draps dey fingahs on de strings—
Bless yo' soul—fu'gits to move 'em,
      When Malindy sings.

2. Tune.   3. Larks.

＊　＊　＊

She jes' spreads huh mouf and follahs,
   "Come to Jesus,"[4] twell you hyeah
Sinnahs' tremblin' steps and voices,
   Timid-lak a-drawlin' neah;
Den she tu'ns to "Rock of Ages,"
   Simply to de cross she clings,
An' you fin' yo' teahs a-drappin'
   When Malindy sings.

Who dat says dat humble praises
   Wif de Master nevah counts?
Heish yo' mouf, I hyeah dat music,
   Ez hit rises up an' mounts—
Floatin' by de hills an' valleys,
   Way above dis buryin' sod,
Ez hit makes its way in glory
   To de very gates of God!

Oh, hit's swetah dan de music
   Of an edicated band;
An' hit's dearah dan de battle's
   Song o' triumph in de lan'.
It seems holier dan evenin'
   When de solemn chu'ch bell rings,
Ez I sit an' ca'mly listen
   While Malindy sings.

Towsah,[5] stop dat ba'kin', hyeah me!
   Mandy, mek dat chile keep still;
Don't yo hyeah de echoes callin'
   F'om de valley to de hill?
Let me listen, I can hyeah it,
   Th'oo de bresh of angels' wings,
Sof' an' sweet, "Swing Low, Sweet Chariot,"[6]
   Ez Malindy sings.

1895

This dialect poem, perhaps Dunbar's most popular, may recall the singing of the poet's mother, Matilda Dunbar.

---

4. Christian hymn, as is "Rock of Ages," below.   6. African-American spiritual.
5. A dog's name.

This poetic tribute is addressed to Frederick Douglass (1817–1895), an escaped slave who went on to a distinguished career as abolitionist writer, orator, and editor. He published *The Narrative of the Life of Frederick Douglass* in 1845, advised President Lincoln during the Civil War, and became a diplomat. The poem expresses a longing for the strength Douglass provided to the African-American community in dark times.

The Debt

This is the debt I pay
Just for one riotous day,
Years of regret and grief,
Sorrow without relief.

Pay it I will to the end—
Until the grave, my friend,
Gives me a true release—
Gives me the clasp of peace.

Slight was the thing I bought,
Small was the debt I thought,
Poor was the loan at best—
God! But the interest!

1903

The Haunted Oak

Pray why are you so bare, so bare,
    Oh bough of the old oak-tree;
And why, when I go through the shade you throw,
    Runs a shudder over me?

My leaves were green as the best, I trow,[1]
    And sap ran free in my veins,
But I saw in the moonlight dim and weird
    A guiltless victim's pains.[2]

I bent me down to hear his sigh;
    I shook with his gurgling moan,
And I trembled sore when they rode away,
    And left him here alone.

1. Believe or trust.
2. That is, a man hanged in the tree. Although the poem nowhere specifies his race, a rash of lynchings of African-American men occurred at the turn of the century. Most savvy readers would have made the connection.

*   *   *

They'd charged him with the old, old crime,
    And set him fast in jail:
Oh why does the dog howl all night long,
    And why does the night wind wail?

He prayed his prayer and he swore his oath,
    And he raised his hand to the sky;
But the beat of hoofs smote[3] on his ear,
    And the steady tread drew nigh.

Who is it rides by night, by night,
    Over the moonlit road?
And what is the spur that keeps the pace,
    What is the galling goad?

And now they beat at the prison door,
    "Ho, keeper, do not stay!
We are friends of him whom you hold within,
    And we fain would take him away.

"From those who ride fast on our heels
    With mind to do him wrong;
They have no care for his innocence,
    And the rope they bear is long."

They have fooled the jailer with lying words,
    They have fooled the man with lies;
The bolts unbar, the locks are drawn,
    And the great door open flies.

Now they have taken him from the jail,
    And hard and fast they ride,
And the leader laughs low down in his throat,
    As they halt my trunk beside.

Oh the judge, he wore a mask of black,
    And the doctor one of white,
And the minister, with his oldest son,
    Was curiously bedight.[4]

3. Struck sharply.
4. Arrayed or dressed. The implication here is that the town's leading white citizens are wearing the hoods and sheets of the Ku Klux Klan.

＊   ＊   ＊

Oh foolish man, why weep you now?
    'Tis but a little space,
And the time will come when these shall dread
    The mem'ry of your face.[5]

I feel the rope against my bark,
    And the weight of him in my grain,
I feel in the throe[6] of his final woe
    The touch of my own last pain.

And never more shall leaves come forth
    On a bough that bears the ban;[7]
I am burned with dread, I am dried and dead,
    From the curse of a guiltless man.

And ever the judge rides by, rides by,
    And goes to hunt the deer,
And ever another rides his soul
    In the guise of a mortal fear.

And ever the man he rides me hard,
    And never a night stays he;
For I feel his curse as a haunted bough,
    On the trunk of a haunted tree.

1903

In this poem, a passing stranger addresses a question to the haunted oak, and the oak's reply composes the rest of the poem. The ABCB rhyme scheme, the alternating lines of four beats and three beats, the language, and the simple, tragic narrative all mark this poem as a ballad, a form that originated in Renaissance Scotland and England.

To Alice Dunbar

All the world is so sweet, dear
And matters so little to me —
You are the whole and the all, dear
The bride for eternity —

5. That is, the members of the lynching party will
receive their just punishment on Judgment Day.
6. Spasm.
7. Curse.

* * *

Life is so gray and so brief, dear
And it is so hard to live.
Why should we neighbor with grief, dear
Better to love and forgive.

E'en tho' I miss you today, dear
Miss you and pass like a breath—
Love is puissant[1] in serving, dear
Far past the portals of death.

1903

Dunbar sent this poem to his wife one year after they had separated and three years before his death.

Compensation

Because I had loved so deeply,
    Because I had loved so long,
God in His great compassion
    Gave me the gift of song.

Because I have loved so vainly,
    And sung with such faltering breath,
The Master in infinite mercy
    Offers the boon[1] of Death.

1905

1. Powerful.   1. Gift or favor.

ABOUT THE EDITORS

Steven Gould Axelrod is Distinguished Professor of English at the University of California, Riverside. He has won his university's Distinguished Teaching Award and has held the McCauley Chair in Teaching Excellence. Among his books are *Robert Lowell: Life and Art* (Princeton University Press, 1978), which was nominated for a Pulitzer Prize, and *Sylvia Plath: The Wound and the Cure of Words* (Johns Hopkins University Press, 1990). He has edited *Robert Lowell: New Essays on the Poetry* (Cambridge University Press, 1986), *Critical Essays on Wallace Stevens* (G. K. Hall, 1988), *Critical Essays on William Carlos Williams* (G. K. Hall/Macmillan, 1995), and *The Critical Response to Robert Lowell* (Greenwood Press, 1999). He is president of the Robert Lowell Society and has published over fifty articles on American poets, including Ralph Waldo Emerson, Emily Dickinson, and James Russell Lowell.

Camille Roman is Visiting Scholar at Brown University and Emeritus Professor of English, Washington State University, Pullman, where she was affiliated with American Studies, Women's Studies, and the Honors College. She is the author of *Elizabeth Bishop's World War II–Cold War View* (Palgrave Macmillan, 2001). With Suzanne Juhasz and Cristanne Miller, she coedited *The Women and Language Debate: A Sourcebook* (Rutgers University Press, 1993). She also cofounded and coedited the Twayne Musical Arts Series with Chris D. Frigon and coedited individual volumes on Sonny Rollins, Lester Young, The Beatles, Black Women Composers, Claude Debussy, Olivier Messiaen, and Downhome Blues Lyrics. She is a former president of The Robert Frost Society and a member of the advisory board of The Elizabeth Bishop Society. She currently sits on the editorial board of *Twentieth-Century Literature* and is a former member of the board of *Tulsa Studies in Women's Literature*, and a former editorial board member of *Frontiers*, where she served as their poetry editor. An Untermeyer poetry fellow, she has won teaching awards at both Brown University and Washington State University, and received a John Cotton Dana Library Public Relations Award for public libraries. She has written and edited extensively on literary, musical, women's, and popular cultures for newspapers, magazines, reviews, and journals.

Thomas Travisano is Professor and Chair of English at Hartwick College. He is the author of *Elizabeth Bishop: Her Artistic Development* (University of Virginia

Press, 1988) and *Midcentury Quartet: Bishop, Lowell, Jarrell, Berryman, and the Making of a Postmodern Aesthetic* (University of Virginia Press, 1999), the principal editor of *Words in Air: The Complete Correspondence Between Elizabeth Bishop and Robert Lowell* (Farrar, Straus & Giroux, 2008) and coeditor of *Gendered Modernisms: American Women Poets and Their Readers* (University of Pennsylvania Press, 1996). He is the founding president of the Elizabeth Bishop Society and the senior advisor to the Robert Lowell Society.

INDEX